M000289321

Essential Readings in Infectious Disease Epidemiology

Manya Magnus, PhD, MPH

The George Washington University
School of Public Health and Health Services
Department of Epidemiology and Biostatistics
Washington, DC

JONES AND BARTLETT PUBLISHERS
Sudbury, Massachusetts
BOSTON   TORONTO   LONDON   SINGAPORE

World Headquarters

Jones and Bartlett Publishers
40 Tall Pine Drive
Sudbury, MA 01776
978-443-5000
info@jbpub.com
www.jbpub.com

Jones and Bartlett Publishers Canada
6339 Ormindale Way
Mississauga, Ontario L5V 1J2
Canada

Jones and Bartlett Publishers
International
Barb House, Barb Mews
London W6 7PA
United Kingdom

Jones and Bartlett's books and products are available through most bookstores and online booksellers. To contact Jones and Bartlett Publishers directly, call 800-832-0034, fax 978-443-8000, or visit our website www.jbpub.com.

Substantial discounts on bulk quantities of Jones and Bartlett's publications are available to corporations, professional associations, and other qualified organizations. For details and specific discount information, contact the special sales department at Jones and Bartlett via the above contact information or send an email to specialsales@jbpub.com.

Production Credits
Publisher: Michael Brown
Production Director: Amy Rose
Production Editor: Tracey Chapman
Associate Production Editor: Kate Stein
Associate Editor: Katey Birtcher
Editorial Assistant: Catie Heverling
Marketing Manager: Sophie Fleck
Manufacturing and Inventory Control Supervisor: Amy Bacus
Composition: Auburn Associates, Inc.
Cover Design: Kristin E. Ohlin
Cover Image: © CDC/Courtesy of Cynthia Goldsmith, Jacqueline Katz, and Sherif R. Zaki
Printing and Binding: Courier Stoughton
Cover Printing: John P. Pow Company

Library of Congress Cataloging-in-Publication Data
Magnus, Manya.
  Essential readings in infectious disease epidemiology / Manya Magnus.
    p. ; cm.
  Includes bibliographical references and index.
  ISBN-13: 978-0-7637-3878-5 (pbk.)
  ISBN-10: 0-7637-3878-6 (pbk.)
  1. Epidemiology. 2. Communicable diseases—Epidemiology. I. Title.
  [DNLM: 1. Communicable Diseases—epidemiology. 2. Epidemiology. 3. Public Health. WA 105 M198e 2009]
  RA651.M25 2009
  614.4—dc22
                                                                                        2008026276

6048
Printed in the United States of America
12 11 10 09 08   10 9 8 7 6 5 4 3 2 1

Acknowledgments

I would like to thank Mike Brown for building a supportive environment for textbook innovation at Jones and Bartlett, LLC. While writing this text, as well as its sibling, *Essentials of Infectious Disease Epidemiology*, I was given creative latitude in their approach—something that is unusual and greatly appreciated. Supporting new modalities of public health education is more essential today than ever before, and Mike's unique approach to educational materials and textbook writing allows the author to explore innovations and methods to their fullest. Dr. Richard Riegelman, the *Essentials* series editor, has been a wonderful support as well, being a proponent for public health education in general and epidemiology in specific. Katey Birtcher and the production team at Jones and Bartlett continue their never-ending assistance at all steps of writing and production. I am indebted to the authors of books, research, and articles who have taught me so much, especially the resources available through the Centers for Disease Control and Prevention, the Health Resources Services Administration, and the National Institutes of Health, without which many of the vivid examples would not be available. I am doubly indebted to my many teachers—formal and informal—encountered along the way, who taught me to delve into not just the "what" but the "how" that this book discusses with you today. Tremendous thanks are given to my father, Dr. Richard E. DeLeon, for sharing with me the joy of questioning and thinking and learning how much fun it can be to avoid the easy answers to questions in science (and life). This text is written in loving memory of my grandmother, Dr. Ida Russakoff Hoos (1912–2007), with gratitude for being an amazing role model, mentor, and friend.

To my husband, Magus Magnus, and children, Hero and Gryphon Magnus: love always, and thanks for everything.

About the Author

Manya Magnus, PhD, MPH, is an Associate Professor in the Department of Epidemiology and Biostatistics, with a secondary appointment as Associate Professor in the Department of Health Policy, at The George Washington University School of Public Health and Health Services. Dr. Magnus is co-director of the School's MPH Epidemiology Program and co-director of the Graduate Certificate in HIV/AIDS Studies. Dr. Magnus received her BA from the University of California, San Diego and her MPH and PhD from Tulane University. Always interested in integrating research with clinical care, Dr. Magnus has collaborated on a variety of epidemiologic studies, including randomized-controlled clinical trials and observational and evaluation studies. She now applies epidemiologic methodology to evaluate national programs in local- and state-level studies, including CDC-sponsored behavioral surveillance, and Special Projects of National Significance funded by the HIV/AIDS Bureau of the Health Services Resources Administration. Dr. Magnus also participates in a variety of other HIV- and STD-related research activities. The primary focus of her research is HIV/AIDS among women, children, adolescents, and other vulnerable populations and includes clinical trials, observational studies, and innovative approaches to evaluation research.

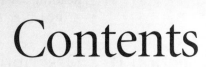

Contents

Series Page		xi
Introduction		xiii
How to Use This Book		xv

Section I	Historical Moments	1
Part I	Public Health, Passion, Persistence	3
Part II	Science and Letters	13
	Reading 1: De Foe and *A Journal of the Plague Year*	15
Part III	What About the Flu?	21
	Reading 2: 1918 Influenza: The Mother of All Pandemics	22
	Reading 3: Public Health Weekly Report for August 15, 1919— The Epidemiology of Influenza	31
	Reading 4: Update: Influenza Activity—United States, September 30, 2007–April 5, 2008, and Composition of the 2008–09 Influenza Vaccine	35
Part IV	Public Health Progress	43
	Reading 5: Achievements in Public Health, 1900–1999: Changes in the Public Health System	44

Part V	Ethics	49
	Reading 6: The Belmont Report	50
	Reading 7: U.S. Public Health Service Syphilis Study at Tuskegee	58
	Reading 8: Failure to Gain Coal-Face Commitment and to Use the Uncertainty Principle	60

Section II Descriptive Epidemiology: Outbreak Investigations 65

Part VI	Descriptive Epidemiology and Outbreak Investigations	67
	Reading 9: Outbreak Investigations—A Perspective	68
	Reading 10: Framework for Evaluating Public Health Surveillance Systems for Early Detection of Outbreaks: Recommendations from the CDC Working Group	74

Part VII	Investigating HIV/AIDS	87
	Reading 11: *Pneumocystis* Pneumonia—Los Angeles	88
	Reading 12: Kaposi's Sarcoma and *Pneumocystis* Pneumonia Among Homosexual Men—New York City and California	90
	Reading 13: Follow-Up on Kaposi's Sarcoma and *Pneumocystis* Pneumonia	92
	Reading 14: A Cluster of Kaposi's Sarcoma and *Pneumocystis carinii* Pneumonia Among Homosexual Male Residents of Los Angeles and Range Counties, California	94

Part VIII	Readily Transmissible and Emerging Infections: Identification, Surveillance, and Control	97
	Reading 15: Outbreak of Severe Acute Respiratory Syndrome—Worldwide, 2003	98
	Reading 16: Preliminary Clinical Description of Severe Acute Respiratory Syndrome	100
	Reading 17: Updated Interim Surveillance Case Definition for Severe Acute Respiratory Syndrome (SARS)—United States, April 29, 2003	101
	Reading 18: Revised U.S. Surveillance Case Definition for Severe Acute Respiratory Syndrome (SARS) and Update on SARS Cases—United States and Worldwide, December 2003	104
	Reading 19: SARS Surveillance Project—Internet-Enabled Multiregion Surveillance for Rapidly Emerging Disease	108
	Reading 20: Excerpt from: Postexposure Prophylaxis, Isolation, and Quarantine to Control an Import-Associated Measles Outbreak—Iowa, 2004	114
	Reading 21: Extensively Drug-Resistant Tuberculosis—United States, 1993–2006	116

Reading 22: Methicillin-Resistant–*Staphylococcus aureus* Hospitalizations, United States   122

Reading 23: Severe Methicillin-Resistant *Staphylococcus aureus* Community-Acquired Pneumonia Associated with Influenza—Louisiana and Georgia, December 2006–January 2007   127

Part IX   Foodborne Diseases   133

Reading 24: Food-Related Illness and Death in the United States   134

Reading 25: Food-Related Illness and Death in the United States: Letters   153

Reading 26: CDC Case Study, Oswego—An Outbreak of Gastrointestinal Illness Following a Church Supper   157

Reading 27: Compendium of Acute Foodborne and Waterborne Diseases   163

Section III   Analytic Methods   169

Part X   Analytic Methods   171

Reading 28: Strengthening the Reporting of Observational Studies in Epidemiology (STROBE): Explanation and Elaboration   172

Part XI   Intention-to-Treat: Tough Idea Made Simple   207

Reading 29: Intention-to-Treat Principle   208

Part XII   Assessing Misclassification: Surveillance Meets Methods   213

Reading 30: Misclassification of the Stages of Syphilis: Implications for Surveillance   214

Reading 31: Interim Within-Season Estimate of the Effectiveness of Trivalent Inactivated Influenza Vaccine—Marshfield, Wisconsin, 2007–08 Influenza Season   221

Part XIII   Understanding Results   227

Reading 32: STD Treatment to Prevent HIV Infection: Implications of Recent Community-Level Studies   229

Part XIV   Different Approaches to Examining Bias in Infectious Disease Epidemiology   233

Reading 33: Excerpt From: Impact of Severity of Illness Bias and Control Group Misclassification Bias in Case–Control Studies of Antimicrobial-Resistant Organisms   234

Reading 34: Excerpt From: An Outbreak of Multidrug-Resistant *Pseudomonas Aeruginosa* Associated with Increased Risk of Patient Death in an Intensive Care Unit   235

Part XV   Challenges in Studying Behavior   237

               Reading 35: Measuring Sexual Behavior: Methodological Challenges
                   in Survey Research   238
               Reading 36: HIV Prevalence, Unrecognized Infection, and
                   HIV Testing Among Men Who Have Sex with Men—
                   Five U.S. Cities, June 2004–April 2005   247

Part XVI   Using Computers to Improve Validity of Data Collection
               while Studying Behavior   253

               Reading 37: A Comparison Between Audio Computer-Assisted
                   Self-Interviews and Clinician Interviews for Obtaining the Sexual History   254
               Reading 38: Randomized Controlled Trial of Audio Computer-
                   Assisted Self-Interviewing: Utility and Acceptability in Longitudinal Studies   255
               Reading 39: Application of Computer-Assisted Interviews to Sexual
                   Behavior Research   256

Exercises

               Exercise 1: Creating an HIV Prevention Program   260
               Exercise 2: Logic Model Development   261
               Exercise 3: Identifying Study Designs   263
               Exercise 4: Getting Started with Critical Evaluation of the Literature   271
               Exercise 5: Name That Study Design   272
               Exercise 6: Evaluating a Public Health Surveillance Program   273

Series Page

See **www.jbpub.com/essentialpublichealth** for the latest information on the series.

TEXTS IN THE *ESSENTIAL PUBLIC HEALTH SERIES*

Essentials of Public Health—Bernard J. Turnock, MD, MPH

Essentials of Environmental Health—Robert H. Friis, PhD

Essentials of Health Policy and Law—Joel Teitelbaum, JD, LLM, and Sara Wilensky, JD, MPP

Essential Readings in Health Policy and Law—Joel Teitelbaum, JD, LLM, and Sara Wilensky, JD, MPP

Essentials of Global Health—Richard Skolnik, MPA

Case Studies in Global Health: Millions Saved—Ruth Levine, PhD, and the What Works Working Group

Essentials of Health Behavior: Social and Behavioral Theory in Public Health—Mark Edberg, PhD

Readings in Health Behavior—Mark Edberg, PhD

Essentials of Biostatistics in Public Health—Lisa Sullivan, PhD

Essentials of Biostatistics Workbook: Statistical Computations Using Excel—Lisa Sullivan, PhD

Epidemiology 101—Robert H. Friis, PhD

Essentials of Infectious Disease Epidemiology—Manya Magnus, PhD, MPH

Essential Readings in Infectious Disease Epidemiology—Manya Magnus, PhD, MPH

Essentials of Health Economics—Diane Dewar, PhD

Essentials of Public Health Biology: A Guide for the Study of Pathophysiology—Constance Urciolo Battle, MD

Fundamentals of Public Health Management and Leadership—Robert E. Burke, PhD

Essentials of Evidence-Based Public Health— Richard Riegelman, MD, MPH, PhD

ABOUT THE EDITOR:

Richard Riegelman, MD, MPH, PhD, is a professor of Epidemiology-Biostatistics, Medicine, and Health Policy and founding dean at The George Washington University School of Public Health and Health Services in Washington, DC.

Introduction

We are born knowing how to perceive; we are not born knowing how to read, interpret, or critically evaluate. Nevertheless, these skills—together with our perception—enable us to move beyond the superficial gleaning of information that is ordinarily done in one's day-to-day life. The difference between reading the newspaper or a relaxing novel and science is the ability to critically evaluate research. This skill informs the development of studies, their implementation, analysis, interpretation, and dissemination. As public health practitioners, you also need to be able to participate in the scientific community, in the science, through an understanding of what research has been conducted in the past. This will enable you to do everything from your own projects—even just a literature review—to understanding and sharing their public health implications. In order to do this, you must be able to understand not only the findings of a given study or report but also understand the methods undertaken to gather the data on which the findings and interpretations are based. This is a skill distinct from just reading, and one that takes practice, much as learning a foreign language.

This is an active text, one designed to engage you in the thinking process as you hone your critical evaluation skills. There aren't any answers; there is only the process of thinking and of thinking deeper. The format of this text is to provide you with focused readings, guiding questions, and exercises based upon the readings; the thinking process you go through for each will give you practice in critical evaluation. The articles in this reader are not all "landmark" articles in infectious disease epidemiology (though some are). Criteria for inclusion in this reader were simple: Each article or exercise was selected to provide you with at least one skill in critical evaluation of the literature. Think of this text as training wheels—articles and pieces of scientific writing in infectious disease epidemiology paired with exercises to get you thinking. Soon you will begin to ask your own questions when reading other articles and resources. All of the facets explored in this reader should enhance your epidemiologic toolkit and allow you to be a better epidemiologist as well as a better reader of the scientific literature.

For those of you using this reader in conjunction with the *Essentials of Infectious Disease Epidemiology* textbook, you will find articles referenced in the text provided here in expanded form. This book should echo and deepen understanding from that more introductory book. For those of you using this reader in conjunction with other epidemiologic textbooks or on its own, you will find that it is self-sufficient in its ability to convey central concepts and exercises and will likely parallel the concepts presented in other epidemiologic educational resources.

How to Use This Book

This reader is designed to be used by individuals but is also a wonderful study guide for pairs or groups; think of the exercises as conversation starters to get your group going. Whether you opt to address the exercises by yourself, in pairs, or in groups, do not stop when you reach the end of the questions: Delve deeper into each article or resource so that you can become an expert in each and every one of these chapters. Like a good book or movie, you will see that each article may be read many times over. At different points in your career—now, 5 years from now, 20 years from now—you will see different things in the methods of each article or resource. The ease with which you will be able to find methodologic flaws, errors, strengths, limitations, and more in each study will grow with the passing years—again, like learning a language. At first it will be harder, but it will become easier, in some ways, with practice. At the same time, you may find that the more subtle aspects—those that you come to with time—are that much harder to reckon with. Thus, the challenges will continue, never cease, as you hone your critical evaluation skills.

Enjoy as you embark on these exciting exercises!

~Manya Magnus, PhD, MPH

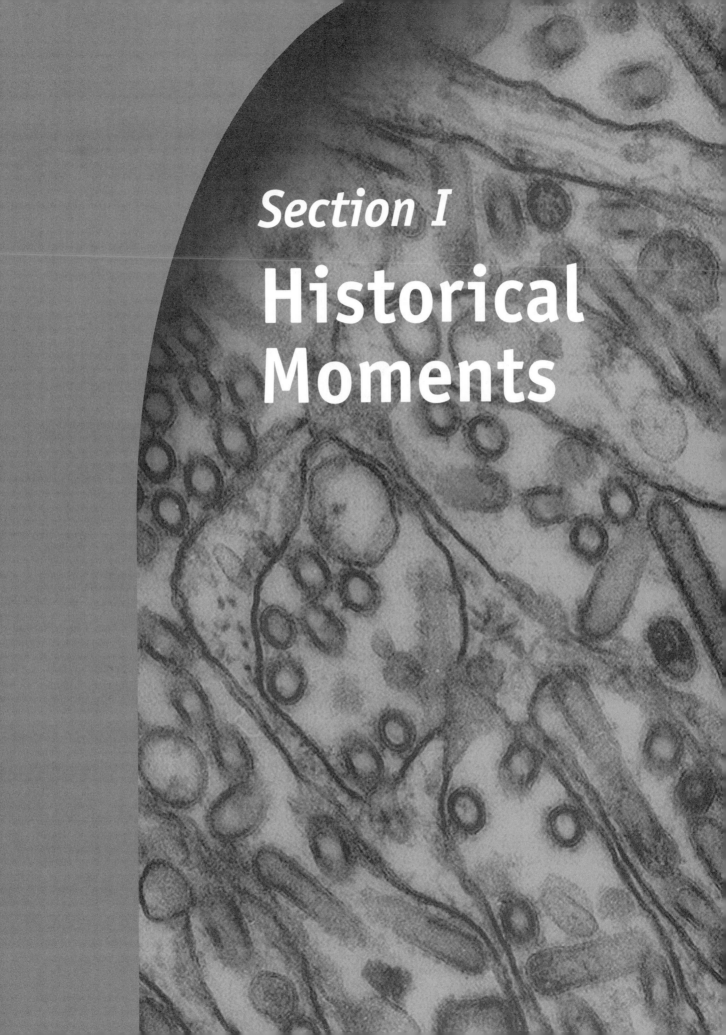

Section I
Historical Moments

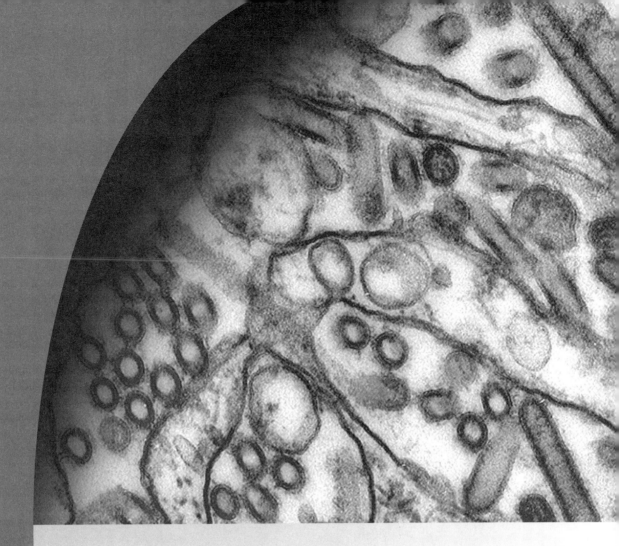

PART I

Public Health, Passion, Persistence

Ignaz Philipp Semmelweis (1818–1865) was a Hungarian obstetrician who studied and practiced medicine with a specialty in obstetrics in Vienna, Austria. It was Semmelweis who was on the forefront of introducing the concept of handwashing into medicine, and who supported the science of contagion with epidemiologic data. This form of antiseptic prophylaxis—lasting to this day as a basic and important tenet in public health and clinical medicine—was at first resisted by Semmelweis' colleagues. Working in a free maternity clinic, the young physician was appalled by the number of maternal deaths that occurred as a result of puerperal fever, also known as childbed fever. This is a bacterial infection that takes place following birth when Group A Streptococcus (GAS, *Streptococcus pyogenes*) bacterium and/or Group B Streptococcus (GBS, *Streptococcus agalactiae*) ascend the vaginal canal and endometrial tissue, following labor and delivery. Not treated, bacterial sepsis can result, inducing shock and death in the new mother, with outbreaks in specific hospitals with case-fatality rates of up to 100% in maternity wards in the absence of prevention and treatment. The first recorded epidemic of puerperal fever occurred at the Hôtel-Dieu de Paris in 1646, and even through the 1800s, hospitals throughout Europe and America consistently reported death rates between 20% and 30% of all women giving birth in their wards. Semmelweis was distressed by his inability to stop his patients from dying at what should be a joyous time in their lives. He also questioned the current medical thinking—that imbalance of the four "humours" resulted in most illnesses—and remained skeptical that this could be the case. That women delivering infants at home seldom died of the disease was further evidence against this theory. But it was his observations, that there were different fatality rates on the two different divisions of the hospital, which generated a key comparison of proportions and helped solve what had been a mystery. Semmelweis saw that the two maternity clinics did not have the same mortality rates: The data are shown here. Between 1841 and 1846, the average mortality rate in the first clinic was 9.92 while that of the second was 3.38. What could be the cause of these differing rates? Semmelweis' data are below:

TABLE 1-1 Annual births, deaths, and mortality rates for all patients at the two clinics of the Vienna maternity hospital from 1841 to 1946.

	First clinic			Second clinic		
	Births	**Deaths**	**Rate**	**Births**	**Deaths**	**Rate**
1841	3036	237	7.7	2442	86	3.5
1842	3287	518	15.8	2659	202	7.5
1843	3060	274	8.9	2739	164	5.9
1844	3157	260	8.2	2956	68	2.3
1845	3492	241	6.8	3241	66	2.03
1846	4010	459	11.4	3754	105	2.7
Total	20,042	1989		17,791	691	
Average			9.92			3.38

Data excerpted from *The Etiology, Concept, and Prophylaxis of Childbed Fever,* by Ignaz Semmelweis, translated by K. Codell Carter, Madison; University of Wisconsin Press, 1983, found in Carol Buck, *The Challenge of Epidemiology: Issues and Selected Readings.* Pan American Health Organization, Scientific Publication No. 505. 1989; 46–60.

FIGURE 1-1 Annual births, deaths, and mortality rates for all patients at the two clinics of the Vienna maternity hospital from 1841 to 1946.

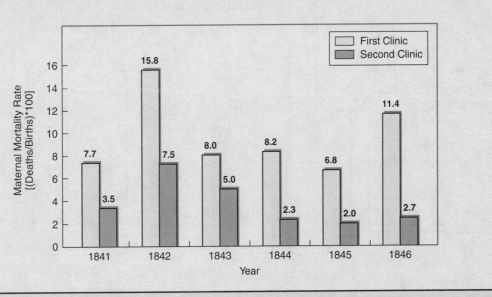

Data excerpted from *The Etiology, Concept, and Prophylaxis of Childbed Fever*, by Ignaz Semmelweis, translated by K. Codell Carter, Madison; University of Wisconsin Press, 1983, found in Carol Buck, *The Challenge of Epidemiology: Issues and Selected Readings*. Pan American Health Organization, Scientific Publication No. 505. 1989; 46–60. Graph created by author.

Semmelweis also noted that many of the newborns of women who died of childbed fever also died, and died with the same types of lesions and symptoms as did their mothers. In fact the rates, parallel those in each clinic:

TABLE 1-2 Annual births, deaths, and mortality rates for newborns at the two clinics of the Vienna maternity hospital from 1841 to 1946.

	First clinic			Second clinic		
	Births	**Deaths**	**Rate**	**Births**	**Deaths**	**Rate**
1841	2813	177	6.2	2252	91	4.04
1842	3037	279	9.1	2414	113	4.06
1843	2828	195	6.8	2570	130	5.05
1844	2917	251	8.6	2739	100	3.06
1845	3201	260	8.1	3017	97	3.02
1846	3533	235	6.5	3398	86	2.05
Total *	18,329	1397		16,390	617	

Data excerpted from *The Etiology, Concept, and Prophylaxis of Childbed Fever*, by Ignaz Semmelweis, translated by K. Codell Carter, Madison; University of Wisconsin Press, 1983, found in Carol Buck, *The Challenge of Epidemiology: Issues and Selected Readings*. Pan American Health Organization, Scientific Publication No. 505. 1989; 46–60.

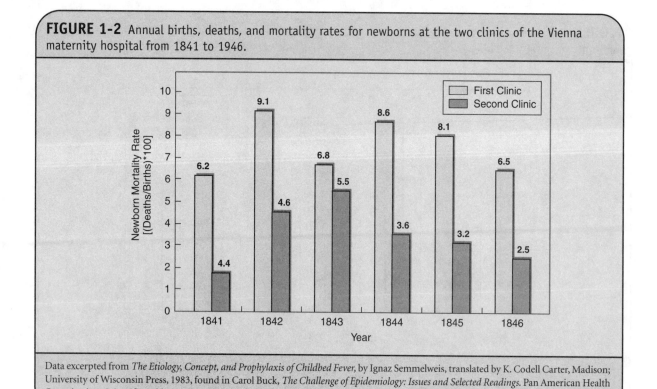

FIGURE 1-2 Annual births, deaths, and mortality rates for newborns at the two clinics of the Vienna maternity hospital from 1841 to 1946.

Data excerpted from *The Etiology, Concept, and Prophylaxis of Childbed Fever*, by Ignaz Semmelweis, translated by K. Codell Carter, Madison; University of Wisconsin Press, 1983, found in Carol Buck, *The Challenge of Epidemiology: Issues and Selected Readings*. Pan American Health Organization, Scientific Publication No. 505. 1989; 46–60. Graph created by author.

(Semmelweis also points out an interesting factor in his writing: that the estimates of mortality for the first clinic probably underestimated the true mortality rate, because women who progressed rapidly with infection were maintained in the clinic ward; others who died subsequently on the general ward were not counted in the first clinic's death counts. In the second clinic, these transfers did not occur. This point illustrates the importance of understanding clinic flow when conducting a study. Had he not known the nature of the clinic flow and its documentation, he would not have been able to describe or estimate the direction of the bias found in his data.)

In addition to the difference in mortality rates between the first and second clinics, Semmelweis was troubled by a variety of other characteristics of the deaths, all which suggested an infectious cause "endemic" to the clinic setting, yet not contagious directly from woman to woman. In searching for the reason behind the difference in mortality between the two clinics, he examined a variety of clinical characteristics between the clinics. Looking to the cause, he noted that "in both clinics these must be equally harmful or harmless and they cannot, therefore, explain the appalling difference in mortality between the clinics." So he was searching for the *predictive* characteristic that could be a clue to what the cause was, as he refused to believe that this was just chance or due to the prevailing medical theories of the day. What did he find? Of women with prolonged periods of dilation (as the cervix opens), nearly all became ill either during the birth process or within 24 or 36 hours after the birth; these women died quickly after developing childbed fever. But the salient factor here was that the same period of dilation in the second clinic was not dangerous. This was a clue. Semmelweis noted many clues about the women, about their deliveries, and his thinking process is impeccable as he reasoned out what could be the cause of these deaths—which he viewed to be preventable, though he did not yet know why.

Semmelweis' experience of mulling all of the information, without epiphany is profound:

> I was convinced that the greater mortality rate at the first clinic was due to an endemic but as yet unknown cause. That the newborn, whether female or male, also contracted childbed fever convinced me that the disease was misconceived. I was aware of many facts for which I had no explanation. Delivery with

prolonged dilation almost inevitably led to death. Patients who delivered prematurely or on the street almost never became ill, and this contradicted my conviction that the deaths were due to endemic causes. The disease appeared sequentially among patients in the first clinic. Patients in the second clinic were healthier, although individuals working there were no more skillful or conscientious in their duties. The disrespect displayed by the employees toward the personnel of the first clinic made me so miserable that life seemed worthless. Everything was in question; everything seemed inexplicable, everything was doubtful. Only the large number of deaths was an unquestionable reality.

Semmelweis also made an important observation that strengthened his impression that there was an infectious cause of the deaths that was intrinsic to the clinic and not passed patient to patient but through some alternate mode. The way the Viennese clinic was structured, women did not have to pay for their care there, provided they submitted to be "available for open instructional purposes, and that those fit to do so serve as wet nurses for the foundling home." Those infants not born at the clinic could not be entered into the foundling home. But a provision was made for women who, in trying to reach the clinic, delivered on the street—they were allowed the privileges of those women who delivered at the hospital. To avail themselves of this access, many women would deliver outside of the hospital, with a midwife or others in attendance, and then immediately after go to the hospital. But despite this situation that could not have been easy on a body or a baby, these women did far better than those women delivered at the first clinic:

As I have noted, women who delivered on the street contracted childbed fever at a significantly lower rate than those who delivered in the hospital. This was in spite of the less favorable conditions in which such births took place. Of course, in most of these cases delivery occurred in a bed with the assistance of a midwife. Moreover, after three hours our patients were obliged to walk to their beds by way of the glass enclosed passageway. However, such inconvenience is certainly less dangerous than being delivered by a midwife, then immediately having to arise, walk down many flights of stairs to the waiting carriage, travel in all weather conditions and over horribly rough pavement to the maternity hospital, and there having to climb up another flight of stairs. For those who really gave birth on the street, the conditions would have been even more difficult.

To me, it appeared logical that patients who experienced street births would become ill at least as frequently as those who delivered in the clinic. I have already expressed my firm conviction that the deaths in the first clinic were not caused by epidemic influences but by endemic and as yet unknown factors, that is, factors whose harmful influences were limited to the first clinic. What protected those who delivered outside the clinic from these destructive unknown endemic influences? In the second clinic, the health of the patients who underwent street births was as good as in the first clinic, but there the difference was not so striking, since the health of the patients was generally much better.

Semmelweis left Vienna for Venice, hoping that "Venetian art treasures would revive my mind and spirits, which had been so seriously affected by my experiences in the maternity hospital." Then arrived the sad news that one of Semmelweis' mentors, Professor Kolletschka, had died. This ushered in an epiphany, an "ah-ha" moment, that catalyzed all of Semmelweis' data. This epiphany allowed him to integrate the data he had collected, yield an interpretation, and lead to a hypothesis. Professor Kolletschka was conducting an autopsy and cut his finger. He became ill with diffuse infection that resembled exactly that of the women (and newborns) with childbed fever. Because they knew the source of his mentor's infection—the cadaverous particles—he was able to at last link it to childbed fever:

Because of the anatomical orientation of the Viennese medical school, professors, assistants, and students have frequent opportunity to contact cadavers. Ordinary washing with soap is not sufficient to remove all adhering cadaverous particles. This is proven by the cadaverous smell that the hands retain for a longer or shorter time. In the examination of pregnant or delivering maternity patients, the hands, contaminated with cadaverous particles, are brought into contact with the genitals of these individuals, creating the possibility of resorption. With resorption, the cadaverous particles are introduced into the vascular system of the patient. In this way, maternity patients contract the same disease that was found in Kolletschka.

This hypothesis provided Semmelweis with an intervention:

> Suppose cadaverous particles adhering to hands cause the same disease among maternity patients that ca-
> daverous particles adhering to the knife caused in Kolletschka. Then if those particles are destroyed chem-
> ically, so that in examinations patients are touched by fingers but not by cadaverous particles, the disease
> must be reduced. This seemed all the more likely since I knew that when decomposing organic material is
> brought into contact with living organisms it may bring on decomposition.
>
> To destroy cadaverous matter adhering to hands I used *chlorina liquida*. This practice began in the mid-
> dle of May 1847; I no longer remember the specific day. Both the students and I were required to wash
> before examinations. After a time, I ceased to use *chlorina liquida* because of its high price, and I adopted
> the less expensive chlorinated lime. In May 1847, during the second half of which chlorine washings were
> first introduced, 36 patients died—this was 12.24 percent of 294 deliveries. In the remaining seven months
> of 1847, the morality rate was below that of the patients in the second clinic.
>
> In these seven months, of the 1841 maternity patients cared for, 56 died (3.04 percent). In 1846, be-
> fore washing with chlorine was introduced, of 4010 patients cared for in the first clinic, 459 died (11.4
> percent). In the second clinic in 1846, of 3754 patients, 105 died (2.7 percent). In 1847, when in approx-
> imately the middle of May I instituted washing with chlorine, in the first clinic of 3490 patients, 176 died
> (5 percent). In the second clinic of 3306 patients, 32 died (0.9 percent). In 1848, chlorine washings were
> employed throughout the year and of 3556 patients, 45 died (1.27 percent). In the second clinic in the
> year 1848, of 3219 patients 43 died (1.33) percent. . . .
>
> In March and August 1848 not a single patient died. In January 1849, of 403 births 9 died (2.23 per-
> cent). In February, of 389 births, 12 died (3.08 percent). March had 406 births, and there were 20 deaths
> (4.9 percent). On 20 March Dr. Carl Braun succeeded me as assistant.

Because of Semmelweis' interventions—which unfortunately were not carried on "conscientiously" by Dr. Braun, who did not subscribe to his theory—the mortality rate in the first clinic (where he was stationed) fell below that of the second. The intervention worked.

As for the newborns, the chlorine washings reduced their mortality as well. Infants whose mothers had died were taken immediately to the "foundling home"; many of these infants there died. As another demonstration of the efficacy of the handwashing, once instituted, newborns ceased to die of childbed fever (i.e., sepsis). In fact, the head of the Imperial Foundling Home in Vienna wrote: "Sepsis of the blood of newborns has become a great rarity. For this we must thank the consequential and most noteworthy discovery of Dr. Semmelweis, emeritus assistant of the Viennese first maternity clinic. His work fortunately explained the cause and the prevention of the formerly murderous ravages of puerperal fever."

Practioners of the time resisted Semmelweis' simple method (handwashing) and understanding of puerperal fever for some years. However, before his death at age 47, he and his work were accepted by the medical establishment in Hungary, where he was from, where he also replicated his success at reducing maternal mortality. It was only after Louis Pasteur's work regarding germ theory, after Semmelweis' death, did his understanding and its implications have widespread impact on public health.

Semmelweis was not the first to consider the cause of childbed fever and imagine it preventable. Other authors, notably among them Oliver Wendell Holmes (1804–1894), also argued for a similar etiology. The year before and an ocean away—though Semmelweis evidently was unaware of Holmes' writings—Holmes used what he had seen to think it through logically. In his essay, *The Contagiousness of Puerperal Fever*, Holmes notes the denial of current medical practitioners that an infection could be the root cause of childbed fever: "In the last edition of Dewees's Treatise on the 'Diseases of Females' it is expressly said, "In this country, under no circumstance that puerperal fever has appeared hitherto, does it afford the slightest ground for the belief that it is contagious." His essay attends his thesis: "The practical point to be illustrated is the following: *The disease known as Puerperal Fever is so far contagious as to be frequently carried from patient to patient by physicians and nurses.*"

Holmes sets forth a numbered list of "incidental questions" that skillfully produce logic that also relates to the general cause of disease as well as puerperal fever in specific:

1. It is granted that all the forms of what is called puerperal fever may not be, and probably are not, equally contagious or infectious. I do not enter into the distinctions which have been drawn by authors, because the facts do not appear to me sufficient to establish any absolute line of demarcation between such forms as may be propagated by contagion and those which are never so propagated. This general result I shall only support by the authority of Dr. Ramsbotham, who gives, as the result of his experience, that the same symptoms belong to what he calls the infectious and the sporadic forms of the disease, and the opinion of Armstrong in his original Essay. If others can show any such distinction, I leave it to them to do it. But there are cases enough that show the prevalence of the disease among the patients of a single practitioner when it was in no degree epidemic, in the proper sense of the term. I may refer to those of Mr. Roberton and of Dr. Peirson, hereafter to be cited, as examples.

2. I shall not enter into any dispute about the particular *mode* of infection, whether it be by the atmosphere the physician carries about him into the sick-chamber, or by the direct application of the virus to the absorbing surfaces with which his hand comes in contact. Many facts and opinions are in favour of each of these modes of transmission. But it is obvious that, in the majority of cases, it must be impossible to decide by which of these channels the disease is conveyed, from the nature of the intercourse between the physician and the patient.

3. It is not pretended that the contagion of puerperal fever must always be followed by the disease. It is true of all contagious diseases that they frequently spare those who appear to be fully submitted to their influence. Even the vaccine virus, fresh from the subject, fails every day to produce its legitimate effect, though every precaution is taken to insure its action. This is still more remarkably the case with scarlet fever and some other diseases.

4. It is granted that the disease may be produced and variously modified by many causes besides contagion, and more especially by epidemic and endemic influences. But this is not peculiar to the disease in question. There is no doubt that smallpox is propagated to a great extent by contagion, yet it goes through the same records of periodical increase and diminution which have been remarked in puerperal fever. If the question is asked how we are to reconcile the great variations in the mortality of puerperal fever in different seasons and places with the supposition of contagion, I will answer it by another question from Mr. Farr's letter to the Registrar-General. He makes the statement that "*five* die weekly of smallpox in the metropolis when the disease is not epidemic," and adds, "The problem for solution is—Why do the five deaths become 10, 15, 20, 31, 58, 88, weekly, and then progressively fall through the same measured steps?"

5. I take it for granted that if it can be shown that great numbers of lives have been and are sacrificed to ignorance or blindness on this point, no other error of which physicians or nurses may be occasionally suspected will be alleged in palliation of this; but that whenever and wherever they can be shown to carry disease and death instead of health and safety, the common instincts of humanity will silence every attempt to explain away their responsibility.

He then quotes the Treatise of a Dr. Gordon, who wrote in 1795,

This disease seized such women only as were visited or delivered by a practitioner, or taken care of by a nurse, who had previously attended patients affected with the disease. I had evident proofs of its infectious nature, and that the infection was as readily communicated as that of the smallpox or measles, and operated more speedily than any other infection with which I am acquainted. I had evident proofs that every person who had been with a patient in the puerperal fever became charged with an atmosphere of infection, which was communicated to every pregnant woman who happened to come within its sphere. This is not an assertion, but a fact, admitting of demonstration, as may be seen by a perusal of the foregoing table.

Referring to a table of seventy-seven cases, in many of which the channel of propagation was evident, he adds: "It is a disagreeable declaration for me to mention, that I myself was the means of carrying the infection to a great number of women." He then enumerates a number of instances in which the disease was conveyed by midwives and others to the neighboring villages and declares that "these facts fully prove that the cause of the puerperal fever, of which I treat, was a specific contagion, or infection, altogether unconnected with a noxious constitution of the atmosphere." But his most terrible evidence is given in these words: "I arrived at that certainty in the matter that I could venture to foretell what women would be affected with the disease, upon hearing by what midwife they were to be delivered, or by what nurse they were to be attended, during their lying-in: and almost in every instance my prediction was verified." (Note how similar these last words are to Semmelweis: "I often pointed out to my students that because these blossoming, vigorously healthy young women had extended periods of dilation, they would die quickly from puerperal fever either during delivery or immediately thereafter. My prognoses were fulfilled.")

Following an in-depth investigation into the works of multiple physicians and midwives that supported his argument, Holmes cites a story similar to that of Semmelweis' mentor, Dr. Kolletschka:

> The first patient, it is stated, was delivered on the 20th of March. "On the 19th Dr. C. made the autopsy of a man who had died suddenly, sick only forty-eight hours; had oedema of the thigh and gangrene extending from a little above the ankle into the cavity of the abdomen." Dr. C. wounded himself very slightly in the right hand during the autopsy. The hand was quite painful the night following, during his attendance on the patient No. 1. He did not see this patient after the 20th, being confined to the house, and very sick from the wound just mentioned, from this time until the 3rd of April. Several cases of erysipelas occurred in the house where the autopsy mentioned above took place, soon after the examination. There were also many cases of erysipelas in town at the time of the fatal puerperal cases which have been mentioned.

And later, "I need not refer to the case lately read before this Society, in which a physician went, soon after performing an autopsy of a case of puerperal fever, to a woman in labor, who was seized with the same disease and perished. The forfeit of that error has been already paid."

Holmes' closes his essay with essential words:

> No tongue can tell the heart-breaking calamity they have caused; they have closed the eyes just opened upon a new world of love and happiness; they have bowed the strength of manhood into the dust; they have cast the helplessness of infancy into the stranger's arms, or bequeathed it, with less cruelty, the death of its dying parent. There is no tone deep enough for regret, and no voice loud enough for warning. The woman about to become a mother or with her new-born infant upon her bosom, should be the object of trembling care and sympathy wherever she bears her tender burden or stretches her aching limbs. The very outcast of the streets has pity upon her sister in degradation when the seal of promised maternity is impressed upon her. The remorseless vengeance of the law, brought down upon its victim by a machinery as sure as destiny, is arrested in its fall at a word which reveals her transient claim for mercy. The solemn prayer of the liturgy singles out her sorrows from the multiplied trials of life, to plead for her in the hour of peril. God forbid that any member of the profession to which she trusts her life, doubly precious at that eventful period, should hazard it negligently, unadvisedly, or selfishly!

> There may be some among those whom I address who are disposed to ask the question, What course are we to follow in relation to this matter? The facts are before them, and the answer must be left to their own judgment and conscience. If any should care to know my own conclusions, they are the following; and in taking the liberty to state them very freely and broadly, I would ask the inquirer to examine them as freely in the light of the evidence which has been laid before him.

> 1. A physician holding himself in readiness to attend cases of midwifery should never take any active part in the post-mortem examination of cases of puerperal fever.
> 2. If a physician is present at such autopsies, he should use thorough ablution, change every article of dress, and allow twenty-four hours or more to elapse before attending to any case of midwifery. It may be well to extend the same caution to cases of simple peritonitis.
> 3. Similar precautions should be taken after the autopsy or surgical treatment of cases of erysipelas, if the physician is obliged to unite such offices with his obstetrical duties, which is in the highest degree inexpedient.

4. On the occurrence of a single case of puerperal fever in his practice, the physician is bound to consider the next female he attends in labor, unless some weeks at least have elapsed, as in danger of being infected by him, and it is his duty to take every precaution to diminish her risk of disease and death.

5. If within a short period two cases of puerperal fever happen close to each other, in the practice of the same physician, the disease not existing or prevailing in the neighborhood, he would do wisely to relinquish his obstetrical practice for at least one month, and endeavor to free himself by every available means from any noxious influence he may carry about with him.

6. The occurrence of three or more closely connected cases, in the practice of one individual, no others existing in the neighborhood, and no other sufficient cause being alleged for the coincidence, is *primâ facie* evidence that he is the vehicle of contagion.

7. It is the duty of the physician to take every precaution that the disease shall not be introduced by nurses or other assistants, by making proper inquiries concerning them, and giving timely warning of every suspected source of danger.

8. Whatever indulgence may be granted to those who have heretofore been the ignorant causes of so much misery, the time has come when the existence of a *private pestilence* in the sphere of a single physician should be looked upon, not as a misfortune, but a crime; and in the knowledge of such occurrences the duties of the practitioner to his profession should give way to his paramount obligations to society.

DISCUSSION QUESTIONS

1. There may be a couple of questions worth asking about the data provided in Semmelweis' table, apart from the hypothesis at hand (i.e., what was causing the elevated death rates in the first clinic?). For example, what was going on in 1842, when the rates at both clinics are about twice their usual? Is there a difference in environmental conditions? Maternal health in the community? Any changes in trends in treatment approaches? Changes in assessment of deaths or their documentation? What else could have made this increase in rates? Give two examples each of a true cause of increase and an artifactual cause.

2. Use the data in narrative form from the excerpt of Semmelweis to create your own table. Then graph these data as you see above, making sure to label each access. What other information would you like to know?

3. Use the data in Tables 1-1 and 1-2 and construct another graph, one to depict both maternal and newborn mortality rates by year and by clinic all on one graph. What does this tell you?

4. Compare and contrast the endeavors of Holmes and Semmelweis, where one uses logic and one uses data. How can these two approaches work together? What do they do the same? What do they do that differs? What are the differences in how each of these may be generalized to other situations? How are they different in the ways in which they may persuade people of different professions and approaches to the problem? What else might you want to know or add to either of their arguments?

SOURCES

Costa CM. The contagiousness of childbed fever: a short history of puerperal sepsis and its treatment. *Medical Journal of Australia* 2002;177: 668–671.

Elek SD. Semmelweis and the Oath of Hippocrates. Proceedings of the Royal Society of Medicine 346–52.

Holmes OW. *The Contagiousness of Puerperal Fever.* Vol. XXXVIII, Part 5. The Harvard Classics. New York: P.F. Collier & Son, 1909–14; Bartleby.com, 2001. www.bartleby.com/38/5/. [Accessed 12/25/07].

Loudon I. Deaths in childbed from the eighteenth century to 1935. Med History 1986;30: 1–41.

Wertz RM, Wertz DC. *Lying-In: A History of Childbirth in America.* New York: New York Free Press, 1977.

Buck C. *The Challenge of Epidemiology: Issues and Selected Readings.* Pan American Health Organization, Scientific Publication No. 505. 1989;46-60. Excerpted from *The Etiology, Concept, and Prophylaxis of Childbed Fever*, by Ignaz Semmelweis, translated by K. Codell Carter, Madison: University of Wisconsin Press, 1983.

http://en.wikipedia.org/wiki/Ignaz_Semmelweis#_note-Mind103 [Accessed 1/20/07].

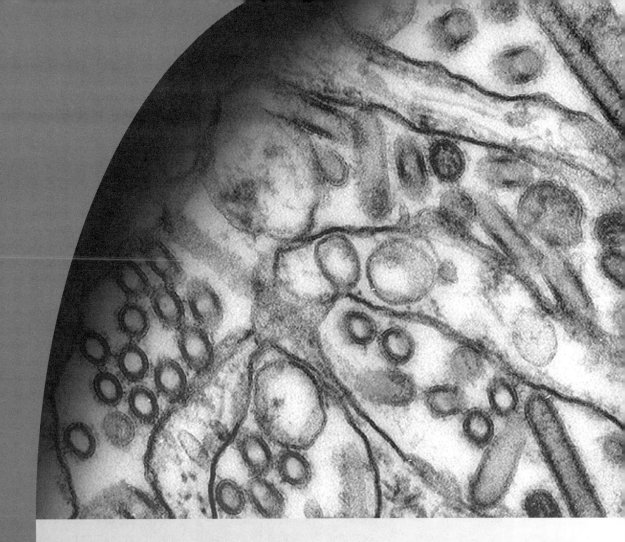

PART II

Science and Letters

It is not only scientists and public health professionals that strive to catalogue and explicate matters of medicine and health. Artists, philosophers, and writers are known to discuss issues in health as a part of their understanding, critical evaluation of, and communication about the world around them. Since health events, both personal and public, have the potential to affect people profoundly, this makes sense. Oliver Wendell Holmes, a man of letters, discussed the logic and causality of childbed fever above, making an intellectual case with argument that was supported later by Semmelweis' (and others') data.

Similarly, Daniel De Foe, known for writing *Robinson Crusoe*, wrote one of the most lasting accounts of the plague that struck Europe in the 1600s. *The Journal of the Plague Year* chronicles his account of London during the year 1665 as he remained in the afflicted city.

The plague, caused by the *Yersinia pestis* bacterium, evokes thoughts of the middle ages, rodents, and some of the worst epidemics in history. A vector-borne illness, plague is transmitted from animal to animal by fleas that are infected with the bacterium. Although mice, voles, rabbits, prairie dogs, and other rodents can carry plague, most outbreaks have house rats as their primary source. This happens particularly when rodent populations die off as a result of the disease, and their flea populations, infected with the bacterium, begin to search for other sources of nourishment in the blood of nearby humans. Sometimes the pets of humans come into contact with vectors and then transmit the disease via fleas to their unsuspecting owners. Plague can also be transmitted through inhalation of droplets as they are coughed by infected animals or people, or via direct contact with infected tissues or fluids. There have been several pandemics associated with plague, from as early as 541 AD (Plague of Justinian) to that in the mid-1300s, which swept through Africa, Asia, and Europe, killing as many as 100 million people including what is thought to be one-third of Europe's populous and half of China's. Additional pandemics occurred in the 1800s throughout India and Asia. Among the many waves of plague, one occurred in 1665 in London about which De Foe writes.

We tend to like to think that plague is gone but in reality, while epidemics are rare, there are cases of plague worldwide, with outbreaks still occurring in developing countries. Like Lyme disease, which happens more and more as nature comes into contact with our society (e.g., with suburban clearings), plague cases continue to emerge.

Fortunately, antibiotics are available and are very effective against the ravages of this disease. CDC (www.cdc.gov) indicates that, globally, there are 1,000 to 2,000 cases each year. During the 1980s epidemic plague occurred each year in Africa, Asia, or South America; these cases were mostly transmitted by rats and in smaller villages or rural areas.

Lymph nodes that are swollen, painful, and hot are called buboes (hence bubonic plague) are the primary sign of the plague, preceded by or together with headache, generalized feeling of illness, exhaustion, and fever. Together with exposure to rodents, plague might be suspected. Onset of the disease ranges from 2 to 6 days following exposure. Rapidly, the bacteria can be spread to the blood (sepsis) and lungs (pneumonic plague or plague pneumonia), and death is the frequent result unless appropriate antibiotic therapy is administered immediately. Plague is an internationally reportable disease, and contacts need to be actively traced to engage them in care.

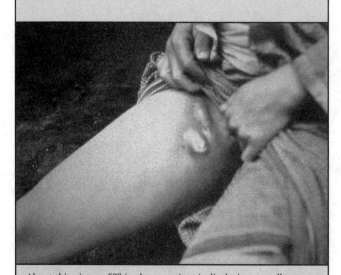

FIGURE 2-1 A picture of a bubo.

About this picture: "This plague patient is displaying a swollen, ruptured inguinal lymph node, or bubo. After the incubation period of 2–6 days, symptoms of the plague appear including severe malaise, headache, shaking chills, fever, and pain and swelling, or adenopathy, in the affected regional lymph nodes, also known as buboes."

Source: CDC Public Health Image Library, 1993.

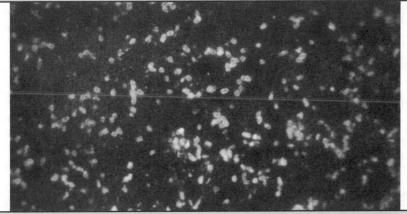

FIGURE 2-2 *Yersinia pestis* bacteria.

About this picture: "This micrograph was stained using a fluorescent antibody staining technique (FA), which uses the specific conjugated antiserum to Fraction 1 (F1) antigen of *Yersinia pestis* to identify the antigens present in animal tissues, and appropriate cultures. Antibody tests, such as this one, are rapid and effective, and though the results are presumptive, they are highly accurate, i.e., greater than 95%. Additional tests used to isolate and to identify *Y. pestis* include animal inoculation (usually mouse), isolation on blood agar or another appropriate medium, and characterization through various biochemical tests. Colonial morphology on culture media, appearance of the organism when stained using Wright's, Wayson's, or Methylene blue stains, and microscopic examination, are other techniques used to pinpoint the diagnosis of plague."

Source: CDC Public Health Library, 1993.

Below are selected pages of De Foe's work, provided by the Google books project. The full scanned original (327 pages) is available at http://books.google.com/ or you can go to your library for a print copy. It is well worth reading in its entirety to gain the full flavor of a first person account of one of the world's worst outbreaks of an infectious disease. Discussion questions are presented following each excerpt.

READING 1
De Foe and *A Journal of the Plague Year*

It was a very ill Time to be sick in, for if any one complain'd, it was immediately said he had the Plague; and tho' I had indeed no Symptoms of that Distemper, yet being very ill, both in my Head and in my Stomach, I was not without Apprehension, that I really was infected; but in about three Days I grew better, the third Night I rested well, sweated a little, and was much refresh'd; the Apprehensions of its being the Infection went also quite away with my Illness, and I went about my Business as usual.

Note here De Foe considers the troubling feeling of being ill during the plague. Later in these excerpts you will see the bills of mortality and they indicate, of course, though easy to forget,

that there are other causes of death besides the plague. And how awful to fall ill, wonder yourself whether you are sick with what is sure to be your last sickness, and fear what is to come! But then the relief that must follow when you recover. . . .

DISCUSSION QUESTIONS

Do you think this experience is pertinent to modern-day epidemics? To the fear one has when having symptoms of other infectious diseases, such as sexually transmitted infectious? Food poisoning? HIV? Tuberculosis? SARS? Influenza or, in particular, avian influenza? What implications are there for symptomatic persons at times of strife and outbreak, even in the absence of the actual disease?

FIGURE 2-3 Title page, Daniel De Foe's *A Journal of the Plague Year*

A JOURNAL

OF

THE PLAGUE YEAR

BEING OBSERVATIONS OR MEMORIALS OF THE MOST
REMARKABLE OCCURRENCES, AS WELL PUBLICK AS PRIVATE,
WHICH HAPPENED IN LONDON DURING THE
LAST GREAT VISITATION IN

1665

WRITTEN BY A CITIZEN WHO CONTINUED ALL THE WHILE IN LONDON
NEVER MADE PUBLICK BEFORE.

By DANIEL DEFOE

WITH AN INTRODUCTION BY HENRY MORLEY.
LL.D., PROFESSOR OF ENGLISH LITERATURE AT
UNIVERSITY COLLEGE, LONDON

LONDON
GEORGE ROUTLEDGE AND SONS
BROADWAY, LUDGATE HILL
NEW YORK: 9 LAFAYETTE PLACE
1884

Source: Daniel De Foe's *A Journal of the Plague Year.*

Journal of the Plague Year, Page 28

The Face of London was now indeed strangely alter'd, I mean the whole Mass of Buildings, City, Liberties, Suburbs, Westminster, Southwark and altogether; for as to the Particular Part called the City, or within the Walls, that was not yet much infected; but in the whole, the Face of Things, I say, was much alter'd; Sorrow and Sadness sat upon every Face; and tho' some Part were not yet overwhelm'd, yet all look'd deeply concern'd; and as we saw it apparently coming on, so every one look'd on himself, and his Family, as in the utmost Danger: were it possible to represent those Times exactly to those that did not see them, and give the Reader due Ideas of the Horror that every where presented it self, it must make just Impressions upon their Minds, and fill them with Surprize. London might well be said to be all in Tears; the Mourners did not go about the Streets indeed, for no Body put on black, or made a formal Dress of Mourning for their nearest Friends; but the Voice of Mourning was truly heard in the Streets; the shrieks of Women and Children at the Windows, and Doors of their Houses, where their dearest Relations were, perhaps dying, or just dead, were so frequent to be heard, as we passed the Streets, that it was enough to pierce the stoutest Heart in the World, to hear them. Tears and Lamentations were seen almost in every House, especially in the first Part of the Visitation; for towards the latter End, Mens Hearts were hardned, and Death was so always before

their Eyes, that they did not so much concern themselves for the Loss of their Friends, expecting, that themselves should be summoned the next Hour.

This description of the times is poignant; imagine the scene, and how you would feel in it.

DISCUSSION QUESTION

The proximity of individuals to the suffering of their neighbors is a critical aspect of disease and its public health implications—not just fear of sickness but actual morbidity and mortality witnessed by all. Describe the impact that this exposure (not just to the disease, which obviously has consequences beyond the psychological) might have on the health of those witnessing it.

Journal of the Plague Year

Orders concerning infected Houses, and Persons
sick of the Plague.

Notice to be given of the Sickness.

"The Master of every House, as soon as any one in his House complaineth, either of Botch, or Purple, or Swelling in any part of his Body, or falleth otherwise dangerously Sick, without apparent Cause of some other Disease, shall give knowledge thereof to the Examiner of Health, within two Hours after the said Sign shall appear.

Sequestration of the Sick.

"As soon as any Man shall be found by this Examiner, Chirurgeon or Searcher to be sick of the Plague, he shall the same Night be sequestred the same House and in case he be so sequestred then though he afterwards die not the House wherein he sickened should be shut up for a Month after the use of the due Preservatives taken the rest.

None to be removed out of infected Houses, but, &c.

"Item, that none be remov'd out of the House where he falleth sick of the Infection, into any other House in the City, (except it be to the Pest-House or a Tent, or unto some such House, which the Owner of the said visited House holdeth in his own Hands, and occupieth by his own Servants) and so as Security be given to the Parish, whither such Remove is made; that the Attendance and Charge about the said visited Persons shall be observed and charged in all the Particularities before expressed, without any Cost of that Parish, to which any such Remove shall happen to be made, and this Remove to be done by Night: And it shall be lawful to any Person that hath two Houses, to remove either his sound or his infected People to his spare House at his choice, so as if he send away first his Sound, he not after send thither the Sick. . . .

"And that no Corps dying of Infection shall be buried, or remain in any Church in time of Common-Prayer, Sermon, or Lecture. And that no Children be suffered at time of burial of any Corps in any Church, Church-yard, or Burying-place to come near the Corps, Coffin, or Grave. And that all the Graves shall be at least six Foot deep.

"And further, all publick Assemblies at other Burials are to be forborn during the Continuance of this Visitation.

No infected Stuff to be uttered.

"That no Clothes, Stuff, Bedding or Garments be suffered to be carried or conveyed out of any infected Houses, and that the Criers and Carriers abroad of Bedding or old Apparel to be sold or pawned, be utterly prohibited and restrained, and no Brokers of Bedding or old Apparel be permitted to make any outward Shew, or hang forth on their Stalls, Shopboards or Windows towards any Street, Lane, Common-way, or Passage, and old Bedding, Apparel, or other Stuff out of any infected House, within Months after the Infection hath been there his House shall be shut up as Infected and so shall continue shut up Twenty Days at the least.

Every visited House to be marked.

"That every House visited, be marked with a red Cross of a Foot long, in the middle of the Door, evident to be seen, and with these usual printed Words, that is to say, 'Lord have Mercy upon us,' to be set close over the same Cross, there to continue until lawful opening of the same House.

Every visited House to be watched.

"That the Constables see every House shut up, and to be attended with Watchmen, which may keep them in, and minister Necessaries unto them at their own Charges (if they be able,) or at the common Charge, if they be unable: The shutting up to be for the space of four Weeks after all be whole.

That precise Order be taken that the Searchers Chirurgeons, Keepers and Buriers are not to pass the Streets without holding a red Rod or Wand of three Foot in Length in their Hands, open and evident to be seen, and are not to go into any other House than into their own, or into that whereunto they are directed or sent for; but to forbear and abstain from Company, especially when they have been lately used in any such Business or Attendance.

Inmates.

That where several Inmates are in one and the same House, and any Person in that House happens to be Infected; no other Person of Family of such House shall be suffered to remove him or themselves without a Certificate from the Examiners of Health of that Parish; or in default thereof, the House whither he or they so remove, shall be shut up as in case of Visitation.

Hackeny-Coaches.

"That care be taken of the Hackney-Coach-men, that they may not (as some of them have been observed to do) after carrying of infected Persons to the Pest-house, and other Places, be admitted to common use, till their Coaches be well aired, and have stood unemploy'd by the Space of five or six Days after such Service."

DISCUSSION QUESTIONS

These public health orders are practical and sensible. Take each of the orders and consider its purpose with regard to the transmission of infectious disease. Are there orders which would be different, now that we have a firmer understanding of the mode of plague transmission? Which would you maintain? Which would you add? Go to www.who.int, www.cdc.gov, or your medical library if you need additional information about *Y pestis* to round out your responses.

This was in many Cases the saving a whole Family, who, if they had been shut up with the sick Person, would inevitably have perished: But on the other Hand, this was another of the Inconveniences of shutting up Houses; for the Apprehensions and Terror of being shut up, made many run away with the rest of the Family, who, tho' it was not publickly known, and they were not quite sick, had yet the Distemper upon them; and who by having an uninterrupted Liberty to go about, but being obliged still to conceal their Circumstances, or perhaps not knowing it themselves, gave the Distemper to others, and spread the Infection in a dreadful Manner, as I shall explain farther hereafter.

And here I may be able to make an Observation or two of my own, which may be of use hereafter to those, into whose Hands this may come, if they should ever see the like dreadful Visitation. (I.) The Infection generally came into the Houses of the Citizens, by the Means of their Servants, who, they were obliged to send up and down the Streets for Necessaries, that is to say, for Food, or Physick, to Bake-houses, Brew-houses, Shops, &c. and who going necessarily thro' the Streets into Shops, Markets, and the like, it was impossible, but that they should one way or other, meet with distempered people, who conveyed the fatal Breath into them, and they brought it Home to the Families, to which they belonged. (2.) It was a great Mistake, that such a great City as this had but one Pest-House; for had their been, instead of one Pest-House, viz. beyond Bunhil-Fields, where, at most, they could receive, perhaps, 200 or 300 People; I say, had there instead of that one been several Pest-Houses, every one able to contain a thousand People without lying two in a Bed, or two Beds in a Room; and had every Master of a Family, as soon as any Servant especially, had been taken sick in his

House, been obliged to send them to the next Pest-House, if they were willing, as many were, and had the Examiners done the like among the poor People, when any had been stricken with the Infection; I say, had this been done where the People were willing, (not otherwise) and the House not been shut, I am perswaded, and was all the While of that Opinion, that not so many, by several Thousands, had the While of that Opinion, that not so many, by several Thousands, had died; for it was observed, and I could give several Instances within the Compass of my own Knowledge, where a Servant had been taken sick, and the Family had either Time to send them out, or retire from the House, and leave the sick Person, as I have said above, they had all been preserved; whereas, when upon one, or more, sickning in a Family, the House has been shut up, the whole Family have perished, and the Bearers been oblig'd to go in to fetch out the Dead Bodies, none being able to bring them to the Door; and at last none left to do it. (2.) This put it out of Question to me, that the Calamity was spread by Infection, that is to say, by some certain Steams, or Fumes, which the Physicians call Effluvia, by the Breath, or by the Sweat, or by the Stench of the Sores of the sick Persons, or some other way, perhaps, beyond even the Reach of the Physicians themselves, which Effluvia affected the Sound, who come within certain Distances of the Sick, immediately penetrating the Vital Parts of the said sound Persons, putting their Blood into an immediate ferment, and agitating their Spirits to that Degree which it was found they were agitated; and so those newly infected Persons communicated it in the same Manner to others; and this I shall give some Instances of, that cannot but convince those who seriously consider it; and I cannot but with some Wonder, find some People, now the Contagion is over, talk of its being an immediate Stroke from Heaven, without the Agency of Means, having Commission to strike this and that particular Person, and non other; which I look upon with Contempt, as the Effect of manifest Ignorance and Enthusiasm; likewise the Opinion of others, who talk of infection being carried on by the Air only, by carrying with it vast Numbers of Insects, and invisible Creatures, who enter into the Body with the Breath, or even at the Pores with the Air, and there generate, or emit most acute Poisons, or poisonous Ovae, or Eggs, which mingle themselves with the Blood, and so infect the Body; a Discourse full of learned Simplicity, and manifested to be so by universal Experience; but I shall say more to this Case in its Order.

DISCUSSION QUESTIONS

De Foe here considers the mode of transmission—augmenting what was known (or believed) about the disease and its spread. What is he saying about the issue of the Pest House (where the ill were sent) and the dangers and futility of having it? How does this relate to stigma? To the issue of latent periods where people are infected and infectious but not yet symptomatic: What suggestions does De Foe make about what can/should be done?

But, this is but one; it is scarce credible what dreadful Cases happened in particular Families every Day; People in the Rage of the Distemper, or in the Torment of their Swellings, which was indeed intolerable, running out of their own Government, raving and distracted, and oftentimes laying violent Hands upon themselves, throwing themselves out at their Windows, shooting themselves, &c. Mothers murthering their own Children, in their Lunacy, some dying of mere Grief, as a Passion, some of mere Fright and Surprize, without any Infection at all; others frighted into Idiotism, and foolish Distractions, some into despair and Lunacy; others into mellancholy Madness.

The Pain of the Swelling was in particular very violent, and to some intolerable; the Physicians and Surgeons may be said to have tortured many poor Creatures, even to Death. The Swellings in some grew hard, and they apply'd violent drawing Plasters, or Pultices, to break them; and if these do not do, they cut and scarified them in a terrible Manner: In some, those Swellings were made hard, partly by the Force of the Distemper, and partly by their being too violently drawn, and were so hard, that no Instrument could cut them, and then they burnt them with Causticks, so that many died raving mad with the Torment; and some in the vary Operation. In these Distresses, some for want of Help to hold them down in their Beds, or to look to them, laid Hands upon themselves, as above. Some broke out into the Streets, perhaps naken, and would run directly down to the River, if they were not stopt by the Watchmen, or other Officers, and plunge themselves into the Water, wherever they found it.

It often pierc'd my very Soul to hear the Groans and Crys of those who were thus tormented, but of the Two, this was counted the most promising Particular in the whole Infection; for, if these Swellings could be brought to a Head, and to break and run, or as the Surgeons call it, to digest, the Patient generally recover'd; whereas those, who like the Gentlewoman's Daughter, were struck with Death at the Beginning, and had the Tokens come out upon them, often went about indifferent easy, till a little before they died, and some till the Moment they dropt down, as in Appoplexies and Epelepsies, is often the Case; such would be taken suddenly very sick, and would run to a Bench or Bulk, or any convenient Place that offer'd it self, or to their own Houses, if possible, as I mentioned before, and there sit down, grow faint and die. This kind of dying was much the same, as it was with those who die of common Mortifications, who die swooning, and as it were, go away in a Dream; such as died thus, had very little Notice of their being infected at all, till the Gangreen was spread thro' their whole Body; nor could Physicians themselves, know certainly how it was with them, till they opened their Breasts, or other parts of their Body, and saw the Tokens.

We had at this Time a great many frightful Stories told us of Nurses and Watchmen, who looked after the dying People, that is to say, hir'd Nurses, who attended infected People, using them barbarously, starving them, smothering them, or by other wicked Means, hastening their End, that is to say, murthering of them: And Watchmen being set to guard Houses that were shut up, when there has been but one person left, and perhaps, that one lying sick, that they have broke in and murthered that Body, and immediately thrown them out into the Dead-Cart! and so they have gone scarce cold to the Grave.

DISCUSSION QUESTIONS

This is a graphic and important description of the severity of the epidemic. Consider public health interventions (then and now) that could be implemented to reduce the tragedy; consider both physical and psychological elements. Extend the terror of this scene to current pandemic flu scenarios: What can we learn? What elements could be incorporated into modern-day emergency preparedness?

It was observable then, that this Calamity of the People made them very humble; for now, for about nine Weeks together, there died near a thousand a-Day, one Day with another, even by the Account of the weekly Bills, which yet I have Reason to be assur'd never gave a full Account, by many thousands; the Confusion being such, and the Carts working in the Dark, when they carried the Dead, that in some Places no Account at all was kept, but they work'd on; the Clerks and Sextons not attending for Weeks together, and not knowing what Number they carried. This Account is verified by the following Bills of Mortality.

	Of all Diseases	Of the Plague
Aug. 8 to Aug. 15	5319	3880
to 22	5568	4237
to 29	7496	6102
Aug. 29 to Sept. 5	8252	6088
to 12	7690	6544
to 19	8297	7165
to 26	6460	5533
Sept. 26 to Oct. 3	5720	4929
to 10	5068	4227
	59870	49705

So that the Gross of the People were carried off in these two Months; for as the whole Number which was brought in, to die of the Plague, was but 68590, here is fifty thousand of them, within a Trifle, in two Months; I say 50000, because as there wants 295 in the Number above, so there wants two Days of two Months in the Account of Time.

DISCUSSION QUESTIONS

Graph these plague mortality data. Be sure to include proper labels for x- and y-axes, units, title, etc. Graph a second figure indicating the proportionate mortality of plague. What do you see?

This was indeed a faithful Monitor to all People, that the Plague is not to be avoided by those that converse promiscu-ously in a Town infected, and People have it when they know it not, and that they likewise give it to others when they know not that they have it themselves; and in this Case, shutting up the WELL or removing the SICK will not do it, unless they can go back and shut up all those that the Sick had Convers'd with, even before they knew themselves to be sick, and none knows how far to carry that back, or where to stop; for none knows when, or where, or how they may have received the Infection, or from whom. This I take to be the Reason, which makes so many People talk of the Air being corrupted and infected, and that they need not be cautious of whom they converse with, for that the Contagion was in the Air. I have seen them in strange Agitations and Surprises on this Account. I have never come near any infected Body! says the disturbed Person, I have Convers'd with none but sound healthy People, and yet I have gotten the Distemper! I am sure I am struck from Heaven, says another, and he falls to the serious Part; again the first goes on exclaiming, I have come near no Infection, or any infected Person, I am sure it is in the Air; We draw in Death when we breath, and there-fore 'tis the Hand of God, there is no withstanding it; and this at last made many People, being hardened to the Danger, grow less concern'd at it, and less cautious towards the lat-ter End of the Time, and when it was come to its height, than they were at first; then with a kind of a Turkish Predestinar-ianism, they would say, if it pleas'd God to strike them, it was all one whether they went Abroad or staid at Home, they cou'd not escape it, and therefore they went boldly about even into infected Houses, and infected Company; visited sick People, and in short, lay in the Beds with their Wives or Relations when they were infected; and what was the Con-sequence? But the same that is the Consequence in Turkey, and in those Countries where they do those Things; namely, that they were infected too, and died by Hundreds and Thousands.

And here I must observe also, that the Plague, as I suppose all Distempers do, operated in a different Manner, on differ-ing Constitutions; some were immediately overwhelm'd with it, and it came to violent Fevers, Vomitings, unsufferable Head-aches, Pains in the Back, and so up to Ravings and Ragings with those Pains: Others with Swellings and Tumours in the Neck or Groyn, or Arm-pits, which till they could be broke put them into insufferable Agonies and Torment; while others, as I have observ'd, were silently infected, the Fever preying upon their Spirits insensibly, and they seeing little of it, till they fell into swooning, and faintings, and Death without pain. . . .

. . . It was very sad to reflect, how such a Person as this last mentioned above, had been a walking Destroyer, perhaps for a Week or Fortnight before that; how he had ruin'd those, that he would have hazarded his Life to save, and had been breathing Death upon them, even perhaps in his tender Kissing and Embracings of his own Children: Yet thus certainly it was, and often has been, and I cou'd give many particular Cases where it has been so; if then the Blow is thus insensibly stricken; if the Arrow flies thus unseen, and cannot be discovered; to what purpose are all the Schemes for shutting up or removing the sick People? those Schemes cannot take place, but upon those that appear to be sick, or to be infected; whereas there are among them, at the same time, Thousands of People, who seem to be well, but are all that while carrying Death with them into all Companies which they come into.

DISCUSSION QUESTIONS

Here De Foe returns to an exploration of asymptomatic infected persons exposing others. What public health intervention does this suggest? Does the fact of plague being transmitted by fleas have an impact on what can be done?

The grateful De Foe closes with:

A dreadful Plague in London was,
In the Year Sixty Five,
Which swept an Hundred Thousand Souls
Away; yet I alive!

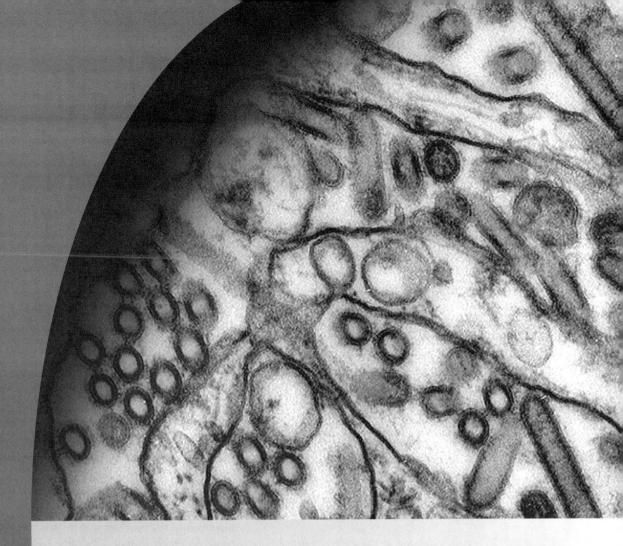

PART III

What About the Flu?

Just when it seems the coast might be clear, along comes another disease, influenza, which in 1918 on the heels of the First World War took hold to cause the illness and deaths of millions around the world. In the following article, authors Taubenberger and Morens explore the influenza pandemic of 1918.

FIGURE 3-1 Influenza virus particles.

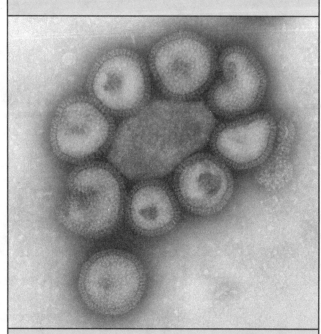

About this picture: "This colorized negative-stained transmission electron micrograph (TEM) depicts the ultrastructural details of a number of influenza virus particles, or 'virions.' A member of the taxonomic family *Orthomyxoviridae*, the influenza virus is a single-stranded RNA organism."

Source: CDC Public Health Image Library 1973; Courtesy of Dr. F. A. Murphy.

The flu is a contagious respiratory illness caused by influenza viruses. It can cause mild to severe illness and can lead to death. The best way to prevent this illness is by getting a flu vaccination each fall.

Every year in the United States, on average:

- 5% to 20% of the population get the flu,
- more than 200,000 people are hospitalized from flu complications, and
- about 36,000 people die from flu.

Some people, such as older people, young children, and people with certain health conditions, are at high risk for serious flu complications.

Influenza A and B are the two types of influenza viruses that cause epidemic human disease. Influenza A viruses are further categorized into subtypes on the basis of two surface antigens: hemagglutinin and neuraminidase. Influenza B viruses are not categorized into subtypes. Since 1977, influenza A (H1N1) viruses, influenza A (H3N2) viruses, and influenza B viruses have been in global circulation. In 2001, influenza A (H1N2) viruses that probably emerged after genetic reassortment between human A (H3N2) and A (H1N1) viruses began circulating widely. Both influenza A and B viruses are further separated into groups on the basis of antigenic characteristics. New influenza virus variants result from frequent antigenic change (i.e., antigenic drift) resulting from point mutations that occur during viral replication. Influenza B viruses undergo antigenic drift less rapidly than influenza A viruses.

READING 2
1918 Influenza: The Mother of All Pandemics

Jeffery K. Taubenberger and David M. Morens

Taubenberger JK, Morens DM. 1918 Influenza: The Mother of All Pandemics. *Emerg Infect Dis* [serial on the Internet]. 2006 Jan [accessed 12/31/07]. Available from http://www.cdc.gov/ncidod/EID/vol12no01/05-0979.htm.

The "Spanish" influenza pandemic of 1918–1919, which caused ≈50 million deaths worldwide, remains an ominous warning to public health. Many questions about its origins, its unusual epidemiologic features, and the basis of its pathogenicity remain unanswered. The public health implications of the pandemic therefore remain in doubt even as we now grapple with the feared emergence of a pandemic caused by H5N1 or other virus. However, new information about the 1918 virus is emerging, for example, sequencing of the entire genome from archival autopsy tissues.

But, the viral genome alone is unlikely to provide answers to some critical questions. Understanding the 1918 pandemic and its implications for future pandemics requires careful experimentation and in-depth historical analysis.

> *"Curiouser and curiouser!"* cried Alice
>
> Lewis Carroll, Alice's Adventures in Wonderland, 1865

An estimated one-third of the world's population (or ~500 million persons) were infected and had clinically apparent illnesses (1, 2) during the 1918–1919 influenza pandemic. The disease was exceptionally severe. Case fatality rates were > 2.5%, compared to < 0.1% in other influenza pandemics (3, 4). Total deaths were estimated at ~50 million (5–7) and were arguably as high as 100 million (7).

The impact of this pandemic was not limited to 1918–1919. All influenza A pandemics since that time, and indeed almost all cases of influenza A worldwide (excepting human infections from avian viruses such as H5N1 and H7N7), have been caused by descendants of the 1918 virus, including "drifted" H1N1 viruses and reassorted H2N2 and H3N2 viruses. The latter are composed of key genes from the 1918 virus, updated by subsequently incorporated avian influenza genes that code for novel surface proteins, making the 1918 virus indeed the "mother" of all pandemics.

In 1918, the cause of human influenza and its links to avian and swine influenza were unknown. Despite clinical and epidemiologic similarities to influenza pandemics of 1889, 1847, and even earlier, many questioned whether such an explosively fatal disease could be influenza at all. That question did not begin to be resolved until the 1930s, when closely related influenza viruses (now known to be H1N1 viruses) were isolated, first from pigs and shortly thereafter from humans. Seroepidemiologic studies soon linked both of these viruses to the 1918 pandemic (8). Subsequent research indicates that descendants of the 1918 virus still persist enzootically in pigs. They probably also circulated continuously in humans, undergoing gradual antigenic drift and causing annual epidemics, until the 1950s. With the appearance of a new H2N2 pandemic strain in 1957 ("Asian flu"), the direct H1N1 viral descendants of the 1918 pandemic strain disappeared from human circulation entirely, although the related lineage persisted enzootically in pigs. But in 1977, human H1N1 viruses suddenly "reemerged" from a laboratory freezer (9). They continue to circulate endemically and epidemically.

Thus in 2006, 2 major descendant lineages of the 1918 H1N1 virus, as well as 2 additional reassortant lineages, persist naturally: a human epidemic/endemic H1N1 lineage, a porcine enzootic H1N1 lineage (so-called classic swine flu), and the reassorted human H3N2 virus lineage, which like the human H1N1 virus, has led to a porcine H3N2 lineage. None of these viral descendants, however, approaches the pathogenicity of the 1918 parent virus. Apparently, the porcine H1N1 and H3N2 lineages uncommonly infect humans, and the human H1N1 and H3N2 lineages have both been associated with substantially lower rates of illness and death than the virus of 1918. In fact, current H1N1 death rates are even lower than those for H3N2 lineage strains (prevalent from 1968 until the present). H1N1 viruses descended from the 1918 strain, as well as H3N2 viruses, have now been cocirculating worldwide for 29 years and show little evidence of imminent extinction.

TRYING TO UNDERSTAND WHAT HAPPENED

By the early 1990s, 75 years of research had failed to answer a most basic question about the 1918 pandemic: why was it so fatal? No virus from 1918 had been isolated, but all of its apparent descendants caused substantially milder human disease. Moreover, examination of mortality data from the 1920s suggests that within a few years after 1918, influenza epidemics had settled into a pattern of annual epidemicity associated with strain drifting and substantially lowered death rates. Did some critical viral genetic event produce a 1918 virus of remarkable pathogenicity and then another critical genetic event occur soon after the 1918 pandemic to produce an attenuated H1N1 virus?

In 1995, a scientific team identified archival influenza autopsy materials collected in the autumn of 1918 and began the slow process of sequencing small viral RNA fragments to determine the genomic structure of the causative influenza virus (10). These efforts have now determined the complete genomic sequence of 1 virus and partial sequences from 4 others. The primary data from the above studies (11–17) and a number of reviews covering different aspects of the 1918 pandemic have recently been published (18–20) and confirm that the 1918 virus is the likely ancestor of all 4 of the human and swine H1N1 and H3N2 lineages, as well as the "extinct" H2N2 lineage. No known mutations correlated with high pathogenicity in other human or animal influenza viruses have been found in the 1918 genome, but ongoing studies to map virulence factors are yielding interesting results. The 1918 sequence data, however, leave unanswered questions about the origin of the virus (19) and about the epidemiology of the pandemic.

WHEN AND WHERE DID THE 1918 INFLUENZA PANDEMIC ARISE?

Before and after 1918, most influenza pandemics developed in Asia and spread from there to the rest of the world.

Confounding definite assignment of a geographic point of origin, the 1918 pandemic spread more or less simultaneously in 3 distinct waves during an ≈12-month period in 1918–1919, in Europe, Asia, and North America (the first wave was best described in the United States in March 1918). Historical and epidemiologic data are inadequate to identify the geographic origin of the virus (21), and recent phylogenetic analysis of the 1918 viral genome does not place the virus in any geographic context (19).

Although in 1918 influenza was not a nationally reportable disease and diagnostic criteria for influenza and pneumonia were vague, death rates from influenza and pneumonia in the United States had risen sharply in 1915 and 1916 because of a major respiratory disease epidemic beginning in December 1915 (22). Death rates then dipped slightly in 1917. The first pandemic influenza wave appeared in the spring of 1918, followed in rapid succession by much more fatal second and third waves in the fall and winter of 1918–1919, respectively (Figure 3-2). Is it possible that a poorly-adapted H1N1 virus was already beginning to spread in 1915, causing some serious illnesses but not yet sufficiently fit to initiate a pandemic? Data consistent with this possibility were reported at the time from European military camps (23), but a counter argument is that if a strain with a new hemagglutinin (HA) was causing enough illness to affect the US national death rates from pneumonia and influenza, it should have caused a pandemic sooner, and when it eventually did, in 1918, many people should have been immune or at least partially immunoprotected. "Herald" events in 1915, 1916, and possibly even in early 1918, if they occurred, would be difficult to identify.

The 1918 influenza pandemic had another unique feature, the simultaneous (or nearly simultaneous) infection of humans and swine. The virus of the 1918 pandemic likely expressed an antigenically novel subtype to which most humans and swine were immunologically naive in 1918 (12, 20). Recently published sequence and phylogenetic analyses suggest that the genes encoding the HA and neuraminidase (NA) surface proteins of the 1918 virus were derived from an avian-like influenza virus shortly before the start of the pandemic

and that the precursor virus had not circulated widely in humans or swine in the few decades before (12, 15, 24). More recent analyses of the other gene segments of the virus also support this conclusion. Regression analyses of human and swine influenza sequences obtained from 1930 to the present place the initial circulation of the 1918 precursor virus in humans at approximately 1915–1918 (20). Thus, the precursor was probably not circulating widely in humans until shortly before 1918, nor did it appear to have jumped directly from any species of bird studied to date (19). In summary, its origin remains puzzling.

WERE THE 3 WAVES IN 1918–1919 CAUSED BY THE SAME VIRUS? IF SO, HOW AND WHY?

Historical records since the 16th century suggest that new influenza pandemics may appear at any time of year, not necessarily in the familiar annual winter patterns of interpandemic years, presumably because newly shifted influenza viruses behave differently when they find a universal or highly susceptible human population. Thereafter, confronted by the selection pressures of population immunity, these pandemic viruses begin to drift genetically and eventually settle into a pattern of annual epidemic recurrences caused by the drifted virus variants.

In the 1918–1919 pandemic, a first or spring wave began in March 1918 and spread unevenly through the United States, Europe, and possibly Asia over the next 6 months (Figure 3-2). Illness rates were high, but death rates in most locales were

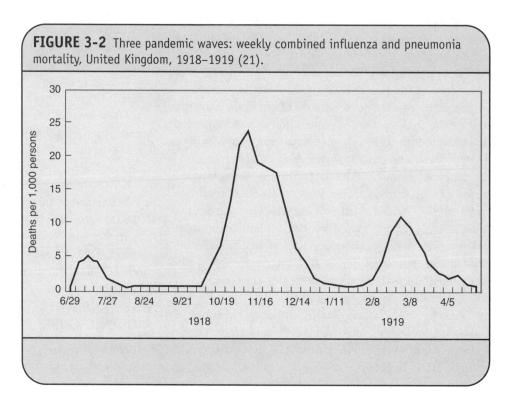

FIGURE 3-2 Three pandemic waves: weekly combined influenza and pneumonia mortality, United Kingdom, 1918–1919 (21).

not appreciably above normal. A second or fall wave spread globally from September to November 1918 and was highly fatal. In many nations, a third wave occurred in early 1919 (21). Clinical similarities led contemporary observers to conclude initially that they were observing the same disease in the successive waves. The milder forms of illness in all 3 waves were identical and typical of influenza seen in the 1889 pandemic and in prior interpandemic years. In retrospect, even the rapid progressions from uncomplicated influenza infections to fatal pneumonia, a hallmark of the 1918–1919 fall and winter waves, had been noted in the relatively few severe spring wave cases. The differences between the waves thus seemed to be primarily in the much higher frequency of complicated, severe, and fatal cases in the last 2 waves.

But 3 extensive pandemic waves of influenza within 1 year, occurring in rapid succession, with only the briefest of quiescent intervals between them, was unprecedented. The occurrence, and to some extent the severity, of recurrent annual outbreaks, are driven by viral antigenic drift, with an antigenic variant virus emerging to become dominant approximately every 2 to 3 years. Without such drift, circulating human influenza viruses would presumably disappear once herd immunity had reached a critical threshold at which further virus spread was sufficiently limited. The timing and spacing of influenza epidemics in interpandemic years have been subjects of speculation for decades. Factors believed to be responsible include partial herd immunity limiting virus spread in all but the most favorable circumstances, which include lower environmental temperatures and human nasal temperatures (beneficial to thermolabile viruses such as influenza), optimal humidity, increased crowding indoors, and imperfect ventilation due to closed windows and suboptimal airflow.

However, such factors cannot explain the 3 pandemic waves of 1918–1919, which occurred in the spring-summer, summer-fall, and winter (of the Northern Hemisphere), respectively. The first 2 waves occurred at a time of year normally unfavorable to influenza virus spread. The second wave caused simultaneous outbreaks in the Northern and Southern Hemispheres from September to November. Furthermore, the interwave periods were so brief as to be almost undetectable in some locales. Reconciling epidemiologically the steep drop in cases in the first and second waves with the sharp rises in cases of the second and third waves is difficult. Assuming even transient postinfection immunity, how could susceptible persons be too few to sustain transmission at 1 point, and yet enough to start a new explosive pandemic wave a few weeks later? Could the virus have mutated profoundly and almost simultaneously around the world, in the short periods between the successive waves? Acquiring viral drift

sufficient to produce new influenza strains capable of escaping population immunity is believed to take years of global circulation, not weeks of local circulation. And having occurred, such mutated viruses normally take months to spread around the world.

At the beginning of other "off season" influenza pandemics, successive distinct waves within a year have not been reported. The 1889 pandemic, for example, began in the late spring of 1889 and took several months to spread throughout the world, peaking in northern Europe and the United States late in 1889 or early in 1890. The second recurrence peaked in late spring 1891 (more than a year after the first pandemic appearance) and the third in early 1892 (21). As was true for the 1918 pandemic, the second 1891 recurrence produced of the most deaths. The 3 recurrences in 1889–1892, however, were spread over > 3 years, in contrast to 1918–1919, when the sequential waves seen in individual countries were typically compressed into ~8–9 months.

What gave the 1918 virus the unprecedented ability to generate rapidly successive pandemic waves is unclear. Because the only 1918 pandemic virus samples we have yet identified are from second-wave patients (16), nothing can yet be said about whether the first (spring) wave, or for that matter, the third wave, represented circulation of the same virus or variants of it. Data from 1918 suggest that persons infected in the second wave may have been protected from influenza in the third wave. But the few data bearing on protection during the second and third waves after infection in the first wave are inconclusive and do little to resolve the question of whether the first wave was caused by the same virus or whether major genetic evolutionary events were occurring even as the pandemic exploded and progressed. Only influenza RNA–positive human samples from before 1918, and from all 3 waves, can answer this question.

WHAT WAS THE ANIMAL HOST ORIGIN OF THE PANDEMIC VIRUS?

Viral sequence data now suggest that the entire 1918 virus was novel to humans in, or shortly before, 1918, and that it thus was not a reassortant virus produced from old existing strains that acquired 1 or more new genes, such as those causing the 1957 and 1968 pandemics. On the contrary, the 1918 virus appears to be an avian-like influenza virus derived in toto from an unknown source (17, 19), as its 8 genome segments are substantially different from contemporary avian influenza genes. Influenza virus gene sequences from a number of fixed specimens of wild birds collected circa 1918 show little difference from avian viruses isolated today, indicating that avian viruses likely undergo little antigenic change in their natural hosts even over long periods (24, 25).

For example, the 1918 nucleoprotein (NP) gene sequence is similar to that of viruses found in wild birds at the amino acid level but very divergent at the nucleotide level, which suggests considerable evolutionary distance between the sources of the 1918 NP and of currently sequenced NP genes in wild bird strains (13, 19). One way of looking at the evolutionary distance of genes is to compare ratios of synonymous to nonsynonymous nucleotide substitutions. A synonymous substitution represents a silent change, a nucleotide change in a codon that does not result in an amino acid replacement. A nonsynonymous substitution is a nucleotide change in a codon that results in an amino acid replacement. Generally, a viral gene subjected to immunologic drift pressure or adapting to a new host exhibits a greater percentage of nonsynonymous mutations, while a virus under little selective pressure accumulates mainly synonymous changes. Since little or no selection pressure is exerted on synonymous changes, they are thought to reflect evolutionary distance.

Because the 1918 gene segments have more synonymous changes from known sequences of wild bird strains than expected, they are unlikely to have emerged directly from an avian influenza virus similar to those that have been sequenced so far. This is especially apparent when one examines the differences at 4-fold degenerate codons, the subset of synonymous changes in which, at the third codon position, any of the 4 possible nucleotides can be substituted without changing the resulting amino acid. At the same time, the 1918 sequences have too few amino acid differences from those of wild-bird strains to have spent many years adapting only in a human or swine intermediate host. One possible explanation is that these unusual gene segments were acquired from a reservoir of influenza virus that has not yet been identified or sampled. All of these findings beg the question: where did the 1918 virus come from?

In contrast to the genetic makeup of the 1918 pandemic virus, the novel gene segments of the reassorted 1957 and 1968 pandemic viruses all originated in Eurasian avian viruses (*26*); both human viruses arose by the same mechanism—reassortment of a Eurasian wild waterfowl strain with the previously circulating human H1N1 strain. Proving the hypothesis that the virus responsible for the 1918 pandemic had a markedly different origin requires samples of human influenza strains circulating before 1918 and samples of influenza strains in the wild that more closely resemble the 1918 sequences.

WHAT WAS THE BIOLOGICAL BASIS FOR 1918 PANDEMIC VIRUS PATHOGENICITY?

Sequence analysis alone does not offer clues to the pathogenicity of the 1918 virus. A series of experiments are under way to model virulence in vitro and in animal models by using viral constructs containing 1918 genes produced by reverse genetics.

Influenza virus infection requires binding of the HA protein to sialic acid receptors on host cell surface. The HA receptor-binding site configuration is different for those influenza viruses adapted to infect birds and those adapted to infect humans. Influenza virus strains adapted to birds preferentially bind sialic acid receptors with α (2–3) linked sugars (27–29). Human-adapted influenza viruses are thought to preferentially bind receptors with α (2–6) linkages. The switch from this avian receptor configuration requires of the virus only 1 amino acid change (30), and the HAs of all 5 sequenced 1918 viruses have this change, which suggests that it could be a critical step in human host adaptation. A second change that greatly augments virus binding to the human receptor may also occur, but only 3 of 5 1918 HA sequences have it (16).

This means that at least 2 H1N1 receptor-binding variants cocirculated in 1918: 1 with high-affinity binding to the human receptor and 1 with mixed-affinity binding to both avian and human receptors. No geographic or chronologic indication exists to suggest that one of these variants was the precursor of the other, nor are there consistent differences between the case histories or histopathologic features of the 5 patients infected with them. Whether the viruses were equally transmissible in 1918, whether they had identical patterns of replication in the respiratory tree, and whether one or both also circulated in the first and third pandemic waves, are unknown.

In a series of in vivo experiments, recombinant influenza viruses containing between 1 and 5 gene segments of the 1918 virus have been produced. Those constructs bearing the 1918 HA and NA are all highly pathogenic in mice (31). Furthermore, expression microarray analysis performed on whole lung tissue of mice infected with the 1918 HA/NA recombinant showed increased upregulation of genes involved in apoptosis, tissue injury, and oxidative damage (32). These findings are unexpected because the viruses with the 1918 genes had not been adapted to mice; control experiments in which mice were infected with modern human viruses showed little disease and limited viral replication. The lungs of animals infected with the 1918 HA/NA construct showed bronchial and alveolar epithelial necrosis and a marked inflammatory infiltrate, which suggests that the 1918 HA (and possibly the NA) contain virulence factors for mice. The viral genotypic basis of this pathogenicity is not yet mapped. Whether pathogenicity in mice effectively models pathogenicity in humans is unclear. The potential role of the other 1918 proteins, singularly and in combination, is also unknown. Experiments to map further the genetic basis of virulence of the 1918 virus in various animal models are planned. These experiments may help define the viral component to the unusual pathogenicity of the 1918 virus but cannot address whether specific host factors in 1918 accounted for unique influenza mortality patterns.

WHY DID THE 1918 VIRUS KILL SO MANY HEALTHY YOUNG ADULTS?

The curve of influenza deaths by age at death has historically, for at least 150 years, been U-shaped (Figure 3-3), exhibiting mortality peaks in the very young and the very old, with a comparatively low frequency of deaths at all ages in between. In contrast, age-specific death rates in the 1918 pandemic exhibited a distinct pattern that has not been documented before or since: a "W-shaped" curve, similar to the familiar U-shaped curve but with the addition of a third (middle) distinct peak of deaths in young adults ≈20–40 years of age. Influenza and pneumonia death rates for those 15–34 years of age in 1918–1919, for example, were > 20 times higher than in previous years (35). Overall, nearly half of the influenza-related deaths in the 1918 pandemic were in young adults 20–40 years of age, a phenomenon unique to that pandemic year. The 1918 pandemic is also unique among influenza pandemics in that absolute risk of influenza death was higher in those < 65 years of age than in those < 65; persons < 65 years of age accounted for > 99% of all excess influenza-related deaths in 1918–1919.

In comparison, the < 65-year age group accounted for 36% of all excess influenza-related deaths in the 1957 H2N2 pandemic and 48% in the 1968 H3N2 pandemic (33).

A sharper perspective emerges when 1918 age-specific influenza morbidity rates (21) are used to adjust the W-shaped mortality curve (Figure 3-4, panels, A, B, and C [35, 37]). Persons < 35 years of age in 1918 had a disproportionately high influenza incidence (Figure 3-4, panel A). But even after adjusting age-specific deaths by age-specific clinical attack rates (Figure 3-4, panel B), a W-shaped curve with a case-fatality peak in young adults remains and is significantly different from U-shaped age-specific case fatality curves typically seen in

other influenza years, e.g., 1928–1929 (Figure 3-4, panel C). Also, in 1918 those 5 to 14 years of age accounted for a disproportionate number of influenza cases, but had a much lower death rate from influenza and pneumonia than other age groups. To explain this pattern, we must look beyond properties of the virus to host and environmental factors, possibly including immunopathology (e.g., antibody-dependent infection enhancement associated with prior virus exposures [38]) and exposure to risk cofactors such as coinfecting agents, medications, and environmental agents.

One theory that may partially explain these findings is that the 1918 virus had an intrinsically high virulence, tempered only in those patients who had been born before 1889, e.g., because of exposure to a then-circulating virus capable of providing partial immunoprotection against the 1918 virus strain only in persons old enough (> 35 years) to have been infected during that prior era (35). But this theory would present an additional paradox: an obscure precursor virus that left no detectable trace today would have had to have appeared and disappeared before 1889 and then reappeared more than 3 decades later.

Epidemiologic data on rates of clinical influenza by age, collected between 1900 and 1918, provide good evidence for the emergence of an antigenically novel influenza virus in 1918 (21). Jordan showed that from 1900 to 1917, the 5- to 15-year age group accounted for 11% of total influenza cases, while the > 65-year

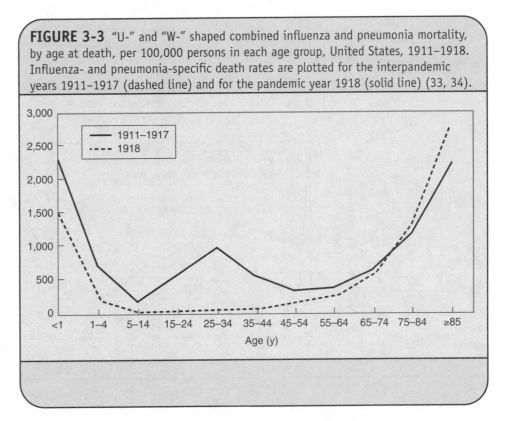

FIGURE 3-3 "U-" and "W-" shaped combined influenza and pneumonia mortality, by age at death, per 100,000 persons in each age group, United States, 1911–1918. Influenza- and pneumonia-specific death rates are plotted for the interpandemic years 1911–1917 (dashed line) and for the pandemic year 1918 (solid line) (33, 34).

FIGURE 3-4 Influenza plus pneumonia (P&I) (combined) age-specific incidence rates per 1,000 persons per age group (panel A), death rates per 1,000 persons, ill and well combined panel B), and case-fatality rates (panel C, solid line), US Public Health Service house-to-house surveys, 8 states, 1918 (36). A more typical curve of age-specific influenza case-fatality (panel C, dotted line) is taken from US Public Health Service surveys during 1928–1929 (37).

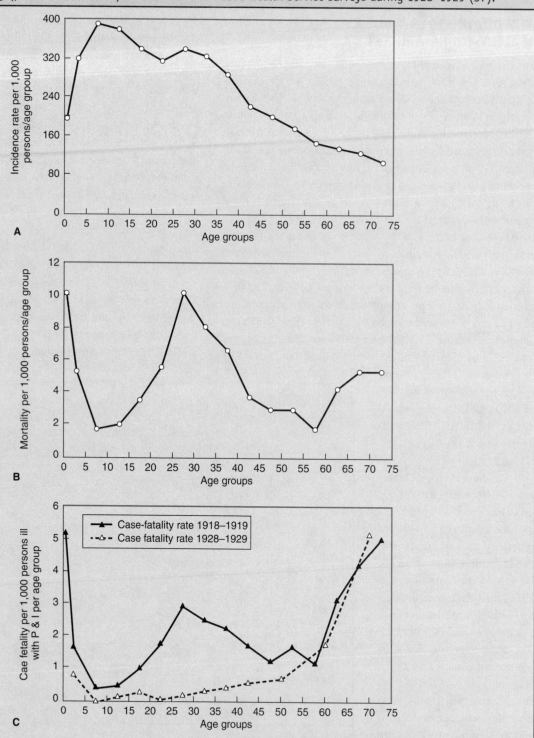

age group accounted for 6 % of influenza cases. But in 1918, cases in the 5 to 15-year-old group jumped to 25% of influenza cases (compatible with exposure to an antigenically novel virus strain), while the > 65-year age group only accounted for 0.6% of the influenza cases, findings consistent with previously acquired protective immunity caused by an identical or closely related viral protein to which older persons had once been exposed. Mortality data are in accord. In 1918, persons > 75 years had lower influenza and pneumonia case-fatality rates than they had during the prepandemic period of 1911–1917. At the other end of the age spectrum (Figure 3-3), a high proportion of deaths in infancy and early childhood in 1918 mimics the age pattern, if not the mortality rate, of other influenza pandemics.

COULD A 1918-LIKE PANDEMIC APPEAR AGAIN? IF SO, WHAT COULD WE DO ABOUT IT?

In its disease course and pathologic features, the 1918 pandemic was different in degree, but not in kind, from previous and subsequent pandemics. Despite the extraordinary number of global deaths, most influenza cases in 1918 (> 95% in most locales in industrialized nations) were mild and essentially indistinguishable from influenza cases today. Furthermore, laboratory experiments with recombinant influenza viruses containing genes from the 1918 virus suggest that the 1918 and 1918-like viruses would be as sensitive as other typical virus strains to the Food and Drug Administration–approved antiinfluenza drugs rimantadine and oseltamivir.

However, some characteristics of the 1918 pandemic appear unique: most notably, death rates were 5–20 times higher than expected. Clinically and pathologically, these high death rates appear to be the result of several factors, including a higher proportion of severe and complicated infections of the respiratory tract, rather than involvement of organ systems outside the normal range of the influenza virus. Also, the deaths were concentrated in an unusually young age group. Finally, in 1918, 3 separate recurrences of influenza followed each other with unusual rapidity, resulting in 3 explosive pandemic waves within a year's time (Figure 3-2). Each of these unique characteristics may reflect genetic features of the 1918 virus, but understanding them will also require examination of host and environmental factors.

Until we can ascertain which of these factors gave rise to the mortality patterns observed and learn more about the formation of the pandemic, predictions are only educated guesses. We can only conclude that since it happened once, analogous conditions could lead to an equally devastating pandemic.

Like the 1918 virus, H5N1 is an avian virus (39), though a distantly related one. The evolutionary path that led to pandemic emergence in 1918 is entirely unknown, but it appears to be different in many respects from the current situation with H5N1. There are no historical data, either in 1918 or in any other pandemic, for establishing that a pandemic "precursor" virus caused a highly pathogenic outbreak in domestic poultry, and no highly pathogenic avian influenza (HPAI) virus, including H5N1 and a number of others, has ever been known to cause a major human epidemic, let alone a pandemic. While data bearing on influenza virus human cell adaptation (e.g., receptor binding) are beginning to be understood at the molecular level, the basis for viral adaptation to efficient human-to-human spread, the chief prerequisite for pandemic emergence, is unknown for any influenza virus. The 1918 virus acquired this trait, but we do not know how, and we currently have no way of knowing whether H5N1 viruses are now in a parallel process of acquiring human-to-human transmissibility. Despite an explosion of data on the 1918 virus during the past decade, we are not much closer to understanding pandemic emergence in 2006 than we were in understanding the risk of H1N1 "swine flu" emergence in 1976.

Even with modern antiviral and antibacterial drugs, vaccines, and prevention knowledge, the return of a pandemic virus equivalent in pathogenicity to the virus of 1918 would likely kill > 100 million people worldwide. A pandemic virus with the (alleged) pathogenic potential of some recent H5N1 outbreaks could cause substantially more deaths.

Whether because of viral, host or environmental factors, the 1918 virus causing the first or 'spring' wave was not associated with the exceptional pathogenicity of the second (fall) and third (winter) waves. Identification of an influenza RNA-positive case from the first wave could point to a genetic basis for virulence by allowing differences in viral sequences to be highlighted. Identification of pre-1918 human influenza RNA samples would help us understand the timing of emergence of the 1918 virus. Surveillance and genomic sequencing of large numbers of animal influenza viruses will help us understand the genetic basis of host adaptation and the extent of the natural reservoir of influenza viruses. Understanding influenza pandemics in general requires understanding the 1918 pandemic in all its historical, epidemiologic, and biologic aspects.

Dr Taubenberger is chair of the Department of Molecular Pathology at the Armed Forces Institute of Pathology, Rockville, Maryland. His research interests include the molecular pathophysiology and evolution of influenza viruses.

Dr Morens is an epidemiologist with a long-standing interest in emerging infectious diseases, virology, tropical medicine, and medical history. Since 1999, he has worked at the National Institute of Allergy and Infectious Diseases.

DISCUSSION QUESTIONS

1. Compare and contrast the 1918 influenza pandemic and the 1665 epidemic of plague. What are similar and dissimilar features?

2. How does the writing approach Taubenberger takes differ from that of De Foe?

3. How does each of these authors wrestle with implications of how the respective diseases should be handled in the future?

REFERENCES FROM THE READING

1. Frost WH. Statistics of influenza morbidity. Public Health Rep. 1920; 35:584–97.

2. Burnet F, Clark E. Influenza: a survey of the last 50 years in the light of modern work on the virus of epidemic influenza. Melbourne: MacMillan; 1942.

3. Marks G, Beatty WK. Epidemics. New York: Scribners, 1976.

4. Rosenau MJ, Last JM. Maxcy-Rosenau preventative medicine and public health. New York: Appleton-Century-Crofts; 1980.

5. Crosby A. America's forgotten pandemic. Cambridge (UK): Cambridge University Press;1989.

6. Patterson KD, Pyle GF. The geography and mortality of the 1918 influenza pandemic. Bull Hist Med. 1991;65:4–21.

7. Johnson NPAS, Mueller J. Updating the accounts: global mortality of the 1918–1920 "Spanish" influenza pandemic. Bull Hist Med 2002;76:105–15.

8. Shope RE. The incidence of neutralizing antibodies for swine influenza virus in the sera of human beings of different ages. J Exp Med. 1936;63:669–84.

9. Kendal AP, Noble GR, Skehel JJ, Dowdle WR. Antigenic similarity of influenza A (H1N1) viruses from epidemics in 1977–1978 to "Scandinavian" strains isolated in epidemics of 1950–1951. Virology. 1978;89:632–6.

10. Taubenberger JK, Reid AH, Krafft AE, Bijwaard KE, Fanning TG. Initial genetic characterization of the 1918 "Spanish" influenza virus. Science. 1997; 275:1793–6.

11. Basler CF, Reid AH, Dybing JK, Janczewski TA, Fanning TG, Zheng H, et al. Sequence of the 1918 pandemic influenza virus nonstructural gene (NS) segment and characterization of recombinant viruses bearing the 1918 NS genes. Proc Natl Acad Sci USA 2001;98:2746–51.

12. Reid AH, Fanning TG, Hultin JV, Taubenberger JK. Origin and evolution of the 1918 "Spanish" influenza virus hemagglutinin gene. Proc Natl Acad Sci U S A 1999;96:1651–6.

13. Reid AH, Fanning TG, Janczewski TA, Lourens RM, and Taubenberger JK. Novel origin of the 1918 pandemic influenza virus nucleoprotein gene segment. J Virol. 2004;78:12462–70.

14. Reid AH, Fanning TG, Janczewski TA, McCall S, Taubenberger JK. Characterization of the 1918 "Spanish" influenza virus matrix gene segment. J Virol. 2002;76:10717–23.

15. Reid AH, Fanning TG, Janczewski TA, Taubenberger JK. Characterization of the 1918 "Spanish" influenza virus neuraminidase gene. Proc Natl Acad Sci U S A 2000;97:6785–90.

16. Reid AH, Janczewski TA, Lourens RM, Elliot AJ, Daniels RS, Berry CL, et al. 1918 influenza pandemic caused by highly conserved viruses with two receptor-binding variants. Emerg Infect Dis. 2003;9:1249–53.

17. Taubenberger JK, Reid AH, Lourens RM, Wang R, Jin G, Fanning TG. Characterization of the 1918 influenza virus polymerase genes. Nature. 2005;437:889–93.

18. Reid AH, Taubenberger JK. The 1918 flu and other influenza pandemics: "over there" and back again. Lab Invest. 1999;79:95–101.

19. Reid AH, Taubenberger JK, Fanning TG. Evidence of an absence: the genetic origins of the 1918 pandemic influenza virus. Nat Rev Microbiol. 2004;2:909–14.

20. Taubenberger JK, Reid AH, Fanning TG. The 1918 influenza virus: a killer comes into view. Virology. 2000;274:241–5.

21. Jordan E. Epidemic influenza: a survey. Chicago: American Medical Association, 1927.

22. Capps J, Moody A. The recent epidemic of grip. JAMA. 1916;67: 1349–50.

23. Oxford JS, Sefton A, Jackson R, Innes W, Daniels RS, Johnson NP. World War I may have allowed the emergence of "Spanish" influenza. Lancet Infect Dis. 2002;2:111–4.

24. Fanning TG, Slemons RD, Reid AH, Janczewski TA, Dean J, Taubenberger JK. 1917 avian influenza virus sequences suggest that the 1918 pandemic virus did not acquire its hemagglutinin directly from birds. J Virol. 2002;76:7860–2.

25. Reid AH, Fanning TG, Slemons RD, Janczewski TA, Dean J, Taubenberger JK. Relationship of pre-1918 avian influenza HA and NP sequences to subsequent avian influenza strains. Avian Dis. 2003;47:921–5.

26. Bean W, Schell M, Katz J, Kawaoka Y, Naeve C, Gorman O, et al. Evolution of the H3 influenza virus hemagglutinin from human and nonhuman hosts. J Virol. 1992;66:1129–38.

27. Weis W, Brown JH, Cusack S, Paulson JC, Skehel JJ, Wiley DC. Structure of the influenza virus haemagglutinin complexed with its receptor, sialic acid. Nature. 1988;333:426–31.

28. Gambaryan AS, Tuzikov AB, Piskarev VE, Yamnikova SS, Lvov DK, Robertson JS, et al. Specification of receptor-binding phenotypes of influenza virus isolates from different hosts using synthetic sialylglycopolymers: non-egg-adapted human H1 and H3 influenza A and influenza B viruses share a common high binding affinity for 6′-sialyl(N-acetyllactosamine). Virology. 1997;232: 345–50.

29. Matrosovich M, Gambaryan A, Teneberg S, Piskarev VE, Yamnikova SS, Lvov DK, et al. Avian influenza A viruses differ from human viruses by recognition of sialyloigosaccharides and gangliosides and by a higher conservation of the HA receptor-binding site. Virology. 1997;233:224–34.

30. Glaser L, Stevens J, Zamarin D, Wilson IA, Garcia-Sastre A, Tumpey TM, et al. Asingle amino acid substitution in the 1918 influenza virus hemagglutinin changes the receptor binding specificity. J Virol. 2005;79:11533–6.

31. Kobasa D, Takada A, Shinya K, Hatta M, Halfmann P, Theriault S, et al. Enhanced virulence of influenza A viruses with the haemagglutinin of the 1918 pandemic virus. Nature. 2004;431:703–7.

32. Kash JC, Basler CF, Garcia-Sastre A, Carter V, Billharz R, Swayne DE, et al. Global host immune response: pathogenesis and transcriptional profiling of type A influenza viruses expressing the hemagglutinin and neuraminidase genes from the 1918 pandemic virus. J Virol. 2004;78:9499–511.

33. Grove RD, Hetzel AM. Vital statistics rates in the United States: 1940–1960. Washington: US Government Printing Office, 1968.

34. Linder FE, Grove RD. Vital statistics rates in the United States: 1900–1940. Washington: US Government Printing Office, 1943.

35. Simonsen L, Clarke MJ, Schonberger LB, Arden NH, Cox NJ, Fukuda K. Pandemic versus epidemic influenza mortality: a pattern of changing age distribution. J Infect Dis 1998;178:53–60.

36. Frost WH. The epidemiology of influenza. Public Health Rep. 1919;34:1823–61.

37. Collins SD. Age and sex incidence of influenza and pneumonia morbidity and mortality in the epidemic of 1928-1929 with comparative data for the epidemic of 1918–1919. Public Health Rep. 1931;46:1909–37.

38. Majde JA. Influenza: Learn from the past. ASM News. 1996;62:514.

39. Peiris JS, Yu WC, Leung CW, Cheung CY, Ng WF, Nicholls JM, et al. Re-emergence of fatal human influenza A subtype H5N1 disease. Lancet. 2004;363:617–9.

More on the Epidemiology of Influenza

Here are some of WH Frost's own words, written in *The Epidemiology of Influenza* in 1919. (Note that Public Health Reports has digitized years' worth of the original reports. This one is available online at the source listed below. This is an incredible boon to those wishing to study public health history!)

READING 3
Public Health Weekly Report for August 15, 1919—
The Epidemiology of Influenza

W.H. Frost, Surgeon, United States Public Health Service

Public Health Weekly Report for August 15, 1919. Public Health Reports, Volume 34(33); August 15, 1919. [Available at http://www.pubmedcentral.nih.gov/tocrender.fcgi?iid=149567; accessed 12/30/07.]

The history of influenza, so far as it is known, that is, for several centuries, comprises a series of long cycles in which great pandemics alternate with periods of relative quiescence, the length of cycles as measured by the intervals between pandemics being usually a matter of decades. The special characteristics of influenza pandemics are their wide and rapid extension, their high attack rates, and their great effect upon general mortality rates. Since these cycles are undoubtedly of fundamental significance in the natural history of influenza, any proper discussion of the epidemiology of the disease should cover at least one full cycle, preferably the last, from 1889 to the present. The material for such a discussion must, however, be collected from many and diverse sources and laboriously fitted together, since there is no concrete, specific, and continuous record of the prevalence or mortality of influenza during such a period of years.

LACK OF SPECIFIC RECORDS

During great epidemics there are abundant, if not exact, records of prevalence, and the resulting mortality can be determined with fair precision, even though a large proportion of the deaths are classified under diagnoses other than influenza. In the intervals between epidemics influenza becomes inextricably confused with other respiratory diseases, having a general clinical resemblance but no definite etiological entity, so that the record of prevalence and even of mortality is virtually lost. The first requisites for epidemiological study, namely, clear differential diagnosis and systematic records of occurrence are therefore lacking in influenza.

In the absence of these essential records, statistics of mortality from the group comprising influenza and all forms of pneumonia afford, perhaps, the nearest approximation to a record of influenza. It is not intended to suggest that the mortality from this group of diseases furnishes in any sense a measure of the prevalence of influenza, but only that it furnishes an index, since it is well established that the epidemic prevalence of influenza markedly affects the mortality from this group of diseases, and since it is at least probable that even in nonepidemic periods there may be some intimate and constant relation between the prevalence of influenza and the mortality from pneumonia.

The following discussion, which is necessarily confined to a few broad outlines, is, accordingly, based on records of mortality from influenza and pneumonia for a series of years, statistics of general mortality during the recent epidemic, and limited morbidity statistics.

Dr. Frost then provides a detailed analysis of previous years' influenza and mortality data.

TABLE 3-1 Death rates per 100,000 of population from Pneumonia (all forms) and from Influenza in Massachusetts, 1887–1916 inclusive.

Year.	Total per year.	Jan.	Feb.	Mar.	Apr.	May.	June.	July.	Aug.	Sept.	Oct.	Nov.	Dec.
1887.....	138.8	19.5	16.7	1.9	22.6	16.1	7.7	5.5	4.1	5.6	9.0	14.8	15.3
1888.....	172.7	24.7	25.1	26.4	21.3	16.4	8.0	5.5	4.0	6.2	11.4	9.8	13.9
1889.....	156.6	17.9	16.3	21.1	19.8	14.9	7.5	5.3	5.2	5.4	10.6	13.2	19.3
1890.....	180.0	47.8	17.7	17.6	20.1	12.7	8.5	6.2	4.8	5.0	9.4	11.8	18.3
1891.....	188.5	20.6	16.4	20.6	25.1	23.9	10.1	5.9	4.0	4.0	7.7	13.8	36.4
1892.....	213.0	61.5	25.2	23.1	21.4	17.0	8.3	5.4	4.2	6.8	8.5	12.5	19.0
1893.....	225.8	27.3	25.4	28.6	33.1	27.3	11.1	8.0	5.0	6.1	9.8	14.3	31.9
1894.....	166.0	32.8	19.9	22.7	18.5	14.0	8.5	5.1	5.1	6.8	8.2	11.3	13.6
1895.....	184.1	19.1	34.4	30.8	20.9	14.4	7.6	5.6	5.3	4.7	10.5	13.4	17.3
1896.....	182.0	19.5	20.7	24.9	25.9	18.7	10.3	7.6	4.5	7.6	10.7	12.7	18.8
1897.....	181.6	21.1	24.9	31.5	19.7	15.2	10.2	7.0	4.5	6.0	11.7	13.1	16.9
1898.....	156.0	18.8	17.1	18.5	18.7	15.7	6.6	6.0	4.8	5.6	10.6	12.8	21.0
1899.....	181.3	37.5	25.8	20.6	18.4	14.0	8.9	5.0	4.8	5.8	8.2	13.2	19.0
1900.....	188.3	22.7	21.1	42.0	30.5	17.6	8.7	5.3	4.3	5.3	6.2	9.9	14.7
1901.....	167.7	22.6	26.6	26.2	19.9	13.9	7.7	3.4	3.4	5.7	9.1	14.2	15.1
1902.....	158.9	15.7	18.9	19.9	16.8	15.5	8.0	6.2	5.3	5.7	11.8	14.5	20.6
1903.....	172.5	25.2	25.8	25.4	18.1	16.8	8.2	7.0	4.5	4.6	7.7	13.3	18.9
1904.....	172.1	22.6	22.7	24.1	21.2	14.2	6.7	5.9	4.4	6.5	9.4	15.9	19.5
1905.....	178.3	24.7	27.7	23.6	17.1	15.5	8.5	5.4	4.8	6.2	8.9	15.8	20.0
1906.....	174.1	22.5	21.9	24.1	21.7	14.9	5.1	6.2	5.0	6.0	9.4	13.8	21.0
1907.....	180.4	25.5	24.4	23.4	18.3	14.3	9.5	5.1	5.1	7.1	9.3	12.7	26.9
1908.....	165.8	26.6	22.2	21.1	19.4	13.5	6.6	4.9	5.8	6.4	9.2	12.4	17.6
1909.....	170.3	22.1	20.0	26.1	20.1	16.0	9.7	5.1	5.0	5.4	8.9	13.6	18.3
1910.....	197.6	24.1	20.7	27.5	23.3	16.9	9.7	7.3	6.3	9.1	12.3	17.0	23.6
1911.....	174.4	22.6	27.1	23.9	20.2	16.9	7.2	6.7	6.1	6.7	9.0	11.8	16.2
1912.....	152.0	19.8	20.2	21.2	16.4	13.3	6.2	5.0	4.1	5.8	9.5	10.5	19.9
1913.....	172.2	23.5	22.8	24.9	19.3	17.1	10.7	6.2	5.4	6.7	8.3	10.4	16.8
1914.....	166.0	22.9	20.1	23.2	20.4	15.2	8.2	5.1	5.5	6.0	10.1	12.6	16.8
1915.....	176.0	17.8	19.3	28.5	27.7	13.6	6.6	7.1	5.8	6.0	8.8	9.8	22.1
1916.....	176.6	35.6	25.5	23.0	17.3	14.0	7.4	5.3	4.1	5.9	7.6	12.8	18.8

Source: W. H. Frost, Surgeon, United States Public Health Service.

Here he provides a graphic of the above data:

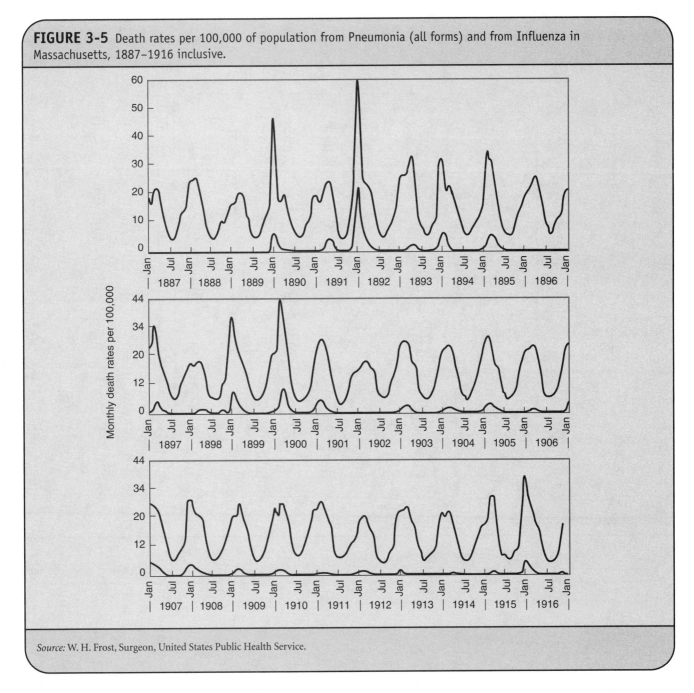

FIGURE 3-5 Death rates per 100,000 of population from Pneumonia (all forms) and from Influenza in Massachusetts, 1887–1916 inclusive.

Source: W. H. Frost, Surgeon, United States Public Health Service.

Using these techniques, he then creates a graph to provide a comparison with the 1918 mortality rates for the three cities under study.

DISCUSSION QUESTIONS

1. What step in an outbreak investigation does Frost's above work most closely represent? Why is it important in general, and in the context of the 1918 influenza pandemic?

2. Compare and contrast the data tables provided by De Foe with Frost's. How are they similar/dissimilar?

3. What are the research questions underlying De Foe's, Frost's, and Semmelweis' works? For each of the above investigations state their:
   a. Research question
   b. Null hypothesis
   c. Alternative hypothesis

FIGURE 3-6 Annual death rates per 100,000 from Influenza and Pneumonia (all forms) by months, (1910–1918).

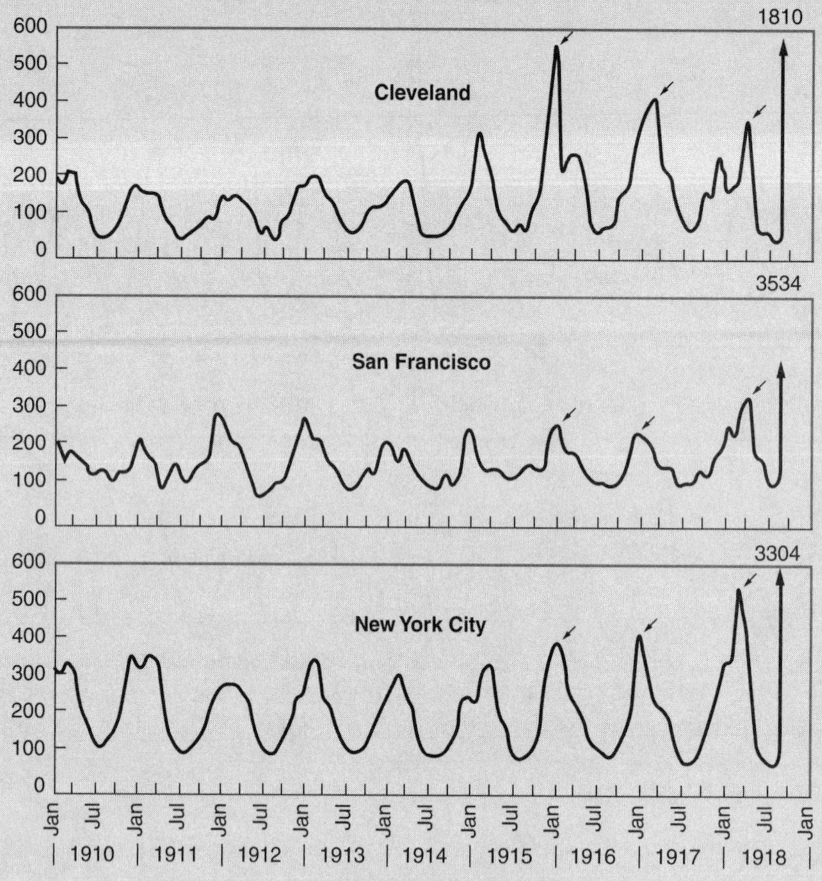

Source: W. H. Frost, Surgeon, United States Public Health Service.

Influenza Today

Even today, even in the absence of the avian influenza we have feared greatly, influenza is nothing to be taken lightly. The following MMWR article describes the relationship between influenza in the 2007–8 season and how it may relate to the composition of the vaccine as well as response to antiviral medications that are administered in response to influenza. Note how many things are related to one another—strain to morbidity and mortality to current and future vaccinations to treatment responses—and then back to the virus itself. When you get to the analytic methods section, be sure to read the case-control study that evaluated influenza and note the unique methods used in that approach.

READING 4
Update: Influenza Activity—United States, September 30, 2007–April 5, 2008, and Composition of the 2008–09 Influenza Vaccine

Centers for Disease Control and Prevention. Update: Influenza Activity—United States, September 30, 2007–April 5, 2008, and Composition of the 2008–09 Influenza Vaccine. *MMWR.* 2008:57;404–9.

This report summarizes U.S. influenza activity* since September 30, 2007, the start of the 2007–08 influenza season, and updates the previous summary (1). Low levels of influenza activity were reported from October through early December. Activity increased from mid-December and peaked in mid-February.

VIRAL SURVEILLANCE

During September 30, 2007–April 5, 2008,[†] World Health Organization (WHO) and National Respiratory and Enteric Virus Surveillance System (NREVSS) collaborating laboratories in the United States reported testing 185,938 specimens for influenza viruses, and 34,380 (18.5%) tested positive (Figure 3-7). Of these, 25,456 (74.0%) were influenza A viruses, and 8,924 (26.0%) were influenza B viruses. A total of 7,715 (30.3%) of the 25,456 influenza A viruses have been subtyped: 2,110 (27.3%) were influenza A (H1N1) viruses, and 5,605 (72.7%) were influenza A (H3N2) viruses. The percentage of specimens testing positive for influenza first exceeded 10% during the week ending January 12 and peaked at 32.0% during the week ending February 16.

For the week ending April 5, 13.2% of specimens tested for influenza were positive. Although influenza A (H1N1) viruses predominated through mid-January, the proportion of reported influenza viruses that were A (H3N2) viruses increased rapidly during January, and during the week ending January 26, influenza A (H3N2) became the predominant virus for the season overall.

This season, more influenza A viruses than influenza B viruses have been identified in all surveillance regions. However, for weeks 13 and 14 (March 23–April 5), more influenza B than influenza A viruses were reported. Among influenza A viruses, influenza A (H3N2) has predominated in

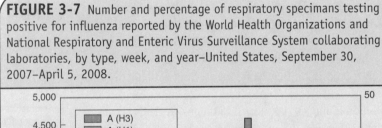

FIGURE 3-7 Number and percentage of respiratory specimens testing positive for influenza reported by the World Health Organizations and National Respiratory and Enteric Virus Surveillance System collaborating laboratories, by type, week, and year–United States, September 30, 2007–April 5, 2008.

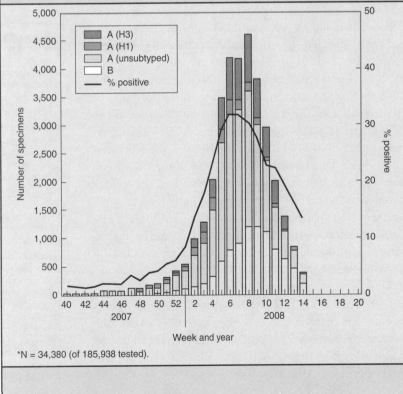

*N = 34,380 (of 185,938 tested).

---

*The CDC influenza surveillance system collects five categories of information from ten data sources. Viral surveillance: U.S. World Health Organization collaborating laboratories, the National Respiratory and Enteric Virus Surveillance System, and novel influenza A virus case reporting. Outpatient illness surveillance: U.S. Influenza Sentinel Provider Surveillance Network and the U.S. Department of Veterans Affairs/U.S. Department of Defense BioSense Outpatient Surveillance System. Mortality: 122 Cities Mortality Reporting System and influenza-associated pediatric mortality reports. Hospitalizations: Emerging Infections Program and New Vaccine Surveillance Network. Summary of geographic spread of influenza: state and territorial epidemiologist reports.

[†]Data as of April 5, 2008.

the East North Central, East South Central, Mid-Atlantic, New England, South Atlantic, West North Central, and West South Central regions, and influenza A (H1N1) has predominated in the Mountain and Pacific regions.

COMPOSITION OF THE 2008–09 INFLUENZA VACCINE

The Food and Drug Administration's Vaccines and Related Biological Products Advisory Committee recommended that the 2008–09 trivalent influenza vaccine for the United States contain A/Brisbane/59/2007-like (H1N1), A/Brisbane/10/2007-like (H3N2), and B/Florida/4/2006-like viruses. This represents a change in all three components from the 2007–08 influenza vaccine formulation used in the United States. These recommendations were based on antigenic analyses of recently isolated influenza viruses, epidemiologic data, post-vaccination serologic studies in humans, and the availability of candidate vaccine strains and reagents.

ANTIGENIC CHARACTERIZATION

States are requested to submit a subset of their influenza virus isolates to CDC for further antigenic characterization. Since September 30, 2007, CDC has antigenically characterized 608 influenza viruses submitted by WHO collaborating laboratories in the United States: 290 influenza A (H1N1), 161 influenza A (H3N2), and 157 influenza B viruses. A total of 200 (69%) of 290 influenza A (H1N1) viruses were characterized as A/Solomon Islands/3/2006-like, the influenza A (H1N1) component of the 2007–08 influenza vaccine for the Northern Hemisphere, and 70 (24%) were characterized as A/Brisbane/59/2007-like, the recommended H1N1 component of the 2008–09 Northern Hemisphere vaccine. Thirty-five (22%) of the 161 influenza A (H3N2) viruses were characterized as A/Wisconsin/67/2005-like, the influenza A (H3N2) component of the 2007–08 influenza vaccine for the Northern Hemisphere. One hundred fifteen (71%) of the 161 viruses were characterized as A/Brisbane/10/2007-like, the recommended influenza A (H3N2) component for the 2008 Southern Hemisphere and 2008–09 Northern Hemisphere vaccines. Influenza B viruses currently circulating can be divided into two antigenically distinct lineages represented by B/Victoria/02/87 and B/Yamagata/16/88. Eight (5%) of the 157 influenza B viruses characterized belong to the B/Victoria lineage of viruses. Six (75%) of these viruses from the B/Victoria lineage were characterized as B/Malaysia/2506/2004-like, the influenza B component of the 2007–08 influenza vaccine. One hundred forty-nine (95%) of the 157 influenza B viruses characterized belong to the B/Yamagata lineage.

OUTPATIENT ILLNESS SURVEILLANCE

For the week ending April 5, 2008, the percentage of outpatient visits for influenza-like illness (ILI)[§] reported by approximately 1,400 U.S. sentinel providers in 50 states, Chicago, the District of Columbia, New York City, and the U.S. Virgin Islands was 1.7%, which was below the national baseline of 2.2%.[¶]

This season, the percentage of outpatient visits for ILI exceeded the national baseline for 13 consecutive weeks. The percentage of outpatient visits for ILI first exceeded baseline during the week ending December 29 and peaked at 5.9% during the week ending February 16. The percentage of outpatient visits for acute respiratory illness (ARI)[**] reported by approximately 350 U.S. Department of Defense (DoD) and 800 Department of Veterans Affairs (VA) BioSense[††] outpatient treatment facilities for the week ending April 5 was 2.2%, which was below the national baseline of 3.2%[§§] (Figure 3-8).

STATE-SPECIFIC ACTIVITY LEVELS

During the week ending April 5, 2008, influenza activity was reported as widespread[¶¶] in six states (Connecticut, Maine,

---

[§]Defined as a temperature of > 100.0°F (> 37.8°C), oral or equivalent, and cough and/or sore throat, in the absence of a known cause other than influenza.

[¶]The national and regional baselines are the mean percentage of visits for ILI during noninfluenza weeks for the previous three seasons plus two standard deviations. A noninfluenza week is a week during which < 10% of specimens tested positive for influenza. National and regional percentages of patient visits for ILI are weighted on the basis of state population. Use of the national baseline for regional data is not appropriate.

[**]Based on *International Classification of Diseases, Ninth Revision* codes for ARI: 460-66 and 480-88.

[††]BioSense is a national surveillance system that receives, analyzes, and evaluates health data from multiple sources, include 1) approximately 1,150 VA/DoD hospitals and ambulatory-care clinics; 2) multihospital systems, local hospitals, and state and regional syndromic surveillance systems in 37 states; and 3) Laboratory Corporation of America (LabCorp) test results.

[§§]The national, regional, and age-specific baselines are the mean percentage of visits for ARI during noninfluenza weeks for the previous three seasons plus two standard deviations. A noninfluenza week is a week during which < 10% of specimens tested positive for influenza. Use of a national baseline for regional data is not appropriate.

[¶¶]Levels of activity are 1) no activity; 2) sporadic: isolated laboratory-confirmed influenza cases or a laboratory-confirmed outbreak in one institution, with no increase in activity; 3) local: increased ILI , or at least two institutional outbreaks (ILI or laboratory-confirmed influenza) in one region with recent laboratory evidence of influenza in that region (virus activity no greater than sporadic in other regions); 4) regional: increased ILI activity or institutional outbreaks (ILI or laboratory-confirmed influenza) in at least two but less than half of the regions in the state with recent laboratory evidence of influenza in those regions; and 5) widespread: increased ILI activity or institutional outbreaks (ILI or laboratory-confirmed influenza) in at least half the regions in the state with recent laboratory evidence of influenza in the state.

FIGURE 3-8 Percentage of outpatient visits for influenza-like illness (ILI) and acute respiratory illness (ARI) reported by the Sentinel Provider Surveillance Network and the U.S. Department of Veterans Affairs/U.S. Department of Defense BioSense Outpatient Surveillance System, by week and year–United States, 2004–05, 2005–06, 2006–07, and 2007–08 influenza seasons.

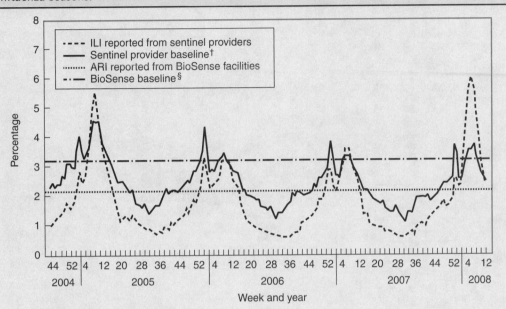

*As of April 5, 2008.

†The national and regional baselines are the mean percentage of visits for ILI during noninfluenza weeks for the preious three seasons plus two standard deviations. A noninfluenza week is a week during which <10% of specimens tested positive for influenza. National and regional percentages of patient visits for ILI are weighted on the basis of state population. Use of the national baseline for regional data is not appropriate.

§The national, regional, and age-specific baselines are the mean percentage of visit for ARI during noninfluenza weeks for the previous three seasons plus two standard deviations. A noninfluenza week is a week during which <10% of specimens tested positive for influenza. Use of national baseline for regional data is not appropriate.

Maryland, New York, Pennsylvania, and Vermont) (Figure 3-9). In addition, regional activity was reported by 11 states (Alaska, California, Colorado, Hawaii, Illinois, Iowa, Massachusetts, New Jersey, North Dakota, Oregon, and Washington); local influenza activity was reported by 23 states (Alabama, Arizona, Georgia, Idaho, Indiana, Kentucky, Louisiana, Michigan, Minnesota, Montana, Nebraska, Nevada, New Hampshire, New Mexico, North Carolina, Ohio, Rhode Island, South Carolina, South Dakota, Texas, Utah, Virginia, and Wyoming); and sporadic activity was reported by the District of Columbia and 10 states (Arkansas, Delaware, Florida, Kansas, Mississippi, Missouri, Oklahoma, Tennessee, West Virginia, and Wisconsin). Activity peaked during weeks 7 and 8 (February 10–23), when 49 states reported widespread influenza activity and one state reported regional activity.

INFLUENZA-ASSOCIATED PEDIATRIC HOSPITALIZATIONS

Pediatric hospitalizations associated with laboratory-confirmed influenza infections are monitored by two population-based surveillance networks, the Emerging Infections Program (EIP) and the New Vaccine Surveillance Network (NVSN). During November 4, 2007–March 22, 2008, the preliminary laboratory-confirmed influenza-associated hospitalization rate reported by NVSN for children aged 0–4 years was 5.61 per 10,000. During September 30, 2007–March 29, 2008, EIP sites reported a preliminary laboratory-confirmed influenza-associated hospitalization rate of 1.32 per 10,000 for children aged 0–17 years. For children aged 0–4 years, the rate was 3.47 per 10,000, and for children aged 5–17 years, the rate was 0.45 per 10,000. Differences in the rate estimates

FIGURE 3-9 Estimated influenza activity levels reported by state epideiologists, by state and level of activity*— United States, week ending April 5, 2008.

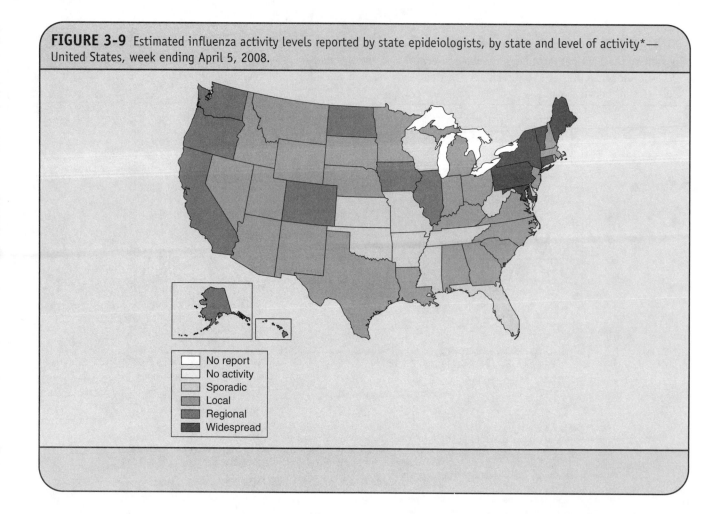

Legend:
- No report
- No activity
- Sporadic
- Local
- Regional
- Widespread

between the NVSN and the EIP systems likely result from the different case-finding methods and the different populations monitored.***

***NVSN conducts surveillance in Monroe County, New York; Hamilton County, Ohio; and Davidson County, Tennessee. NVSN provides population-based estimates of laboratory-confirmed influenza hospitalization rates in children aged < 5 years admitted to NVSN hospitals with fever or respiratory symptoms. Children are prospectively enrolled, and respiratory samples are collected and tested by viral culture and reverse transcription–polymerase chain reaction (RT-PCR). EIP conducts surveillance in 60 counties associated with 12 metropolitan areas: San Francisco, California; Denver, Colorado; New Haven, Connecticut; Atlanta, Georgia; Baltimore, Maryland; Minneapolis/St. Paul, Minnesota; Albuquerque, New Mexico; Las Cruces, New Mexico; Albany, New York; Rochester, New York; Portland, Oregon; and Nashville, Tennessee. EIP conducts surveillance for laboratory-confirmed, influenza-related hospitalizations in persons aged < 18 years. Hospital laboratory and admission databases and infection-control logs are reviewed to identify children with a positive influenza test (i.e., viral culture, direct fluorescent antibody assays, RT-PCR, or a commercial rapid antigen test) from testing conducted as a part of their routine care.

PNEUMONIA AND INFLUENZA-RELATED MORTALITY

Pneumonia and influenza (P&I) was listed as an underlying or contributing cause of death for 8.9% of all deaths reported through the 122 Cities Mortality Reporting System for the week ending April 5, 2008. This percentage was above the epidemic threshold of 6.9% for the week††† and marked the thirteenth consecutive week that the proportion of all deaths attributed to P&I was above the epidemic threshold (Figure 3-10). The proportion of deaths from P&I exceeded the epidemic threshold during week ending January 5 and peaked at 9.1% during the week ending March 15.

†††The expected seasonal baseline proportion of P&I deaths reported by the 122 Cities Mortality Reporting System is projected using a robust regression procedure in which a periodic regression model is applied to the observed percentage of deaths from P&I that occurred during the preceding 5 years. The epidemic threshold is 1.645 standard deviations above the seasonal baseline.

FIGURE 3-10 Percentage of all deaths attributed to pneumonia and influenza (P & I) reported by the 122 Cities Mortality Reporting System, by week and year, 2003–2008.

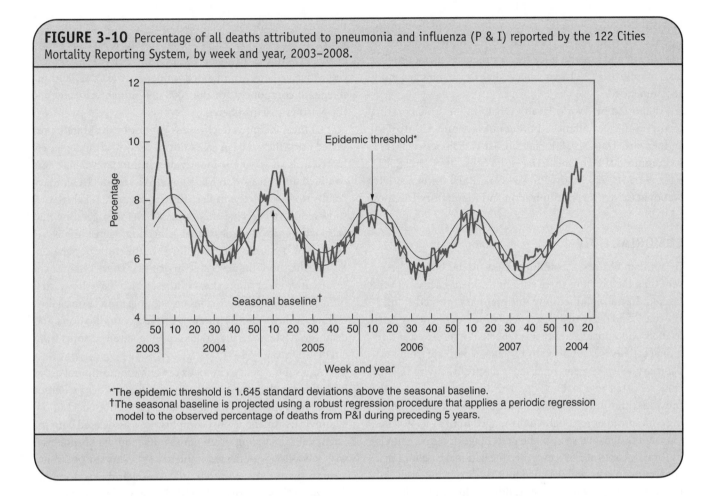

*The epidemic threshold is 1.645 standard deviations above the seasonal baseline.
†The seasonal baseline is projected using a robust regression procedure that applies a periodic regression model to the observed percentage of deaths from P&I during preceding 5 years.

INFLUENZA-RELATED PEDIATRIC MORTALITY

During September 30, 2007–April 5, 2008, a total of 65 pediatric deaths among children aged < 18 years associated with laboratory-confirmed influenza were reported from 26 states, New York City, and Chicago through the National Notifiable Diseases Surveillance System. The median age of decedents was 4.5 years (range: 1 month to 17.8 years). During the preceding three influenza seasons, the total number of influenza-related pediatric deaths reported to CDC ranged from 46 to 74.

RESISTANCE TO ANTIVIRAL MEDICATIONS

During this influenza season, an increase in the number of influenza viruses resistant to the neuraminidase inhibitor, oseltamivir, has been observed. Among the 1,153 influenza A and B viruses tested during the 2007–08 influenza season, to date, 84 (8.3%) have been found to be resistant to oseltamivir. All the oseltamivir-resistant viruses have been influenza A (H1N1) viruses and have been determined to share the same genetic mutation that confers oseltamivir resistance. These 84 viruses represent 10.2% of the 824 influenza A (H1N1) viruses that have been tested, an increase from four (0.7%) of 588 influenza A (H1N1) viruses tested during the 2006–07 season. No resistance to oseltamivir has been identified among the 194 influenza A (H3N2) or the 135 influenza B viruses tested, and no antiviral resistance to zanamivir has been detected in any influenza A or B viruses. Resistance to adamantanes (amantadine and rimantadine) continues to be high among influenza A viruses. Of 261 influenza A (H3N2) viruses tested, 260 (99.6%) were resistant to adamantanes. Adamantane resistance among influenza A (H1N1) viruses also has been detected, but at a lower level. Of 729 influenza A (H1N1) viruses tested, 81 (11.1%) were resistant to adamantanes. The adamantanes have no activity against influenza B viruses.

Based on the level of oseltamivir resistance observed in only one influenza A subtype (H1N1), persisting high levels of resistance to adamantanes in A (H3N2) viruses, and the predominance of A (H3N2) viruses circulating in the United

States during the 2007–08 season with co-circulation of influenza B viruses, CDC continues to recommend the use of oseltamivir and zanamivir for the treatment or chemoprophylaxis of influenza (2). Use of amantadine or rimantadine is not recommended.

Reported by: World Health Organization Collaborating Center for Surveillance, Epidemiology, and Control of Influenza; C Dao, MPH, L Blanton, MPH, S Epperson, MPH, L Brammer, MPH, L Finelli, DrPH, T Wallis, MS, T Uyeki, MD, J Bresee, MD, A Klimov, PhD, N Cox, PhD, Influenza Div, National Center for Immunization and Respiratory Diseases, CDC.

EDITORIAL NOTE

By some indicators, this influenza season has been more severe than the previous three seasons. Influenza activity in the United States remained low until January, peaked in mid-February, and decreased thereafter. For the week ending April 5, 2008, widespread activity was reported in six states, and regional activity was reported in 11 states, a decrease from mid-February, when 49 states reported widespread activity and one state reported regional activity. During peak activity of the previous three influenza seasons, the number of states reporting widespread or regional activity ranged from 41 to 49 states. During the 2007–08 season, the percentage of outpatient visits for ILI peaked at 5.9%, exceeded the national baseline for 13 consecutive weeks, and declined to 1.7% during the week ending April 5. During the previous three influenza seasons, the peak percentage of visits for ILI ranged from 3.2% to 5.4% and exceeded baseline levels for 14 to 16 consecutive weeks. To date, the percentage of deaths attributable to P&I peaked at 9.1% and exceeded the epidemic threshold for 13 consecutive weeks this season. For the week ending April 5, the proportion of deaths attributable to P&I was 8.9%. During the previous three seasons, the peak percentage of deaths attributable to P&I ranged from 7.7% to 8.9%, and the total number of weeks above the epidemic threshold ranged from 1 to 11 consecutive weeks. P&I mortality is higher this season than the previous three seasons, which were mild. The 2007–08 season is similar to the 2003–04 season, when the percentage of deaths attributable to P&I peaked at 10.4% and the number of consecutive weeks above the epidemic threshold was 9 weeks.

Influenza A (H1N1) viruses predominated through mid-January, but influenza A (H3N2) viruses were more frequently identified than influenza A (H1N1) viruses since late January and have predominated overall. The majority of influenza A (H1N1) viruses were characterized as A/Solomon Islands/3/2006, the influenza A (H1N1) component of the 2007–08 in-

fluenza vaccine for the Northern Hemisphere. To date, the majority of influenza A (H3N2) and influenza B viruses were characterized as A/Brisbane/10/2007 and B/Florida/04/2006, respectively, the recommended influenza A (H3N2) and influenza B components of the 2008–09 influenza vaccine for the Northern Hemisphere.

Clinical vaccine effectiveness cannot be accurately predicted using these data. A case-control study to estimate the effectiveness of trivalent inactivated influenza vaccine was conducted this season in Marshfield, Wisconsin. Preliminary results from subjects enrolled during January 21–February 8 show an overall vaccine effectiveness of 44%, suggesting that vaccination provided substantial protection against influenza-associated, medically attended illness in the study population, despite the suboptimal vaccine match (3). These preliminary results are similar to previous studies, which have shown that influenza vaccination provides measurable protection against influenza illness and influenza-related complications and death, even when vaccine strains are antigenically distinct from circulating strains (4–7).

As a supplement to influenza vaccination, antiviral drugs have aided in the control and prevention of influenza. Recent studies have identified a considerable protective effect of oseltamivir treatment against complications associated with influenza (8), including death among older adults hospitalized with laboratory-confirmed influenza (9). This season, resistance to the influenza antiviral drug oseltamivir among influenza A (H1N1) viruses (84 [10.2%] of 824 tested) has been detected. All 84 resistant influenza A (H1N1) viruses identified in the United States this season share the same genetic mutation; this mutation is the most common mutation in this subtype that confers resistance to oseltamivir. Increased resistance to oseltamivir among influenza A (H1N1) viruses has been reported from many countries this season (10). No oseltamivir resistance has been detected among influenza A (H3N2) or B viruses currently circulating in the United States. Given the low level of resistance to oseltamivir, the finding of resistance only in some influenza A (H1N1) viruses, and no resistance to zanamivir, these drugs continue to be recommended for the treatment and prophylaxis of influenza (2). Although recommendations for use of antiviral medications have not changed, enhanced surveillance for detection of oseltamivir-resistant influenza viruses is ongoing and will enable continued monitoring of changing trends over time. In addition to vaccination and antivirals, other means of decreasing the spread and impact of influenza include staying home from work or school when ill, avoiding others who are sick, covering the nose or mouth with a tissue when coughing or sneezing, and frequent hand washing. Additional information is available at http://www.cdc.gov/flu/protect/habits.htm.

Influenza surveillance reports for the United States are posted online weekly during October–May and are available at http://www.cdc.gov/flu/weekly/fluactivity.htm. Additional information regarding influenza viruses, influenza surveillance, the influenza vaccine, and avian influenza is available at http://www.cdc.gov/flu.

ACKNOWLEDGMENTS

This report is based on data contributed by participating state and territorial health departments and state public health laboratories, World Health Organization collaborating laboratories, National Respiratory and Enteric Virus Surveillance System collaborating laboratories, the U.S. Influenza Sentinel Provider Surveillance System, the U.S. Department of Veterans Affairs/U.S. Department of Defense BioSense Outpatient Surveillance System, the New Vaccine Surveillance Network, the Emerging Infections Program, and the 122 Cities Mortality Reporting System.

DISCUSSION QUESTIONS

1. Go to www.cdc.gov and seek the influenza reports from at least three previous years; compare these to the 2007–8 season described above. What is the same? What is different?

2. What is a consequence of human action on the distribution of influenza described here? Could it have been anticipated? What might be done in the future to limit negative consequences of necessary public health interventions?

3. Do you think that a heightened influenza season will increase or decrease public response to the need for vaccination? Do you think that the difficulty in determining the correct composition of the vaccine that took place in this season will have a negative or positive impact on an individual's decision to vaccinate in future seasons? Why? What might be confounders that could obscure our understanding in the relationship between these issues? Design a study that could evaluate how this influenza season may impact future healthcare utilization with regard to this virus.

REFERENCES FROM THE READING

1. CDC. Update: influenza activity—United States, September 30–February 9, 2008. MMWR 2008;57:179–83.

2. CDC. Health Advisory: influenza antiviral use for persons at high risk for influenza complications or who have severe influenza illness. Atlanta, GA: US Department of Health and Human Services, CDC; 2008 Available at http://www2a.cdc.gov/han/archivesys/viewmsgv.asp?alertnum=00271.

3. CDC. Interim within-season estimate of the effectiveness of trivalent inactivated influenza vaccine—Marshfield, Wisconsin, 2007–08 influenza season. MMWR 2008;57:393–8.

4. Edwards KM, Dupont WD, Westrich MK, Plummer WD Jr, Palmer PS, Wright PF. A randomized controlled trial of cold-adapted and inactivated vaccines for the prevention of influenza A disease. J Infect Dis 1994;169:68–76.

5. Nichol KL, Nordin JD, Nelson DB, Mullooly JP, Hak E. Effectiveness of influenza vaccine in the community-dwelling elderly. N Engl J Med 2007;357:1373–81.

6. Shuler CM, Iwamoto M, Bridges CB. Vaccine effectiveness against medically attended, laboratory-confirmed influenza among children aged 6 to 59 months, 2003–2004. Pediatrics 2007;119:e587–95.

7. Russell KL, Ryan MA, Hawksworth A, et al. Effectiveness of the 2003–2004 influenza vaccine among U.S. military basic trainees: a year of suboptimal match between vaccine and circulating strain. Vaccine 2005;23:1981–5.

8. Kaiser L, Wat C, Mills T, Mahoney P, Ward P, Hayden F. Impact of oseltamivir treatment on influenza-related lower respiratory tract complications and hospitalizations. Arch Intern Med 2003;163:1667–72.

9. McGeer A, Green KA, Plevneshi A, et al. Antiviral therapy and outcomes of influenza requiring hospitalization in Ontario, Canada. Clin Infect Dis 2007;45:1568–75.

10. World Health Organization. Influenza A (H1N1) virus resistance to oseltamivir—last quarter 2007 to 4 April 2008. Geneva, Switzerland: World Health Organization; 2008. Available at http://www.who.int/csr/disease/influenza/H1N1ResistanceWeb20080403.pdf.

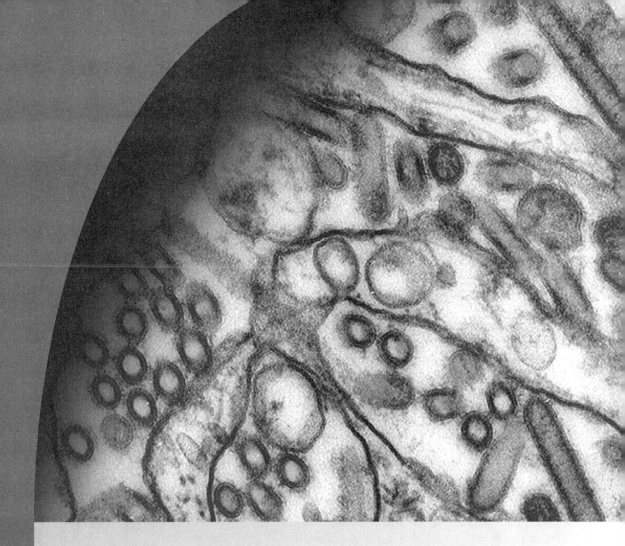

PART **IV**

Public Health Progress

In 1999, on the edge of the new millennium, authors at CDC noted the progress that has been made in public health during the preceding century. These included the following:

Ten Great Public Health Achievements—United States, 1900–1999

- Vaccination
- Motor-vehicle safety
- Safer workplaces
- Control of infectious diseases
- Decline in deaths from coronary heart disease and stroke
- Safer and healthier foods
- Healthier mothers and babies

- Family planning
- Fluoridation of drinking water
- Recognition of tobacco use as a health hazardHow was the progress made, however? In the below article, the authors outline key ways that advances could be possible and several landmark moments in public health.

How was the progress made, however? In the below article, the authors outline key ways that advances could be possible and several landmark moments in public health.

READING 5
Achievements in Public Health, 1900–1999: Changes in the Public Health System

Centers for Disease Control and Prevention. Achievements in Public Health, 1900–1999: Changes in the Public Health System. *MMWR*. 1999;48:1141–7. [www.cdc.gov/mmwr; accessed 10/1/2005.]

The 10 public health achievements highlighted in this *MMWR* series reflect the successful response of public health to the major causes of morbidity and mortality of the 20th century. In addition, these achievements demonstrate the ability of public health to meet an increasingly diverse array of public health challenges. This report highlights critical changes in the U.S. public health system this century.

In the early 1900s in the United States, many major health threats were infectious diseases associated with poor hygiene and poor sanitation (e.g., typhoid), diseases associated with poor nutrition (e.g., pellagra and goiter), poor maternal and infant health, and diseases or injuries associated with unsafe workplaces or hazardous occupations (4, 5, 7, 8). The success of the early public health system to incorporate biomedical advances (e.g., vaccinations and antibiotics) and to develop interventions such as health education programs resulted in decreases in the impact in these diseases. However, as the incidence of these diseases decreased, chronic diseases (e.g., cardiovascular disease and cancer) increased (6, 10). In the last half of the century, public health identified the risk factors for many chronic diseases and intervened to reduce mortality. Public efforts also led to reduced deaths attributed to a new

technology, the motor vehicle (3). These successes demonstrated the value of community action to address public health issues and have fostered public support for the growth of institutions that are components of the public health infrastructure.* The focus of public health research and programs shifted to respond to the effects of chronic diseases on the public's health (12–17). While continuing to develop and refine interventions, enhanced morbidity and mortality surveillance helped to maintain these earlier successes. The shift in focus led to improved capacity of epidemiology and to changes in public health training and programs.

QUANTITATIVE ANALYTIC TECHNIQUES

Epidemiology, the population-based study of disease and an important part of the scientific foundation of public health, acquired greater quantitative capacity during the 20th century. Improvements occurred in both study design and periodic standardized health surveys (12, 18–21). Methods of data collection evolved from simple measures of disease prevalence (e.g., field surveys) to complex studies of precise analyses (e.g., cohort studies, case-control studies, and randomized clinical trials) (12). The first well-developed, longitudinal cohort study was conducted in 1947 among the 28,000 residents of Framingham,

---

*The government, community, professional, voluntary, and academic institutions and organizations that support or conduct public health research or programs.

Massachusetts, many of whom volunteered to be followed over time to determine incidence of heart disease (12). The Framingham Heart Study served as the model for other longitudinal cohort studies and for the concept that biologic, environmental, and behavioral risk factors exist for disease (6, 12).

In 1948, modern clinical trials began with publication of a clinical trial of streptomycin therapy for tuberculosis, which employed randomization, selection criteria, pre-determined evaluation criteria, and ethical considerations (19, 21). In 1950, the case-control study gained prominence when this method provided the first solidly scientific evidence of an association between lung cancer and cigarette smoking (22). Subsequently, high-powered statistical tests and analytic computer programs enabled multiple variables collected in large-scale studies to be measured and to the development of tools for mathematical modeling. Advances in epidemiology permitted elucidation of risk factors for heart disease and other chronic diseases and the development of effective interventions.

PERIODIC STANDARDIZED HEALTH SURVEYS

In 1921, periodic standardized health surveys began in Hagerstown, Maryland (12). In 1935, the first national health survey was conducted among U.S. residents (12, 23). In 1956, these efforts resulted in the National Health Survey, a population-based survey that evolved from focusing on chronic disease to estimating disease prevalence for major causes of death, measuring the burden of infectious diseases, assessing exposure to environmental toxicants, and measuring the population's vaccination coverage. Other population-based surveys (e.g., Behavioral Risk Factor Surveillance System, Youth Risk Behavior Survey, and the National Survey of Family Growth) were developed to assess risk factors for chronic diseases and other conditions (24–26). Methods developed by social scientists and statisticians to address issues such as sampling and interviewing techniques have enhanced survey methods used in epidemiologic studies (12).

MORBIDITY AND MORTALITY SURVEILLANCE

National disease monitoring was first conducted in the United States in 1850, when mortality statistics based on death registrations were first published by the federal government (23, 27). During 1878–1902, Congress authorized the collection of morbidity reports on cholera, smallpox, plague, and yellow fever for use in quarantine measures, to provide funds to collect and disseminate these data, to expand authority for weekly reporting from states and municipal authorities, and to provide forms for collecting data and publishing reports (15, 23, 27). The first annual summary of *The Notifiable Diseases* in 1912 included reports of 10 diseases from 19 states, the District of Columbia, and Hawaii. By 1928, all states, the District of Columbia,

Hawaii, and Puerto Rico were participating in the national reporting of 29 diseases. In 1950, state and territorial health officers authorized the Council of State and Territorial Epidemiologists (CSTE) to determine which diseases should be reported to the U.S. Public Health Service (PHS) (27). In 1961, the Centers for Disease Control and Prevention (CDC) assumed responsibility for collecting and publishing nationally notifiable diseases data. As of January 1, 1998, 52 infectious diseases were notifiable at the national level.

In the early 1900s, efforts at surveillance focused on tracking persons with disease; by mid-century, the focus had changed to tracking trends in disease occurrence (28, 29). In 1947, Alexander Langmuir at the newly formed Communicable Disease Center, the early name for CDC, began the first disease surveillance system (27). In 1955, surveillance data helped to determine the cause of poliomyelitis among children recently vaccinated with an inactivated vaccine (28). After the first polio cases were recognized, data from the national polio surveillance program confirmed that the cases were linked to one brand of vaccine contaminated with live wild poliovirus. The national vaccine program continued by using supplies from other polio vaccine manufacturers (28). Since these initial disease surveillance efforts, morbidity tracking has become a standard feature of public health infectious disease control (29).

PUBLIC HEALTH TRAINING

In 1916, with the support of the Rockefeller Foundation, the Johns Hopkins School of Hygiene and Public Health was started (30, 31). By 1922, Columbia, Harvard, and Yale universities had established schools of public health. In 1969, the number of schools of public health had increased to 12, and in 1999, 29 accredited schools of public health enrolled approximately 15,000 students (31, 32). Besides the increase in the number of schools and students, the types of student in public health schools changed. Traditionally, students in public health training already had obtained a medical degree. However, increasing numbers of students entered public health training to obtain a primary postgraduate degree. In 1978, 3753 (69%) public health students enrolled with only baccalaureates. The proportion of students who were physicians declined from 35% in 1944–1945 to 11% in 1978 (28, 31). Thus, public health training evolved from a second degree for medical professionals to a primary health discipline (33). Schools of public health initially emphasized the study of hygiene and sanitation; subsequently, the study of public health has expanded into five core disciplines: biostatistics, epidemiology, health services administration, health education/ behavioral science, and environmental science (30, 34).

Programs also were started to provide field training in epidemiology and public health. In 1948, a board was established to certify training of physicians in public health administration, and by 1951, approximately 40 local health departments had accredited preventive medicine and public residency programs. In 1951, CDC developed the Epidemic Intelligence Service (EIS) to guard against domestic acts of biologic warfare during the Korean conflict and to address common public health threats. Since 1951, more than 2000 EIS officers have responded to requests for epidemiologic assistance within the United States and throughout the world. In 1999, 149 EIS officers are on duty.

NONGOVERNMENT AND GOVERNMENT ORGANIZATIONS

At the beginning of the century, many public health initiatives were started and supported by nongovernment organizations. However, as federal, state, and local public health infrastructure expanded, governments' role increased and assumed more responsibility for public health research and programs. Today, public health represents the work of both government and nongovernment organizations.

Nongovernment Organizations

The Rockefeller Sanitary Committee's Hookworm Eradication Project conducted during 1910–1920 was one of the earliest voluntary efforts to engage in a campaign for a specific disease (35). During 1914–1933, the Rockefeller Foundation also provided $2.6 million to support county health departments and sponsored medical education reform. Other early efforts to promote community health include the National Tuberculosis Association work for TB treatment and prevention, the National Consumers League's support of maternal and infant health in the 1920s, the American Red Cross' sponsorship of nutrition programs in the 1930s, and the March of Dimes' support of research in the 1940s and 1950s that led to a successful polio vaccine. Mothers Against Drunk Driving started in 1980 by a group of women in California after a girl was killed by an intoxicated driver and grew into a national campaign for stronger laws against drunk driving.

Professional organizations and labor unions also worked to promote public heath. The American Medical Association advocated better vital statistics and safer foods and drugs (17). The American Dental Association endorsed water fluoridation despite the economic consequences to its members (9). Labor organizations worked for safer workplaces in industry (4). In the 1990s, nongovernment organizations sponsor diverse public health research projects and programs (e.g., family planning, human immunodeficiency virus prevention, vaccine development, and heart disease and cancer prevention).

State Health Departments

The 1850 Report of the Sanitary Commission of Massachusetts, authored by Lemuel Shattuck (13, 14), outlined many elements of the modern public health infrastructure including a recommendation for establishing state and local health boards. Massachusetts formed the first state health department in 1889. By 1900, 40 states had health departments that made advances in sanitation and microbial sciences available to the public. Later, states also provided other public health interventions: personal health services (e.g., disabled children and maternal and child health care, and sexually transmitted disease treatment), environmental health (e.g., waste management and radiation control), and health resources (e.g., health planning, regulation of health care and emergency services, and health statistics). All states have public health laboratories that provide direct services and oversight functions (36).

County Health Departments

Although some cities had local public health boards in the early 1900s, no county health departments existed (33). During 1910–1911, the success of a county sanitation campaign to control a severe typhoid epidemic in Yakima County, Washington, created public support for a permanent health service, and a local health department was organized on July 1, 1911 (33). Concurrently, the Rockefeller Sanitary Commission began supporting county hookworm eradication efforts (17, 35). By 1920, 131 county health departments had been established; by 1931, 599 county health departments were providing services to one fifth of the U.S. population (33); in 1950, 86% of the U.S. population was served by a local health department, and 34,895 persons were employed full-time in public health agencies (37).

Local Health Departments

In 1945, the American Public Health Association proposed six minimum functions of local health departments (38). In 1988, the Institute of Medicine defined these functions as assessment, policy development, and assurance, and PHS has proposed 10 organizational practices to implement the three core functions (39, 40). The national health objectives for 2000, released in 1990, provided a framework to monitor the progress of local health departments (41). In 1993, 2888 local health departments,** representing county, city, and district health organizations operated in 3042 U.S. counties. Of the 2079 local health departments surveyed in 1993, nearly all provided vaccination services (96%) and tuberculosis treatment (86%); fewer provided family planning (68%) and cancer prevention programs (54%) (42).

**A local health department is an administrative or service unit of local or state government responsible for the health of a jurisdiction smaller than the state.

Federal Government

In 1798, the federal government established the Marine Hospital Service to provide health services to seamen (15). To recognize its expanding quarantine duties, in 1902, Congress changed the service's name to the Public Health and Marine Hospital Service and, in 1912, to the Public Health Service. In 1917, PHS' support of state and local public health activities began with a small grant to study rural health (35). During World War I, PHS received resources from Congress to assist states in treating venereal diseases. The Social Security Act of 1935, which authorized health grants to states, and a second Federal Venereal Diseases Control Act in 1938 (13, 14), expanded the federal government's role in public health (15, 35). In 1939, PHS and other health, education, and welfare agencies were combined in the Federal Security Agency, forerunner of the Department of Health and Human Services. In the 1930s, the federal government began to provide resources for specific conditions, beginning with care for crippled children. After World War II, the federal role in public health continued to expand with the Hospital Services and Construction Act (Hill-Burton) of 1946*** (15). In 1930, Congress established the National Institutes of Health [formerly the Hygiene Laboratories of the Public Health Service] and the Food and Drug Administration. CDC was established in 1946 (29). Legislation to form Medicare and Medicaid was enacted in 1965, and the Occupational Safety and Health Administration and the Environmental Protection Agency were organized in 1970.

Although federal, state, and local health agencies and services have increased throughout the century, public health resources represent a small proportion of overall health-care costs. In 1993, federal, state, and local health agencies spent an estimated $14. 4 billion on core public health functions, 1%-2% of the $903 billion in total health-care expenditure (43).

CONCLUSION

The public health infrastructure changed to provide the elements necessary for successful public health interventions: organized and systematic observations through morbidity and mortality surveillance, well-designed epidemiologic studies and other data to facilitate the decision-making process, and individuals and organizations to advocate for resources and to ensure that effective policies and programs were implemented and conducted properly. In 1999, public health is a complex partnership among federal agencies, state and local governments, nongovernment organizations, academia, and community members. In the 21st century, the success of the U.S. public health system will depend on its ability to change to meet new threats to the public's health.

***T = P.L. 79-725.

DISCUSSION QUESTIONS

1. The advances discussed above concern a range of health-related activities, from vehicles to infectious disease to chronic disease to behavior, yet the methods and structural/environmental progress apply to all of them similarly. How does our ability to study threats to public health inform the structural changes that need to be made? Are there differences in how these are made on the basis of the domain that is being focused on?

2. How do health-related behaviors in one domain (e.g., infectious) relate to those in another? For example, smoking is a distinct risk behavior but is associated with other risk behaviors. How do constellations of change affect one another?

3. The article references that the first annual summary of *The Notifiable Diseases* was released in 1912. Why was this reporting and recording an important step toward reduction of infectious diseases?

REFERENCES FROM THE READING

1. CDC. Ten great public health achievements—United States, 1900–1999. MMWR 1999;48:241–3.
2. CDC. Impact of vaccines universally recommended for children—United States, 1990–1998. MMWR 1999;48:243–8.
3. CDC. Motor-vehicle safety: a 20th century public health achievement. MMWR 1999;48:369–74.
4. CDC. Improvements in workplace safety—United States, 1900–1999. MMWR 1999;48:461–9.
5. CDC. Control of infectious diseases. MMWR 1999;48:621–9.
6. CDC. Decline in deaths from heart disease and stroke—United States, 1900–1999. MMWR 1999;48:649–56.
7. CDC. Healthier mothers and babies. MMWR 1999;48:849–57.
8. CDC. Safer and healthier foods. MMWR 1999;48:905–13.
9. CDC. Fluoridation of drinking water to prevent dental caries. MMWR 1999;48:933–40.
10. CDC. Tobacco use—United States, 1900–1999. MMWR 1999;48:986–93.
11. CDC. Family planning. MMWR 1999;48:1073–80.
12. Susser M. Epidemiology in the United States after World War II: the evolution of technique. Epid Reviews 1985;7:147–77.
13. Turnock BJ. The organization of public health in the United States. In: Turnock BJ, ed. Public health: What it is and how it works. Gaithersburg, Maryland: Aspen Publication, 1997:1121–68.
14. Last JM. Scope and method of prevention. In: Last JM, Wallace RB, eds. Maxcy-Rosenau-Last Public health and preventive medicine. 13th ed. Norwalk, Connecticut: Appleton & Lange, 1992:11–39.
15. Hanlon JJ, Pickett GE. Public health: administration and practice. 8th ed. St. Louis, Missouri: Times Mirror/Mosby College Publishing, 1984:22–44.
16. Koplan JP, Thacker SB, Lezin NA. Epidemiology in the 21st century: calculation, communication, and intervention. Am J Public Health 1999;89:1153–5.
17. Terris M. Evolution of public health and preventive medicine in the United States. Am J Public Health 1975;65:161–9.
18. Vandenbroucke JP. Clinical investigation in the 20th century: the ascendency of numerical reasoning. Lancet 1998;352(suppl 2):12–6.

19. Vandenbroucke JP. A short note on the history of the randomized controlled trial. J Chronic Dis 1987;40:985–6.

20. Doll R. Clinical trials: retrospect and prospect. Statistics in Medicine 1982;1:337–44.

21. Armitage P. The role of randomization in clinical trials. Statistics in Medicine 1982;1:345–52.

22. Doll R, Hill AB. Smoking and carcinoma of the lung. Br Med J 1950; 2:740–8.

23. Teutsch SM, Churchill RE, eds. Principles and practice of public health surveillance. New York: Oxford University Press, 1994.

24. Remington PL, Smith MY, Williamson DF, Anda RF, Gentry EM, Hogelin GC. Design, characteristics and usefulness of state-based behavioral risk factor surveillance, 1981–87. Public Health Rep 1988;103:366–75.

25. Kann L, Kinchen SA, Williams BI, et al. Youth risk behavior surveillance—United States, 1997. In: CDC surveillance summaries (August 14). MMWR 47(no. SS-3).

26. Mosher WD. Design and operation of the 1995 national survey of family growth. Fam Plann Perspect 1998;43–6.

27. CDC. Summary of notifiable diseases, United States, 1997. MMWR 1997;46(no. SS-54).

28. Langmuir AD. The surveillance of communicable diseases of national importance. N Engl J Med 1963;268:182–92.

29. CDC. History perspectives: history of CDC. MMWR 1996;45:526–8.

30. Roemer MI. Preparing public health leaders for the 1990s. Public Health Rep 1988;103:443–51.

31. Winkelstein W, French FE. The training of epidemiologists in schools of public health in the United States: a historical note. Int J Epidemiol 1973;2:415–6.

32. Association of Schools of Public Health. Enrollment of U.S. schools of public health 1987–1997. Available at http://www.asph.org/webstud1.gif. Accessed December 14, 1999.

33. Crawford BL. Graduate students in U.S. schools of public health: comparison of 3 academic years. Public Health Rep 1979;94:67–72.

34. Association of Schools of Public Health. Ten most frequently asked questions by perspective students. Available at http://www.asph.org/10quest.htm. Accessed December 14, 1999.

35. US Treasury Department/Public Health Service. History of county health organizations in the United States 1908–1933. In: Public health bulletin (No. 222). Washington, DC: Public Health Service, 1936.

36. Altman D, Morgan DH. The role of state and local government in health. Health Affairs 1983;2;7–31.

37. Mountin JW, Flook E. Guide to health organization in the United States, 1951. Washington, DC: Public Health Service, Federal Security Agency, Bureau of State Services, 1951; PHS publication no. 196.

38. Emerson H, Luginbuhl M. 1200 local public school departments for the United States. Am J Public Health 1945;35:898–904.

39. Dyal WW. Ten organizational practices of public health: a historical perspective. Am J Prev Med 1995;11(suppl 2):6–8.

40. Institute of Medicine. The future of public health. Washington, DC: National Academy Press, 1988.

41. Public Health Service. Healthy people 2000: national health promotion and disease prevention objectives—full report, with commentary. Washington, DC: US Department of Health and Human Services, Public Health Service, 1991; DHHS publication no. (PHS)91-50212.

42. CDC. Selected characteristics of local health departments—United States, 1992–1993. MMWR 1994;43:839–43.

43. CDC. Estimated expenditures for core public health functions—selected states, October 1992–September 1993. MMWR 1995;44:421,427–9.

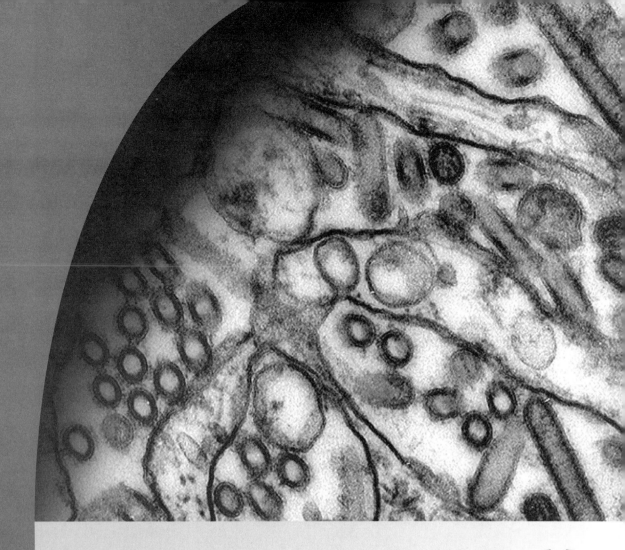

PART **V**

Ethics

In the United States, the Belmont Report is one of the most important guiding documents as we conduct research in any realm; other countries have their own documents of guiding ethical principles. After reading it in its entirety, outline and discuss the basic ethical principles. Take one of the many online ethics courses (one your institution has, www.CITItraining.org, or http://cme.cancer.gov/clinicaltrials/learning/humanparticipant-protections. asp, for example) and extract one of the many examples of ethically compromised studies. (For example, Tuskegee syphilis study.) Dissect the study and note where each of the principles was violated and how. Then design a study that could examine the same research question—if possible—in an ethical manner.

It is easy to assume *we* are ethical—*they* are not. But it is important to always bear in mind that we can all make the wrong research choices, even when we think they are in the best interest of individual or public health. This is one critical reason why it is essential to gain the insights and input from a multidisciplinary team as you develop your research. It takes experts of all disciplines to be able to identify potential ethical violations and ensure that your study is ethical in all aspects. No one researcher knows it all, or can see all potential challenges or limitations—we need to work as a team. Also in that team must be members of the target population who can advise and highlight issues that others may miss. All institutions have Institutional Review Boards (IRB) or ethics committees charged to oversee research for the institution, state, agency, country, or other organizational level such as a clinic. These are not administrative exercises: Research review is there to ensure through a rigorous process the protection of research subjects' rights. Boards exist to provide expert and multidisciplinary review of all protocols and instrumentation and protect subject rights and the institution conducting the research; their approval must be sought prior to study implementation and prior to any changes or modifications to previously approved studies. As you progress in your public health career, make it a priority to get to know those overseeing research in your workplace so that you understand the importance of protecting the rights of participants. Doing so is everyone's job: from data entry clerk to nurse to data manager to principal investigator. The basic tenets of protecting subject rights are outlined in the following Belmont Report.

READING 6
The Belmont Report

Department of Health, Education, and Welfare. Ethical Principles and Guidelines for the Protection of Human Subjects of Research. http://ohsr.od.nih.gov/guidelines/belmont.html.

Office of the Secretary

Ethical Principles and Guidelines for the Protection of Human Subjects of Research
The National Commission for the Protection of Human Subjects of Biomedical and Behavioral Research
April 18, 1979

AGENCY: Department of Health, Education, and Welfare.

ACTION: Notice of Report for Public Comment.

SUMMARY: On July 12, 1974, the National Research Act (Pub. L. 93-348) was signed into law, thereby creating the National Commission for the Protection of Human Subjects of Biomedical and Behavioral Research. One of the charges to the Commission was to identify the basic ethical principles that should underlie the conduct of biomedical and behavioral research involving human subjects and to develop guidelines which should be followed to assure that such research is conducted in accordance with those principles. In carrying out the above, the Commission was directed to consider: (i) the boundaries between biomedical and behavioral research and the accepted and routine practice of medicine, (ii) the role of assessment of risk-benefit criteria in the determination of the appropriateness of research involving human subjects, (iii) appropriate guidelines for the selection of human subjects for participation in such research and (iv) the nature and definition of informed consent in various research settings.

The Belmont Report attempts to summarize the basic ethical principles identified by the Commission in the course of its deliberations. It is the outgrowth of an intensive four-day period of discussions that were held in February 1976 at the Smithsonian Institution's Belmont Conference Center supplemented by the monthly deliberations of the Commission that were held over a period of nearly four years. It is a statement of basic ethical principles and guidelines that should assist in resolving the ethical problems that surround the conduct of research with human subjects. By publishing the Report in the Federal Register, and providing reprints upon request, the Secretary intends that it may be made readily available to scientists, members of Institutional Review Boards, and Federal employees. The two-volume Appendix, containing the lengthy reports of experts and specialists who assisted the Commission in fulfilling this part of its charge, is available as DHEW Publication No. (OS) 78-0013 and No. (OS) 78-0014, for sale by the Superintendent of Documents, U.S. Government Printing Office, Washington, D.C. 20402.

Unlike most other reports of the Commission, the Belmont Report does not make specific recommendations for administrative action by the Secretary of Health, Education, and Welfare. Rather, the Commission recommended that the Belmont Report be adopted in its entirety, as a statement of the Department's policy. The Department requests public comment on this recommendation.

NATIONAL COMMISSION FOR THE PROTECTION OF HUMAN SUBJECTS OF BIOMEDICAL AND BEHAVIORAL RESEARCH: MEMBERS OF THE COMMISSION

Kenneth John Ryan, M.D., Chairman, Chief of Staff, Boston Hospital for Women.

Joseph V. Brady, Ph.D., Professor of Behavioral Biology, Johns Hopkins University.

Robert E. Cooke, M.D., President, Medical College of Pennsylvania.

Dorothy I. Height, President, National Council of Negro Women, Inc.

Albert R. Jonsen, Ph.D., Associate Professor of Bioethics, University of California at San Francisco.

Patricia King, J.D., Associate Professor of Law, Georgetown University Law Center.

Karen Lebacqz, Ph.D., Associate Professor of Christian Ethics, Pacific School of Religion.

***David W. Louisell, J.D., Professor of Law, University of California at Berkeley.

Donald W. Seldin, M.D., Professor and Chairman, Department of Internal Medicine, University of Texas at Dallas.

***Eliot Stellar, Ph.D., Provost of the University and Professor of Physiological Psychology, University of Pennsylvania.

***Robert H. Turtle, LL.B., Attorney, VomBaur, Coburn, Simmons & Turtle, Washington, D.C.

***Deceased.

TABLE OF CONTENTS

Ethical Principles and Guidelines for Research Involving Human Subjects

A. Boundaries Between Practice and Research
B. Basic Ethical Principles
    1. Respect for Persons
    2. Beneficence
    3. Justice
C. Applications
    1. Informed Consent
    2. Assessment of Risk and Benefits
    3. Selection of Subjects

ETHICAL PRINCIPLES AND GUIDELINES FOR RESEARCH INVOLVING HUMAN SUBJECTS

Scientific research has produced substantial social benefits. It has also posed some troubling ethical questions. Public attention was drawn to these questions by reported abuses of human subjects in biomedical experiments, especially during the Second World War. During the Nuremberg War Crime Trials, the Nuremberg code was drafted as a set of standards for judging physicians and scientists who had conducted biomedical experiments on concentration camp prisoners. This code became the prototype of many later codes (1) intended to assure that research involving human subjects would be carried out in an ethical manner.

The codes consist of rules, some general, others specific, that guide the investigators or the reviewers of research in their work. Such rules often are inadequate to cover complex situations; at times they come into conflict, and they are frequently difficult to interpret or apply. Broader ethical principles will provide a basis on which specific rules may be formulated, criticized and interpreted.

Three principles, or general prescriptive judgments, that are relevant to research involving human subjects are identified in this statement. Other principles may also be relevant. These three are comprehensive, however, and are stated at a level of generalization that should assist scientists, subjects, reviewers and interested citizens to understand the ethical issues inherent in research involving human subjects. These principles cannot always be applied so as to resolve beyond dispute particular ethical problems. The objective is to provide an analytical framework that will guide the resolution of ethical problems arising from research involving human subjects.

This statement consists of a distinction between research and practice, a discussion of the three basic ethical principles, and remarks about the application of these principles.

PART A: BOUNDARIES BETWEEN PRACTICE & RESEARCH

A. Boundaries Between Practice and Research

It is important to distinguish between biomedical and behavioral research, on the one hand, and the practice of accepted therapy on the other, in order to know what activities ought to undergo review for the protection of human subjects of research. The distinction between research and practice is blurred partly because both often occur together (as in research designed to evaluate a therapy) and partly because notable departures from standard practice are often called "experimental" when the terms "experimental" and "research" are not carefully defined.

For the most part, the term "practice" refers to interventions that are designed solely to enhance the well-being of an individual patient or client and that have a reasonable expectation of success. The purpose of medical or behavioral practice is to provide diagnosis, preventive treatment or therapy to particular individuals (2). By contrast, the term "research" designates an activity designed to test a hypothesis, permit conclusions to be drawn, and thereby to develop or contribute to generalizable knowledge (expressed, for example, in theories, principles, and statements of relationships). Research is usually described in a formal protocol that sets forth an objective and a set of procedures designed to reach that objective.

When a clinician departs in a significant way from standard or accepted practice, the innovation does not, in and of itself, constitute research. The fact that a procedure is "experimental," in the sense of new, untested or different, does not automatically place it in the category of research. Radically new procedures of this description should, however, be made the object of formal research at an early stage in order to determine whether they are safe and effective. Thus, it is the responsibility of medical practice committees, for example, to insist that a major innovation be incorporated into a formal research project (3).

Research and practice may be carried on together when research is designed to evaluate the safety and efficacy of a therapy. This need not cause any confusion regarding whether or not the activity requires review; the general rule is that if there is any element of research in an activity, that activity should undergo review for the protection of human subjects.

PART B: BASIC ETHICAL PRINCIPLES

B. Basic Ethical Principles

The expression "basic ethical principles" refers to those general judgments that serve as a basic justification for the many particular ethical prescriptions and evaluations of human actions. Three basic principles, among those generally accepted in our cultural tradition, are particularly relevant to the ethics of research involving human subjects: the principles of respect of persons, beneficence and justice.

1. **Respect for Persons.**—Respect for persons incorporates at least two ethical convictions: first, that individuals should be treated as autonomous agents, and second, that persons with diminished autonomy are entitled to protection. The principle of respect for persons thus divides into two separate moral requirements: the requirement to acknowledge autonomy and the requirement to protect those with diminished autonomy.

An autonomous person is an individual capable of deliberation about personal goals and of acting under the direction of such deliberation. To respect autonomy is to give weight to autonomous persons' considered opinions and choices while refraining from obstructing their actions unless they are clearly detrimental to others. To show lack of respect for an autonomous agent is to repudiate that person's considered judgments, to deny an individual the freedom to act on those considered judgments, or to withhold information necessary to make a considered judgment, when there are no compelling reasons to do so.

However, not every human being is capable of self-determination. The capacity for self-determination matures during an individual's life, and some individuals lose this capacity wholly or in part because of illness, mental disability, or circumstances that severely restrict liberty. Respect for the immature and the incapacitated may require protecting them as they mature or while they are incapacitated.

Some persons are in need of extensive protection, even to the point of excluding them from activities which may harm them; other persons require little protection beyond making sure they undertake activities freely and with awareness of possible adverse consequence. The extent of protection afforded should depend upon the risk of harm and the likelihood of benefit. The judgment that any individual lacks autonomy should be periodically reevaluated and will vary in different situations.

In most cases of research involving human subjects, respect for persons demands that subjects enter into the research voluntarily and with adequate information. In some situations, however, application of the principle is not obvious. The involvement of prisoners as subjects of research provides an instructive example. On the one hand, it would seem that the principle of respect for persons requires that prisoners not be deprived of the opportunity to volunteer for research. On the other hand, under prison conditions they may be subtly coerced or unduly influenced to engage in research activities for which they would not otherwise volunteer. Respect for persons would then dictate that prisoners be protected. Whether to allow prisoners to "volunteer" or to "protect" them presents a dilemma. Respecting persons, in most hard cases, is often a matter of balancing competing claims urged by the principle of respect itself.

2. **Beneficence.**—Persons are treated in an ethical manner not only by respecting their decisions and protecting them from harm, but also by making efforts to secure their well-being. Such treatment falls under the principle of beneficence. The term "beneficence" is often understood to cover acts of kindness or charity that go beyond strict obligation. In this document, beneficence is understood in a stronger sense, as an obligation. Two general rules have been formulated as complementary expressions of beneficent actions in this sense: (1) do not harm and (2) maximize possible benefits and minimize possible harms.

The Hippocratic maxim "do no harm" has long been a fundamental principle of medical ethics. Claude Bernard extended it to the realm of research, saying that one should not injure one person regardless of the benefits that might come to others. However, even avoiding harm requires learning what is harmful; and, in the process of obtaining this information, persons may be exposed to risk of harm. Further, the Hippocratic Oath requires physicians to benefit their patients "according to their best judgment." Learning what will in fact benefit may require exposing persons to risk. The problem posed by these imperatives is to decide when it is justifiable to seek certain benefits despite the risks involved, and when the benefits should be foregone because of the risks.

The obligations of beneficence affect both individual investigators and society at large, because they extend both to particular research projects and to the entire enterprise of research. In the case of particular projects, investigators and members of their institutions are obliged to give forethought to the maximization of benefits and the reduction of risk that might occur from the research investigation. In the case of scientific research in general, members of the larger so-

ciety are obliged to recognize the longer term benefits and risks that may result from the improvement of knowledge and from the development of novel medical, psychotherapeutic, and social procedures.

The principle of beneficence often occupies a well-defined justifying role in many areas of research involving human subjects. An example is found in research involving children. Effective ways of treating childhood diseases and fostering healthy development are benefits that serve to justify research involving children—even when individual research subjects are not direct beneficiaries. Research also makes it possible to avoid the harm that may result from the application of previously accepted routine practices that on closer investigation turn out to be dangerous. But the role of the principle of beneficence is not always so unambiguous. A difficult ethical problem remains, for example, about research that presents more than minimal risk without immediate prospect of direct benefit to the children involved. Some have argued that such research is inadmissible, while others have pointed out that this limit would rule out much research promising great benefit to children in the future. Here again, as with all hard cases, the different claims covered by the principle of beneficence may come into conflict and force difficult choices.

3. **Justice.**—Who ought to receive the benefits of research and bear its burdens? This is a question of justice, in the sense of "fairness in distribution" or "what is deserved." An injustice occurs when some benefit to which a person is entitled is denied without good reason or when some burden is imposed unduly. Another way of conceiving the principle of justice is that equals ought to be treated equally. However, this statement requires explication. Who is equal and who is unequal? What considerations justify departure from equal distribution? Almost all commentators allow that distinctions based on experience, age, deprivation, competence, merit and position do sometimes constitute criteria justifying differential treatment for certain purposes. It is necessary, then, to explain in what respects people should be treated equally. There are several widely accepted formulations of just ways to distribute burdens and benefits. Each formulation mentions some relevant property on the basis of which burdens and benefits should be distributed. These formulations are (**1**) to each person an equal share, (**2**) to each person according to individual need, (**3**) to each person according to individual effort, (**4**) to each person according to societal contribution, and (**5**) to each person according to merit.

Questions of justice have long been associated with social practices such as punishment, taxation and political representation. Until recently these questions have not generally been associated with scientific research. However, they are foreshadowed even in the earliest reflections on the ethics of research involving human subjects. For example, during the 19th and early 20th centuries the burdens of serving as research subjects fell largely upon poor ward patients, while the benefits of improved medical care flowed primarily to private patients. Subsequently, the exploitation of unwilling prisoners as research subjects in Nazi concentration camps was condemned as a particularly flagrant injustice. In this country, in the 1940s, the Tuskegee syphilis study used disadvantaged, rural black men to study the untreated course of a disease that is by no means confined to that population. These subjects were deprived of demonstrably effective treatment in order not to interrupt the project, long after such treatment became generally available.

Against this historical background, it can be seen how conceptions of justice are relevant to research involving human subjects. For example, the selection of research subjects needs to be scrutinized in order to determine whether some classes (e.g., welfare patients, particular racial and ethnic minorities, or persons confined to institutions) are being systematically selected simply because of their easy availability, their compromised position, or their manipulability, rather than for reasons directly related to the problem being studied. Finally, whenever research supported by public funds leads to the development of therapeutic devices and procedures, justice demands both that these not provide advantages only to those who can afford them and that such research should not unduly involve persons from groups unlikely to be among the beneficiaries of subsequent applications of the research.

PART C: APPLICATIONS

C. Applications

Applications of the general principles to the conduct of research leads to consideration of the following requirements: informed consent, risk/benefit assessment, and the selection of subjects of research.

1. **Informed Consent.**—Respect for persons requires that subjects, to the degree that they are capable, be given the opportunity to choose what shall or shall not happen to them. This opportunity is provided when adequate standards for informed consent are satisfied.

While the importance of informed consent is unquestioned, controversy prevails over the nature and possibility of an informed consent. Nonetheless, there is widespread agreement that the consent process can be analyzed as containing three elements: information, comprehension and voluntariness.

Information. Most codes of research establish specific items for disclosure intended to assure that subjects are given sufficient information. These items generally include: the research procedure, their purposes, risks and anticipated benefits, alternative procedures (where therapy is involved), and a statement offering the subject the opportunity to ask questions and to withdraw at any time from the research. Additional items have been proposed, including how subjects are selected, the person responsible for the research, etc.

However, a simple listing of items does not answer the question of what the standard should be for judging how much and what sort of information should be provided. One standard frequently invoked in medical practice, namely the information commonly provided by practitioners in the field or in the locale, is inadequate since research takes place precisely when a common understanding does not exist. Another standard, currently popular in malpractice law, requires the practitioner to reveal the information that reasonable persons would wish to know in order to make a decision regarding their care. This, too, seems insufficient since the research subject, being in essence a volunteer, may wish to know considerably more about risks gratuitously undertaken than do patients who deliver themselves into the hand of a clinician for needed care. It may be that a standard of "the reasonable volunteer" should be proposed: the extent and nature of information should be such that persons, knowing that the procedure is neither necessary for their care nor perhaps fully understood, can decide whether they wish to participate in the furthering of knowledge. Even when some direct benefit to them is anticipated, the subjects should understand clearly the range of risk and the voluntary nature of participation.

A special problem of consent arises where informing subjects of some pertinent aspect of the research is likely to impair the validity of the research. In many cases, it is sufficient to indicate to subjects that they are being invited to participate in research of which some features will not be revealed until the research is concluded. In all cases of research involving incomplete disclosure, such research is justified only if it is clear that (1) incomplete disclosure is truly necessary to accomplish the goals of the research, (2) there are no undisclosed risks to subjects that are more than minimal, and (3) there is an adequate plan for debriefing subjects, when appropriate, and for dissemination of research results to them. Information about risks should never be withheld for the purpose of eliciting the cooperation of subjects, and truthful answers should always be given to direct questions about the research. Care should be taken to distinguish cases in which disclosure would destroy or invalidate the research from cases in which disclosure would simply inconvenience the investigator.

Comprehension. The manner and context in which information is conveyed is as important as the information itself. For example, presenting information in a disorganized and rapid fashion, allowing too little time for consideration or curtailing opportunities for questioning, all may adversely affect a subject's ability to make an informed choice.

Because the subject's ability to understand is a function of intelligence, rationality, maturity and language, it is necessary to adapt the presentation of the information to the subject's capacities. Investigators are responsible for ascertaining that the subject has comprehended the information. While there is always an obligation to ascertain that the information about risk to subjects is complete and adequately comprehended, when the risks are more serious, that obligation increases. On occasion, it may be suitable to give some oral or written tests of comprehension.

Special provision may need to be made when comprehension is severely limited—for example, by conditions of immaturity or mental disability. Each class of subjects that one might consider as incompetent (e.g., infants and young children, mentally disable patients, the terminally ill and the comatose) should be considered on its own terms. Even for these persons, however, respect requires giving them the opportunity to choose to the extent they are able, whether or not to participate in research. The objections of these subjects to involvement should be honored, unless the research entails providing them a therapy unavailable elsewhere. Respect for persons also requires seeking the permission of other parties in order to protect the subjects from harm. Such persons are thus respected both by acknowledging their own wishes and by the use of third parties to protect them from harm.

The third parties chosen should be those who are most likely to understand the incompetent subject's situation and to act in that person's best interest. The person authorized to act on behalf of the subject should be given an opportunity to observe the research as it proceeds in order to be able to withdraw the subject from the research, if such action appears in the subject's best interest.

Voluntariness. An agreement to participate in research constitutes a valid consent only if voluntarily given. This element of informed consent requires conditions free of coercion and undue influence. Coercion occurs when an overt threat of harm is intentionally presented by one person to another in order to obtain compliance. Undue influence, by contrast, occurs through an offer of an excessive, unwarranted, inappropriate or improper reward or other overture in order to obtain compliance. Also, inducements that would ordinarily be acceptable may become undue influences if the subject is especially vulnerable.

Unjustifiable pressures usually occur when persons in positions of authority or commanding influence—especially where possible sanctions are involved—urge a course of action for a subject. A continuum of such influencing factors exists, however, and it is impossible to state precisely where justifiable persuasion ends and undue influence begins. But undue influence would include actions such as manipulating a person's choice through the controlling influence of a close relative and threatening to withdraw health services to which an individual would otherwise be entitled.

2. **Assessment of Risks and Benefits.**—The assessment of risks and benefits requires a careful arrary of relevant data, including, in some cases, alternative ways of obtaining the benefits sought in the research. Thus, the assessment presents both an opportunity and a responsibility to gather systematic and comprehensive information about proposed research. For the investigator, it is a means to examine whether the proposed research is properly designed. For a review committee, it is a method for determining whether the risks that will be presented to subjects are justified. For prospective subjects, the assessment will assist the determination whether or not to participate.

The Nature and Scope of Risks and Benefits. The requirement that research be justified on the basis of a favorable risk/benefit assessment bears a close relation to the principle of beneficence, just as the moral requirement that informed consent be obtained is derived primarily from the principle of respect for persons. The term "risk" refers to a possibility that harm may occur. However, when expressions such as "small risk" or "high risk" are used, they usually refer (often ambiguously) both to the chance (probability) of experiencing a harm and the severity (magnitude) of the envisioned harm.

The term "benefit" is used in the research context to refer to something of positive value related to health or welfare. Unlike, "risk," "benefit" is not a term that expresses probabilities. Risk is properly contrasted to probability of benefits, and benefits are properly contrasted with harms rather than risks of harm. Accordingly, so-called risk/benefit assessments are concerned with the probabilities and magnitudes of possible harm and anticipated benefits. Many kinds of possible harms and benefits need to be taken into account. There are, for example, risks of psychological harm, physical harm, legal harm, social harm and economic harm and the corresponding benefits. While the most likely types of harms to research subjects are those of psychological or physical pain or injury, other possible kinds should not be overlooked.

Risks and benefits of research may affect the individual subjects, the families of the individual subjects, and society at large (or special groups of subjects in society). Previous codes and Federal regulations have required that risks to subjects be outweighed by the sum of both the anticipated benefit to the subject, if any, and the anticipated benefit to society in the form of knowledge to be gained from the research. In balancing these different elements, the risks and benefits affecting the immediate research subject will normally carry special weight. On the other hand, interests other than those of the subject may on some occasions be sufficient by themselves to justify the risks involved in the research, so long as the subjects' rights have been protected. Beneficence thus requires that we protect against risk of harm to subjects and also that we be concerned about the loss of the substantial benefits that might be gained from research.

The Systematic Assessment of Risks and Benefits. It is commonly said that benefits and risks must be "balanced" and shown to be "in a favorable ratio." The metaphorical character of these terms draws attention to the difficulty of making precise judgments. Only on rare occasions will quantitative techniques be available for the scrutiny of research protocols. However, the idea of systematic, nonarbitrary analysis of risks and benefits should be emulated insofar as possible. This ideal requires those making decisions about the justifiability of research to be thorough in the accumulation and assessment of information about all aspects of the research, and to consider alternatives systematically. This procedure renders the assessment of research more rigorous and precise, while making communication between review board members and investigators less subject to misinterpretation, misinformation and conflicting judgments. Thus, there should first be a determination of the validity of the presuppositions of the research; then the nature, probability and magnitude of risk should be distinguished with as much clarity as possible. The method of ascertaining risks should be explicit, especially where there is no alternative to the use of such vague categories as small or slight risk. It should also be determined whether an investigator's estimates of the probability of harm or benefits are reasonable, as judged by known facts or other available studies.

Finally, assessment of the justifiability of research should reflect at least the following considerations: (**i**) Brutal or inhumane treatment of human subjects is never morally justified. (**ii**) Risks should be reduced to those necessary to achieve the research objective. It should be determined whether it is in fact necessary to use human subjects at all. Risk can perhaps never be entirely eliminated, but it can often be reduced by careful attention to alternative procedures. (**iii**) When research involves significant risk of serious impairment, review committees should be extraordinarily insistent on the justification of the risk (looking usually to the likelihood of benefit to the subject—or, in some rare cases, to the manifest voluntariness of the participation). (**iv**) When vulnerable populations are involved in research, the appropriateness of involving them should itself be demonstrated. A number of variables go into such judgments, including the nature and degree of risk, the condition of the particular population involved, and the nature and level of the anticipated benefits. (**v**) Relevant risks and benefits must be thoroughly arrayed in documents and procedures used in the informed consent process.

3. **Selection of Subjects.**—Just as the principle of respect for persons finds expression in the requirements for consent, and the principle of beneficence in risk/benefit assessment, the principle of justice gives rise to moral

requirements that there be fair procedures and outcomes in the selection of research subjects.

Justice is relevant to the selection of subjects of research at two levels: the social and the individual. Individual justice in the selection of subjects would require that researchers exhibit fairness: thus, they should not offer potentially beneficial research only to some patients who are in their favor or select only "undesirable" persons for risky research. Social justice requires that distinction be drawn between classes of subjects that ought, and ought not, to participate in any particular kind of research, based on the ability of members of that class to bear burdens and on the appropriateness of placing further burdens on already burdened persons. Thus, it can be considered a matter of social justice that there is an order of preference in the selection of classes of subjects (e.g., adults before children) and that some classes of potential subjects (e.g., the institutionalized mentally infirm or prisoners) may be involved as research subjects, if at all, only on certain conditions.

Injustice may appear in the selection of subjects, even if individual subjects are selected fairly by investigators and treated fairly in the course of research. Thus injustice arises from social, racial, sexual and cultural biases institutionalized in society. Thus, even if individual researchers are treating their research subjects fairly, and even if IRBs are taking care to assure that subjects are selected fairly within a particular institution, unjust social patterns may nevertheless appear in the overall distribution of the burdens and benefits of research. Although individual institutions or investigators may not be able to resolve a problem that is pervasive in their social setting, they can consider distributive justice in selecting research subjects.

Some populations, especially institutionalized ones, are already burdened in many ways by their infirmities and environments. When research is proposed that involves risks and does not include a therapeutic component, other less burdened classes of persons should be called upon first to accept these risks of research, except where the research is directly related to the specific conditions of the class involved. Also, even though public funds for research may often flow in the same directions as public funds for health care, it seems unfair that populations dependent on public health care constitute a pool of preferred research subjects if more advantaged populations are likely to be the recipients of the benefits.

One special instance of injustice results from the involvement of vulnerable subjects. Certain groups, such as racial minorities, the economically disadvantaged, the very sick, and the institutionalized may continually be sought as research subjects, owing to their ready availability in settings where research is conducted. Given their dependent status and their frequently compromised capacity for free consent, they should be protected against the danger of being involved in research solely for administrative convenience, or because they are easy to manipulate as a result of their illness or socioeconomic condition.

NOTES

(1) Since 1945, various codes for the proper and responsible conduct of human experimentation in medical research have been adopted by different organizations. The best known of these codes are the Nuremberg Code of 1947, the Helsinki Declaration of 1964 (revised in 1975), and the 1971 Guidelines (codified into Federal Regulations in 1974) issued by the U.S. Department of Health, Education, and Welfare Codes for the conduct of social and behavioral research have also been adopted, the best known being that of the American Psychological Association, published in 1973.

(2) Although practice usually involves interventions designed solely to enhance the well-being of a particular individual, interventions are sometimes applied to one individual for the enhancement of the well-being of another (e.g., blood donation, skin grafts, organ transplants) or an intervention may have the dual purpose of enhancing the well-being of a particular individual, and, at the same time, providing some benefit to others (e.g., vaccination, which protects both the person who is vaccinated and society generally). The fact that some forms of practice have elements other than immediate benefit to the individual receiving an intervention, however, should not confuse the general distinction between research and practice. Even when a procedure applied in practice may benefit some other person, it remains an intervention designed to enhance the well-being of a particular individual or groups of individuals; thus, it is practice and need not be reviewed as research.

(3) Because the problems related to social experimentation may differ substantially from those of biomedical and behavioral research, the Commission specifically declines to make any policy determination regarding such research at this time. Rather, the Commission believes that the problem ought to be addressed by one of its successor bodies.

One of the most horrific biomedical ethical violations in the United States, the "Tuskegee Study of Untreated Syphilis in the Negro Male" was conducted in the United States from 1932 to 1972. Known now simply as "Tuskegee," this study is synonymous with racism and unethical research conduct—and an awful moment in the history of research in the United States. Some research studies have suggested that Tuskegee is a contributing factor to difficulties in enrolling African Americans in biomedical research including clinical trials, as well as possibly a barrier to health care seeking altogether. Below you will find a CDC summary and timeline, as well as a brief discussion of research implications regarding Tuskegee.

READING 7
U.S. Public Health Service Syphilis Study at Tuskegee

Centers for Disease Control and Prevention. U.S. Public Health Service Syphilis Study at Tuskegee. http://www.cdc.gov/tuskegee/timeline.htm and http://www.cdc.gov/tuskegee/after.htm [accessed 2-8-08].

The American people are sorry—for the loss, for the years of hurt.

You did nothing wrong, but you were grievously wronged.

I apologize and I am sorry that this apology has been so long in coming.

President William J. Clinton, May 16, 1997

Nearly 65 years after the U.S. Public Health Service Syphilis Study at Tuskegee began, President Clinton apologized for the U.S. government's role in the research study, which was carried out in Macon County, Alabama, from 1932 to 1972.

The United States Public Health Service, in trying to learn more about syphilis and justify treatment programs for blacks, withheld adequate treatment from a group of poor black men who had the disease, causing needless pain and suffering for the men and their loved ones.

In the wake of the Tuskegee Study and other studies, the federal government took a closer look at research involving human subjects and made changes to prevent the moral breaches that occurred in Tuskegee from happening again.

THE TUSKEGEE TIMELINE
The Study Begins
In 1932, the Public Health Service, working with the Tuskegee Institute, began a study to record the natural history of syphilis in hopes of justifying treatment programs for blacks. It was called the "Tuskegee Study of Untreated Syphilis in the Negro Male."

The study involved 600 black men—399 with syphilis, 201 who did not have the disease. The study was conducted with-

out the benefit of patients' informed consent. Researchers told the men they were being treated for "bad blood," a local term used to describe several ailments, including syphilis, anemia, and fatigue. In truth, they did not receive the proper treatment needed to cure their illness. In exchange for taking part in the study, the men received free medical exams, free meals, and burial insurance. Although originally projected to last 6 months, the study actually went on for 40 years.

What Went Wrong?

In July 1972, an Associated Press story about the Tuskegee Study caused a public outcry that led the Assistant Secretary for Health and Scientific Affairs to appoint an Ad Hoc Advisory Panel to review the study. The panel had nine members from the fields of medicine, law, religion, labor, education, health administration, and public affairs.

The panel found that the men had agreed freely to be examined and treated. However, there was no evidence that researchers had informed them of the study or its real purpose. In fact, the men had been misled and had not been given all the facts required to provide informed consent.

The men were never given adequate treatment for their disease. Even when penicillin became the drug of choice for syphilis in 1947, researchers did not offer it to the subjects. The advisory panel found nothing to show that subjects were ever given the choice of quitting the study, even when this new, highly effective treatment became widely used.

The Study Ends and Reparation Begins

The advisory panel concluded that the Tuskegee Study was "ethically unjustified"—the knowledge gained was sparse when compared with the risks the study posed for its subjects. In October 1972, the panel advised stopping the study at once. A month later, the Assistant Secretary for Health and Scientific Affairs announced the end of the Tuskegee Study.

In the summer of 1973, a class-action lawsuit was filed on behalf of the study participants and their families. In 1974, a $10 million out-of-court settlement was reached. As part of the settlement, the U.S. government promised to give lifetime medical benefits and burial services to all living participants. The Tuskegee Health Benefit Program (THBP) was established to provide these services. In 1975, wives, widows and offspring were added to the program. In 1995, the program was expanded to include health as well as medical benefits. The Centers for Disease Control and Prevention was given responsibility for the program, where it remains today in the National Center for HIV/AIDS, Viral Hepatitis, STD, and TB Prevention. As of May 2007, 19 widows, children and grandchildren are receiving medical and health benefits.

TIMELINE

1895   Booker T. Washington at the Atlanta Cotton Exposition, outlines his dream for black economic development and gains support of northern philanthropists, including Julius Rosenwald (President of Sears, Roebuck and Company).

1900   Tuskegee educational experiment gains widespread support. Rosenwald Fund provides monies to develop schools, factories, businesses, and agriculture.

1915   Booker T. Washington dies; Robert Motin continues work.

1926   Health is seen as inhibiting development and major health initiative is started. Syphilis is seen as major health problem. Prevalence of 35 percent observed in reproductive age population.

1929   Aggressive treatment approach initiated with mercury and bismuth. Cure rate is less than 30 percent; treatment requires months and side effects are toxic, sometimes fatal.

1929   "Wall Street Crash"—economic depression begins.

1931   Rosenwald Fund cuts support to development projects. Clark and Vondelehr decide to follow men left untreated due to lack of funds in order to show need for treatment program.

1932   Follow-up effort organized into study of 399 men with syphilis and 201 without. The men would be given periodic physical assessments and told they were being treated. Motin agrees to support study if "Tuskegee gets its full share of the credit" and black professionals are involved (Dr. Dibble and Nurse Rivers are assigned to study).

1934   First papers suggest health effects of untreated syphilis.

1936   Major paper published. Study criticized because it is not known if men are being treated. Local physicians asked to assist and asked not to treat men. It was also decided to follow the men until death.

1940   Efforts made to hinder men from getting treatment ordered under the military draft effort.

1945   Penicillin accepted as treatment of choice for syphilis.

1947   USPHS establishes "Rapid Treatment Centers" to treat syphilis; men in study are not treated, but syphilis declines.

1962   Beginning in 1947, 127 black medical students are rotated through unit doing the study.

1968   Concern is raised about ethics of study by Peter Buxtun and others.

1969   CDC reaffirms need for study and gains local medical societies' support (AMA and NMA chapters officially support continuation of study).

1972   First news articles condemn studies.

1972   Study ends.

1973   Congress holds hearings and a class-action lawsuit is filed on behalf of the study participants.

1974   A $10 million out-of-court settlement is reached and the U.S. government promised to give lifetime medical benefits and burial services to all living participants. The Tuskegee Health Benefit Program (THBP) was established to provide these services.

1975   Wives, widows and offspring were added to the program.

1995   The program was expanded to include health as well as medical benefits.

1997   On May 16th President Clinton apologizes on behalf of the Nation.

Content Source: National Center for HIV/AIDS, Viral Hepatitis, STD, and TB Prevention.

RESEARCH IMPLICATIONS

How Tuskegee Changed Research Practices

After the Tuskegee Study, the government changed its research practices to prevent a repeat of the mistakes made in Tuskegee.

In 1974, the National Research Act was signed into law, creating the National Commission for the Protection of Human Subjects of Biomedical and Behavioral Research. The group identified basic principles of research conduct and suggested ways to ensure those principles were followed.

In addition to the panel's recommendations, regulations were passed in 1974 that required researchers to get voluntary informed consent from all persons taking part in studies done or funded by the Department of Health, Education, and Welfare (DHEW). They also required that all DHEW-supported studies using human subjects be reviewed by Institutional Review Boards, which read study protocols and decide whether they meet ethical standards.

The rules and policies for human subjects research have been reviewed and revised many times since they were first approved. From 1980–1983, the President's Commission for the Study of Ethical Problems in Medicine and Biomedical and Behavioral Research looked at federal rules for doing research on human subjects to see how well those rules were being followed. An Ethics Advisory Board was formed in the late 1970s to review ethical issues of biomedical research. In 1991, federal departments and agencies (16 total) adopted the Federal Policy for the Protection of Human Subjects.

Efforts to promote the highest ethical standards in research are still going on today. In October 1995, President Bill Clinton created a National Bioethics Advisory Commission, funded and led by the Department of Health and Human Services. The commission's task was to review current regulations, policies, and procedures to ensure all possible safeguards are in place to protect research volunteers. It was succeeded by the President's Council on Bioethics, which was established in 2001.

DISCUSSION QUESTIONS

1. There are three basic principles outlined in The Belmont Report: the principles of respect of persons, beneficence, and justice. Discuss how Tuskegee violates each of these (may do so in more than one way).

2. What was the moment when the study became unequivocally unethical?

3. Design a study that would examine the natural history of syphilis without being unethical in any way.

4. Design a study that would examine the effect of Tuskegee on willingness to access preventive health care among an urban population of African American youth. Is it possible that different screening activities are affected differently? If so, how can you measure the effects? What if there are effect modifiers—how might they be measured?

Randomized Controlled Trials: Design Is Easy, Implementation Not Always

In the following article, Sackett discusses his own personal relationship to conducting a randomized controlled trial: the bedside issues that are frequently taken for granted. It is relatively easy to design a study, but ensuring that each and every facet of the study is conducted according to the protocol is another story entirely. In every study, implementation relies upon front line staff: Individuals who did the thinking are seldom the ones doing all the work. Understanding their view, their level of "buy-in," their needs, is critical. This is part of the reason that working in an interdisciplinary/multidisciplinary team to write studies (randomized or otherwise) is a necessary step in all research, as is obtaining input from the people in whose hands the study's success will ultimately lie. The below is a first-hand account of some of the issues a physician faces when implementing a clinical trial. Dr. Sackett's analysis of the need for care in the conduct of clinical trials—really, in all studies—is crucial if we want (as we do) to be able to believe their findings.

READING 8
Failure to Gain Coal-Face Commitment and to Use the Uncertainty Principle

David L Sackett

Sackett DL. Why randomized controlled trials fail but needn't: 1. Failure to gain "coal-face" commitment and to use the uncertainty principle. *CMAJ*. 2000;162(9):1311–14.

Dr. Sackett is Director of the Trout Research & Education Centre at Irish Lake, Markdale, Ont.

This article has been peer reviewed.

FROM THE UNDERSIDE

My pager went off as I was half-dozing, half-reading the newspaper. Yuri Gagarin, born the same year as me, had just become the first man to orbit the earth; Nelson Mandela, not yet imprisoned, had gone underground; and John F. Kennedy had just signed the bill creating the Peace Corps. An hour later, back on the charity ward and feeling the effects of too much acrid coffee and too little sleep, achalasia hit me when I found the lancet-shaped diplococci in her sputum. It was 3 am and the research protocol, appearing unannounced on our workroom wall, declared that, as the front-line clinician (the British call this "working at the coal face"), I had to enter her into the trial.

She was single, poor, the sole supporter of 3 children and now so sick after 10 days of cough, fever and sputum that she'd risked losing her menial job by leaving it early to struggle through Chicago's filthy March slush to our emergency room. My boss was testing one of the first synthetic penicillins against the then standard penicillin G in patients with pneumococcal pneumonia, and she fit the entry criteria. But she had classic signs of hepatization and already had suffered an episode of the euphoria and cyanosis we'd been taught was characteristic of bacteremia and interlobar spread. The last patient I'd seen this sick from pneumococcal pneumonia, a strapping 18-year-old basketball player, was also the first patient on whom I'd conducted fruitless open-chest cardiac massage.

With the fear, hopelessness and trust I'd come to expect from my patients, she consented at once to take part in the trial. But by the time I completed her entry form I knew what I had to do. Blocking the view of the ward nurse, I took the syringe containing the study drug from the refrigerator, loaded a second syringe with penicillin G and injected her with both.

I have never discussed this decision with anyone, nor admitted it until now. I don't know how many of my fellow house officers did the same thing for their sickest patients. I believe that my action was right in particular, wrong in general (I've never cheated since), and doubly preventable.

EFFECT

To the extent that other house officers were doing their best to care for similar patients responded as I did, patients in both arms of this randomized controlled trial (RCT) would have been given penicillin G. As a result, it was a trial of the effect of *adding* synthetic penicillin *to* penicillin G, rather than the comparison of the 2 drugs that our boss had intended. In the absence of a negative interaction between the 2 penicillins, any lack of efficacy of synthetic penicillin when given alone would have remained undetected. The effect was a "false-equivalence" RCT.

I don't know how often this type of RCT failure occurs, and I've never encountered anyone who does know. Ken Schulz (1) collected anecdotes of attempts to "break the code" to find out what treatment a patient would be assigned to if they entered an RCT, from transilluminating a sealed envelope to rifling through the files of the principal investigator.

CAUSES

There were 2 underlying causes for the failure (at least in my contribution to it) of this RCT. The first was failure to gain "coal-face" commitment. I was an underling who had never been party to any discussion of the study question and how it would best be answered. It was not "my trial," and I had only a general stake, not a personal one, in guaranteeing that it generated a valid answer. The second cause was failure to use the uncertainty principle: I was certain that my patient needed penicillin G, and my responsibility to her welfare was in direct conflict with my responsibility to the internal validity of the RCT. Moreover, this possibility was neither acknowledged nor accommodated in the protocol posted on the wall. I could not serve both my patient and the RCT, and in serving the former I cheated the latter because this was preferable to serving the latter and thereby cheating the former, my patient. This conflict arose from my "knowing" that my patient needed penicillin G, and such convictions are just as relevant when they are wrong as when they are right.

PRINCIPLES

Coal-Face Commitment

Only collaborators and patients who consider an RCT "theirs" should be expected to follow its protocol. Although this principle has to do with human behaviour, not research methods, it is a key determinant of the internal validity and efficiency of every RCT. Given the increasing variety and magnitude of the competing demands placed on front-line clinicians, no one should be surprised to discover these clinicians neglecting any task they deem nonessential. The more detailed the entry form and eligibility criteria for "somebody else's" RCT, the greater the risk the criteria will be ignored, misunderstood or misapplied by distracted clinicians who regard them as further intrusions into an overfull call schedule.

Uncertainty Principle

Patient entry into RCTs should be governed by the uncertainty principle. What is "ethical" in one culture or era may be "unethical" in another; therefore, in this series I will avoid pronouncements on good and evil. However, when the set of ethical principles that are in vogue at a certain place and time impinge on the design and conduct of contemporaneous RCTs, I will examine the evidence on which the principles are based and their effects on RCTs. In the example I present in this essay, we need to consider both the waning North American principle of "equipoise" and the principle of "uncertainty" that is being increasingly adopted in most other parts of the world.

Equipoise is a "state of balance or equilibrium between two alternative therapies" (2) such that "there is no preference between treatments, i.e., it is thought equally likely that treatment A or B will turn out to be superior. At this point we may be said to be 'agnostic' . . . we would take odds of 1:1 on a bet."

(3) In certain times and places, equipoise has been considered a prerequisite for an ethical RCT. And in some of these times and places, the individual clinician and patient had to be free of any "hunch" or preference ("theoretical" equipoise) (4), while in others, individual clinicians and patients could have a preference as long as they "recognize that their less-favored treatment is preferred by colleagues whom they consider to be responsible and competent" (5) ("clinical" equipoise).

Opponents of the equipoise construct (including me) argue that it has three fatal flaws. First, it is incapable of application: equipoise is lost as soon as the first pair of patients given the alternative treatments finishes the trial and the allocation code is broken. Second, it treats hunches (preferences) as point-estimates and ignores the uncertainty with which those hunches are held. Put another way, and linking the constructs of equipoise and uncertainty, equipoise demands a "confidence interval" of zero, whereas uncertainty permits and works with confidence intervals of 50%, 99%, or any other magnitude. Third, and as a result of the first 2, equipoise is almost never possessed by trialists or explored by ethics committees. For example, in the great majority of the more than 200 RCTs in which I have played a role, neither I nor my patients nor my collaborators nor the nonparticipants we encountered from the relevant profession were in equipoise, and our hunches frequently were strong ones (indeed, some potential clinical collaborators were so convinced that the experimental treatment was efficacious or useless that they refused to have anything to do with a trial of it). It isn't that we have no hunches and are indifferent to the alternative treatments in our RCTs; it's that we are uncertain about whether our hunches are correct.

The "uncertainty" construct rejects the indifference of equipoise and builds on the notion that clinicians and patients are often uncertain whether their hunches about a treatment's effectiveness are true. That is, although their hunch about a specific treatment may be that it is probably effective, the boundaries ("confidence interval") around that hunch may run all the way from extremely effective (a wonder drug), across zero (ineffective) and into the realm of frank harm. When the uncertainty boundaries of a group of clinicians and patients include or cross zero (such that they recognize that the treatment they prefer might, in fact, be useless or even harmful), it is time for a trial, and that trial is ethical. Similarly, in equivalence trials such as the one that opened this essay, uncertainty exists as long as the confidence interval around the hunch that one of the treatments is actually superior includes or crosses zero. As I'll show you in the following section, this uncertainty principle helps decision-making not only by individual clinicians and individual patients, but also by trialists and trial monitors.

PREVENTIVE STRATEGIES

Achieve Commitment to the Trial in the Front Lines

Application of the "coal-face" principle (only clinicians and patients who consider an RCT "theirs" should be expected to follow its protocol) should begin with the first draft of the question to be answered by the RCT (fighting through the question to be posed by an RCT deserves much of the total effort expended on it, and will be discussed in greater detail in future essays in this series). The question should be shown, discussed and argued over with an ever-widening array of clinical and methodological collaborators, and ultimately with the front-line physicians, research assistants and study nurses who will effect its success or failure. In multicentre RCTs, part of each centre's responsibility should be to educate and involve those who are admitting and following the study patients and responding to their questions and concerns throughout the trial. The benefits of this time-consuming activity are 4. First, the attendant discussion and debate improves the specificity and clinical usefulness of the question. Second, when this process draws in other scientists, including bench researchers, it improves the science used to answer the question (and explain it). Third, these discussions permit collaborators and front-line participants to "buy in" to the trial and develop both the ownership and commitment that are essential for the successful assembly, care and follow-up of study patients and for adherence to the study protocol. Finally, the discussions provide the forum in which to understand the uncertainty principle and to gain confidence in the front lines in its ability to preserve patient choice and clinical judgement while protecting study validity.

Apply the Uncertainty Principle When Entering Patients Into RCTs

My contribution to the failure of the penicillin trial would have been prevented if its eligibility criteria had incorporated the general principle of uncertainty as it applies to the individual patient. I find this incorporation best articulated by Richard Peto and Colin Baigent: (6)

> A patient should not be entered if the responsible clinician or the patient are for any medical or non-medical reasons reasonably certain that one of the treatments that might be allocated would be inappropriate for this particular individual (in comparison with either no treatment or some other treatment that could be offered to the patient in or outside the trial).

I was reasonably certain that the synthetic penicillin was inappropriate for my patient. Had the uncertainty principle been in effect, my patient would never have entered the trial, and its internal validity would have been protected. Yes, one less patient would have entered the trial. But the consequent loss in the study's precision could have been made up by prolonging its recruitment phase, while the loss in its validity was irreparable.

There are several supplemental benefits to this preventive strategy. First, making patients equal partners in the application of the uncertainty principle legitimizes their hunches, respects their autonomy and reinforces the need for their informed consent. Second, its application can reduce complexity, confusion and waste in the generation and application of eligibility and ineligibility criteria. When exclusion criteria try to anticipate all of the real-world situations in which a reasonable clinician might not want to invite an eligible patient to join an RCT, they swell in size and complexity, confound the patient's risk and responsiveness with the clinician's responsibility and can result in unnecessarily strict entry criteria (e.g., age) and decreased patient numbers. Third, the application of the uncertainty principle to individual patients acts synergistically with the deliberations of the trial monitors, who examine the accumulating unblinded results. Their prime duty is to monitor the boundaries of uncertainty at the group level, alerting the trialists when it shrinks (for all patients or sensible subgroups) to the point where the more effective treatment becomes clear (and if this clarity emerges for some prespecified subgroups but not others, the trial can be stopped for the former but continued for the latter, all on the basis of the uncertainty principle). Finally, while respecting the clinical judgement that keeps some patients and clinicians from entering RCTs, the uncertainty principle is impervious to the validity of their hunches; even when the hunches are wildly wrong, acting on them will not damage the internal validity of the trial result.

The uncertainty principle acknowledges that most clinicians and patients do have hunches about a treatment's effectiveness but that the boundaries ("confidence interval") around their hunches may run all the way from extremely effective (a wonder drug), across zero (ineffective) and into the realm of frank harm.

Equipoise is a "state of balance or equilibrium between two alternative therapies" such that "there is no preference between treatments; i.e., it is thought equally likely that treatment A or B will turn out to be superior." Some definitions require each individual clinician and patient to be free of any "hunch" or preference ("theoretical" equipoise), while others permit individual clinicians and patients to have hunches as long as they "recognize that their less-favored treatment is preferred by colleagues whom they consider responsible and competent" ("clinical" equipoise).

PREVENTING RCT FAILURE

When the success or failure of the RCT depends on the recruitment of patients who are appropriate in type and number, achieve commitment to the trial in the front lines (the "coal face"). This will

- improve adherence to the protocol
- improve the study question
- improve the science
- provide a forum for incorporating values into research

When clinicians and patients have hunches about efficacy (i.e., always), apply the uncertainty principle when entering patients into RCTs. This will

- recognize and reinforce clinical judgment and patients' values and autonomy
- reduce complex eligibility criteria and paper work
- act synergistically with the deliberations of the trial monitors
- protect internal validity regardless of whether hunches are correct or wildly wrong

I thank 22 colleagues who offered encouragement and suggestions on drafts of this essay.

DISCUSSION QUESTIONS

1. In which direction (in favor of or against the study drug) might the author's decision to add the penicillin shot bias the study's findings? Describe why in narrative form and develop a mathematical example.

2. Differentiate equipoise and the uncertainty principle. Why does the author advocate for the latter?

3. Does provider lack of equipoise impact the three basic principles outlined in The Belmont Report? If so, how? If not, why not?

REFERENCES FROM THE READING

1. Schulz KF. Subverting randomization in controlled trials. *JAMA* 1995;274:1456–8.
2. Singer PA, Lantos JD, Whitington PF, Broelsch CE, Siegler M. Equipoise and the ethics of segmental liver resection. *Clin Res* 1988;36:539–45.
3. Lilford RJ, Jackson J. Equipoise and the ethics of randomisation. *J R Soc Med* 1995;88:552–9.
4. Hellman S, Hellman DS. Of mice but not men—problems of the randomized trial. *N Engl J Med* 1991;324:1585–9.
5. Freedman B. Equipoise and the ethics of clinical research. *N Engl J Med* 1987;317:141–5.
6. Peto R, Baigent C. Trials: the next 50 years. *BMJ* 1998;317:1170–1.

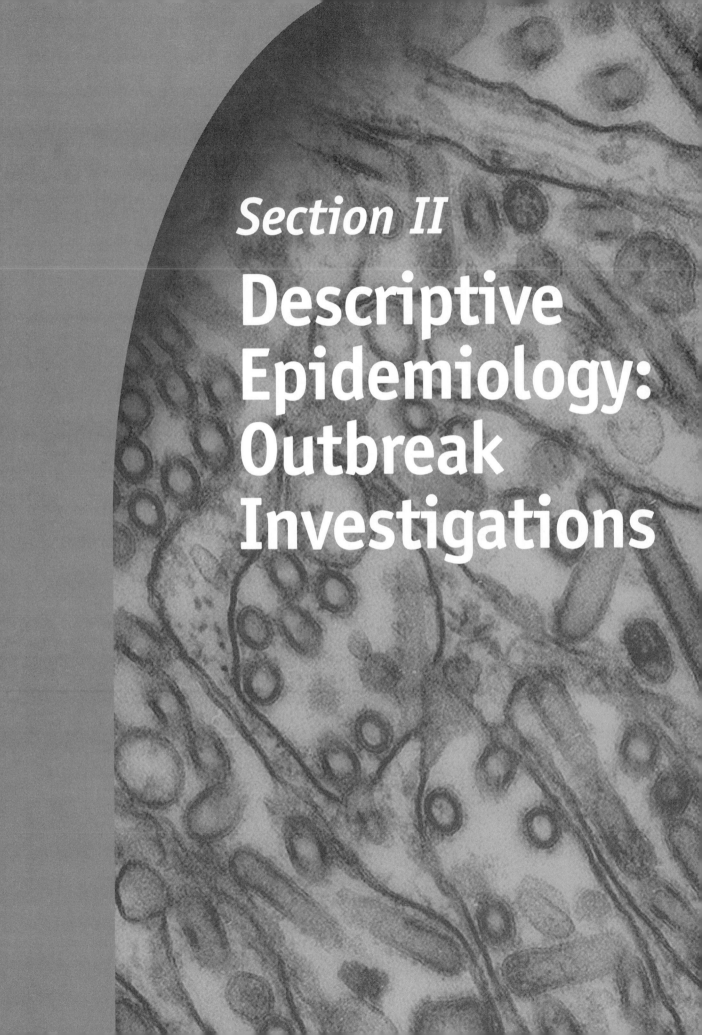

Section II

Descriptive Epidemiology: Outbreak Investigations

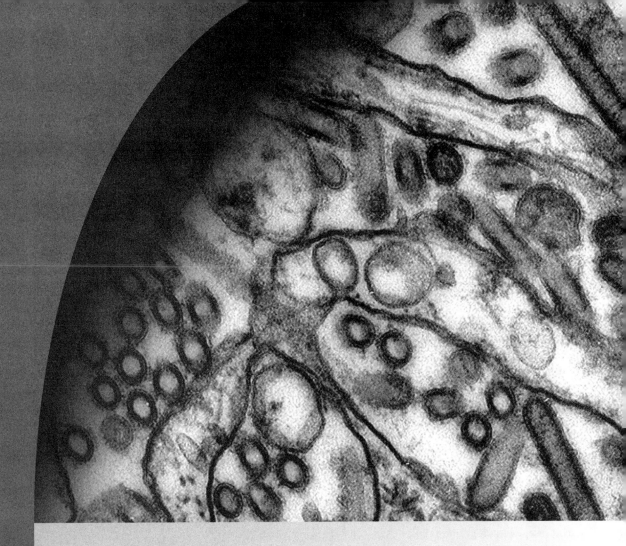

PART VI

Descriptive Epidemiology and Outbreak Investigations

Learning how to describe information is one of the most critical epidemiologic skills in our toolkit. Computers have enabled a wealth of methods to adjust for confounders, effect modifiers, and mathematical complexities of topics under study. However, simply *describing* information—although one of the first epidemiologic techniques developed—remains today one of our most powerful tools. In order to be able to understand the data under study, we need to be able to understand what is happening on the most basic level. How do we define the food poisoning case under study? How many cases of it were there? When did their symptoms occur? How many persons had each of the symptoms under investigation? How many went to the hospital? Where did the cases occur? Where had the individuals eaten prior to becoming symptomatic? What did each of the sick individuals eat? What did each of the non-sick individuals eat? And so forth. We open this section with a summary of outbreak investigations, refreshing you about the key issues in this critical form of epidemiologic and public health study.

READING 9
Outbreak Investigations—A Perspective

Arthur L. Reingold

Reingold AL, Outbreak Investigations—A Perspective. *Emerg Inf Dis*. 1998;4:21–7.

Outbreak investigations, an important and challenging component of epidemiology and public health, can help identify the source of ongoing outbreaks and prevent additional cases. Even when an outbreak is over, a thorough epidemiologic and environmental investigation often can increase our knowledge of a given disease and prevent future outbreaks. Finally, outbreak investigations provide epidemiologic training and foster cooperation between the clinical and public health communities.

Investigations of acute infectious disease outbreaks are very common, and the results of such investigations are often published; however, surprisingly little has been written about the actual procedures followed during such investigations (1,2). Most epidemiologists and public health officials learn the procedures by conducting investigations with the initial assistance of more experienced colleagues. This article outlines the general approach to conducting an outbreak investigation. The approach applies not only to infectious disease outbreaks but also to outbreaks due to noninfectious causes (e.g., toxic exposure).

HOW OUTBREAKS ARE RECOGNIZED

Possible outbreaks of disease come to the attention of public health officials in various ways. Often, an astute clinician, infection control nurse, or clinical laboratory worker first notices an unusual disease or an unusual number of cases of a disease and alerts public health officials. For example, staphylococcal toxic shock syndrome and eosinophilia myalgia syndrome were

first noted by clinicians (3,4). Frequently, it is the patient (or someone close to the patient) who first suspects a problem, as is often the case in food-borne outbreaks after a shared meal and as was the case in the investigation of a cluster of cases of apparent juvenile rheumatoid arthritis near Lyme, Connecticut, which led to the discovery of Lyme disease (5). Review of routinely collected surveillance data can also detect outbreaks of known diseases, as in the case of hepatitis B infection among the patients of an oral surgeon in Connecticut and patients at a weight reduction clinic (6,7). The former outbreak was first suspected when routinely submitted communicable disease report forms for several patients from one small town indicated that all of the patients had recently had oral surgery.

However, it is relatively uncommon for outbreaks to be detected in this way and even more uncommon for them to be detected in this way while they are still in progress. Finally, sometimes public health officials learn about outbreaks of disease from the local newspaper or television news.

REASONS FOR INVESTIGATING OUTBREAKS

The most compelling reason to investigate a recognized outbreak of disease is that exposure to the source(s) of infection may be continuing; by identifying and eliminating the source of infection, we can prevent additional cases. For example, if cans of mushrooms containing botulinum toxin are still on store shelves or in homes or restaurants, their recall and destruction can prevent further cases of botulism. However, even if an outbreak is essentially over by the time the epidemiologic investigation begins—that is, if no one is being further exposed to the source of infection—investigating the outbreak may still be indicated for many reasons.

Foremost is that the results of the investigation may lead to recommendations or strategies for preventing similar future outbreaks. For example, a Legionnaires' disease outbreak investigation may produce recommendations for grocery store misting machine use that may prevent other outbreaks (8). Other reasons for investigating outbreaks are the opportunity to 1) describe new diseases and learn more about known diseases; 2) evaluate existing prevention strategies, e.g., vaccines; 3) teach (and learn) epidemiology; and 4) address public concern about the outbreak.

Once a decision is made to investigate an outbreak, three types of activities are generally involved—the epidemiologic investigation; the environmental investigation; and the interaction with the public, the press, and, in many instances, the legal system. While these activities often occur simultaneously throughout the investigation, it is conceptually easier to consider each of them separately.

EPIDEMIOLOGIC INVESTIGATION

Outbreak investigations are, in theory, indistinguishable from other epidemiologic investigations; however, outbreak investigations encounter more constraints. 1) If the outbreak is ongoing at the time of the investigation, there is great urgency to find the source and prevent additional cases. 2) Because outbreak investigations frequently are public, there is substantial pressure to conclude them rapidly, particularly if the outbreak is ongoing. 3) In many outbreaks, the number of cases available for study is limited; therefore, the statistical power of the investigation is limited. 4) Early media reports concerning the outbreak may bias the responses of persons subsequently interviewed. 5) Because of legal liability and the financial interests of persons and institutions involved, there is pressure to conclude the investigation quickly, which may lead to hasty decisions regarding the source of the outbreak. 6) If detection of the outbreak is delayed, useful clinical and environmental samples may be very difficult or impossible to obtain. Outbreak investigations have essential components as follows: 1) establish case definition(s); 2) confirm that cases are "real"; 3) establish the background rate of disease; 4) find cases, decide if there is an outbreak, define scope of the outbreak; 5) examine the descriptive epidemiologic features of the cases; 6) generate hypotheses; 7) test hypotheses; 8) collect and test environmental samples; 9) implement control measures; and 10) interact with the press, inform the public. While the first seven components are listed in logical order, in most outbreak investigations, many occur more or less simultaneously. The importance of these components may vary depending on the circumstances of a specific outbreak.

CASE DEFINITION

In some outbreaks, formulating the case definition(s) and exclusion criteria is straightforward; for example, in an outbreak of gastroenteritis caused by Salmonella infection, a laboratory-confirmed case would be defined as a culture-confirmed infection with Salmonella or perhaps with Salmonella of the particular serotype causing the outbreak, while a clinical case definition might be new onset of diarrhea. In other outbreaks, the case definition and exclusion criteria are complex, particularly if the disease is new and the range of clinical manifestations is unknown (e.g., in a putative outbreak of chronic fatigue syndrome). In many outbreak investigations, multiple case definitions are used (e.g., laboratory-confirmed case vs. clinical case; definite vs. probable vs. possible case; outbreak-associated case vs. non–outbreak-associated case; primary case vs. secondary case), and the resulting data are analyzed by using different case definitions.

When the number of cases available for study is not a limiting factor and a case-control study is being used to examine risk factors for becoming a case, a strict case definition is often preferable to increase specificity and reduce misclassification of disease status (i.e., reduce the chance of including cases of unrelated illness or no illness as outbreak-related cases).

CASE CONFIRMATION

In certain outbreaks, clinical findings in reported cases should be reviewed closely, either directly, by examining the patients, or indirectly, by detailed review of the medical records and discussion with the attending health-care provider(s), especially when a new disease appears to be emerging (e.g., in the early investigations of Legionnaires' disease, AIDS, eosinophilia myalgia syndrome, and hantavirus pulmonary syndrome) (4, 9–11). Clinical findings should also be examined closely when some or all of the observed cases may be factitious, perhaps because of laboratory error (12); a discrepancy between the clinical and laboratory findings generally exists, which may be discernible only by a detailed review of the clinical findings.

ESTABLISHING THE BACKGROUND RATE OF DISEASE AND FINDING CASES

Once it is clear that a suspected outbreak is not the result of laboratory error, a set of activities should be undertaken to establish the background rate of the disease in the affected population and to find all the cases in a given population in a certain period. This set of activities should prove that the observed number of cases truly is in excess of the "usual" number (i.e., that an outbreak has occurred), define the scope of the outbreak geographically and temporally, find cases to describe the epidemiologic features of those affected and to include them in analytic epidemiologic studies (see below) or, most often, accomplish a combination of these goals.

When hundreds of acute onset diarrhea cases are suddenly seen daily in a single outpatient setting (10), an outbreak is clearly occurring. On the other hand, when too many hospitalized patients are dying unexpectedly of cardiac arrest (13) or the number of cases of listeriosis in a given county in recent months is moderately elevated, it may be necessary to establish the background rates in the population to determine whether an outbreak is occurring. In such situations, the period and geographic areas involved would provide the most useful baseline data, keeping in mind that the labor and time required to collect such information is often directly proportional to the length of the period and the size of the geographic area selected. Because disease incidence normally fluctuates by season, data from comparable seasons in earlier years should be included.

Establishing the background rate of a disease is generally more straightforward if confirmatory tests are available than if laboratory tests are unavailable or infrequently used. The rate of certain invasive bacterial infections (e.g., listeriosis and meningococcal infections) in a given area can be easily documented by reviewing the records of hospital clinical microbiology laboratories; however, cases for which specimens were not submitted to these laboratories for testing will go undetected. When a disease is less frequently laboratory-confirmed because health-care providers may not have considered the diagnosis or ordered the appropriate laboratory tests (e.g., for Legionnaires' disease), establishing the background rate of disease in a community or a hospital suspected of having an outbreak generally requires alternative case-finding strategies and is almost invariably more labor intensive. In an outbreak of a new disease, substantial effort is often necessary to determine whether or not cases of that disease had been occurring but had gone unrecognized.

Once data concerning the background rate of a disease (including case-finding for the current period) have been collected, it is generally possible to determine whether or not an outbreak is occurring or has occurred, although in some situations it may remain unclear whether or not the number of cases observed exceeds the background rate. In part, the problem may relate to how an outbreak is defined. To paraphrase a U.S. Supreme Court justice speaking about pornography, "I can't define an outbreak, but I know one when I see one." Thus, it may be difficult to detect and prove the existence of small outbreaks, but large ones are self-evident.

An outbreak can also be difficult to identify when during the period under study changes occur in the care-seeking behavior and access to care of patients; the level of suspicion, referral patterns, and test-ordering practices of healthcare providers; the diagnostic tests and other procedures used by laboratories; and the prevalence of underlying immunosuppressive conditions or other host factors in the population.

All these factors, which can affect the apparent incidence of a disease and produce artifactual changes perceived as increases (or decreases) in the actual incidence, need to be considered when interpreting the findings.

DESCRIPTIVE EPIDEMIOLOGY

By collecting patient data, the case-finding activities provide extremely important information concerning the descriptive epidemiologic features of the outbreak. By reviewing and plotting on an "epidemic curve" the times of onset of the cases and by examining the characteristics (e.g., age, sex, race/ethnicity, residence, occupation, recent travel, or attendance at events) of the ill persons, investigators can often generate hypotheses concerning the cause(s)/source(s) of the outbreak. While linking the sudden onset of gastroenteritis among scores of persons who attended a church supper to the single common meal they shared is generally not a challenge, an otherwise cryptic source can be at least hinted at by the descriptive epidemiologic features of the cases involved. For example, in a particularly perplexing outbreak of Salmonella Muenchen infections ultimately traced to contaminated marijuana, the age distribution of the affected persons and of their households was markedly different from that typically seen for salmonellosis (14). Or, similarly, in the outbreak of legionellosis due to contaminated misting machines in the produce section of a grocery store, before the link to this exposure was even suspected, it was noted that women constituted a substantially higher proportion of the cases usually seen with this disease (5). The shape of the epidemic curve can also be very instructive, suggesting a point-source epidemic, ongoing transmission, or a combination of the two.

GENERATING A HYPOTHESIS

The source(s) and route(s) of exposure must be determined to understand why an outbreak occurred, how to prevent similar outbreaks in the future, and, if the outbreak is ongoing, how to prevent others from being exposed to the source(s) of infection. In some outbreaks, the source and route are obvious to those involved in the outbreak and to the investigators. However, even when the source of exposure appears obvious at the outset, a modicum of skepticism should be retained because the obvious answer is not invariably correct. For example, in an outbreak of nosocomial legionellosis in Rhode Island, the results of an earlier investigation into a small number of hospital-acquired cases at the same hospital had demonstrated that Legionella pneumophila was in the hospital potable water supply, and a sudden increase in new cases was strongly believed to be related to the potable water (15). However, a detailed epidemiologic investigation implicated a new cooling tower at the hospital as the source of the second outbreak.

While the true source of exposure, or at least a relatively short list of possibilities, is apparent in many outbreaks, this is not the case in the more challenging outbreaks. In these instances, hypotheses concerning the source/route of exposure can be generated in a number of ways beyond a detailed review of the descriptive epidemiologic findings. A review of existing epidemiologic, microbiologic, and veterinary data is very useful for learning about known and suspected sources of previous outbreaks or sporadic cases of a given infection or disease, as well as the ecologic niche of an infectious agent. Thus, in an outbreak of invasive Streptococcus zooepidemicus infections in New Mexico due to consumption of soft cheese made from contaminated raw milk, the investigation focused on exposure to dairy products and animals because of previous microbiologic and veterinary studies (16).

A review of existing data generally only helps confirm what is already known about a particular disease and is far less helpful in identifying totally new and unsuspected sources or routes of infection (i.e., marijuana as a source of Salmonella). When neither review of the descriptive epidemiologic features of the cases nor review of existing scientific information yields the correct hypothesis, other methods can be used to generate hypotheses about what the patients have in common. Open-ended interviews of those infected (or their surrogates) are one such method in which investigators try to identify all possibly relevant exposures (e.g., a list of all foods consumed) during a given period. For example, in an investigation of Yersinia enterocolitica infections in young children in Belgium, open-ended interviews of the mothers of some of the ill children showed that many gave their children raw pork sausage as a weaning food, providing the first clue as to the source of these infections (17). Similarly, in two outbreaks of food-borne listeriosis, a variant of this process led to the identification of the source of the outbreak. In one of these outbreaks, a search of the refrigerator of one of the case-patients who, as a visitor to the area, had had very limited exposure to foods there, suggested cole slaw as a possible vehicle of infection (18). In the other outbreak, an initial case-control study found no differences between cases and controls regarding exposure to a number of specific food items but showed that case households were more likely than control households to buy their food at a particular foodstore chain. To generate a list of other possible food sources of infection, in-

vestigators shopped with persons who did the shopping for case households and compiled a list of foods purchased at that foodstore chain that had not been reported in the previous study. This approach implicated pasteurized milk from that chain as the source of the outbreak (19).

In some particularly perplexing outbreaks, bringing together a subset of the patients to discuss their experiences and exposures in a way that may reveal unidentified links can be useful.

TESTING THE HYPOTHESIS

Whether a hypothesis explaining the occurrence of an outbreak is easy or difficult to generate, an analytic epidemiologic study to test the proposed hypothesis should be considered. While in many instances a case-control study is used, other designs, including retrospective cohort and cross-sectional studies, can be equally or more appropriate. The goal of all these studies is to assess the relationship between a given exposure and the disease under study. Thus, each exposure of interest (e.g., each of the meals eaten together by passengers on a cruise ship and each of the foods and beverages served at those meals) constitutes a separate hypothesis to be tested in the analytic study. In outbreaks where generating the correct hypothesis is difficult, multiple analytic studies, with additional hypothesis-generating activities in between, are sometimes needed before the correct hypothesis is formed and tested (19).

In interpreting the results of such analytic studies, one must consider the possibility that "statistically significant" associations between one or more exposures and the disease may be chance findings, not indicative of a true relationship. By definition, any "statistically significant" association may have occurred by chance. (When the standard cut point of $p < 0.05$ is used, this occurs 5% of the time.) Because many analytic epidemiologic studies of outbreaks involve testing many hypotheses, the problem of "multiple comparisons" arises often.

While there are statistical methods for adjusting for multiple comparisons, when and even whether to use them is controversial. At a minimum, it is important to go beyond the statistical tests and examine the magnitude of the effect observed between exposure and disease (e.g., the odds ratio, relative risk) and the 95% confidence intervals, as well as biologic plausibility in deciding whether or not a given "statistically significant" relationship is likely to be biologically meaningful. Evidence of a dose response effect between a given exposure and illness (i.e., the greater the exposure, the greater the risk for illness) makes a causal relationship between exposure and disease more likely.

Whether the time interval between a given exposure and onset of illness is consistent with what is known about the incubation period of the disease under study must also be assessed. When illness is "statistically significantly" related to more than one exposure (e.g., to eating each of several foods at a common meal), it is important to determine whether multiple sources of infection (perhaps due to cross-contamination) are plausible and whether some of the noted associations are due to confounding (e.g., exposure to one potential source is linked to exposure to other sources) or to chance.

When trying to decide if a "statistically significant" exposure is the source of an outbreak, it is important to consider what proportion of the cases can be accounted for by that exposure. One or more of the patients may be classified as "nonexposed" for various reasons: incorrect information concerning exposure status (due to poor memory, language barriers); multiple sources of exposure or routes of transmission (perhaps due to cross-contamination); secondary person-to-person transmission that followed a common source exposure; or patients without the suspected exposure, representing background cases of the disease unrelated to the outbreak. The plausibility of each of these explanations varies by outbreak. While there is no cutoff point above or below which the proportion of exposed case-patients should fall before an exposure is thought to account for an outbreak, the lower this proportion, the less likely the exposure is, by itself, the source.

Other possibilities need to be considered when the analytic epidemiologic study finds no association between the hypothesized exposures and risk for disease. The most obvious possibility is that the real exposure was not among those examined, and additional hypotheses should be generated. However, other possibilities should also be considered, particularly when the setting of the outbreak makes this first explanation unlikely (e.g., when it is known that those involved in the outbreak shared only a single exposure or set of exposures, such as eating a single common meal). Two other explanations for failing to find a "statistically significant" link between one or more exposures and risk for illness also need to be considered—the number of persons available for study and the accuracy of the available information concerning the exposures.

Thus, if the outbreak involves only a small number of cases (and non-ill persons), the statistical power of the analytic study to find a true difference in exposure between the ill and the non-ill (or a difference in the rate of disease among the exposed and the unexposed) is very limited. If the persons involved in the outbreak do not provide accurate information about their exposure to suspected sources or vehicles of infection because of lack of knowledge, poor memory, language difficulty, mental impairment, or other reasons, the resulting misclassification of exposure status also can prevent the epidemiologic study from implicating the source of infection. Studies have documented that even under ideal circumstances, memory concerning such exposures is faulty (20). However, given the usually enormous differences in rates of disease between those exposed and those not exposed to the source of the outbreak, even small studies or studies with substantial misclassification of exposure can still correctly identify the source.

ENVIRONMENTAL INVESTIGATION

Samples of foods and beverages served at a common meal believed to be the source of an outbreak of gastroenteritis or samples of the water or drift from a cooling tower believed to be the source of an outbreak of Legionnaires' disease can support epidemiologic findings. In the best scenario, the findings of the epidemiologic investigation would guide the collection and testing of environmental samples. However, environmental specimens often need to be obtained as soon as possible, either before they are no longer available, as in the case of residual food from a common meal, or before environmental interventions are implemented, as in the case of treating a cooling tower to eradicate Legionella. Because laboratory testing of environmental samples is often expensive and labor intensive, it is sometimes reasonable to collect and store many samples but test only a limited number. Collaborating with a sanitarian, environmental engineer, or other professional during an environmental inspection or collection of specimens is always beneficial.

While finding or not finding the causative organism in environmental samples is often perceived by the public, the media, and the courts as powerful evidence implicating or exonerating an environmental source, either positive or negative findings can be misleading for several reasons. For example, finding Legionella in a hospital potable water system does not prove that the potable water (rather than a cooling tower or some other source) is responsible for an outbreak of Legionnaires' disease (21). Similarly, not finding the causative organism in an environmental sample does not conclusively rule out a source as the cause of the problem, in part because the samples obtained and tested may not represent the source (e.g., because of error in collecting the specimens, intervening changes in the environmental source) and in part because the samples may have been mishandled. Furthermore, in some outbreaks caused by well-characterized etiologic agents, laboratory methods of detecting the agent in environmental samples are insensitive, technically difficult, or not available, as in the case of recent outbreaks of Cyclospora infections associated with eating imported berries (22, 23).

CONTROL MEASURES

Central to any outbreak investigation is the timely implementation of appropriate control measures to minimize further illness and death. At best, the implementation of control measures would be guided by the results of the epidemiologic investigation and possibly (when appropriate) the testing of environmental specimens. However, this approach may delay prevention of further exposure to a suspected source of the outbreak and is, therefore, unacceptable from a public health perspective. Because the recall of a food product, the closing of a restaurant, or similar interventions can have profound economic and legal implications for an institution, a manufacturer or owner, and the employees of the establishments involved, acting precipitously can also have substantial negative effects. The recent attribution of an outbreak of Cyclospora infections to strawberries from California demonstrates the economic impact that can result from releasing and acting on incorrect information (22, 23). Thus, the timing and nature of control measures are difficult. Balancing the responsibility to prevent further disease with the need to protect the credibility and reputation of an institution is very challenging.

INTERACTIONS WITH THE PUBLIC AND PRESS

While the public and the press are not aware of most outbreak investigations, media attention and public concern become part of some investigations. Throughout the course of an outbreak investigation, the need to share information with public officials, the press, the public, and the population affected by the outbreak must be assessed. While press, radio, and television reports can at times be inaccurate, overall the media can be a powerful means of sharing information about an investigation with the public and disseminating timely information about product recalls.

Dr. Reingold worked as an epidemiologist at the Centers for Disease Control and Prevention for 8 years before joining the faculty of the School of Public Health at the University of California, Berkeley. He is currently professor of epidemiology and head of the Division of Public Health Biology and Epidemiology.

REFERENCES FROM THE READING

1. Goodman RA, Buehler JW, Koplan JP. The epidemiologic field investigation: science and judgment in public health practice. Am J Epidemiol 1990;132:9–16.

2. MacKenzie WR, Goodman RA. The public health response to an outbreak. Current Issues in Public Health1996;2:1–4.

3. Chesney PJ, Chesney RW, Purdy W, Nelson D, McPherson T, W and P, et al. Epidemiologic notes and reports: toxic-shock syndrome—United States. MMWR Morb Mortal Wkly Rep 1980;29:229–30.

4. Hertzman PA, Blevins WL, Mayer J, Greenfield B, Ting M, Gleich GJ, et al. Association of eosinophilia myalgia syndrome with the ingestion of tryptophan. N Engl J Med 1980;322:871.

5. Steere AC, Malawista SE, Syndman DR, Shope RF, Andman WA, Ross MR, Steele FM. Lyme arthritis: an epidemic of oligoarticular arthritis in children and adults in three Connecticut communities. Arthritis Rheum 1977; 20:7.

6. Reingold AL, Kane MA, Murphy BL, Checko P, Francis DP, Maynard JE. Transmission of Hepatitis B by an oral surgeon. J Infect Dis 1982;145: 262.

7. Canter J, Mackey K, Good LS, Roberto RR, Chin J, Bond WW, et al. An outbreak of hepatitis B associated with jet injections in a weight reduction clinic. Arch Intern Med 1990;150:1923–7.

8. Mahoney FJ, Hoge CW, Farley TA, Barbaree JM, Breiman RF, Benson RF, McFarland LM. Community-wide outbreak of Legionnaires' disease associated with a grocery store mist machine. J Infect Dis 1992;165:736.

9. Fraser DW, Tsai TR, Orenstein W, Parkin WE, Beecham HJ, Sharrar RG, et al. Legionnaires' disease: description of an epidemic of pneumonia. N Engl J Med 1977;297:1189–97.

10. Kriedman-Kien A, Laubenstein L, Marmor M, Hymes K, Green J, Ragaz A, et al. Kaposi's sarcoma and Pneumocystis pneumonia among homosexual men—New York City and California. MMWR Morb Mortal Wkly Rep 1981;30:305–8.

11. Koster F, Levy H, Mertz G, Young S, Foucar K, McLaughlin J, et al. Outbreak of acute illness— southwestern United States. MMWR Morb Mortal Wkly Rep 1993;42:421–4.

12. Weinstein RA, Bauer FW, Hoffman RD, Tyler PG, Anderson RL, Stamm WE. Factitious meningitis: diagnostic error due to nonviable bacteria in commercial lumbar puncture trays. JAMA 1975;233:878.

13. Buehler JW, Smith LF, Wallace EM, Heath CW, Rusiak R, Herndon JL. Unexplained deaths in a children's hospital: an epidemiologic assessment. N Engl J Med 1985;313:211.

14. Taylor DN, Wachsmuth IK, Shangkuan Y-H, Schmidt EV, Barrett TJ, Schrader JS, et al. Salmonellosis associated with marijuana: a multistate outbreak traced by plasmid fingerprinting. N Engl J Med 1982;306:1249.

15. Garbe PL, Davis BJ, Weisfeld JS, Markowitz L, Miner P, Garrity F, et al. Nosocomial Legionnaires' disease: epidemiologic demonstration of cooling towers as a source. JAMA 1985;254:521.

16. Espinosa FH, Ryan WM, Vigil PL, Gregory DF, Hilley RB, Romig DA, et al. Group C streptococcal infections associated with eating homemade cheese: New Mexico. MMWR Morb Mortal Wkly Rep 1983;32:514.

17. Tauxe RV, Walters G, Goossen V, VanNoyer R, Vandepitte J, Martin SM, et al. Yersinia enterocolitica infections and pork: the missing link. Lancet 1987;5:1129.

18. Schlech WF, Lavigne PM, Bortolussi RA, Allen AC, Haldane EV, Wort AJ, et al. Epidemic listeriosis: evidence for transmission by food. N Engl J Med 1983;308:203.

19. Fleming DW, Cochi SL, MacDonald KL, Brondum J, Hayes PS, Plikaytis BD, et al. Pasteurized milk as a vehicle of infection in an outbreak of listeriosis. N Engl J Med 1985;312:404.

20. Decker MD, Booth AL, Dewey MJ, Fricker RS, Hutcheson RH, Schaffner W. Validity of food consumption histories in a foodborne outbreak investigation. Am J Epidemiol 1986;124:859.

21. Hayes EB, Matte TD, O'Brien TR, McKinley TW, Logsdon GS, Rose JB, et al. Large community outbreak of cryptosporidiosis due to contamination of a filtered public water supply. N Engl J Med 1989;390:1372.

22. Chambers J, Somerfieldt S, Mackey L, Nichols S, Ball R, Roberts D, et al. Outbreaks of Cyclospora cayetanensis infection—United States, 1996. MMWR Morb Mortal Wkly Rep 1996;45:549–51.

23. Hofman J, Liu Z, Genese C, Wolf G, Manley W, Pilot K, et al. Update: outbreaks of Cyclospora cayetanensis infection—United States and Canada, 1996. MMWR Morb Mortal Wkly Rep 1996;45:611–2.

The following recommendations outline a framework for assessment of surveillance systems that address outbreaks. This framework allows information about outbreaks to effectively inform development and maintenance of surveillance systems—an essential step toward recognition and control.

READING 10
Framework for Evaluating Public Health Surveillance Systems for Early Detection of Outbreaks: Recommendations from the CDC Working Group

James W. Buehler, Richard S. Hopkins, J. Marc Overhage, Daniel M. Sosin, Van Tong

Beuhler JW, Hopkins RS, Overhage JM, et al. Framework for Evaluating Public Health Surveillance Systems for Early Detection of Outbreaks: Recommendations from the CDC Working Group. *MMWR*. 2004;53 (No. RR-5).

SUMMARY

The threat of terrorism and high-profile disease outbreaks has drawn attention to public health surveillance systems for early detection of outbreaks. State and local health departments are enhancing existing surveillance systems and developing new systems to better detect outbreaks through public health surveillance. However, information is limited about the usefulness of surveillance systems for outbreak detection or the best ways to support this function. This report supplements previous guidelines for evaluating public health surveillance systems. Use of this framework is intended to improve decision-making regarding the implementation of surveillance for outbreak detection. Use of a standardized evaluation methodology, including description of system design and operation, also will enhance the exchange of information regarding methods to improve early detection of outbreaks. The framework directs particular attention to the measurement of timeliness and validity for outbreak detection. The evaluation framework is designed to support assessment and description of all surveillance approaches to early detection, whether through traditional disease reporting, specialized analytic routines for aberration detection, or surveillance using early indicators of disease outbreaks, such as syndromic surveillance.

INTRODUCTION

Public health surveillance is the ongoing, systematic collection, analysis, interpretation, and dissemination of data about a health-related event for use in public health action to reduce morbidity and mortality and to improve health (1). Surveillance serves at least eight public health functions. These include supporting case detection and public health interventions, estimating the impact of a disease or injury, portraying the natural history of a health condition, determining the distribution and spread of illness, generating hypotheses and stimulating research, evaluating prevention and control measures, and facilitating planning (2). Another important public health function of surveillance is outbreak detection (i.e., identifying an increase in frequency of disease above the background occurrence of the disease).

Outbreaks typically have been recognized either based on accumulated case reports of reportable diseases or by clinicians and laboratorians who alert public health officials about clusters of diseases. Because of the threat of terrorism and the increasing availability of electronic health data, enhancements are being made to existing surveillance systems, and new surveillance systems have been developed and implemented in public health jurisdictions with the goal of early and complete detection of outbreaks (3). The usefulness of surveillance systems for early detection and response to outbreaks has not been established, and substantial costs can be incurred in developing or enhancing and managing these surveillance systems and investigating false alarms (4). The measurement of the performance of public health surveillance systems for outbreak detection is needed to establish the relative value of different approaches and to provide information needed to improve their efficacy for detection of outbreaks at the earliest stages.

This report supplements existing CDC guidelines for evaluating public health surveillance systems (1). Specifically, the report provides a framework to evaluate timeliness for outbreak detection and the balance among sensitivity, predictive value positive (PVP), and predictive value negative (PVN) for detecting outbreaks. This framework also encourages detailed description of system design and operations and of their experience with outbreak detection.

The framework is best applied to systems that have data to demonstrate the attributes of the system under consideration.

Nonetheless, this framework also can be applied to systems that are in early stages of development or in the planning phase by using citations from the published literature to support conclusions. Ideally, the evaluation should compare the performance of the surveillance system under scrutiny to alternative surveillance systems and produce an assessment of the relative usefulness for early detection of outbreaks.

BACKGROUND

Early detection of outbreaks can be achieved in three ways: 1) by timely and complete receipt, review, and investigation of disease case reports, including the prompt recognition and reporting to or consultation with health departments by physicians, health-care facilities, and laboratories consistent with disease reporting laws or regulations; 2) by improving the ability to recognize patterns indicative of a possible outbreak early in its course, such as through analytic tools that improve the predictive value of data at an early stage of an outbreak or by lowering the threshold for investigating possible outbreaks; and 3) through receipt of new types of data that can signify an outbreak earlier in its course. These new types of data might include health-care product purchases, absences from work or school, presenting symptoms to a health-care provider, or laboratory test orders (5).

DISEASE CASE REPORTS

The foundation of communicable disease surveillance in the United States is the state and local application of the reportable disease surveillance system known as the National Notifiable Disease Surveillance System (NNDSS), which includes the listing of diseases and laboratory findings of public health interest, the publication of case definitions for their surveillance, and a system for passing case reports from local to state to CDC. This process occurs best where two-way communication occurs between public health agencies and the clinical community: clinicians and laboratories report cases and clusters of reportable and unusual diseases, and health departments consult on case diagnosis and management, alerts, surveillance summaries, and clinical and public health recommendations and policies. Faster, more specific and affordable diagnostic methods and decision-support tools for diseases with substantial outbreak potential could improve the timely recognition of reportable diseases. On-going health-care provider and laboratory outreach, education, and 24-hour access to public health professionals are needed to enhance reporting of urgent health threats. Electronic laboratory reporting (i.e., the automated transfer of designated data from a laboratory database to a public health data repository using a defined message structure) also will improve the timeliness and completeness of reporting notifiable conditions (6–8) and

can serve as a model for electronic reporting of a wider range of clinical information. A comprehensive surveillance effort supports timely investigation (i.e., tracking of cases once an outbreak has been recognized) and data needs for managing the public health response to an outbreak or terrorist event.

PATTERN RECOGNITION

Statistical tools for pattern recognition and aberration detection can be applied to screen data for patterns warranting further public health investigation and to enhance recognition of subtle or obscure outbreak patterns (9). Automated analysis and visualization tools can lessen the need for frequent and intensive manual analysis of surveillance data.

NEW DATA TYPES

Many new surveillance systems, loosely termed syndromic surveillance systems, use data that are not diagnostic of a disease but that might indicate the early stages of an outbreak. The scope of this framework is broader than these novel systems, yet the wide-ranging definitions and expectations of syndromic surveillance require clarification. Syndromic surveillance for early outbreak detection is an investigational approach where health department staff, assisted by automated data acquisition and generation of statistical signals, monitor disease indicators continually (real-time) or at least daily (near real-time) to detect outbreaks of diseases earlier and more completely than might otherwise be possible with traditional public health methods (e.g., by reportable disease surveillance and telephone consultation). The distinguishing characteristic of syndromic surveillance is the use of indicator data types. For example, a laboratory is a data source that can support traditional disease case reporting by submitting reports of confirmatory laboratory results for notifiable conditions; however, test requests are a type of laboratory data that might be used as an outbreak indicator by tracking excess volume of test requests for diseases that typically cause outbreaks. New data types have been used by public health to enhance surveillance, reflecting events that might precede a clinical diagnosis (e.g., patient's chief complaints in emergency departments, clinical impressions on ambulance log sheets, prescriptions filled, retail drug and product purchases, school or work absenteeism, and constellations of medical signs and symptoms in persons seen in various clinical settings).

Outbreak detection is the overriding purpose of syndromic surveillance for terrorism preparedness. Enhanced casefinding and monitoring the course and population characteristics of a recognized outbreak also are potential benefits of syndromic surveillance (4). A manual syndromic surveillance system was used to detect additional anthrax cases in the fall of 2001 when the outbreak was recognized (10). Complicating the understanding of syndromic surveillance is that syndromes have been used for case detection and management of diseases when the condition is infrequent and the syndrome is relatively specific for the condition of interest. Acute flaccid paralysis is a syndromic marker for poliomyelitis and is used to detect single cases of suspected polio in a timely way to initiate investigation and control measures. In this case, the syndrome is relatively uncommon and serious and serves as a proxy for polio (11). Syndromes also have been used effectively for surveillance in resource-poor settings for sexually transmitted disease detection and control where laboratory confirmation is not possible or practical (12). However, syndromic surveillance for terrorism is not intended for early detection of single cases or limited outbreaks because the early clinical manifestations of diseases that might be caused by terrorism are common and nonspecific (13).

FRAMEWORK

This framework is intended to support the evaluation of all public health surveillance systems for the timely detection of outbreaks. The framework is organized into four categories: system description, outbreak detection, experience, and conclusions and recommendations. A comprehensive evaluation will address all four categories.

A. System Description

1. **Purpose.** The purpose(s) of the system should be explicitly and clearly described and should include the intended uses of the system. The evaluation methods might be prioritized differently for different purposes. For example, if terrorism is expected to be rare, reassurance might be the primary purpose of the terrorism surveillance system. However, for reassurance to be credible, negative results must be accurate and the system should have a demonstrated ability to detect outbreaks of the kind and size being dismissed. The description of purpose should include the indications for implementing the system; whether the system is designed for short-term, high-risk situations or long-term, continuous use; the context in which the system operates (whether it stands alone or augments data from other surveillance systems); what type of outbreaks the system is intended to detect; and what secondary functional value is desired. Designers of the system should specify the desired sensitivity and specificity of the system and whether it is intended to capture small or large events.

2. **Stakeholders.** The stakeholders of the system should be listed. Stakeholders include those who provide data for the system and those who use the information generated by the system (e.g., public health practitioners; healthcare providers; other health-related data providers; public safety officials; government officials at local, state, and federal levels; community residents; nongovernmental organizations; and commercial systems developers). The stakeholders might vary among different systems and might change as conditions change. Listing stakeholders helps define who the system is intended to serve and provides context for the evaluation results.

3. **Operation.** All aspects of the operation of the syndromic surveillance system should be described in detail to allow stakeholders to validate the description of the system and for other interested parties to understand the complexity and resources needed to operate such a system. Detailed system description also will facilitate evaluation by highlighting variations in system operation that are relevant to variations in system performance (Figure 6-1). Such a conceptual model can facilitate the description of the system. The description of the surveillance process should address 1) systemwide characteristics (data flow [Figure 6-2]), including data and transmission standards to facilitate interoperability and data sharing between information systems, security, privacy, and confidentiality; 2) data sources (used broadly in this framework to include the data-producing facility [i.e., the entity sharing data with the public health surveillance system], the data type [e.g., chief complaint, discharge diagnosis, laboratory test order], and the data format [e.g., electronic or paper, text descriptions of events or illnesses, or structured data reworded or stored in standardized format]); 3) data processing before analysis (the data collation, filtering, transformation, and routing functions required for public health to use the data, including the classification and assigning of syndromes); 4) statistical analysis (tools for automated screening of data for potential outbreaks); and 5) epidemiologic analysis, interpretation, and investigation (the rules, procedures, and tools that support decision-making in response to a system signal, including adequate staffing with trained epidemiologists who can review, explore, and interpret the data in a timely manner).

B. Outbreak Detection

The ability of a system to reliably detect an outbreak at the earliest possible stage depends on the timely capture and processing of the data produced by transactions of health behaviors (e.g., over-the-counter pharmaceutical sales, emergency depart-

FIGURE 6-1 Process model for early outbreak detection.

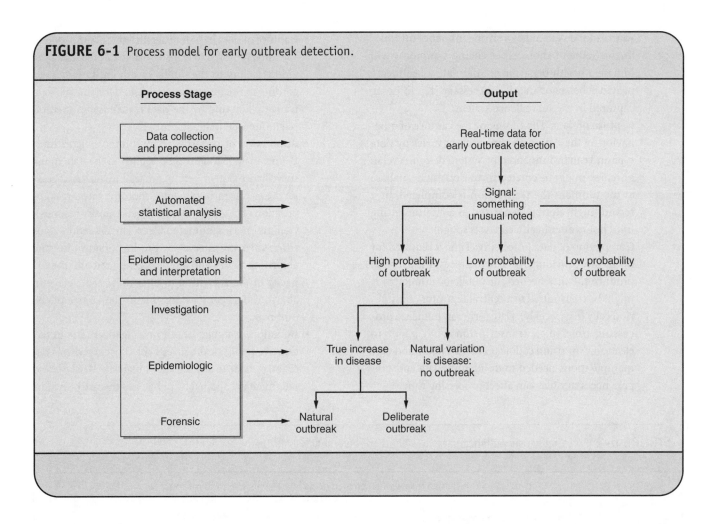

ment visits, and nurse call-line volume) or health-care activities (e.g., laboratory test volume and triage categorization of chief complaint) that might indicate an outbreak; the validity of the data for measuring the conditions of interest at the earliest stage of illness and the quality of those data; and the detection methods applied to these processed surveillance data to distinguish expected events from those indicative of an outbreak.

1. **Timeliness.** The timeliness of surveillance approaches for outbreak detection is measured by the lapse of time from exposure to the disease agent to the initiation of a public health intervention. A timeline with interim milestones is proposed to improve the specificity of timeliness measures (Figure 6-3). Although measuring all of the time points that define the intervals might be impractical or inexact in an applied outbreak setting, measuring intervals in a consistent way can be used to compare alternative outbreak-detection approaches and specific surveillance systems.

   • Onset of exposure: By anchoring the timeline on exposure, the timeliness advantage of different data

sources can be assessed and compared. Exposure can most easily be estimated in a point-source outbreak. Time of exposure is often inferred from knowledge of the agent (e.g., incubation period) and the epidemiology of the outbreak.

   • Onset of symptoms: The interval to symptom onset in each case is defined by the incubation period for the agent. Time of symptom onset might be estimated using case interviews or existing knowledge of the agent and the time of exposure. The incubation period might vary according to host factors and the route and dose of the exposure.

   • Onset of behavior: Following symptom onset, several health behaviors can occur (e.g., purchasing over-the-counter medication from a store, calling in sick to work, or visiting an urgent-care center). When an affected person interacts with the health-care system, a variety of health-care provider behaviors might be performed (e.g., order of a laboratory test and admission to a hospital). The selection of data sources for a system has a strong influence on time-liness. Some of those experiencing symptoms will initiate a health behavior or stimulate a healthcare provider behavior that is a necessary step to being captured in the surveillance system.

- Capture of data: The timing of the capture of a behavior by the data-providing facility varies by data type and can be influenced by system design. A retail purchase might be entered in an electronic database at the moment the transaction is completed, or a record might not be generated in a clinical setting until hours after health care was sought.
- Completion of data processing: Time is required for the facility providing the data to process the data and produce the files needed for public health. Records might be transmitted to a central repository only periodically (e.g., weekly). Data form can influence processing time (e.g., transcription from paper to electronic form and coding text-based data), and data manipulations needed to de-identify data and prepare necessary files can affect processing time.

- Capture of data in public health surveillance system: The time required to transfer data from the data providing facility to the public health entity varies according to the frequency established for routine data transmission and by the data transmission method (e.g., Internet, mail, or courier).
- Application of pattern recognition tools/algorithms: Before analytic tools can be applied to the data in the surveillance system, certain processing steps are necessary (e.g., categorization into syndrome categories, application of case definition, and data transformations).
- Generation of automated alert: The detection algorithm's alerting interval is a product of how often the algorithm is run and a report generated and the capacity of the algorithm to filter noise and detect an aberration as early as possible in the course of the outbreak.
- Initiation of public health investigation: The initiation of a public health investigation occurs when a decision is made to acquire additional data. Analysis and judgment are applied by public health-care providers

FIGURE 6-2 Prototypical surveillance data flow chart for emergency department encounters.

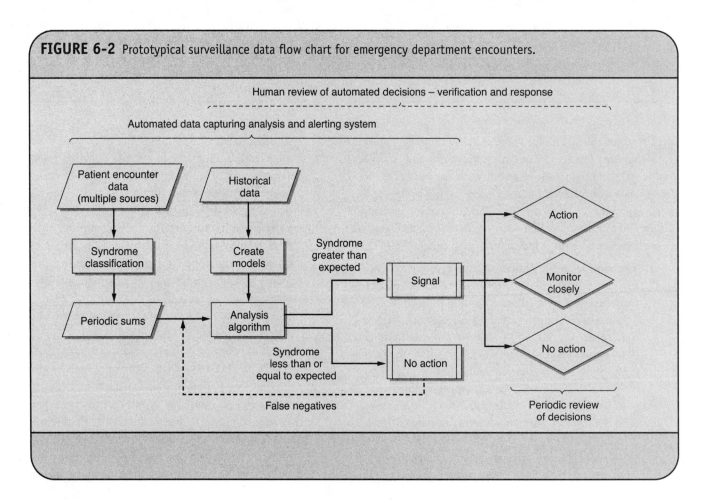

to the processed surveillance data and other available information to decide whether new data collection is warranted to confirm the existence of an outbreak. The challenge of interpreting data from multiple surveillance systems could diminish potential advantages in timeliness. The focus on outbreak detection allows for investigations of potential outbreaks to proceed before a specific clinical diagnosis is obtained.

- Initiation of public health intervention: When an outbreak of public health significance is confirmed, interventions can be implemented to control the severity of disease and prevent further spread. Interventions might be of a general nature directed to the recognition of an outbreak (e.g., apply respiratory infection precautions and obtain clinical specimens for diagnosis) or can be specific to the diagnosis (e.g., antibiotic prophylaxis or vaccination).

2. **Validity.** Measuring the validity of a system for outbreak detection requires an operational definition of an outbreak. Although a statistical deviation from a baseline rate can be useful for triggering further investigation, it is not sufficient for defining an outbreak. In practice, the confirmation of an outbreak is a judgment that depends on past experience with the condi-

tion, the severity of the condition, the communicability of the condition, confidence in the diagnosis of the condition, public health concern about outbreaks at the time, having options for effective prevention or control, and the resources required and available to respond. Operationally, an outbreak is defined by the affected public health jurisdiction when the occurrence of a condition has changed sufficiently to warrant public health attention.

The validity of a surveillance system for outbreak detection varies according to the outbreak scenario and surveillance system factors. These factors can confound the comparison of systems and must be carefully described in the evaluation. For example, the minimum size of an outbreak that can be detected by a system cannot be objectively compared among systems unless they are identical or differences are accounted for in several ways.

- Case definitions: Establish the specificity and sensitivity for the condition of interest on the basis of the data source, data type, and response criteria.
- Baseline estimation: Determine the stability of the background occurrence of cases. Estimations are affected by factors such as population size and

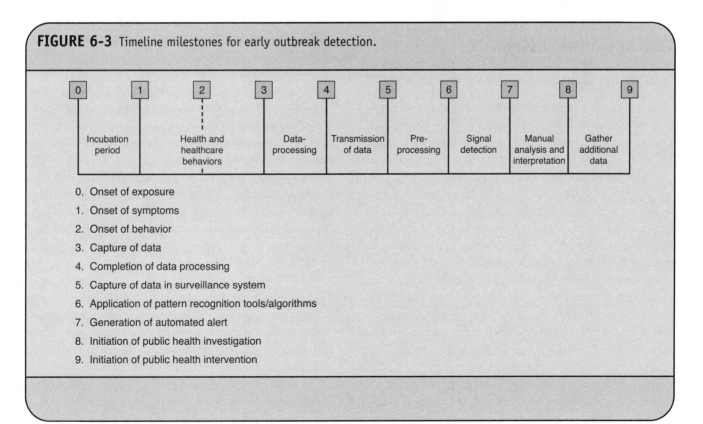

FIGURE 6-3 Timeline milestones for early outbreak detection.

| 0 | 1 | 2 | 3 | 4 | 5 | 6 | 7 | 8 | 9 |

| Incubation period | Health and healthcare behaviors | Data-processing | Transmission of data | Pre-processing | Signal detection | Manual analysis and interpretation | Gather additional data |

0. Onset of exposure
1. Onset of symptoms
2. Onset of behavior
3. Capture of data
4. Completion of data processing
5. Capture of data in surveillance system
6. Application of pattern recognition tools/algorithms
7. Generation of automated alert
8. Initiation of public health investigation
9. Initiation of public health intervention

geographic distribution. The performance of detection algorithms will vary by the quality and duration and inherent variability of baseline data.

- Reporting delays: Result in incomplete data, introducing bias that will diminish the performance of detection algorithms.
- Data characteristics: Includes underlying patterns in the data (e.g., seasonal variation) and systematic errors inherent in the data (e.g., product sales that influence purchasing behaviors unrelated to illness).
- Outbreak characteristics: Results from agent, host, and environmental factors that affect the epidemiology of the outbreak. For example, a large aerosol exposure with an agent causing serious disease in a highly susceptible population will have different detection potential than an outbreak of similar size spread person-to-person over a longer time and dispersed distribution.
- Statistical analysis: Defines how data are screened for outbreak detection. Detection algorithms have different performance characteristics under different outbreak conditions.
- Epidemiologic analysis, interpretation, and investigation: The procedures, resources, and tools for analysis, interpretation, and response that can substantially affect the ability to detect and respond to outbreaks.

VALIDATION APPROACHES

Different approaches to outbreak detection need to be evaluated under the same conditions to isolate the unique features of the system (e.g., data type) from the outbreak characteristics and the health department capacity. The data needed to evaluate and compare the performance of surveillance systems for early outbreak detection can be obtained from naturally occurring outbreaks or through simulation.

Controlled comparisons of surveillance systems for detection of deliberately induced outbreaks will be difficult because of the infrequency of such outbreaks and the diversity of systems and outbreak settings. However, understanding the value of different surveillance approaches to early detection will increase as descriptions of their experience with detecting and missing naturally occurring outbreaks accumulate. Accumulation of experience descriptions is made more difficult by not having standard methods for measuring outbreak detection successes and failures across systems and by the diversity of surveillance system and outbreak factors that influence performance. Standardized classification of system and outbreak factors will enable comparison of experiences across systems. Pending the development of classification standards,

descriptive evaluation should include as much detail as possible. Proxy outbreak scenarios reflect the types of naturally occurring outbreaks that should not be missed to instill confidence in the ability of these systems to detect outbreaks caused by terrorism.

Examples of proxy events or outbreaks include seasonal events (e.g., increases in influenza, norovirus gastroenteritis, and other infectious respiratory agents) and community outbreaks (e.g., foodborne, waterborne, hepatitis A, child-care–associated shigellosis, legionellosis, and coccidioidomycosis and histoplasmosis in areas where the diseases are endemic).

The measurement of outbreaks detected, false alarms, and outbreaks missed or detected late should be designed as a routine part any system workflow and conducted with minimal effort or complexity. Routine reporting should be automated where possible. Relevant information needs include: the number of statistical aberrations detected at a set threshold in a defined period of time (e.g., frequency per month at a given p-value); the action taken as a result of the signals (e.g., review for data errors, in-depth follow-up analysis of the specific conditions within the syndrome category, manual epidemiologic analysis to characterize a signal, examining data from other systems, and increasing the frequency of reporting from affected sites); resources directed to the follow-up of the alert; public health response that resulted (e.g., an alert to clinicians, timely dissemination of information to other health entities, a vaccination campaign, or no further response); documentation of how every recognized outbreak in the jurisdiction was detected; an assessment of the value of the follow-up effort (e.g., the effort was an appropriate application of public health resources); a detailed description of the agent, host, and environmental conditions of the outbreak; and the number of outbreaks detected only late in their course or in retrospect. To evaluate the relative value of different methods for outbreak detection, a direct comparison approach is needed. For example, if a health department detects a substantial number of its outbreaks through telephone consultations, then a phone call tracking system might produce the data needed to compare telephone consults with other approaches for early detection of outbreaks.

As an alternative to naturally occurring outbreaks, simulations can allow for the control and modification of agent, host, and environmental factors to study system performance across a range of common scenarios. However, simulations are limited in their ability to mimic the diversity and unpredictability of real-life events. Whenever possible, simulated outbreaks should be superimposed on historical trend data. To evaluate detection algorithms comparatively, a shared challenge problem and data set would be helpful. Simulation is limited by the availability of well-documented outbreak scenarios (e.g., organism or agent characteristics, transmission characteristics, and population characteristics). Simulations should incorporate data for each of the factors described previously. Multiple simulation runs should be used to test algorithm performance in different outbreak scenarios, allowing for generation of operating characteristic curves that reflect performance in a range of conditions.

Focused studies to validate the performance of limited aspects of systems (e.g., data sources, case definitions, statistical methods, and timeliness of reporting) can provide indirect evidence of system performance. Component studies also can test assumptions about outbreak scenarios and support better data simulation. Syndrome case definitions for certain specific data sources need to be validated. Component validation studies should emphasize outbreak detection over case detection.

These studies contain explicit hypotheses and research questions and should be shared in a manner to advance the development of outbreak detection systems without unnecessary duplication.

STATISTICAL ASSESSMENT OF VALIDITY

Surveillance systems must balance the risk for an outbreak, the value of early intervention, and the finite resources for investigation. Perceived high risk and high value of timely detection support high sensitivity and low thresholds for investigation. A low threshold can prompt resource-intensive investigations and occupy vital staff, and a high threshold might delay detection and intervention. The perceived threat of an outbreak, the community value attached to early detection, and the investigation resources available might vary over time. As a result, specifying a fixed relation between optimal sensitivity and predictive value for purposes of evaluation might be difficult.

The sensitivity and PVP and PVN are closely linked and considered together in this framework. Sensitivity is the percentage of outbreaks occurring in the jurisdiction detected by the system. PVP reflects the probability of a system signal being an outbreak. PVN reflects the probability that no outbreak is occurring when the system does not yield a signal. The calculation of sensitivity and predictive value is described in detail in the updated guidelines for evaluating public health surveillance systems (1). Measurement of sensitivity requires an alternative data source of high quality (e.g., "gold" standard) to confirm outbreaks in the population that were missed by the surveillance system. Sensitivity for outbreak detection could be assessed through capture-recapture techniques with two independent data sources (14). The high costs associated with responding to false alarms and with delayed response to out-

breaks demand efforts to quantify and limit the impact of both. As long as the likelihood of terrorism is extremely low, PVP will remain near zero and a certain level of nonterrorism signals will be a necessary part of conducting surveillance for the detection of terrorism. Better performance can be achieved in one attribute (e.g., sensitivity) without a performance decrement in another (e.g., PVP) by changing the system (e.g., adding a data type or applying a better detection algorithm).

Improving sensitivity by lowering the cut-off for signaling an outbreak will reduce PVP. Sensitivity and PVP for these surveillance systems will ultimately be calibrated in each system to balance the secondary benefits (e.g., detection of naturally occurring outbreaks, disease case finding and management, reassurance of no outbreak during periods of heightened risk, and a stronger reporting and consultation relation between public health and clinical medicine) with the locally acceptable level of false alarms.

DATA QUALITY

The validity of syndromic surveillance system data is dependent on data quality. Error-prone systems and data prone to inaccurate measurement can negatively affect detection of unusual trends. Although data quality might be a less critical problem for screening common, nonspecific indicators for statistical aberrations, quality should be evaluated and improved to the extent possible. Measuring data quality is dependent on a standard (e.g., medical record review or fabricated test data with values known to the evaluator). The updated guidelines for evaluating public health surveillance systems (1) describe data quality in additional detail.

- Representativeness: When case ascertainment within a population is incomplete (e.g., in a sentinel system or a statistically based sample), representativeness reflects whether a system accurately describes the distribution of cases by time, place, and person. Geographic representativeness is particularly important for detecting outbreaks of infectious diseases.
- Completeness of data: The frequency of unknown or blank responses to data items in the system can be used to measure the level of completeness. For systems that update data from previous transmissions, time should be factored into measurement by indicating the percentage of records that are complete (i.e., all variables are captured for a record) on initial report and within an appropriate interval (e.g., 48 hours) of submission. Sites with substantial reporting delays can be flagged for reliability concerns and targeted for improvement. Incomplete data can require follow-up before analysis,

with associated decreases in timeliness and increase in cost. When multiple data providers contribute to a common data store for statistical analysis, the percentage of reporting sources that submit their data on a routine interval (e.g., every 24 hours) conveys the completeness of the aggregate database for routine analysis. Evaluation of completeness should include a description of the problems experienced with manual data management (e.g., coding errors or loss of data) and the problems with automated data management (e.g., programming errors or inappropriate filtering of data).

C. System Experience

The performance attributes described in this section convey the experience that has accrued in using the system.

1. **System usefulness.** A surveillance system is useful for outbreak detection depending on its contribution to the early detection of outbreaks of public health significance that leads to an effective intervention. An assessment of usefulness goes beyond detection to address the impact or value added by its application. Measurement of usefulness is inexact. As with validity, measurement will benefit from common terminology and standard data elements. In the interim, detailed efforts to describe and illustrate the consequences of early detection efforts will improve understanding of their usefulness.

   Evaluation should begin with a review of the objectives of the system and should consider the priorities. To the extent possible, usefulness should be described by the disease prevention and control actions taken as a result of the analysis and interpretation of the data from the system.

   The impact of the surveillance system should be contrasted with other mechanisms available for outbreak detection. An assessment of usefulness should list the outbreaks detected and the role that different methods played in the identification of each one. Examples of how the system has been used to detect or track health problems other than outbreaks in the community should be included. The public health response to the outbreaks and health problems detected should be described as well as how data from new or modified surveillance systems support inferences about disease patterns that would not be possible without them.

   Surveillance systems for early outbreak detection are sometimes justified for the reassurance they provide when aberrant patterns are not apparent during a heightened risk period or when the incidence of cases declines during an outbreak. When community reassurance is claimed as a benefit of the surveillance system, reassurance should be defined and the measurement quantified (e.g., number of phone calls from the public on a health department hotline, successful press conferences, satisfaction of public health decision-makers, or resources to institutionalize the new surveillance system). A description should include who is reassured and of what they are reassured, and reassurance should be evaluated for validity by estimating the PVN.

2. **Flexibility.** The flexibility of a surveillance system refers to the system's ability to change as needs change. The adaptation to changing detection needs or operating conditions should occur with minimal additional time, personnel, or other resources. Flexibility generally improves the more data processing is handled centrally rather than distributed to individual data-providing facilities because fewer system and operator behavior changes are needed. Flexibility should address the ability of the system to apply evolving data standards and code sets as reflected in Public Health Information Network (PHIN) standards (http://www.cdc.gov/phin). Flexibility includes the adaptability of the system to shift from outbreak detection to outbreak management. The flexibility of the system to meet changing detection needs can include the ability to add unique data to refine signal detection, to capture exposure and other data relevant to managing an outbreak, to add data providers to increase population coverage and detect or track low frequency events, to modify case definitions (the aggregation of codes into syndrome groupings), to improve the detection algorithm to filter random variations in trends more efficiently, and to adjust the detection threshold. Flexibility also can be reflected by the ability of the system to detect and monitor naturally occurring outbreaks in the absence of terrorism. System flexibility is needed to balance the risk for an outbreak, the value of early intervention, and the resources for investigation as understanding of these factors changes.

3. **System acceptability.** As with the routine evaluation of public health surveillance systems (1), the acceptability of a surveillance system for early outbreak detection is reflected by the willingness of participants and stakeholders to contribute to the data collection and analysis. This concept includes the authority and willingness to share electronic health data and should in-

clude an assessment of the legal basis for the collection of prediagnosis data and the implications of privacy laws (e.g., Health Insurance Portability and Accountability Act Privacy Rule) (15). All states have broad disease-reporting laws that require reporting of diseases of public health importance, and many of these laws appear compatible with the authority to receive syndromic surveillance data (16). The authority to require reporting of indicator data for persons who lack evidence of a reportable condition and in the absence of an emergency is less clear and needs to be verified by jurisdictions. Acceptability can vary over time as the threat level, perceived value of early detection, support for the methods of surveillance, and resources fluctuate.

Acceptability of a system can be inferred from the extent of its adoption. Acceptability is reflected by the participation rate of potential reporting sources, by the completeness of data reporting, and by the timeliness of person-dependent steps in the system (e.g., manual data entry from emergency department logs as distinguished from electronic data from the normal clinical workflow).

4. **Portability.** The portability of a surveillance system addresses how well the system could be duplicated in another setting. Adherence to the PHIN standards can enhance portability by reducing variability in the application of information technology between sites. Reliance on person-dependent steps, including judgment and action criteria (e.g., for analysis and interpretation) should be fully documented to improve system portability. Portability also is influenced by the simplicity of the system. Examples should be provided of the deployment of similar systems in other settings, and the experience of those efforts should be described. In the absence of examples, features of the system that might support or detract from portability should be described.

5. **System stability.** The stability of a surveillance system refers to its resilience to system changes (e.g., change in coding from International Classifications of Disease, Ninth Revision [ICD-9] to ICD-10). Stability can be demonstrated by the duration and consistent operation of the system. System stability is distinguished from the reliability of data elements within the system. The consistent representation of the condition under surveillance (reliability) is an aspect of data quality. Stability can be measured by the frequency of system outages or downtime for servicing during periods of

need, including downtime of data providers, the frequency of personnel deficiencies from staff turnover, and budget constraints. Ongoing support by system designers and evolving software updates might improve system stability. Stability also can be reflected in the extent of control over costs and system changes that the sponsoring agency maintains.

6. **System costs.** Cost is a vital factor in assessing the relative value of surveillance for terrorism preparedness. Cost-effectiveness analyses and data modeling are needed under a range of scenarios to estimate the value of innovations in surveillance for outbreak detection and terrorism preparedness (17). Improved methods of measuring cost and impact are needed. Costs borne by data providers should be noted; however, the cost perspective should be that of the community (societal perspective) to account for costs of prevention and treatment born by the community. Direct costs include the fees paid for software and data, the personnel salary and support expenses (e.g., training, equipment support, and travel), and other resources needed to operate the system and produce information for public health decisions (e.g. office supplies, Internet and telephone lines, and other communication equipment). Fixed costs for running the system should be differentiated from the variable costs of responding to system alarms. Variable costs include the cost of follow-up activities (e.g., for diagnosis, case-management, or community interventions). The cost of responding to false alarms represents a variable but inherent inefficiency of an early detection system that should be accounted for in the evaluation. Similarly, variable costs include the financial and public health costs of missing outbreaks entirely or recognizing them late. Costs vary because the sensitivity and timeliness of the detection methods can be modified according to changes in tolerance for missing outbreaks and for responding to false alarms. Similarly, the threshold and methods for investigating system alarms can vary with the perceived risk and need to respond. Costs from public health response to false alarms with traditional surveillance systems need to be measured in a comparable way when assessing the relative value of new surveillance methods. Cost savings should be estimated by assessing the impact of prevention and control efforts (e.g., health-care costs and productivity losses averted) Questions to answer include the following:

• How many investigations were initiated as a result of these data?

- What response was made and what cost was incurred through follow-up of flagged events?
- What were the indications for responding?
- How much staff time was required for follow-up?
- Was anxiety raised unnecessarily by false alarms?
- Was benefit obtained (e.g., through improved communication and confidence in the responsibility and performance of public health) when false alarms were investigated?
- Who was affected?
- What costs did partners incur in follow-up of signals (e.g., medical record staff work and clinical staff efforts)?

Follow-up costs for false alarms should be distinguished from costs related to investigations that uncover real outbreaks that warrant a public health response.

- Did the health department fail to respond to a true event because of complacency or the response burden resulting from false alarms?
- Did late recognition of an outbreak result in unnecessary morbidity?
- Have lessons learned from earlier events reduced costs as the system has continued to operate?

D. Conclusions and Recommendations for Use and Improvement of Systems for Early Outbreak Detection

The evaluation should be summarized to convey the strengths and weaknesses of the system under scrutiny. Summarizing and reporting evaluation findings should facilitate the comparison of systems for those making decisions about new or existing surveillance methods. These conclusions should be validated among stakeholders of the system and modified accordingly. Recommendations should address adoption, continuation, or modification of the surveillance system so that it can better achieve its intended purposes. Recommendations should be disseminated widely and actively interpreted for all appropriate audiences.

An Institute of Medicine study concluded that although innovative surveillance methods might be increasingly helpful in the detection and monitoring of outbreaks, a balance is needed between strengthening proven approaches (e.g., diagnosis of infectious illness and strengthening the liaison between clinical-care providers and health departments) and the exploration and evaluation of new approaches (17). Guidance for the evaluation of surveillance systems for outbreak detection is on-going. Many advances are needed in understanding of systems and outbreak characteristics to improve performance metrics. For example, research is needed to understand the personal health and clinical health care behaviors that might serve as early indicators of priority diseases; analytic methods are needed to improve pattern recognition and to integrate multiple streams of data; a shared vocabulary is needed for describing outbreak conditions, managing text-based information, and supporting case definitions; and evaluation research is needed, including cost-effectiveness of different surveillance models for early detection, both in real-life comparisons and in simulated data environments, to characterize the size and nature of epidemics that can be detected through innovative surveillance approaches. Pending more robust measures of system performance, the goal of this framework is to improve public health surveillance systems for early outbreak detection by providing practical guidance for evaluation.

ACKNOWLEDGMENTS

This report includes contributions by Daniel S. Budnitz, M.D., National Center for Injury Prevention and Control; Richard L. Ehrenberg, M.D., National Institute for Occupational Safety and Health; Timothy Doyle, Robert R. German, Dr.P.H., Timothy A. Green, Ph.D., Samuel L. Groseclose, D.V.M., Division of Public Health Surveillance and Informatics, Denise Koo, M.D., Division of Applied Public Health Training, Carol A. Pertowski, M.D., Stephen B. Thacker M.D., Epidemiology Program Office; José G. Rigau-Pérez, M.D., National Center for Infectious Diseases, CDC, Atlanta, Georgia. Melvin A. Kohn, M.D., State Epidemiologist, Oregon Department of Human Services, Portland. Steven C. Macdonald, Ph.D., Office of Epidemiology, Washington State Department of Health, Olympia. Nkuchia M. M'ikanatha, Dr.P.H., Pennsylvania Department of Health and Department, Harrisburg. Kelly Henning, M.D., New York City Department of Health and Mental Hygiene. Dan E. Peterson, M.D., Cereplex, Inc., Gaithersburg, Maryland. Michael L. Popovich, Scientific Technologies Corporation, Tucson, Arizona. Scott F. Wetterhall, M.D., DeKalb County Board of Health, Decatur, Georgia. Christopher W. Woods, M.D., Division of Infectious Diseases, Duke University Medical Center, Durham, North Carolina.

REFERENCES FROM THE READING

1. CDC. Updated guidelines for evaluating public health surveillance systems: recommendations from the guidelines working group. MMWR 2001;50 (No. RR-13).

2. Teutsch SM, Churchill RE. Principles and practice of public health surveillance. 2nd ed. Oxford, New York: Oxford University Press, 2000.

3. Lober WB, Karras BT, Wagner MM, et al. Roundtable on bioterrorism detection: information system-based surveillance. J Am Med Inform Assoc 2002;9:105–15.

4. Reingold A. If syndromic surveillance is the answer, what is the question? Biosecurity and Bioterrorism: Biodefense Strategy, Practice, and Science 2003;1:1–5.

5. Wagner MM, Tsui FC, Espino JU, et al. The emerging science of very early detection of disease outbreaks. J Pub Health Mgmt Pract 2001;6:51–9.

6. Effler P, Ching-Lee M, Bogard A, Ieong MC, Nekomoto T, Jernigan D. Statewide system of electronic notifiable disease reporting from clinical laboratories: comparing automated reporting with conventional methods. JAMA 1999;282:1845–50.

7. Panackal AA, M'ikanatha NM, Tsui FC, et al. Automatic electronic laboratory-based reporting of notifiable infectious diseases at a large health system. Emerg Infect Dis. 2002;8:685–91.

8. Hoffman MA, Wilkinson TH, Bush A, et al. Multijurisdictional approach to biosurveillance, Kansas City. Emerg Infect Dis. 2003:9;1281–6.

9. Hutwagner L, Thompson W, Seeman GM, Treadwell, T. The bioterrorism preparedness and response early aberration reporting system (EARS). J Urban Health 2003;80:89–96.

10. Tan CG, Sandhu HS, Crawford DC, et al. Surveillance for anthrax cases associated with contaminated letters, New Jersey, Delaware, and Pennsylvania, 2001. Emerg Infect Dis. 2002;8:1073–6.

11. Robertson SE, Suleiman AJM, Mehta FR, Al-Dhahry SHS, El-Bualy MS. Poliomyelitis in Oman: acute flaccid paralysis surveillance leading to early detection and rapid response to a type 3 outbreak. Bull WHO 1994;72:907–14.

12. Grosskurth H, Mosha F, Todd J, et al. Impact of improved treatment of sexually transmitted diseases on HIV infection in rural Tanzania: randomized controlled trial. Lancet 1995;346:530–6.

13. Zeng X, Wagner M. Modeling the effects of epidemics on routinely collected data. Proc AMIA Annu Symp 2001:781–5.

14. Bishop YNM, Fienberg SE, Holland PW. Estimating the size of a closed population. In: Discrete multivariate analysis: theory and practice. Cambridge, MA: MIT Press, 1975.

15. CDC. HIPAA privacy rule and public health: guidance from CDC and the U.S. Department of Health and Human Services. MMWR Supplement 2003;52:1–12.

16. Broome CV, Horton HH, Tress D, Lucido SJ, Koo D. Statutory basis for public health reporting beyond specific diseases. J Urban Health 2003:80: 14–22.

17. Smolinski MS, Hamburg MA, Lederberg J. Microbial threats to health: emergence, detection, and response. Washington, DC: National Academies Press, 2003.

CDC Evaluation Working Group on Public Health Surveillance Systems for Early Detection of Outbreaks.

Chair: Dan Sosin, M.D., Division of Public Health Surveillance and Informatics, Epidemiology Program Office, CDC.

Members: Claire Broome, M.D., Office of the Director; Richard Hopkins, M.D., Henry Rolka, M.S., Division of Public Health Surveillance and Informatics; Van Tong, M.P.H., Epidemiology Program Office, CDC Atlanta, Georgia. James W. Buehler, MD, Dept of Epidemiology, Rollins School of Public Health, Emory University, Atlanta, Georgia. Louise Gresham, Ph.D., San Diego Health and Human Services, Public Health Services, San Deigo, California. Ken Kleinman, Sc.D., Harvard Pilgrim Health Care, Cambridge, Massachusetts. Farzad Mostashari, M.D., New York City Department of Health and Mental Hygiene, New York. J. Marc Overhage, M.D., Indiana University School of Medicine, Indianapolis. Julie Pavlin, M.D., Division of Preventive Medicine, Walter Reed Army Institute of Research, Silver Springs, Maryland. Robert Rolfs, M.D., Utah Department of Health, Salt Lake City. David Siegrist, M.S., Potomac Institute for Policy Studies, Arlington, Virginia.

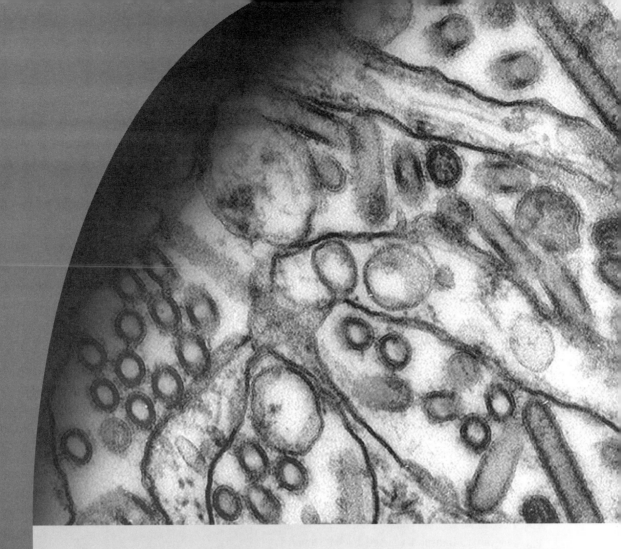

PART VII

Investigating HIV/AIDS

In 1981, the first cases of an unusual occurrence of *Pneumocystis carinii* pneumonia in healthy, young individuals were reported. With the words below, the era of HIV/AIDS was introduced—a new epidemic, a new pandemic, a new impact on individual and public health. Much of what we know now was gained by the process of outbreak investigation and application of our epidemiologic toolkit: case reports, case series, case-control studies, and cohort studies. Research in the lab simultaneously endeavored to search out the pathogen responsible for what later became known to be the virus that renders the immune system incompetent. The causal agent was discovered to be a retrovirus named human immunodeficiency virus (HIV), the virus that causes acquired immune deficiency syndrome (AIDS). On the heels of the first PCP cases were cases of Kaposi's sarcoma, a type of cancer rare in healthy younger individuals, usually only found in older or immunocompromised persons. The following articles are the first published in the United States *Morbidity and Mortality Weekly Report* by the CDC. How do we go from knowing nothing to knowing something? Transport yourself back in time to 1981, and read this first signs of the public health threat that became known as HIV/AIDS. Then consider the questions at the end. Imagine you are an outbreak investigator on the case; what would you have done?

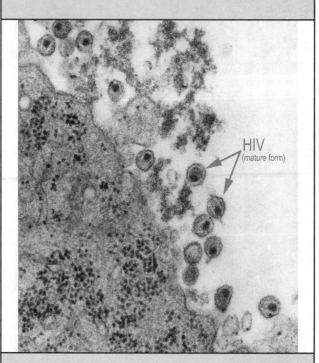

FIGURE 7-1 HIV.

HIV (mature form)

About this picture: "The human immunodeficiency virus (HIV), a retrovirus, was identified in 1983 as the etiologic agent for the acquired immunodeficiency syndrome (AIDS). AIDS is characterized by changes in the population of T-cell lymphocytes that play a key role in the immune defense system. In the infected individual, the virus causes a depletion of subpopulation of T-cells, called T-helper cells, which leaves these patients susceptible to opportunistic infections, as well as certain malignancies."

Source: Public Health Image Library CDC, 2006.

READING 11
Pneumocystis Pneumonia—Los Angeles

Centers for Disease Control and Prevention. *Pneumocystis* Pneumonia—Los Angeles. *MMWR.* 1981;5:230–2.

In the period October 1980–May 1981, 5 young men, all active homosexuals, were treated for biopsy-confirmed *Pneumocystis carinii* pneumonia at 3 different hospitals in Los Angeles, California. Two of the patients died. All 5 patients had laboratory-confirmed previous or current cytomegalovirus (CMV) infection and candidal mucosal infection. Case reports of these patients follow.

Patient 1: A previously healthy 33-year-old man developed *P. carinii* pneumonia and oral mucosal candidiasis in March 1981 after a 2-month history of fever associated with el-

evated liver enzymes, leukopenia, and CMV viruria. The serum complement-fixation CMV titer in October 1980 was 256; in May 1981 it was 32.* The patient's condition deteriorated despite courses of treatment with trimethoprim-sulfamethoxazole (TMP/SMX), pentamidine, and acyclovir. He died May 3, and postmortem examination showed residual *P. carinii* and CMV pneumonia, but no evidence of neoplasia.

Patient 2: A previously healthy 30-year-old man developed *p. carinii* pneumonia in April 1981 after a 5-month history of fever each day and of elevated liver-function tests, CMV viruria, and documented seroconversion to CMV, i.e., an acute-

---

*Paired specimens not run in parallel.

phase titer of 16 and a convalescent-phase titer of 28* in anti-complement immunofluorescence tests. Other features of his illness included leukopenia and mucosal candidiasis. His pneumonia responded to a course of intravenous TMP/SMX, but, as of the latest reports, he continues to have a fever each day.

Patient 3: A 30-year-old man was well until January 1981 when he developed esophageal and oral candidiasis that responded to Amphotericin B treatment. He was hospitalized in February 1981 for *P. carinii* pneumonia that responded to TMP/SMX. His esophageal candidiasis recurred after the pneumonia was diagnosed, and he was again given Amphotericin B. The CMV complement-fixation titer in March 1981 was 8. Material from an esophageal biopsy was positive for CMV.

Patient 4: A 29-year-old man developed *P. carinii* pneumonia in February 1981. He had had Hodgkin's disease 3 years earlier, but had been successfully treated with radiation therapy alone. He did not improve after being given intravenous TMP/SMX and corticosteroids and died in March. Postmortem examination showed no evidence of Hodgkin's disease, but *P. carinii* and CMV were found in lung tissue.

Patient 5: A previously healthy 36-year-old man with clinically diagnosed CMV infection in September 1980 was seen in April 1981 because of a 4-month history of fever, dyspnea, and cough. On admission he was found to have *P. carinii* pneumonia, oral candidiasis, and CMV retinitis. A complement-fixation CMV titer in April 1981 was 128. The patient has been treated with 2 short courses of TMP/SMX that have been limited because of a sulfa-induced neutropenia. He is being treated for candidiasis with topical nystatin.

The diagnosis of *Pneumocystis* pneumonia was confirmed for all 5 patients antemortem by closed or open lung biopsy. The patients did not know each other and had no known common contacts or knowledge of sexual partners who had had similar illnesses. Two of the 5 reported having frequent homosexual contacts with various partners. All 5 reported using inhalant drugs, and 1 reported parenteral drug abuse. Three patients had profoundly depressed *in vitro* proliferative responses to mitogens and antigens. Lymphocyte studies were not performed on the other 2 patients.

Reported by MS Gottlieb, MD, HM Schanker, MD, PT Fan, MD, A Saxon, MD, JD Weisman, DO, Div of Clinical Immunology-Allergy, Dept of Medicine, UCLA School of Medicine; I Pozalski, MD, Cedars-Mt. Sinai Hospital, Los Angeles; Field Services Div, Epidemiology Program Office, CDC.

Editorial Note: *Pneumocystis* pneumonia in the United States is almost exclusively limited to severely immunosuppressed patients (1). The occurrence of pneumocystosis in these 5 previously healthy individuals without a clinically apparent underlying immunodeficiency is unusual. The fact that these patients were all homosexuals suggests an association between some aspect of a homosexual lifestyle or disease acquired through sexual contact and *Pneumocystis* pneumonia in this population. All 5 patients described in this report had laboratory-confirmed CMV disease or virus shedding within 5 months of the diagnosis of *Pneumocystis* pneumonia. CMV infection has been shown to induce transient abnormalities of *in vitro* cellular-immune function in otherwise healthy human hosts (2, 3). Although all 3 patients tested had abnormal cellular-immune function, no definitive conclusion regarding the role of CMV infection in these 5 cases can be reached because of the lack of published data on cellular-immune function in healthy homosexual males with and without CMV antibody. In 1 report, 7 (3.6%) of 194 patients with pneumocystosis also had CMV infection; 40 (21%) of the same group had at least 1 other major concurrent infection (1). A high prevalence of CMV infections among homosexual males was recently reported: 179 (94%) had CMV viruria; rates for 101 controls of similar age who were reported to be exclusively heterosexual were 54% for seropositivity and zero fro viruria (4). In another study of 64 males, 4 (6.3%) had positive tests for CMV in semen, but none had CMV recovered from urine. Two of the 4 reported recent homosexual contacts. These findings suggest not only that virus shedding may be more readily detected in seminal fluid than urine, but also that seminal fluid may be an important vehicle of CMV transmission (5).

All the above observations suggest the possibility of a cellular-immune dysfunction related to a common exposure that predisposes individuals to opportunistic infections such as pneumocystosis and candidiasis. Although the role of CMV infection in the pathogenesis of pneumocystosis remains unknown, the possibility of *P. carinii* infection must be carefully considered in a differential diagnosis for previously healthy homosexual males with dyspnea and pneumonia.

REFERENCES FROM THE READING

1. Walzer PD, Perl DP, Krogstad DJ, Rawson G, Schultz MG. *Pneumocystis carinii* pneumonia in the United States. Epidemiologic, diagnostic, and clinical features. Ann Intern Med 1974;80:83–93.

2. Rinaldo CR, Jr, Black PH, Hirsh MS. Interaction of cytomegalovirus with leukocytes from patients with mononucleosis due to cytomegalovirus. J Infect Dis 1977;136:667–78.

3. Rinaldo CR, Jr, Carney WP, Richter BS, Black PH, Hirsh MS. Mechanisms of immunosuppression in cytomegaloviral mononucleosis. J Infect Dis 1980;141:488–95.

4. Drew WL, Mintz L, Miner RC, Sands M, Ketterer B. Prevalence of cytomegalovirus infection in homosexual men. J Infect Dis 1981;143: 188–92.

5. Lang DJ, Kummer JF. Cytomegalovirus in semen: observations in selected populations,. J Infect Dis 1975; 132:472–3.

*Paired specimens not run in parallel.

READING 12
Kaposi's Sarcoma and *Pneumocystis* Pneumonia Among Homosexual Men—New York City and California

Centers for Disease Control and Prevention. Kaposi's Sarcoma and *Pneumocystis* Pneumonia Among Homosexual Men—New York City and California. *MMWR*. 1981;30:306–8.

During the past 30 months, Kaposi's sarcoma (KS), an uncommonly reported malignancy in the United State, has been diagnosed in 26 homosexual men (20 in New York City [NYC]; 6 in California). The 26 patients range in age from 26–51 years (mean 39 years). Eight of these patients died (7 in NYC, 1 in California)—all 8 within 24 months after KS was diagnosed. The diagnoses in all 26 cases were based on histopathological examination of skin lesions, lymph nodes, or tumor in other organs. Twenty-five of the 26 patients were white, 1 was black. Presenting complaints from 20 of these patients are shown in Table 7-1.

Skin or mucous membrane lesions, often dark blue to violaceous plaques or nodules, were present in most of the patients on their initial physician visit. However, these lesions were not always present and often were considered benign by the patient and his physician.

A review of the New York University Coordinated Cancer Registry for KS in men under age 50 revealed no cases from 1970–1979 at Bellevue Hospital and 3 cases in this age group at the New York University Hospital from 1961–1979.

Seven KS patients had serious infections diagnosed after their initial physician visit. Six patients had pneumonia (4 biopsy confirmed as due to *Pneumocystis carinii* [PC]), and one had necrotizing toxoplasmosis of the central nervous system. One of the patients with *Pneumocystis* pneumonia also experienced severe, recurrent, herpes simplex infection; extensive candidiasis; and cryptococcal meningitis. The results of tests for cytomegalovirus (CMV) infection were available for 12 patients. All 12 had serological evidence of past or present CMV infection. In 3 patients for whom culture results were available, CMV was isolated from blood, urine and/or lung of all 3. Past infections with amebiasis and hepatitis were commonly reported.

Since the previous report of 5 cases or *Pneumocystis* pneumonia in homosexual men from Los Angeles (1), 10 additional cases (4 in Los Angeles and 6 in the San Francisco Bay are) of biopsy-confirmed PC pneumonia have been identified in homosexual men in the state. Two of the 10 patients also have KS. This brings the total number of *Pneumocystis* cases among homosexual men in California to 15 since September 1979. Patients range in age from 25 to 46 years.

Reported by A Friedman-Kien, MD, L Laubenstein, MD, M Marmor, PhD, K Hymes, MD, J Green, MD, A Ragaz, MD, J Gottleib, BD, F Muggia, MD, R Demopolous, MD, M Weintraub, MD, D Williams, MD, New York University Medical Center, NYC; R Oliveri, MD, J Marmer, MD, NYC; J Wallace, MD, I Halperin, MD, JF Gillooley, MD, St. Vincent's Hospital and Medical Center, NYC; N Prose, MD, Downstate Medical Center, NYC; E Klein, MD, Roosevelt Hospital, NYC; J Vogel, MD, B Safai, MD, P Myskowski, MD, C Urmacher, MD, B Koziner, MD, L Nisce, MD, M Kris, MD, D Armstrong, MD, J Gold, MD, Sloan-Kettering Memorial Institute, NYC; D Mildran, MD, Beth Israel Hospital, NYC; M Tapper, MD, Lenox Hill Hospital, NYC; JB Weissman, MD, Columbia Presbyterian Hospital, NYC; R Rothenberg, MD, State Epidemiologist, New York State Dept of Health; SM Friedman, MD, Acting Director, Bur of Preventable Diseases, New York City Dept of Health; FP Siegal, MD, Dept of Medicine, Mount Sinai School of Medicine, City College of New York, NYC; J Groundwater, MD, J Gilmore, MD, San Francisco; D Coleman, MD, S Follensbee, MD, J Gullett, MD, SJ Stegman, MD, University of California at San Francisco; C Wofsy, MD, San Francisco General Hospital, San Francisco; D Bush, MD, Franklin Hospital, San Francisco; L Drew, MD, PhD, Mt. Zion Hospital, E Braff, MD, S Dritz, MD, City/County Health Dept, San Francisco; M Klein, MD, Valley Memorial Hospital, Selinas; JK Preiksaitis, MD, Stanford University Medical Center, Palo Alto; MS Gottlieb, MD, University of California at Los Angeles; R Jung, MD, University of Southern California Medical Center,

TABLE 7-1 Presenting complaints in 20 patients with Kaposi's sarcoma.

Presenting complaint	Number (percentage) of patients
Skin lesion(s) only	10 (50%)
Skin lesions plus lymphadenopathy	4 (20%)
Oral mucosal lesion only	1 (5%)
Inguinal adenopathy plus perirectal abscess	1 (5%)
Weight loss and fever	2 (10%)
Weight loss, fever, and pneumonia (one due to *Pneumocystis carinii*)	2 (10%)

Los Angeles; J Chin, MD, State Epidemiologist, California Dept of Health Services; J Goedert, MD, National Cancer Institute, National Institute of Health; Parasitic Diseases Div, Center for Infectious Diseases, VD Control Division, Center for Prevention Services, Chronic Diseases Div, Center for Environmental Health, CDC.

Editorial Note: KS is a malignant neoplasm manifested primarily by multiple vascular nodules in the skin and other organs. The disease is multifocal, with a course ranging from indolent, with only skin manifestations, to fulminant, with extensive visceral involvement (2).

Accurate incidence and morality rates for KS are not available for the United States, but the annual incidence has been estimated to be between 0.02–0.06 per 100,000; it affects primarily elderly males (3, 4). In a series of 92 patients treated between 1949 and 1975 at the Memorial Sloan-Kettering Cancer Institute in NYC, 76% were male, and the mean age was 63 years (range 23–90 years) at the time of diagnosis (5).

The disease in elderly men is usually manifested by skin lesions and a chronic clinical course (mean survival time is 8–13 years) (2). Two exceptions to this epidemiologic pattern have been noted previously. The first occurs in an endemic belt across equatorial Africa, where KS commonly affects children and young adults and accounts for up to 9% of all cancers (3). Secondly, the disease appears to have a higher incidence in renal transplant recipients (6–9) and in others receiving immunosuppressive therapy (10–12).

The occurrence of this number of KS cases during a 30-month period among young, homosexual men is considered highly unusual. No previous association between KS and sexual preference has been reported. The fulminant clinical course reported in many of these patients also differs from that classically described for elderly persons.

The histopathologic diagnosis of KS may be difficult for 2 reasons. Changes in some lesions may be interpreted as nonspecific, and other cutaneous and soft tissue sarcomas, such as angiosarcoma of the skin, may be confused with KS (13, 14).

That 10 new cases of *Pneumocystis* pneumonia have been identified in homosexual men suggests that the 5 previously reported cases were not an isolated phenomenon (1). In addition, CDC has a report of 4 homosexual men in NYC who developed severe, progressive, perianal herpes simplex infections and had evidence of cellular immunodeficiencies. Three died, 1 with systemic CMV infection (1). Furthermore, serologic evidence of past CMV infection and active shedding of CMV have been shown to be much more common among homosexual men than heterosexual men attending a sexually transmitted disease clinic (15). A specific serologic association with CMV infection has been demonstrated among American and European patients with KS (16, 17) and herpes-type virus particles have

been demonstrated in tissue culture cell lines from African cases of KS (18). It has been hypothesized that activation of oncogenic virus during periods of immunosuppression may result in the development of KS (19). Although immunosuppression often results in CMV infection, it is not yet clear whether CMV infection precedes or follows the above-mentioned disorders.

Although it is not certain that the increase in KS and PC pneumonia is restricted to homosexual men, the vast majority of recent cases have been reported from this group. Physicians should be alert for Kaposi's sarcoma, PC pneumonia, and other opportunistic infections associated with immunosuppression in homosexual men.

REFERENCES FROM THE READING

1. CDC. *Pneumocystis* pneumonia—Los Angeles. MMWR 1981;30:250.
2. Safai B, Good RA. Kaposi's sarcoma: a review and recent developments. CA 1981;31:1–12.
3. Oettle AG. Geographical and racial differences in the frequency of Kaposi's sarcoma as evidence of environmental or genetic causes. Acta Un Int Cancr 1962;18:330–63.
4. Rothman S. Remarks on sex, age, and racial distribution of Kaposi's sarcoma and on possible pathogenetic factors. Acta Un Int Cancer 1962;18:326–9.
5. Safai B, Miké V, Giraldo G, Beth E, Good RA. Association of Kaposi's sarcoma with second primary malignancies: possible etiopathogenic implications. Cancer 1980;45:1472–9.
6. Harwood AR, Osoba D, Hostader SL, et al. Kaposi's sarcoma in recipients of renal transplants. Am J Med 1979;67:759–65.
7. Stribling J, Weitzner S, Smith GV. Kaposi sarcoma in renal allograft recipients. Cancer 1978;42:442–6.
8. Myers BD, Kessler E, Levi J, Pick A, Rosenfeld JB, Tikvah P. Kaposi sarcoma in kidney transplant recipients. Arch Intern Med 1974;133:307–11.
9. Penn I. Kaposi's sarcoma in organ transplant recipients: report of 20 cases. Transplantation 1979;27:8–11.
10. Gange RW, Jones EW. Kaposi's sarcoma and immunosuppressive therapy: an appraisal. Clin Exp Dermatol 1978;3:135–46.
11. Klepp O, Dahl O, Stenwig JT. Association of Kaposi's sarcoma and prior immunosuppressive therapy: a 5-year material of Kaposi's sarcoma in Norway. Cancer 1978;42:2626–30.
12. Hoshaw RA, Schwartz RA. Kaposi's sarcoma after immunosuppressive therapy with prednisone. Arch Dermatol 1980:116;1280–2.
13. Girard C, Johnson EC, Graham JH. Cutaneous angiosarcoma. Cancer 1970;26:868–83.
14. Rosai J, Sumner HW, Kostianovsky M, Perez-Mesa C. Angiosarcoma of the skin. A clinicopathologic and fine structural study. Hum Pathol 1976;7:83–109.
15. Drew WL, Mintz L, Miner RC, Sands M, Ketterer B. Prevalence of cytomegalovirus infection in homosexual men. J Infect Dis 1981;143:188–92.
16. Giraldo G, Beth E, Kourilsky FM, et al. Antibody patterns to herpesvirus in Kaposi's sarcoma: serologic association of European Kaposi's sarcoma with cytomegalovirus. Int J Cancer 1975;15:839–48.
17. Giraldo G, Beth E, Henle W, et al. Antibody patterns to herpesvirus in Kaposi's sarcoma. II. serological association of American Kaposi's sarcoma with cytomegalovirus. Int J Cancer 1978;22:126–31.
18. Giraldo G, Beth E, Haguenau F. Herpes-type virus particles in tissue culture of Kaposi's sarcoma from different geographic regions. J Natl Cancer Inst 1972;49:1509–26.
19. Kapedia SB, Krause JR. Kaposi's sarcoma after long-term alkylating agent therapy for multiple myeloma. South Med J 1977;70:1011–3.

READING 13
Follow-Up on Kaposi's Sarcoma and
Pneumocystis Pneumonia

Centers for Disease Control and Prevention. Follow-Up on Kaposi's Sarcoma and *Pneumocystis* Pneumonia. *MMWR*. 1981;30:409-10.

Twenty-six cases of Kaposi's sarcoma (KS) and 15 cases of *Pneumocystis carinii* pneumonia (PCP) among previously healthy homosexual men were recently reported (1, 2). Since July 3, 1981, CDC has received reports of an additional 70 cases of these 2 conditions in persons without known underlying disease. The sex, race, sexual preference, and mortality data known for 108 persons with either or both conditions are summarized in Table 7-2.

The majority of the reported cases of KS and/or PCP have occurred in white men. Patients ranged in age from 15–52 years; over 95% were men 25-49 years of age. Ninety-four percent (95/101) of the men for whom sexual preference was known were homosexual or bisexual. Forty percent of the reported cases were fatal. Of the 82 cases for which the month of diagnosis is known, 75 (91%) have occurred since January 1980, with 55 (67%) diagnosed from January through July 1981. Although physicians from several states have reported cases of KS and PCP among previously healthy homosexual

men, the majority of cases have been reported from New York and California.

Reported by SM Friedman, MD, YM Feldman, MD, New York City Dept of Health; R Rothenberg, MD, State Epidemiologist, New York State Dept of Health; S Dritz, MD, E Braff, MD, City/County Health Dept, San Francisco; S Fannin, MD, Los Angeles County Dept of Health Svcs; I Heindl, MD, California Dept of Health Svcs; RK Sikes, DVM, State Epidemiologist, Georgia Dept of Human Resources; RA Gunn, MD, State Epidemiologist, Florida State Dept of Health and Rehabilitative Svcs; MA Roberts, PhD, State Epidemiologist, Oklahoma State Dept of Health; Task Force on Kaposi's Sarcoma and Opportunistic Infections, Center for Prevention Svcs, Center for Infectious Diseases, Center for Environmental Health, Field Svcs Div, Consolidated Surveillance and Communications Activities, Epidemiology Program Office, CDC.

Editorial Note: KS is a rare, malignant neoplasm seen predominantly in elderly men in this country. In elderly men, the disease is manifested by skin lesions and a chronic clinical course; it is rarely fatal (3). In contrast, the persons currently reported to have KS are young to middle-aged men, and 20% of the cases have been fatal. Although some of the patients

TABLE 7-2 Cases of Kaposi's sarcoma (KS) and *Pneumocystis carinii* pneumonia (PCP) reported to CDC with dates of onset between January 1976 and July 1981.

Diagnosis (number of patients)	Sex		Race of men				Sexual preference of men			Fatality (percentage)
	Male	Female	White	Black	Hispanic	Unknown	Homosexual or bisexual	Heterosexual	Unknown	
KS and PCP (N=7)	7	0	5	0	1	1	7	0	0	3/7 (43%)
KS only (N=47)	47	0	41	3	3	0	44	1	2	8/47 (17%)
PCP only (N=54)	53	1	33	9	7	4	44	5	4	32/54 (59%)
Total (N=108)	107	1	79	12	11	5	95	6	6	43/108 (40%)

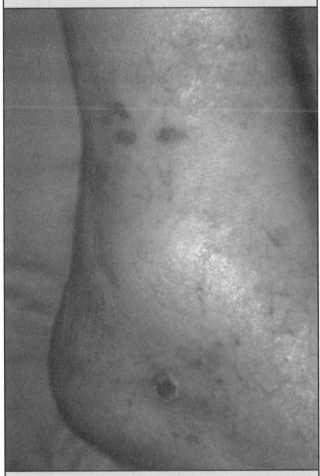

FIGURE 7-2 Kaposi's sarcoma lesions.

About this picture: "This photograph shows the cutaneous brown Kaposi's sarcoma lesions located over the medial left ankle and foot.

In more recent years, the vast majority of cases of Kaposi's sarcoma are found in patients with AIDS. The most common site for KS is on the skin, but it may also affect internal organs, particularly the lymph nodes, the lungs and digestive system."

Source: Public Health Image Library CDC/Dr. Steve Kraus; 1981.

skin, lymph node, or visceral-lesion tissue has been difficult even in specialized hands.

The occurrence of *Pneumocystis carinii* pneumonia in patients who are not immunosuppressed as a result of known underlying disease or therapy is also highly unusual (4). Although 7 (11%) of the 61 patients with PCP also had KS, in many instances pneumonia preceded the tumor. Although most of the patients with PCP reported recent respiratory symptoms, some gave a history of weeks to months of systemic symptoms including weight loss and general malaise, similar to the prodrome described by patients who developed lymphadenopathic KS. Several of the patients with PCP had other serious infections, including gastrointestinal candidiasis, cryptococcal meningitis, and disseminated infections with Mycobacteriaceae and herpes simplex. Many of the PCP and KS patients have had positive cultures or serologic evidence of infection with cytomegalovirus.

The apparent clustering of both *Pneumocystis carinii* pneumonia and KS among homosexual men suggests a common underlying factor. Both diseases have been associated with host immunosuppression (4–6), and studies in progress are showing immunosuppression in some of these cases. The extent of cause of immune suppression is not known. Physicians should be aware of the possible occurrence of these diseases and other opportunistic infections, particularly among men with symptoms suggestive of these disorders or their prodromes, since therapy is specific and verification of the diagnosis requires biopsy.

Several state and local health departments and CDC are conducting active surveillance for KS, PCP, and opportunistic infections in persons without known predisposing underlying disease. A national case-control study will be implemented shortly.

REFERENCES FROM THE READING

1. CDC. *Pneumocystis* pneumonia—Los Angeles. MMWR 1981;30:250–2.

2. CDC. Kaposi's sarcoma and *Pneumocystis* pneumonia among homosexual men—New York City and California. MMWR 1981;30:305–8.

3. Safai B, Good RA. Kaposi's sarcoma: a review and recent developments. CA 1981;31:1–12.

4. Walzer PD, Peri DP, Krogstad DJ, Rawson PG, Schultz MG. *Pneumocystis carinii* pneumonia in the United States. Epidemiologic, diagnostic, and clinical features. Ann Intern Med 1974;80:83–93.

5. Penn I. Kaposi's sarcoma in organ transplant recipients: report of 20 cases. Transplantation 1979;27:8–11.

6. Gange RW, Jones EW. Kaposi's sarcoma and immunosuppressive therapy: an appraisal. Clin Exp Dermatol 1978;3:135–46.

have presented with the violaceous skin or mucous membrane lesions typical of KS, many such lesions have been initially overlooked. Other patients have been diagnosed by lymph node biopsy after a prodrome consisting of fever, weight loss, and lymphadenopathy. Seven (13%) of fifty-four KS patients also had PCP. In many cases the histopathologic diagnosis from

READING 14
A Cluster of Kaposi's Sarcoma and *Pneumocystis carinii* Pneumonia Among Homosexual Male Residents of Los Angeles and Range Counties, California

Centers for Disease Control and Prevention. A Cluster of Kaposi's Sarcoma and Pneumocystis carinii Pneumonia among Homosexual Male Residents of Los Angeles and range Counties, California. *MMWR*. 1982;31:305–7.

In the period June 1, 1981–April 12, 1982, CDC received reports of 19 cases of biopsy-confirmed Kaposi's sarcoma (KS) and/or Pneumocystis carinii pneumonia (PCP) among previously healthy homosexual male residents of Los Angeles and Orange counties, California. Following an unconfirmed report of possible associations among cases in southern California, interviews were conducted with all 8 of the patients still living and with the close friends of 7 of the other 11 patients who had died.

Data on sexual partners were obtained for 13 patients, 8 with KS and 5 with PCP. For any patient to be considered as a sexual contact of another person, the reported exposures of that patient had to be either substantiated or not denied by the other person involved in the relationship (or by a close friend of that person).

Within 5 years of the onset of symptoms, 9 patients (6 with KS and 3 with PCP) had had sexual contact with other patients with KS or PCP. Seven patients from Los Angeles County had had sexual contact with other patients from Los Angeles County, and 2 from Orange County had had sexual contact with 1 patient who was not a resident of California. Four of the 9 patients had been exposed to more than 1 patient who had KS or PCP. Three of the 6 patients with KS developed their symptoms after sexual contact with persons who already had symptoms of KS. One of these 3 patients developed symptoms of KS 9 months after sexual contact, another patient developed symptoms 13 months after contact, and a third patient developed symptoms 22 months after contact.

The other 4 patients in the group of 13 had no known sexual contact with reported cases. However, 1 patient with KS had an apparently healthy sexual partner in common with 2 persons with PCP; 1 patient with KS reported having had sexual contact with 2 friends of the non-Californian with KS; and 2 patients with PCP had most of their anonymous contacts (greater than or equal to 80%) with persons in bathhouses attended frequently by other persons in Los Angeles with KS or PCP.

The 9 patients from Los Angeles and Orange counties directly linked to other patients are part of an interconnected series of cases that may include 15 additional patients (11 with KS and 4 with PCP) from 8 other cities. The non-Californian with KS mentioned earlier is part of this series. In addition to having had sexual contact with 2 patients with KS from Orange County, this patient said he had sexual contact with 1 patient with KS and 1 patient with PCP from New York City and 2 of the 3 patients with PCP from Los Angeles County. Reported by S Fannin, MD, County of Los Angeles Dept of Health Svcs, MS Gottlieb, MD, UCLA School of Medicine, JD Weisman, DO, E Rogolsky, MD, Los Angeles, T Prendergast, MD, County of Orange Dept of Public Health and Medical Svcs, J Chin, MD, State Epidemiologist, California Dept of Health Svcs; AE Friedman-Kien, MD, L Laubenstein, MD, New York University Medical Center, S Friedman, MD, New York City Dept of Health, R Rothenberg, MD, State Epidemiologist, New York Health Dept; Task Force on Kaposi's Sarcoma and Opportunistic Infections, CDC.

Editorial Note: An estimated 185,000–415,000 homosexual males live in Los Angeles County.* Assuming that they had a median of 13.5 to 50 different sexual partners per year over the past 5 years,** the probability that 7 of 11 patients with KS or PCP would have sexual contact with any one of the other 16 reported patients in Los Angeles County would seem to be remote. The probability that 2 patients with KS living in different parts of Orange County would have sexual contact with the same non-Californian with KS would appear to be even

---

*Estimates of the homosexual male population are derived from Kinsey et al. (1) who reported that 8% of adult males are exclusively homosexual and that 18% have at least as much homosexual as heterosexual experience for at least 3 years between the ages of 16 and 55 years; and the U. S. Bureau of the Census, which reported that approximately 2,304,000 males between the ages of 18 and 64 years lived in Los Angeles County in 1980.

**Estimates of sexual activity are derived from data collected by Jay and Young (2), indicating that 130 homosexual male respondents in Los Angeles had a median of 13.5 different sexual partners in 1976, and from CDC data showing that 13 patients with KS and/or PCP in the Los Angeles area tended to report having more sexual partners in the year before onset of symptoms (median = 50) than did homosexual males surveyed by Jay and Young.

lower. Thus, observations in Los Angeles and Orange counties imply the existence of an unexpected cluster of cases.

The cluster in Los Angeles and Orange counties was identified on the basis of sexual contact. One hypothesis consistent with the observations reported here is that infectious agents are being sexually transmitted among homosexually active males. Infectious agents not yet identified may cause the acquired cellular immunodeficiency that appears to underlie KS and/or PCP among homosexual males (3–6). If infectious agents cause these illnesses, sexual partners of patients may be at increased risk of developing KS and/or PCP.

Another hypothesis to be considered is that sexual contact with patients with KS or PCP does not lead directly to acquired cellular immunodeficiency, but simply indicates a certain style of life. The number of homosexually active males who share this lifestyle may be much smaller than the number of homosexual males in the general population.

Exposure to some substance (rather than an infectious agent) may eventually lead to immunodeficiency among a subset of the homosexual male population that shares a particular style of life. For example, Marmor et al. recently reported that exposure to amyl nitrite was associated with an increased risk of KS in New York City (7). Exposure to inhalant sexual stimulants, central-nervous-system stimulants, and a variety of other "street" drugs was common among males belonging to the cluster of cases of KS and PCP in Los Angeles and Orange counties.

DISCUSSION QUESTIONS

1. Recall the steps we undertake in an outbreak investigation. List those that you see in the above reports, those you feel are missing, and what you might have done differently had you known then what we know now.

2. Do you note any signs of stigma about the patients or the disease under investigation? What are they? How might they have impacted the investigation at hand?

3. In the initial PCP report, what do you think the authors think could be going on, that is, what do you first hypothesize? What might be an alternate explanation for what they found, given what we now understand about HIV?

4. Name the study design type for each of the above four reports. State the strengths and limitations for each study design in general and in each report specifically. Which biases are most common for each of these designs? Can you spot any present in these write-ups?

5. What step or steps would you recommend taking after the last report?

6. Discuss the *Editorial Note* in the final of the four articles. What are the authors saying? Why is it important enough to mention in this report? On the basis of this information, how will your interpretation of the information differ from what it might have in the absence of this information?

REFERENCES FROM THE READING

1. Kinsey AC, Pomeroy WB, Martin CE. Sexual behavior in the human male. Philadelphia: WB Saunders, 1948:650–1.

2. Jay K, Young A. The gay report. New York: Summit, 1979.

3. Friedman-Kien AE. Disseminated Kaposi's sarcoma syndrome in young homosexual men. Am Acad Dermatol 1981;5:468–71.

4. Gottlieb MS, Schroff R, Schanker HM, et al. Pneumocystis carinii pneumonia and mucosal candidiasis in previously healthy homosexual men. N Engl J Med 1981;305:1425–3l.

5. Masur H, Michelis MA, Greene JB, et al. An outbreak of community-acquired Pneumocystis carinii pneumonia. N Engl J Med 1981;305: 1431–8.

6. Siegal FP, Lopez C, Hammer GS, et al. Severe acquired immunodeficiency in male homosexuals, manifested by chronic perianal ulcerative herpes simplex lesions. N Engl J Med 1981;305:1439–44.

7. Marmor M, Friedman-Kien AE, Laubenstein L., et al. Risk factors for Kaposi's sarcoma in homosexual men. Lancet 1982;1:1083–7.

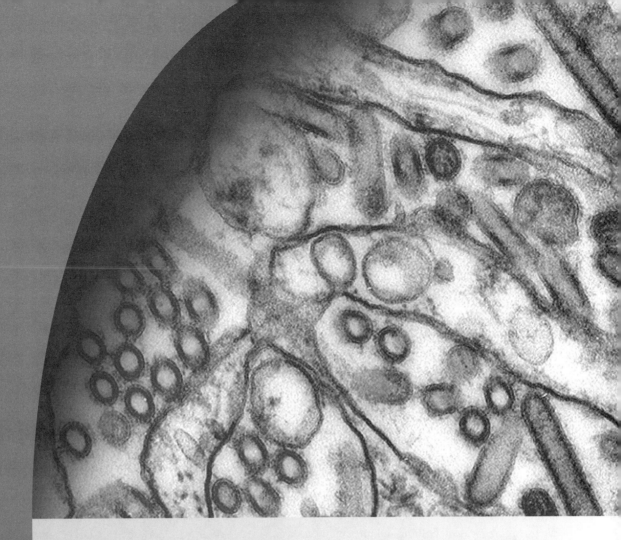

PART VIII

Readily Transmissible and Emerging Infections: Identification, Surveillance, and Control

In late 2002 or early 2003, another previously unknown disease emerged, an acute respiratory syndrome that became known as Severe Acute Respiratory Syndrome (SARS). This is an excellent example of the effect rapid public health action can take: Spread of the disease was rapidly halted and the disease has not yet become the danger that it threatened to be. Here is the first description of the disease.

READING 15
Outbreak of Severe Acute Respiratory Syndrome—Worldwide, 2003

CDC SARS Investigative Team; AT Fleischauer, PhD, EIS Officer, CDC

CDC SARS Investigative Team; Fleischauer AT, PhD, EIS Officer, CDC . Outbreak of Severe Acute Respiratory Syndrome—Worldwide, 2003. *MMWR*. 2003;52:226–228.

Since late February 2003, CDC has been supporting the World Health Organization (WHO) in the investigation of a multi-country outbreak of atypical pneumonia of unknown etiology. The illness is being referred to as severe acute respiratory syndrome (SARS). This report describes the scope of the outbreak, preliminary case definition, and interim infection control guidance for the United States.

On February 11, the Chinese Ministry of Health notified WHO that 305 cases of acute respiratory syndrome of unknown etiology had occurred in six municipalities in Guangdong province in southern China during November 16, 2002–February 9, 2003. The disease was characterized by transmission to health-care workers and household contacts; five deaths were reported (1). On February 26, a man aged 47 years who had traveled in mainland China and Hong Kong became ill with a respiratory illness and was hospitalized shortly after arriving in Hanoi, Vietnam. Health-care providers at the hospital in Hanoi subsequently developed a similar illness. The patient died on March 13 after transfer to an isolation facility in Hong Kong. During late February, an outbreak of a similar respiratory illness was reported in Hong Kong among workers at another hospital; this cluster was linked to a patient who had traveled previously to southern China. On March 12, WHO issued a global alert about the outbreak and instituted worldwide surveillance.

As of March 19, WHO has received reports of 264 patients from 11 countries with suspected and probable* SARS (see Table 8-1). Areas with reported local transmission include Hong Kong and Guangdong province, China; Hanoi, Vietnam; and Singapore. More limited transmission has been reported in Taipei, Taiwan, and Toronto, Canada. The initial cases reported in Singapore, Taiwan, and Toronto were among persons who all had traveled to China.

On March 15, after issuing a preliminary case definition for suspected cases (see Table 8-2), CDC initiated enhanced domestic surveillance for SARS. CDC also issued a travel advisory suggesting that persons planning nonessential travel to Hong Kong, Guangdong, or Hanoi consider postponing their travel (http://www.cdc.gov/travel/other/acute_resp_syn_multi.htm). On March 16, CDC began advising passengers arriving on direct flights from these three locations to seek medical attention if they have symptoms of febrile respiratory illness. As of March 18, approximately 12,000 advisory notices

TABLE 8-1 Number of suspected and probable cases and deaths from severe acute respiratory syndrome, by location—Worldwide, 2003.*

Location	No. Cases	Deaths	
		No.	(%)
Hong Kong	150	5	(3)
Vietnam	56	2	(4)
Singapore	31	0	—
Canada	8	2	(25)
Taiwan	3	0	—
Germany	1	0	—
Thailand	1	0	—
Slovenia	1	0	—
United Kingdom	1	0	—
United States	11	0	—
Spain	1	0	—
Total	**264**	**9**	**(3)**

*As of March 19, 2003.
Source: Data from World Health Organization

*Suspected cases (Table 8-2) with either a) radiographic evidence of pneumonia or respiratory distress syndrome or b) evidence of unexplained respiratory distress syndrome by autopsy are designated probable cases by the WHO case definition.

had been distributed to airline passengers. In addition, surveillance is being heightened for suspected cases of SARS among arriving passengers. As of March 19, a total of 11 suspected cases of SARS in the United States are under investigation by CDC and state health authorities.

Among patients reported worldwide as of March 19, the disease has been characterized by rapid onset of high fever, myalgia, chills, rigor, and sore throat, followed by shortness of breath, cough, and radiographic evidence of pneumonia. The incubation period has generally been 3–5 days (range: 2–7 days). Laboratory findings have included thrombocytopenia and leukopenia. Many patients have had respiratory distress or severe pneumonia requiring hospitalization, and several have required mechanical ventilation. Of the 264 suspected and probable cases reported by WHO, nine (3%) persons have died. In addition, secondary attack rates of > 50% have been observed among health-care workers caring for patients with SARS in both Hong Kong and Hanoi. Additional clinical and epidemiologic details are available from WHO at http://www. who.int/wer/pdf/2003/wer7812.pdf.

In the United States, initial diagnostic testing for persons with suspected SARS should include chest radiograph, pulse oximetry, blood cultures, sputum Gram stain and culture, and

TABLE 8-2 CDC preliminary case definition for severe acute respiratory syndrome (SARS).*

Suspected case

Respiratory illness of unknown etiology with onset since February 1, 2003, and the following criteria:

- Documented temperature > 100.4°F (≤ 38.0°C)
- One or more symptoms of respiratory illness (e.g., cough, shortness of breath, difficulty breathing, or radiographic findings of pneumonia or acute respiratory distress syndrome)
- Close contact[†] within 10 days of onset symptoms with a person under investigation for or suspected of having SARS or travel within 10 days of onset symptoms to an area with documents transmission of SARS as defined by the World Health Organization (WHO).

*As of March 19, 2003.
[†]Defined as having cared for, having lived with, or having had direct contact with respiratory secretions and/or body fluids of a person suspected of having SARS.
Source: CDC.

testing for viral respiratory pathogens, particularly influenza types A and B and respiratory syncytial virus. Clinicians should save any available clinical specimens (e.g., respiratory samples, blood, serum, tissue, and biopsies) for additional testing until diagnosis is confirmed. Instructions for specimen collection are available from CDC at http://www.cdc.gov/ncidod/sars/pdf/specimen collection-sars.pdf. Specimens should be forwarded to CDC by state health departments after consultation with the SARS State Support Team at the CDC Emergency Operations Center.

Clinicians evaluating suspected cases should use standard precautions (e.g., hand hygiene) together with airborne (e.g., N-95 respirator) and contact (e.g., gowns and gloves) precautions http:// www.cdc. gov/ncidod/sars/infection control.htm). Until the mode of transmission has been defined more precisely, eye protection also should be worn for all patient contact. As more clinical

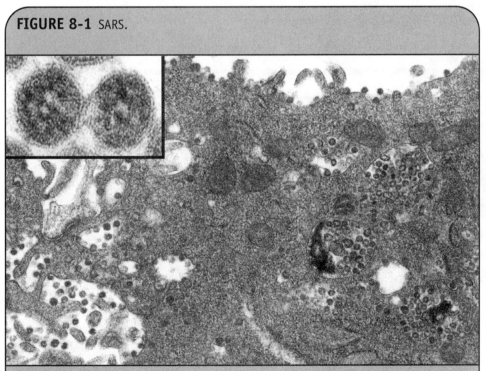

FIGURE 8-1 SARS.

"Note the coronaviruses contained within cytoplasmic membrane-bound vacuoles, and cisternae of the rough endoplasmic reticulum.

This thin section electron micrograph of an infected Vero E6 cell reveals particles of coronavirus. The coronavirus is now recognized as the etiologic agent of the 2003 SARS (Severe Acute Respiratory Syndrome) outbreak."

Source: Public Health Image Library CDC/C.S. Goldsmith/T.G. Ksiazek/S.R. Zaki, 2003.

and epidemiologic information becomes available, interim recommendations will be updated.

Editorial Note: During 2000, approximately 83 million nonresident passengers arrived in China, 13 million in Hong Kong, and 2 million in Vietnam, and approximately 460,000 residents of China, Hong Kong, and Vietnam traveled to the United States (2). "During January 1, 1997–March 18, 2003, an estimated 5% of ill tourists worldwide who sought post-travel care from one of 25 worldwide GeoSentinel travel clinics had pneumonia (International Society of Travel Medicine, unpublished data, 2003). In the United States, approximately 500,000 persons with pneumonia require hospitalization each year; in approximately half of these cases, no etiologic agent is identified despite intensive investigation (3, 4). On the basis of these data and the broad and necessarily nonspecific case definition, cases meeting the criteria for SARS are anticipated worldwide and in the United States. However, most of the anticipated cases are expected to be unrelated to the current outbreak.

Electron microscopic identification of paramyxovirus-like particles has been reported from Germany and Hong Kong (5). This family of viruses includes measles, mumps, human parainfluenza viruses, and respiratory syncytial virus in addition to the recently identified henipaviruses and metapneumovirus. Additional testing is under way to confirm a definitive etiology. Identification of the causative agent should lead to

specific diagnostic tests, simplify surveillance, and focus treatment guidelines and infection control guidance.

Clinicians and public health officials who suspect cases of SARS are requested to report such cases to their state health departments. CDC requests that reports of suspect cases from state health departments, international airlines, cruise ships, or cargo carriers be directed to the SARS Investigative Team at the CDC Emergency Operations Center, telephone 770-488-7100. Additional information about SARS (e.g., infection control guidance and procedures for reporting suspected cases) is available at http://www.cdc.gov/ncidod/sars. Global case counts are available at http://www.who.int.

REFERENCES FROM THE READING

1. World Health Organization. Disease outbreak reported: acute respiratory syndrome in China—update 3. Available at http://www.who.int/csr/don/2003_2_20/en.

2. World Tourism Organization. Yearbook of Tourism Statistics. Madrid, Spain: World Tourism Organization, 2002.

3. Martson BJ, Plouffe JF, File TM, et al. Incidence of community-acquired pneumonia requiring hospitalization: results of a population-based active surveillance study in Ohio. Arch Intern Med 1997;157:1709–18.

4. Marrie TJ, Durant H, Yates L. Community-acquired pneumonia requiring hospitalization: 5-year prospective study. Rev Infect Dis 1989;11:586–98.

5. World Health Organization. Disease outbreak reported: acute respiratory syndrome in China—update 4. Available at http://www.who.int/csr/don/2003_03_19/en.

This more general dispatch went out at the same time.

READING 16
Preliminary Clinical Description of Severe Acute Respiratory Syndrome

World Health Organization, Geneva, Switzerland.
Immunization and Respiratory Infections Division, Centre for Infectious Disease Prevention and Control, Health Canada, Ottawa, Canada. CDC SARS Investigation Team; TA Clarke, MD, and B Park, MD, EIS officers, CDC.

CDC SARS Investigation Team; TA Clarke, MD, and B Park, MD, EIS officers, CDC. Preliminary Clinical Description of Severe Acute Respiratory Syndrome. MMWR. Dispatch Vol. 52, March F21, 2003.

Severe acute respiratory syndrome (SARS) is a condition of unknown etiology that has been described in patients in Asia,

North America, and Europe. This report summarizes the clinical description of patients with SARS based on information collected since mid-February 2003 by the World Health Organization (WHO), Health Canada, and CDC in collaboration with health authorities and clinicians in Hong Kong, Taiwan, Bangkok, Singapore, the United Kingdom, Slovenia, Canada, and the United States. This information is preliminary and limited by the broad and necessarily nonspecific case definition.

As of March 21, 2003, the majority of patients identified as having SARS have been adults aged 25–70 years who were previously healthy. Few suspected cases of SARS have been reported among children aged < 15 years. The incubation period for SARS is typically 2–7 days; however, isolated reports have suggested an incubation period as long as 10 days. The illness begins generally with a prodrome of fever (> 100.4°F [> 38.0°C]). Fever often is high, sometimes is associated with chills and rigors, and might be accompanied by other symptoms, including headache, malaise, and myalgia. At the onset of illness, some persons have mild respiratory symptoms. Typically, rash and neurologic or gastrointestinal findings are absent; however, some patients have reported diarrhea during the febrile prodrome. After 3–7 days, a lower respiratory phase begins with the onset of a dry, nonproductive cough or dyspnea, which might be accompanied by or progress to hypoxemia. In 10%–20% of cases, the respiratory illness is severe enough to require intubation and mechanical ventilation. The case-fatality rate among persons with illness meeting the current WHO case definition of SARS is approximately 3%. Chest radiographs might be normal during the febrile prodrome and throughout the course of illness. However, in a substantial proportion of patients, the respiratory phase is characterized by early focal interstitial infiltrates progressing to more generalized, patchy, interstitial infiltrates. Some chest radiographs from patients in the late stages of SARS also have shown areas of consolidation. Early in the course of disease, the absolute lymphocyte count is often decreased. Overall white blood cell counts have generally been normal or decreased. At the peak of the respiratory illness, approximately 50% of patients have leucopenia and thrombocytopenia or low-normal platelet counts (50,000–150,000/μL). Early in the respiratory phase, elevated creatine phosphokinase levels (as high as 3,000 IU/L) and hepatic transaminases (two to six times the upper limits of normal) have been noted. In the majority of patients, renal function has remained normal. The severity of illness might be highly variable, ranging from mild illness to death. Although a few close contacts of patients with SARS have developed a similar illness, the majority have remained well. Some close contacts have reported a mild, febrile illness without respiratory signs or symptoms, suggesting the illness might not always progress to the respiratory phase. Treatment regimens have included several antibiotics to presumptively treat known bacterial agents of atypical pneumonia. In several locations, therapy also has included antiviral agents such as oseltamivir or ribavirin. Steroids have also been administered orally or intravenously to patients in combination with ribavirin and other antimicrobials. At present, the most efficacious treatment regimen, if any, is unknown.

In the United States, clinicians who suspect cases of SARS are requested to report such cases to their state health departments. CDC requests that reports of suspected cases from state health departments, international airlines, cruise ships, or cargo carriers be directed to the SARS Investigative Team at the CDC Emergency Operations Center, telephone 770-488-7100. Outside the United States, clinicians who suspect cases of SARS are requested to report such cases to their local public health authorities. Additional information about SARS (e.g., infection control guidance and procedures for reporting suspected cases) is available at http://www.cdc.gov/ncidod/sars. Global case counts are available at http://www.who.int.

As more information became known, the case definition was updated accordingly.

READING 17
Updated Interim Surveillance Case Definition for Severe Acute Respiratory Syndrome (SARS)—United States, April 29, 2003

Centers for Disease Control and Prevention. Updated Interim Surveillance Case Definition for Severe Acute Respiratory Syndrome (SARS)—United States, April 29, 2003. *MMWR*. April 29, 2003;52(Dispatch):1–3.

CDC's interim surveillance case definition for severe acute respiratory syndrome (SARS) has been updated to include laboratory criteria for evidence of infection with the SARS-associated coronavirus (SARS-CoV) (Figure 8-2, Table 8-3). In addition, clinical criteria have been revised to reflect the possible spectrum of respiratory illness associated with SARS-CoV. Epidemiologic criteria have been retained. The majority of U.S. cases of SARS continue to be associated with travel,* with only limited secondary spread to household members or health-care providers (1).

*In this updated case definition, Taiwan has been added to the areas with documented or suspected community transmission of SARS; Hanoi, Vietnam, is now an area with recently documented or suspected community transmission of SARS.

SARS has been associated etiologically with a novel coronavirus, SARS-CoV (2, 3). Evidence of SARS-CoV infection has been identified in patients with SARS in several countries, including the United States. Several new laboratory tests can be used to detect SARS-CoV. Serologic testing for coronavirus antibody can be performed by using indirect fluorescent antibody or enzyme-linked immunosorbent assays that are specific for antibody produced after infection. Although some patients have detectable coronavirus antibody during the acute phase (i.e., within 14 days of illness onset), definitive interpretation of negative coronavirus antibody tests is possible only for specimens obtained > 21 days after onset of symptoms. A reverse transcriptase polymerase chain reaction (RT-PCR) test specific for viral RNA has been positive within the first 10 days after onset of fever in specimens from some SARS patients, but the duration of detectable viremia or viral shedding is unknown. RT-PCR testing can detect SARS-CoV in clinical specimens, including serum, stool, and nasal secretions. Finally, viral culture and isolation have both been used to detect SARS-CoV. Absence of SARS-CoV antibody in serum obtained < 21 days after illness onset, a negative PCR test, or a negative viral culture does not exclude coronavirus infection.

Reported U.S. cases of SARS still will be classified as suspect or probable; however, these cases can be further classified as laboratory-confirmed or -negative if laboratory data are available and complete, or as laboratory-indeterminate if specimens are not available or testing is incomplete. Obtaining convalescent serum samples to make a final determination about infection with SARS-CoV is critical.

No instances of SARS-CoV infection have been detected in persons who are asymptomatic. However, data are insufficient to exclude the possibility of asymptomatic infection with SARS-CoV and the possibility that such persons can transmit the virus. Investigations of close contacts and health-care workers exposed to SARS patients might provide information about the occurrence of asymptomatic infected persons. Similarly, the clinical manifestations of SARS might extend beyond respiratory illness. As more is learned about SARS-CoV infection, clinical and laboratory criteria will provide a framework for classifying the full spectrum of infection (Figure 8-2).

This surveillance case definition should be used for reporting and classification purposes only. It should not be used for clinical management or as the only criterion for identifying or testing patients who might have SARS or for instituting infection-control precautions (4, 5). This definition will be updated as new data become available or if changes in the epidemiology of SARS occur in the United States.

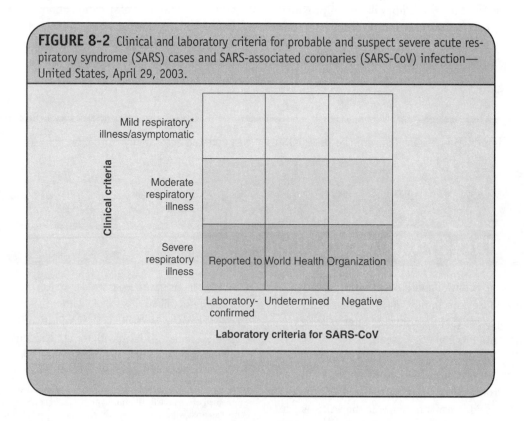

FIGURE 8-2 Clinical and laboratory criteria for probable and suspect severe acute respiratory syndrome (SARS) cases and SARS-associated coronaries (SARS-CoV) infection—United States, April 29, 2003.

TABLE 8-3 Updated interim U.S. surveillance case definition for severe acute respiratory syndrome (SARS)—United States, April 29, 2003.

Clinical criteria
- Asymptomatic or mild respiratory illness
- Moderate respiratory illness
  — Temperature of > 100.4° F (> 38° C)*, and
  — One or more clinical findings of respiratory illness (e.g., cough, shortness of breath, difficulty breathing, or hypoxia)
- Severe respiratory illness
  — Temperature of > 100.4° F (> 38° C)*, and
  — One or more clinical findings of respiratory illness (e.g., cough, shortness of breath, difficulty breathing, or hypoxia), and
    — radiographic evidence of pneumonia, or
    — respiratory distress syndrome, or
    — autopsy findings consistent with pneumonia or respiratory distress syndrome without an identifiable cause

Epidemiologic criteria
- Travel (including transit in an airport) within 10 days of onset symptoms to an area with current or recently documented or suspected community transmission of SARS[†], or
- Close contact[§] within 10 days of onset symptoms with a person known or suspected to have SARS infection

Laboratory criteria[♦]
- Confirmed
  — Detection of antibody to SARS-CoV in specimens obtained during acute illness or > 21 days after illness onset, or
  — Detection of SARS-CoV RNA by RT-PCR confirmed by a second PCR assay, by using a second aliquot of the specimen and a different set of PCR primers, or
  — Isolation of SARS-CoV
- Negative
  — Absence of antibody to SARS-CoV in convalescent serum obtained > 21 days after symptom onset
- Undetermined: laboratory testing either not performed or incomplete

Case classification[**]
- Probable case: meets the clinical criteria for severe respiratory illness of unknown etiology with onset since February 1, 2003, and epidemiologic criteria; laboratory criteria confirmed, negative, or undetermined
- Suspect case: meets the clinical criteria for moderate respiratory illness of unknown etiology with onset since February 1, 2003, and epidemiologic criteria; laboratory criteria confirmed, negative, or undetermined

---

*A measured documented temperature of > 100.4° F (> 38° C) is preferred. However, clinical judgment should be used when evaluating patients for whom a measured temperature of > 100.4° F (> 38° C) has not been documented. Factors that might be considered include patient self-report of fever, use of antipyretics, presence of immunocompromising conditions or therapies, lack of access to health care, or inability to obtain a measured temperature. Reporting authorities might consider these factors when classifying patients who do not strictly meet the clinical criteria for this case definition.

[†]Areas with current documented or suspected community transmission of SARS include mainland China and Hong Kong Special Administrative Region, People's Republic of China; Singapore; Taiwan; and Toronto, Canada. Hanoi, Vietnam, is an area with recently documented or suspected community transmission of SARS.

[§]Close contact is defined as having cared for or lived with a person known to have SARS or having a high likelihood of direct contact with respiratory secretions and/or body fluids of a patient known to have SARS. Examples of close contact include kissing or embracing, sharing eating or drinking utensils, close conversation (< 3 feet), physical examination, and any other direct physical contact between persons. Close contact does not include activities such as walking by a person or sitting across a waiting room or office for a brief period of time.

[♦]Assays for the laboratory diagnosis of SARS-CoV infection include enzyme-linked immunosorbent assay, indirect fluorescent-antibody assay, and reverse transcription polymerase chain reaction (RT-PCR) assays of appropriately collected clinical specimens (Source: CDC. Guidelines for collection of specimens from potential cases of SARS. Available at http://www.cdc.gov/ncidod/sars/specimen_collection_sars2.htm). Absence of SARS-CoV antibody from serum obtained < 21 days after illness onset, a negative PCR test, or a negative viral culture does not exclude coronavirus infection and is not considered a definitive laboratory result. In these instances, a convalescent serum specimen obtained > 21 days after illness is needed to determine infection with SARS-CoV. All SARS diagnostic assays are under evaluation.

[**]Asymptomatic SARS-CoV infection or clinical manifestations other than respiratory illness might be identified as more is learned about SARS-CoV infection.

REFERENCES FROM THE READING

1. CDC. Update: Severe acute respiratory syndrome—United States, 2003. MMWR 2003;52:357–60.

2. Ksiazek TG, Erdman D, Goldsmith C, et al. A novel coronavirus associated with severe acute respiratory syndrome. N Engl J Med. Available at http://content.nejm.org/cgi/reprint/NEJMoa030781v3.pdf.

3. Drosten C, Gunther S, Preiser W, et al. Identification of a novel coronavirus in patients with severe acute respiratory syndrome. N Engl J Med. Available at http://content.nejm.org/cgi/reprint/NEJMoa030747v2.pdf.

4. CDC. Updated interim domestic guidelines for triage and disposition of patients who may have severe acute respiratory distress syndrome (SARS). Available at http://www.cdc.gov/ncidod/sars/triage_interim_guidance.htm.

5. CDC. Interim guidance on infection control precautions for patients with suspected severe acute respiratory syndrome (SARS) and close contacts in households. Available at http://www.cdc.gov/ncidod/sars/ic-closecontacts.htm.

By year's end, the following update was provided.

READING 18
Revised U.S. Surveillance Case Definition for Severe Acute Respiratory Syndrome (SARS) and Update on SARS Cases— United States and Worldwide, December 2003

SARS Team and Executive Committee, Council of State and Territorial Epidemiologists. SARS Investigative Team, CDC.

SARS Team and Executive Committee, Council of State and Territorial Epidemiologists, SARS Investigative Team, CDC. Revised U.S. Surveillance Case Definition for Severe Acute Respiratory Syndrome (SARS) and Update on SARS Cases— United States and Worldwide, December 2003. *MMWR.* 2003;52:1202–1206.

During the 2003 epidemic of severe acute respiratory syndrome (SARS), CDC and the Council of State and Territorial Epidemiologists (CSTE) developed surveillance criteria to identify persons with SARS. The surveillance case definition changed throughout the epidemic as understanding of the clinical, laboratory, and transmission characteristics of SARS-associated coronavirus (SARS-CoV) increased (1–5). On June 26, CSTE adopted a position statement to add SARS-CoV disease to the National Notifiable Disease Surveillance System (NNDSS). The position statement included criteria for defining a SARS case for national reporting. On November 3, CSTE issued a new interim position statement* with a revised SARS case definition. This report summarizes the new U.S. surveillance case definition for SARS and updates reported cases of SARS worldwide and in the United States.

SUMMARY OF CHANGES TO CASE DEFINITION

The revised SARS case definition (Table 8-4) modifies the clinical, epidemiologic, laboratory, and case-exclusion criteria in the U.S. surveillance case definition used during the 2003 epidemic. In the clinical criteria, "early" illness replaces "asymptomatic" or "mild" illness. The epidemiologic criteria include the following new categories: 1) possible exposure to SARS-CoV and 2) likely exposure to SARS-CoV. Laboratory criteria for evidence of SARS-CoV infection reflect advances in testing technology. The case-exclusion criteria have been changed to allow for exclusion when a serum sample collected >28 days after onset of symptoms is negative for antibody to SARS-CoV.

The revised case definition also classifies each SARS case as either a SARS report under investigation (SARS RUI) or SARS-CoV disease. SARS RUI is a sensitive, nonspecific case classification based solely on clinical or epidemiologic criteria and includes cases classified previously as probable or suspect. SARS-CoV disease is a more specific case classification based on selected clinical and epidemiologic criteria or laboratory confirmation. SARS RUIs might subsequently meet the definition for SARS-CoV disease based on results from laboratory testing (Tables 8-5 and 8-6).

UPDATE ON SARS CASES

During November 2002–July 2003, a total of 8,098 probable SARS cases were reported to the World Health Organization (WHO) from 29 countries, including 29 cases from the United States; 774 SARS-related deaths (case-fatality rate: 9.6%) were reported, none of which occurred in the United States (6). Eight U.S. cases had serologic evidence of SARS-CoV infection; these eight cases have been described previously (7–10).

TABLE 8-4 Revised Council of State and Territorial Epidemiologists surveillance case definition for severe acute respiratory syndrome (SARS), December 2003.

Clinical criteria

Early illness

- Presence of two or more of the following features: fever (might be subjective), chills, rigors, myalgia, headache, diarrhea, sore throat, or rhinorrhea

Mild-to-moderate respiratory illness

- Temperature of > 100.4° F (> 38° C)* **and**
- One or more clinical findings of lower respiratory illness (e.g., cough, shortness of breath, or difficulty breathing)

Severe respiratory illness

- Meets clinical criteria of mild-to-moderate respiratory illness **and**
- One or more of the following findings:
  — Radiographic evidence of pneumonia, **or**
  — Acute respiratory distress syndrome, **or**
  — Autopsy findings consistent with pneumonia or acute respiratory distress syndrome without an identifiable cause

Epidemiologic criteria

Possible exposure to SARS-associated coronavirus (SARS-CoV)

One or more of the following exposures in the 10 days before onset of symptoms:

- Travel to a foreign or domestic location with documented or suspected recent transmission of SARS-CoV[†] or
- Close contact[§] with a person with mild-to-moderate or severe respiratory illness and history of travel in the 10 days before onset of symptoms to a foreign or domestic location with documented or suspected recent transmission of SARS-CoV[†]

Likely exposure to SARS-CoV

One or more of the following exposures in the 10 days before onset of symptoms:

- Close contact[§] with a person with confirmed SARS-CoV disease or
- Close contact[§] with a person with mild-to-moderate or severe respiratory illness for whom a chain of transmission can be linked to a confirmed case of SARS-CoV disease in the 10 days before onset of symptoms

Laboratory criteria

Tests to detect SARS-CoV are being refined and their performance characteristics assessed[♦]; therefore, criteria for laboratory diagnosis of SARS-CoV are changing. The following are general criteria for laboratory confirmation of SARS-CoV:

- Detection of serum antibody to SARS-CoV by a test validated by CDC (e.g., enzyme immunoassay), or
- Isolation in cell culture of SARS-CoV from a clinical specimen, or
- Detection of SARS-CoV RNA by a reverse transcription polymerase chain reaction test validated by CDC and with subsequent confirmation in a reference laboratory (e.g., CDC).

Information about the current criteria for laboratory diagnosis of SARS-CoV is available at http://www.cdc.gov/ncidod/sars/labdiagnosis.htm.

Exclusion criteria

A case may excluded as a SARS report under investigation (SARS RUI), including as a CDC-defined probable SARS-CoV case, if any of the following apply:

- An alternative diagnosis can explain the illness fully**, **or**
- Antibody to SARS-CoV is undetectable in a serum specimen obtained > 28 days after onset of illness[††], **or**
- The case was reported on the basis of contact with a person who was excluded subsequently as a case of SARS-CoV disease; then the reported case also is excluded, provided other epidemiologic or laboratory criteria are not present.

Case classification

SARS RUI

Reports in persons from areas where SARS is not known to be active

- SARS RUI-1: Cases compatible with SARS in groups likely to be first affected by SARS-CoV[§§] if SARS-CoV is introduced from a person without clear epidemiologic links to known cases of SARS-CoV disease or places with known ongoing transmission of SARS-CoV

Reports in persons from areas where SARS activity is occurring

- SARS RUI-2: Cases meeting the clinical criteria for mild-to-moderate illness and the epidemiologic criteria for possible exposure (spring 2003 CDC definition for suspect cases[♦♦])

continues

TABLE 8-4 Revised Council of State and Territorial Epidemiologists surveillance case definition for severe acute respiratory syndrome (SARS), December 2003 (continued).

- SARS RUI-3: Cases meeting the clinical criteria for severe illness and the epidemiologic criteria for possible exposure (spring 2003 CDC definition for probable cases◆◆)
- SARS RUI-4: Cases meeting the clinical criteria for early or mild-to-moderate illness and the epidemiologic criteria for likely exposure to SARS-CoV

SARS-CoV disease
- Probable case of SARS-CoV disease: meets the clinical critera for severe respiratory illness and the epidemiologic criteria for likely exposure to SARS-CoV
- Confirmed case of SARS-CoV disease: clinically compatible illness (i.e., early, mild-to-moderate, or severe) that is laboratory confirmed

---

*A measured documented temperature of > 100.4° F (> 38° C) is expected. However, clinical judgment may allow a small proportion of patients without a documented fever to meet this criterion. Factors that might be considered include patient's self-report of fever, use of antipyretics, presence of immuno-compromising conditions or therapies, lack of access to health care, or inability to obtain a measured temperature. Initial case classification based on reported information might change, and reclassification might be required.

†Types of locations specified will vary (e.g., country, airport, city, building, or floor of building). The last date a location may be a criterion for exposure is 10 days (one incubation period) after removal of that location from CDC travel alert status. The patient's travel should have occurred on or before the last date the travel alert was in place. Transit through a foreign airport meets the epidemiologic criteria for possible exposure in a location for which a CDC travel advisory is in effect. Information about CDC travel alerts and advisories and assistance in determining appropriate dates are available at http://www.cdc.gov/ncidod/sars/travel.htm.

§Close contact is defined as having cared for or lived with a person with SARS or having a high likelihood of direct contact with respiratory secretions and/or body fluids of a person with SARS (during encounters with the patient through contact with materials contaminated by the patient) either during the period the person was clinically ill or within 10 days of resolution of symptoms. Examples of close contact include kissing or embracing, sharing eating or drinking utensils, close (i.e., < 3 feet) conversation, physical examination, and any other direct physical contact between persons. Close contact does not include activities such as walking by a person or sitting across a waiting room or office for a brief time.

◆The identification of the etiologic agent of SARS (i.e., SARS-CoV) led to the rapid development of enzyme immunoassays and immunofluorescence assays for serologic diagnosis and reverse transcription polymerase chain reaction assays for detection of SARS-CoV RNA in clinical samples. These assays can be very sensitive and specific for detecting antibody and RNA, respectively, in the later stages of SARS-CoV disease. However, both are less sensitive for detecting infection early in illness. The majority of patients in the early stages of SARS-CoV disease have a low titer of virus in respiratory and other secretions and require time to mount an antibody response. SARS-CoV antibody tests might be positive as early as 8–10 days after onset of illness and often by 14 days after onset of illness, but sometimes not until 28 days after onset of illness. Information about the current criteria for laboratory diagnosis of SARS-CoV is available at http://www.cdc.gov/ncidod/sars/labdiagnosis.htm.

**Factors that may be considered in assigning alternate diagnoses include the strength of the epidemiologic exposure criteria for SARS-CoV disease, the specificity of the alternate diagnostic test, and the compatibility of the clinical presentation and course of illness with the alternative diagnosis.

††Current data indicate that > 95% of patients with SARS-CoV disease mount an antibody response to SARS-CoV. However, health officials may choose not to exclude a case on the basis of lack of serologic response if reasonable concern exists that an antibody response could not be mounted.

§§Consensus guidance is in development between CDC and CSTE on which groups are most likely to be affected first by SARS-CoV if it reemerges. SARS-CoV disease should be considered at a minimum in the differential diagnoses for persons requiring hospitalization for pneumonia confirmed radiographically or acute respiratory distress syndrome without identifiable etiology and who have one of the following risk factors in the 10 days before the onset of illness:
- Travel to mainland China, Hong Kong, or Taiwan, or close contact with an ill person with a history of recent travel to one of these areas, or
- Employment in an occupation associated with a risk for SARS-CoV exposure (e.g., health-care worker with direct patient contact or a worker in a laboratory that contains live SARS-CoV), or
- Part of a cluster of cases of atypical pneumonia without an alternative diagnosis.

Guidelines for the identification, evaluation, and management of these patients are available at http://www.cdc.gov/ncidod/sars/absenceofsars.htm.

◆◆During the 2003 SARS epidemic, CDC case definitions were the following:
Suspect case
- Meets the clinical criteria for mild-to-moderate respiratory illness and the epidemiologic criteria for possible exposure to SARS-CoV but does not meet any of the laboratory criteria and exclusion criteria or
- Unexplained acute respiratory illness that results in death of a person on whom an autopsy was not performed and that meets the epidemiologic criteria for possible exposure to SARS-CoV but does not meet any of the laboratory criteria and exclusion criteria.
Probable case
- Meets the clinical criteria for severe respiratory illness and the epidemiologic criteria for possible exposure to SARS-CoV but does not meet any of the laboratory criteria and exclusion criteria.

TABLE 8-5 Severe acute respiratory syndrome- associated coronavirus (SARS-CoV) case classification before laboratory testing, by clinical and epidemiologic criteria.

Epidemiologic criteria	Clinical criteria for degree of illness		
	Early	Mild to moderate	Severe
Unknown	—	—	SARS RUI*-1
Possible	—	SARS RUI-2	SARS RUI-3
Likely	SARS RUI-4	SARS RUI-4	Probable case of SARS-CoV disease

*Report under investigation.

TABLE 8-6 Severe acute respiratory syndrome—associated coronavirus (SARS-CoV) case classification after laboratory testing, by initial report category.

Initial report category	Laboratory testing results		
	Negative*	Positive	Not performed
SARS RUI†-1 to SARS RUI-4	Excluded	Confirmed case of SARS-CoV disease	Undetermined§
Probable case of SARS-CoV disease	Excluded	Confirmed case of SARS-CoV disease	Probable case of SARS-CoV disease

*Negative test as defined by negative antibody titer taken > 28 days after the onset of symptoms. A negative polymerase chain reaction result does not rule out SARS-CoV disease.
†Report under investigation.
§Collection and/or laboratory testing of specimen was not completed.

A total of 156 reported U.S. SARS cases from the 2003 epidemic remain under investigation, with 137 (88%) cases classified according to previous surveillance criteria as suspect SARS and 19 (12%) classified as probable SARS. Because convalescent serum specimens have not been obtained from the 19 probable and 137 suspect cases that remain under investigation, whether these persons had SARS-CoV disease is unknown.

Editorial Note: The revised surveillance case definition for SARS reflects an improved understanding of the clinical and laboratory characteristics of SARS-CoV. The revision differentiates patients with nonspecific clinical illness or less definitive epidemiologic associations (i.e., SARS RUIs) from those with laboratory-confirmed SARS-CoV infection or more definitive epidemiologic links (i.e., cases of SARS-CoV disease). Local and state health departments will monitor SARS RUIs to ensure implementation of prompt public health measures for preventing disease transmission if SARS-CoV is confirmed subsequently. Numerous SARS RUIs probably will be excluded as SARS cases as laboratory results become available during the course of illness. Surveillance data for cases meeting the

SARS-CoV disease case definition will be reported to NNDSS and included in the weekly statistical summary of notifiable infectious diseases in the United States published in *MMWR* (Table 1 [Summary of Provisional Cases of Selected Notifiable Diseases, United States]).

Reporting of cases meeting previous SARS definitions ended in late July 2003. However, case numbers continue to change as new clinical information or results of additional laboratory testing on cases reported previously become available. Updated case counts reflecting these changes are available from CDC at http://www.cdc.gov/od/oc/media/sars/cases.htm.

Efforts are under way to prepare for a possible reappearance of SARS-CoV. CDC, in collaboration with other federal partners, state and local health officials, professional organizations and societies, and representatives of the health-care industry, has developed a guidance document to help public health and health-care officials detect the reappearance of SARS-CoV in the United States quickly and implement a decisive and effective public health response. The document, "Public Health Guidance for Community-Level Preparedness and Response to Severe Acute Respiratory Syndrome (SARS)," is available at http://www.cdc. gov/ncidod/sars/sarsprepplan.htm.

REFERENCES FROM THE READING

1. CDC. Outbreak of severe acute respiratory syndrome—worldwide, 2003. MMWR 2003;52:226–8.

2. CDC. Updated interim surveillance case definition for severe acute respiratory syndrome (SARS)—United States, April 29, 2003. MMWR 2003;52:391–3.

3. CDC. Update: severe acute respiratory syndrome—United States, May 21, 2003. MMWR 2003;52:466—8.

4. CDC. Update: severe acute respiratory syndrome—United States, June 4, 2003. MMWR 2003;52:525–6.

5. CDC. Update: severe acute respiratory syndrome—worldwide and United States, 2003. MMWR 2003;52:664–5.

6. World Health Organization. Summary table of SARS cases by country, November 1, 2002–August 7, 2003. Available at http://www.who.int/csr/sars/country/2003_08_15/en/.

7. CDC. Severe acute respiratory syndrome (SARS) and coronavirus testing—United States, 2003. MMWR 2003;52:297–302.

8. CDC. Update: severe acute respiratory syndrome—United States, 2003. MMWR 2003;52:357–60.

9. CDC. Update: severe acute respiratory syndrome—United States, May 28, 2003. MMWR 2003;52:500–1.

10. CDC. Update: severe acute respiratory syndrome—United States, June 11, 2003. MMWR 2003;52:550.

In 2004, MMWR reported on the SARS surveillance project, described here. This use of technology to perform surveillance over a wide geographical region becomes increasingly important as human society travels more rapidly from place to place. Infectious diseases do not observe borders, making the coordination of surveillance across counties, states, countries, or continents that much more important.

READING 19
SARS Surveillance Project—Internet-Enabled Multiregion Surveillance for Rapidly Emerging Disease

Seth L. Foldy, E. Barthell, J. Silva, P. Biedrzycki, D. Howe, M. Erme, B. Keaton, C. Hamilton, L. Brewer, G. Miller, E. Eby, R. Coles, K. Pemble, and C. Felton

Foldy SL, Barthell E, Silva J, et al. SARS Surveillance Project—Internet-Enabled Multiregion Surveillance for Rapidly Emerging Disease. *MMWR*. 2004;53(Suppl):215–220.

ABSTRACT

Introduction: On March 15, 2003, CDC requested health-care and public health agencies to conduct surveillance for severe acute respiratory syndrome (SARS). The SARS Surveillance Project (SARS-SP) was established to rapidly implement multi-regional SARS surveillance in emergency departments (EDs) by using existing Internet-based tools.

Objectives: The objectives of SARS-SP were to 1) disseminate and update SARS screening forms for ED triage, 2) establish surveillance for SARS syndrome elements by using Regional Emergency Medicine Internet (REMI), 3) expand surveillance to multiple regions, and 4) evaluate the usefulness of Internet tools for agile surveillance during a rapidly emerging global epidemic.

Methods: SARS-SP developed, distributed, and updated an Internet-based triage form to identify patients for infection control and public health reporting. EDs then were invited to report visit frequencies with various SARS syndrome elements to local public health authorities by using the REMI Internet application (first in one metropolitan area, and later in four). After pilot-testing in one metropolitan area, the surveillance system was implemented in three others.

Results: Active syndromic surveillance was established by health departments in Milwaukee, Wisconsin; Denver, Colorado; Akron, Ohio; and Fort Worth, Texas. A total of 27 EDs reported syndrome frequencies from > 146,000 patient encounters.

Conclusions: ED and public health partners reported being satisfied with the system, confirming the usefulness of Internet tools in the rapid establishment of multiregion syndromic surveillance during an emerging global epidemic.

INTRODUCTION

On March 15, 2003, CDC urgently requested health-care and public health agencies to conduct surveillance for severe acute respiratory syndrome (SARS) (1), a pneumonia later attributed to a newly discovered coronavirus (SARS-CoV). SARS had spread rapidly by air travel to three continents and appeared to be highly infectious to health-care workers and patients in health-care settings (1). The cause of SARS was then unknown, and diagnostic tests were lacking. Basic epidemiologic facts (e.g., the range of clinical symptomatology, whether persons with mild or asymptomatic infection could transmit disease, and the range of possible routes of infection) were unknown. Minimal assurance could be given that SARS was not already circulating in the United States. As a result, public health systems had to deploy complex, rapidly changing measures to protect health-care facilities and to take an agile approach to surveillance.

Frontlines of Medicine (http://www.frontlinesmed.org/) is a collaborative of emergency medicine, public health, and informatics professionals organized to enable better public health surveillance of emergency department (ED) information (2). Frontlines of Medicine created the SARS Surveillance Project (SARS-SP) workgroup to develop, disseminate, and update a practical screening (case-finding) form for potential SARS pa-

FIGURE 8-3 EMSystem® and SARS Surveillance Project sites—United States, 2003.

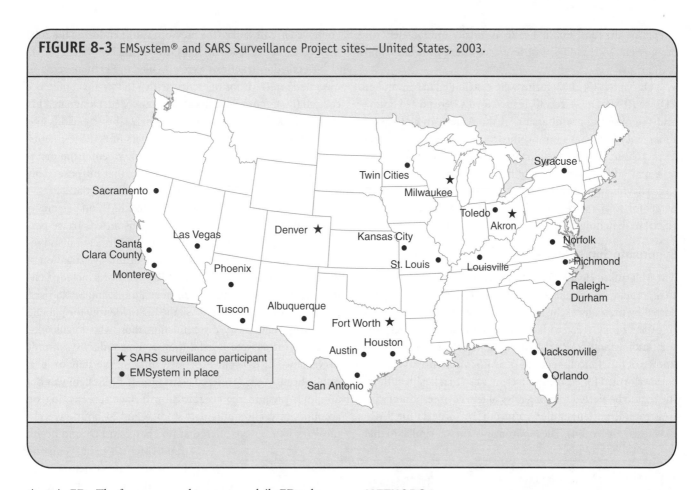

★ SARS surveillance participant
● EMSystem in place

tients in EDs. The form was used to measure daily ED volumes of SARS syndrome elements. These counts were transmitted and assembled regionally by using EMSystem® Regional Emergency Medicine Internet (REMI).* Because EMSystem was in use in 26 cities (Figure 8-3), syndromic surveillance developed in one city was presumed to be portable to multiple urban areas quickly and inexpensively.

The objectives of SARS-SP were to 1) create, disseminate, and update SARS screening forms for ED triage, 2) conduct SARS surveillance by using REMI, 3) expand surveillance to multiple regions, and 4) evaluate the usefulness of Internet tools for agile surveillance during a rapidly emerging global epidemic. SARS triage forms and surveillance were field-tested in Milwaukee, Wisconsin. The form was then distributed over the Internet, and three other urban regions initiated surveillance.

*EMSystem is an Internet-served REMI that allows restricted viewing of Internet screens protected by standard Secure Sockets Layer (SSL) with 128-bit encryption, and can alert participants using text mail messages. EMSystem and similar networked REMI applications were developed to improve situational awareness of emergency departments regarding ambulance diversions, mass casualty events, and other emergency medical services system changes. They have since been used for other functions including public health alerting, monitoring health-care utilization and readiness, and syndromic surveillance (3).

METHODS

Case-Finding Triage Forms

A single-page screening form was created for ED triage personnel (available at http://www.frontlinesmed.org/SARS-SP). The form was designed to 1) identify patients requiring immediate infection control and public health notification (case finding) and 2) facilitate counting and reporting to public health officials the number of daily visits featuring SARS syndrome elements for time-trend surveillance. Three check boxes recorded the presence or absence of the following elements of the SARS case definition (hereafter referred to as "SARS elements"): fever (history or finding of temperature > 38°C); respiratory findings (i.e., cough, shortness of breath, difficulty breathing, pneumonia, or respiratory distress syndrome); and either recent travel to locations associated with SARS transmission or contact with a suspected SARS patient (hereafter referred to as "SARS risks"). Pulse oximetry < 95% was recorded separately.

Screening was originally recommended only for patients with fever; later, after CDC recommended assessing patients for possible SARS on the basis of either fever or respiratory symptoms, triage personnel were instructed to screen patients with either complaint. The screening form encouraged ED staff to telephone the local public health authority immediately for any patient with the triad of fever, respiratory findings, and SARS risks.

On March 17, 2003, forms were distributed to Milwaukee EDs via REMI. On March 30, revised forms were posted online and the national membership of the American College of Emergency Physicians was notified by e-mail of the screening form website. Persons downloading forms were invited to enter an e-mail address to receive notification of updated forms and to participate in the voluntary syndromic surveillance effort. Screening forms were revised twice (and registered users notified) to matching changing CDC recommendations.

Syndromic Surveillance

The Milwaukee Health Department (MHD) invited local EDs to report daily visit totals and the numbers of screened patients sorted by mutually exclusive combinations of SARS elements (e.g., fever only, fever with respiratory findings only, respiratory findings with SARS risks only, etc.). Because little was then known of the clinical spectrum of SARS infection, surveillance was performed for each clinical element so that health authorities could be alerted to rising rates of febrile or respiratory illness even if patients failed to meet CDC criteria for SARS diagnosis (Figure 8-4). The reporting system was similar to that

employed in Milwaukee the previous summer during the 2002 Major League Baseball All-Star Game using EMSystem (4, 5).

Detailed instructions were e-mailed to ED managers and mounted on REMI for reference, with a follow-up conference call. MHD staff provided assistance as needed. Designated ED staff collected all screening forms for 24-hour periods and sorted them into mutually exclusive sets of SARS elements. REMI automatically reminded EDs daily to enter the previous day's totals on a screen designed for that purpose. Only authorized staff could enter or view surveillance data.

Only visit counts were entered into REMI; no personally identifiable health information was transmitted. Triage personnel stamped each form with patient identification and retained completed forms in case public health investigation of a particular patient was needed. If REMI reports included visits with the triad of fever, respiratory illness, and SARS risks, public health officials could ask the ED to identify the patient.

During nationwide dissemination, those who downloaded screening forms were asked if they would conduct syndromic surveillance. If ED staff expressed interest, the state or local public health agency offered assistance. If EMSystem was not already in use in the area, local interface screens, log-on accounts, server accounts, data storage, and 24-hour/day technical assistance were offered at no charge to EDs and health departments, using existing EMSystem infrastructure.

Participating public health staff used password-protected accounts to download daily jurisdiction-specific data from REMI as a tab-delimited spreadsheet. Each health department had exclusive access to its local data and controlled how it was analyzed and acted on. Milwaukee data were also downloaded remotely at CDC for analysis with the Early Aberration Reporting System (EARS) to test the feasibility of remote analysis (6).

Surveys

Participating health department surveillance coordinators provided summary statistics and impressions of the project. In July 2003, surveys were also sent to nurse managers at the 13 participating Milwaukee-area EDs.

FIGURE 8-4 Workflow for the SARS Surveillance Project.

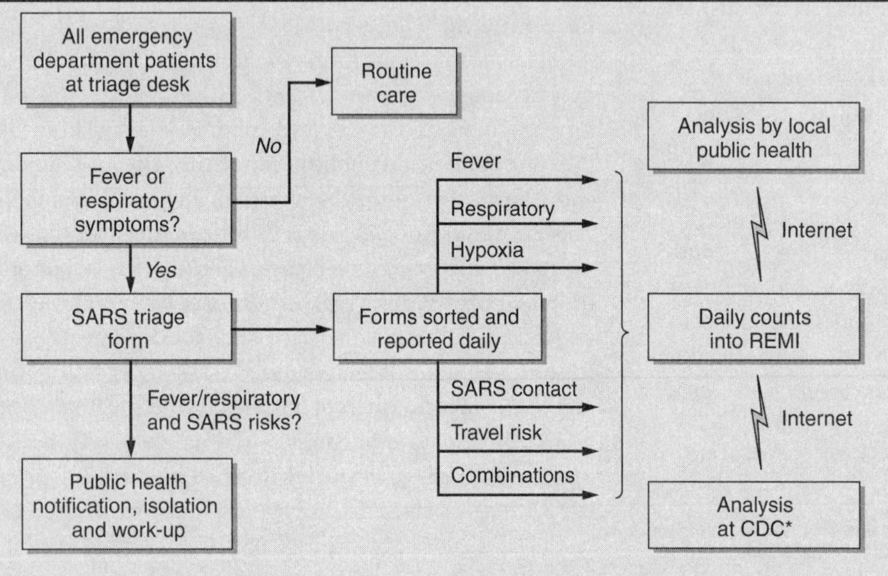

*CDC analysis conducted for short-term proof of concept in Milwaukee only.

RESULTS

During May–September 2003, a total of > 500 SARS-SP website hits were logged, and 257 persons requested e-mail notification of screening-form changes. Much smaller numbers visited the site after receiving e-mail notification of revised forms. The total number of EDs or clinics that used the screening form is not known.

During March 19–June 25, 2003, a total of 13 Milwaukee-area EDs participated in syndromic surveillance of 105,669 visits. Three other metropolitan areas (Denver, Colorado; Akron, Ohio; and Fort Worth, Texas) established ED syndromic surveillance with reporting to health authorities. During April 23–May 31, 2003, nine EDs in Denver, Colorado, that already used REMI sent surveillance information on 16,997 encounters to the Colorado Department of Public Health and Environment (CDPHE). During May 1–June 1, 2003, three EDs in Akron, Ohio, reported information from 12,939 encounters to the Akron Health Department (AHD). Neither the hospitals nor AHD had previously used REMI. During May 12–October 12, 2003, two hospitals in Fort Worth, Texas, that already used REMI reported on 10,941 encounters to Tarrant County Public Health (TCPH), with surveillance continuing beyond October. EDs in eight other cities expressed interest in daily syndromic surveillance, but efforts to recruit a public health agency failed in seven. The eighth city initiated a surveillance pilot in fall 2003.

Only one person in all four cities ultimately met the CDC criteria for possible SARS, and no confirmed cases were reported. Thus, neither case-finding sensitivity nor specificity can be measured. During March 15–October 1, 2003, three of the four jurisdictions investigated 42 potential SARS cases, of which 22 (52%) were prompted by the triage form. In Milwaukee, five investigations originated from telephone calls about positive ED triage forms; four originated from REMI electronic reports; and five originated outside EDs. All 13 investigations by CDPHE began with REMI reports. All 15 TCPH investigations began before initiation of SARS-SP surveillance and originated from nonmedical settings (e.g. from airlines). No patient investigated for possible SARS visited a participating ED but failed detection by the screening form.

The median percentage of surveillance period days for which participating EDs reported syndrome frequencies electronically by using REMI was 89% (range: 52%–100%). The most common data-quality problems cited by public health surveillance coordinators were nonreporting, reports lacking total ED visit census, and errors in the date of surveillance; telephone calls were sufficient to resolve these concerns. In Milwaukee, questions and data-quality concerns required frequent calls (7–9 daily) to and from EDs early in the project but only 1–2 calls by the end.

Resources did not permit on-site chart review to validate the accuracy of SARS element frequency reporting. Also, the standard ED record would not necessarily collect SARS risk history (travel or contact) and thus is not an ideal standard for comparison.

Each city performed its own analyses of syndromic time-series data. Cross-city analysis was not performed. In Milwaukee, staff graphed time series of SARS elements as crude counts, proportions of total ED census, and standard scores (i.e., the difference of daily counts from the cumulative mean, divided by the standard deviation) to display significant aberrations from the mean (Figure 8-5). The overall incidence rate of ED visits with each SARS element varied widely between cities, which is not surprising given the different geographic areas and date ranges of surveillance. Local surveillance-period incidence rates of ED patients reporting fever plus respiratory illness ranged from 0.33% in Akron to 1.4% in Denver. Two cities (Milwaukee and Fort Worth) investigated increasing syndrome trends; in both cases, telephone queries and record reviews by ED staff proved sufficient to exclude SARS as the cause.

During March 22–April 20, 2003, CDC easily downloaded daily Milwaukee data for EARS analysis, but these files did not include corrections made by local public health staff after telephone contact with EDs. Permitting online correction of data files on REMI would enable more accurate remote analysis.

Six of 13 participating Milwaukee ED managers returned nonanonymous surveys. Four of six believed SARS screening was performed as requested during all shifts. On a five-point scale ("strongly agree," "somewhat agree," "neutral," "somewhat disagree," and "strongly disagree,") five of six managers at least somewhat agreed they felt more secure knowing screening was being performed and also that screening increased the index of suspicion for SARS in their ED (one response to each item was neutral). Four at least somewhat agreed that data tabulation and data entry were easy (with one respondent neutral and the other somewhat disagreeing to both items). The average estimate for the time to complete the form at triage was 2.6 minutes (range: 1–5 minutes; median: 3 minutes), and the average estimate for daily tabulation and reporting was 17 minutes (range: 5–45 minutes; median: 15 minutes). These compared favorably with estimated time spent on syndromic surveillance during the 2002 All-Star Game project, further validating that surveillance from the controlled confines of the triage desk was more manageable. Two managers had participated in syndromic surveillance during the previous summer; both strongly agreed that triage-based surveillance was superior, and both at least

FIGURE 8-5 Daily Emergency Department (ED) visits by patients with severe acute respiratory syndrome (SARS) elements (fever plus respiratory symptoms plus hypoxia)—Milwaukee, Wisconsin, Wisconsin, 2003.

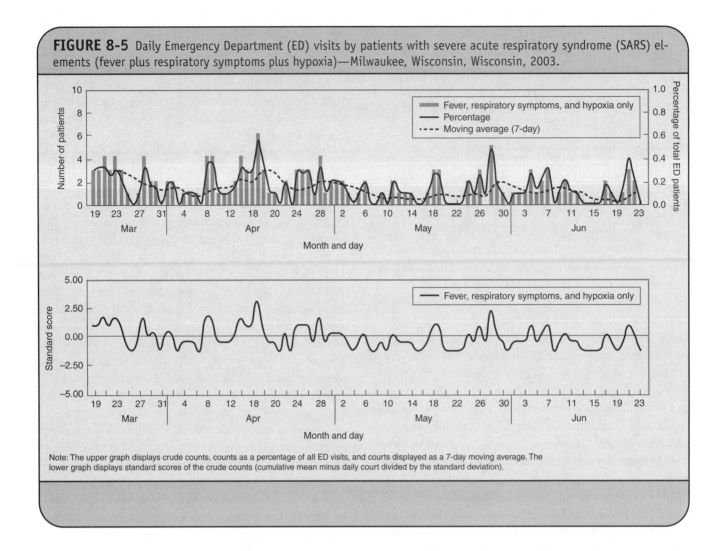

Note: The upper graph displays crude counts, counts as a percentage of all ED visits, and courts displayed as a 7-day moving average. The lower graph displays standard scores of the crude counts (cumulative mean minus daily court divided by the standard deviation).

somewhat agreed that prior experience with REMI surveillance facilitated the rapid start-up of SARS surveillance.

The four public health surveillance coordinators all reported that they were glad they had participated and were interested in similar surveillance opportunities. Queried on ways to improve the system, two coordinators stated that they wished they had recruited additional EDs to participate, and two stated that they desired better communications between public health agencies and ED staff.

DISCUSSION

SARS traveled extremely quickly, and new information about the disease evolved at a similar pace. SARS-SP, a rapidly organized, voluntary response, leveraged three capabilities to help clinicians and health officials keep pace: 1) interdisciplinary collaboration between emergency medicine, public health, and informatics; 2) an always-on, secure REMI net-

work used in > 24 metropolitan areas, and 3) rapid Internet information dissemination to clinicians. These were applied to two critical tasks: 1) helping ED staff detect possible SARS cases (case-finding) so they could protect patients, staff, and the community and 2) establishing syndromic surveillance to warn local health officials if illness consistent with SARS was increasing in their communities. The latter was deployed because CDC's surveillance focused on identifying known or suspected SARS risks but might not alert authorities to illness from unsuspected SARS contact (e.g., from asymptomatic transmission or unreported cases).

Ready-to-use screening forms helped busy ED staff to consistently meet complex, rapidly changing CDC guidance. ED triage (through which every patient passes early in an ED visit) was selected for case-finding and syndromic surveillance on the basis of ED workflow and previous experience. The 2002 All-Star Game surveillance project determined that relying on treating staff to record syndrome data produced poor-quality surveillance data and substantial staff-time demands (4, 5). In contrast, triage nurses equipped with a well-crafted case-finding form could consistently "Screen—Isolate—Call Public Health." Although the sample size was limited, ED managers in Milwaukee reported higher satisfaction, greater confidence in data collection, and more reasonable time demands from triage-based surveillance than from the earlier 2002 All-Star Game surveillance program.

Paper-based forms have important limitations. Manual data check-off, tabulation, and entry each multiply the risk of data error and consume staff time. However, surveillance methods relying exclusively on mined data from existing registration, discharge, or other routine data sets would miss relevant information (e.g., recent travel), and they would not provide a real-time alert to ED personnel to implement infection control, diagnostic testing, and public health reporting. Therefore, data mining alone does not replace intelligent tools at the point of service for agile surveillance and response. Ideally, future triage information systems could be modified rapidly to collect and analyze newly important information (e.g., travel) alongside other routinely collected data (e.g., chief complaints) as part of routine workflow. The right combinations of data would automatically alert staff and public health authorities of a potential case while data for ongoing syndromic surveillance are collected with no additional human effort. Intelligent, programmable, and interoperable electronic medical record systems, linked through clinical networks such as REMI, could result in automated yet agile surveillance.

Milwaukee had used REMI previously to facilitate drop-in ED surveillance. Resulting experience and relationships helped MHD rapidly implement SARS surveillance. EDs in other cities appeared more prone to participate when they already used REMI in their day-to-day work (as was the case in 24 of the 27 participating EDs). Staff used the same application for surveillance that they used daily for other purposes, eliminating the need for new hardware and simplifying training. By contrast, public health agencies that were unfamiliar with the REMI application appeared more reluctant to participate.

Existing experience, servers, and 24-hour technical assistance capability that already supported the REMI system were leveraged to support rapid, multiregional surveillance. The project demonstrated that remote CDC specialists could use aberration analysis on remote REMI data. Ideally, such data should be quality-checked locally before analysis.

Rapid dissemination and updating of the screening form was enabled by ACEP's membership e-mail list and Internet tools. Because SARS-SP anticipated rapid evolution of case definitions, clinicians were encouraged to subscribe for updates. However, not surprisingly, busy clinicians often failed to return for updated forms after downloading the original form. Ideally, REMI-networked clinical information systems would automatically incorporate updates and eliminate outdated tools from the point of service.

EDs in 12 urban areas expressed willingness to submit syndromic surveillance information to public health authorities, but only four health departments participated. The Council of State and Territorial Epidemiologists and the National Association of County and City Health Officials did not promote the project among their members because it lacked formal CDC endorsement. Such endorsement might be a precondition to participation, particularly in a fast-moving emergency with competing time demands.

Although this was a successful proof of concept of multiregional REMI-enabled surveillance, it had limitations. First, sensitivity and specificity of the triage screening and reporting cannot be calculated without SARS cases. Second, data were not validated by chart review. Third, ED records do not routinely record all information (e.g., travel) solicited. Finally, the system emphasized sensitivity over specificity.

With sufficient proportion of EDs involved, a sharp or sustained increase in community incidence of febrile and respiratory illness would likely be detected. Stamping and storing complete screening forms simplified rapid public health investigation. Because all four health departments reported being satisfied that they had participated in the surveillance project, it appears that a low positive predictive value for SARS was nevertheless practically manageable. Surveillance did not exhaust the patience of either EDs or public health agencies in springtime, but the outcome might have been different if the incidence rate of influenza and other common respiratory viruses were rising rather than falling.

CONCLUSION

SARS syndromic surveillance was rapidly established under emergency conditions by a loose network of collaborators using the tools available. It was handicapped by the lack of a legal or practical framework for sharing surveillance information across jurisdictions, and resources did not allow rigorous evaluation of the system's performance. Nevertheless, the ability to share surveillance tools across communities in a rapidly evolving outbreak illustrates how networked tools (e.g., REMI), which now reach > 18% of the nation's EDs, have become practical instruments for agile surveillance across multiple regions. This is enhanced when clinicians and public health agencies are familiar with the applications from regular use. State and federal public health involvement might elicit participation by more agencies and could exploit untapped potential of these applications, such as integrating data across multiple regions and employing more sophisticated aberration algorithms.

ACKNOWLEDGMENTS

Lori Hutwagner, National Center for Infectious Diseases, CDC, provided advice and EARS analysis; American College of Emergency Physicians publicized the screening tool and promoted participation in surveillance; Infinity HealthCare, Inc., developed and deployed new surveillance screens, accounts, and technical assistance without charge; and the staffs of participating hospitals and health departments established local procedures to transmit and review surveillance data. Milwaukee Health Department staff were supported in part by Lynde Uihlein through the Milwaukee Center for Emergency Public Health Preparedness, and by the Wisconsin Division of Public Health/CDC Cooperative Agreement #U90/CCU517002-03-02.

REFERENCES FROM THE READING

1. CDC. Outbreak of severe acute respiratory syndrome—worldwide, 2003. MMWR 2003;52:226–82.

2. Barthell EN, Cordell WH, Moorhead JC, et al. The Frontlines of Medicine Project: a proposal for the standardized communication of emergency department data for public health uses including syndromic surveillance for biological and chemical terrorism. Ann Emerg Med 2002;39:422–9.

3. Barthell EN, Foldy SL, Pemble KR, et al. Assuring community emergency capacity with collaborative Internet tools: the Milwaukee experience. J Public Health Manag Pract 2003;9:35–42.

4. Foldy S, Biedryzcki P, Barthell E, et al. The Milwaukee Biosurveillance Project: real time syndromic surveillance using secure regional Internet. [Abstract]. J Urban Health 2003;80(2 Suppl 1):i126.

5. Foldy S, Biedrzycki P, Barthell E, et al. Syndromic surveillance using Regional Emergency Medicine Internet. Ann Emerg Med 2004 (in press).

6. Hutwagner L, Thompson W, Seeman GM, Treadwell T. The bioterrorism preparedness and response Early Aberration Reporting System (EARS). J Urban Health 2003;80(2 Suppl 1):i89–96.

These basic tenets are referenced in an interesting case of a person with measles who traveled from India to the United States (see source below and in *Essentials of Infectious Disease Epidemiology*).

READING 20
Excerpt from: Postexposure Prophylaxis, Isolation, and Quarantine to Control an Import-Associated Measles Outbreak— Iowa, 2004

Centers for Disease Control and Prevention. Postexposure Prophylaxis, Isolation, and Quarantine to Control an Import-Associated Measles Outbreak—Iowa, 2004. *MMWR*. 2004;53:969–71.

An essential public health tool, rarely used in the last half century in the United States, quarantine is often confused with isolation, which is the restriction of movement of persons who are known to be infected with a communicable disease and who often are symptomatic. Quarantine reduces the risk of exposure to disease by separating and restricting the movement of persons who are not yet ill but who have been exposed to an infectious agent and might become infectious. Quarantine is more difficult to implement than isolation because the persons under quarantine are not symptomatic and thus have greater difficulty understanding the need for staying at home when compared with ill persons who need to be isolated.

Before antibiotics and vaccines, quarantine was used when direct medical countermeasures were not routinely available. However, quarantine often was implemented in a manner that equated disease with crime; consequently, quarantine acquired negative connotations associated with stigma and discrimination. For quarantine to be an effective and acceptable public health tool, these negative connotations must be overcome by applying the measure equally and fairly among all persons who have been exposed, and by using other approaches. These include providing education about the rationale for using quarantine; offering acceptable alternatives to quarantine, when feasible, such as postexposure vaccination or obtaining serologic proof of immunity; and applying due process measures, such as written notice and opportunities to appeal.

The use of quarantine to address public health problems demands a balancing of individual civil liberties with the collective needs of the public's health. Additional focus on the health, welfare, and social needs of persons subjected to quarantine is required. During the 2003 epidemic of severe acute respiratory syndrome (SARS), CDC listed 10 principles for modern quarantine (3, 4). In the United States, as in most countries of the world, government has the duty and legal power to address risks associated with persons whose freedom of movement might endanger the public's health. Under circumstances described in federal statute,* the U.S. government has the authority to detain persons for the control of communicable diseases. In particular, the U.S. government has the authority to isolate and quarantine persons to control the spread of selected communicable diseases specified by presidential executive order (5, 6). In addition, all 50 states and the District of Columbia have the authority to detain persons under their own quarantine laws. In the event of an epidemic resulting from natural transmission or from deliberate introduction, both state and federal quarantine laws could be invoked to stem the spread of disease.

REFERRING TO SARS

In 2003, the SARS outbreak triggered the widest use of quarantine globally since the influenza pandemic of 1917. Largely voluntary quarantine was used in Canada to keep approximately 20,000 persons in their homes for 10 days (8). For 27 persons who refused voluntary quarantine, public health officials issued legally enforceable quarantine orders. In certain cities in Asia (e.g., Beijing, Hong Kong, Singapore, and Taipei), quarantine authority was used to order thousands of persons to remain in their homes, an intervention that has been credited with helping to contain the outbreak (3). Although SARS did not spread within the United States, certain jurisdictions used quarantine authority to minimize the risk of spreading the virus (e.g., via unprotected health-care workers exposed to infectious SARS patients).

The scope and specifics of laws authorizing quarantine vary substantially by state. States that have not reviewed their quarantine laws might consider doing so by using a systematic approach covering essential features (e.g., quarantine, jurisdictional aspects, and due process). State and local health officials also might consider reviewing quarantine-related laws with their agencies' legal counsels, in coordination with law enforcement officials and the judiciary.

Ten Principles of Modern Quarantine

Modern quarantine is a collective action for the common good predicated on aiding persons infected or exposed to infectious agents while protecting others from the dangers of inadvertent exposure.

1. Used when exposed to highly dangerous and contagious diseases, when resources are available to implement and maintain, and when less restrictive means cannot accomplish the public health objectives.
2. Encompasses a wide range of strategies, from passive self-monitoring for symptoms to use of barriers limiting entry and exit to authorized persons.
3. Used in combination with other interventions and countermeasures to ensure that persons in quarantine or isolation are among the first to receive all supportive interventions available.
4. Ensures rapid isolation of infectious persons and separation from those merely exposed.
5. Lasts only as long as necessary to achieve epidemic control but no longer than the disease incubation period.
6. Does not have to be absolute to be effective; therefore, favors voluntary over compulsory approaches.
7. More likely to involve limited numbers of exposed persons in small areas than in a widespread geographic locale.
8. Requires clear understanding of the roles of jurisdictions and legal authorities.
9. Requires coordination and planning with multiple partners.
10. Requires education, trust, and participation of the general public.

Essential Questions to Review Regarding Quarantine Authority

Modern quarantine is a collective action for the common good predicated on aiding persons infected or exposed to infectious agents while protecting others from the dangers of inadvertent exposure.

1. Used when exposed to highly dangerous and contagious diseases, when resources are available to implement and maintain, and when less restrictive means cannot accomplish the public health objectives.
2. Encompasses a wide range of strategies, from passive self-monitoring for symptoms to use of barriers limiting entry and exit to authorized persons.
3. Used in combination with other interventions and countermeasures to ensure that persons in quarantine or isolation are among the first to receive all supportive interventions available.
4. Ensures rapid isolation of infectious persons and separation from those merely exposed.
5. Lasts only as long as necessary to achieve epidemic control but no longer than the disease incubation period.
6. Does not have to be absolute to be effective; therefore, favors voluntary over compulsory approaches.
7. More likely to involve limited numbers of exposed persons in small areas than in a widespread geographic locale.
8. Requires clear understanding of the roles of jurisdictions and legal authorities.
9. Requires coordination and planning with multiple partners.
10. Requires education, trust, and participation of the general public.

One thing that is intriguing about infectious diseases is that infectious organisms seldom remain static. Microbes we once tamed remain tame until, often, they become affected by our methods of control. A good example is that of tuberculosis. Requiring diligent and long-term therapy even in the absence of drug resistance, extensively drug-resistant tuberculosis has emerged, resulting in TB that is not sensitive to the drugs we use to treat it. Below is a summary of XDR-TB's emergence, including a provisional case definition, followed by a description of the problem of lack of treatment and potential for cross-border disease sharing.

Reading 21
Extensively Drug-Resistant Tuberculosis—United States, 1993–2006

NS Shah, MD, Albert Einstein College of Medicine, Bronx, New York. R Pratt, S Althomsons, T Navin, MD, KG Castro, MD, VA Robison, DDS, PhD, JP Cegielski, MD, Div of Tuberculosis Elimination, National Center for HIV/AIDS, Viral Hepatitis, STD, and TB Prevention (proposed), CDC.

Shah NS, Pratt R, Althomsons S, et al. Extensively Drug-Resistant Tuberculosis—United States, 1993–2006. MMWR. 2007;56:250–3.

The worldwide emergence of extensively drug-resistant tuberculosis (XDR TB) and a provisional definition* for this form of TB were first reported in November 2005 (1, 2). A more detailed description of these findings and preliminary data from the U.S. National TB Surveillance System (NTSS) were published in 2006 (3). The U.S. data indicated that 74 TB cases reported during 1993–2004 met the case definition for XDR TB (3). Subsequent reports suggested different definitions for XDR TB (4, 5). In October 2006, the World Health Organization convened an Emergency Global Task Force on XDR TB, which revised the case definition to specify resistance to at least isoniazid and rifampin among first-line anti-TB drugs, resistance to any fluoroquinolone, and resistance to at least one second-line injectable drug (amikacin, capreomycin, or kanamycin) (6). This report updates the 2006 report on XDR TB in the United States, using the revised case definition and provisional data for 2006. NTSS data were analyzed for reported XDR-TB cases during 1993–2006; a total of 49 cases (3% of evaluable multidrug-resistant [MDR] TB cases) met the revised case definition for XDR TB. Of these, 17 (35%) were reported during 2000–2006. Compared with 1993–1999, cases from 2000–2006 were more likely to be in persons who were foreign born and less likely to be in persons with human immunodeficiency virus (HIV) infection. XDR TB presents a global threat and a challenge to TB-control activities in the United States. To prevent the spread of XDR TB, renewed vigilance is needed through drug-susceptibility testing, case reporting, specialized care, infection control, and expanded capacity for outbreak detection and response.

TB cases reported to NTSS from 50 states and the District of Columbia (DC) were analyzed for the period 1993–2006.[†]

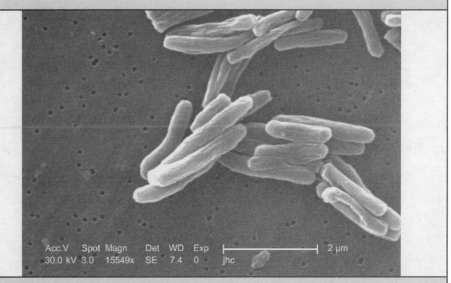

FIGURE 8-6 Mycobacterium tuberculosis.

About this picture: "Under a high magnification of 15549x, this colorized scanning electron micrograph (SEM) depicted some of the ultrastructural details seen in the cell wall configuration of a number of Gram-positive *Mycobacterium tuberculosis* bacteria. As an obligate aerobic organism *M. tuberculosis* can only survive in an environment containing oxygen. This bacterium ranges in length between 2 and 4 microns, and a width between 0.2 and 0.5 microns. See PHIL 8438 for a black and white version of this image.

TB bacteria become active, and begin to multiply, if the immune system can't stop them from growing. The bacteria attack the body and destroy tissue. If in the lungs, the bacteria can actually create a hole in the lung tissue. Some people develop active TB disease soon after becoming infected, before their immune system can fight off the bacteria. Other people may get sick later, when their immune system becomes weak for another reason.

Babies and young children often have weak immune systems. People infected with HIV, the virus that causes AIDS, have very weak immune systems. Other people can have weak immune systems, too, especially people with any of these conditions: substance abuse; diabetes mellitus; silicosis; cancer of the head or neck; leukemia or Hodgkin's disease; severe kidney disease; low body weight; certain medical treatments (such as corticosteroid treatment or organ transplants); specialized treatment for rheumatoid arthritis, or Crohn's disease."

Source: Public Health Image Library CDC/Dr. Ray Butler; Janice Carr; 2006.

All culture-confirmed cases with initial drug-susceptibility test (DST) results reported for at least isoniazid and rifampin were included in the analysis. Because susceptibility testing is time consuming, especially for second-line drugs, initial DST results are reported separately to avoid delaying reporting of routine TB case data. At the end of treatment, the outcome is reported in a second follow-up report. The HIV status of TB cases reported to NTSS was available through 2006, except in California, where only data on positive HIV test results[§] were available through 2004.

TB cases reported during 1993–1999, a period of rapidly decreasing incidence of both TB and MDR TB, were compared with cases reported during 2000–2006, a period of slower decline in TB and MDR-TB rates. During 1993–2006, a total of 202,436 culture-confirmed TB cases were reported to NTSS; 190,312 of these cases had initial DST results for at least iso-niazid and rifampin, including 2,927 (2%) with initial resistance to both drugs (i.e., MDR TB). Of the 2,927 MDR-TB cases, 1,665 (57%) had DST results reported for at least one fluoroquinolone and one injectable second-line drug. Of these, 49 cases (3%) met the revised definition of XDR TB, including 32 cases reported during 1993–1999 and 17 cases during 2000–2006 (Table 8-7).

The 49 XDR-TB cases were reported from nine states and one city, with the largest numbers in New York City (19 cases) and California (11 cases) (Figure 8-7). HIV status was known for 29 (59%) of the 49 persons with XDR TB (Table 8-7); 16 (55%) were HIV positive. During 1993–1999, a total of 19 persons with XDR TB had known HIV status, of whom 14 (74%) were HIV positive; during 2000–2006, 10 persons had known HIV status, of whom two (20%) were HIV positive. The number and percentage of persons with XDR TB in the group aged

FIGURE 8-7 Number of reported cases of extensively drug-resistant tuberculosis (XDR TB)*—United States, 1993–2006.

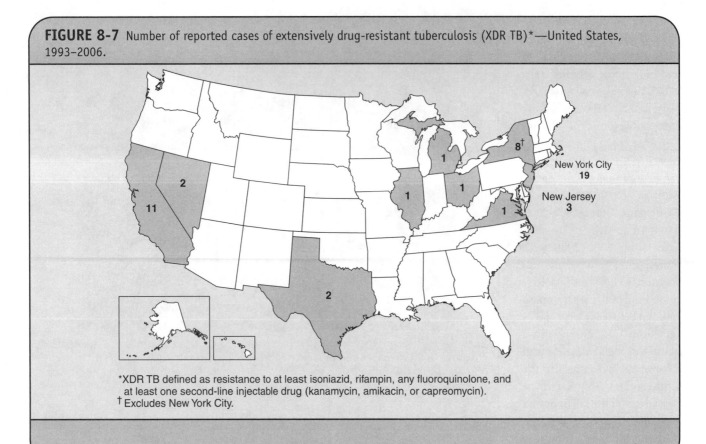

*XDR TB defined as resistance to at least isoniazid, rifampin, any fluoroquinolone, and at least one second-line injectable drug (kanamycin, amikacin, or capreomycin).
† Excludes New York City.

TABLE 8-7 Reported cases of tuberculosis (TB), multidrug resistant (MDR) TB, and extensively drug-resistant (XDR)* TB—U.S. National TB Surveillance Systems,† 1993–1999 and 2000–2006.

Characteristic	1993–1999		2000–2006	
	No.	(%)§	No.	(%)§
Total number of culture-confirmed TB cases with initial drug-susceptibility test (DST) results reported for at least isoniazid and rifampin	111,758	—	78,554	—
No. of cases with initial resistance to at least isoniazid and rifampin (i.e., MDR TB♦) (% of total TB cases)	2,005	(2)	922	(1)
No. of cases with reported initial DST results sufficient to rule in XDR TB** (% of MDR-TB cases)	1,069	(53)	596	(65)
No. of cases with reported initial DST results sufficient to rule out XDR TB** (% of MDR-TB cases)	360	(18)	291	(32)
No. of XDR-TB cases under revised definition (% of MDR-TB cases)	32	(2)	17	(2)
Country of origin (% of XDR-TB cases)				
U.S. born	19	(59)	4	(24)
Foreign born	12	(38)	13	(76)
Unknown	1	(3)	0	—

continues

Characteristic	1993–1999		2000–2006	
	No.	(%)[§]	No.	(%)[§]
Human immunodeficiency virus (HIV) status[††] (% of XDR-TB cases)				
HIV positive	14	(44)	2	(12)
HIV negative	5	(16)	8	(47)
HIV test not administered or status unknown	13	(40)	7	(41)
Age group (yrs) (% of XDR-TB cases)				
0–14	1	(3)	0	—
15–24	1	(3)	4	(24)
25–44	21	(66)	6	(35)
45–64	3	(9)	6	(35)
≥ 65	6	(19)	1	(6)
Race/ethinicity (% of XDR-TB cases)				
Hispanic	11	(34)	5	(29)
Asian, non-Hispanic	3	(9)	7	(41)
Black, non-Hispanic	9	(28)	2	(12)
White, non-Hispanic	8	(25)	3	(18)
Other race, non-Hispanic	1	(3)	0	—
Sex (% of XDR-TB cases)				
Female	9	(28)	9	(53)
Male	23	(72)	8	(47)
TB history (% of XDR–TB cases)				
Previous TB[§§]	4	(13)	3	(18)
No previous TB	27	(84)	14	(82)
Unknown	1	(3)	0	—
Results of sputum microscopy for acid-fast bacilli (% of XDR-TB cases)				
Positive	15	(47)	12	(71)
Negative	9	(28)	3	(18)
Not done/Unknown	8	(25)	2	(12)
Treatment outcome (% of XDR-TB cases)				
Completed treatment	11	(34)	6	(35)
Died during treatment	10	(31)	2	(12)
Outcome not yet reported	3	(9)	5	(29)
Moved, lost to follow-up, or other	8	(25)	4	(24)

*Defined as resistance to at least isoniazid, rifampin, any fluoroquinoione, and to at least one second-line injectable drug (amikacin, capreomycin, or kanamycin).

[†]On the basis of cases reported from 50 states and the District of Columbia (DC), through February 8, 2007. Cases reported from U.S.-affiliated island territories excluded.

[§]Percentage might not add to 100% because of rounding.

[♦]Defined as resistance to at least isoniazid and rifampin.

**On the basis of DST results in the U.S. National TB Surveillance System for drugs included in the definition of XDR TB: isoniazid, rifampin, ciprofloxacin, ofloxacin, kanamycin, amikacin, and capreomycin.

[††]HIV reporting for California, which only reports HIV-positive results, completed through 2004; no HIV positives were reported from California. HIV reporting for 49 states other than California and DC completed through 2005, provisional for 2006.

[§§]Persons who had verified TB disease in the past, were discharged (e.g., completed therapy) or lost to supervision for .12 consecutive months, and had verified disease again.

25–44 years decreased from 21 (66%) during 1993–1999 to six (35%) during 2000–2006.

When the two periods were compared, the number of XDR-TB cases among foreign-born persons did not change substantially, but the percentage of XDR-TB cases among foreign-born persons increased from 39% (12 cases) in 1993–1999 to 76% (13 cases) in 2000–2006 as the number of XDR-TB cases among U.S.-born cases decreased (Table 8-7). Among racial/ethnic populations, nine (28%) of 32 XDR-TB cases during 1993–1999 were reported among non-Hispanic blacks, decreasing to two (12%) of 17 cases during 2000–2006. Conversely, the number and percentage of cases among Asians increased from three (9%) during 1993–1999 to seven (41%) during 2000–2006. Sputum microscopy for acid-fast bacilli was positive in 27 (69%) of the 39 cases with known results. Mortality in XDR-TB cases was strongly associated with HIV infection. Among 41 persons with XDR TB and known outcomes, 12 (29%) persons died; 10 of those had HIV infection, and the other two did not have HIV test results reported.

Editorial Note: After approximately 30 years of declining trends, a TB epidemic occurred in the United States during 1985–1992. From 22,201 cases in 1985 (9.3 per 100,000 population), reported TB increased to 26,673 cases in 1992 (10.4 per 100,000 population) (7). Although the incidence of MDR TB in the United States was largely unknown before 1993, the number of cases began increasing in New York City in the early 1980s (8), and numerous outbreaks of MDR TB were described in the late 1980s and early 1990s (9). With implementation of elements of the 1992 National Action Plan to Combat Multidrug-Resistant Tuberculosis, reported MDR-TB cases declined rapidly (10). TB-control activities included improving laboratory services for rapid, accurate culture and DST, improving infection control, and strengthening NTSS to include DST and HIV test results beginning in 1993. The rapid decrease in MDR-TB cases during 1993–1999 likely correlated with the 34% decline in TB cases overall in the United States to 17,501 (6.3 per 100,000) in 1999 (7).

Effective treatment of MDR TB requires administration, for 18–24 months, of four to six drugs to which the infecting organism is susceptible, including multiple second-line drugs. Beginning in the 1980s, the use of second-line drugs increased substantially as physicians and TB-control programs treated growing numbers of MDR-TB cases. Increased use of these drugs resulted in MDR-TB strains with extensive resistance to both first- and second-line drugs. Thus, XDR TB in the 1990s likely represented the legacy of the 1985–1992 TB epidemic in the United States and treatments to combat the spike in MDR-TB cases.

Characteristics of XDR-TB cases changed during 2000–2006 in parallel with the changing epidemiology of TB in general and MDR TB in particular. These changes included an overall decrease in the number of cases, a decrease in the proportion of cases in HIV-infected persons, an increase in the proportion of cases among foreign-born persons, and an increase in the proportion of Asians among persons with XDR TB, compared with 1993–1999 (7).

The findings in this report are subject to at least five limitations. First, the number of XDR-TB cases is a minimum estimate because of incomplete DST data. Although 57% of MDR-TB cases had DST results reported for at least one fluoroquinolone and at least one of the three second-line injectable drugs, only 22% had DST results reported for all drug combinations in the definition of XDR TB, taking into consideration cross-resistance among drugs and data available in NTSS. Initial TB isolates with any resistance to rifampin or resistance to any two first-line drugs should be tested for susceptibility to a full panel of anti-TB drugs, and the results should be reported accordingly. Second, aggregate reporting of drug resistance traditionally has been based only on initial DST results, not on drug resistance that develops during treatment. Because of the complexity of second-line DST, results can be delayed by several months and might not be included in the report of initial DST results. Third, approximately 20% of reported TB cases do not have positive cultures that would enable DSTs to be performed. Fourth, NTSS data for 2006 are provisional, and final case counts, including XDR-TB cases, are subject to revision. Finally, HIV test results usually are reported to NTSS after both TB and HIV surveillance systems have verified their annual case counts. Thus, HIV test results lag behind TB case counts, and data on HIV status are complete through 2005 but provisional for 2006, except for California, which provided data only through 2004. In addition, HIV test results from California are less complete.

The NTSS surveillance data summarized in this report represent an updated measurement of XDR TB in the United States. However, surveillance data do not enable a detailed understanding of how most XDR-TB cases arise. For example, the relative importance of person-to-person XDR-TB transmission compared with the emergence of XDR TB in individual patients as a consequence of inadequate treatment cannot be determined.

Use of second-line drugs to treat drug-resistant TB is increasing throughout the world, presaging substantial increases in XDR TB internationally. Accurate measures of the incidence, prevalence, and determinants of XDR TB are needed to target public health responses. Attention to fundamental aspects of TB control (e.g., surveillance, prompt culture and DST, directly observed treatment, contact investigation, rapid containment of outbreaks, and infection control) is needed to control XDR TB in the United States in the same manner that MDR TB was addressed during the previous decade. The Federal TB Task Force is developing a domestic and international response for U.S. government agencies regarding XDR TB. A senior-level interagency meeting will be convened to formulate a comprehensive response and to assign responsibilities for a unified strategic approach. Additional information regarding XDR TB is available at http://www.who.int/tb/xdr/en/index.html.

REFERENCES FROM THE READING

1. Shah NS, Wright A, Drobniewski F, et al. Extreme drug resistance in tuberculosis ("XDR-TB"): global survey of supranational reference laboratories for Mycobacterium tuberculosis with resistance to second-line drugs. Int J Tuberc Lung Dis 2005;9(Suppl 1):S77.

2. Holtz TH, Riekstina V, Zarovska E, Laserson KF, Wells CD, Leimane V. XDR-TB: extreme drug-resistance and treatment outcome under DOTS-Plus, Latvia, 2000–2002. Int J Tuberc Lung Dis 2005;9(Suppl 1):S258.

3. CDC. Emergence of Mycobacterium tuberculosis with extensive resistance to second-line drugs—worldwide, 2000–2004. MMWR 2006;55:301–5.

4. Gandhi NR, Moll A, Sturm AW, et al. Extensively drug-resistant tuberculosis as a cause of death in patients co-infected with tuberculosis and HIV in a rural area of South Africa. Lancet 2006;368:1575–80.

5. Leimane V, Holtz TH. MDR-TB and XDR-TB management in Latvia. Global XDR-TB Task Force, Geneva, Switzerland; 2006. Available at http://whqlibdoc.who.int/hq/2007/who_htm_tb_2007.375_eng.pdf.

6. CDC. Revised definition of extensively drug-resistant tuberculosis. MMWR 2006;55:1176.

7. CDC. Reported tuberculosis in the United States, 2005: Mycobacterium tuberculosis. Atlanta, GA: US Department of Health and Human Services, CDC; 2006. Available at http://www.cdc.gov/nchstp/tb/surv/surv2005/pdf/tbsurvfullreport.pdf.

8. Frieden TR, Sterling T, Pablos-Mendez A, Kilburn JO, Cauthen GM, Dooley SW. The emergence of drug-resistant tuberculosis in New York City. N Engl J Med 1993;328:521–6.

9. Moore M, McCray E, Onorato I. The interaction of human immunodeficiency virus and multidrug-resistant Mycobacterium tuberculosis [Chapter 4]. In: Bastian I, Portaels F, eds. Multidrug-resistant tuberculosis. Dordrecht, the Netherlands: Kluwer Academic Publishers; 2000:45–57.

10. CDC. National Action Plan to Combat Multidrug-Resistant Tuberculosis. MMWR 1992;41(No. RR-11):5–48.

In view of the preceding reading, consider the situation that took place in June 2007.

EXHIBIT 8-1

A Timeline of Andrew Speaker's Infection

by Vikki Valentine

June 06, 2007—Officials were summoned to two separate hearings on Capitol Hill Wednesday to explain how Atlanta attorney Andrew Speaker was able to leave and re-enter the United States despite a diagnosis of drug-resistant tuberculosis.

Speaker, 31, was placed under a federal isolation order on May 28 after traveling to Europe against the recommendations of public health officials.

Speaker is now undergoing treatment at the National Jewish Medical and Research Center in Denver. By telephone, he told a Senate subcommittee Wednesday that he was never told by local and federal health officials he was contagious until he returned to the United States from a European honeymoon. Health officials contend they repeatedly told Speaker he should not to fly.

"We gave the patient the benefit of the doubt, and in retrospect we made a mistake," said Dr. Julie Gerberding, head of the Centers for Disease Control and Prevention. "We failed to take the aggressive actions we could have."

Source: Accessed at www.npr.org, 12/31/07.

Methicillin-resistant *Staphylococcus aureus* (MRSA) is increasingly in the news. The ubiquitous bacteria *S. aureus* is a common cause of infections among non-hospitalized and hospitalized persons alike; in recent years, we have seen a proliferation of *S. aureus* increasingly resistant to penicillin (introduced in the 1940s) and newer synthetic penicillinase medications—our front-line drugs to treat it. The following article describes the epidemiology of MRSA and the one immediately after it describes an outbreak investigation in 2007.

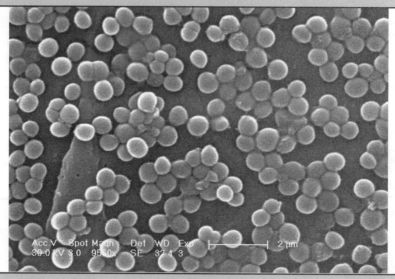

FIGURE 8-8 Methicillin-resistant *Staphylococcus aureus* bacteria.

About this picture: This 2005 scanning electron micrograph (SEM) depicted numerous clumps of methicillin-resistant *Staphylococcus aureus* bacteria, commonly referred to by the acronym, MRSA; Magnified 9560x.

Recently recognized outbreaks, or clusters of MRSA in community settings have been associated with strains that have some unique microbiologic and genetic properties, compared with the traditional hospital-based MRSA strains, which suggests some biologic properties, e.g., virulence factors like toxins, may allow the community strains to spread more easily, or cause more skin disease. A common strain named USA300-0114 has caused many such outbreaks in the United States. See PHIL 10046 for a colorized version of this micrograph.

Methicillin-resistant *Staphylococcus aureus* infections, e.g., bloodstream, pneumonia, bone infections, occur most frequently among persons in hospitals and healthcare facilities, including nursing homes, and dialysis centers. Those who acquire a MRSA infection usually have a weakened immune system, however, the manifestation of MRSA infections that are acquired by otherwise healthy individuals, who have not been recently hospitalized or had a medical procedure such as dialysis, or surgery, first began to emerge in the mid- to late-1990s. These infections in the community are usually manifested as minor skin infections such as pimples and boils. Transmission of MRSA has been reported most frequently in certain populations, e.g., children, sports participants, or jail inmates."

Source: Public Health Image Library CDC/Janice Haney Carr/Jeff Hageman, M.H.S./Janice Haney Carr, 2005.

READING 22
Methicillin-Resistant–*Staphylococcus aureus* Hospitalizations, United States

Matthew J. Kuehnert, Holly A. Hill, Benjamin A. Kupronis, Jerome I. Tokars, Steven L. Solomon, and Daniel B. Jernigan

Kuehnert JM, Hill HA, Kupronis BA, et al. Methicillin-resistant– Staphylococcus aureus Hospitalizations, United States. *Emerg Inf Dis*. 2005;11:868–72.

Methicillin-resistant *Staphylococcus aureus* (MRSA) is increasingly a cause of nosocomial and community-onset infection with unknown national scope and magnitude. We used the National Hospital Discharge Survey to calculate the number of US hospital discharges listing *S. aureus*–specific diagnoses, defined as those having at least 1 International Classification of Diseases (ICD)-9 code specific for *S. aureus* infection. The number of hospital discharges listing *S. aureus*–specific diagnoses was multiplied by the proportion of methicillin resistance for each corresponding infection site to determine the number of MRSA infections.

From 1999 to 2000, an estimated 125,969 hospitalizations with a diagnosis of MRSA infection occurred annually, including 31,440 for septicemia, 29,823 for pneumonia, and 64,706 for other infections, accounting for 3.95 per 1,000 hospital discharges. The method used in our analysis may provide a simple way to assess trends of the magnitude of MRSA infection nationally.

Staphylococcus aureus is a major cause of infection in both healthcare and community settings. It is one of the most common causes of healthcare-associated infections reported to the National Nosocomial Infections Surveillance (NNIS) System, including ventilator-associated pneumonia, surgical site infection, and catheter-associated bloodstream infection (1). *S. aureus* is also a frequent cause of community-associated infections, particularly skin and soft tissue infections. Although most community-onset infections are treated in the outpatient setting, some invasive infections, including bacteremia, septic arthritis, toxic shock syndrome, osteomyelitis, and endocarditis, have devastating complications and may require hospitalization (2).

Antimicrobial resistance in *S. aureus* emerged soon after penicillin came into common use in the 1940s. During the next 2 decades, resistance of this pathogen to penicillin became widespread, followed by increasing resistance to the new semisynthetic penicillinase-resistant antimicrobial drugs (e.g., methicillin, oxacillin, nafcillin) (3). In the last 20 years, methicillin-resistant *S. aureus* (MRSA) has spread throughout the world in healthcare settings, leading to an increased reliance on vancomycin for empiric treatment (4). Recently, *S. aureus* resistance to vancomycin, the last commonly used antimicrobial drug to which this organism was considered uniformly susceptible, has emerged (5). In addition, serious MRSA infection has been increasingly reported in persons without identified predisposing risk, including recent healthcare exposure (6).

MRSA infections are thought to cause substantial illness and contribute to healthcare costs in the United States. However, published estimates vary widely and have been based on single-center or local data with limited applicability (4, 7). Accurate estimates of the incidence of MRSA infection are essential to determine effects on health and healthcare expenditures. Since most patients with serious MRSA infections are hospitalized, we focused our estimate on hospitalized patients.

METHODS

The incidence of *S. aureus* infection was estimated from the number of hospitalizations with *S. aureus*–related discharge diagnoses in a national surveillance database. We used 1999 and 2000 public-use data from the National Hospital Discharge Survey (NHDS) to calculate the number of hospital discharges with at least 1 *S. aureus*–related discharge diagnosis. All acute-care hospitalizations, except infants whose hospital stay began at their own birth, were included. The NHDS is a nationally representative annual sample of discharge records from ≈ 475

nonfederal shortstay hospitals (8). The survey is based on a stratified, multistage probability design; the sampled hospital discharge records are weighted to produce national estimates. The database includes ≤ 7 principal discharge diagnoses. We identified *S. aureus*–related discharge diagnoses by using the International Classification of Diseases, Ninth Revision, Clinical Modification (ICD-9-CM) codes specific for *S. aureus* infection: 038.11 (*S. aureus* septicemia), 482.41 (*S. aureus* pneumonia), and 041.11 (*S. aureus* infection in conditions classified elsewhere or of unspecified site). A discharge record listing multiple *S. aureus*–related diagnoses was counted only once. Septicemia was preferentially included, followed by *S. aureus*–related pneumonia.

Next, the percentage of isolates resistant to oxacillin was determined. To simplify terminology, resistance to methicillin and oxacillin hereafter are used interchangeably. Oxacillin is used as a proxy for testing of susceptibility to all β-lactam antimicrobials, including methicillin. The Surveillance Network (TSN) Database-USA (Focus Technologies, Herndon, VA, USA) was the source of antimicrobial susceptibility testing results. TSN is a repository of quantitative and qualitative susceptibility results collected from > 200 microbiology laboratories in the United States. These laboratories make up a nationally representative sample based on associated hospital bed size, patient population, and geographic region as determined by the US Bureau of the Census (9, 10). Susceptibility testing of patient isolates is conducted on site by each participating laboratory as part of routine diagnostic testing; only isolates judged as clinically significant are included. Data are generated by using Food and Drug Administration–approved testing methods. *S. aureus* antimicrobial susceptibility to oxacillin was classified as susceptible, intermediate, or resistant according to NCCLS breakpoint criteria; we classified intermediate isolates as methicillin-susceptible *S. aureus* for purposes of this analysis. Data were stratified by site of infection, i.e., bloodstream, lung, and other sites. Duplicate isolates were removed if the initial and subsequent isolates were cultured within 30 days of each other. The number of hospital discharges listing *S. aureus*–specific diagnoses was multiplied by the proportion of methicillin resistance at each corresponding infection site to determine the total number of MRSA infections. Infections also were stratified by geographic region and age. The frequency of primary diagnosis and the 10 most frequent secondary (all-listed) diagnoses were abstracted from hospitalizations that included *S. aureus*–specific diagnoses. Results for the years 1999–2000 were determined by calculating data specific to each year and then averaging. Data on resistance rates were stratified first by region and then by age; for each stratification, a chi-square test was used to determine whether differences were significant. The

Cochran-Armitage test, a nonparametric method, was used to determine the trend in MRSA hospitalization rate by age category. The effects of region and age on the incidence rate of MRSA were assessed by calculating relative rates and their associated 95% confidence intervals, with the lowest rates designated as comparison groups. Since the rate of *S. aureus* and the MRSA proportion were estimated separately and then multiplied to obtain the MRSA hospitalization rate, the variance of the MRSA rate was calculated by using the delta method (11). The variance of the methicillin resistance proportions was determined under the assumption that the antimicrobial susceptibility data reflected those that would have been derived from a random sample of all *S. aureus* isolates in the United States in that time period. Variance estimates were calculated using SUDAAN software (Research Triangle Institute, Research Triangle Park, NC, USA). For both *S. aureus* rates and methicillin resistance proportions, variances were estimated separately for 1999 and 2000, and the larger of the variance estimates was used in subsequent calculation of 95% confidence intervals for relative rates.

RESULTS

We estimate that 291,542 hospital discharges with *S. aureus* infection-related diagnoses occurred annually from 1999 to 2000 (Table 8-8). A diagnosis of *S. aureus* infection occurred in 9.13 of every 1,000 hospital discharges. The overall rate of methicillin resistance for all *S. aureus* infections was reported to be 43.2%. MRSA rates for septicemia, pneumonia, and other infections increased with patient age. An estimated 125,969 hospitalizations with 1 or more discharge diagnoses associ-

ated with MRSA infection occurred annually, accounting for 3.95 of every 1,000 hospital discharges. For all sites, most diagnoses occurred in persons > 65 years of age.

In hospitalizations in which *S. aureus* septicemia and pneumonia were listed as discharge diagnoses, these conditions were primary diagnoses in 34.3% and 49.3% of discharges, respectively. For *S. aureus* infection in conditions classified elsewhere and in an unspecified site, a diagnosis intended only for secondary listing, the most frequent primary diagnoses were postoperative (e.g., wound) infection (10.1%), cellulitis or abscess (9.9%), infection from an implanted device or graft (7.3%), and urinary tract infection (3.6%). The largest proportion of *S. aureus*–related discharge diagnoses occurred in patients from the South, followed by the Midwest, Northeast, and West (Table 8-9). For both, the rate of *S. aureus* discharge diagnoses and methicillin resistance proportion, significant differences were seen by geographic region. *S. aureus* discharge diagnoses were significantly higher for the South than the Northeast, while for methicillin resistance proportion, the Northeast, Midwest, and South were significantly higher than the West (p < 0.05 for all comparisons). The South had the highest MRSA hospitalization rate, reflecting both the *S. aureus* rate and methicillin resistance proportion, which was significantly higher than the MRSA rate estimated for the West (South vs. West, relative risk 1.57, 95% confidence interval 1.29–1.91).

Most *S. aureus*–related discharge diagnoses occurred in patients > 65 years of age. When *S. aureus* diagnoses by rate were examined, a bimodal distribution was seen, with highest rates occurring in children and the elderly (Table 8-10). Patients ≤ 14 and 15–44 years of age had higher MRSA hos-

TABLE 8-8 *Staphylococcus aureus*-related discharge diagnoses, United States, 1999–2000, by patient age and infection site.*

Discharge diagnosis	Age (y)				
	≤ 14	15–44	45–64	≥ 65	Total[†]
S. aureus septicemias	2,918	12,272	20,028	38,948	74,166
Proportion of methicillin-resistant isolates from blood culture	0.144	0.317	0.392	0.495	0.424
MRSA septicemias	420	3,890	7,851	19,279	31,440
S. aureus pneumonias	2,328	5,582	6,926	41,427	56,263
Proportion of methicillin-resistant isolates from lower respiratory culture	0.195	0.333	0.467	0.586	0.530
MRSA pneumonias	454	1,859	3,234	24,276	29,823
Other *S. aureus* infections	14,290	39,222	40,496	67,105	161,113
Proportion of methicillin-resistant isolates from other culture sites	0.160	0.279	0.378	0.539	0.402
Other MRSA infections	2,286	10,943	15,307	36,170	64,706

*MRSA, methicillin-resistant *S. aureus*.
[†]Because of rounding of methicillin-resistant proportions, total MRSA infections may differ slightly when estimates are calculated across category groups by row (i.e., age) compared with column (i.e., infection site).

TABLE 8-9 *Staphylococcus aureus*-related hospitalizations, United States, 1999–2000, by geographic region.*

Region	S. aureus (%)	Discharge diagnosis		
		S. aureus rate[†]	MR (%)	MRSA rate[†]
West	17.4	9.04	31.4	2.84
Northeast	20.5	8.51	41.3	3.52
Midwest	22.6	9.06	43.5	3.94
South	39.5	9.58	46.5	4.45

*MR, methicillin resistant; MRSA, methicillin-resistant *S. aureus*.
[†]Rate, hospitalizations with *S. aureus*—or MRSA—related discharge diagnoses per 1,000 discharges.

TABLE 8-10 *Staphylococcus aureus*-related hospitalizations, United States, 1999–2000, by patient age.*

Age (y)	S. aureus (%)	Discharge diagnosis			MRSA RR (95% CI)
		S. aureus rate[†]	MR (%)	MRSA rate[†]	
≤ 14	6.7	80.8	16.2	13.1	Referent
15–44	19.6	56.9	29.3	16.7	1.2 (0.94–1.6)
45–64	23.1	97.4	39.1	38.1	2.9 (2.2–3.8)
≥ 65	50.6	117.6	54.1	63.6	4.8 (3.7–6.2)

*MR, methicillin resistant; MRSA, methicillin-resistant *S. aureus*; RR, relative risk; CI, confidence interval.
[†]Rate, hospitalizations with *S. aureus* or MRSA-related discharge diagnoses per 1,000 discharges.

pitalization rates compared with patients 45–64 and ≥ 65 years of age ($p < 0.01$). Overall, the MRSA rate increased with patient age ($p < 0.05$ for trend).

DISCUSSION

Infectious diseases cause many hospitalizations each year in the United States; these diseases include syndromes commonly associated with *S. aureus*. In 1994, the rate of hospitalization for infectious disease was 15 per 1,000 US population, with a total of 4 million hospitalizations, including 1,480,000 pneumonias, 335,000 skin infections, and 302,000 septicemias; yearly rates for these disease syndromes were similar from 1999 to 2000 (12–14). Gram-positive organisms are an increasingly recognized cause of systemic infection, including sepsis (12, 15). More than half of all sepsis cases are estimated to be caused by gram-positive organisms, including *S. aureus* (16). In the Calgary Health Region in Canada, the annual incidence of invasive *S. aureus* infection was estimated to be 28.4 cases per 100,000 population from 1999 to 2000, which is comparable with the rate of invasive pneumococcal disease and exceeds the rate of invasive streptococcal infection (17). Drug resistance in *S. aureus*, including the emergence of MRSA in healthcare

and community settings, is an increasingly reported event that makes treating serious infection difficult. Extrapolating from our estimates and those of Simonsen et al. (12), a rate of ≈ 47 diagnoses per 100,000 population, making up 3% of all infectious disease hospitalizations, were associated with laboratory-confirmed MRSA infection from 1999 to 2000, and ≈ 10% of septicemias were caused by MRSA.

Although the burden of MRSA infection has not been systematically estimated nationally, past estimates have been based on single-center or selected population-based studies in the United States. Based on ICD-9-CM data from the New York City metropolitan area, an estimated 1.0% of hospital discharges are associated with *S. aureus* infection, and 0.21% of discharges are estimated to be associated with MRSA (18). In 1995, based on extrapolation of hospital discharge data from NHDS and nosocomial infection data from the NNIS System, an estimated 206,504 *S. aureus* infections (0.58% of admissions) and 70,270 MRSA infections (0.20% of admissions) were acquired in the healthcare setting (Centers for Disease Control and Prevention, unpub. data). Our estimates for 1999 to 2000 are similar for *S. aureus* infections but are higher for MRSA.

Although ICD-9-CM coding accuracy for *S. aureus* infections has not been specifically examined, the accuracy of coding for sepsis from all causes has been reviewed, and has demonstrated a sensitivity > 75% for any septicemia or bacteremia code and positive and negative predictive values > 80% for the code specific for *Staphylococcus* spp. septicemia (ICD-9-CM 038) (16, 19). However, the relationship between true *S. aureus* infections and ICD-9 discharge coding should be further assessed to validate this method as a tool for monitoring national trends.

We found associations between MRSA rate and both region and age. This finding is consistent with previously published data showing an association between age and both the incidence of invasive *S. aureus* infection and the rate of methicillin resistance (17, 20). We also demonstrated a significant difference in MRSA discharge rates between the South and

West. Although past microbiologic surveys also have reported higher rates of methicillin resistance in the South compared with other regions, the reasons for this variation are unclear (21, 22). These differences may need to be assessed as community-associated MRSA infection becomes more common.

Our estimate is subject to a number of limitations that most likely underestimated hospitalizations associated with MRSA infection. First, *S. aureus* infections may not have been accurately represented by the ICD-9-CM discharge code; colonization may have been inadvertently included; and more likely, true infections may not have been identified, since these diagnoses require laboratory culture confirmation. Since only 7 principal diagnoses are included in NHDS, infections listed less prominently may have been excluded. Duplicate isolates were excluded when identified within 30 days of each other; thus, unusual scenarios, such as multiple infections during a hospitalization or infections present for > 30 days, were not included. We were not able to distinguish between community- and healthcare-acquired infection. However, this analysis was designed to measure the overall incidence of disease associated with acute care hospitalization, regardless of acquisition site, and did not include disease managed in the outpatient setting. Although previously published region and age stratification groups were used, which reduces risk of bias, unmeasured confounders may have affected calculated trends. Finally, although both NHDS and TSN data aim to represent nationally representative samples based on similar factors, methods may have differed, which could have skewed our results. For all data used, institutional settings, such as long-term care or correctional facilities, were not included.

In summary, our estimates indicate that the national burden of serious MRSA disease is quantifiable and substantial. Measurement of trends in *S. aureus* disease, such as the increasing incidence of antimicrobial resistance associated with certain age groups and geographic regions, will have implications in the development of prevention programs, both in the healthcare and community settings. Our method provides a simple way to estimate trends of magnitude of hospitalization associated with *S. aureus* infection in the United States and could complement methods currently in place for national surveillance.

ACKNOWLEDGMENTS

We appreciate invaluable technical assistance provided by Maria Owings, Jean Kozak, Ron Master, and Daniel Sahm. Dr. Kuehnert is a medical epidemiologist at the National Center for Infectious Diseases, Centers for Disease Control and Prevention. His research interests have included antimicrobial resistance surveillance and now focus on improvement of blood, organ, and other tissue safety.

REFERENCES FROM THE READING

1. National Nosocomial Infections Surveillance (NNIS) system report, data summary from January 1992–June 2001, issued June 2001. Am J Infect Control. 2001;29;404–21.

2. Lowy FD. *Staphylococcus aureus* infections. N Engl J Med. 1998; 339: 520–32.

3. Finland M. Emergence of antibiotic resistance in hospitals. Rev Infect Dis. 1979;1:4–21.

4. Jernigan JA, Clemence MA, Stott GA, Titus MG, Alexander CH, Palumbo CM, et al. Control of methicillin-resistant *Staphylococcus aureus* at a university hospital: one decade later. Infect Control Hosp Epidemiol. 1995;16:686–96.

5. Chang S, Sievert DM, Hageman JC, Boulton ML, Tenover FC, Downes FP, et al. Infection with vancomycin-resistant *Staphylococcus aureus* containing the *vanA* resistance gene. N Engl J Med. 2003;348:1342–7.

6. Herold BC, Immergluck LC, Maranan MC, Lauderdale DS, Gaskin RE, Boyle-Vavra S, et al. Community-acquired methicillin-resistant *Staphylococcus aureus* in children with no identified predisposing risk. JAMA. 1998;279:593–8.

7. Petti CA, Fowler VG Jr. *Staphylococcus aureus* bacteremia and endocarditis. Infect Dis Clin North Am. 2002;16:413–35.

8. Dennison C, Pokras R. Design and operation of the National Hospital Discharge Survey: 1988 redesign. Vital Health Stat. 2000;1:1–42.

9. Jones ME, Mayfield DC, Thornsberry C, Karlowsky JA, Sahm DF, Peterson D. Prevalence of oxacillin resistance in *Staphylococcus aureus* among inpatients and outpatients in the United States during 2000. Antimicrob Agents Chemother. 2002;46:3104–5.

10. U.S. Bureau of the Census. Census 2000 geographic terms and concepts. Washington; 2000.

11. Oehlert GW. A note on the delta method. Am Stat. 1992;46:27–9.

12. Simonsen L, Conn LA, Pinner RW, Teutsch S. Trends in infectious disease hospitalizations in the United States, 1980–1994. Arch Intern Med. 1998;158:1923–8.

13. Popovic JR, Hall MJ. 1999 National Hospital Discharge Survey. Advance data from vital and health statistics. No. 319. Hyattsville (MD): National Center for Health Statistics; 2001.

14. Hall MJ, Owings MF. 2000 National Hospital Discharge Survey. Advance data from vital and health statistics. No. 329. Hyattsville (MD): National Center for Health Statistics; 2002.

15. Bone RC. Gram-positive organisms and sepsis. Arch Intern Med. 1994; 154:26–34.

16. Martin GS, Mannino DM, Eaton S, Moss M. The epidemiology of sepsis in the United States from 1979 through 2000. N Engl J Med. 2003; 348: 1546–54.

17. Laupland KB, Church DL, Mucenski M, Sutherland LR, Davies HD. Population-based study of the epidemiology of and the risk factors for invasive *Staphylococcus aureus* infections. J Infect Dis. 2003;187:1452–9.

18. Rubin RJ, Harrington CA, Poon A, Dietrich K, Greene JA, Moiduddin A. The economic impact of *Staphylococcus aureus* infection in New York City hospitals. Emerg Infect Dis. 1999;5:9–17.

19. Ollendorf DA, Fendrick AM, Massey K, Williams GR, Oster G. Is sepsis accurately coded on hospital bills? Value Health. 2002;5:79–81.

20. Diekema DJ, Pfaller MA, Jones RN, and the SENTRY Participants Group. Age-related trends in pathogen frequency and antimicrobial susceptibility of bloodstream isolates in North America. Int J Antimicrob Agents. 2002;20:412–8.

21. Wakefield DS, Pfaller M, Massanari RM, Hammons GT. Variation in methicillin-resistant *Staphylococcus aureus* occurrence by geographic location and hospital characteristics. Infect Control. 1987;8:151–7.

22. 1997 ASCP Susceptibility Testing Group. United States geographic bacteria susceptibility patterns. Diag Microbiol Infect Dis. 1999;35: 143–51.

READING 23
Severe Methicillin-Resistant *Staphylococcus aureus* Community-Acquired Pneumonia Associated with Influenza— Louisiana and Georgia, December 2006–January 2007

Reported by: M Pogue, S Burton, MPH, P Kreyling, MPH, J Naponick, MD, J Stefanski, MD, R Ratard, MD, Louisiana Office of Public Health. S Bulens, MPH, J Cope, MPH, J Tuttle, MD, J Ladson, MPH, M Tobin-D'Angelo, MD, K Arnold, MD, Georgia Div of Public Health. J Hageman, MHS, R Gorwitz, MD, G Fosheim, MPH, S McAllister, K Anderson, J Patel, PhD, B Limbago, PhD, Div of Healthcare Quality Promotion, National Center for Preparedness, Detection, and Control of Infectious Diseases; A Fry, MD, L Brammer, MPH, R Dhara, MPH, D Shay, MD, Influenza Div, National Center for Immunization and Respiratory Diseases; J Guarner, MD, S Zaki, MD, PhD, Infectious Disease Pathology Activity, National Center for Zoonotic, Vector-Borne, and Enteric Diseases; J Brunkard, PhD, A Kallen, MD, EIS officers, and CDC.

Pogue M, Burton S, Kreyling P, et al. Severe Methicillin-Resistant Staphylococcus aureus Community-Acquired Pneumonia Associated with Influenza—Louisiana and Georgia, December 2006–January 2007. *MMWR.* 2007; 56:325–9.

Staphylococcus aureus infection has been reported infrequently as a cause of community-acquired pneumonia (CAP) and typically has been associated with influenza virus infection or influenza-like illness (ILI).* During the 2003–04 influenza season, methicillin-resistant *S. aureus* (MRSA) gained attention as a cause of 15 cases of influenza-associated CAP[†] (1). No formal surveillance has been conducted, and few additional cases of MRSA CAP were reported to CDC during the 2004–05 and 2005–06 influenza seasons. However, in January 2007, CDC received reports of 10 cases of severe MRSA CAP, including six deaths, among previously healthy children and adults in Louisiana and Georgia during December 2006–January 2007. These were the first reported cases of severe MRSA CAP during the 2006–07 influenza season in the two states, and 10 was a higher number than expected for the 2-month period. A case of severe MRSA CAP was defined as pneumonia requiring hospitalization or resulting in the death of a patient from whom a specimen (i.e., sterile site or sputum sample) yielded MRSA when collected < 48 hours after hospitalization or arrival at an emergency department (ED).

Association with influenza was determined by either a positive result on a laboratory test or a diagnosis of ILI. This report describes three of the MRSA CAP cases as examples and summarizes all 10 of the reported cases. These cases underscore the need for health-care providers to be vigilant, especially during the influenza season, for severe cases of CAP that might be caused by MRSA.

CASE REPORTS
Louisiana Case 1
A previously healthy boy aged 10 years (Table 8-11) became ill with fever, cough, sore throat, and bilateral earache on December 6, 2006, and was treated with acetaminophen at home. The next day, his symptoms worsened and he was taken to a local ED in respiratory distress with a fever of 104°F (40°C). A chest radiograph was performed and revealed mutlilobar pneumonia. The patient was transferred to another hospital and admitted to the pediatric intensive care unit (PICU), where he required endotracheal intubation and mechanical ventilation. He was treated initially on December 7 with intravenous (IV) ceftriaxone; vancomycin was started the next day. On December 8, a rapid immunochromatographic assay for the qualitative detection of influenza A or B was performed on nasopharyngeal secretions and was positive for influenza A. A sputum culture obtained the same day grew MRSA; blood cultures were negative. The patient had leukopenia and worsening hypotension and hypoxia. He died on December 9, approximately 42 hours after admission to the PICU. The cause of death was reported as bilateral pneumonia. The patient had no documented history of MRSA; no documentation of influenza vaccination was present in either his medical record or the statewide immunization database, Louisiana Immunization Network for Kids Statewide (LINKS).

Louisiana Case 2
An adolescent boy aged 14 years (Table 8-11) had ILI symptoms on December 26, 2006, and was taken to a local ED, where he was treated with clarithromycin and penicillin for atypical pneumonia and pharyngitis. A rapid test for group A streptococcus was negative. The following day, the patient was taken to his primary-care provider with worsening symptoms and

TABLE 8-11 Demographic and clinical characteristics of patients with severe methicillin-resistant *Staphylococcus aureus* (MRSA) community-acquired pneumonia associated with influenza or influenza-like illness* —Louisiana and Georgia, December 2006–January 2007.

State and case no.	Age	Sex	Comorbidities	Previous MRSA skin disease (self or contact)	Sites of positive MRSA cultures	Respiratory symptom onset to collection of MRSA sample (days)	Initial radiologic findings	Laboratory influenza test	Influenza vaccination documented by medical record or immunization registry	Empiric antimicrobials before *S. aureus* Culture	Outcome (cause of death)	Respiratory symptom onset to death (days)
Louisiana												
1	10 yrs	M	None	Unknown	Sputum	2	Multiple lobar infiltrate	Rapid test positive	No	Ceftriaxone	Died (bilateral pneumonia)	3
2	14 yrs	M	None	Yes (self)	Blood, sputum, tonsillar swab	2	Multiple lobar infiltrate	Rapid test positive	No	Ceftriaxone	Died (sepsis, pneumonia, DIC†)	2
3	43 yrs	M	Hepatitis C, hypertension	Yes (self)	Blood, sputum	3	Multiple lobar infiltrate	Test not performed	No	Vancomycin, gentamicin	Survived	Not applicable
4	26 yrs	M	None	Yes (self)	Sputum	5	Multiple lobar infiltrate	Rapid test negative§	No	Trimethoprim-sulfamethoxazole	Survived	Not applicable
5	21 yrs	M	None	Yes (contact)	Blood, sputum	6	Multiple lobar infiltrate	Rapid test positive	No	Ceftriaxone	Survived	Not applicable
6	4 mos	F	None	No	Pleural rind	3	Single lobar infiltrate, pleural effusion	Test not performed	No	Ceftriaxone	Survived	Not applicable
Georgia												
1	8 yrs	F	None	None known in last year	Sputum	3	Single lobar infiltrate	Viral culture positive	No	Azithromycin, ceftriaxone, vancomycin	Died (hypoxia, pneumonia, respiratory distress, MRSA sepsis)	25

2	48 yrs	F	Current smoker	None known in last year	Sputum, blood, nares	3	Multiple lobar infiltrate	Rapid test negative§	Ceftriaxone, azithromycin, levofloxacin, pipercillin/ tazobactam	No	4	Died (MRSA sepsis)
3	27 yrs	F	Current smoker	None known	Sputum, blood	2	Single lobar infiltrate	Rapid test positive	Ceftriaxone, azithromycin	No	19	Died (necrotizing pneumonia)
4	22 yrs	F	None	None known	Blood	2	Multiple lobar infiltrate	Rapid test positive	Ceftriaxone, vancomycin	No	2	Died (MRSA pneumonia)

*Defined as a temperature of ≥ 100.0° F (≥ 37.8° C), oral or equivalent, with cough and/or sore throat, in the absence of a known cause other than influenza.
†Disseminated intravascular coagulation.
§Patient had influenza-like illness, and influenza test was conducted outside the 4-day reliability window from respiratory symptom onset to test.

was prescribed oseltamivir for suspected influenza. On December 28, the youth returned to the ED in respiratory distress and was noted to have bloody, frothy sputum; a fever of 104°F (40°C); and hypoxia. In the ED, the patient was intubated, placed on mechanical ventilation, and administered IV ceftriaxone and vancomycin. A chest radiograph revealed diffuse bilateral infiltrates, and a computed tomography scan of his chest revealed extensive bilateral lung consolidation and small anterior mediastinal and posterior pneumothoraces. A rapid immunochromatographic assay performed on nasopharyngeal secretions was positive for influenza A, and a blood culture grew MRSA. The patient died on December 28, approximately 6 hours after arrival in the ED; cause of death was recorded as pneumonia, sepsis, and disseminated intravascular coagulation. At autopsy, the lungs displayed necrotizing pneumonia. Immunohistochemical assay in the lung revealed evidence of *S. aureus* (positive antigens using monoclonal and polyclonal anti-S. aureus antibodies) in the areas of pneumonia; however, the tissues did not indicate evidence of influenza A or B by immunohistochemistry. MRSA was recovered from a tonsillar swab and lung specimen. Influenza vaccination had not been documented in the patient's medical record or in LINKS. His medical history was unremarkable except for a culture-confirmed axillary MRSA abscess that was diagnosed on October 9, 2006, and treated with trimethoprim-sulfamethoxazole for 7 days.

Georgia Case 1

A previously healthy girl aged 8 years (Table 8-11) was taken to her primary-care provider on December 17, 2006, after 3 days of fever (maximum: 103.0°F [39.4°C]), cough, and posttussive emesis. She was treated in the provider's office with azithromycin, dexamethasone, and aerosolized albuterol. Her condition worsened, and she was transported to a local ED, where she received IV ceftriaxone and nebulized albuterol. A chest radiograph revealed a right lower lobe pneumonia. She was transported to a referral hospital, where she was noted to be hypotensive and hypoxemic. She was intubated on arrival and placed on extracorporeal membrane oxygenation. During intubation, she had cardiac arrest and was resuscitated. Also on December 17, viral and sputum cultures were collected that tested positive for influenza A and MRSA, respectively; blood cultures were negative for MRSA. After a long hospital course complicated by renal and hepatic failure and a subpulmonic abscess, the patient died on January 7, 2007, a total of 25 days after onset of symptoms. Cause of death was listed as hypoxia, pneumonia, respiratory distress, and MRSA sepsis. Influenza vaccination was not documented in the medical record or in the Georgia Registry of Immunization Transactions and Services.

SUMMARY OF 10 CASES

Ten cases of severe MRSA CAP were reported during December 2006–January 2007 from Louisiana and Georgia (Table 8-11). Median age of the 10 patients was 17.5 years (range: 4 months to 48 years), and eight were aged <30 years. Five of the patients were female. One patient had a history of chronic hepatitis C and hypertension, and two were current smokers; none of the other patients had any relevant medical history. Four patients had documentation of either recent MRSA skin and soft tissue infection (SSTI) or living with someone with a history of MRSA SSTI. In all 10 cases, clinicians diagnosed ILI either preceding or concurrent with CAP. Six patients had laboratory-confirmed influenza. Influenza vaccination status for the 2006–07 influenza season was available for six of the patients; none had documentation of vaccination. Radiologic information on the initial evaluation was available for all patients; three had unilobar infiltrates, and seven had multilobar infiltrates. In three patients, MRSA was isolated only from sputum. Respiratory symptoms for the 10 patients began a median of 3 days (range: 2–6 days) before collection of specimens that grew MRSA. Of the six (60%) patients who died, the median period from respiratory symptom onset to death was 3.5 days (range: 2–25 days).

LABORATORY FINDINGS

Among the 10 cases, MRSA isolates from five of the six Louisiana cases were available for microbiologic characterization by CDC. All isolates were resistant to beta-lactams and erythromycin, two had inducible resistance to clindamycin, and two were not susceptible to levofloxacin. All isolates were positive for Panton-Valentine leukocidin (PVL) toxin genes by polymerase chain reaction and carried the staphylococcal cassette chromosome mec (SCCmec) type IVa resistance gene cassette. Pulsed-field gel electrophoresis analysis revealed that the five isolates had indistinguishable patterns and were designated USA 300-0114.

Notes

*Defined as a temperature of >100.0°F (>37.8°C), oral or equivalent, with cough and/or sore throat, in the absence of a known cause other than influenza.

†Defined as pneumonia occurring during the 2003–04 influenza season in a person with either laboratory-confirmed influenza virus infection, clinician determined ILI (e.g., fever plus sore throat or cough), or both, from whom a specimen (i.e., blood, sputum, or pleural fluid) that was collected within 48 hours after hospitalization yielded S. aureus.

Editorial Note: As demonstrated by the cases in this report, secondary S. aureus pneumonia is a potentially catastrophic complication of influenza. S. aureus respiratory coinfections often develop into severe, necrotizing pneumonia with a relatively high case-fatality rate (33% during the influenza epidemic of 1968–1969) and rapid clinical progression (e.g., death within 24 hours after admission) (2). S. aureus pneumonia has been complicated further by the emergence of MRSA as a cause of infection among persons in the community without traditionally recognized MRSA risk factors (3). During the 2003–04 influenza season, 15 cases of influenza-associated

CAP caused by MRSA and four deaths (fatality rate: 26.7%) were reported to CDC, generally in persons with no medical problems (1, 4).

Reports of pediatric mortality associated with bacterial coinfections with influenza virus infection have been uncommon. During the 2003–04 influenza season, 153 influenza-associated pediatric deaths were reported through state health departments to CDC; 102 of these had bacterial cultures obtained, and 11 were positive for S. aureus, primarily CAP infections (5). Pediatric influenza deaths were made nationally notifiable in 2004. During October 1, 2004–January 19, 2007, a total of 99 pediatric deaths associated with influenza were reported to CDC. Of these, 13 were tested for concomitant invasive bacterial infections, and only four had invasive S. aureus coinfection; two of those four deaths are reported here.

Particularly notable in the 10 cases described in this report is the short period between any respiratory symptom onset and either death or recovery of MRSA from the patient. Respiratory symptoms began a median of 3 days before recovery of MRSA, and four (67%) of six patients who died did so within 4 days of respiratory symptom onset. These short durations suggest that, in these cases, the influenza virus and MRSA infections likely occurred concomitantly rather than in the more classically described biphasic clinical course of CAP symptoms after influenza illness (6).

In the United States, the majority of community-associated MRSA infections have been SSTIs caused by a single pulsed-field type, termed USA300. USA300 isolates typically are resistant only to beta-lactam and macrolide antimicrobial agents and contain genes for the PVL toxin, which lyses white blood cells; these genes typically are not present in strains of health-care–associated MRSA (7). A recent study with an acute pneumonia animal model determined that PVL was associated with the development of necrotizing pneumonia (8). In general, diagnostic testing for CAP is encouraged if the results might affect clinical decisions (e.g., antimicrobial management). In 30% of the cases in this report, MRSA was recovered only from sputum. The recently released Infectious Disease Society of America/American Thoracic Society CAP guidelines for adults recommend sputum cultures along with blood cultures and other diagnostic tests for certain patients (e.g., those with severe disease). Other indications for sputum culture include pleural effusion, cavitary infiltrates, and failure of outpatient therapy; all of these indications were observed among the MRSA patients described in this report.

The guidelines also note that sputum Gram stain is useful for quickly identifying pathogens such as S. aureus that are not the most common causes of CAP and might not be covered by routine empiric therapy (9). Beginning optimal therapy quickly can reduce mortality (9). Four patients in this report had a documented history of MRSA skin infection in themselves or in a close contact before contracting pneumonia. The presence of preceding staphylococcal skin disease among persons with staphylococcal pneumonia has been described previously during an influenza pandemic (10). The index of suspicion for MRSA CAP, therefore, should be increased in patients with a history of MRSA infection or close contact with an MRSA-infected person or in communities where MRSA infections have been identified. If MRSA CAP is suspected, clinicians should add vancomycin or linezolid to the empiric regimen (9). These cases serve to remind health-care providers that CAP can be caused by MRSA. Although uncommon, MRSA CAP has few obvious characteristics that differentiate it from other bacterial infections or from influenza virus infection alone; MRSA CAP often affects young, otherwise healthy persons and can be rapidly fatal. MRSA should be suspected in persons with severe pneumonia, especially during the influenza season, in those with cavitary infiltrates, and in those with a history of MRSA infection. Fatal cases of MRSA CAP or cases requiring hospitalization or ICU admission should be reported through state health departments to CDC's Division of Healthcare Quality Promotion by telephone (800-893-0485) or e-mail (search@cdc.gov).

ACKNOWLEDGMENTS

This report is based, in part, on contributions by C Jones-Nazar, MD, D Robertson, J Eavey, MPH, Louisiana Office of Public Health; L Kravet, Louisiana State Public Health Laboratory; F Brian, MD, Rapides Parish Coroner's Office; LJ Mayeux, MD, Avoyelles Parish Coroner's Office; and C Trant, MD, Lafayette Parish Coroner's Office, Louisiana.

DISCUSSION QUESTIONS

1. What do think the primary intent of the March 21, 2003, dispatch on SARS was?

2. Following initial identification of SARS' symptoms (prior to laboratory identification), what would be appropriate next steps?

3. On the basis of what was communicated in the first notice and then the MMWR dispatch, could you create a case definition for SARS?

4. When the Dispatch says "necessarily nonspecific case definition," what does it mean? Why "necessarily" and how "nonspecific"?

5. Describe the evolution of the case definition for SARS and the chronology of events. What role did the case definition play in halting the spread of the disease?

6. Describe the communication of events through the MMWR. Is there additional information you would have liked to know? Go to www.cdc.gov and research SARS to find out additional information about the disease and flesh out the events that took place.

7. Discuss the SARS surveillance project, and comment on the different modes of data collection (e.g., syndromic surveillance, surveys). What are the goals of the project? What methods might be undertaken to ensure that the system expands and is maintained into the future, and remains responsive to changes in SARS over time? Go to Frontlines of Medicine (http://www.frontlinesmed.org/) and learn about emergency preparedness for infectious diseases.

8. Describe the public health actions taken to slow the spread of SARS described in the early reports. Were they effective? What steps in the outbreak investigation were critical to have this impact? Consider the following diseases: Could these same public health actions be effective for them? Why? Why not? Look up information about these diseases using textbooks, a Medline or PubMed search, or using reliable internet sources. When you consider this question, do not forget to incorporate each disease's characteristics into your assessment. What about each disease makes it relatively easier or more difficult to identify and halt? Consider the basic principles of modern day quarantine: Can/should these be incorporated into your approach for any of the below diseases? Can you make generalizations about diseases and what makes them easier to slow?

9. a. Influenza [consider both general current strains as well as potential for Avian (H5N1)]
   b. Polio (consider both vaccine-associated and wild-type)
   c. Measles
   d. Drug-resistant tuberculosis
   e. HIV/AIDS
   f. Chlamydia
   g. Malaria
   h. MRSA

10. Consider the XDR TB MMWR you read and also the reporting of the individual with it in June 2007. Discuss the ethics involved in quarantine as well as individuals' rights. Consult other sources (www.who.int, www.cdc.gov, media outlets) to paint a picture of the situation at hand. What could have been done differently?

11. What are possible methods for studying the spread of and characteristics associated with MRSA? What do you think may need to be done to enhance its surveillance and control?

REFERENCES FROM THE READING

1. Hageman JC, Uyeki TM, Francis JS, et al. Severe community-acquired pneumonia due to Staphylococcus aureus, 2003–04 influenza season. Emerg Infect Dis 2006;12:894–9.

2. Schwarzmann SW, Adler JL, Sullivan RJ, Marine WM. Bacterial pneumonia during the Hong Kong influenza epidemic of 1968–1969. Arch Intern Med 1971;127:1037–41.

3. Fridkin SK, Hageman JC, Morrison M, et al. Methicillin-resistant Staphylococcus aureus disease in three communities. N Engl J Med 2005; 352:1436–44.

4. Francis JS, Doherty MC, Lopatin U, et al. Severe community-onset pneumonia in healthy adults caused by methicillin-resistant Staphylococcus aureus carrying the Panton-Valentine leukocidin genes. Clin Infect Dis 2005;40:100–7.

5. Bhat N, Wright JG, Broder KR, et al. Influenza-associated deaths among children in the United States, 2003–2004. N Engl J Med 2005; 353:2559–67.

6. Treanor JJ. Influenza virus. In: Mandell GL, Bennett JE, Dolin R, eds. The principles and practice of infectious diseases, 6th ed. Philadelphia, PA: Elsevier Inc. 2005:2060–85.

7. Tenover FC, McDougal LK, Goering RV, et al. Characterization of a strain of community-associated methicillin-resistant Staphylococcus aureus widely disseminated in the United States. J Clin Microbiol 2006;44:108–18.

8. Labandeira-Rey M, Couzon F, Boisset S, et al. Staphylococcus aureus Panton-Valentine leukocidin causes necrotizing pneumonia. Science 2007;315:1130–3.

9. Mandell LA, Wunderink RG, Anzueto A, et al. Infectious Diseases Society of America/American Thoracic Society consensus guidelines on the management of community-acquired pneumonia in adults. Clin Infect Dis 2007;44(Suppl 2):S27–72.

10. Goslings WR, Mulder J, Djajadiningrat J, Masurel J. Staphylococcal pneumonia in influenza in relation to antecedent staphylococcal skin infection. Lancet 1959;2:428–30.

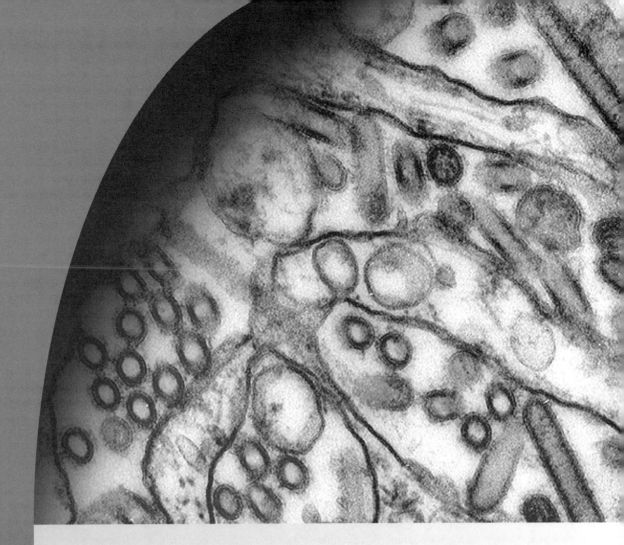

PART IX

Foodborne Diseases

Although there are emerging and reemerging infectious diseases still to be identified, controlled, and conquered, those with whom we are well-acquainted cannot be ignored. Foodborne diseases are responsible for an enormous burden of disease globally, and knowledge about how to prevent and treat them does not always reduce their spread. Thousands of people become ill each year from foodborne disease. The following article describes the estimated prevalence of common foodborne pathogens, while the interesting correspondence that follows discusses the authors' methods.

READING 24
Food-Related Illness and Death in the United States

Paul S. Mead, Laurence Slutsker, Vance Dietz, Linda F. McCaig, Joseph S. Bresee, Craig Shapiro, Patricia M. Griffin, and Robert V. Tauxe

Mead PS, Slutsker L, Dietz V, et al. Food-Related Illness and Death in the United States. *Emerg Inf Dis*. 1999;5:607–25.

To better quantify the impact of foodborne diseases on health in the United States, we compiled and analyzed information from multiple surveillance systems and other sources. We estimate that foodborne diseases cause approximately 76 million illnesses, 325,000 hospitalizations, and 5,000 deaths in the United States each year. Known pathogens account for an estimated 14 million illnesses, 60,000 hospitalizations, and 1,800 deaths. Three pathogens, Salmonella, Listeria, and Toxoplasma, are responsible for 1,500 deaths each year, more than 75% of those caused by known pathogens, while unknown agents account for the remaining 62 million illnesses, 265,000 hospitalizations, and 3,200 deaths. Overall, foodborne diseases appear to cause more illnesses but fewer deaths than previously estimated.

More than 200 known diseases are transmitted through food (1). The causes of foodborne illness include viruses, bacteria, parasites, toxins, metals, and prions, and the symptoms of foodborne illness range from mild gastroenteritis to life-threatening neurologic, hepatic, and renal syndromes. In the United States, foodborne diseases have been estimated to cause 6 million to 81 million illnesses and up to 9,000 deaths each year (2–5). However, ongoing changes in the food supply, the identification of new foodborne diseases, and the availability of new surveillance data have made these figures obsolete. New, more accurate estimates are needed to guide prevention efforts and assess the effectiveness of food safety regulations.

Surveillance of foodborne illness is complicated by several factors. The first is underreporting. Although foodborne illnesses can be severe or even fatal, milder cases are often not detected through routine surveillance. Second, many pathogens transmitted through food are also spread through water or from person to person, thus obscuring the role of foodborne transmis-sion. Finally, some proportion of foodborne illness is caused by pathogens or agents that have not yet been identified and thus cannot be diagnosed. The importance of this final factor cannot be overstated. Many of the pathogens of greatest concern today (e.g., Campylobacter jejuni, Escherichia coli O157:H7, Listeria monocytogenes, Cyclospora cayetanensis) were not recognized as causes of foodborne illness just 20 years ago. In this article, we report new estimates of illnesses, hospitalizations, and deaths due to foodborne diseases in the United States. To ensure their validity, these estimates have been derived by using data from multiple sources, including the newly established Foodborne Diseases Active Surveillance Network (FoodNet). The figures presented include estimates for specific known pathogens, as well as overall estimates for all causes of foodborne illness, known, unknown, infectious, and noninfectious.

DATA SOURCES

Data sources for this analysis include the Foodborne Diseases Active Surveillance Network (FoodNet) (6), the National Notifiable Disease Surveillance System (7), the Public Health Laboratory Information System (8), the Gulf Coast States Vibrio Surveillance System (9), the Foodborne Disease Outbreak Surveillance System (10), the National Ambulatory Medical Care Survey (11), the National Hospital Ambulatory Medical Care Survey (12–14), the National Hospital Discharge Survey (15), the National Vital Statistics System (16), and selected published studies.

Established in 1996, FoodNet is a collaborative effort by the Centers for Disease Control and Prevention, the U.S. Department of Agriculture, the U.S. Food and Drug Administration, and selected state health departments. FoodNet conducts active surveillance for seven bacterial and two parasitic foodborne diseases within a defined population of 20.5 million Americans (6). Additional surveys conducted within the FoodNet catchment area provide information on the frequency of diarrhea in the general population, the proportion of ill persons seeking care, and the frequency of stool culturing by physicians and laboratories for selected foodborne pathogens.

common food) (10). As components of the National Health Care Survey, the National Ambulatory Medical Care Survey and the National Hospital Ambulatory Medical Care Survey measure health care use in various clinical settings, including physician offices and hospital emergency and outpatient departments (11–14). These surveys collect information on patient characteristics, patient symptoms or reasons for visit, provider diagnosis, and whether the patient was hospitalized. Up to three symptoms are recorded using a standard classification (17), and up to three provider diagnoses are recorded according to the International Classification of Diseases, 9th Revision, Clinical Modifications (ICD-9-CM,18) (Table 9-1).

FIGURE 9-1 *Escherichia coli* bacteria of the strain O157:H7.

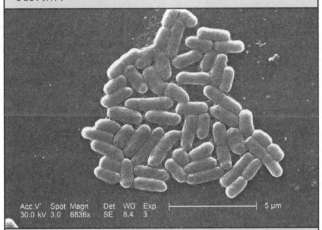

Acc.V Spot Magn   Det WD   Exp   5 µm
30.0 kV 3.0 6836x   SE   8.4   3

About this picture: "Under a magnification of 6836x, this colorized scanning electron micrograph (SEM) depicted a number of Gram-negative *Escherichia coli* bacteria of the strain O157:H7, which is one of hundreds of strains of this bacterium. Although most strains are harmless, and live in the intestines of healthy humans and animals, this strain produces a powerful toxin, which can cause severe illness.

E. coli O157:H7 was first recognized as a cause of illness in 1982 during an outbreak of severe bloody diarrhea; the outbreak was traced to contaminated hamburgers. Since then, most infections have come from eating undercooked ground beef.

The combination of letters and numbers in the name of the bacterium refers to the specific markers found on its surface, which distinguishes it from other types of *E. coli*. See PHIL 8800 for a black and white version of this image.

Escherichia coli O157:H7 is an emerging cause of foodborne illness. An estimated 73,000 cases of infection and 61 deaths occur in the United States each year. Infection often leads to bloody diarrhea, and occasionally to kidney failure. Most illness has been associated with eating undercooked, contaminated ground beef. Person-to-person contact in families and child care centers is also an important mode of transmission. Infection can also occur after drinking raw milk, and after swimming in, or drinking sewage-contaminated water.

Consumers can prevent *E. coli* O157:H7 infection by thoroughly cooking ground beef, avoiding unpasteurized milk, and washing hands carefully. Because the organism lives in the intestines of healthy cattle, preventive measures on cattle farms and during meat processing are being investigated."

Source: CDC/National Escherichia, Shigella, Vibrio Reference Unit at CDC/ Janice Haney Carr, 2006.

The National Notifiable Disease Surveillance System (7) and the Public Health Laboratory Information System (8) collect passive national surveillance data for a wide range of diseases reported by physicians and laboratories. The Gulf Coast States Vibrio Surveillance System collects reports of Vibrio infections from selected states (9), and the Foodborne Disease Outbreak Surveillance System receives data from all states on recognized foodborne illness outbreaks (defined as two or more cases of a similar illness resulting from ingestion of a

TABLE 9-1 ICD-9-CM codes and associated conditions.

Code	Condition
001	Cholera
002	Typhoid fever
003	*Salmonella*
004	Shigellosis
005.0	Staphyloccocal food poisoning
005.1	Botulism
005.2-005.3	Other *Clostridia*
005.4	*Vibrio parahaemolyticus*
005.8-005.9	Other and unspecified bacterial food poisoning
006	Amebiasis
007.1	Giardiasis
007.0, 007.2-007.9	Other protozoal intestinal infections
008.00, 008.09	Misc. *Escherichia coli*
008.01	Enteropathogenic *E. coli*
008.02	Enterotoxigenic *E. coli*
008.03	Enteroinvasive *E. coli*
008.04	Enterohemorrhagic *E. coli*
008.43	*Campylobacter*
008.44	*Yersinia*
008.41-2, 008.46-9, 008.5	Misc. bacterial
008.61	Rotavirus
008.62	Adenovirus
008.63	Norwalk virus
008.64	Other small round structured viruses
008.65	Calicivirus
008.66	Astrovirus
008.67	Enterovirus
008.69, 008.8	Other virus
009.	Ill-defined intestinal infections
558.9	Other noninfectious gastroenteritis

FIGURE 9-2 *Campylobacter jejuni.*

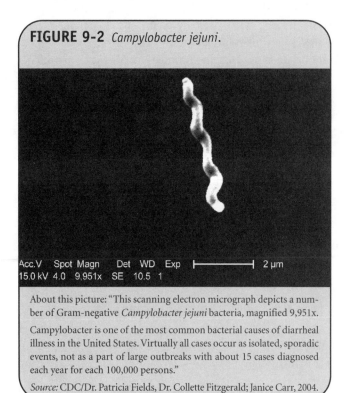

Acc.V   Spot Magn   Det   WD   Exp ⊢————⊣ 2 μm
15.0 kV 4.0 9.951x   SE   10.5 1

About this picture: "This scanning electron micrograph depicts a number of Gram-negative *Campylobacter jejuni* bacteria, magnified 9,951x.

Campylobacter is one of the most common bacterial causes of diarrheal illness in the United States. Virtually all cases occur as isolated, sporadic events, not as a part of large outbreaks with about 15 cases diagnosed each year for each 100,000 persons."

Source: CDC/Dr. Patricia Fields, Dr. Collette Fitzgerald; Janice Carr, 2004.

The National Hospital Discharge Survey, another component of the National Health Care Survey, is a representative annual sample of discharge records from approximately 475 nonfederal short-stay hospitals (15). The information collected includes up to seven principal discharge diagnoses classified by ICD- 9-CM codes (18). Because these data include information on condition at discharge, they can be used as a source of information on in-hospital deaths. Additional information on food-related deaths was obtained from the National Vital Statistics System, which collects death certificate data on causes of death classified by 3- or 4- digit ICD-9 codes (16).

In addition to information from these formal surveillance systems, we used data from two published population-based studies. The Tecumseh study was conducted from 1965 through 1971 in 850 households in Tecumseh, Michigan, with an emphasis on households with young children (19). Households were telephoned weekly to identify incident cases of self-defined diarrhea, vomiting, nausea, or stomach upset. The Cleveland study was conducted among a selected group of 86 families followed from 1948 through 1957 (20). A family member recorded occurrences of gastrointestinal illnesses and associated symptoms on a monthly tally sheet. Both studies also collected information on extraintestinal illnesses (e.g., respiratory illness). Other studies with similar designs were not included in our analysis, either because they were relatively small or because they did not provide information on the desired endpoints.

THE STUDY

Food-Related Illness and Death from Known Pathogens

Total Cases

To estimate the total number of foodborne illnesses caused by known pathogens, we determined the number of reported cases for each pathogen, adjusted the figures to account for underreporting, and estimated the proportion of illnesses specifically attributable to foodborne transmission. Although data from various periods were used, adjustments for changes in population size had minimal effect on the final estimates and were therefore omitted. Cases may be reported in association with documented foodborne outbreaks, through passive surveillance systems (e.g., the National Notifiable Disease Surveillance System, the Public Health Laboratory Information System), or through active surveillance systems (e.g., FoodNet). Sporadic illness caused by some pathogens (e.g., Bacillus cereus, Clostridium perfringens, Staphylococcus aureus) is not reportable through passive or active systems; hence, the only cases reported are those related to outbreaks. For these pathogens, we have assumed that if diagnosed sporadic cases were reported, the total number would be 10 times the number of outbreak-related cases. This multiplier is based on experience with pathogens for which data are available on both sporadic and outbreak-associated cases (e.g., reported cases of Salmonella or Shigella, Table 9-2). For all pathogens, the number of outbreak-related cases was calculated as the average annual number of such cases reported to CDC from 1983 to 1992, the most recent years for which published outbreak data are available. For pathogens also under passive surveillance, we used the average number of cases reported to CDC from 1992 through 1997, and for pathogens under active surveillance through FoodNet, we used the average rate observed for the surveillance population from 1996 to 1997 and applied this to the total 1997 U.S. population (with some modification for E. coli O157:H7; Appendix).

Irrespective of the surveillance system, many cases of foodborne illness are not reported because the ill person does not seek medical care, the health-care provider does not obtain a specimen for diagnosis, the laboratory does not perform the necessary diagnostic test, or the illness or laboratory findings are not communicated to public health officials. Therefore, to calculate the total number of illnesses caused by each pathogen, it is necessary to account for underreporting, i.e., the difference between the number of reported cases and the number of cases that actually occur in the community. For Salmonella, a pathogen that typically causes nonbloody diarrhea, the degree of underreporting has been estimated at ~38 fold (Voetsch, manuscript in preparation) (21). For E. coli O157:H7, a pathogen that typically causes bloody diarrhea, the degree of

TABLE 9-2 Reported and estimated[a] illnesses, frequency of foodborne transmission, and hospitalization and case fatality rates for known foodborne pathogens, United States.

Disease or Agent	Estimated total cases	Reported Cases by Surveillance Type			% Foodborne transmission	Hospitalization rate	Case-fatality rate
		Active	Passive	Outbreak			
Bacterial							
Bacillus cereus	27,360		720	72	100	0.006	0.0000
Botulism, foodborne	58		29		100	0.800	0.0769
Brucell, spp.	1,554		111		50	0.550	0.0500
Campylobacter spp.	2,453,926	64,577	37,496	146	80	0.102	0.0010
Clostridium perfringens	248,520		6,540	654	100	0.003	0.0005
Escherichia coli O157:H7	73,480	3,674	2,725	500	85	0.295	0.0083
E. coli, non-O157 STEC	36,740	1,837			85	0.295	0.0083
E. coli, enterotoxigenic	79,420		2,090	209	70	0.005	0.0001
E. coli, other diarrheogenic	79,420		2,090		30	0.005	0.0001
Listeria monocytogenes	2,518	1,259	373		99	0.922	0.2000
Salmonella typhi[b]	824		412		80	0.750	0.0040
Salmonella, nontyphoidal	1,412,498	37,171	37,842	3,640	95	0.221	0.0078
Shigella spp.	448,240	22,412	17,324	1,476	20	0.139	0.0016
Staphylococcus food poisoning	185,060		4,870	487	100	0.180	0.0002
Streptococcus, foodborne	50,920		1,340	134	100	0.133	0.0000
Vibrio cholerae, toxigenic	54		27		90	0.340	0.0060
V. vulnificus	94		47		50	0.910	0.3900
Vibrio, other	7,880	393	112		65	0.126	0.0250
Yersinia enterocolitica	96,368	2,536			90	0.242	0.0005
Subtotal	5,204,934						
Parasitic							
Cryptosporidium parvum	300,000	6,630	2,788		10	0.150	0.005
Cyclospora cayetanensis	16,264	428	98		90	0.020	0.0005
Giardia lamblia	2,000,000	107,000	22,907		10	n/a	n/a
Taxoplasma gondii	225,000		15,000		50	n/a	n/a
Trichinella spiralis	52		26		100	0.081	0.003
Subtotal	2,541,316						
Viral							
Norwalk-like viruses	23,000,000				40	n/a	n/a
Rotavirus	3,900,000				1	n/a	n/a
Astrovirus	3,900,000				1	n/a	n/a
Hepatitis A	83,391		27,797		5	0.130	0.0030
Subtotal	30,883,391						
Grand Total	**38,629,641**						

[a]Numbers in italics are estimates; others are measured.
[b]> 70% of cases acquired abroad.

underreporting has been estimated at ~20 fold (22). Because similar information is not available for most other pathogens, we used a factor of 38 for pathogens that cause primarily nonbloody diarrhea (e.g., Salmonella, Campylobacter) and 20 for pathogens that cause bloody diarrhea (e.g., E. coli O157:H7, Shigella). For pathogens that typically cause severe illness (i.e., Clostridium botulinum, Listeria monocytogenes), we arbitrarily used a far lower multiplier of 2, on the assumption that most cases come to medical attention. Details of the calculations for each specific pathogen and rationale are provided in the Appendix.

Where information from both active and passive reporting was available, we used the figure from active surveillance when estimating the total number of cases. Having estimated the number of cases caused by each pathogen, the final step was to estimate for each the percentage of illness attributable to foodborne transmission. The total number of cases was then multiplied by this percentage to derive the total number of illnesses attributable to foodborne transmission. The rationale for each estimate is presented in the Appendix; although precise percentages are generally difficult to justify, in most instances there is ample support for the approximate value used. Results are presented in Tables 9-2 and 9-3.

TABLE 9-3 Estimated illnesses, hospitalizations, and deaths caused by known foodborne pathogens, United States.

Disease or agent	Illnesses			Hospitalizations			Deaths		
	Total	Food-borne	% of total food-borne	Total	Food-borne	% of total food-borne	Total	Food-borne	% of total food-borne
Bacterial									
Bacillus cereus	27,360	27,360	0.2	8	8	0.0	0	0	0.0
Botulism, foodborne	58	58	0.0	46	46	0.1	4	4	0.2
Brucella, spp.	1,554	777	0.0	122	61	0.1	11	6	0.3
Campylobacter spp.	2,453,926	1,963,141	14.2	13,174	10,539	17.3	124	99	5.5
Clostridium perfringens	248,520	248,520	1.8	41	41	0.1	7	7	0.4
Escherichia coli O157:H7	73,480	62,458	0.5	2,168	1,843	3.0	61	52	2.9
E. coli, non-O157 STEC	36,740	31,229	0.2	1,084	921	1.5	30	26	1.4
E. coli, enterotoxigenic	79,420	55,594	0.4	21	15	0.0	0	0	0.0
E. coli, other diarrheogenic	79,420	23,826	0.2	21	6	0.0	0	0	0.0
Listeria monocytogenes	2,518	2,493	0.0	2,322	2,298	3.8	504	499	27.6
Salmonella typhi	824	659	0.0	618	494	0.8	3	3	0.1
Salmonella, nontyphoidal	1,412,498	1,341,873	9.7	16,430	15,608	25.6	582	553	30.6
Shigella spp.	448,240	89,648	0.6	6,231	1,246	2.0	70	14	0.8
Staphylococcus food poisoning	185,060	185,060	1.3	1,753	1,753	2.9	2	2	0.1
Streptococcus, foodborne	50,920	50,920	0.4	358	358	0.6	0	0	0.0
Vibrio cholerae, toxigenic	54	49	0.0	18	17	0.0	0	0	0.0
V. vulnificus	94	47	0.0	86	43	0.1	37	18	1.0
Vibrio, other	7,880	5,122	0.0	99	65	0.1	20	13	0.7
Yersinia enterocolitica	96,368	86,731	0.6	1,228	1,105	1.8	3	2	0.1
Subtotal	5,204,934	4,175,565	30.2	45,826	36,466	59.9	1,458	1,297	71.7
Parasitic									
Cryptosporidium parvum	300,000	30,000	0.2	1,989	199	0.3	66	7	0.4
Cyclospora cayetanensis	16,264	14,638	0.1	17	15	0.0	0	0	0.0
Giardia lamblia	2,000,000	200,000	1.4	5,000	500	0.8	10	1	0.1
Taxoplasma gondii	225,000	112,500	0.8	5,000	2,500	4.1	750	375	20.7
Trichinella spiralis	52	52	0.0	4	4	0.0	0	0	0.0
Subtotal	2,541,316	357,190	2.6	12,010	3,219	5.3	827	383	21.2
Viral									
Norwalk-like viruses	23,000,000	9,200,000	66.6	50,000	20,000	32.9	310	124	6.9
Rotavirus	3,900,000	39,000	0.3	50,000	500	0.8	30	0	0.0
Astrovirus	3,900,000	39,000	0.3	12,500	125	0.2	10	0	0.0
Hepatitis A	83,391	4,170	0.0	10,841	90	0.9	83	4	0.2
Subtotal	30,883,391	9,282,170	67.2	123,341	21,167	34.8	433	129	7.1
Grand Total	**38,629,641**	**13,814,924**	**100.0**	**181,177**	**60,854**	**100.0**	**2,718**	**1,809**	**100.0**

FIGURE 9-3 *Salmonella infantis.*

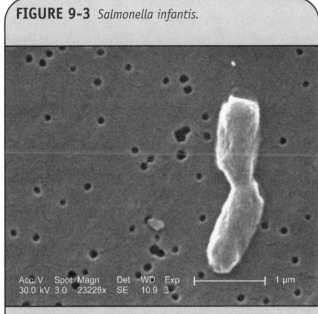

Acc. V   Spot Magn   Det   WD   Exp   1 μm
30.0 kV   3.0   23228x   SE   10.9   3

About this picture: "This scanning electron micrograph (SEM) depicts two highly magnified rod-shaped, motile, Gram-negative *Salmonella infantis* bacteria, which are attached; Magnification 23228x.

Clinical features of "Salmonellosis" include fever, abdominal cramps, and diarrhea, which is sometimes bloody. Occasionally these bacteria can establish a localized infection such as septic arthritis, or can even progress to sepsis, which occurs due to the systemic spread of these pathogens. The etiologic agents are members of the Gram-negative family of bacteria Enterobacteriaceae, of which approximately 2000 serotypes cause human disease, including Salmonella infantis. The incidence of salmonellosis is estimated at 1.4 million cases occurring annually in the United States, and of these, approximately 30,000 are culture-confirmed cases reported to CDC."

Source: Public Health Image Library CDC /Janice Carr, 2005.

Known pathogens account for an estimated 38.6 million illnesses each year, including 5.2 million (13%) due to bacteria, 2.5 million (7%) due to parasites, and 30.9 million (80%) due to viruses (Table 9-2). Overall, foodborne transmission accounts for 13.8 million of the 38.6 million illnesses (Table 9-3). Excluding illness caused by Listeria, Toxoplasma, and hepatitis A virus (three pathogens that typically cause nongastrointestinal illness), 38.3 million cases of acute gastroenteritis are caused by known pathogens, and 13.6 million (36%) of these are attributable to foodborne transmission. Among all illnesses attributable to foodborne transmission, 30% are caused by bacteria, 3% by parasites, and 67% by viruses.

Hospitalizations

To estimate the number of hospitalizations due to foodborne transmission, we calculated for each pathogen the expected number of hospitalizations among reported cases by multiplying the number of reported cases by pathogen-specific hospitalization rates from FoodNet data (23, 24), reported outbreaks

(10, 25), or other published studies (Appendix). Not all illnesses resulting in hospitalization are diagnosed or reported. Healthcare providers may not order the necessary diagnostic tests, patients may have already taken antibiotics that interfere with diagnostic testing, or the condition leading to hospitalization may be a sequela that develops well after resolution of the actual infection (e.g., Campylobacter-associated Guillain-Barré syndrome). Therefore, to account for underreporting, we doubled the number of hospitalizations among reported cases to derive for each pathogen an estimate of the total number of hospitalizations. Finally, we multiplied this figure by the proportion of infections attributable to foodborne transmission. Because of gaps in the available data, this approach could not be used for some parasitic and viral diseases (Appendix).

Overall, the pathogens listed in Table 9-2 cause an estimated 181,177 hospitalizations each year, of which 60,854 are attributable to foodborne transmission (Table 9-3). Excluding hospitalizations for infection with Listeria, Toxoplasma, and hepatitis A virus, 163,015 hospitalizations for acute gastroenteritis are caused by known pathogens, of which 55,512 (34%) are attributable to foodborne transmission. Overall, bacterial pathogens account for 60% of hospitalizations attributable to foodborne transmission, parasites for 5%, and viruses for 34%.

Deaths

Like illnesses and hospitalizations, deaths are also underreported. Precise information on food-related deaths is especially difficult to obtain because pathogen-specific surveillance systems rarely collect information on illness outcome, and outcome-specific surveillance systems (e.g., death certificates) grossly underreport many pathogen-specific conditions. To estimate the number of deaths due to bacterial pathogens, we used the same approach described for hospitalizations: first calculating the number of deaths among reported cases, then doubling this figure to account for unreported deaths, and finally multiplying by the percentage of infections attributable to foodborne transmission. As with hospitalization, this approach could not be used for some parasitic and viral diseases. Overall, the specified pathogens cause an estimated 2,718 deaths each year, of which 1,809 are attributable to foodborne transmission (Table 9-3). Excluding death due to Listeria, Toxoplasma, and hepatitis A virus, the number of deaths due to pathogens that cause acute gastroenteritis is 1,381, of which 931 (67%) are attributable to foodborne transmission. Bacteria account for 72% of deaths associated with foodborne transmission, parasites for 21%, and viruses for 7%. Five pathogens account for over 90% of estimated food-related deaths: Salmonella (31%), Listeria (28%), Toxoplasma (21%), Norwalk-like viruses (7%), Campylobacter (5%), and E. coli O157:H7 (3%).

Food-Related Illness and Death from Unknown Pathogens

Some proportion of gastrointestinal illness is caused by foodborne agents not yet identified. This conclusion is supported by well-documented foodborne outbreaks of distinctive illness for which the causative agent remains unknown (e.g., Brainerd diarrhea) (26), by the large percentage of foodborne outbreaks reported to CDC for which no pathogen is identified (25), and by the large number of new foodborne pathogens identified in recent years.

To estimate food-related illness and death from unknown pathogens, we used symptom-based data to estimate the total number of acute gastrointestinal illnesses and then subtracted from this total the number of cases accounted for by known pathogens; this difference represents the illness due to acute gastroenteritis of unknown etiology. To determine how much of this illness was due to foodborne transmission, we used the percentages of foodborne transmission as determined above for acute gastroenteritis caused by known pathogens.

Total Cases

To determine the rate of acute gastroenteritis in the general population, we used data on the frequency of diarrhea from the 1996 to 1997 FoodNet population survey. This survey did not collect data on the rate of vomiting among persons without diarrhea, however, so we relied on the Tecumseh and Cleveland studies for information on the frequency of this symptom. Because young children were overrepresented in the Tecumseh and Cleveland studies relative to the current U.S. population, rates of illness for these studies were age-adjusted. For the Tecumseh data, we used the reported age- and symptom-specific rates. For the Cleveland study, we used the method described by Garthright (27) to derive an overall age-adjusted rate of gastrointestinal illness; we then multiplied this rate by the relative frequency of symptoms to derive age-adjusted rates for specific symptoms. In the 1996–97 FoodNet population survey, the overall rate of diarrhea was 1.4 episodes per person per year, and the rate of diarrheal illness, defined as diarrhea (3 loose stools per 24-hour period) lasting > 1 day or interfering with normal activities, was 0.75 episodes per person per year (H. Herikstad, manuscript in preparation). We used the lower 0.75 rate for our analysis. To this we added the average age-adjusted rate of vomiting without diarrhea from the Tecumseh and Cleveland studies (0.30, Table 9-4) to derive an overall estimate of 1.05 episodes per person per year of acute gastrointestinal illness characterized by diarrhea, vomiting, or both. Previous studies have shown that some cases of acute gastrointestinal illness are accompanied by respiratory symptoms; although the causes of these illnesses are generally unknown, such cases have traditionally been attributed to respiratory pathogens (20, 27). Data on the frequency of concomitant respiratory symptoms were not collected in the 1996–97 FoodNet survey but were 20% to 27% among patients with acute gastroenteritis in the Tecumseh and Cleveland studies. Therefore, we adjusted downward our estimate of acute gastroenteritis by 25%, yielding a final estimate of 0.79 (1.05 × 0.75) episodes of acute gastroenteritis per person per year. Extrapolated to a population of 267.7 million persons, the U.S. resident population in 1997 (28), this rate is equivalent to 211 million episodes each year in the United States.

As determined previously, 38.3 million of these 211 million episodes of acute gastroenteritis are attributable to known pathogens. A small proportion of the remaining 173 million episodes can be accounted for by known, noninfectious agents (e.g., mycotoxins, marine biotoxins); however, most are attributable to unknown agents. Because we cannot directly ascertain how many of these illnesses of unknown etiology are due to foodborne transmission, we used the relative frequency of foodborne transmission for known pathogens as a guide. For illnesses of known etiology, foodborne transmission accounts for 36% of total cases. Applying this percentage yields an estimate of 62 million cases of acute gastroenteritis of unknown etiology (36% of 173 million) due to foodborne transmission each year.

TABLE 9-4 Frequency of gastrointestinal illness in the general population, in episodes per person per year, as determined by three studies.

Symptom	FoodNet Population Survey Age adjusted	Tecumseh Study		Cleveland Study	
		Crude	Age adjusted	Crude	Age adjusted
Diarrhea or vomiting	—	0.98	0.81	1.28	0.87
Diarrhea, any	0.75	0.63	0.52	0.83	0.56
Without vomiting	0.61	0.40	0.33	0.48	0.33
With vomiting	0.14	0.23	0.19	0.35	0.23
Vomiting without diarrhea	—	0.35	0.29	0.45	0.31

Hospitalizations

The National Ambulatory Medical Care Survey/the National Hospital Ambulatory Medical Care Survey data were searched for visits due to symptoms of diarrhea, vomiting, or gastrointestinal infection (reason for visit classification {RVC} codes 1595, 1530, 1540) (17) and for visits resulting in a diagnosis of infectious enteritis (ICD-9-CM codes 001-009.3; Table 9-1). Visits associated with respiratory symptoms (RVC codes 1400-1499) or a diagnosis of

TABLE 9-5 Average annual hospitalizations and deaths for gastrointestinal illness by diagnostic category, National Hospital Discharge Survey, 1992–1996.

	1st diagnosis		All diagnoses	
Cause of enteritis[a]	Hospitalizations	Deaths	Hospitalizations	Deaths
Bacterial (001–005, 008–008.5)	27,987	148[b]	54,953	1,139
Viral (008.6–008.8)	82,149	0[b]	132,332	194[b]
Parasitic (006–007)	2,806	82[b]	5,799	127[b]
Unknown etiology (009, 558.9)	186,537	868[b]	423,293	5,148
Total	299,479	1,898	616,377	6,608

[a]ICD-9-CM code.
[b]Estimate unreliable as a result of small sample size.

influenza (ICD-9-CM code 487) were excluded. Data for the years 1992 to 1996 were combined before analysis. Overall, these criteria yielded an average of 15,810,905 visits annually from 1992 through 1996, of which an average of 1,246,763, or 7.9%, resulted in hospitalization. This figure is equivalent to a rate of 4.7 hospitalizations per 1,000 person-years.

The National Hospital Discharge Survey data were searched by using diagnostic codes for infectious gastroenteritis of known cause (ICD-9-CM codes 001-008; Table 9-1), with the exception of the code for Clostridium difficile colitis (ICD9 008.45), a common form of nosocomially acquired diarrhea. In addition, we included the nonspecific ICD-9-CM diagnosis codes 009 (infectious gastroenteritis) and 558.9 (other and unspecified noninfectious gastroenteritis and colitis). Despite the description, many of the illnesses attributed to ICD-9-CM code 558.9 are likely to be either infectious or due to agents possibly transmitted by food. For example, in the absence of laboratory testing, sporadic cases of viral gastroenteritis may be coded as 558.9. Under the previous ICD-8 classification, these same cases would have been assumed to be infectious and coded as 009 (29, 30). Data for the years 1992 to 1996 were weighted according to National Center for Health Statistics criteria and averaged to derive national estimates of annual hospitalizations. Records with a diagnosis of respiratory illness were not excluded because of the high incidence of respiratory infections among hospitalized patients.

Considering all listed diagnoses, the National Hospital Discharge Survey data for the years 1992 to 1996 yielded an annual average of 616,337 hospital discharges with a diagnosis of gastrointestinal illness. Included in this figure are 193,084 cases of gastroenteritis with an identified pathogen and an additional 423,293 cases of gastroenteritis of unknown etiology (Table 9-5). Converted to a rate, the total number is equivalent to 2.3 hospitalizations per 1,000 person-

years. Because these data depend on the recording of a diagnosis and not just a symptom, it is likely that they underestimate the rate of hospitalization for acute gastroenteritis. This view is supported by FoodNet population survey data indicating a rate of approximately 7.2 hospitalizations per 1,000 person-years for diarrheal illness (H. Herikstad, manuscript in preparation). These data were not included here because they omit hospitalizations for vomiting alone and are not easily adjusted for concomitant respiratory symptoms. Averaging the rates from the National Ambulatory Medical Care Survey/ National Hospital Ambulatory Medical Care Survey and National Hospital Discharge Survey yields a final estimate of 3.5 hospitalizations per 1,000 person-years, equivalent to 936,726 hospitalizations annually for acute gastroenteritis. As noted previously, 163,153 of these hospitalizations can be attributed to known causes of acute gastroenteritis, yielding an estimated 773,573 hospitalizations for acute gastroenteritis caused by unknown agents. Applying the relative frequency of foodborne transmission as determined for known pathogens yields an estimated 263,015 hospitalizations (34% of 773,573) for acute gastroenteritis due to foodborne transmission of unknown agents.

Deaths

Multiple-cause-of-death data (16) and information on in-hospital-death data (National Hospital Discharge Survey) were used. ICD-9-CM codes 001-008 were employed to identify deaths due to diagnosed infectious gastroenteritis and ICD-9-CM codes 009 and 558 to identify deaths due to gastroenteritis of unknown etiology. Death certificate data for the years 1992 to 1996 yielded an annual average of 6,195 total deaths, of which 1,432 (23%) were due to specific causes of gastroenteritis and 4,763 (77%) to undiagnosed causes of gastroenteritis. For the same years and ICD-9-CM codes, the average annual in-hospital deaths for all-listed diagnoses totaled 6,608, of which 1,460 were due to specific and 5,148 (77%) undiagnosed causes of gastroenteritis (Table 9-5). Averaging the totals for all causes from death certificate and National Hospital Discharge Survey data and adjusting to the 1997 U.S. census estimates, we estimated that gastroenteritis contributed to the death of 6,402 persons in the United States in 1997. A total of 1,386 of these deaths can be explained by known causes of acute gastroenteritis (see above). Thus an estimated 5,016 deaths from acute gastroenteritis are caused by unknown agents. Applying the relative frequency of foodborne transmission as determined for known pathogens yields an estimated 3,360 deaths (67% of 5,016) due to acute gastroenteritis caused by foodborne transmission of unknown agents.

OVERALL FOOD-RELATED ILLNESS AND DEATH

We summed illness attributable to foodborne gastroenteritis caused by known and unknown pathogens, yielding an estimate of 76 million illnesses, 318,574 hospitalizations, and 4,316 deaths. Adding to these figures the nongastrointestinal illness caused by Listeria, Toxoplasma, and hepatitis A virus, we arrived at a final national estimate of 76 million illnesses, 323,914 hospitalizations, and 5,194 deaths each year (Figure 9-4).

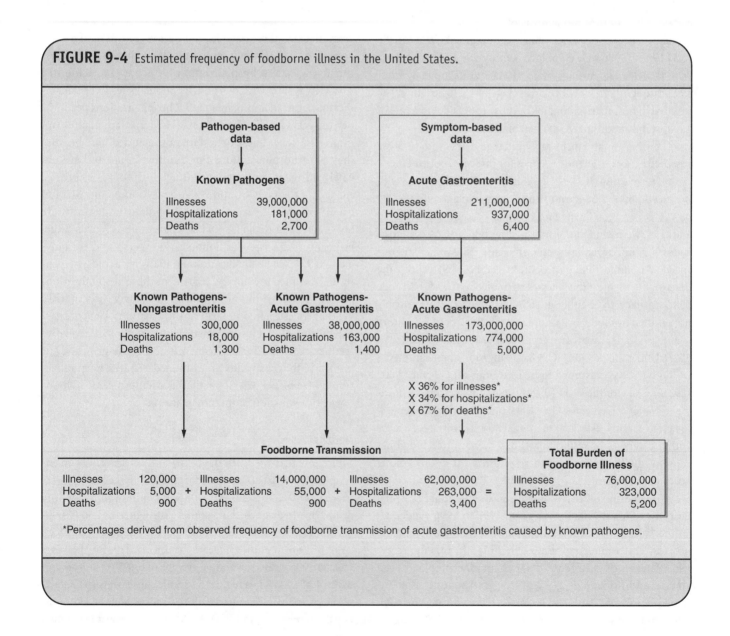

FIGURE 9-4 Estimated frequency of foodborne illness in the United States.

*Percentages derived from observed frequency of foodborne transmission of acute gastroenteritis caused by known pathogens.

CONCLUSIONS

The nature of food and foodborne illness has changed dramatically in the United States over the last century. While technological advances such as pasteurization and proper canning have all but eliminated some disease, new causes of foodborne illness have been identified. Researchers have used various methods to estimate the illnesses and deaths due to foodborne diseases in the United States. In 1985, Archer and Kvenberg coupled information on underreporting of salmonellosis with data on other foodborne pathogens to derive estimates of 8.9 million illnesses due to known pathogens and 24 million to 81 million illnesses due to all foodborne agents (2). In 1987, Bennett et al. computed incidence figures for all known infectious diseases and determined the proportion of each due to various modes of transmission. Summing these figures, they concluded that foodborne transmission of known pathogens caused 6.5 million illnesses and up to 9,000 deaths each year (3). In 1989, Todd used a combination of methods, including extrapolation from Canadian surveillance data, to derive an estimate of 12.5 million foodborne illnesses and 522 related deaths each year (4). Finally, in 1994, a task force convened by the Council for Agricultural Science and Technology (CAST) reviewed available studies and estimated the overall number of food-related illnesses at 33 million cases per year (5). These various estimates often refer to different entities. The estimates of 6.5 million and 8.9 million refer to illness caused by known pathogens, whereas the estimate of 33 million refers to all causes of foodborne illnesses, known and unknown, infectious and noninfectious.

Our estimates are based on data from a wide variety of sources and differ from previous estimates in several respects. For known pathogens, our estimate of 13.8 million illnesses per year is substantially higher than the previous estimates of 6.5 million and 8.9 million (2, 3), an increase attributable largely to our inclusion of foodborne illness caused by Norwalk-like viruses. For foodborne illness of all etiologies, our estimate of 76 million illnesses is within the range proposed by Archer and Kvenberg (2) but considerably higher than the point estimate of 33 million presented in the CAST report (5). Both our estimate and the CAST estimate assume that foodborne transmission accounts for ~35% of acute gastroenteritis cases caused by unknown agents. The disparity between the two stems from differences in the estimated annual frequency of acute gastroenteritis overall: 211 million cases for our estimate, 99 million for the CAST estimate. Whereas our estimates of illness are generally higher than those of previous studies, our estimates of death are generally lower. We estimate that foodborne illness causes 5,020 deaths annually (1,810 deaths due to known pathogens and 3,210 deaths due to unknown agents), a total that is slightly more than half the 9,000 deaths estimated by Bennett et al. (3). The Bennett estimate includes 2,100 deaths due to campylobacteriosis, 1,200 deaths due to staphylococcal food poisoning, and 1,000 deaths due to trichinosis: our total for all three of these diseases is 101 deaths. Our estimated case fatality rates for several other diseases are also lower than those used in the Bennett report, either because better data are available or perhaps because treatment has improved. Our analysis suggests that unknown agents account for approximately 81% of foodborne illnesses and hospitalizations and 64% of deaths. Among cases of foodborne illness due to known agents, Norwalk-like viruses account for over 67% of all cases, 33% of hospitalizations, and 7% of deaths. The assumptions underlying the Norwalk-like viruses figures are among the most difficult to verify, and these percentages should be interpreted with caution (Appendix). Other important causes of severe illness are Salmonella and Campylobacter, accounting for 26% and 17% of hospitalizations, respectively. The leading causes of death are Salmonella, Listeria, and Toxoplasma, which together account for 1,427, or more than 75% of foodborne deaths caused by known pathogens. Many of the deaths due to toxoplasmosis occur in HIV-infected patients; recent advances in HIV treatment may greatly reduce deaths due to toxoplasmosis. Of necessity, our analysis entails a number of assumptions. The first major assumption concerns the degree of underreporting. Well documented estimates of underreporting are not available for most pathogens; therefore, we relied on multipliers derived for salmonellosis and other diseases. For salmonellosis, the multiplier of 38 has been independently derived by investigators in the United States using different data sources. The U.S. figure is five to tenfold higher than multipliers for Salmonella and Campylobacter recently derived in Great Britain (31). However, this difference is nearly or wholly offset by far higher per capita rates of reported infections in Great Britain. Nevertheless, when extrapolated to other pathogens, these multipliers may result in under- or overestimates, and clearly studies such as those conducted for Salmonella are needed to develop better multipliers for these other diseases. However, in our analysis, changing the multipliers for individual diseases has a minimal effect on the overall estimate of foodborne illness. Our second set of assumptions concerns the frequency of foodborne transmission for individual pathogens. We have used published studies when available, but these are rare. As with underreporting multipliers, errors affect estimates for individual pathogens but have minimal effect on the estimate of overall illness and death from foodborne diseases. The one notable exception is the estimate for Norwalk-like viruses. Because these viruses account for an especially large number of illnesses, changes in the percentage attributed to foodborne transmission have a major effect on our overall estimates. For example, if the actual number of infections due to foodborne transmission were 30% rather than 40%, the overall estimate would decrease from 76 million to 63 million illnesses per year. Interestingly, our overall estimate is influenced far less by the Norwalk-like virus case estimate itself. It would require a 100-fold reduction in the estimated number of Norwalk-like virus cases to reduce the overall estimate from 76 million to 63 million.

A third assumption concerns the frequency of acute gastroenteritis in the general population. The rate we used is based in part on recent data from the FoodNet population survey, a retrospective survey involving more than 9,000 households. The overall rate of diarrhea as recorded by the survey was 1.4 episodes per person per year; however, we used the survey is far lower rate of 0.75 episodes of diarrheal illness per person per year. Furthermore, we limited our definition of acute gastroenteritis to symptoms of diarrhea or vomiting and reduced the rate to account for concomitant respiratory symptoms. As a result, our final assumed rate of 0.79 episodes of acute gastroenteritis per person per year is very similar to respiratory-adjusted estimates derived from the prospectively conducted Tecumseh (0.74) and Cleveland (0.71) studies (27). All three studies are based on household surveys, and thus the rates of illness are not influenced by changes in health-care delivery. Compared with rates of diarrheal illness from studies conducted in Great Britain, our estimated rate is higher than in one recent study (31) but lower than another (32).

In addition to these assumptions, our analysis has several limitations. Differences in available surveillance information prevented us from using the same method to estimate illness and death from bacterial, parasitic, and viral pathogens. Furthermore, because of a paucity of surveillance information, we did not include specific estimates for some known, occasionally foodborne pathogens (e.g., Plesiomonas, Aeromonas, or Edwardsiella), nor did we develop specific estimates for known noninfectious agents, such as mushroom or marine biotoxins, metals, and other inorganic toxins. However, many of these agents cause gastroenteritis and are therefore captured in our overall estimate of foodborne illness. With the exception of a few important pathogens (Appendix), we have not estimated the number of cases of chronic sequelae, although these may be part of the overall burden of foodborne diseases. Finally, future research will refine our assumptions and allow for more precise estimates. Methodologic differences between our analysis and previously published studies make it difficult to draw firm conclusions regarding overall trends in the incidence of foodborne illness. In general, the differences between our estimates and previously published figures appear to be due primarily to the availability of better information and new analyses rather than real changes in disease frequency over time. For example, E. coli O157:H7 was estimated to cause 10,000 to 20,000 illnesses annually, based on studies of patients visiting a physician for diarrhea. Recent FoodNet data have allowed a more detailed estimation of mild illnesses not resulting in physician consultation. Our estimate of nearly 74,000 illnesses per year incorporates these milder illnesses and should not be misconstrued as demonstrating a recent increase in E. coli O157:H7 infections. Whatever the limitations on retrospective comparisons, the estimates presented here provide a more reliable benchmark with which to judge the effectiveness of ongoing and future prevention efforts.

Further refinements of foodborne disease estimates will require continued and improved active surveillance. Beginning in 1998, the FoodNet population survey was modified to capture cases of vomiting not associated with diarrhea; further enhancement to capture concomitant respiratory symptoms should refine the FoodNet survey data. Expansion of laboratory diagnostic capacity could lead to better detection of certain pathogens, estimates of the degree of underreporting for additional diseases, and estimates of the proportion of specific diseases transmitted through food.

Heightened surveillance for acute, noninfectious foodborne diseases, such as mushroom poisoning and other illnesses caused by biotoxins, could further improve estimates of illness and death from foodborne illness. Emergency department-based surveillance systems (33) or poison control center-based surveillance might provide such information. Finally, identifying new causes of enteric illness and defining the public health importance of known agents (e.g., enteroaggregative E. coli) would improve foodborne disease prevention efforts.

APPENDIX

Methods, assumptions, and references for pathogen-specific estimates

Bacterial Pathogens

Pathogen: *Bacillus cereus*

Reported cases: Cases not routinely reported. Because it is a mild illness, reported cases assumed to be 10 times the average annual number of outbreak-related cases reported to CDC, 1983–1992 (10, 25).

Total cases: Assumed to be 38 times the number of reported cases by extrapolation from studies of salmonellosis.

Hospitalization rate: Determined from outbreaks reported to CDC, 1982–1992 (10, 25) and (CDC, unpub. data).

Case-fatality rates: Determined from outbreaks reported to CDC, 1982–1992 (10, 25), including those associated with nursing homes (34).

Percent foodborne: Although infection occasionally occurs through other routes, case estimates presented are based on foodborne outbreaks and are therefore assumed to reflect only foodborne transmission.

Pathogen: *Clostridium botulinum*

Reported cases: Average annual number of cases of foodborne botulism reported to CDC, 1992–1997 (7).

Total cases: Because it is a severe illness, assumed to be two times the number of reported cases.

Hospitalization rate: Determined from outbreaks reported to CDC, 1982–1992 (10, 25) and (CDC, unpub. data).

Case-fatality rate: Based on outbreaks reported to CDC, 1982–1992 (10, 25).

Percent foodborne: 100% by definition.

Pathogen: *Brucella* spp.

Reported cases: Average annual number of cases reported to CDC, 1992–1997 (7).

Total cases: Assumed to be 14 times reported cases, based on published estimates that 4% to 10% of cases are reported (35).

Hospitalization rate: Determined from outbreaks reported to CDC, 1982–1992 (10, 25) and (CDC, unpub. data).

Case-fatality rate: Historically 2% to 5% (36).

Percent foodborne: Overall, consumption of milk or cheese products from Mexico implicated in 45% of cases reported from California from 1973 to 1992 (37). Because the proportion of cases due to foodborne transmission was higher in the latter half of this period, we assumed that currently 50% of cases are foodborne.

Comments: Reports from California or Texas account for most of cases in recent years.

Pathogen: *Campylobacter* spp.

Reported cases: Outbreak-related cases based on reports to CDC, 1983–1992 (10, 25). Passive surveillance estimate based on average number of cases reported to CDC, 1992–1994 (CDC, unpub. data). Active surveillance estimate based on extrapolation of average 1996–1997 FoodNet rate (24.1 cases per 100,000 population) to 1997 U.S. population (23).

Total cases: Assumed to be 38 times the number of reported cases, based on studies of salmonellosis. Resulting estimate is roughly comparable with midpoint rate estimate from Tauxe

(38) for C. jejuni (1,020 cases per 100,000 population), applied to 1997 population. Assumes minimal contribution from nonjejuni Campylobacter.

Hospitalization rate: Based on hospitalization rate for culture-confirmed cases reported to FoodNet, 1996–1997 (23, 24).

Case-fatality rate: Based on case-fatality rate for culture-confirmed cases reported to FoodNet, 1996–1997 (23, 24).

Percent foodborne: Although waterborne outbreaks occur, foodborne transmission accounts for most of the sporadic cases (38).

Comments: Guillain-Barré syndrome (GBS) is an acute flaccid paralysis that can occur several weeks after infection with various agents, including Campylobacter. The incidence of GBS has been estimated at 1.7 cases per 100,000 population, and serologic studies suggest that ~30% of patients with GBS have evidence of recent infection with Campylobacter (39). Based on these figures, we estimate that ~1,360 cases of Campylobacter-associated GBS occurred in the United States in 1997.

Pathogen: *Clostridium perfringens*

Reported cases: Cases not routinely reported. Because it is a mild illness, number of reported cases assumed to be 10 times the average annual number of outbreak-related cases reported to CDC, 1983–1992 (10, 25).

Total cases: Assumed to be 38 times the number of reported cases, by extrapolation from studies of salmonellosis. Hospitalization rate: Determined from outbreaks reported to CDC, 1982–1992 (10, 25) and (CDC, unpub. data).

Case-fatality rate: Based on reported outbreaks, 1983–1992 (10, 25).

Percent foodborne: 100% (40). Case estimates presented are based on foodborne outbreaks and therefore reflect foodborne transmission of C. perfringens, type A.

Pathogen: *Escherichia coli* O157:H7

Reported cases: Passive surveillance estimate based on average number of cases reported to CDC through the National Electronic Telecommunications System for Surveillance (NETSS), 1995–1998; data from the Public Health Laboratory Information System (PHLIS) were used for those states not reporting to NETSS during this time period (7). Passive surveillance data for 1998 are provisional. Active surveillance estimate based on an extrapolation of a weighted average of the FoodNet rate for the years 1996–1997 to the 1997 U.S. population (23, 24). A weighted average was used because the overall FoodNet rate is disproportionately influenced by a high rate in a single northern state with a relatively small population. Because the incidence of infection is thought to be generally higher in northern states (41), we weighted the crude rate derived from FoodNet by the total population of each participating state. The weighted rate (1.34 cases per 100,000 population) was used when extrapolating the FoodNet rate to the total U.S. population.

Total cases: Studies conducted in FoodNet sites suggest that 13–27 cases of E. coli O157:H7 infection occur in the community for each confirmed case that is reported (22). To estimate total cases, we multiplied the number of reported cases, as determined through active surveillance, by 20, the midpoint of this estimate.

Hospitalization rate: Based on the hospitalization rate for culture-confirmed cases reported to FoodNet, 1996–1997 (23, 24).

Case-fatality rate: Case-fatality rate based on mortality associated with sporadic cases reported to FoodNet, 1996–1997 (23, 24).

Percent foodborne: Based on outbreaks of known source reported to CDC, 1982–1997 (CDC, unpub. data). Person-to-person transmission assumed to be secondary to foodborne transmission (2).

Comments: Our estimate of total cases is considerably higher than previous estimates based on patients seeking care for diarrhea. Our estimate includes patients with far milder illness and should not be interpreted as indicating an increase in incidence. Hemolytic uremic syndrome (HUS) occurs in ~4% of all reported cases. Based on our estimate of total cases and active surveillance cases, between 2,954 and 147 patients are expected to contract HUS each year.

Pathogen: *E. coli*, Shiga toxin-producing serogroups other than O157 (STEC)

Reported cases: Cases not routinely reported; many clinical laboratories cannot identify.

Total cases: Assumed to be half as common as infection with E. coli O157:H7. Early studies suggest that the incidence of non-O157 STEC infections is 20%–30% that of E. coli O157:H7 in North America (42, 43); however, more recent studies using different techniques suggest that this figure should be 50% (44, 45).

Hospitalization rate: Assumed to be comparable with E. coli O157:H7, but may be lower (46).

Case-fatality rate: Assumed to be comparable with E. coli O157:H7, but may be lower (46).

Percent foodborne: Assumed to be comparable with E. coli O157:H7.

Comment: Although non-O157 STEC can cause hemolytic uremic syndrome, the relative frequency of this complication is unknown. Reports from Canada suggest that non-

O157 STEC are the cause of at least 7% (47) and possibly as many as 20% (48) of HUS cases.

Pathogen: *E. coli*, enterotoxigenic
Reported cases: Not routinely reported. Outbreak-related cases based on average for 18 outbreaks reported to CDC from 1975 through 1997 (CDC, unpub. data). Reported cases assumed to be 10 times the number of outbreak-related cases.

Total cases: Assumed to be 38 times the number of reported cases by extrapolation from studies of salmonellosis.

Hospitalization rate: Low; assumed to be 0.5% of cases.

Case-fatality rate: Serious illness is generally restricted to infants in developing countries. Based on experience with reported outbreaks, assumed to be 1 in 10,000 cases in the United States.

Percent foodborne: Nearly all outbreaks reported to CDC from 1975 through 1997 have been foodborne (CDC, unpub. data); many sporadic cases are associated with travel to other countries where both water and foodborne exposures are likely.

Pathogen: *E. coli*, other diarrheogenic
Reported cases: Not routinely reported. Assumed to be at least as common as enterotoxigenic E. coli (ETEC) based on limited information from studies in North America and Europe (49).

Total cases: Assumed equal to ETEC.

Hospitalization rate: Assumed equal to ETEC.

Case-fatality rate: Assumed equal to ETEC.

Percent foodborne: Very little data available. As few foodborne outbreaks have been reported, it is assumed that only 30% of cases are foodborne.

Comment: This category includes enteropathogenic, enteroaggregative, and enteroinvasive E. coli, as well as poorly defined pathogenic groups (50). Although little is known about the incidence of these infections in the United States, these pathogens have been linked to both outbreaks and sporadic illnesses. Limited studies suggest that the importance of some of these organisms in the United States is seriously underestimated (see Nataro and Kaper [49]). Although clearly a heterogeneous collection of organisms, we assume that these pathogens as a group have similar modes of transmission and mortality rates as ETEC.

Pathogen: *Listeria monocytogenes*
Reported cases: Rates from FoodNet, 1996–1997 (23, 24) and comparable sentinel site surveillance (51), extrapolated to the 1997 U.S. population.

Total cases: Because it is a severe illness, assumed to be 2 times the number of reported cases.

Hospitalization rate: Based on hospitalization rate for culture-confirmed cases reported to FoodNet, 1996–1997 (23, 24).

Case-fatality rate: Based on published reports (51), 1996–1997 FoodNet data (23, 24), and recent outbreaks (CDC, unpub. data).

Percent foodborne: Although foodborne transmission accounts for all reported domestic outbreaks (52), the potential for nosocomial transmission has been demonstrated (53).

Comments: Figures include both perinatal and nonperinatal disease. FoodNet data on hospitalization indicate that nearly 90% of reported cases result in hospitalization (24).

Pathogen: *Salmonella* Typhi

Reported cases: Average number of cases reported to CDC, 1992–1997 (7).

Total cases: Because it is a severe illness, assumed to be two times the number of reported cases.

Hospitalization rate: Rate of hospitalization based on published outbreak reports (54, 55).

Case-fatality rate: Based on outcomes of 2,254 cases reviewed by Mermin (56).

Percent foodborne: Although waterborne outbreaks have been reported in the United States, foodborne transmission is believed to account for most cases (3).

Comments: Over 70% percent of reported cases are associated with foreign travel (56).

Pathogen: *Salmonella,* nontyphoidal

Reported cases: Outbreak-related cases based on reports to CDC, 1983–1992 (10, 25). Passive surveillance estimate based on average number of cases reported to CDC, 1992–1997 (57). Active surveillance estimate based on extrapolation of the average 1996–1997 FoodNet rate to the 1997 U.S. population (23).

Total cases: Assumed to be 38 times the number of reported cases based on FoodNet data (Voetsch, manuscript in preparation) and the sequential surveillance artifact multiplier derived by Chalker and Blaser (21).

Hospitalization rate: Based on hospitalization rate for culture-confirmed cases reported to FoodNet, 1996–1997 (23, 24).

Case-fatality rate: Average case-fatality rate among cases reported to FoodNet, 1996–1997 (23, 24). This rate is lower than the previously published rate of 1.3% (58). Percent foodborne: Although occasionally associated with exposure to pets, reptiles, and contaminated water, salmonellosis is primarily a foodborne disease (59).

Pathogen: *Shigella* spp.

Reported cases: Outbreak-related cases based on reports to CDC, 1983–1992 (10, 25). Passive surveillance estimate based on average number of cases reported annually to CDC, 1992–1997 (57). Active surveillance estimate based on extrapolation of average 1996–1997 FoodNet rate to the 1997 U.S. population (23).

Total cases: Because Shigella frequently causes bloody diarrhea, total cases assumed to be 20 times the number of reported cases, based on similarity to E. coli O157:H7.

Hospitalization rate: Based on hospitalization rate for culture-confirmed cases reported to FoodNet, 1996–1997 (23, 24).

Case-fatality rate: Average case-fatality rate among cases reported to FoodNet, 1996–1997 (23, 24).

Percent foodborne: Assumed to be 20%. Although most cases are due to person-to-person transmission (60), foodborne outbreaks are responsible for a substantial number of cases (61).

Pathogen: *Staphylococcus aureus* (enterotoxin)

Reported cases: Not routinely reported. Assumed to be 10 times the number of foodborne outbreak-related cases reported to CDC, 1983–1992 (10, 25).

Total cases: Assumed to be 38 times the number of reported cases, by extrapolation from studies of salmonellosis.

Hospitalization rate: Determined from outbreaks reported to CDC, 1982–1992 (10, 25), (CDC, unpub. data), and published reports (62).

Case-fatality rate: Determined from reported outbreaks to CDC, 1977–1992 (10, 25, 63).

Percent foodborne: 100% by definition. Case estimates presented are based on foodborne outbreaks and therefore reflect foodborne transmission.

Comment: The number of outbreak-associated cases of staphylococcal food poisoning reported to CDC has decreased substantially since 1973 (Bean and Griffin, 1990). This decrease is unlikely to be an artifact of decreased recognition: there has been no compensatory increase in the number of foodborne outbreaks of unknown etiology with an incubation period consistent with staphylococcal food poisoning (CDC, unpub. data).

Pathogen: *Streptococcus,* Group A

Reported cases: Not routinely reported. Assumed to be 10 times the number of foodborne outbreak-related cases reported to CDC, 1982–1992 (10, 25).

Total cases: Assumed to be 38 times the number of reported cases, by extrapolation from studies of salmonellosis.

Hospitalization rate: Determined from outbreaks reported to CDC, 1982–1992 (10, 25) and CDC, unpub. data.

Case-fatality rate: Determined from outbreaks reported to CDC, 1982–1992 (10).

Percent foodborne: 100% foodborne by definition. Case estimates presented are based on foodborne outbreaks and therefore reflect foodborne transmission.

Pathogen: *Vibrio cholerae*, toxigenic O1 or O139.

Reported cases: Based on cases reported to CDC, 1988–1997 (7).

Total cases: Assumed that the number of clinically significant illnesses is two times the number of reported cases.

Hospitalization rate: Based on cases reported to CDC, 1992–1994 (64).

Case-fatality rate: Based on cases reported to CDC, 1992–1994 (64).

Percent foodborne: Assumed to be primarily foodborne. Most reported cases linked to foodborne outbreaks, and at least 65% of sporadic cases may be foodborne (64).

Comments: 96% of cases acquired abroad (64).

Pathogen: *Vibrio vulnificus*

Reported cases: Cases reported to CDC from 22 states, 1988–1996 (65).

Total cases: Because it is a severe illness, assumed to be two times the number of reported cases.

Hospitalization rate: Based on overall rate among cases reported to CDC, 1988–1996 (65).

Case-fatality rate: Based on overall rate among cases reported to CDC, 1988–1996; death rate higher among cases due to foodborne transmission (65).

Percent foodborne: Based on Shapiro et al. (65).

Comment: Most cases are reported by Gulf States (Florida, Alabama, Louisiana, Texas).

Pathogen: *Vibrio*, other spp.

Reported cases: Passive surveillance estimate based on cases reported to CDC, 1988–1996 (CDC, unpub. data). Active surveillance estimate based on 1996 FoodNet rate extrapolated to the 1997 U.S. population (23). FoodNet data from 1997 not included because of a large outbreak of Vibrio parahaemolyticus infections that could falsely elevate the overall rate.

Total cases: Because it is a moderately severe illness, total cases assumed to equal 20 times the reported cases, a degree of underreporting comparable with E. coli O157:H7 infections.

Hospitalization rate: Based on rate among non-vulnificus, non-cholerae O1 cases reported by Hlady (66).

Case-fatality rate: Based on rate among non-vulnificus, non-cholerae O1 cases reported by Hlady (66).

Percent foodborne: Based on history of shellfish consumption for cases reported by Hlady (66).

Comment: Because of larger sample size, data from Hlady (66) used in preference to FoodNet data for hospitalization and death rates.

Pathogen: *Yersinia enterocolitica*

Reported cases: Active surveillance estimate based on extrapolation of average 1996–1997 FoodNet rate to the 1997 U.S. population (23, 24).

Total cases: Assumed to be 38 times the number of reported cases, based on studies of salmonellosis.

Hospitalization rate: Based on the hospitalization rate for culture-confirmed cases reported to FoodNet, 1996–1997 (23, 24).

Case-fatality rate: Low, assumed to be 0.5% (23). Percent foodborne: Assumed to be 90%. Nearly all reported outbreaks in United States have been linked to contaminated foods, and pork is specifically believed to be the source of most infections (67).

PARASITIC PATHOGENS

Pathogen: *Cryptosporidium parvum*

Reported cases: Passive surveillance estimate based on the average annual number of cases reported to CDC, 1995–1997 (7). Active surveillance estimate based on extrapolation of the average 1997–98 FoodNet rate to the 1997 U.S. population (6, 24). Total cases: Published studies suggest that ~2% of all stools tested for Cryptosporidium are positive (68, 69). We assume this rate of infection applies to all patients visiting a healthcare provider for acute gastroenteritis. Using an estimate of ~15 million physician visits for diarrhea each year (see text), we estimate there are approximately 300,000 cases of cryptosporidiosis per year. This figure is 45-fold higher than the estimated number of reported cases based on FoodNet active surveillance, a multiplier only slightly larger than the one used for salmonellosis.

Hospitalization rate: Based on the hospitalization rate for culture-confirmed cases reported to FoodNet, 1997–1998 (6, 24).

Case-fatality rate: Average case-fatality rate among cases reported to FoodNet, 1997–1998 (6, 24).

Percent foodborne: Based on very limited information (70–72), we assume that 10% of cases are attributable to foodborne transmission, with the rest due to consumption of contaminated water or person-to-person transmission.

Comment: Cryptosporidiosis in AIDS is associated with a severe protracted course of diarrhea (73).

Pathogen: *Cyclospora cayetanensis*

Reported cases: Passive surveillance estimate based on average annual number of cases reported to CDC, 1995–1997 (7). Active surveillance estimate based on extrapolation of average 1997–1998 FoodNet rate to the 1997 U.S. population (6, 24).

Total cases: Assumed to be 38 times the number of reported cases based on studies of salmonellosis.

Hospitalization rate: Based on the hospitalization rate for culture-confirmed cases reported to FoodNet, 1997 (24).

Case-fatality rate: Very low (74, 75). Assumed to be 0.05%, comparable with Clostridium perfringens.

Percent foodborne: Assumed 90% foodborne, based on recent reported outbreaks (74, 75).

Pathogen: *Giardia lamblia*

Reported cases: Not routinely reported.

Total cases: Sensitive surveillance in two sites (Vermont and Wisconsin) suggests a rate of 40 cases per 100,000 persons per year (76, 77). In addition, an estimated 5% of all cases are reported. Thus, approximately 100,000 cases will be detected each year, representing 2,000,000 actual cases.

Hospitalization rate: An estimated 5,000 cases per year are severe enough to require hospitalization.

Case-fatality rate: Exceedingly low. Assumed to be no more than 10 deaths annually.

Percent foodborne: Assumed to be 10%. Recreational water is probably the major source of transmission (76–78); however, several foodborne outbreaks have been reported (79, 80).

Pathogen: *Toxoplasma gondii*

Reported cases: Not routinely reported.

Total cases: Based on national serologic data collected during the 1994 NHANES, approximately 40% of persons ≥ 60 years old are seropositive for toxoplasmosis (CDC, unpub. data). Assuming equal rates of infection over time, at least 0.6% of the population experiences an acute infection each year, representing approximately 1,500,000 infections per year. Approximately 15% of infections are symptomatic. Hospitalization rate: Varies widely according to host immune status. Data from NHDS indicate that from 1992 to 1996, toxoplasmosis was the first listed diagnosis for approximately 5,000 hospital discharges each year. We have used this figure as a conservative estimate of the number of actual hospitalizations.

Case-fatality rate: Varies widely according to host immune status. Of the approximately 5,000 hospital discharges annually for which toxoplasmosis is the first listed diagnosis, approximately 750 involve a deceased patient. We have used this figure as a conservative estimate of the number of actual deaths.

Percent foodborne: Although the proportion associated with eating contaminated food varies by geographic region, we assume an overall average of 50%. Recent unpublished data from Europe suggest that 60% of acute infections are from contaminated food (Ruth Gilbert, pers. comm.).

Comment: Typically, infection with Toxoplasma gondii produces an asymptomatic illness or a mild viral-like febrile illness with lymphadenopathy. Acute diarrhea is not commonly associated with acute infection. Estimates from the Massachusetts Department of Health suggest that one case of congenital toxoplasmosis occurs for every 10,000 births (81). Extrapolating to 4,000,000 live births in the United States, an estimated 400 children are born with congenital toxoplasmosis. Based on calculations by investigators from Stanford University, each year approximately 6,000 women who experience an acute infection during pregnancy and who do not receive treatment give birth to a child with congenital toxoplasmosis, which results in chronic sequelae (82). During an outbreak of toxoplasmosis in British Columbia, of an estimated 2,900–7,700 infections, 19 cases of retinitis were reported. If there are at least 150,000 symptomatic cases annually, from 300 to 1,050 cases (0.2% to 0.7%, respectively) of ocular toxoplasmosis could occur. If there are 300,000 cases, from 600 to 2,100 ocular cases could occur. Thus, there could be from 300 to 2,100 ocular cases of toxoplasmosis annually. An estimated 4,000 persons with AIDS develop Toxoplasma encephalitis annually. In summary, from (400 + 300 + 4,000) = 4,700 to (6,000 + 2,100 + 4,000) = 12,100 persons develop chronic sequelae due to toxoplasmosis each year.

Pathogen: *Trichinella spiralis*

Reported cases: Based on NETSS surveillance data, approximately 40 cases are reported annually.

Total cases: Because it can be a severe illness, assumed to be two times the number of reported cases.

Hospitalization rate: Based on outbreak-related cases reported to CDC, 1982–1992 (10).

Case-fatality rate: Assumed to be 0.3% based on data from a large series in Europe.

Percent foodborne: 100% (83)

Comment: Clinically, acute trichinosis may be asymptomatic or may have acute gastrointestinal symptoms, followed by a parenteral phase of fever and myalgias. In 10% to 20% of cases neurologic or cardiac symptoms develop, many severe and potentially leading to chronic illness.

VIRAL PATHOGENS

Pathogen: Rotavirus

Reported cases: Not routinely reported.

Total cases: Because every child has at least one symptomatic infection (84–86), the number of cases is assumed to equal the 1997 U.S. birth cohort (3.9 million).

Hospitalizations: 50,000 (87, 88).

Case-fatality rate: Very low: 20 to 40 deaths per year (89).

Percent foodborne: probably very low (< 1%) (90).

Pathogen: Astrovirus

Reported cases: Not routinely reported.

Total cases: Because every child has at least one symptomatic infection, the number of cases is assumed to equal the 1997 US birth cohort (3.9 million).

Hospitalizations: Assumed to equal 25% of number of hospitalizations for rotavirus (= 12,500) (91).

Case-fatality rate: Very low (< 10 deaths per year).

Percent foodborne: Probably very low (< 1%) (91).

Pathogen: Norwalk-like viruses (NLV).

Reported cases: Not routinely reported.

Total cases: Very few data are available for assessing the disease burden associated with Norwalk-like viruses, and very few studies have been conducted using the most sensitive diagnostics for NLVs. One community-based study from the Netherlands found 17% of cases of acute gastroenteritis were associated with Norwalk-like viruses, compared with 6% of controls, using reverse transcriptase polymerase chain reaction (RT-PCR) for detection of NLVs (92). An Australian study detected NLVs in 15% of hospitalized patients using immune electron microscopy (93). Studies have generally been conducted exclusively among young children or used less sensitive detection methods (electron microscopy); in these studies, NLVs have been detected in ~1% to 5% of participants (94–98). However, a recent study incorporating RT-PCR for viral detection among children 2 months to 2 years of age found that 21% of cases of acute gastroenteritis were associated with NLVs (99). Given these data, we assume that 11% of all episodes of acute primary gastroenteritis are due to NLVs (using the data from the best of the studies) (92).

Hospitalizations: NLV assumed to account for 11% of 452,000 annual hospitalizations for viral gastroenteritis (100).

Case-fatality rate: Low. NLV assumed to account for 11% of an estimated 2,800 fatal cases of viral gastroenteritis each year (100).

Percent foodborne: We assume that the proportion of all NLV-associated illness that is foodborne is 40%. This estimate is based on a recent report which found that 47% of NLV-associated acute gastroenteritis outbreaks in the United States in which the modes of transmission were known were foodborne (101). Since we would assume that foodborne-associated outbreaks might be more likely to be reported than Norwalk-like virus-associated outbreaks with other mechanisms of spread, the proportion was lowered to 40%.

This estimate is in general agreement with other reviews (102–104). No data are available to directly determine the proportion of cases of NLV-associated disease attributable to foodborne transmission.

Pathogen: Hepatitis A

Reported cases: Based on cases reported to CDC, 1992–1997 (7).

Total cases: Assumed to be three times the number of reported cases (105).

Hospitalizations: Thirteen percent; based on data from CDC Sentinel Counties Studies (106);

Case-fatality rate: 0.3%; based on data from the viral Hepatitis Surveillance Program and the CDC Sentinel Counties Studies (105, 107). Deaths calculated by applying the case-fatality rate to reported cases.

Percent foodborne: Foodborne transmission accounts for approximately 5% of outbreaks of known source (105). Note that the source is not determined in approximately 50% of hepatitis A outbreaks, and foodborne transmission could account for a far higher percentage of cases.

ACKNOWLEDGMENTS

We thank Fred Angulo, Beth Bell, Thomas Breuer, Cindy Friedman, Roger Glass, Eric Mintz, Steven Ostroff, Morris Potter, David Swerdlow, Tom Van Gilder, and two anonymous reviewers for their comments. Dr. Mead is a medical epidemiologist with the Foodborne and Diarrheal Diseases Branch, CDC, in Atlanta, Georgia. His professional interests include infectious diseases surveillance, outbreak investigations, and interventions to prevent foodborne illness.

REFERENCES FROM THE READING

1. Bryan FL. Diseases transmitted by foods. Atlanta: Centers for Disease Control; 1982.

2. Archer DL, Kvenberg JE. Incidence and cost of foodborne diarrheal disease in the United States. J Food Protect 1985;48:887–94.

3. Bennett J, Holmberg S, Rogers M, Solomon S. Infectious and parasitic diseases. In: Amler R, Dull H, editors. Closing the gap: the burden of unnecessary illness. New York: Oxford Univ Press; 1987:102–14.

4. Todd ECD. Preliminary estimates of costs of foodborne disease in the United States. J Food Protect 1989;52:595–601.

5. Foodborne pathogens: risks and consequences. Ames, IA: Council of Agricultural Science and Technology; 1994.

6. 1998 FoodNet Surveillance Results. Preliminary Report. Atlanta: Centers for Disease Control and Prevention; 1999.

7. Summary of notifiable diseases, United States, 1997. MMWR Morb Mortal Wkly Rep 1997;46(54).

8. Bean NH, Martin SM, Bradford H. PHLIS: an electronic system for reporting public health data from remote sites. Am J Public Health 1992; 82:1273–76.

9. Levine W, Griffin P, Gulf Coast Vibrio Working Group. Vibrio infections on the Gulf Coast: results of first year regional surveillance. J Infect Dis 1993;167:479–83.

10. Foodborne disease outbreaks, 5-year summary, 1983–1987. MMWR 1992;39(SS-1):15–57.

11. Woodwell DA. National Ambulatory Medical Care Survey: 1996 Summary. Advance data from vital and health statistics; no. 295. Hyattsville, Maryland: National Center for Health Statistics; 1997.

12. McCaig LF, McLemore T. Plan and operation of the National Hospital Ambulatory Medical Care Survey. Hyattsville: National Center for Health Statistics; 1994.

13. McCaig LF. National Hospital Ambulatory Medical Care Survey: 1996 Outpatient Department Summary. Advance data from vital and health statistics: no. 294. Hyattsville, Maryland: National Center for Health Statistics; 1997.

14. McCaig LF, Stussman BJ. National Hospital Ambulatory Medical Care Survey: 1996 Emergency Department Summary. Advance data from vital and health statistics: no. 293. Hyattsville, Maryland: National Center for Health Statistics; 1997.

15. Graves EJ, Gillium BS. Detailed diagnoses and procedures, National Hospital Discharge Survey, 1995. National Center for Health Statistics. Vital Health Stat 1997;13.

16. NCHS. Public use data tape documentation. Multiple cause of death for ICD-9. Hyattsville, Maryland: Public Health Service; 1998.

17. Schneider D, Appleton L, McLemore T. A reason for visit classification for ambulatory care. Hyattsville, Maryland: National Center for Health Statistics; 1979.

18. Public Health Service and Health Care Financing Administration. International classification of diseases, 9th Revision, Clinical Modification. Washington D.C.: Public Health Service; 1991.

19. Monto AS, Koopman JS. The Tecumseh Study. XI. Occurrence of acute enteric illness in the community. Am J Epidemiol 1980;112:323–333.

20. Dingle JH, Badger GF, Jordan W. Gastrointestinal illness. In: Illness in the home. A study of 25,000 illness in a group of Cleveland families. Cleveland: The Press of Western Reserve University; 1964:129–61.

21. Chalker R, Blaser M. A review of human salmonellosis: III. Magnitude of Salmonella infection in the United States. Rev Infect Dis 1988;10:111–24.

22. Hedberg C, Angulo F, Townes J, Vugia D, Farley M, FoodNet. Differences in Escherichia coli O157:H7 annual incidence among FoodNet active surveillance sites. Baltimore, MD; 1997 June 22–26, 1997.

23. 1996 Final FoodNet surveillance report. Atlanta: Centers for Disease Control and Prevention; 1998.

24. 1997 Final FoodNet surveillance report. Atlanta: Centers for Disease Control and Prevention; 1998.

25. Surveillance for foodborne-disease outbreaks—United States, 1988–1992. MMWR 1996;45(No. SS-5):2–55.

26. Parsonnet J, Wanke CA, Hack H. Idiopathic chronic diarrhea. In: Blaser MJ, Smith PD, Ravdin JI, Greenberg HB, Guerrant RL, editors. Infections of the gastrointestinal tract. New York: Raven Press, Ltd; 1995: 311–23.

27. Garthright WE, Archer DL, Kvenberg JE. Estimates of incidence and cost of infectious diseases in the United States. Pub Health Reports 1988; 103:107–15.

28. Population estimates. Available at http://www.census.gov/population/www/estimates/popest.html ed: Bureau of the Census, Economics and Statistics Administration, US Department of Commerce.

29. Helmick CG, Griffin PM, Addiss DG, Tauxe RV, Juranek DD. Infectious diarrhea. In: Everhart JE, editor. Digestive diseases in the United States: epidemiology and impact. U.S. Department of Health and Human Service, National Institutes of Health, National Institute of Diabetes and Digestive Diseases. Washington, D.C.: U.S. Government Printing Office; 1994: 85–123.

30. Dugger BC, Lewis WF. Comparability of diagnostic data coded by the 8th and 9th revisions of the international classification of diseases. Washington, D.C.: U.S. Government Printing Office 1987: DHHS publication no. (PHS) 87-1378. (Vital and health statistics: series 2, no. 104).

31. Wheeler JG, Sethi D, Cowden JM, Wall PG, Rodrigues LC, Tompkins DS, et al. Study of infectious intestinal disease in England: rates in the community, presenting to general practice, and reported to national surveillance. The Infectious Intestinal Disease Study Executive. BMJ 1999;318:1046–50.

32. Feldman RA, Banatvala N. The frequency of culturing stools from adults with diarrhea in Great Britain. Epidemiol Infect 1994;113:41–4.

33. Talan DA, Moran GJ, Mower WR, Newdow M, Ong S, Slutsker L, et al. Emergency ID NET: an emergency department-based emerging infections sentinel network. Ann Emerg Med 1998;32:703–11.

34. Levine W, Smart J, Archer D, Bean N, Tauxe R. Foodborne disease outbreaks in nursing homes, 1975 through 1987. JAMA 1991;266:2105–09.

35. Taylor JP, Perdue JN. The changing epidemiology of human brucellosis in Texas. Am J Epidemiol 1989;130:160–5.

36. Dalrymple-Champneys W. Brucella infection and undulant fever in man. London: Oxford University Press; 1960.

37. Chomel B, DeBess E, Mangiamele D, Reilly K, Farver T, Sun R, et al. Changing trends in the epidemiology of human brucellosis in California from 1973 to 1992: a shift toward foodborne transmission. J Infect Dis 1994;170: 1216–23.

38. Tauxe R. Epidemiology of Campylobacter jejuni infections in the United States and other industrialized nations. In: Nachamkin, Blaser M, Tompkins L, editors. Campylobacter jejuni: current status and future trends; 1992. p. 9–19.

39. Mishu B, Blaser MJ. Role of infection due to Campylobacter jejuni in the initiation of Guillain-Barré syndrome. Clin Infec Dis 1993;17:104–8.

40. Bartlett JG. Gas gangrene (other Clostridium-associated diseases). In: Mandell GL, Douglas RG, Bennett JE, editors. Principles and practice of infectious diseases. Third ed. New York: Churchill Livingstone; 1990: 1850–60.

41. Slutsker L, Ries AA, Greene KD, Wells JG, Hutwagner L, Griffin PM. Escherichia coli O157:H7 diarrhea in the United States: clinical and epidemiologic features. Ann Intern Med 1997;126:505–13.

42. Pai CH, Ahmed N, Lior H, Johnson WM, Sims HV, Woods DE. Epidemiology of sporadic diarrhea due to verocytotoxin-producing Escherichia coli: a two-year prospective study. J Infect Dis 1988;157:1054–7.

43. Bokete TN, O'Callahan CM, Clausen CR, Tang NM, Tran N, Moseley SL, et al. Shiga-like toxin-producing Escherichia coli in Seattle children: a prospective study. Gastroenterology 1993;105:1724–31.

44. Acheson DWK, Breuker SD, Donohue-Rolfe A, Kozak K, Yi A, Keusch GT. Development of a clinically useful diagnostic enzyme immunoassay for enterohemorrhagic Escherichia coli infection. In: Karmali MA, Goglio AG, editors. Recent advances in verocytotoxin-producing Escherichia coli infections. Amsterdam: Elsevier Science B. V.; 1994:109–12.

45. Park CH, Gates KM, Vandel NM, Hixon DL. Isolation of Shiga-like toxin producing Escherichia coli (O157 and non-O157) in a community hospital. Diagn Microbiol Infect Dis 1996;26:69–72.

46. Tarr PI, Neill MA. Perspective: the problem of non- O157:H7 shiga toxin (Verocytotoxin)-producing Escherichia coli [comment]. J Infect Dis 1996;174:1136–9.

47. Rowe PC, Orrbine E, Lior H, Wells GA, McLaine PN. A prospective study of exposure to verotoxin-producing Escherichia coli among Canadian children with haemolytic uraemic syndrome. The CPKDRC coinvestigators. Epidemiol Infect 1993;110:1–7.

48. Johnson R, Clark R, Wilson J, Read S, Rhan K, Renwick S, et al. Growing concerns and recent outbreaks involving non-O157:H7 serotypes of verocytogenic Escherichia coli. J Food Protect 1996;59:1112–22.

49. Nataro JP, Kaper JB. Diarrheogenic Escherichia coli. Clin Microbiol Rev 1998;11:1–60.

50. Hedberg CW, Savarino SJ, Besser JM, Paulus CJ, Thelen VM, Myers LJ, et al. An outbreak of foodborne illness caused by Escherichia coli O39:NM, an agent not fitting into the existing scheme for classifying diarrheogenic E. coli. J Infect Dis 1997;176:1625–8.

51. Tappero J, Schuchat A, Deaver K, Mascola L, Wenger J. Reduction in the incidence of human listeriosis in the United States. Effectiveness of prevention efforts. JAMA 995;273:1118–22.

52. Slutsker L, Schuchat A. Listeriosis in Humans. In: Ryser E, Marth E, editors. Listeria, listeriosis, and food safety. New York: Marcel Dekker; 1999: 75–96.

53. Schuchat A, Lizano C, Broome C, Swaminathan B, Kim C, Winn K. Outbreak of neonatal listeriosis associated with mineral oil. Pediatr Infect Dis J 1991;10:183–9.

54. Hoffman TA, Ruiz CJ, Counts GW, Sachs JM, Nitzkin JL. Waterborne typhoid fever in Dade County, Florida. Clinical and therapeutic evaluation of 105 bacteremic patients. Am J Med 1975;59:481–7.

55. Klotz SA, Jorgensen JH, Buckwold FJ, Craven PC. Typhoid fever. An epidemic with remarkably few clinical signs and symptoms. Arch Intern Med 1984;144:533–7.

56. Mermin J, Townes J, Gerber M, Dolan N, Mintz E, Tauxe R. Typhoid fever in the United States,1985-1994. Arch Intern Med 1998;158:633–638.

57. Laboratory confirmed Salmonella surveillance. Annual Summary, 1997. Atlanta, Georgia: Centers for Disease Control and Prevention; 1999.

58. Cohen M, Tauxe R. Drug-resistant Salmonella in the United States: an epidemiologic perspective. Science 1986;234:964–9.

59. Tauxe R. Salmonella: a postmodern pathogen. J Food Protect 1991;54:563–8.

60. DuPont HL. Shigella species. In: Mandell GL, Douglas RG, Bennett JE, editors. Principles and practice of infectious diseases. 3rd ed. New York: Churchill Livingstone; 1990:1716–22.

61. Black RE, Craun GF, Blake PA. Epidemiology of common-source outbreaks of shigellosis in the United States, 1961-1975. Am J Epidemiol 1978;108:47–52.

62. Levine WC, Bennett RW, Choi Y, Henning KJ, Rager JR, Hendricks KA, et al. Staphylococcal food poisoning caused by imported canned mushrooms. J Infect Dis 1996;173:1263–7.

63. Holmberg S, Blake P. Staphylococcal food poisoning in the United States. JAMA 1984;251:487–9.

64. Mahon B, Mintz E, Greene K, Wells J, Tauxe R. Reported cholera in the United States, 1992–1994. JAMA 1996;276:307–12.

65. Shapiro RL, Altekruse S, Hutwagner L, Bishop R, Hammond R, Wilson S, et al. The role of Gulf Coast oysters harvested in warmer months in Vibrio vulnificus infections in the United States, 1988-1996. Vibrio Working Group. J Infect Dis 1998;178:752–9.

66. Hlady W, Klontz K. The epidemiology of Vibrio infections in Florida, 1981–1993. J Infect Dis 1996;173:1176–83.

67. Ostroff S. Yersinia as an emerging infection: epidemiologic aspects of Yersiniosis. Contributions to Microbiology & Immunology 1995;13:5–10.

68. Skeels MR, Sokolow R, Hubbard CV, Andrus JK, Baisch J. Cryptosporidium infection in Oregon public health clinic patients, 1985–88: the value of statewide laboratory surveillance. Am J Public Health 1990;80:305–8.

69. Roberts CL, Morin C, Addiss DG, Wahlquist SP, Mshar PA, Hadler JL. Factors influencing Cryptosporidium testing in Connecticut. J Clin Microbiol 1996;34:2292–3.

70. Petersen C. Cryptosporidium and the food supply. Lancet 1995;345:1128–9.

71. Djuretic T, Wall PG, Nichols G. General outbreaks of infectious intestinal disease associated with milk and dairy products in England and Wales: 1992 to 1996. Commun Dis Rep CDR Wkly 1997;7:R41–5.

72. Outbreaks of Escherichia coli O157:H7 infection and cryptosporidiosis associated with drinking unpasteurized apple cider—Connecticut and New York, October 1996. MMWR 1997;46:4–8.

73. Petersen C. Cryptosporidiosis in patients infected with the human immunodeficiency virus [see comments]. Clin Infect Dis 1992;15:903–9.

74. Herwaldt BL, Ackers ML. An outbreak in 1996 of cyclosporiasis associated with imported raspberries. The Cyclospora Working Group [see comments]. N Engl J Med 1997;336:1548–56.

75. Herwaldt BL, Beach MJ. The return of Cyclospora in 1997: another outbreak of cyclosporiasis in North America associated with imported raspberries. Cyclospora Working Group [see comments]. Ann Intern Med 1999; 130:210–20.

76. Addiss DG, Davis JP, Roberts JM, Mast EE. Epidemiology of giardiasis in Wisconsin: increasing incidence of reported cases and unexplained seasonal trends. Am J Trop Med Hyg 1992;47:13–9.

77. Birkhead G, Vogt RL. Epidemiologic surveillance for endemic Giardia lamblia infection in Vermont. The roles of waterborne and person-to-person transmission. Am J Epidemiol 1989;129:762–8.

78. Dennis DT, Smith RP, Welch JJ, Chute CG, Anderson B, Herndon JL, et al. Endemic giardiasis in New Hampshire: a case-control study of environmental risks. J Infect Dis 1993;167:1391–5.

79. Petersen LR, Cartter ML, Hadler JL. A food-borne outbreak of Giardia lamblia. J Infect Dis 1988;157:846–848.

80. Osterholm MT, Forfang JC, Ristinen TL, Dean AG, Washburn JW, Godes JR, et al. An outbreak of foodborne giardiasis. N Engl J Med 1981;304: 24-8.

81. Guerina NG, Hsu HW, Meissner HC, Maguire JH, Lynfield R, Stechenberg B, et al. Neonatal serologic screening and early treatment for congenital Toxoplasma gondii infection. The New England Regional Toxoplasma Working Group [see comments]. N Engl J Med 1994;330:1858–63.

82. Wong SY, Remington JS. Toxoplasmosis in pregnancy [see comments]. Clin Infect Dis 1994;18:853–61.

83. Capo V, Despommier DD. Clinical aspects of infection with Trichinella spp. Clinical Microbiology Reviews 1996;9:47–54.

84. Tucker A, Haddix A, Bresee J, Holman R, Parashar U, Glass R. Cost-effectiveness analysis of a rotavirus immunization program for the United States. JAMA 1998;279:1371–76.

85. Rodriguez WJ, Kim HW, Brandt CD, Schwartz RH, Gardner MK, Jeffries B, et al. Longitudinal study of rotavirus infection and gastroenteritis in families served by a pediatric medical practice: clinical and epidemiologic observations. Pediatr Infect Dis J 1987;6:170–6.

86. Gurwith M, Wenman W, Hinde D, Feltham S, Greenberg H. A prospective study of rotavirus infection in infants and young children. J Infect Dis 1981;144:218–24.

87. Parashar UD, Holman RC, Clarke MJ, Bresee JS, Glass RI. Hospitalizations associated with rotavirus diarrhea in the United States, 1993 through 1995: surveillance based on the new ICD-9-CM rotavirus-specific diagnostic code. J Infect Dis 1998;177:13–7.

88. Jin S, Kilgore PE, Holman RC, Clarke MJ, Gangarosa EJ, Glass RI. Trends in hospitalizations for diarrhea in United States children from 1979 through 1992: estimates of the morbidity associated with rotavirus. Pediatr Infect Dis J 1996;15:397–404.

89. Kilgore PE, Holman RC, Clarke MJ, Glass RI. Trends of diarrheal disease-associated mortality in US children, 1968 through 1991. JAMA 1995; 274:1143–48.

90. Kapikian AZ, Chanock RM. Rotaviruses. In: Fields BN, DM DMK, Howley PM, et al, editors. Fields Virology. 3rd ed. Philadelphia: Lippincott-Raven; 1996: 1657–708.

91. Glass RI, Noel J, Mitchell D, Herrmann JE, Blacklow NR, Pickering LK, et al. The changing epidemiology of astrovirus-associated gastroenteritis: a review. Arch Virol Suppl 1996;12:287–300.

92. Koopmans M, van Duynhoven Y, van de Heide R, et al. Molecular detection and epidemiology of Norwalk-like viruses and Sapporo-like viruses in the Netherlands. Presented at the International Workshop on Human Caliciviruses, Atlanta, Georgia, USA; 1999 Mar 29–31.

93. Grohman G. Viral diarrhoea in children in Australia. In: Tzipori S, et al, editors. Infectious diarrhoea of the young. New York: Elsevier Science Publishers; 1985.

94. Wolfaardt M, Taylor MB, Booysen HF, Englebrecht L, Grabow WOK, Jiang X. Incidence of human calicivirus and rotavirus infection in patients with gastroenteritis in South Africa. J Med Virol 1997;51:290–6.

95. Vial P, Kotloff KL, Tall BD, Morris JG, Levine MM. Detection by immune electron microscopy of 27-nm viral particles associated with community-acquired diarrhea in children. J Infect Dis 1989;161:571–3.

96. Donneli G, Ruggeri FM, Tinari A, Marziano ML, Menichella D, Caione D, et al. A three-year diagnostic and epidemiologic study on viral infantile diarrhoea in Rome. Epidemiol Infect 1988;100:311–20.

97. Riepenhoff-Talty M, Saif LJ, Barrett HJ, Suzuki H, Ogra PL. Potential spectrum of etiologic agents of viral enteritis in hospitalized patients. J Clin Microbiol 1983;17:352–6.

98. Suzuki H, Konno T, Kutsuzawa T, Imai A, Tazawa F, Ishida N, et al. The occurrence of calicivirus in infants with acute gastroenteritis. J Med Virol 1979;4:321–6.

99. Pang X, Joensuu J, Vesikari T. Human calicivirus-associated sporadic gastroenteritis in Finnish children less than 2 years of age followed prospectively during a rotavirus vaccine trial. Pediatr Infect Dis J 1999;18:420–6.

100. Mounts A, Holman R, Clarke M, Bresee J, Glass R. Trends in hospitalizations associated with gastroenteritis among adults in the United States, 1979-1995. Epi Infect . In press 1999.

101. Fankhauser RL NJ, Monroe SS, Ando T, Glass RI. Molecular epidemiology of "Norwalk-like viruses" in outbreaks of gastroenteritis in the United States. J Infect Dis 1998;178:1571–8.

102. Kaplan JE, Feldman R, Campbell DS, Lookabaugh C, Gary WG. The frequency of a Norwalk-like pattern of illness in outbreaks of acute gastroenteritis. Am J Pub Health 1982;72:1329–2.

103. Sekine S, Okada S, Hayashi Y. Prevalence of small round structured virus infections in acute gastroenteritis outbreaks in Tokyo. Microbiol Immunol 1989;33:207–17.

104. Viral Gastroenteritis Sub-Committee of the PHLS Virology Committee. Outbreaks of gastroenteritis associated with SRSVs. PHLS Microbiol Digest 1998;10:1–8.

105. Hepatitis surveillance report no. 56. Atlanta: U.S. Department of Health and Human Services, Public Health Service, CDC. 1996.

106. Bell BP, Shapiro CN, Alter MJ, Moyer LA, Judson FN, Mottram K, et al. The diverse patterns of hepatitis A epidemiology in the United States. Implications for vaccination strategies. J Infect Dis 1998;178:1579–84.

107. Hoofnagle JH, Carithers RL, Shapiro C, Ascher N. Fulminant hepatic failure. Summary of a workshop. Hepatology 1995;21:240–252.

Note the correspondence which followed.

READING 25
Food-Related Illness and Death in the United States: Letters

Centers for Disease Control and Prevention. Letters. *Emerg Infect Dis*. 1999;5:143–146. Available from http://www.cdc.gov/ncidod/eid/vol5no6/letters.htm.

To the Editor: Dr. Mead and colleagues should be commended for attempting to estimate the prevalence of foodborne disease in the United States (1). Their study provides more complete estimates than previous studies in terms of the number of foodborne pathogens included; for example, it includes the first realistic estimate of the number of cases of disease due to Norwalk-like caliciviruses. However, the publication of these estimates raises some important issues.

Even though "accurate estimates of disease burden are the foundation of sound public health policy" (2), most of these estimates (in particular, the assumption that unknown agents are transmitted by food in the same proportion as known agents) were derived from assumptions rather than data. Known foodborne agents clearly cannot account for most gastrointestinal illnesses (1). However, illnesses from unknown agents may be as likely to have the transmission characteristics of rotavirus (1% foodborne) or *Cryptosporidium* (10% foodborne) as those of the Norwalk-like viruses (40% foodborne). Furthermore, it was assumed that detecting outbreaks or cases of toxin-mediated illnesses (e.g., due to *Bacillus cereus*, *Staphylococcus aureus*, or *Clostridium perfringens)* follows the model of *Salmonella*. In the authors' entire list of known food-

borne agents, data are presented for cases identified both from outbreaks and active surveillance for only three agents: *Salmonella, Shigella*, and *Campylobacter*. *Salmonella* is clearly the most highly characterized, hence the most attractive as a model. However, the ratios of the numbers of cases detected through active surveillance to the numbers of cases detected through outbreaks range from 10 for *Salmonella* to more than 400 for *Campylobacter*. What if the ratios for toxin-mediated illnesses were more similar to *Campylobacter* than to *Salmonella* ratios? The total estimated cases of these illnesses would increase by a factor of 40. The inadequacy of simply applying a *Salmonella*-based multiplier to the number of cases reported from outbreaks can be demonstrated by applying that multiplier to the total number of cases reported in all foodborne disease outbreaks, typically 15,000 to 20,000 per year (3, 4). On the basis of these estimates, the number of foodborne illnesses would range from 5.7 million to 7.6 million, including illnesses caused by unknown agents.

The authors make similar assumptions for hospitalizations and deaths: unknown agents are estimated to account for 81% of hospitalizations and 65% of deaths due to foodborne illnesses. In a retrospective review of death certificate data similar to that used by Mead and colleagues, Perkins et al. projected the number of unexplained deaths possibly due to infectious diseases they expected to find in the Emerging Infections Program sites (5). Prospectively, a much smaller number of unexplained deaths was actually found, because known causes were identified through a detailed review of the death certificates and cases (6). A prospective examination of death certificates for foodborne diseases might also result in a smaller than expected yield.

The need to rely on assumptions to generate estimates highlights the gaps in our understanding of foodborne diseases. A dozen different studies could address these data gaps. However, once the 76 million figure is agreed upon, the perceived need for these studies will decrease.

Finally, if these estimates are accepted as reasonable, do current food safety efforts represent sound public policy? If 82% of foodborne illnesses, 81% of hospitalizations, and 65% of deaths are caused by agents we have not yet identified, where is the commitment of resources needed to identify them? If eradicating *Campylobacter*, *Salmonella*, *Escherichia coli* O157:H7, and *Listeria* would reduce the number of foodborne illnesses by only 5%, hospitalizations by 10%, and deaths by 25%, why are these agents the primary focus of our national foodborne disease control efforts? Overestimating the occurrence of foodborne diseases caused by unknown agents may lead us to undervalue the public health importance of these and other well-known agents.

Estimating the occurrence of foodborne diseases is daunting. The numerous efforts, including this one by Mead et al., to provide estimates have serious shortcomings. The real challenge is to identify the gaps in our knowledge so that they can be systematically addressed and updated estimates of foodborne illness can be provided to guide prevention efforts and assess the effectiveness of current food safety measures (2).

Craig Hedberg
University of Minnesota,
Minneapolis, Minnesota, USA

REFERENCES

1. Mead PS, Slutsker L, Dietz V, McCaig LF, Bresee JS, Shapiro C, et al. Food-related illness and death in the United States. Emerg Infect Dis 1999;5:607–25.

2. Centers for Disease Control and Prevention. CDC data provides the most complete estimate on foodborne disease in the United States. Press release available at URL: http://www.cdc.gov/od/oc/media/pressrel/r990917.htm

3. Foodborne disease outbreaks, 5-year summary, 1983–1987. MMWR Morb Mortal Wkly Rep 1992;39(SS-1):1–15.

4. Surveillance for foodborne disease outbreaks. United States, 1988–92. MMWR Morb Mortal Wkly Rep 1996;45(SS-5):2–55.

5. Perkins BA, Flood JM, Danila R, Holman RC, Reingold AL, Klug LA, et al. Unexplained deaths due to possibly infectious causes in the United States: defining the problem and designing surveillance and laboratory approaches. Emerg Infect Dis 1996;2:47–53.

6. Minnesota Department of Health. Annual summary of communicable diseases reported to the Minnesota Department of Health, 1998. Disease Control Newsletter 1999;27:29–30.

FOOD-RELATED ILLNESS AND DEATH IN THE UNITED STATES REPLY TO DR. HEDBERG

To the Editor: Like all scientific undertakings, our estimates require assumptions. Because the actual frequency of foodborne transmission of unknown agents cannot be measured directly, it must be assumed. If unknown agents had transmission characteristics similar to those of rotavirus (1% foodborne transmission) or cryptosporidium (10% foodborne transmission), as Dr. Hedberg suggests, the number of cases of foodborne illness caused by unknown agents would be substantially lower than we estimated. However, unknown agents could just as easily have the transmission characteristics of *Escherichia coli* O157:H7 or *Campylobacter* (80% foodborne transmission), which just 30 years ago were "unknown agents." For the sake of objectivity, we based our assumption on the aggregate of information for known pathogens rather than on "expert opinion." Interestingly, however, the Council of Science and Technology's "expert opinion" of the percentage of diarrheal illness due to foodborne transmission was 35% (1), nearly identical to the figure we developed.

As noted in our article, pathogen-specific multipliers for underreporting are needed for many diseases. For lack of a better model, we assumed that the underreporting of toxin-mediated diseases follows the model of *Salmonella*. The alternative Dr. Hedberg suggests, *Campylobacter*, is also a nontoxin-mediated bacterial infection like *Salmonella*, but one for which the degree of underreporting is less well documented. Extrapolating from outbreak data to the number of sporadic cases does indeed have limitations, which is the reason we used it for only the few diseases for which other surveillance data were not available.

Regarding deaths attributed to unknown agents, prospective studies may show that some of these deaths are in fact caused by known agents. However, this would not necessarily lessen the overall impact of foodborne illness: it would merely shift the number of deaths from the unknown category to the known category. The possibility that some deaths attributed to unknown agents are in fact caused by *Salmonella* and other known pathogens supports our use of data on known pathogens to estimate the frequency of foodborne transmission for unknown agents.

Improved estimates will require expanded research into the etiologic spectrum of undiagnosed illness. In the meantime, documenting the substantial impact of foodborne illness neither devalues current surveillance and prevention efforts nor undermines future efforts to determine the causes and impact of foodborne diseases. Our estimates help define gaps in existing knowledge and provide a more rational basis for public health policy than reliance on decades-old data.

Paul S. Mead, Laurence Slutsker,
Patricia M. Griffin, Robert V. Tauxe
Centers for Disease Control and Prevention,
Atlanta, Georgia, USA

DISCUSSION QUESTIONS

1. This is an important article that demonstrates methods used to assess the burden of food-related illness. Discuss the letter writer's objection; what do you think about that?

2. Go to more updated sources available today. Use the same methods Mead et al. used to characterize one (or more) foodborne diseases of your choice. Are you able to find the statistics you need from more than two sources?

REFERENCES FROM THE READING

1. Bryan FL. Diseases transmitted by foods. Atlanta: Centers for Disease Control; 1982.

2. Archer DL, Kvenberg JE. Incidence and cost of foodborne diarrheal disease in the United States. J Food Protect 1985;48:887–94.

3. Bennett J, Holmberg S, Rogers M, Solomon S. Infectious and parasitic diseases. In: Amler R, Dull H, editors. Closing the gap: the burden of unnecessary illness. New York: Oxford Univ Press; 1987: 102–14.

4. Todd ECD. Preliminary estimates of costs of foodborne disease in the United States. J Food Protect 1989;52:595–601.

5. Foodborne pathogens: risks and consequences. Ames, IA: Council of Agricultural Science and Technology; 1994.

6. 1998 FoodNet Surveillance Results. Preliminary Report. Atlanta: Centers for Disease Control and Prevention; 1999.

7. Summary of notifiable diseases, United States, 1997. MMWR Morb Mortal Wkly Rep 1997;46(54).

8. Bean NH, Martin SM, Bradford H. PHLIS: an electronic system for reporting public health data from remote sites. Am J Public Health 1992;82:1273–76.

9. Levine W, Griffin P, Gulf Coast Vibrio Working Group. Vibrio infections on the Gulf Coast: results of first year regional surveillance. J Infect Dis 1993;167:479–83.

10. Foodborne disease outbreaks, 5-year summary, 1983–1987. MMWR 1992;39 (SS-1):15–57.

11. Woodwell DA. National Ambulatory Medical Care Survey: 1996 Summary. Advance data from vital and health statistics; no. 295. Hyattsville, Maryland: National Center for Health Statistics; 1997.

12. McCaig LF, McLemore T. Plan and operation of the National Hospital Ambulatory Medical Care Survey. Hyattsville: National Center for Health Statistics; 1994.

13. McCaig LF. National Hospital Ambulatory Medical Care Survey: 1996 Outpatient Department Summary. Advance data from vital and health statistics: no. 294. Hyattsville, Maryland: National Center for Health Statistics; 1997.

14. McCaig LF, Stussman BJ. National Hospital Ambulatory Medical Care Survey: 1996 Emergency Department Summary. Advance data from vital and health statistics: no. 293. Hyattsville, Maryland: National Center for Health Statistics; 1997.

15. Graves EJ, Gillium BS. Detailed diagnoses and procedures, National Hospital Discharge Survey, 1995. National Center for Health Statistics. Vital Health Stat 1997;13.

16. NCHS. Public use data tape documentation. Multiple cause of death for ICD-9. Hyattsville, Maryland: Public Health Service; 1998.

17. Schneider D, Appleton L, McLemore T. A reason for visit classification for ambulatory care. Hyattsville, Maryland: National Center for Health Statistics; 1979.

18. Public Health Service and Health Care Financing Administration. International classification of diseases, 9th Revision, Clinical Modification. Washington D.C.: Public Health Service; 1991.

19. Monto AS, Koopman JS. The Tecumseh Study. XI. Occurrence of acute enteric illness in the community. Am J Epidemiol 1980;112:323–333.

20. Dingle JH, Badger GF, Jordan W. Gastrointestinal illness. In: Illness in the home. A study of 25,000 illness in a group of Cleveland families. Cleveland: The Press of Western Reserve University; 1964: 129–61.

21. Chalker R, Blaser M. A review of human salmonellosis: III. Magnitude of Salmonella infection in the United States. Rev Infect Dis 1988;10:111–24.

22. Hedberg C, Angulo F, Townes J, Vugia D, Farley M, FoodNet. Differences in Escherichia coli O157:H7 annual incidence among FoodNet active surveillance sites. Baltimore, MD; 1997 June 22–26, 1997.

23. 1996 Final FoodNet surveillance report. Atlanta: Centers for Disease Control and Prevention; 1998.

24. 1997 Final FoodNet surveillance report. Atlanta: Centers for Disease Control and Prevention; 1998.

25. Surveillance for foodborne-disease outbreaks United States, 1988–1992. MMWR 1996;45(No. SS-5):2–55.

26. Parsonnet J, Wanke CA, Hack H. Idiopathic chronic diarrhea. In: Blaser MJ, Smith PD, Ravdin JI, Greenberg HB, Guerrant RL, editors. Infections of the gastrointestinal tract. New York: Raven Press, Ltd; 1995: 311–23.

27. Garthright WE, Archer DL, Kvenberg JE. Estimates of incidence and cost of infectious diseases in the United States. Pub Health Reports 1988;103: 107–15.

28. Population estimates. Available at http://www.census.gov/population/www/estimates/popest.html ed: Bureau of the Census, Economics and Statistics Administration, US Department of Commerce.

29. Helmick CG, Griffin PM, Addiss DG, Tauxe RV, Juranek DD. Infectious diarrheas. In: Everhart JE, editor. Digestive diseases in the United States: epidemiology and impact. U.S. Department of Health and Human Service, National Institutes of Health, National Institute of Diabetes and Digestive Diseases. Washington, D.C.: U.S. Government Printing Office; 1994: 85–123.

30. Dugger BC, Lewis WF. Comparability of diagnostic data coded by the 8th and 9th revisions of the international classification of diseases. Washington, D.C.: U.S. Government Printing Office 1987: DHHS publication no. (PHS) 87-1378. (Vital and health statistics: series 2, no. 104).

31. Wheeler JG, Sethi D, Cowden JM, Wall PG, Rodrigues LC, Tompkins DS, et al. Study of infectious intestinal disease in England: rates in the community, presenting to general practice, and reported to national surveillance. The Infectious Intestinal Disease Study Executive. BMJ 1999;318:1046–50.

32. Feldman RA, Banatvala N. The frequency of culturing stools from adults with diarrhea in Great Britain. Epidemiol Infect 1994;113:41–4.

33. Talan DA, Moran GJ, Mower WR, Newdow M, Ong S, Slutsker L, et al. Emergency ID NET: an emergency department-based emerging infections sentinel network. Ann Emerg Med 1998;32:703–11.

34. Levine W, Smart J, Archer D, Bean N, Tauxe R. Foodborne disease outbreaks in nursing homes, 1975 through 1987. JAMA 1991;266:2105–09.

35. Taylor JP, Perdue JN. The changing epidemiology of human brucellosis in Texas. Am J Epidemiol 1989;130:160–5.

36. Dalrymple-Champneys W. Brucella infection and undulant fever in man. London: Oxford University Press; 1960.

37. Chomel B, DeBess E, Mangiamele D, Reilly K, Farver T, Sun R, et al. Changing trends in the epidemiology of human brucellosis in California from 1973 to 1992: a shift toward foodborne transmission. J Infect Dis 1994;170: 1216–23.

38. Tauxe R. Epidemiology of Campylobacter jejuni infections in the United States and other industrialized nations. In: Nachamkin, Blaser M, Tompkins L, editors. Campylobacter jejuni: current status and future trends; 1992. p. 9–19.

39. Mishu B, Blaser MJ. Role of infection due to Campylobacter jejuni in the initiation of Guillain-Barré syndrome. Clin Infec Dis 1993;17:104–8.

40. Bartlett JG. Gas gangrene (other Clostridium-associated diseases). In: Mandell GL, Douglas RG, Bennett JE, editors. Principles and practice of infectious diseases. Third ed. New York: Churchill Livingstone; 1990: 1850–60.

41. Slutsker L, Ries AA, Greene KD, Wells JG, Hutwagner L, Griffin PM. Escherichia coli O157:H7 diarrhea in the United States: clinical and epidemiologic features. Ann Intern Med 1997;126:505–13.

42. Pai CH, Ahmed N, Lior H, Johnson WM, Sims HV, Woods DE. Epidemiology of sporadic diarrhea due to verocytotoxin-producing Escherichia coli: a two-year prospective study. J Infect Dis 1988;157:1054–7.

43. Bokete TN, O'Callahan CM, Clausen CR, Tang NM, Tran N, Moseley SL, et al. Shiga-like toxin-producing Escherichia coli in Seattle children: a prospective study. Gastroenterology 1993;105:1724–31.

44. Acheson DWK, Breuker SD, Donohue-Rolfe A, Kozak K, Yi A, Keusch GT. Development of a clinically useful diagnostic enzyme immunoassay for enterohemorrhagic Escherichia coli infection. In: Karmali MA, Goglio AG, editors. Recent advances in verocytotoxin-producing Escherichia coli infections. Amsterdam: Elsevier Science B. V.; 1994: 109–12.

45. Park CH, Gates KM, Vandel NM, Hixon DL. Isolation of Shiga-like toxin producing Escherichia coli (O157 and non-O157) in a community hospital. Diagn Microbiol Infect Dis 1996;26:69–72.

46. Tarr PI, Neill MA. Perspective: the problem of non-O157:H7 shiga toxin (Verocytotoxin)-producing Escherichia coli [comment]. J Infect Dis 1996;174:1136–9.

47. Rowe PC, Orrbine E, Lior H, Wells GA, McLaine PN. A prospective study of exposure to verotoxin-producing Escherichia coli among Canadian children with haemolytic uraemic syndrome. The CPKDRC co-investigators. Epidemiol Infect 1993;110:1–7.

48. Johnson R, Clark R, Wilson J, Read S, Rhan K, Renwick S, et al. Growing concerns and recent outbreaks involving non-O157:H7 serotypes of verocytoxigenic Escherichia coli. J Food Protect 1996;59:1112–22.

49. Nataro JP, Kaper JB. Diarrheogenic Escherichia coli. Clin Microbiol Rev 1998;11:1–60.

50. Hedberg CW, Savarino SJ, Besser JM, Paulus CJ, Thelen VM, Myers LJ, et al. An outbreak of foodborne illness caused by Escherichia coli O39:NM, an agent not fitting into the existing scheme for classifying diarrheogenic E. coli. J Infect Dis 1997;176:1625–8.

51. Tappero J, Schuchat A, Deaver K, Mascola L, Wenger J. Reduction in the incidence of human listeriosis in the United States. Effectiveness of prevention efforts. JAMA 1995;273:1118–22.

52. Slutsker L, Schuchat A. Listeriosis in Humans. In: Ryser E, Marth E, editors. Listeria, listeriosis, and food safety. New York: Marcel Dekker; 1999: 75–96.

53. Schuchat A, Lizano C, Broome C, Swaminathan B, Kim C, Winn K. Outbreak of neonatal listeriosis associated with mineral oil. Pediatr Infect Dis J 1991;10:183–9.

54. Hoffman TA, Ruiz CJ, Counts GW, Sachs JM, Nitzkin JL. Waterborne typhoid fever in Dade County, Florida. Clinical and therapeutic evaluation of 105 bacteremic patients. Am J Med 1975;59:481–7.

55. Klotz SA, Jorgensen JH, Buckwold FJ, Craven PC. Typhoid fever. An epidemic with remarkably few clinical signs and symptoms. Arch Intern Med 1984;144:533–7.

56. Mermin J, Townes J, Gerber M, Dolan N, Mintz E, Tauxe R. Typhoid fever in the United States,1985–1994. Arch Intern Med 1998;158:633–638.

57. Laboratory confirmed Salmonella surveillance. Annual Summary, 1997. Atlanta, Georgia: Centers for Disease Control and Prevention; 1999.

58. Cohen M, Tauxe R. Drug-resistant Salmonella in the United States: an epidemiologic perspective. Science 1986;234:964–9.

59. Tauxe R. Salmonella: a postmodern pathogen. J Food Protect 1991; 54:563–8.

60. DuPont HL. Shigella species. In: Mandell GL, Douglas RG, Bennett JE, editors. Principles and practice of infectious diseases. 3rd ed. New York: Churchill Livingstone; 1990: 1716–22.

61. Black RE, Craun GF, Blake PA. Epidemiology of common-source outbreaks of shigellosis in the United States, 1961–1975. Am J Epidemiol 1978; 108:47–52.

62. Levine WC, Bennett RW, Choi Y, Henning KJ, Rager JR, Hendricks KA, et al. Staphylococcal food poisoning caused by imported canned mushrooms. J Infect Dis 1996;173:1263–7.

63. Holmberg S, Blake P. Staphylococcal food poisoning in the United States. JAMA 1984;251:487–9.

64. Mahon B, Mintz E, Greene K, Wells J, Tauxe R. Reported cholera in the United States, 1992–1994. JAMA 1996;276:307–12.

65. Shapiro RL, Altekruse S, Hutwagner L, Bishop R, Hammond R, Wilson S, et al. The role of Gulf Coast oysters harvested in warmer months in Vibrio vulnificus infections in the United States, 1988–1996. Vibrio Working Group. J Infect Dis 1998;178:752–9.

66. Hlady W, Klontz K. The epidemiology of Vibrio infections in Florida, 1981–1993. J Infect Dis 1996;173:1176–83.

67. Ostroff S. Yersinia as an emerging infection: epidemiologic aspects of Yersiniosis. Contributions to Microbiology & Immunology 1995;13:5–10.

68. Skeels MR, Sokolow R, Hubbard CV, Andrus JK, Baisch J. Cryptosporidium infection in Oregon public health clinic patients, 1985–88: the value of statewide laboratory surveillance. Am J Public Health 1990;80: 305–8.

69. Roberts CL, Morin C, Addiss DG, Wahlquist SP, Mshar PA, Hadler JL. Factors influencing Cryptosporidium testing in Connecticut. J Clin Microbiol 1996;34:2292–3.

70. Petersen C. Cryptosporidium and the food supply. Lancet 1995;345: 1128–9.

71. Djuretic T, Wall PG, Nichols G. General outbreaks of infectious intestinal disease associated with milk and dairy products in England and Wales: 1992 to 1996. Commun Dis Rep CDR Wkly 1997;7:R41–5.

72. Outbreaks of Escherichia coli O157:H7 infection and cryptosporidiosis associated with drinking unpasteurized apple cider—Connecticut and New York, October 1996. MMWR 1997;46:4–8.

73. Petersen C. Cryptosporidiosis in patients infected with the human immunodeficiency virus [see comments]. Clin Infect Dis 1992;15:903–9.

74. Herwaldt BL, Ackers ML. An outbreak in 1996 of cyclosporiasis associated with imported raspberries. The Cyclospora Working Group [see comments]. N Engl J Med 1997;336:1548–56.

75. Herwaldt BL, Beach MJ. The return of Cyclospora in 1997: another outbreak of cyclosporiasis in North America associated with imported raspberries. Cyclospora Working Group [see comments]. Ann Intern Med 1999; 130:210–20.

76. Addiss DG, Davis JP, Roberts JM, Mast EE. Epidemiology of giardiasis in Wisconsin: increasing incidence of reported cases and unexplained seasonal trends. Am J Trop Med Hyg 1992;47:13–9.

77. Birkhead G, Vogt RL. Epidemiologic surveillance for endemic Giardia lamblia infection in Vermont. The roles of waterborne and person-to-person transmission. Am J Epidemiol 1989;129:762–8.

78. Dennis DT, Smith RP, Welch JJ, Chute CG, Anderson B, Herndon JL, et al. Endemic giardiasis in New Hampshire: a case-control study of environmental risks. J Infect Dis 1993;167:1391–5.

79. Petersen LR, Cartter ML, Hadler JL. A food-borne outbreak of Giardia lamblia. J Infect Dis 1988;157:846–848.

80. Osterholm MT, Forfang JC, Ristinen TL, Dean AG, Washburn JW, Godes JR, et al. An outbreak of foodborne giardiasis. N Engl J Med 1981; 304:24–8.

81. Guerina NG, Hsu HW, Meissner HC, Maguire JH, Lynfield R, Stechenberg B, et al. Neonatal serologic screening and early treatment for congenital Toxoplasma gondii infection. The New England Regional Toxoplasma Working Group [see comments]. N Engl J Med 1994;330:1858–63.

82. Wong SY, Remington JS. Toxoplasmosis in pregnancy [see comments]. Clin Infect Dis 1994;18:853–61.

83. Capo V, Despommier DD. Clinical aspects of infection with Trichinella spp. Clinical Microbiology Reviews 1996;9:47–54.

84. Tucker A, Haddix A, Bresee J, Holman R, Parashar U, Glass R. Cost-effectiveness analysis of a rotavirus immunization program for the United States. JAMA 1998;279:1371–76.

85. Rodriguez WJ, Kim HW, Brandt CD, Schwartz RH, Gardner MK, Jeffries B, et al. Longitudinal study of rotavirus infection and gastroenteritis in families served by a pediatric medical practice: clinical and epidemiologic observations. Pediatr Infect Dis J 1987;6:170–6.

86. Gurwith M, Wenman W, Hinde D, Feltham S, Greenberg H. A prospective study of rotavirus infection in infants and young children. J Infect Dis 1981;144:218–24.

87. Parashar UD, Holman RC, Clarke MJ, Bresee JS, Glass RI. Hospitalizations associated with rotavirus diarrhea in the United States, 1993 through 1995: surveillance based on the new ICD-9-CM rotavirus-specific diagnostic code. J Infect Dis 1998;177:13–7.

88. Jin S, Kilgore PE, Holman RC, Clarke MJ, Gangarosa EJ, Glass RI. Trends in hospitalizations for diarrhea in United States children from 1979 through 1992: estimates of the morbidity associated with rotavirus. Pediatr Infect Dis J 1996;15:397–404.

89. Kilgore PE, Holman RC, Clarke MJ, Glass RI. Trends of diarrheal disease-associated mortality in US children, 1968 through 1991. JAMA 1995; 274: 1143–48.

90. Kapikian AZ, Chanock RM. Rotaviruses. In: Fields BN, DM DMK, Howley PM, et al, editors. Fields Virology. 3rd ed. Philadelphia: Lippincott-Raven; 1996: 1657–708.

91. Glass RI, Noel J, Mitchell D, Herrmann JE, Blacklow NR, Pickering LK, et al. The changing epidemiology of astrovirus-associated gastroenteritis: a review. Arch Virol Suppl 1996;12:287–300.

92. Koopmans M, van Duynhoven Y, van de Heide R, et al. Molecular detection and epidemiology of Norwalk-like viruses and Sapporo-like viruses in the Netherlands. Presented at the International Workshop on Human Caliciviruses, Atlanta, Georgia, USA; 1999 Mar 29–31.

93. Grohman G. Viral diarrhoea in children in Australia. In: Tzipori S, et al, editors. Infectious diarrhoea of the young. New York: Elsevier Science Publishers; 1985.

94. Wolfaardt M, Taylor MB, Booysen HF, Englebrecht L, Grabow WOK, Jiang X. Incidence of human calicivirus and rotavirus infection in patients with gastroenteritis in South Africa. J Med Virol 1997;51:290–6.

95. Vial P, Kotloff KL, Tall BD, Morris JG, Levine MM. Detection by immune electron microscopy of 27-nm viral particles associated with community-acquired diarrhea in children. J Infect Dis 1989;161:571–3.

96. Donneli G, Ruggeri FM, Tinari A, Marziano ML, Menichella D, Caione D, et al. A three-year diagnostic and epidemiologic study on viral infantile diarrhoea in Rome. Epidemiol Infect 1988;100:311–20.

97. Riepenhoff-Talty M, Saif LJ, Barrett HJ, Suzuki H, Ogra PL. Potential spectrum of etiologic agents of viral enteritis in hospitalized patients. J Clin Microbiol 1983;17:352–6.

98. Suzuki H, Konno T, Kutsuzawa T, Imai A, Tazawa F, Ishida N, et al. The occurrence of calicivirus in infants with acute gastroenteritis. J Med Virol 1979;4:321–6.

99. Pang X, Joensuu J, Vesikari T. Human calicivirus-associated sporadic gastroenteritis in Finnish children less than 2 years of age followed prospectively during a rotavirus vaccine trial. Pediatr Infect Dis J 1999;18:420–6.

100. Mounts A, Holman R, Clarke M, Bresee J, Glass R. Trends in hospitalizations associated with gastroenteritis among adults in the United States, 1979–1995. Epi Infect. In press 1999.

101. Fankhauser RL NJ, Monroe SS, Ando T, Glass RI. Molecular epidemiology of "Norwalk-like viruses" in outbreaks of gastroenteritis in the United States. J Infect Dis 1998;178:1571–8.

102. Kaplan JE, Feldman R, Campbell DS, Lookabaugh C, Gary WG. The frequency of a Norwalk-like pattern of illness in outbreaks of acute gastroenteritis. Am J Pub Health 1982;72:1329–2.

103. Sekine S, Okada S, Hayashi Y. Prevalence of small round structured virus infections in acute gastroenteritis outbreaks in Tokyo. Microbiol Immunol 1989;33:207–17.

104. Viral Gastroenteritis Sub-Committee of the PHLS Virology Committee. Outbreaks of gastroenteritis associated with SRSVs. PHLS Microbiol Digest 1998;10:1–8.

105. Hepatitis surveillance report no. 56. Atlanta: U.S. Department of Health and Human Services, Public Health Service, CDC. 1996.

106. Bell BP, Shapiro CN, Alter MJ, Moyer LA, Judson FN, Mottram K, et al. The diverse patterns of hepatitis A epidemiology in the United States. Implications for vaccination strategies. J Infect Dis 1998;178:1579–84.

107. Hoofnagle JH, Carithers RL, Shapiro C, Ascher N. Fulminant hepatic failure. Summary of a workshop. Hepatology 1995;21:240–252.

One of the most well-known foodborne outbreaks is characterized in the *CDC Case Study, Oswego—An Outbreak of Gastrointestinal Illness Following a Church Supper*. Here is the student case study, a wonderful example of an outbreak with questions for you to work on as you hone your epidemiology skills.

The following table describes the basic characteristics of some of the most common foodborne diseases. There are many other sources, however, on line as well as at your library. Be sure to check them out!

READING 26
CDC Case Study, Oswego—An Outbreak of Gastrointestinal Illness Following a Church Supper

Centers for Disease Control and Prevention. CDC Case Study, Oswego—An Outbreak of Gastrointestinal Illness Following a Church Supper. Epidemiology Program Office *Case Studies in Applied Epidemiology* No. 401-303 [accessed 1/1/08]. Available from http://www.cdc.gov/eis/casestudies/xoswego.401-303.student.pdf.

This case study is based on an investigation conducted by the New York State Department of Public Health Division. The case study was developed by Wendell Ames, MD, Stafford Wheeler, MD, and Alexander Langmuir, MD in the early 1940s. It has been substantially updated and edited since then by Philip Brachman, Michael Gregg, and Richard Dicker, with input from the many instructors who have reviewed and taught "Oswego" as part of the EIS Summer Course each year.

Centers for Disease Control and Prevention Epidemiology Program Office

Case Studies in Applied Epidemiology No. 401-303

Oswego—An Outbreak of Gastrointestinal Illness Following a Church Supper

Student's Guide

LEARNING OBJECTIVES

After completing this case study, the participant should be able to:

- Define the terms "cluster," "outbreak," and "epidemic";
- List the steps in the investigation of an outbreak;
- Draw, interpret, and describe the value of an epidemic curve;
- Calculate and compare food-specific attack rates to identify possible vehicles;
- List reasons for investigating an outbreak that has apparently ended.

PART I—BACKGROUND

On April 19, 1940, the local health officer in the village of Lycoming, Oswego County, New York, reported the occurrence of an outbreak of acute gastrointestinal illness to the District Health Officer in Syracuse. Dr. A. M. Rubin, epidemiologist-in-training, was assigned to conduct an investigation.

When Dr. Rubin arrived in the field, he learned from the health officer that all persons known to be ill had attended a church supper held on the previous evening, April 18. Family members who did not attend the church supper did not become ill. Accordingly, Dr. Rubin focused the investigation on the supper. He completed Interviews with 75 of the 80 persons known to have attended, collecting information about the occurrence and time of onset of symptoms, and foods consumed. Of the 75 persons interviewed, 46 persons reported gastrointestinal illness.

Question 1: Would you call this an epidemic? Would you call it an outbreak?

Question 2: Review the steps of an outbreak investigation.

Clinical Description

The onset of illness in all cases was acute, characterized chiefly by nausea, vomiting, diarrhea, and abdominal pain. None of the ill persons reported having an elevated temperature; all recovered within 24 to 30 hours. Approximately 20% of the ill persons visited physicians. No fecal specimens were obtained for bacteriologic examination.

Question 3: List the broad categories of diseases that must be considered in the differential diagnosis of an outbreak of gastrointestinal illness.

The investigators suspected that this was a vehicle-borne outbreak, with food as the vehicle.

Question 4: In epidemiologic parlance, what is a vehicle? What is a vector? What are other modes of transmission?

Question 5: If you were to administer a questionnaire to the church supper participants, what information would you collect? Group the information into categories.

Dr. Rubin put his data into a line listing.

Question 6: What is a line listing? What is the value of a line listing?

PART II—DESCRIPTION OF THE SUPPER

The supper was held in the basement of the village church. Foods were contributed by numerous members of the congregation. The supper began at 6:00 p.m. and continued until 11:00 p.m. Food was spread out on a table and consumed over a period of several hours. Data regarding onset of illness and food eaten or water drunk by each of the 75 persons interviewed are provided in the attached line listing. The approximate time of eating supper was collected for only about half the persons who had gastrointestinal illness.

Question 7: What is the value of an epidemic curve?

Question 8: Using graph paper, graph the cases by time of onset of illness (include appropriate labels and title). What does this graph tell you?

Question 9: Are there any cases for which the times of onset are inconsistent with the general experience? How might they be explained?

Question 10: How could the data in the line listing be better presented?

PART III

Attached is the line listing sorted by illness status (ill or well), and by time of onset.

Question 11: Where possible, using the new line listing, calculate incubation periods and illustrate their distribution with an appropriate graph.

Question 12: Determine the range and median of the incubation period.

Question 13: How does the information on incubation period, combined with the data on clinical symptoms, help in the differential diagnosis of the illness? (If necessary, refer to the Compendium of Acute Foodborne Gastrointestinal Disease).

TABLE 9-6 Line listing from investigation of outbreak of gastroenteritis, Oswego, New York, 1940 (two pages).

ID	Age	Sex	Time of Meal	ILL	Date of Onset	Time of Onset	Baked ham	Spinach	Mashed potatoes	Cabbage salad	Jello	Rolls	Brown bread	Milk	Coffee	Water	Cakes	Van ice cream	Choc ice cream	Fruit salad
1	11	M	unk	N			N	N	N	N	N	N	N	N	N	N	N	N	Y	N
2	52	F	8:00 PM	Y	4/19	12:30 AM	Y	Y	Y	N	N	Y	N	N	Y	N	N	Y	N	N
3	65	M	6:30 PM	Y	4/19	12:30 AM	Y	Y	N	N	N	N	N	N	Y	N	N	Y	Y	N
4	59	F	6:30 PM	Y	4/19	12:30 AM	N	N	N	Y	N	N	N	N	Y	N	Y	Y	Y	N
5	13	F	unk	N			N	N	N	N	N	N	N	N	N	N	N	Y	Y	N
6	63	F	7:30 PM	Y	4/18	10:30 PM	Y	N	N	N	Y	Y	Y	N	N	Y	N	Y	N	N
7	70	M	7:30 PM	Y	4/18	10:30 PM	Y	N	N	N	N	N	N	N	N	Y	N	N	Y	N
8	40	F	7:30 PM	Y	4/19	2:00 AM	N	N	N	N	N	Y	N	N	Y	N	Y	Y	Y	N
9	15	F	10:00 PM	Y	4/19	1:00 AM	Y	N	N	N	N	N	N	N	N	N	N	N	Y	N
10	33	F	7:00 PM	Y	4/18	11:00 PM	Y	N	N	N	N	N	N	Y	Y	Y	N	Y	Y	N
11	65	M	unk	N			N	N	N	N	N	N	N	N	N	N	N	N	Y	Y
12	38	F	unk	N			Y	N	N	N	N	Y	N	Y	Y	Y	Y	Y	Y	N
13	62	F	unk	N			Y	N	N	N	N	N	N	N	N	N	N	Y	Y	N
14	10	M	7:30 PM	Y	4/19	2:00 AM	N	N	N	N	N	Y	N	N	N	N	N	Y	Y	N
15	25	M	unk	N			Y	N	N	N	N	N	N	N	N	N	N	N	Y	N
16	32	F	unk	Y	4/19	10:30 AM	Y	N	N	N	N	Y	N	N	N	N	N	Y	Y	N
17	62	F	unk	Y	4/19	12:30 AM	Y	N	N	N	N	N	N	N	N	N	N	Y	Y	N
18	36	M	unk	Y	4/18	10:15 PM	Y	N	N	N	N	Y	N	N	Y	Y	N	Y	Y	N
19	11	M	unk	N			N	N	?	N	N	N	N	N	N	N	N	N	Y	N
20	33	F	unk	Y	4/18	10:00 PM	Y	N	N	N	N	N	N	N	N	N	N	Y	Y	Y
21	13	F	10:00 PM	Y	4/19	1:00 AM	N	N	N	N	N	N	N	N	N	N	N	Y	Y	N
22	7	M	unk	Y	4/18	11:00 PM	N	N	N	N	N	N	Y	N	N	Y	Y	Y	N	N
23	64	M	unk	N			N	N	N	N	N	N	N	N	N	N	N	Y	Y	N
24	3	M	unk	Y	4/18	9:45 PM	N	N	N	N	N	N	N	N	Y	N	N	Y	Y	N
25	65	F	unk	N			N	N	N	N	N	N	N	N	N	N	N	Y	Y	N
26	59	F	unk	Y	4/18	9:45 PM	N	N	N	N	N	N	Y	N	N	N	Y	Y	Y	N
27	15	F	10:00 PM	Y	4/19	1:00 AM	Y	Y	N	N	N	N	N	N	N	N	N	Y	Y	N
28	62	M	unk	N			N	N	N	Y	N	N	Y	N	Y	Y	Y	N	Y	N

continues

TABLE 9-6 Line listing from investigation of outbreak of gastroenteritis, Oswego, New York, 1940 (two pages) (continued).

ID	Age	Sex	Time of Meal	ILL	Date of Onset	Time of Onset	Baked ham	Spinach	Mashed potatoes	Cabbage salad	Jello	Rolls	Brown bread	Milk	Coffee	Water	Cakes	Van ice cream	Choc ice cream	Fruit salad
29	37	F	unk	Y	4/18	11:00 PM	Y	Y	Y	N	Y	Y	Y	N	Y	N	Y	Y	N	N
30	17	M	10:00 PM	N			N	N	N	N	N	Y	N	N	Y	N	Y	Y	Y	N
31	35	M	unk	Y	4/18	9:00 PM	Y	Y	Y	N	N	Y	Y	N	Y	N	Y	Y	N	Y
32	15	M	10:00 PM	Y	4/19	1:00 AM	N	N	N	N	N	N	Y	N	Y	N	N	Y	N	N
33	50	F	10:00 PM	Y	4/19	1:00 AM	N	N	N	Y	N	Y	Y	N	Y	N	Y	Y	N	N
34	40	M	unk	N			Y	N	N	N	N	N	Y	N	Y	N	Y	N	Y	N
35	35	F	unk	N			N	N	N	N	N	N	Y	N	Y	N	N	Y	Y	N
36	35	F	unk	Y	4/18	9:15 PM	Y	Y	Y	N	N	Y	Y	N	Y	N	Y	Y	Y	N
37	36	M	unk	N			N	N	N	N	N	N	N	N	Y	N	N	Y	Y	N
38	57	F	unk	Y	4/18	11:30 PM	Y	Y	Y	N	N	Y	N	N	Y	N	N	Y	Y	N
39	16	F	10:00 PM	Y	4/19	1:00 AM	N	N	N	N	N	N	N	N	Y	N	N	Y	Y	N
40	68	M	unk	Y	4/18	9:30 PM	N	N	N	N	N	N	N	N	Y	N	Y	Y	Y	N
41	54	F	unk	N			Y	Y	N	N	N	Y	Y	N	N	N	Y	N	N	N
42	77	M	unk	Y	4/19	2:30 AM	Y	Y	Y	N	N	N	N	N	Y	N	Y	Y	N	N
43	72	F	unk	Y	4/19	2:00 AM	N	N	N	N	N	N	N	N	Y	N	N	Y	N	N
44	58	M	unk	Y	4/18	9:30 PM	N	Y	Y	N	N	N	N	Y	Y	N	N	Y	N	N
45	20	M	10:00 PM	N			N	N	N	N	N	N	N	N	N	N	N	N	?	N
46	17	M	unk	N			N	N	N	N	N	N	N	N	Y	N	N	Y	Y	N
47	62	F	unk	Y	4/19	12:30 AM	Y	Y	Y	N	N	Y	N	N	Y	Y	Y	Y	N	N
48	20	F	7:00 PM	Y	4/19	1:00 AM	N	N	N	N	N	N	N	N	Y	Y	N	Y	N	N
49	52	F	unk	Y	4/18	10:30 PM	Y	Y	Y	N	N	N	N	N	Y	N	Y	Y	N	N
50	9	F	unk	N			N	N	N	N	N	N	N	N	Y	N	N	Y	Y	N
51	50	M	unk	N			N	N	N	N	N	N	N	N	Y	N	N	Y	N	N
52	8	M	11:00 AM	Y	4/18	3:00 PM	Y	Y	Y	N	N	Y	N	N	Y	N	Y	Y	N	N
53	35	F	unk	N			N	N	N	N	N	N	N	N	N	N	N	Y	N	N
54	48	F	unk	Y	4/19	12:00 AM*	Y	Y	Y	N	N	N	N	N	N	N	Y	Y	N	N
55	25	M	unk	Y	4/18	11:00 PM	N	N	N	N	N	N	N	N	N	Y	Y	Y	Y	N
56	11	F	unk	N			N	N	N	N	N	N	N	N	N	N	N	N	N	N
57	74	M	unk	Y	4/18	10:30 PM	Y	Y	Y	N	Y	Y	Y	N	N	N	Y	Y	N	N
58	12	F	10:00 PM	Y	4/19	1:00 AM	N	N	N	N	N	N	N	N	N	N	Y	Y	Y	N

#	Age	Sex	Time		Date	Time											
59	44	F	7:30 PM	Y	4/19	2:30 AM	Y	Y	N	Y	N	N	Y	Y	N	Y	N	N
60	53	F	7:30 PM	Y	4/19	11:30 PM	Y	Y	N	Y	N	Y	Y	Y	Y	Y	Y	N
61	37	M	unk	N			N	N	N	N	N	N	N	N	N	N	N	N
62	24	F	unk	N			Y	Y	Y	Y	Y	Y	Y	Y	N	N	N	N
63	69	F	unk	N			N	Y	Y	Y	Y	Y	N	Y	Y	Y	Y	N
64	7	M	unk	N			Y	Y	Y	Y	Y	N	Y	Y	Y	N	N	N
65	17	F	10:00 PM	Y	4/19	1:00 AM	N	N	N	N	N	N	N	N	Y	N	N	N
66	8	F	unk	Y	4/19	12:30 AM	Y	N	Y	Y	Y	Y	Y	Y	Y	Y	Y	N
67	11	F	7:30 PM	N			Y	Y	Y	Y	Y	Y	N	Y	N	N	N	N
68	17	M	7:30 PM	N			N	N	N	N	N	N	N	N	N	N	N	N
69	36	F	unk	N			N	N	N	N	N	N	N	N	N	N	N	N
70	21	F	unk	Y	4/19	12:30 AM	Y	N	N	Y	Y	Y	N	N	Y	Y	Y	N
71	60	M	7:30 PM	Y	4/19	1:00 AM	N	N	N	N	N	N	N	N	Y	N	N	N
72	18	F	7:30 PM	Y	4/19	12:00 AM*	Y	Y	Y	Y	Y	Y	Y	Y	Y	Y	Y	N
73	14	F	10:00 PM	N			N	N	N	N	N	N	N	N	N	N	N	N
74	52	M	unk	Y	4/19	2:15 AM	Y	Y	Y	Y	Y	Y	Y	Y	Y	Y	Y	N
75	45	F	unk	Y	4/18	11:00 PM	Y	Y	Y	Y	Y	Y	Y	Y	Y	N	N	Y

*Midnight between 4/18 and 4/19.

Question 14: Using the data in the attached line listing, complete the table below. Which food is the most likely vehicle of infection?

Question 15: Outline further investigations that should be pursued.

Question 16: What control measures would you suggest?

Question 17: Why was it important to work up this outbreak?

Question 18: Refer to the steps of an outbreak investigation you listed in Question 2. How does this investigation fit that outline?

PART IV—CONCLUSION

The following is quoted verbatim from the report prepared by Dr. Rubin:

"The ice cream was prepared by the Petrie sisters as follows:

"On the afternoon of April 17 raw milk from the Petrie farm at Lycoming was brought to boil over a water bath, sugar and eggs were then added and a little flour to add body to the mix. The chocolate and vanilla ice cream were prepared separately. Hershey's chocolate was necessarily added to the chocolate mix. At 6 p.m. the two mixes were taken in covered containers to the church basement and allowed to stand overnight. They were presumably not touched by anyone during this period.

"On the morning of April 18, Mr. Coe added five ounces of vanilla and two cans of condensed milk to the vanilla mix, and three ounces of vanilla and one can of condensed milk to the chocolate mix. Then the vanilla ice cream was transferred to a freezing can and placed in an electrical freezer for 20 minutes, after which the vanilla ice cream was removed from the freezer can and packed into another can which had been previously washed with boiling water. Then the chocolate mix was put into the freezer can which had been rinsed out with tap water and allowed to freeze for 20 minutes. At the conclusion of this both cans were covered and placed in large wooden receptacles which were packed with ice. As noted, the chocolate ice cream remained in the one freezer can.

"All handlers of the ice cream were examined. No external lesions or upper respiratory infections were noted. Nose and throat cultures were taken from two individuals who prepared the ice cream.

"Bacteriological examinations were made by the Division of Laboratories and Research, Albany, on both ice creams. Their report is as follows:

'Large numbers of *Staphylococcus aureus* and *albus* were found in the specimen of vanilla ice cream. Only a few staphylococci were demonstrated in the chocolate ice cream.'

"Report of the nose and throat cultures of the Petries who prepared the ice cream read as follows:

'*Staphylococcus aureus* and hemolytic streptococci were isolated from nose culture and

Staphylococcus albus from throat culture of Grace Petrie. *Staphylococcus albus* was isolated from the nose culture of Marian Petrie. The hemolytic streptococci were not of the type usually associated with infections in man.'

TABLE 9-7 [Tracking table]									
	Number of persons who ATE specfied food				Number of persons who did NOT eat specified food				
Food Items Served	Ill	Not Ill	Total	Percent Ill (Attack rate)	Ill	Not Ill	Total	Percent Ill (Attack rate)	Attack Rate Ratio
Baked ham									
Spinach									
Mashed potato									
Cabbage salad									
Jello									
Rolls									
Brown bread									
Milk									
Coffee									
Water									
Cakes									
Ice cream, vanilla									
Ice cream, chocolate									
Fruit salad									

"Discussion as to Source: The source of bacterial contamination of the vanilla ice cream is not clear. Whatever the method of the introduction of the staphylococci, it appears reasonable to assume it must have occurred between the evening of April 17 and the morning of April 18. No reason for contamination peculiar to the vanilla ice cream is known.

"In dispensing the ice creams, the same scooper was used. It is therefore not unlikely to assume that some contamination to the chocolate ice cream occurred in this way. This would appear to be the most plausible explanation for the illness in the three individuals who did not eat the vanilla ice cream.

"Control Measures: On May 19, all remaining ice cream was condemned. All other food at the church supper had been consumed.

"Conclusions: An attack of gastroenteritis occurred following a church supper at Lycoming. The cause of the outbreak was contaminated vanilla ice cream. The method of contamination of ice cream is not clearly understood. Whether the positive *Staphylococcus* nose and throat cultures occurring in the Petrie family had anything to do with the contamination is a matter of conjecture."

Note: Patient #52 was a child who while watching the freezing procedure was given a dish of vanilla ice cream at 11:00 a.m. on April 18.

Addendum:

Certain laboratory techniques not available at the time of this investigation might prove very useful in the analysis of a similar epidemic today. These are phage typing, which can be done at CDC, and identification of staphylococcal enterotoxin in food by immuno-diffusion or by enzyme-linked immunosorbent assay (ELISA), which is available through the Food and Drug Administration (FDA).

One would expect the phage types of staphylococci isolated from Grace Petrie's nose and the vanilla ice cream and vomitus or stool samples from ill persons associated with the church supper to be identical had she been the source of contamination. Distinctly different phage types would mitigate against her as the source (although differences might be observed as a chance phenomenon of sampling error) and suggest the need for further investigation, such as cultures of others who might have been in contact with the ice cream in preparation or consideration of the possibility that contamination occurred from using a cow with mastitis and that the only milk boiled was that used to prepare chocolate ice cream. If the contaminated food had been heated sufficiently to destroy staphylococcal organisms but not toxin, analysis for toxin (with the addition of urea) would still permit detection of the cause of the epidemic. A Gram stain might also detect the presence of nonviable staphylococci in contaminated food.

REFERENCE TO THE READING

Gross MB. Oswego County revisited. *Public Health Reports* 1976;91:160–70.

Reading 27
Compendium of Acute Foodborne and Waterborne Diseases

Centers for Disease Control and Prevention. Compendium of Acute Foodborne and Waterborne Diseases. 2003. Available from http://www.cdc.gov/eis/casestudies/xoswego.401.303.compendium.pdf.

I. Diseases typified by vomiting after a short incubation period with little or no fever

Agent	Incubation Period	Clinical Syndrome	Pathophysiology	Characteristic Foods	Specimens
A. *Staphylococcus aureus*	30 min–8 hours; usually 2–4 hours	Vomiting, diarrhea	preformed enterotoxin	sliced/chopped ham and meats, custards, cream fillings	Food: enterotoxin assay (FDA), culture for quantitation and phage typing of staph, gram stain

continues

Agent	Incubation Period	Clinical Syndrome	Pathophysiology	Characteristic Foods	Specimens
					<u>Handlers:</u> culture nares, skin, skin lesions, and phage type Staph. <u>Cases:</u> culture stool and vomitus, phage type Staph.
B. *Bacillus cereus*	1–6 hours	Vomiting, some patients with diarrhea; fever uncommon	? preformed enterotoxin	cooked rice	<u>Food:</u> culture for quantitation <u>Cases:</u> stool culture
C. Heavy metals • Antimony • Cadmium • Copper • Iron • Tin • Zinc	5 min–8 hours; usually < 1 hour	Vomiting, often metallic taste		foods and beverages prepared/stored/cooked in containers coated/lined/ contaminated with offending metal	Toxicologic analysis of food container, vomitus, stomach contents, urine, blood, feces

II. Diseases typified by diarrhea after a moderate to long incubation period, often with fever

Agent	Incubation Period	Clinical Syndrome	Pathophysiology	Characteristic Foods	Specimens
A. *Clostridium perfringens*	6–24 hours	Diarrhea, abdominal cramps; vomiting and fever uncommon	enterotoxin formed *in vivo*	meat, poultry	<u>Food:</u> enterotoxin assay done as research procedure by FDA, culture for quantitation and serotyping <u>Cases:</u> culture stool for quantitation and serotyping of *C. perfringens*; test for enterotoxin in stool. <u>Controls:</u> culture stool for quantitation and serotyping of *C. perfringens*
B. *Bacillus cereus*	6–24 hours	Diarrhea, abdominal cramps, and vomiting in some patients; fever uncommon	? enterotoxin	custards, cereals, puddings, sauces, meat loaf	<u>Food:</u> culture <u>Cases:</u> stool culture
C. *Vibrio parahemolyticus*	4–30 hours	Diarrhea	tissue invasion, ? enterotoxin	seafood	Food: culture on TCBS, serotype, Kanagawa test <u>Cases:</u> stool cultures on TCBS, serotype, Kanagawa test

continues

Agent	Incubation Period	Clinical Syndrome	Pathophysiology	Characteristic Foods	Specimens
D. Salmonella (nontyphoid)	6 hours–10 days; usually 6–48 hours	Diarrhea, often with fever and abdominal cramps	tissue invasion	poultry, eggs, meat, raw milk (cross-contamination important)	<u>Food:</u> culture with serotyping <u>Cases:</u> stool culture with serotyping <u>Handlers:</u> stool culture with serotyping as secondary consideration
E. Norovirus (formerly, "Norwalk-like viruses")	15–77 hours; usually 24–48 hours	Vomiting, cramps, diarrhea, headache, fever	unknown	raw or undercooked shellfish, water, many others	Detection of viral RNA in stool or vomitus by reverse transcriptase-polymerase chain reaction (RT-PCR)
F. Rotavirus	16–48 hours	Vomiting, chills, and diarrhea, especially in infants and children	unknown	foodborne transmission not well documented	<u>Cases:</u> stool examination by EM or ELISA; serology <u>Food:</u> culture and serotype
G. Escherichia coli enterotoxigenic (ETEC)	6–48 hours	Diarrhea, abdominal cramps, nausea; vomiting and fever less common	enterotoxin	uncooked vegetables, salads, water, cheese	<u>Cases:</u> stool culture; serotype and demonstration of enterotoxin production; invasiveness assay
H. Escherichia coli enteroinvasive (EIEC)	Variable	diarrhea (might be bloody), fever, abdominal cramps	tissue invasion	same as ETEC above	same as ETEC above
I. Listeria monocytogenes —Invasive Disease	2–6 weeks	Meningitis, neonatal sepsis, fever	?	Milk, soft cheeses	<u>Food:</u> culture, serotype <u>Cases:</u> stool/blood cultures, serotype, serology
Listeria monocytogenes, —Diarrheal Disease	Unknown (3–70 days?)	Diarrhea, fever, abdominal cramps	?	Milk, soft cheeses	same as above
J. Vibrio cholerae non-01 and non-0139	1–5 days	Watery diarrhea	enterotoxin formed in vivo, ? tissue invasion	shellfish	<u>Food:</u> culture on TCBS, serotype <u>Cases:</u> stool cultures on TCBS, serotype
K. Vibrio cholerae O1 or 0139	1–5 days	Watery diarrhea, often accompanied by vomiting	enterotoxin formed in vivo	shellfish, water or foods contaminated by infected person or obtained from contaminated environmental source	<u>Food:</u> culture on TCBS, serotype <u>Cases:</u> stool culture on TCBS, serotype
L. Shigella spp.	12 hours–6 days; usually 2–4 days	Diarrhea (often bloody), often accompanied by fever and abdominal cramps	tissue invasion	foods contaminated by infected foodhandler; usually not foodborne	<u>Food:</u> culture and serotype <u>Cases:</u> stool culture and serotype <u>Handlers:</u> stool culture and serotype

Agent	Incubation Period	Clinical Syndrome	Pathophysiology	Characteristic Foods	Specimens
M. *Escherichia coli* enterohemorrhagic (*E. coli* O157:H7 and others)	1–10 days; usually 3–4 days	Diarrhea (often bloody), abdominal cramps (often severe), little or no fever	cytotoxin	beef, raw milk, water, apple cider, lettuce	<u>Cases:</u> stool culture on sorbitol-MacConkey; isolation of *E. coli* O157:H7 or other Shiga-like toxin-producing *E. coli* from clinical specimen
N. *Yersinia enterocolitica*	1–10 days; usually 4–6 days	Diarrhea abdominal pain (often severe)	tissue invasion, ? enterotoxin	pork products, milk, food contaminated by infected human or animal	<u>Food:</u> culture on CIN agar, cold enrichment <u>Cases:</u> stool culture on CIN
O. *Cyclospora cayetanensis*	1–11 days; median: 7 days	Fatigue, protracted diarrhea, often relapsing	tissue invasion	raw produce, water	<u>Food/water:</u> consult DPD <u>Cases:</u> stool examination for organisms; PCR (developmental) and testing for oocyste sporulation at DPD
P. *Cryptosporidium parvum*	2–28 days; median: 7 days	Diarrhea, nausea, vomiting; fever	tissue invasion	uncooked foods, water	<u>Food/water:</u> consult DPD <u>Cases:</u> stool examination for organisms or antigen; PCR and serologic test developmental (consult DPD)
Q. *Giardia lamblia*	3–25 days; median: 7 days	Diarrhea, gas, cramps, nausea, fatigue	?	uncooked foods, water	<u>Food/water:</u> consult DPD <u>Cases:</u> detection of antigen or organism in stool, duodenal contents, or small-bowel biopsy specimen

III. Botulism

Agent	Incubation Period	Clinical Syndrome	Pathophysiology	Characteristic Foods	Specimens
Clostridium botulinum	2 hours–8 days; usually 12–48 hours	Illness of variable severity; common symptoms include diplopia, blurred vision, and bulbar weakness; paralysis, which is usually descending and bilateral, might progress rapidly	preformed toxin	improperly canned or similarly preserved foods	<u>Food:</u> toxin assay <u>Cases:</u> serum and stool for toxin assay; stool culture for *C. botulinum*

continues

Agent	Incubation Period	Clinical Syndrome	Pathophysiology	Characteristic Foods	Specimens
M. *Escherichia coli* enterohemorrhagic (*E. coli* O157:H7 and others)	1–10 days; usually 3–4 days	Diarrhea (often bloody), abdominal cramps (often severe), little or no fever	cytotoxin	beef, raw milk, water, apple cider, lettuce	<u>Cases:</u> stool culture on sorbitol-MacConkey; isolation of *E. coli* 0157:H7 or other Shiga-like toxin-producing *E. coli* from clinical specimen
N. *Yersinia enterocolitica*	1–10 days; usually 4–6 days	Diarrhea abdominal pain (often severe)	tissue invasion, ? enterotoxin	pork products, milk, food contaminated by infected human or animal	<u>Food:</u> culture on CIN agar, cold enrichment <u>Cases:</u> stool culture on CIN
O. *Cyclospora cayetanensis*	1–11 days; median: 7 days	Fatigue, protracted diarrhea, often relapsing	tissue invasion	raw produce, water	<u>Food/water:</u> consult DPD <u>Cases:</u> stool examination for organisms; PCR (developmental) and testing for oocyste sporulation at DPD
P. *Cryptosporidium parvum*	2–28 days; median: 7 days	Diarrhea, nausea, vomiting; fever	tissue invasion	uncooked foods, water	<u>Food/water:</u> consult DPD <u>Cases:</u> stool examination for organisms or antigen; PCR and serologic test developmental (consult DPD)
Q. *Giardia lamblia*	3–25 days; median: 7 days	Diarrhea, gas, cramps, nausea, fatigue	?	uncooked foods, water	<u>Food/water:</u> consult DPD <u>Cases:</u> detection of antigen or organism in stool, duodenal contents, or small-bowel biopsy specimen

Section III
Analytic Methods

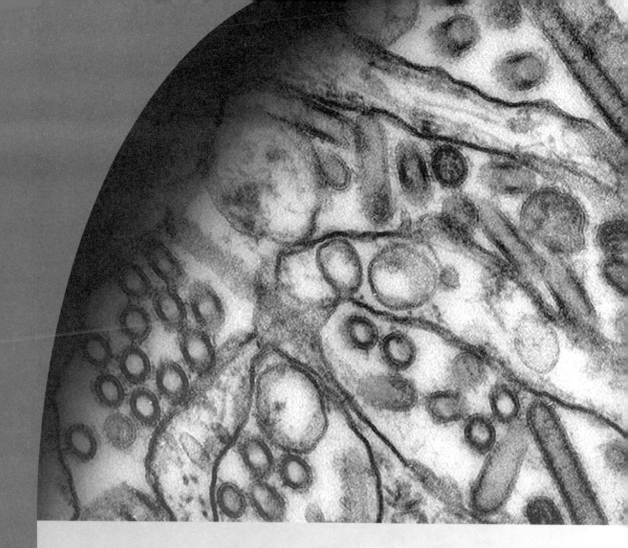

PART X

Analytic Methods

Methods are critical: How we do what we do and how we study what we study are directly related to what our research findings mean and what we can do with them. Critical evaluation—assessing methods, biases, analysis, interpretation, and more—is a skill worth building. It takes practice, but the more you read the easier it will become. The articles in this section are intended to do two things: provide you with papers that hone in on specific methodological issues and skills (e.g., biases, writing) as well as give you practice in reading epidemiologic literature. These skills can and should be applied to all of the reading you do in your educational program, or as you teach yourself. One way of building these skills beyond this Reader is to take any article available from your favorite peer-reviewed journal and go through it looking at its study design and writeup. The discussion questions following the articles in this section will help you do this, and over time, your skills will improve dramatically. For those of you who wish to develop your own studies, this practice will ultimately assist you as you design, analyze, interpret, and communicate your own work.

In October 2007, a monumental boon to epidemiologists was released in the form of the STROBE statement (see source below). This statement contains guidelines that are a veritable recipe for writing up studies that can be used by students and practitioners of epidemiology alike. The statement assists us in communicating our methods systematically, consistently, and effectively. It also gives an excellent primer on basic epidemiologic methods.

READING 28
Strengthening the Reporting of Observational Studies in Epidemiology (STROBE): Explanation and Elaboration

Jan P. Vandenbroucke, MD; Erik von Elm, MD; Douglas G. Altman, DSc; Peter C. Gøtzsche, MD; Cynthia D. Mulrow, MD; Stuart J. Pocock, PhD; Charles Poole, ScD; James J. Schlesselman, PhD; and Matthias Egger, MD, for the STROBE initiative

Vandenbroucke JP, von Elm E, Altman DG, et al. Strengthening the Reporting of Observational Studies in Epidemiology (STROBE): Explanation and Elaboration. *PLoS Medicine* Vol. 4, No. 10. [accessed 12/1/2007]. Available from http://medicine.plosjournals.org/perlserv/?request=get-document&doi=10.1371/journal.pmed.0040297.

Editor's Note: In order to encourage dissemination of the STROBE Statement, this article is being published simultaneously in *Annals of Internal Medicine*, *Epidemiology*, and *PLoS Medicine*. It is freely accessible on the *Annals of Internal Medicine* Web site (www.annals.org) and will also be published on the Web sites of *Epidemiology* and *PLoS Medicine*. The authors jointly hold the copyright of this article. For details on further use, see the STROBE Web site (www.strobe-statement.org).

Much medical research is observational. The reporting of observational studies is often of insufficient quality. Poor reporting hampers the assessment of the strengths and weaknesses of a study and the generalizability of its results. Taking into account empirical evidence and theoretical considerations, a group of methodologists, researchers, and editors developed the Strengthening the Reporting of Observational Studies in Epidemiology (STROBE) recommendations to improve the quality of reporting of observational studies.

The STROBE Statement consists of a checklist of 22 items, which relate to the title, abstract, introduction, methods, results, and discussion sections of articles. Eighteen items are common to cohort studies, case-control studies, and cross-sectional studies, and 4 are specific to each of the 3 study designs. The STROBE Statement provides guidance to authors about how to improve the reporting of observational studies and facilitates critical appraisal and interpretation of studies by reviewers, journal editors, and readers.

This explanatory and elaboration document is intended to enhance the use, understanding, and dissemination of the STROBE Statement. The meaning and rationale for each checklist item are presented. For each item, 1 or several published examples and, where possible, references to relevant empirical studies and methodological literature are provided. Examples of useful flow diagrams are also included. The STROBE Statement, this document, and the associated Web site (www.strobe-statement.org) should be helpful resources to improve reporting of observational research.

Rational health care practices require knowledge about the etiology and pathogenesis, diagnosis, prognosis, and treatment of diseases. Randomized trials provide valuable evidence about treatments and other interventions. However, much of clinical or public health knowledge comes from observational research (1). About 9 of 10 research papers published in clinical specialty journals describe observational research (2, 3).

THE STROBE STATEMENT

Reporting of observational research is often not detailed and clear enough to assess the strengths and weaknesses of the investigation (4, 5). To improve the reporting of observational research, we developed a checklist of items that should be addressed: the Strengthening the Reporting of Observational Studies in Epidemiology (STROBE) Statement (Table 10-1).

Items relate to the title, abstract, introduction, methods, results, and discussion sections of articles. The STROBE Statement has recently been published in several journals (6). Our aim is to ensure clear presentation of what was planned, done, and found in an observational study. We stress that the recommendations are not prescriptions for setting up or conducting studies, nor do they dictate methodology or mandate a uniform presentation.

STROBE provides general reporting recommendations for descriptive observational studies and studies that investigate associations between exposures and health outcomes. STROBE addresses the 3 main types of observational studies: cohort, case-control, and cross-sectional studies. Authors use diverse terminology to describe these study designs. For instance, "follow-up study" and "longitudinal study" are used as synonyms for

TABLE 10-1 The Strengthening the Reporting of Observational Studies in Epidemiology (STROBE) Statement: Checklist of Items that Should Be Addressed in Reports of Observational Studies.

Item	Item Number	Recommendation
Title and abstract	1	(a) Indicate the study's design with a commonly used term in the title or the abstract.
		(b) Provide in the abstract an informative and balanced summary of what was done and what was found.
Introduction		
Background/ rationale	2	Explain the scientific background and rationale for the investigation being reported.
Objectives	3	State specific objectives, including and prespecified hypotheses.
Methods		
Study design	4	Present key elements of study design early in the paper.
Setting	5	Describe the setting, locations, and relevant dates, including periods of recruitment, exposure, follow-up, and data collection.
Participants	6	(a) *Cohort study*: Give the eligibility criteria, and the sources and methods of selection participants. Describe methods of follow-up.
		Case-control study: Give the eligibility criteria, and the sources and methods of case ascertainment and control selection. Give the rationale for the choice of cases and controls.
		Cross-sectional study: Give the eligibility criteria, and the sources and methods of the selection of participants.
		(b) *Cohort study*: For matched studies, give matching criteria and the number of exposed and unexposed.
		Case-control study: For matched studies, give matching criteria and the number of controls per case.
Variables	7	Clearly define all outcomes, exposures, predictors, potential confounders, and effect modifiers. Give diagnostic criteria, if applicable.
Data sources/ measurements	8*	For each variable of interest, give sources of data and details of methods of assessment (measurement). Describe comparability of assessment methods if there is more than one group.
Bias	9	Describe any efforts to address potential sources of bias.

continues

TABLE 10-1 *(continued)*

Item	Item Number	Recommendation
Study size	10	Explain how the study size was arrived at.
Quantitative variables	11	Explain how quantitative variables were handled in the analyses. If applicable, describe which groupings were chosen and why.

Statistical methods	12	(a) Describe all statistical methods, including those used to control for confounding.
		(b) Describe any methods used to examine subgroups and interactions.
		(c) Explain how missing data were addressed.
		(d) *Cohort study*: If applicable, explain how loss to follow-up was addressed.
		    Case-control study: If applicable, explain how matching of cases and controls was addressed.
		    Cross-sectional study: If applicable, describe analytical methods taking account of sampling strategy.
		(e) Describe any sensitivity analyses.

Results		
Participants	13*	(a) Report the numbers of individuals at each stage of the study—e.g., numbers potentially eligible, examined for eligibility, confirmed eligible, included in the study, completing follow-up, and analyzed. (b) Give reasons for nonparticipation at each stage. (c) Consider use of a flow diagram.
Descriptive data	14*	(a) Give characteristics of study participants (e.g., demographic, clinical, social) and information on exposures and potential confounders. (b) Indicate the number of participants with missing data for each variable of interest. (c) *Cohort study*: Summarize follow-up time—e.g., average and total amount.
Outcome data	15*	*Cohort study*: Report numbers of outcome events of summary measures over time. *Case-control study*: Report numbers in each exposure category or summary measures of exposure. *Cross-sectional study*: Report numbers of outcome events or summary measures.
Main results	16	(a) Give unadjusted estimates and, if applicable, confounder-adjusted estimates and their precision (e.g., 95% confidence intervals). Make clear which confounders were adjusted for and why they were included. (b) Report category boundaries when continuous variables were categorized. (c) If relevant, consider translating estimates of relative risk into absolute risk for a meaningful time period.
Other analyses	17	Report other analyses done—e.g., analyses of subgroups and interactions and sensitivity analyses.
Discussion		
Key results	18	Summarize key results with reference to study objectives.
Limitations	19	Discuss limitations of the study, taking into account sources of potential bias or imprecision. Discuss both direction and magnitude of any potential bias.
Interpretations	20	Give a cautious overall interpretation of results considering objectives, limitations, multiplicity of analyses, results from similar studies, and other relevant evidence.
Generalizability	21	Discuss the generalizability (external validity) of the study results.
Other information		
Funding	22	Give the source of funding and the role of the funders for the present study and, if applicable, for the original study on which the present article is based.

*Give such information separately for cases and controls in case-control studies, and, if applicable, for exposed and unexposed groups in cohort and cross-sectional studies.

Separate versions of the checklist for cohort, case-control, and cross-sectional studies are available on the STROBE Web site (www.strobe-statement.org).

"cohort study," and "prevalence study" as a synonym for "cross-sectional study." We chose the present terminology because it is in common use. Unfortunately, terminology is often used incorrectly (7) or imprecisely (8). In Table 10-2, we describe the hallmarks of the 3 study designs.

THE SCOPE OF OBSERVATIONAL RESEARCH

Observational studies serve a wide range of purposes, from reporting a first hint of a potential cause of a disease to veri-

fying the magnitude of previously reported associations. Ideas for studies may arise from clinical observations or from biological insight. Ideas may also arise from informal looks at data that lead to further explorations. Like a clinician who has seen thousands of patients and notes 1 that strikes her attention, the researcher may note something special in the data. Adjusting for multiple looks at the data may not be possible or desirable (9), but further studies to confirm or refute initial observations are often needed (10). Existing data may be used to examine new ideas about potential causal factors, and may be sufficient for rejection or confirmation. In other instances, studies follow that are specifically designed to overcome potential problems with previous reports. The latter studies will gather new data and will be planned for that purpose, in contrast to analyses of existing data. This leads to diverse viewpoints, for example, on the merits of looking at subgroups or the importance of a predetermined sample size. STROBE tries to accommodate these diverse uses of observational research—from discovery to refutation or confirmation. Where necessary, we will indicate in what circumstances specific recommendations apply.

HOW TO USE THIS PAPER

This paper is linked to the shorter STROBE paper that introduced the items of the checklist in several journals (6), and forms an integral part of the STROBE Statement. Our intention is to explain how to report research well, not how research should be done. We offer a detailed explanation for each checklist item. Each explanation is preceded by an example of what we consider transparent reporting. This does not mean

TABLE 10-2 Main Study Designs Covered by STROBE.

Cohort, case-control, and cross-sectional designs represent different approaches of investigating the occurrence of health-related events in a given population and time period. These studies may address many types of health-related events, including disease or disease remission, disability or complications, death or survival, and the occurrence of risk factors.

In *cohort studies*, the investigators follow people over time. They obtain information about people and their exposures at baselines, let time pass, and then assess the occurrence of outcomes. Investigators commonly make contrasts between individuals who are exposed and not exposed or among groups of individuals with different categories of exposure. Investigators may assess several different outcomes, and examine exposure and outcome variables at multiple points during follow-up. Closed cohorts (for example, birth cohorts) enroll a defined number of participants at study onset and follow them from that time forward, often at set intervals up to a fixed end date. In open cohorts, the study population is dynamic; people enter and leave the population at different points in time (for example, inhabitants of a town). Open cohorts change due to deaths, births, and migration, but the composition of the population with regard to variables such as age and gender may remain approximately constant, especially over a short period of time. In a closed cohort, cumulative incidences (risks) and incidence rates can be estimated; when exposed and unexposed groups are compared, this leads to risk ratio or rate ratio estimates. Open cohorts estimate incidence rates and rate ratios.

In *case-control studies*, investigators compare exposures between people with a particular disease outcome (cases) and people without that outcome (controls). Investigators aim to collect cases and controls that are representative of an underlying cohort or a cross-section of a population. That population can be defined geographically, but also more loosely as the catchment area of health care facilities. The case sample may be 100% or a large fraction of available cases, while the control sample usually is only a small fraction of the people who do not have the pertinent outcome. Controls represent the cohort or population of people from which the cases arose. Investigators calculate the ratio of the odds of exposures to putative causes of the disease among cases and controls. Depending on the sampling strategy for cases and controls and the nature of the population studied, the odds ratio obtained in a case-control study is interpreted as the risk ratio, rate ratio, or (prevalence) odds ratio (16, 17). The majority of published case-control studies sample open cohorts and so allow direct estimations of rate ratios.

In *cross-sectional studies*, investigators assess all individuals in a sample at the same point in time, often to examine the prevalence of exposures, risk factors, or disease. Some cross-sectional studies are analytical and aim to quantify potential causal associations between exposures and disease. Such studies may be analyzed like a cohort study by comparing disease prevalence between exposure groups. They may also be analyzed like a case-control study by comparing the odds of exposure between groups with and without disease. A difficulty that can occur in any design but is particularly clear in cross-sectional studies is establishing that an exposure preceded the disease, although the time order of exposure and outcome may sometimes be clear. In a study in which the exposure variable is congenital or genetic, for example, we can be confident that the exposure preceded the disease, even if we are measuring both at the same time.

that the study from which the example was taken was uniformly well reported or well done; nor does it mean that its findings were reliable, in the sense that they were later confirmed by others: It only means that this particular item was well reported in that study. In addition to explanations and examples, we included boxes with supplementary information. These are intended for readers who want to refresh their memories about some theoretical points or be quickly informed about technical background details. A full understanding of these points may require studying the textbooks or methodological papers that are cited.

STROBE recommendations do not specifically address topics, such as genetic linkage studies, infectious disease modeling, or case reports and case series (11, 12). As many of the key elements in STROBE apply to these designs, authors who report such studies may nevertheless find our recommendations useful. For authors of observational studies that specifically address diagnostic tests, tumor markers, and genetic associations, STARD (13), REMARK (14), and STREGA (15) recommendations may be particularly useful.

THE ITEMS IN THE STROBE CHECKLIST

We now discuss and explain the 22 items in the STROBE checklist (Table 10-1) and give published examples for each item. Some examples have been edited by removing citations or spelling out abbreviations. Eighteen items apply to all 3 study designs, whereas 4 are design-specific. Starred items (for example, item 8*) indicate that the information should be given separately for cases and controls in case-control studies, or exposed and unexposed groups in cohort and cross-sectional studies. We advise authors to address all items somewhere in their paper, but we do not prescribe a precise location or order. For instance, we discuss the reporting of results under a number of separate items, while recognizing that authors might address several items within a single section of text or in a table.

TITLE AND ABSTRACT

1(a) Indicate the study's design with a commonly used term in the title or the abstract.

EXAMPLE

"Leukaemia incidence among workers in the shoe and boot manufacturing industry: a case-control study" (18).

EXPLANATION

Readers should be able to easily identify the design that was used from the title or abstract. An explicit, commonly used

term for the study design also helps ensure correct indexing of articles in electronic databases (19, 20).

1(b) Provide in the abstract an informative and balanced summary of what was done and what was found.

EXAMPLE

"Background: The expected survival of HIV-infected patients is of major public health interest.

Objective: To estimate survival time and age-specific mortality rates of an HIV-infected population compared with that of the general population.

Design: Population-based cohort study.

Setting: All HIV-infected persons receiving care in Denmark from 1995 to 2005.

Patients: Each member of the nationwide Danish HIV Cohort Study was matched with as many as 99 persons from the general population according to sex, date of birth, and municipality of residence.

Measurements: The authors computed Kaplan-Meier life tables with age as the time scale to estimate survival from age 25 years. Patients with HIV infection and corresponding persons from the general population were observed from the date of the patient's HIV diagnosis until death, emigration, or 1 May 2005.

Results: 3990 HIV-infected patients and 379 872 persons from the general population were included in the study, yielding 22 744 (median, 5.8 y/person) and 2 689 287 (median, 8.4 y/person) person-years of observation. Three percent of participants were lost to follow-up. From age 25 years, the median survival was 19.9 years (95% CI, 18.5 to 21.3) among patients with HIV infection and 51.1 years (CI, 50.9 to 51.5) among the general population. For HIV-infected patients, survival increased to 32.5 years (CI, 29.4 to 34.7) during the 2000 to 2005 period. In the subgroup that excluded persons with known hepatitis C coinfection (16%), median survival was 38.9 years (CI, 35.4 to 40.1) during this same period. The relative mortality rates for patients with HIV infection compared with those for the general population decreased with increasing age, whereas the excess mortality rate increased with increasing age.

Limitations: The observed mortality rates are assumed to apply beyond the current maximum observation time of 10 years.

Conclusions: The estimated median survival is more than 35 years for a young person diagnosed with HIV infection in the late highly active antiretroviral therapy era. However, an ongoing effort is still needed to further reduce mortality rates for these persons compared with the general population" (21).

EXPLANATION

The abstract provides key information that enables readers to understand a study and decide whether to read the article. Typical components include a statement of the research question, a short description of methods and results, and a conclusion (22). Abstracts should summarize key details of studies and should only present information that is provided in the article. We advise presenting key results in a numerical form that includes numbers of participants, estimates of associations, and appropriate measures of variability and uncertainty (for example, odds ratios with confidence intervals). We regard it insufficient to state only that an exposure is or is not significantly associated with an outcome.

A series of headings pertaining to the background, design, conduct, and analysis of a study may help readers acquire the essential information rapidly (23). Many journals require such structured abstracts, which tend to be of higher quality and more readily informative than unstructured summaries (24, 25).

INTRODUCTION

The Introduction section should describe why the study was done and what questions and hypotheses it addresses. It should allow others to understand the study's context and judge its potential contribution to current knowledge.

2 Background/rationale: Explain the scientific background and rationale for the investigation being reported.

EXAMPLE

"Concerns about the rising prevalence of obesity in children and adolescents have focused on the well-documented associations between childhood obesity and increased cardiovascular risk and mortality in adulthood. Childhood obesity has considerable social and psychological consequences within childhood and adolescence, yet little is known about social, socioeconomic, and psychological consequences in adult life. A recent systematic review found no longitudinal studies on the outcomes of childhood obesity other than physical health outcomes and only two longitudinal studies of the socioeconomic effects of obesity in adolescence. Gortmaker et al. found that US women who had been obese in late adolescence in 1981 were less likely to be married and had lower incomes seven years later than women who had not been overweight, while men who had been overweight were less likely to be married. Sargent et al. found that UK women, but not men, who had been obese at 16 years in 1974 earned 7.4% less than their nonobese peers at age 23. . . . We used longitudinal data from the 1970 British birth cohort to examine the adult socioeco-

nomic, educational, social, and psychological outcomes of childhood obesity" (26).

EXPLANATION

The scientific background of the study provides important context for readers. It sets the stage for the study and describes its focus. It gives an overview of what is known on a topic and what gaps in current knowledge are addressed by the study. Background material should note recent pertinent studies and any systematic reviews of pertinent studies.

3 Objectives: State specific objectives, including any prespecified hypotheses.

EXAMPLE

"Our primary objectives were to 1) determine the prevalence of domestic violence among female patients presenting to four community-based, primary care, adult medicine practices that serve patients of diverse socioeconomic background and 2) identify demographic and clinical differences between currently abused patients and patients not currently being abused" (27).

EXPLANATION

Objectives are the detailed aims of the study. Well-crafted objectives specify populations, exposures and outcomes, and parameters that will be estimated. They may be formulated as specific hypotheses or as questions that the study was designed to address. In some situations, objectives may be less specific, for example, in early discovery phases. Regardless, the report should clearly reflect the investigators' intentions. For example, if important subgroups or additional analyses were not the original aim of the study but arose during data analysis, they should be described accordingly (see items 4, 17, and 20).

METHODS

The Methods section should describe what was planned and what was done in sufficient detail to allow others to understand the essential aspects of the study, to judge whether the methods were adequate to provide reliable and valid answers, and to assess whether any deviations from the original plan were reasonable.

4 Study design: Present key elements of study design early in the paper.

EXAMPLE

"We used a case-crossover design, a variation of a case-control design that is appropriate when a brief exposure (driver's phone use) causes a transient rise in the risk of a rare outcome (a crash). We compared a driver's use of a mobile phone at the estimated time of a crash with the same driver's use during another suitable time period. Because drivers are their own controls, the design controls for characteristics of the driver that may affect the risk of a crash but do not change over a short period of time. As it is important that risks during control periods and crash trips are similar, we compared phone activity during the hazard interval (time immediately before the crash) with phone activity during control intervals (equivalent times during which participants were driving but did not crash) in the previous week" (28).

EXPLANATION

We advise presenting key elements of study design early in the methods section (or at the end of the introduction) so that readers can understand the basics of the study. For example, authors should indicate that the study was a cohort study, which followed people over a particular time period, and describe the group of persons that comprised the cohort and their exposure status. Similarly, if the investigation used a case-control design, the cases and controls and their source population should be described. If the study was a cross-sectional survey, the population and the point in time at which the cross-section was taken should be mentioned. When a study is a variant of the 3 main study types, there is an additional need for clarity. For instance, for a case-crossover study, 1 of the variants of the case-control design, a succinct description of the principles was given in the example above (28).

We recommend that authors refrain from simply calling a study "prospective" or "retrospective," because these terms are ill defined (29). One usage sees cohort and prospective as synonymous and reserves the word retrospective for case-control studies (30). A second usage distinguishes prospective and retrospective cohort studies according to the timing of data collection relative to when the idea for the study was developed (31). A third usage distinguishes prospective and retrospective case-control studies depending on whether the data about the exposure of interest existed when cases were selected (32). Some advise against using these terms (33), or adopting the alternatives "concurrent" and "historical" for describing cohort studies (34). In STROBE, we do not use the words prospective and retrospective or alternatives, such as concurrent and historical. We recommend that, whenever authors use these words, they define what they mean. Most importantly, we recommend that authors describe exactly how and when data collection took place.

The first part of the methods section might also be the place to mention whether the report is 1 of several from a study. If a new report is in line with the original aims of the study, this is usually indicated by referring to an earlier publication and by briefly restating the salient features of the study. However, the aims of a study may also evolve over time. Researchers often use data for purposes for which they were not originally intended, including, for example, official vital statistics that were collected primarily for administrative purposes, items in questionnaires that originally were only included for completeness, or blood samples that were collected for another purpose. For example, the Physicians' Health Study, a randomized controlled trial of aspirin and carotene, was later used to demonstrate that a point mutation in the factor V gene was associated with an increased risk of venous thrombosis, but not of myocardial infarction or stroke (35). The secondary use of existing data is a creative part of observational research and does not necessarily make results less credible or less important. However, briefly restating the original aims might help readers understand the context of the research and possible limitations in the data.

5 Setting: Describe the setting, locations, and relevant dates, including periods of recruitment, exposure, follow-up, and data collection.

EXAMPLE

"The Pasitos Cohort Study recruited pregnant women from Women, Infant, and Child clinics in Socorro and San Elizario, El Paso County, Texas and maternal-child clinics of the Mexican Social Security Institute in Ciudad Juarez, Mexico from April 1998 to October 2000. At baseline, prior to the birth of the enrolled cohort children, staff interviewed mothers regarding the household environment. In this ongoing cohort study, we target follow-up exams at 6-month intervals beginning at age 6 months" (36).

EXPLANATION

Readers need information on setting and locations to assess the context and generalizability of a study's results. Exposures, such as environmental factors and therapies, can change over time. Also, study methods may evolve over time. Knowing when a study took place and over what period participants were recruited and followed up places the study in historical context and is important for the interpretation of results.

Information about setting includes recruitment sites or sources (for example, electoral roll, outpatient clinic, cancer registry, or tertiary care center). Information about location may refer to the countries, towns, hospitals, or practices where the investigation took place. We advise stating dates rather than only describing the length of time periods. There may be different sets of dates for exposure, disease occurrence, recruitment, beginning and end of follow-up, and data collection. Of note, nearly 80% of 132 reports in oncology journals that used survival analysis included the starting and ending dates for accrual of patients, but only 24% also reported the date on which follow-up ended (37).

6 Participants:

6(a) Cohort study: Give the eligibility criteria, and the sources and methods of selection of participants. Describe methods of follow-up.

EXAMPLE

"Participants in the Iowa Women's Health Study were a random sample of all women ages 55 to 69 years derived from the state of Iowa automobile driver's license list in 1985, which represented approximately 94% of Iowa women in that age group. . . . Follow-up questionnaires were mailed in October 1987 and August 1989 to assess vital status and address changes. . . . Incident cancers, except for nonmelanoma skin cancers, were ascertained by the State Health Registry of Iowa. . . . The Iowa Women's Health Study cohort was matched to the registry with combinations of first, last, and maiden names, zip code, birth date, and social security number" (38).

6(a) Case-control study: Give the eligibility criteria, and the sources and methods of case ascertainment and control selection. Give the rationale for the choice of cases and controls.

EXAMPLE

"Cutaneous melanoma cases diagnosed in 1999 and 2000 were ascertained through the Iowa Cancer Registry. . . . Controls, also identified through the Iowa Cancer Registry, were colorectal cancer patients diagnosed during the same time. Colorectal cancer controls were selected because they are common and have a relatively long survival, and because arsenic exposure has not been conclusively linked to the incidence of colorectal cancer" (39).

6(a) Cross-sectional study: Give the eligibility criteria, and the sources and methods of selection of participants.

EXAMPLE

"We retrospectively identified patients with a principal diagnosis of myocardial infarction (code 410) according to the International Classification of Diseases, 9th Revision, Clinical Modification, from codes designating discharge diagnoses, excluding the codes with a fifth digit of 2, which designates a subsequent episode of care. . . . A random sample of the entire Medicare cohort with myocardial infarction from February 1994 to July 1995 was selected. . . . To be eligible, patients had to present to the hospital after at least 30 minutes but less than 12 hours of chest pain and had to have ST-segment elevation of at least 1 mm on 2 contiguous leads on the initial electrocardiogram" (40).

EXPLANATION

Detailed descriptions of the study participants help readers understand the applicability of the results. Investigators usually restrict a study population by defining clinical, demographic, and other characteristics of eligible participants. Typical eligibility criteria relate to age, gender, diagnosis, and comorbid conditions. Despite their importance, eligibility criteria often are not reported adequately. In a survey of observational stroke research, 17 of 49 reports (35%) did not specify eligibility criteria (5).

Eligibility criteria may be presented as inclusion and exclusion criteria, although this distinction is not always necessary or useful. Regardless, we advise authors to report all eligibility criteria and also to describe the group from which the study population was selected (for example, the general population of a region or country) and the method of recruitment (for example, referral or self-selection through advertisements).

Knowing details about follow-up procedures, including whether procedures minimized nonresponse and loss to follow-up and whether the procedures were similar for all participants, informs judgments about the validity of results. For example, in a study that used IgM antibodies to detect acute infections, readers needed to know the interval between blood tests for IgM antibodies so that they could judge whether some infections likely were missed because the interval between blood tests was too long (41). In other studies where follow-up procedures differed between exposed and unexposed groups, readers might recognize substantial bias due to unequal ascertainment of events or differences in nonresponse or loss to follow-up (42). Accordingly, we advise that researchers describe the methods used for following participants and whether those methods were the same for all participants, and that they describe the completeness of ascertainment of variables (see also item 14).

In case-control studies, the choice of cases and controls is crucial to interpreting the results, and the method of their selection has major implications for study validity. In general, controls should reflect the population from which the cases arose. Various methods are used to sample controls, all with advantages and disadvantages. For cases that arise from a general population, population roster sampling, random-digit dialing, or neighborhood or friend controls are used. Neighborhood or friend controls may present intrinsic matching on exposure (17). Controls with other diseases may have advantages over population-based controls, in particular for hospital-based cases, because they better reflect the catchment population of a hospital and have greater comparability of recall and ease of recruitment. However, they can present problems if the exposure of interest affects the risk of developing or being hospitalized for the control condition(s) (43, 44). To remedy this problem, often a mixture of the best defensible control diseases is used (45).

6(b) Cohort study: For matched studies, give matching criteria and number of exposed and unexposed.

EXAMPLE

"For each patient who initially received a statin, we used propensity-based matching to identify 1 control who did not receive a statin according to the following protocol. First, propensity scores were calculated for each patient in the entire cohort on the basis of an extensive list of factors potentially related to the use of statins or the risk of sepsis. Second, each statin user was matched to a smaller pool of nonstatin users by sex, age (plus or minus 1 year), and index date (plus or minus 3 months). Third, we selected the control with the closest propensity score (within 0.2 SD) to each statin user in a 1:1 fashion and discarded the remaining controls" (46).

6(b) Case-control study: For matched studies, give matching criteria and the number of controls per case.

EXAMPLE

"We aimed to select 5 controls for every case from among individuals in the study population who had no diagnosis of autism or other pervasive developmental disorders (PDD) recorded in their general practice record and who were alive and registered with a participating practice on the date of the PDD diagnosis in the case. Controls were individually matched to cases by year of birth (up to 1 year older or younger), sex, and general practice. For each of 300 cases, 5 controls could be identified who met all the matching criteria. For the remaining 994, 1 or more controls was excluded. . . ." (47).

EXPLANATION

Matching is much more common in case-control studies, but occasionally, investigators use matching in cohort studies to make groups comparable at the start of follow-up. Matching in cohort studies makes groups directly comparable for potential confounders and presents fewer intricacies than with case-control studies. For example, it is not necessary to take the matching into account for the estimation of the relative risk (48). Because matching in cohort studies may increase sta-

tistical precision, investigators might allow for the matching in their analyses and thus obtain narrower confidence intervals.

In case-control studies, matching is done to increase a study's efficiency by ensuring similarity in the distribution of variables between cases and controls, in particular the distribution of potential confounding variables (48, 49). Because matching can be done in various ways, with 1 or more controls per case, the rationale for the choice of matching variables and the details of the method used should be described. Commonly used forms of matching are frequency matching (also called group matching) and individual matching. In frequency matching, investigators choose controls so that the distribution of matching variables becomes identical or similar to that of cases. Individual matching involves matching 1 or several controls to each case. Although intuitively appealing and sometimes useful, matching in case-control studies has a number of disadvantages, is not always appropriate, and needs to be taken into account in the analysis (see Table 10-3).

Even apparently simple matching procedures may be poorly reported. For example, authors may state that controls were matched to cases "within 5 years," or using "5-year age bands." Does this mean that, if a case was 54 years old, the respective control needed to be in the 5-year age band 50 to 54, or aged 49 to 59, which is within 5 years of age 54? If a wide (for example, 10-year) age band is chosen, there is a danger of residual confounding by age (see Table 10-4), for example, because controls may then be younger than cases on average.

7 Variables: Clearly define all outcomes, exposures, predictors, potential confounders, and effect modifiers. Give diagnostic criteria, if applicable.

EXAMPLE

"Only major congenital malformations were included in the analyses. Minor anomalies were excluded according to the exclusion list of European Registration of Congenital Anomalies (EUROCAT). If a child had more than 1 major congenital malformation of 1 organ system, those malformations were treated as 1 outcome in the analyses by organ system. . . . In the statistical analyses, factors considered potential confounders were maternal age at delivery and number of previous parities. Factors considered potential effect modifiers were maternal age at reimbursement for antiepileptic medication and maternal age at delivery" (55).

EXPLANATION

Authors should define all variables considered for and included in the analysis, including outcomes, exposures, predictors, potential confounders, and potential effect modifiers. Disease outcomes require adequately detailed description of the diagnostic

TABLE 10-3 Matching in Case-Control Studies.

In any case-control study, sensible choices need to be made on whether to use matching of controls to cases, and if so, what variables to match on, the precise method of matching to use, and the appropriate method of statistical analysis. Not to match at all may mean that the distribution of some key potential confounders (for example, age, sex) is radically different between cases and controls. Although this could be adjusted for in the analysis, there could be a major loss in statistical efficiency.

The use of matching in case-control studies and its interpretation are fraught with difficulties, especially if matching is attempted on several risk factors, some of which may be linked to exposure of prime interest. For example, in a case-control study of myocardial infarction and oral contraceptives nested in a large pharmacoepidemiologic database, with information about thousands of women that are available as potential controls, investigators may be tempted to choose matched controls who had similar levels of risk factors to each case of myocardial infarction. One objective is to adjust for factors that might influence the prescription of oral contraceptives and thus to control for *confounding by indication*. However, the result will be a control group that is *no longer representative* of the oral contraceptive use in the source population; controls will be older than the source population because patients with myocardial infarction tend to be older. This has several implications. A crude analysis of the data will produce odds ratios that are usually biased toward unity of the matching factor is associated with the exposure. The solution is to perform a matched or stratified analysis. In addition, because the matched control group ceases to be representative for the population at large, the exposure distribution among the controls can no longer be used to estimate the population attributable fraction. Also, the effect of the matching factor can no longer be studied, and the search for well-matched controls can be cumbersome—making a design with a nonmatched control group preferable because the nonmatched controls will be easier to obtain and the control group can be larger. Overmatching is another problem, which may reduce the efficiency of matched case-control studies, and, in some situations, introduce bias. Information is lost and the power of the study is reduced if the matching system variable is closely associated with the exposure. Then many individuals in the same matched sets will tend to have identical or similar levels of exposures and therefore not contribute relevant information. Matching will introduce irremediable bias if the matching variable is not a confounder but in the causal pathway between exposure and disease. For example, in vitro fertilization is associated with an increased risk of perinatal death, due to an increase in multiple births and low-birth-weight infants. Matching on plurality or birth weight will bias results toward the null, and this cannot be remedied in the analysis.

Matching is intuitively appealing, but the complexities involved have led methodologists to advise against routine matching in case-control studies. They recommend instead a careful and judicious consideration of each potential matching factor, recognizing that it could instead be measured and used as an adjustment variable without matching on it. In response, there has been a reduction in the number of matching factors employed; an increasing use of frequency matching, which avoids some of the problems discussed above; and more case-control studies with no matching at all. Matching remains most desirable, or even necessary, when the distributions of the confounder (for example, age) might differ radically between the unmatched comparison groups.

times use "dependent variable" for an outcome and "independent variable" or "explanatory variable" for exposure and confounding variables. The latter is not precise, as it does not distinguish exposures from confounders.

If many variables have been measured and included in exploratory analyses in an early discovery phase, consider providing a list with details on each variable in an appendix, additional table, or separate publication. Of note, the *International Journal of Epidemiology* recently launched a new section with "cohort profiles," that includes detailed information on what was measured at different points in time in particular studies (56, 57). Finally, we advise that authors declare all "candidate variables" considered for statistical analysis, rather than selectively reporting only those included in the final models (see item 16a) (58, 59).

8 Data sources/measurement: For each variable of interest, give sources of data and details of methods of assessment (measurement). Describe comparability of assessment methods if there is more than one group.

EXAMPLE 1

"Total caffeine intake was calculated primarily using U.S. Department of Agriculture food composition sources. In these calculations, it was assumed that the content of caffeine was 137 mg per cup of coffee, 47 mg per cup of tea, 46 mg per can or bottle of cola beverage, and 7 mg per serving of chocolate candy. This method of measuring (caffeine) intake was shown to be valid in both the NHS I cohort and a similar cohort study of male health professionals...Self-reported diagnosis of hypertension was found to be reliable in the NHS I cohort" (60).

criteria. This applies to criteria for cases in a case-control study, disease events during follow-up in a cohort study, and prevalent disease in a cross-sectional study. Clear definitions and steps taken to adhere to them are particularly important for any disease condition of primary interest in the study.

For some studies, "determinant" or "predictor" may be appropriate terms for exposure variables and outcomes may be called "end points." In multivariable models, authors some-

TABLE 10-4 Grouping.

There are several reasons why continuous data may be grouped. When collecting data, it may be better to use an ordinal variable than to seek an artificially precise continuous measure for an exposure based on recall over several years. Categories may also be helpful for presentation, for example, to present all variables in a similar style, or to show a dose-response relationship.

Grouping may also be done to simplify the analysis, for example to avoid an assumption of linearity. However, grouping loses information and may reduce statistical power, especially when dichotomization is used. If a continuous confounder is grouped, residual confounding may occur, whereby some of the variable's confounding effect remains unadjusted for. Increasing the number of categories can diminish power loss and residual confounding and is especially appropriate in large studies. Small studies may use few groups because of limited numbers.

Investigators may choose cut-points for groupings based on commonly used values that are relevant for diagnosis or prognosis, for practicality, or on statistical grounds. They may choose equal numbers of individuals in each group using quantiles. On the other hand, one may gain more insight into the association with the outcome by choosing more extreme outer groups and having the middle group(s) larger than the outer groups. In case-control studies, deriving a distribution from the control group is preferred because it is intended to reflect the source population. Readers should be informed if cut-points are selected post hoc from several alternatives. In particular, if the cut-points were chosen to minimize a P value, the true strength of an association will be exaggerated.

When analyzing grouped variables, it is important to recognize their underlying continuous nature. For instance, a possible trend in risk across ordered groups can be investigated. A common approach is to model the rank of the groups as a continuous variable. Such linearity across group scores will approximate an actual linear relation if groups are equally spaced (for example, 10-year age groups) but not otherwise. Il'yasova et al. (92) recommend publication of both the categorical and the continuous estimates of effect, with their standard errors, in order to facilitate meta-analysis, as well as providing intrinsically valuable information on dose-response. One analysis may inform the other, and neither is assumption-free. Authors often ignore the ordering and consider the estimates (and P values) separately for each category compared to the reference category. This may be useful for description, but may fail to detect a real trend in risk groups. If a trend is observed, a confidence interval for a slope might indicate the strength of the observation.

ing validation studies (as in the first example), we advise that authors give the estimated validity or reliability, which can then be used for measurement error adjustment or sensitivity analyses (see items 12e and 17).

In addition, it is important to know if groups being compared differed with respect to the way in which the data were collected. This may be important for laboratory examinations (as in the second example) and other situations. For instance, if an interviewer first questions all the cases and then the controls, or vice versa, bias is possible because of the learning curve; solutions such as randomizing the order of interviewing may avoid this problem. Information bias may also arise if the compared groups are not given the same diagnostic tests or if 1 group receives more tests of the same kind than another (see item 9).

9 Bias: Describe any efforts to address potential sources of bias.

EXAMPLE 1

"In most case-control studies of suicide, the control group comprises living individuals, but we decided to have a control group of people who had died of other causes. . . . With a control group of deceased individuals, the sources of information used to assess risk factors are informants who have recently experienced the death of a family member or close associate—and are therefore more comparable to the sources of information in the suicide group than if living controls were used" (64).

EXAMPLE 2

"Detection bias could influence the association between Type 2 diabetes mellitus (T2DM) and primary open-angle glaucoma (POAG) if women with T2DM were under closer ophthalmic surveillance than women without this condition. We compared the mean number of eye examinations reported by women with and without diabetes. We also recalculated the

EXAMPLE 2

"Samples pertaining to matched cases and controls were always analyzed together in the same batch and laboratory personnel were unable to distinguish among cases and controls" (61).

EXPLANATION

The way in which exposures, confounders, and outcomes were measured affects the reliability and validity of a study. Measurement error and misclassification of exposures or outcomes can make it more difficult to detect cause–effect relationships, or may produce spurious relationships. Error in measurement of potential confounders can increase the risk of residual confounding (62, 63). It is helpful, therefore, if authors report the findings of any studies of the validity or reliability of assessments or measurements, including details of the reference standard that was used. Rather than simply cit-

relative risk for POAG with additional control for covariates associated with more careful ocular surveillance (a self-report of cataract, macular degeneration, number of eye examinations, and number of physical examinations)" (65).

EXPLANATION

Biased studies produce results that differ systematically from the truth (see Table 10-5). It is important for a reader to know what measures were taken during the conduct of a study to reduce the potential of bias. Ideally, investigators carefully consider potential sources of bias when they plan their study. At the stage of reporting, we recommend that authors always assess the likelihood of relevant biases. Specifically, the direction and magnitude of bias should be discussed and, if possible, estimated. For instance, in case-control studies, information bias can occur, but may be reduced by selecting an appropriate control group, as in the first example (64). Differences in the medical surveillance of participants were a problem in the second example (65). Consequently, the authors provide more detail about the additional data they collected to tackle this problem. When investigators have set up quality control programs for data collection to counter a possible "drift" in measurements of variables in longitudinal studies, or to keep variability at a minimum when multiple observers are used, these should be described.

Unfortunately, authors often do not address important biases when reporting their results. Among 43 case-control and cohort studies published from 1990 to 1994 that investigated the risk of second cancers in patients with a history of cancer, medical surveillance bias was mentioned in only 5 articles (66). A survey of reports of mental health research published during 1998 in 3 psychiatric journals found that only 13% of 392 articles mentioned response bias (67). A survey of cohort studies in stroke research found that 14 of 49 (28%) articles published from 1999 to 2003 addressed potential selection bias in the recruitment of study participants and 35 (71%) mentioned the possibility that any type of bias may have affected results (5).

10 Study size: Explain how the study size was arrived at.

EXAMPLE 1

"The number of cases in the area during the study period determined the sample size" (73).

TABLE 10-5 Bias.

Bias is a systematic deviation of a study's result from a true value. Typically, it is introduced during the design or implementation of a study and cannot be remedied later. Bias and confounding are not synonymous. Bias arises from flawed information or subject selection so that a wrong association is found. Confounding produces relations that are factually right, but that cannot be interpreted causally because some underlying, unaccounted-for factor is associated with both exposure and outcome. Also, bias needs to be distinguished from random error, a deviation from a true value caused by statistical fluctuations (in either direction) in the measured data. Many possible sources of bias have been described, and a variety of terms are used. We find 2 simple categories helpful: information bias and selection bias.

Information bias occurs when systematic differences in the completeness or the accuracy of data lead to differential misclassification of individuals regarding exposures or outcomes. For instance, if diabetic women receive more regular and thorough eye examinations, the ascertainment of glaucoma will be more complete than in women without diabetes. Patients receiving a drug that causes nonspecific stomach discomfort may undergo gastroscopy more often and have more ulcers detected than patients not receiving the drug—even if the drug does not cause more ulcers. This type of information bias is also called "detection bias" or "medical surveillance bias." One way to assess its influence is to measure the intensity of medical surveillance in the different study groups and to adjust for it in statistical analyses. In case-control studies, information bias occurs if cases recall past exposures more or less accurately than controls without that disease, or if they are more or less willing to report then (also called "recall bias"). "Interviewer bias" can occur if interviewers are aware of the study hypothesis and subconsciously or consciously gather data selectively. Some form of blinding of study participants and researchers is therefore often valuable.

Selection bias may be introduced in case-control studies if the probability of including cases or controls is associated with exposure. For instance, a doctor recruiting participants for a study on seep-vein thrombosis might diagnose this disease in a woman who has leg complaints and takes oral contraceptives. But she might not diagnose deep-vein thrombosis in a woman with similar complaints who is not taking such medication. Such bias may be countered by using cases and controls that were referred in the same way to the diagnostic service. Similarly, the use of disease registers may introduce selection bias: If a possible relationship between an exposure and a disease is known, cases may be more likely to be submitted to a register if they have been exposed to the suspected causative agent. "Response bias" is another type of selection bias that occurs if differences in characteristics between those who respond and those who decline participation in a study affect estimates of prevalence, incidence, and, in some circumstances, associations. In general, selection bias affects the internal validity of a study. This is different from problems that may arise with the selection of participants for a study in general, which affects the external rather than the internal validity of a study.

EXAMPLE 2

"A survey of postnatal depression in the region had documented a prevalence of 19.8%. Assuming depression in mothers with normal-weight children to be 20% and an odds ratio of 3 for depression in mothers with a malnourished child, we needed 72 case-control sets (1 case to 1 control) with an 80% power and 5% significance" (74).

EXPLANATION

A study should be large enough to obtain a point estimate with a sufficiently narrow confidence interval to meaningfully answer a research question. Large samples are needed to distinguish a small association from no association. Small studies often provide valuable information, but wide confidence intervals may indicate that they contribute less to current knowledge in comparison with studies providing estimates with narrower confidence intervals. Also, small studies that show "interesting" or "statistically significant" associations are published more frequently than small studies that do not have "significant" findings. While these studies may provide an early signal in the context of discovery, readers should be informed of their potential weaknesses.

The importance of sample size determination in observational studies depends on the context. If an analysis is performed on data that were already available for other purposes, the main question is whether the analysis of the data will produce results with sufficient statistical precision to contribute substantially to the literature, and sample size considerations will be informal. Formal, a priori calculation of sample size may be useful when planning a new study (75, 76). Such calculations are associated with more uncertainty than is implied by the single number that is generally produced. For example, estimates of the rate of the event of interest or other assumptions central to calculations are commonly imprecise, if not guesswork (77). The precision obtained in the final analysis can often not be determined beforehand because it will be reduced by inclusion of confounding variables in multivariable analyses (78), the degree of precision with which key variables can be measured (79), and the exclusion of some individuals.

Few epidemiologic studies explain or report deliberations about sample size (4, 5). We encourage investigators to report pertinent formal sample size calculations if they were done. In other situations, they should indicate the considerations that determined the study size (for example, a fixed available sample, as in the first example above). If the observational study was stopped early when statistical significance was achieved, readers should be told. Do not bother readers with post hoc justifications for study size or retrospective power

calculations (77). From the point of view of the reader, confidence intervals indicate the statistical precision that was ultimately obtained. It should be realized that confidence intervals reflect statistical uncertainty only, and not all uncertainty that may be present in a study (see item 20).

11 Quantitative variables: Explain how quantitative variables were handled in the analyses. If applicable, describe which groupings were chosen, and why.

EXAMPLE

"Patients with a Glasgow Coma Scale less than 8 are considered to be seriously injured. A GCS of 9 or more indicates less serious brain injury. We examined the association of GCS in these two categories with the occurrence of death within 12 months from injury" (80).

EXPLANATION

Investigators make choices regarding how to collect and analyze quantitative data about exposures, effect modifiers, and confounders. For example, they may group a continuous exposure variable to create a new categorical variable (see Table 10-4). Grouping choices may have important consequences for later analyses (81, 82). We advise that authors explain why and how they grouped quantitative data, including the number of categories, the cut-points, and category mean or median values. Whenever data are reported in tabular form, the counts of cases, controls, persons at risk, person-time at risk, etc., should be given for each category. Tables should not consist solely of effect-measure estimates or results of model fitting.

Investigators might model an exposure as continuous in order to retain all the information. In making this choice, one needs to consider the nature of the relationship of the exposure to the outcome. As it may be wrong to assume a linear relation automatically, possible departures from linearity should be investigated. Authors could mention alternative models they explored during analyses (for example, using log transformation, quadratic terms, or spline functions). Several methods exist for fitting a nonlinear relation between the exposure and outcome (82–84). Also, it may be informative to present both continuous and grouped analyses for a quantitative exposure of prime interest.

In a recent survey, two thirds of epidemiologic publications studied quantitative exposure variables (4). In 42 of 50 articles (84%), exposures were grouped into several ordered categories, but often without any stated rationale for the choices made. Fifteen articles used linear associations to model continuous exposure, but only 2 reported checking for linearity. In another survey, of the psychological literature, dichotomization was justified in only 22 of 110 articles (20%) (85).

12 Statistical methods:

12(a) Describe all statistical methods, including those used to control for confounding.

EXAMPLE

"The adjusted relative risk was calculated using the Mantel-Haenszel technique, when evaluating if confounding by age or gender was present in the groups compared. The 95% confidence interval (CI) was computed around the adjusted relative risk, using the variance according to Greenland and Robins and Robins et al." (93).

EXPLANATION

In general, there is no one correct statistical analysis but, rather, several possibilities that may address the same question but make different assumptions. Regardless, investigators should predetermine analyses at least for the primary study objectives in a study protocol. Often additional analyses are needed, either instead of, or as well as, those originally envisaged, and these may sometimes be motivated by the data. When a study is reported, authors should tell readers whether particular analyses were suggested by data inspection. Even though the distinction between prespecified and exploratory analyses may sometimes be blurred, authors should clarify reasons for particular analyses.

If groups being compared are not similar with regard to some characteristics, adjustment should be made for possible confounding variables by stratification or by multivariable regression (see Table 10-6) (94). Often, the study design determines which type of regression analysis is chosen. For instance, Cox proportional hazard regression is commonly used in cohort studies (95), whereas logistic regression is often the method of choice in case-control studies (96, 97). Analysts should fully describe specific procedures for variable selection and not only present results from the final model (98, 99). If model comparisons are made to narrow down a list of potential confounders for inclusion in a final model, this process should be described. It is helpful to tell readers if 1 or 2 covariates are responsible for a great deal of the apparent confounding in a data analysis. Other statistical analyses, such as imputation procedures, data transformation, and calculations of attributable risks, should also be described. Nonstandard or novel approaches should be referenced, and the statistical software used reported. As a guiding principle, we advise statistical methods be described "with enough detail to enable a knowledgeable reader with access to the original data to verify the reported results" (100).

In an empirical study, only 93 of 169 articles (55%) reporting adjustment for confounding clearly stated how continuous and multicategory variables were entered into the statistical

---

> **TABLE 10-6** Confounding.
>
> "Confounding" literally means "confusion of effects." A study might seem to show either an association or no association between an exposure and the risk of a disease. In reality, the seeming association or lack of association is due to another factor that determines the occurrence of the disease but that is also associated with the exposure. The other factor is called the *confounding factor* or *confounder*. Confounding thus gives a wrong assessment of the potential "causal" association of an exposure. For example, if women who approach middle age and develop elevated blood pressure are less often prescribed oral contraceptives, a simple comparison of the frequency of cardiovascular disease between those who use contraceptives and those who do not might give the wrong impression that contraceptives protect against heart disease.
>
> Investigators should think beforehand about potential confounding factors. This will inform the study design and allow proper data collection by identifying the confounders for which detailed information should be sought. Restriction or matching may be used. In the example above, the study might be restricted to women who do not have the confounder, elevated blood pressure. Matching on blood pressure might also be possible, though not necessarily desirable. In the analysis phase, investigators may use stratification or multivariable analysis to reduce the effect of confounders. Stratification consists of dividing the data in strata for the confounder (for example, strata of blood pressure), assessing estimates of association within each stratum, and calculating the combined estimate of association as a weighted average over all strata. Multivariable analysis achieves the same result but permits one to take more variables into account simultaneously. It is more flexible but may involve additional assumptions about the mathematical form of the relationship between exposure and disease.
>
> Taking confounders into account is crucial in observational studies, but readers should not assume that analyses adjusted for confounders establish the "causal part" of an association. Results may still be distorted by residual confounding (the confounding that remains after unsuccessful attempts to control for it), random sampling error, selection bias, and information bias.

model (101). Another study found that among 67 articles in which statistical analyses were adjusted for confounders, it was mostly unclear how confounders were chosen (4).

12(b) Describe any methods used to examine subgroups and interactions.

EXAMPLE

"Sex differences in susceptibility to the 3 lifestyle-related risk factors studied were explored by testing for biologic interaction according to Rothman: a new composite variable with 4 categories (a–b–, a–b+, a+b–, and a+b+) was redefined for sex and a dichotomous exposure of interest, where a– and b– denote absence of exposure. RR was calculated for each category after adjustment for age. An interaction effect is defined as departure from additivity of absolute effects, and excess RR caused by interaction (RERI) was calculated:

$$\text{RERI}=\text{RR}(a^+b^+)-\text{RR}(a^-b^+)-\text{RR}(a^+b^-)-1$$

where RR(a+b+) denotes RR among those exposed to both factors where RR(a–b–) is used as reference category (RR = 1.0). Ninety-five percent CIs were calculated as proposed by Hosmer and Lemeshow. RERI of 0 means no interaction" (103).

EXPLANATION

As discussed in detail under item 17, many debate the use and value of analyses restricted to subgroups of the study population (4, 104). Subgroup analyses are nevertheless often done (4). Readers need to know which subgroup analyses were planned in advance, and which arose while analyzing the data. Also, it is important to explain what methods were used to examine whether effects or associations differed across groups (see item 17).

Interaction relates to the situation when one factor modifies the effect of another (therefore also called "effect modification"). The joint action of 2 factors can be characterized in 2 ways: on an additive scale, in terms of risk differences; or on a multiplicative scale, in terms of relative risk (see Table 10-7). Many authors and readers may have their own preference about the way interactions should be analyzed. Still, they may be interested to know to what extent the joint effect of exposures differs from the separate effects. There is consensus that the additive scale, which uses absolute risks, is more appropriate for public health and clinical decision making (105). Whatever view is taken, this should be clearly presented to the reader, as is done in the example above (103). A layout presenting separate effects of both exposures as well as their joint effect, each

relative to no exposure, might be most informative. It is presented in the example for interaction under item 17, and the calculations on the different scales are explained in Table 10-7.

12(c) Explain how missing data were addressed.

EXAMPLE

"Our missing data analysis procedures used missing at random (MAR) assumptions. We used the MICE (multivariate imputation by chained equations) method of multiple multivariate imputation in STATA. We independently analysed 10 copies of the data, each with missing values suitably imputed, in the multivariate logistic regression analyses. We averaged estimates of the variables to give a single mean estimate and adjusted standard errors according to Rubin's rules" (106).

EXPLANATION

Missing data are common in observational research. Questionnaires posted to study participants are not always filled in completely, participants may not attend all follow-up visits, and routine data sources and clinical databases are often incomplete. Despite its ubiquity and importance, few papers report in detail on the problem of missing data (5, 107). Investigators may use any of several approaches to address missing data. We describe some strengths and limitations of various approaches in Table 10-8. We advise that authors report the number of missing values for each variable of interest (exposures, outcomes, confounders) and for each step in the analysis. Authors should give reasons for missing values if possible and indicate how many individuals were excluded because of missing data when describing the flow of participants through the study (see item 13). For analyses that account for missing data, authors should describe the nature of the analysis (for example, multiple imputation) and the assumptions that were made (for example, missing at random, see Table 10-8).

12(d) Cohort study: If applicable, describe how loss to follow-up was addressed.

EXAMPLE

"In treatment programmes with active follow-up, those lost to follow-up and those followed up at 1 year had similar baseline CD4 cell counts (median 115 cells per μL and 123 cells per μL), whereas patients lost to follow-up in programmes with no active follow-up procedures had considerably lower CD4 cell counts than those followed up (median 64 cells per μL and 123 cells per μL).... Treatment programmes with passive follow-up were excluded from subsequent analyses" (116).

> **TABLE 10-7** Interaction (Effect Modification): The Analysis of Joint Effects.
>
> Interaction exists when the association of an exposure with the risk of disease differs in the presence of another exposure. One problem in evaluating and reporting interactions is that the effect of an exposure can be measured in 2 ways: as a relative risk (or rate ratio) or as a risk difference (or rate difference). The use of relative risk leads to a multiplicative model, whereas the use of the risk of difference corresponds to an additive model. A distinction is sometimes made between "statistical interaction," which can be a departure from either a multiplicative or additive model, and a "biologic interaction," which is measured by departure from an additive model. However, neither additive nor multiplicative models point to a particular biologic mechanism.
>
> Regardless of the model choice, the main objective is to understand how the joint effect of 2 exposures differs from their separate effects (in the absence of the exposure). The Human Genomic Epidemiology Network (HuGENet) proposed a layout for transparent presentation of separate and joint effects that permits evaluation of different types of interaction. Data from the study on oral contraceptives and factor V Leiden mutation were used to explain to explain the proposal, and this example is also used in item 17. Oral contraceptives and factors V Leiden mutation each increase the risk of venous thrombosis; their separate and joint effects can be calculated from the 2 × 4 table, where the odds of ratio of 1 denotes the baseline of women without factor V Leiden who do not use oral contraceptives.
>
> A difficulty is that some study designs, such as case-control studies, and several statistical models, such as logistic or Cox regression models, estimate relative risks (or rate ratios) and intrinsically lead to multiplicative modeling. In these instances, relative risks can be translated to an additive scale. In example 1 of item 17, the separate odds ratios are 3.7 and 6.9; the joint odds ratio is 34.7. When these data are analyzed under a multiplicative model, a joint odds ratio of 25.7 is expected (3.7 × 6.9). The observed joint effect of 34.7 is 1.4 times greater than expected on a multiplicative scale (34.7 − 25.7). This quantity (1.4) is the odds ratio of the multiplicative interaction. It would be equal to the antilog of the estimated interaction coefficient from a logistic regression model. Under an additive model, the joint odds ratio is expected to be 9.6 (3.7 + 6.9 − 1). The observed joint effect departs strongly from additivity: The difference is 25.1 (34.7 − 9.6). When odds ratios are interpreted as relative risks (or rate ratios), the latter quantity (25.1) is the relative excess risk from interaction (RERI). This can be understood more easily when imagining that the reference value (equivalent to OR = 1) represents a baseline incidence of venous thrombosis of, say, 1/10 000 women-years, which ten increases in the presence of separate and joint exposures.

CD4 helper cells than those remaining under observation and were therefore at higher risk of dying (116).

It is important to distinguish persons who reach the end of the study from those lost to follow-up. Unfortunately, statistical software usually does not distinguish between the 2 situations: in both cases, follow-up time is automatically truncated ("censored") at the end of the observation period. Investigators therefore need to decide, ideally at the stage of planning the study, how they will deal with loss to follow-up. When few patients are lost, investigators may either exclude individuals with incomplete follow-up, or treat them as if they withdrew alive at either the date of loss to follow-up or the end of the study. We advise authors to report how many patients were lost to follow-up and what censoring strategies they used.

12(d) Case-control study: If applicable, explain how matching of cases and controls was addressed.

EXPLANATION

Cohort studies are analyzed using life table methods or other approaches that are based on the person-time of follow-up and time to developing the disease of interest. Among individuals who remain free of the disease at the end of their observation period, the amount of follow-up time is assumed to be unrelated to the probability of developing the outcome. This will be the case if follow-up ends on a fixed date or at a particular age. Loss to follow-up occurs when participants withdraw from a study before that date. This may hamper the validity of a study if loss to follow-up occurs selectively in exposed individuals, or in persons at high risk of developing the disease ("informative censoring"). In the example above, patients lost to follow-up in treatment programs with no active follow-up had fewer

EXAMPLE

"We used McNemar's test, paired *t* test, and conditional logistic regression analysis to compare dementia patients with their matched controls for cardiovascular risk factors, the occurrence of spontaneous cerebral emboli, carotid disease, and venous to arterial circulation shunt" (117).

EXPLANATION

In individually matched case-control studies, a crude analysis of the odds ratio, ignoring the matching, usually leads to an estimation that is biased toward unity (see Table 10-3). A matched analysis is therefore often necessary. This can intuitively be understood as a stratified analysis: each case is seen as 1 stratum with his or her set of matched controls. The analysis rests on

TABLE 10-8 Missing Data: Problems and Possible Solutions.

A common approach to dealing with missing data is to restrict analyses to individuals with complete data on all variables required for a particular analysis. Although such "complete case" analyses are unbiased in many circumstances, they can be biased and are always inefficient. Bias arises if individuals with missing data are not typical of the whole sample. Inefficiency arises because of the reduced sample size for analysis.

Using the last observation carried forward for repeated measures can distort trends over time if persons who experience a foreshadowing of the outcome selectively drop out. Inserting a missing category indicator for a confounder may increase residual confounding. Imputation, in which each missing value is replaced with an assumed or estimated value, may lead to attenuation or exaggeration of the association of interest, and without the use of sophisticated methods described below may produce standard errors that are too small.

Rubin developed a typology of missing data problems, based on a model for the probability of an observation being missed. Data are described as missing completely at random (MCAR) if the probability that a particular observation is missing does not depend on the value of any observable variable(s). Data are missing at random (MAR) if, given the observed data, the probability that observations are missing is independent of the actual values of the missing data. For example, suppose younger children are more prone to missing spirometry measurements, but that the probability of missing is unrelated to the true unobserved lung function, after accounting for age. Then, the missing lung function measurement would be MAR in models including age. Data are missing not at random (MNAR) if the probability of missing still depends on the missing value even after taking the available data into account. When the data are MNAR, valid inferences require explicit assumptions about the mechanisms that led to missing data. Methods to deal with data missing at random (MAR) fall into 3 broad classes: likelihood-based approaches, weighted estimation, and multiple imputation. Of these 3 approaches, multiple imputation is the most commonly used and flexible, particularly when multiple variables have missing values. Results using any of these approaches should be compared with those from complete case analyses, and important differences discussed. The plausibility of assumptions made in missing data analyses is generally unverifiable. In particular, it is impossible to prove that data are MAR, rather than MNAR. Such analyses are therefore best viewed in the spirit of sensitivity analysis.

---

considering whether the case is more often exposed than the controls, despite having made them alike regarding the matching variables. Investigators can do such a stratified analysis using the Mantel-Haenszel method on a "matched" 2 × 2 table. In its simplest form, the odds ratio becomes the ratio of pairs that are discordant for the exposure variable. If matching was done for variables like age and sex that are universal attributes, the analysis needs not retain the individual, person-to-person matching; a simple analysis in categories of age and sex is sufficient (50). For other matching variables, such as neighborhood, sibship, or friendship, however, each matched set should be considered its own stratum.

In individually matched studies, the most widely used method of analysis is conditional logistic regression, in which each case and their controls are considered together. The conditional method is necessary when the number of controls varies among cases, and when, in addition to the matching variables, other variables need to be adjusted for. To allow readers to judge whether the matched design was appropriately taken into account in the analysis, we recommend that authors describe in detail what statistical methods were used to analyze the data. If taking the matching into account does have little effect on the estimates, authors may choose to present an unmatched analysis.

12(d) Cross-sectional study: If applicable, describe analytical methods taking account of sampling strategy.

EXAMPLE

"The standard errors (SE) were calculated using the Taylor expansion method to estimate the sampling errors of estimators based on the complex sample design. . . . The overall design effect for diastolic blood pressure was found to be 1.9 for men and 1.8 for women, and for systolic blood pressure, it was 1.9 for men and 2.0 for women" (118).

EXPLANATION

Most cross-sectional studies use a prespecified sampling strategy to select participants from a source population. Sampling may be more complex than taking a simple random sample, however. It may include several stages and clustering of participants (for example, in districts or villages). Proportionate stratification may ensure that subgroups with a specific characteristic are correctly represented. Disproportionate stratification may be useful to oversample a subgroup of particular interest.

An estimate of association derived from a complex sample may be more or less precise than that derived from a simple random sample. Measures of precision, such as standard error or confidence interval, should be corrected using the design effect, a ratio measure that describes how much precision is gained or lost if a more complex sampling strategy is used instead of simple random sampling (119). Most complex sampling techniques lead to a decrease of precision, resulting in a design effect greater than 1.

We advise that authors clearly state the method used to adjust for complex sampling strategies so that readers may understand how the chosen sampling method influenced the precision of the obtained estimates. For instance, with clustered sampling, the implicit trade-off between easier data collection and loss of precision is transparent if the design effect is reported. In the example, the calculated design effect of 1.9 for men indicates that the actual sample size would need to be 1.9 times greater than with simple random sampling for the resulting estimates to have equal precision.

12(e) Describe any sensitivity analyses.

EXAMPLE

"Because we had a relatively higher proportion of 'missing' dead patients with insufficient data (38/148 = 25.7%) as compared to live patients (15/437 = 3.4%) . . . , it is possible that this might have biased the results. We have, therefore, carried out a sensitivity analysis. We have assumed that the proportion of women using oral contraceptives in the study group applies to the whole (19.1% for dead, and 11.4% for live patients), and then applied two extreme scenarios: either all the exposed missing patients used second-generation pills or they all used third-generation pills" (120).

EXPLANATION

Sensitivity analyses are useful to investigate whether the main results are consistent with those obtained with alternative analysis strategies or assumptions (121). Issues that may be examined include the criteria for inclusion in analyses, the definitions of exposures or outcomes (122), which confounding variables merit adjustment, the handling of missing data (120, 123), possible selection bias or bias from inaccurate or inconsistent measurement of exposure, disease, and other variables; and specific analysis choices, such as the treatment of quantitative variables (see item 11). Sophisticated methods are increasingly used to simultaneously model the influence of several biases or assumptions (124–126).

In 1959, Cornfield and colleagues famously showed that a relative risk of 9 for cigarette smoking and lung cancer was extremely unlikely to be due to any conceivable confounder, because the confounder would need to be at least 9 times as

prevalent in smokers as in nonsmokers (127). This analysis did not rule out the possibility that such a factor was present, but it did identify the prevalence such a factor would need to have. The same approach was recently used to identify plausible confounding factors that could explain the association between childhood leukemia and living near electric power lines (128). More generally, sensitivity analyses can be used to identify the degree of confounding, selection bias, or information bias required to distort an association. One important, perhaps underrecognized, use of sensitivity analysis is when a study shows little or no association between an exposure and an outcome and it is plausible that confounding or other biases toward the null are present.

RESULTS

The Results section should give a factual account of what was found, from the recruitment of study participants, the description of the study population, to the main results and ancillary analyses. It should be free of interpretations and discursive text reflecting the authors' views and opinions.

13 Participants:

13(a) Report the numbers of individuals at each stage of the study—e.g., numbers potentially eligible, examined for eligibility, confirmed eligible, included in the study, completing follow-up, and analyzed.

EXAMPLE

"Of the 105 freestanding bars and taverns sampled, 13 establishments were no longer in business and 9 were located in restaurants, leaving 83 eligible businesses. In 22 cases, the owner could not be reached by telephone despite 6 or more attempts. The owners of 36 bars declined study participation. . . . The 25 participating bars and taverns employed 124 bartenders, with 67 bartenders working at least 1 weekly daytime shift. Fifty-four of the daytime bartenders (81%) completed baseline interviews and spirometry; 53 of these subjects (98%) completed follow-up" (129).

EXPLANATION

Detailed information on the process of recruiting study participants is important for several reasons. Those included in a study often differ in relevant ways from the target population to which results are applied. This may result in estimates of prevalence or incidence that do not reflect the experience of the target population. For example, people who agreed to participate in a postal survey of sexual behavior attended church less often, had less conservative sexual attitudes and earlier age at first sexual intercourse, and were more likely to smoke cigarettes and drink alcohol than people who refused (130). These differences suggest that postal surveys may overestimate sexual liberalism and activity in the population. Such response bias (see Table 10-5) can distort exposure–disease associations if associations differ between those eligible for the study and those included in the study. As another example, the association between young maternal age and leukemia in offspring, which has been observed in some case-control studies (131, 132), was explained by differential participation of young women in case and control groups. Young women with healthy children were less likely to participate than those with unhealthy children (133). Although low participation does not necessarily compromise the validity of a study, transparent information on participation and reasons for nonparticipation is essential. Also, as there are no universally agreed definitions for participation, response, or follow-up rates, readers need to understand how authors calculated such proportions (134).

Ideally, investigators should give an account of the numbers of individuals considered at each stage of recruiting study participants, from the choice of a target population to the inclusion of participants' data in the analysis. Depending on the type of study, this may include the number of individuals considered to be potentially eligible, the number assessed for eligibility, the number found to be eligible, the number included in the study, the number examined, the number followed up, and the number included in the analysis. Information on different sampling units may be required, if sampling of study participants is carried out in 2 or more stages as in the example above (multistage sampling). In case-control studies, we advise that authors describe the flow of participants separately for case and control groups (135). Controls can sometimes be selected from several sources, including, for example, hospitalized patients and community dwellers. In this case, we recommend a separate account of the numbers of participants for each type of control group. Olson and colleagues proposed useful reporting guidelines for controls recruited through random-digit dialing and other methods (136).

A recent survey of epidemiologic studies published in 10 general epidemiology, public health, and medical journals found that some information regarding participation was provided in 47 of 107 case-control studies (59%), 49 of 154 cohort studies (32%), and 51 of 86 cross-sectional studies (59%) (137). Incomplete or absent reporting of participation and nonparticipation in epidemiologic studies was also documented in 2 other surveys of the literature (4, 5). Finally, there is evidence that participation in epidemiologic studies may

have declined in recent decades (137, 138), which underscores the need for transparent reporting (139).

13(b) Give reasons for nonparticipation at each stage.

EXAMPLE

"The main reasons for nonparticipation were the participant was too ill or had died before interview (cases 30%, controls < 1%), nonresponse (cases 2%, controls 21%), refusal (cases 10%, controls 29%), and other reasons (refusal by consultant or general practitioner, non-English speaking, mental impairment) (cases 7%, controls 5%)" (140).

EXPLANATION

Explaining the reasons why people no longer participated in a study or why they were excluded from statistical analyses helps readers judge whether the study population was representative of the target population and whether bias was possibly introduced. For example, in a cross-sectional health survey, nonparticipation due to reasons unlikely to be related to health status (for example, the letter of invitation was not delivered because of an incorrect address) will affect the precision of estimates but will probably not introduce bias. Conversely, if many individuals opt out of the survey because of illness or perceived good health, results may underestimate or overestimate the prevalence of ill health in the population.

13(c) Consider use of a flow diagram.

EXAMPLE

See the Figure.

EXPLANATION

An informative and well-structured flow diagram can readily and transparently convey information that might otherwise require a lengthy description (142), as in the example above. The diagram may usefully include the main results, such as the number of events for the primary outcome. While we recommend the use of a flow diagram, particularly for complex observational studies, we do not propose a specific format for the diagram.

14 Descriptive data:

14(a) Give characteristics of study participants (e.g., demographic, clinical, social) and information on exposures and potential confounders.

FIGURE 10-1 Example of a Flow Diagram.

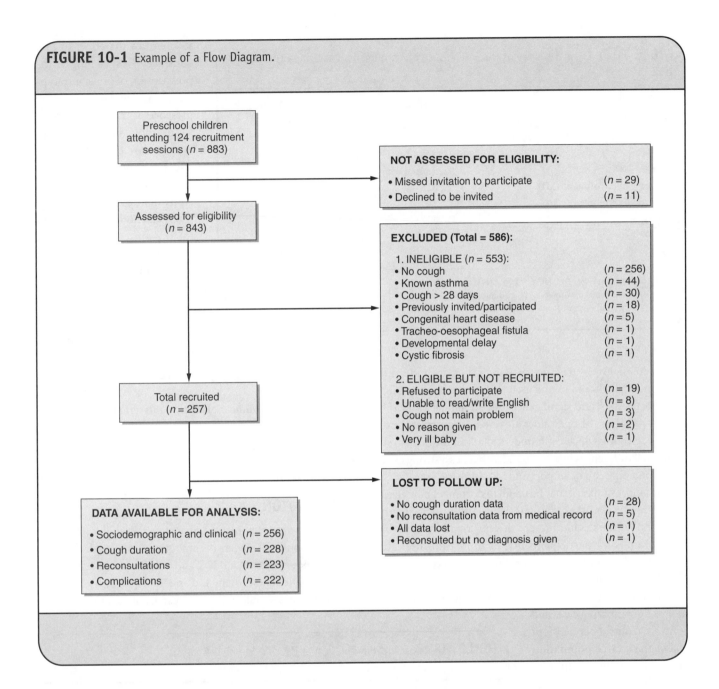

EXAMPLE

See Table 10-9.

EXPLANATION

Readers need descriptions of study participants and their exposures to judge the generalizability of the findings. Information about potential confounders, including whether and how they were measured, influences judgments about study validity. We advise authors to summarize continuous variables for each study group by giving the mean and standard deviation, or, when the data have an asymmetrical distribution (as is often the case), the median and percentile range (for example, 25th and 75th percentiles). Variables that make up a small number of ordered categories (such as stages of disease I to IV) should not be presented as continuous variables; it is preferable to give numbers and proportions for each category (see Table 10-4). In studies that compare groups, the descriptive characteristics and numbers should be given by group, as in the example above.

TABLE 10-9 Characteristics of the Study Base at Enrollment, Castellana G (Italy), 1985–1986.*

Characteristic	HCV Negative ($n = 1458$)	HCV Positive ($n = 511$)	Unknown ($n = 513$)
Sex, n (%)			
Male	936 (64)	296 (58)	197 (39)
Female	522 (36)	215 (42)	306 (61)
Mean age at enrollment (SD), y	45.7 (10.5)	52.0 (9.7)	52.5 (9.8)
Daily alcohol intake, n (%)			
None	250 (17)	129 (25)	119 (24)
Moderate[†]	853 (59)	272 (53)	293 (58)
Excessive[±]	355 (24)	110 (22)	91 (18)

*Adapted from reference 143. HCV = hepatitis C virus.
[†]Men, < 60 g ethanol/d; women, < 30 g ethanol/d.
[±]Men, > 60 g ethanol/d; women > 30 g ethanol/d.

Inferential measures such as standard errors and confidence intervals should not be used to describe the variability of characteristics, and significance tests should be avoided in descriptive tables. Also, P values are not an appropriate criterion for selecting which confounders to adjust for in analysis; even small differences in a confounder that has a strong effect on the outcome can be important (144, 145).

In cohort studies, it may be useful to document how an exposure relates to other characteristics and potential confounders. Authors could present this information in a table with columns for participants in 2 or more exposure categories, which permits to judge the differences in confounders between these categories.

In case-control studies, potential confounders cannot be judged by comparing cases and controls. Control persons represent the source population and will usually be different from the cases in many respects. For example, in a study of oral contraceptives and myocardial infarction, a sample of young women with infarction more often had risk factors for that disease, such as high serum cholesterol, smoking, and a positive family history, than the control group (146). This does not influence the as-

sessment of the effect of oral contraceptives, as long as the prescription of oral contraceptives was not guided by the presence of these risk factors-for example, because the risk factors were only established after the event (see Table 10-6). In case-control studies, the equivalent of comparing exposed and nonexposed controls for the presence of potential confounders (as is done in cohorts) can be achieved by exploring the source population of the cases: if the control group is large enough and represents the source population, exposed and unexposed controls can be compared for potential confounders (121, 147).

14(b) Indicate the number of participants with missing data for each variable of interest.

EXAMPLE

See Table 10-10.

EXPLANATION

As missing data may bias or affect generalizability of results, authors should tell readers the amounts of missing data for exposures, potential confounders, and other important characteristics of patients (see item 12c and Table 10-8). In a cohort study, authors should report the extent of loss to follow-up

TABLE 10-10 Symptom End Points Used in Survival Analysis.*

End Point	Cough, n (%)	Shortness of Breath, n (%)	Sleeplessness, n (%)
Symptom resolved	201 (79)	138 (54)	171 (67)
Censored	27 (10)	21 (8)	24 (9)
Never symptomatic	0	46 (18)	11 (4)
Data missing	28 (11)	51 (20)	50 (20)
Total	256 (100)	256 (100)	256 (100)

*Adapted from reference 141.

(with reasons), because incomplete follow-up may bias findings (see items 12d and 13) (148). We advise authors to use their tables and figures to enumerate amounts of missing data.

14(c) Cohort study: Summarize follow-up time-e.g., average and total amount.

EXAMPLE

"During the 4366 person-years of follow-up (median 5.4, maximum 8.3 years), 265 subjects were diagnosed as having dementia, including 202 with Alzheimer's disease" (149).

EXPLANATION

Readers need to know the duration and extent of follow-up for the available outcome data. Authors can present a summary of the average follow-up with either the mean or median follow-up time or both. The mean allows a reader to calculate the total number of person-years by multiplying it with the number of study participants. Authors also may present minimum and maximum times or percentiles of the distribution to show readers the spread of follow-up times. They may report total person-years of follow-up or some indication of the proportion of potential data that was captured (148). All such information may be presented separately for participants in 2 or more exposure categories. Almost one half

of 132 articles in cancer journals (mostly cohort studies) did not give any summary of length of follow-up (37).

15 Outcome data:

Cohort study: Report numbers of outcome events or summary measures over time.

EXAMPLE

See Table 10-11.

Case-control study: Report numbers in each exposure category or summary measures over time.

EXAMPLE

See Table 10-12.

Cross-sectional study: Report numbers of outcome events or summary measures.

EXAMPLE

See Table 10-13.

EXPLANATION

Before addressing the possible association between exposures (risk factors) and outcomes, authors should report relevant descriptive data. It may be possible and meaningful to present measures of association in the same table that presents the descriptive data (see item 14a). In a cohort study with events as outcomes, report the numbers of events for each outcome of interest. Consider reporting the event rate per person-year of follow-up. If the risk of an event changes over follow-up time, present the numbers and rates of events in appropriate intervals of follow-up or as a Kaplan-Meier life table or plot. It might be preferable to show plots as cumulative incidence that go up from 0% rather than down from 100%, especially if the event rate is lower than, say,

TABLE 10-11 Rates of HIV-1 Serconversion by Selected Sociodemographic Variables, 1990–1993.*

Variable	Person-Years	Seroconverted, *n*	Rate/1000 Person-Years (95% CI)
Calendar year			
1990	2197.5	18	8.2 (4.4–12.0)
1991	3210.7	22	6.9 (4.0–9.7)
1992	3162.6	18	5.7 (3.1–8.3)
1993	2912.9	26	8.9 (5.5–12.4)
1994	1104.5	5	4.5 (0.6–8.5)
Tribe			
Bagandan	8433.1	48	5.7 (4.1–7.3)
Other Ugandan	578.4	9	15.6 (5.4–25.7)
Rwandese	2318.6	16	6.9 (3.5–10.3)
Other tribe	866.0	12	13.9 (6.0–21.7)
Religion			
Muslim	3313.5	9	2.7 (0.9–4.5)
Other	8882.7	76	8.6 (6.6–10.5)

*Adapted from reference 150.

TABLE 10-12 Exposure Among Liver Cirrhosis Cases and Controls.*

Exposure	Cases ($n = 40$), n (%)	Controls ($n = 139$), n (%)
Vinyl chloride monomer (cumulative exposure)		
< 160 ppm	7 (18)	38 (27)
160–500 ppm	7 (18)	40 (29)
500–2500 ppm	9 (23)	37 (27)
> 2500 ppm	17 (43)	24 (17)
Alcohol consumption		
< 30 g/d	1 (3)	82 (59)
30–60 g/d	7 (18)	46 (33)
> 60 g/d	32 (80)	11 (8)
HBsAg/HCV status		
Negative	33 (83)	136 (98)
Positive	7 (18)	3 (2)

*Adapted from reference 151. HBsAG = hepatitis B surface antigen; HCV = hepatitis C virus.

30% (153). Consider presenting such information separately for participants in different exposure categories of interest. If a cohort study is investigating other time-related outcomes (for example, quantitative disease markers such as blood pressure), present appropriate summary measures (for example, means and standard deviations) over time, perhaps in a table or figure.

For cross-sectional studies, we recommend presenting the same type of information on prevalent outcome events or summary measures. For case-control studies, the focus will be on reporting exposures separately for cases and controls as frequencies or quantitative summaries (154). For all designs, it may be helpful also to tabulate continuous outcomes or exposures in categories, even if the data are not analyzed as such.

16 Main results:

16 (a) Give unadjusted estimates and, if applicable, confounder-adjusted estimates and their pre-

cision (e.g., 95% confidence intervals). Make clear which confounders were adjusted for and why they were included.

EXAMPLE 1

"We initially considered the following variables as potential confounders by Mantel-Haenszel stratified analysis: . . . The variables we included in the final logistic regression models were those . . . that produced a 10% change in the odds ratio after the Mantel-Haenszel adjustment" (155).

EXAMPLE 2

See Table 10-13.

EXPLANATION

In many situations, authors may present the results of unadjusted or minimally adjusted analyses and those from fully adjusted analyses. We advise giving the unadjusted analyses together with the main data, for example, the number of cases and controls that were exposed or not. This allows the reader to understand the data behind the measures of association (see item 15). For adjusted analyses, report the number of persons in the analysis, as this number may differ because of missing values in covariates (see item 12c). Estimates should be given with confidence intervals.

Readers can compare unadjusted measures of association with those adjusted for potential confounders and judge by how much, and in what direction, they changed. Readers may think that "adjusted" results equal the causal part of the measure of association, but adjusted results are not necessarily free of random sampling error, selection bias, information bias, or residual confounding (see Table 10-6). Thus, great care should be exercised when interpreting adjusted results, as the

TABLE 10-13 Prevalence of Current Asthma and Diagnosed Hay Fever, by Average *Alternaria alternata* Antigen Level in the Household.*

Categorized *Alternaria* Level[†]	Current Asthma		Diagnosed Hay Fever	
	Patients, n	Prevalence (95% CI)[±]	Patients, n	Prevalence (95% CI)[±]
1st tertile	40	4.8 (3.3–6.9)	93	16.4 (13.0–20.5)
2nd tertile	61	7.5 (5.2–10.6)	122	17.1 (12.8–22.5)
3rd tertile	73	8.7 (6.7–11.3)	93	15.2 (12.1–18.9)

*Adapted from reference 152.
[†]First tertile, 3.90 g/g; second tertile, 3.906.27 g/g; third tertile, 6.28 g/g.
[±]Percentage (95% CI) weighted for the multistage sampling design of the National Survey of Lead and Allergens in Housing.

validity of results often depends crucially on complete knowledge of important confounders, their precise measurement, and appropriate specification in the statistical model (see item 20) (157, 158).

Authors should explain all potential confounders considered, and the criteria for excluding or including variables in statistical models. Decisions about excluding or including variables should be guided by knowledge, or explicit assumptions, on causal relations. Inappropriate decisions may introduce bias, for example, by including variables that are in the causal pathway between exposure and disease (unless the aim is to assess how much of the effect is carried by the intermediary variable). If the decision to include a variable in the model was based on the change in the estimate, it is important to report what change was considered sufficiently important to justify its inclusion. If a "backward deletion" or "forward inclusion" strategy was used to select confounders, explain that process and give the significance level for rejecting the null hypothesis of no confounding. Of note, we and others do not advise selecting confounders based solely on statistical significance testing (147, 159, 160).

Recent studies of the quality of reporting of epidemiologic studies found that confidence intervals were reported in most articles (4). However, few authors explained their choice of confounding variables (4, 5).

16(b) Report category boundaries when continuous variables were categorized.

EXAMPLE

See Table 10-14.

EXPLANATION

Categorizing continuous data has several important implications for analysis (see Table 10-4) and also affects the presentation of results. In tables, outcomes should be given for each exposure category, for example, as counts of persons at risk, person-time at risk, if relevant separately for each group (for example, cases and controls). Details of the categories used may aid comparison of studies

and meta-analysis. If data were grouped using conventional cut-points, such as body mass index thresholds (162), group boundaries (that is, range of values) can be derived easily, except for the highest and lowest categories. If quantile-derived categories are used, the category boundaries cannot be inferred from the data. As a minimum, authors should report the category boundaries; it is helpful also to report the range of the data and the mean or median values within categories.

16(c) If relevant, consider translating estimates of relative risk into absolute risk for a meaningful time period.

EXAMPLE

"10 years' use of HRT [hormone replacement therapy] is estimated to result in five (95% CI 3-7) additional breast cancers per 1000 users of oestrogen-only preparations and 19 (15-23) additional cancers per 1000 users of oestrogen-progestogen combinations" (163).

EXPLANATION

The results from studies examining the association between an exposure and a disease are commonly reported in relative terms, as ratios of risks, rates, or odds (see Table 10-15).

TABLE 10-14 Relative Rates of Rehospitalization, by Treatment in Patients in Community Care after First Hospitalization Due to Schizophrenia and Schizoaffective Disorder.*

Treatment	Relapses, n	Person-Years	Crude Relative Rate (95% CI)	Adjusted Relative Rate (95% CI)[†]	Fully Adjusted Relative Rate (95% CI)[†]
Perphenazine	53	187	0.41 (0.29–0.59)	0.45 (0.32–0.65)	0.32 (0.22-0.49)
Olanzapine	329	822	0.59 (0.45–0.75)	0.55 (0.43–0.72)	0.54 (0.41–0.71)
Clozapine	336	804	0.61 (0.47–0.79)	0.53 (0.41–0.69)	0.64 (0.48–0.85)
Chlorprothixene	79	146	0.79 (0.58–1.09)	0.83 (0.61–1.15)	0.64 (0.45-0.91)
Thioridazine	115	201	0.84 (0.63–1.12)	0.82 (0.61–1.10)	0.70 (0.51–0.96)
Perphenazine	155	327	0.69 (0.58–0.82)	0.78 (0.59–1.03)	0.85 (0.63-1.13)
Risperidone	343	651	0.77 (0.60–0.99)	0.80 (0.62–1.03)	0.89 (0.69–1.16)
Haloperidol	73	107	1.00	1.00	1.00
Chlorpromazine	82	127	0.94 (0.69–1.29)	0.97 (0.71–1.33)	1.06 (0.76–1.47)
Levomepromazine	52	63	1.21 (0.84–1.73)	0.82 (0.58–1.18)	1.09 (0.76–1.57)
No antipsychotic drugs	2248	3362	0.98 (0.77–1.23)	1.01 (0.80–1.27)	1.16 (0.91–1.47)

*Adapted from reference 156.
[†]Adjusted for sex, calendar year, age at onset of follow-up, number of previous relapses, duration of first hospitalization, and length of follow-up (adjusted column), and additionally for a score of the propensity to start a treatment other than haloperidol (fully adjusted column).

TABLE 10-15 Polychlorinated Biphenyls in Cord Serum.*

Quartile	Range, *ng/g*	Number
1	0.07–0.24	180
2	0.24–0.38	181
3	0.38–0.60	181
4	0.61–18.14	180

*Adapted from reference 161.

Relative measures capture the strength of the association between an exposure and disease. If the relative risk is a long way from 1, it is less likely that the association is due to confounding (164, 165). Relative effects or associations tend to be more consistent across studies and populations than absolute measures, but what often tends to be the case may be irrelevant in a particular instance. For example, similar relative risks were obtained for the classic cardiovascular risk factors for men living in Northern Ireland, France, the United States, and Germany, despite the fact that the underlying risk of coronary heart disease varies substantially among these countries (166, 167). In contrast, in a study of hypertension as a risk factor for cardiovascular disease mortality, the data were more compatible with a constant rate difference than with a constant rate ratio (168).

Widely used statistical models, including logistic (169) and proportional hazards (Cox) regression (170) are based on ratio measures. In these models, only departures from constancy of ratio effect measures are easily discerned. Nevertheless, measures which assess departures from additivity of risk differences, such as the Relative Excess Risk from Interaction (RERI; see item 12b and Table 10-7), can be estimated in models based on ratio measures.

In many circumstances, the absolute risk associated with an exposure is of greater interest than the relative risk. For example, if the focus is on adverse effects of a drug, one will want to know the number of additional cases per unit time of use (for example, days, weeks, or years). The example gives the additional number of breast cancer cases per 1000 women who used hormone-replacement therapy for 10 years (163). Measures such as the attributable risk or population attributable fraction may be useful to gauge how much disease can be prevented if the exposure is eliminated. They should preferably be presented together with a measure of statistical uncertainty (for example, confidence intervals as in the example). Authors should be aware of the strong assumptions made in this context, including a causal relationship between a risk factor and disease (see Table 10-16) (171). Because of the semantic ambiguity and complexities involved, authors should report in detail what methods were used to calculate attributable risks, ideally giving the formulae used (172).

A recent survey of abstracts of 222 articles published in leading medical journals found that in 62% of abstracts of randomized trials including a ratio measure absolute risks were given, but only in 21% of abstracts of cohort studies (173). A free text search of MEDLINE 1966 to 1997 showed that 619 items mentioned attributable risks in the title or abstract, compared to 18 955 using relative risk or odds ratio, for a ratio of 1 to 31 (174).

17 Other analyses: Report other analyses done—e.g., analyses of subgroups and interactions and sensitivity analyses.

EXAMPLE 1

See Table 10-16.

EXAMPLE 2

See Table 10-17.
See Table 10-18.

EXPLANATION

In addition to the main analysis, other analyses are often done in observational studies. They may address specific subgroups, the potential interaction between risk factors, the calculation of attributable risks, or use alternative definitions of study variables in sensitivity analyses.

There is debate about the dangers associated with subgroup analyses, and multiplicity of analyses in general (4, 104). In our opinion, there is too great a tendency to look for evidence of subgroup-specific associations, or effect-measure modification, when overall results appear to suggest little or no effect. On the other hand, there is value in exploring whether an overall association appears consistent across several preferably prespecified subgroups, especially when a study is large enough to have sufficient data in each subgroup. A second area of debate is about interesting subgroups that arose during the data analysis. They might be important findings, but might also arise by chance. Some argue that it is neither possible nor necessary to inform the reader about all subgroup analyses done, as future analyses of other data will tell to what extent the early exciting findings stand the test of time (9). We advise authors to report which analyses were planned, and which were

TABLE 10-16 Measures of Association, Effect, and Impact.

Observational studies may be solely done to describe the magnitude and distribution of a health problem in the population. They may examine the number of people who have a disease at a particular time (prevalence) or who develop a disease over a defined period (incidence). The incidence may be expressed as the proportion of people developing the disease (cumulative incidence) or as a rate per person-time of follow-up (incidence rate). Specific terms are used to describe different incidences: among others, mortality rate, birth rate, attack rate, or case-fatality rate. Similarly, terms like point *prevalence* and *period, annual,* or *lifetime prevalence* are used to describe different types of prevalence.

Other observational studies address cause-effect relationships. Their focus is the comparison of the risk, rate, or prevalence of the event of interest between those exposed and those not exposed to the risk factor under investigation. These studies often estimate a "relative risk," which may stand for risk ratios (ratios of cumulative incidences) as well as rate ratios (ratios of incidence rates). In case-control studies, only a fraction of the source population (the controls) are included. Results are expressed as the ratio of the odds of exposure among cases and controls. This odds ratio provides an estimate of the risk or rate ratio depending on the sampling of cases and controls. The prevalence ratio or prevalence odds ratio from cross-sectional studies may be useful in some situations.

Expressing results both in relative and absolute terms may often be helpful. For example, in a study of male British doctors, the incidence rate of death from lung cancer over 50 years of follow-up was 249 per 100,000 per year among smokers, compared to 17 per 100 000 per year among nonsmokers: a rate ratio of 14.6 (249 − 17). For coronary heart disease (CHD), the corresponding rates were 1001 and 619 per 100 000 per year, for a rate ratio of 1.61 (1001 − 619). The effect of smoking on death appears much stronger for lung cancer than for CHD. The picture changes when we consider the absolute effects of smoking. The difference in incidence rates was 232 per 100,000 per year (249 − 17) for lung cancer and 382 for CHD (1001 − 619). Therefore, among doctors who smoked, smoking was more likely to cause death from CHD than from lung cancer.

How much of the disease burden in a population could be prevented by eliminating exposure? Global estimates have been published for smoking. According to one study, 91% of all lung cancers, 40% of CHD, and 33% of all deaths among men in 2000 were attributed to smoking. The population attributable fraction is generally defined as the proportion of cases caused by a particular exposure, but several concepts (and no unified terminology) exist, and incorrect approached to adjust for other factors are sometimes used. What are the implications for reporting? The relative measures emphasize the strength of an association, and are most useful in etiologic research. If a causal relationship with an exposure is documented and associations are interpreted as *effects*, estimates of relative risk may be translated into suitable measures of absolute risk in order to gauge the possible impact of public health policies. However, authors should be aware of the strong assumptions made in this context. Care is needed in deciding which concept and method is appropriate for a particular situation.

A sensible approach is to report the separate effect of each exposure as well as the joint effect-if possible in a table, as in the first example above (183) or in the study by Martinelli and associates (185). Such a table gives the reader sufficient information to evaluate additive as well as multiplicative interaction (how these calculations are done is shown in Table 10-7). Confidence intervals for separate and joint effects may help the reader to judge the strength of the data. In addition, confidence intervals around measures of interaction, such as the Relative Excess Risk from Interaction (RERI) relate to tests of interaction or homogeneity tests. One recurrent problem is that authors use comparisons of *P* values across subgroups, which lead to erroneous claims about an effect modifier. For instance, a statistically significant association in one category (for example, men) but not in the other (women) does not in itself provide evidence of effect modification. Similarly, the confidence intervals for each point estimate are sometimes inappropriately used to infer that there is no interaction when intervals overlap. A more valid inference is achieved by directly evaluating whether the magnitude of an association

not (see items 4, 12b, and 20). This will allow readers to judge the implications of multiplicity, taking into account the study's position on the continuum from discovery to verification or refutation.

A third area of debate is how joint effects and interactions between risk factors should be evaluated: on additive or multiplicative scales, or should the scale be determined by the statistical model that fits best? (See item 12b and Table 10-7.)

differs across subgroups.

Sensitivity analyses are helpful to investigate the influence of choices made in the statistical analysis, or to investigate the robustness of the findings to missing data or possible biases (see item 12b). Judgment is needed regarding the level of reporting of such analyses. If many sensitivity analyses were performed, it may be impractical to present detailed findings for them all. It may sometimes be sufficient to report

TABLE 10-17 Analysis of Oral Contraceptive Use, Presence Factor V Leiden Allele, and Risk for Venous Thromboembolism.*

Factor V Leiden	Oral Contraceptives	Patients, n	Controls, n	Odds Ratio
Yes	Yes	25	2	34.7
Yes	No	10	4	6.9
No	Yes	84	63	3.7
No	No	36	100	1.0 (reference)

*Modified from reference 182.

that sensitivity analyses were carried out and that they were consistent with the main results presented. Detailed presentation is more appropriate if the issue investigated is of major concern, or if effect estimates vary considerably (59, 186).

Pocock and colleagues found that 43 out of 73 articles reporting observational studies contained subgroup analyses. The majority claimed differences across groups but only 8 articles reported a formal evaluation of interaction (see item 12b) (4).

DISCUSSION

The Discussion section addresses the central issues of validity and meaning of the study (191). Surveys have found that discussion sections are often dominated by incomplete or biased assessments of the study's results and their implications, and rhetoric supporting the authors' findings (192, 193). Structuring

the discussion may help authors avoid unwarranted speculation and overinterpretation of results while guiding readers through the text (194, 195). For example, *Annals of Internal Medicine* (196) recommends that authors structure the discussion section by presenting the following: 1) a brief synopsis of the key findings; 2) consideration of possible mechanisms and explanations; 3) comparison with relevant findings from other published studies; 4) limitations of the study; and 5) a brief section that summarizes the implications of the work for practice and research. Others have made similar suggestions (191, 194). The section on research recommendations and the section on limitations of the study should be closely linked to each other. Investigators should suggest ways in which subsequent research can improve on their studies rather than blandly stating "more research is needed" (197, 198). We recommend that authors structure their discussion sections, perhaps also using suitable subheadings.

18 Key results: Summarize key results with reference to study objectives.

EXAMPLE

"We hypothesized that ethnic minority status would be associated with higher levels of cardiovascular disease (CVD) risk factors, but that the associations would be explained substantially by socioeconomic status (SES). Our hypothesis was not confirmed. After adjustment for age and SES, highly significant differences in body mass index, blood pressure, diabetes, and physical inactivity remained between white women and both black and Mexican-American women. In addition, we found large differences in CVD risk factors by SES, a finding that illustrates the high-risk status of both ethnic minority women as well as white women with low SES" (199).

TABLE 10-18 Sensitivity of the Rate Ratio for Cardiovascular Outcome to an Unmeasured Confounder.*

Prevalence of Unmeasured Binary Confounder in the Exposed Group, %	Prevalence of Unmeasured Binary Confounder in the Comparator Group, %	Unmeasured Binary Confounder Rate Ratio	High Exposure Rate Ratio (95% CI)†
90	10	1.5	1.20 (1.01–1.42)
90	50	1.5	1.43 (1.22–1.67)
50	10	1.5	1.39 (1.18–1.63)
90	10	2	0.96 (0.81–1.13)
90	50	2	1.27 (1.11–1.45)
50	10	2	1.21 (1.03–1.42)
90	50	3	1.18 (1.01–1.38)
50	10	3	0.99 (0.85–1.16)
90	50	5	1.08 (0.85–1.26)

*Adapted from reference 184.
†Adjusted for age, sex, cardiovascular drug use, and unmeasured binary confounder.

EXPLANATION

It is good practice to begin the discussion with a short summary of the main findings of the study. The short summary reminds readers of the main findings and may help them assess whether the subsequent interpretation and implications offered by the authors are supported by the findings.

19 Limitations: Discuss limitations of the study, taking into account sources of potential bias or imprecision. Discuss both direction and magnitude of any potential bias.

EXAMPLE

"Since the prevalence of counseling increases with increasing levels of obesity, our estimates may overestimate the true prevalence. Telephone surveys also may overestimate the true prevalence of counseling. Although persons without telephones have similar levels of overweight as persons with telephones, persons without telephones tend to be less educated, a factor associated with lower levels of counseling in our study. Also of concern is the potential bias caused by those who refused to participate as well as those who refused to respond to questions about weight. Furthermore, because data were collected cross-sectionally, we cannot infer that counseling preceded a patient's attempt to lose weight" (200).

EXPLANATION

The identification and discussion of the limitations of a study are an essential part of scientific reporting. It is important not only to identify the sources of bias and confounding that could have affected results, but also to discuss the relative importance of different biases, including the likely direction and magnitude of any potential bias (see Table 10-5 and item 9).

Authors should also discuss any imprecision of the results. Imprecision may arise in connection with several aspects of a study, including the study size (item 10) and the measurement of exposures, confounders, and outcomes (item 8). The inability to precisely measure true values of an exposure tends to result in bias toward unity: the less precisely a risk factor is measured, the greater the bias. This effect has been described as "attenuation" (201, 202) or more recently as "regression dilution bias" (203). However, when correlated risk factors are measured with different degrees of imprecision, the adjusted relative risk associated with them can be biased toward or away from unity (204–206).

When discussing limitations, authors may compare the study being presented with other studies in the literature in terms of validity, generalizability, and precision. In this approach, each study can be viewed as a contribution to the literature, not as a stand-alone basis for inference and action (207). Surprisingly, the discussion of important limitations of a study is sometimes omitted from published reports. A survey of authors who had published original research articles in *The Lancet* found that important weaknesses of the study were reported by the investigators in the survey questionnaires, but not in the published article (192).

20 Interpretation: Give a cautious overall interpretation considering objectives, limitations, multiplicity of analyses, results from similar studies, and other relevant evidence.

EXAMPLE

"Any explanation for an association between death from myocardial infarction and use of second generation oral contraceptives must be conjectural. There is no published evidence to suggest a direct biologic mechanism, and there are no other epidemiologic studies with relevant results. . . . The increase in absolute risk is very small and probably applies predominantly to smokers. Due to the lack of corroborative evidence, and because the analysis is based on relatively small numbers, more evidence on the subject is needed. We would not recommend any change in prescribing practice on the strength of these results" (120).

EXPLANATION

The heart of the discussion section is the interpretation of a study's results. Overinterpretation is common and human; even when we try hard to give an objective assessment, reviewers often rightly point out that we went too far in some respects. When interpreting results, authors should consider the nature of the study on the discovery to verification continuum and potential sources of bias, including loss to follow-up and nonparticipation (see items 9, 12, and 19). Due consideration should be given to confounding (item 16a), the results of relevant sensitivity analyses, and the issue of multiplicity and subgroup analyses (item 17). Authors should also consider residual confounding due to unmeasured variables or imprecise measurement of confounders. For example, socioeconomic status (SES) is associated with many health outcomes and often differs between groups being compared. Variables used to measure SES (income, education, or occupation) are surrogates for other undefined and unmeasured exposures, and the true confounder will by definition be measured with error (208). Authors should address the real range of uncertainty in estimates, which is larger than the statistical uncertainty reflected in confidence intervals. The latter do not take into account other uncertainties that arise from a study's design, implementation, and methods of measurement (209).

To guide thinking and conclusions about causality, some may find criteria proposed by Hill in 1965 helpful (164). How strong is the association with the exposure? Did it precede the onset of disease? Is the association consistently observed in different studies and settings? Is there supporting evidence from experimental studies, including laboratory and animal studies? How specific is the exposure's putative effect, and is there a dose-response relationship? Is the association biologically plausible? These criteria should not, however, be applied mechanically. For example, some have argued that relative risks below 2 or 3 should be ignored (210, 211). This is a reversal of the point by Cornfield and colleagues about the strength of large relative risks (see item 12b) (127). Although a causal effect is more likely with a relative risk of 9, it does not follow that one below 3 is necessarily spurious. For instance, the small increase in the risk of childhood leukemia after intrauterine irradiation is credible because it concerns an adverse effect of a medical procedure for which no alternative explanations are obvious (212). Moreover, the carcinogenic effects of radiation are well established. The doubling in the risk of ovarian cancer associated with eating 2 to 4 eggs per week is not immediately credible, because dietary habits are associated with a large number of lifestyle factors as well as SES (213). In contrast, the credibility of much-debated epidemiologic findings of a difference in thrombosis risk between different types of oral contraceptives was greatly enhanced by the differences in coagulation found in a randomized crossover trial (214). A discussion of the existing external evidence from different types of studies should always be included, but may be particularly important for studies reporting small increases in risk. Further, authors should put their results in context with similar studies and explain how the new study affects the existing body of evidence, ideally by referring to a systematic review.

21 Generalizability: Discuss the generalizability (external validity) of the study results.

EXAMPLE

"How applicable are our estimates to other HIV-1-infected patients? This is an important question because the accuracy of prognostic models tends to be lower when applied to data other than those used to develop them. We addressed this issue by penalizing model complexity, and by choosing models that generalized best to cohorts omitted from the estimation procedure. Our database included patients from many countries from Europe and North America who were treated in different settings. The range of patients was broad: men and women from teenagers to elderly people were included, and the major expo-

sure categories were well represented. The severity of immunodeficiency at baseline ranged from not measurable to very severe, and viral load from undetectable to extremely high" (215).

EXPLANATION

Generalizability, also called external validity or applicability, is the extent to which the results of a study can be applied to other circumstances (216). There is no external validity per se; the term is meaningful only with regard to clearly specified conditions (217). Can results be applied to an individual, groups, or populations that differ from those enrolled in the study with regard to age, sex, ethnicity, severity of disease, and comorbid conditions? Are the nature and level of exposures comparable, and the definitions of outcomes relevant to another setting or population? Are data that were collected in longitudinal studies many years ago still relevant today? Are results from health services research in one country applicable to health systems in other countries?

The question of whether the results of a study have external validity is often a matter of judgment that depends on the study setting, the characteristics of the participants, the exposures examined, and the outcomes assessed. Thus, it is crucial that authors provide readers with adequate information about the setting and locations, eligibility criteria, the exposures and how they were measured, the definition of outcomes, and the period of recruitment and follow-up. The degree of nonparticipation and the proportion of unexposed participants in whom the outcome develops are also relevant. Knowledge of the absolute risk and prevalence of the exposure, which will often vary across populations, are helpful when applying results to other settings and populations (see Table 10-16).

OTHER INFORMATION

22 Funding: Give the source of funding and the role of the funders for the present study and, if applicable, for the original study on which the present article is based.

EXPLANATION

Some journals require authors to disclose the presence or absence of financial and other conflicts of interest (100, 218). Several investigations show strong associations between the source of funding and the conclusions of research articles (219–222). The conclusions in randomized trials recommended the experimental drug as the drug of choice much more often (odds ratio, 5.3) if the trial was funded by for-profit organizations, even after adjustment for the effect size (223). Other studies document the influence of the tobacco and telecommunication industries on the research they funded (224–227).

There are also examples of undue influence when the sponsor is governmental or a nonprofit organization.

Authors or funders may have conflicts of interest that influence any of the following: the design of the study (228); choice of exposures (228, 229), outcomes (230), statistical methods (231); and selective publication of outcomes (230) and studies (232). Consequently, the role of the funders should be described in detail: in what part of the study they took direct responsibility (for example, design, data collection, analysis, drafting of manuscript, decision to publish) (100). Other sources of undue influence include employers (for example, university administrators for academic researchers and government supervisors, especially political appointees, for government researchers), advisory committees, litigants, and special interest groups.

CONCLUDING REMARKS

The STROBE Statement aims to provide helpful recommendations for reporting observational studies in epidemiology. Good reporting reveals the strengths and weaknesses of a study and facilitates sound interpretation and application of study results. The STROBE Statement may also aid in planning observational studies, and may guide peer reviewers and editors in their evaluation of manuscripts.

We wrote this explanatory article to discuss the importance of transparent and complete reporting of observational studies, to explain the rationale behind the different items included in the checklist, and to give examples from published articles of what we consider good reporting. We hope that the material presented here will assist authors and editors in using STROBE.

We stress that STROBE and other recommendations on the reporting of research (13, 233, 234) should be seen as evolving documents that require continual assessment, refinement, and, if necessary, change (235, 236). For example, the CONSORT statement for the reporting of parallel-group randomized trials was first developed in the mid-1990s (237). Since then, members of the group have met regularly to review the need to revise the recommendations; a revised version appeared in 2001 (233) and a further version is in development. Similarly, the principles presented in this article and the STROBE checklist are open to change as new evidence and critical comments accumulate. The STROBE Web site (www.strobe-statement.org) provides a forum for discussion and suggestions for improvements of the checklist, this explanatory document, and information about the good reporting of epidemiologic studies.

Several journals ask authors to follow the STROBE Statement in their instructions to authors (see Web site for current list). We invite other journals to adopt the STROBE Statement and contact us through our Web site to let us know. The journals publishing the STROBE recommendations provide open access. The STROBE Statement is therefore widely accessible to the biomedical community.

Author and Article Information

From Leiden University Medical Center, Leiden, the Netherlands; Institute of Social and Preventive Medicine, University of Bern, Bern, Switzerland; University Medical Centre, Freiburg, Germany; Cancer Research UK/NHS Centre for Statistics in Medicine, Oxford, United Kingdom; Nordic Cochrane Centre, Rigshospitalet, Copenhagen, Denmark; University of Texas Health Science Center, San Antonio, Texas; London School of Hygiene and Tropical Medicine, London, United Kingdom; University of North Carolina School of Public Health, Chapel Hill, North Carolina; University of Pittsburgh Graduate School of Public Health and University of Pittsburgh Cancer Institute, Pittsburgh, Pennsylvania; and University of Bristol, Bristol, United Kingdom.

Note: The following individuals have contributed to the content and elaboration of the STROBE Statement: Douglas G. Altman, Maria Blettner, Paolo Boffetta, Hermann Brenner, Geneviève Chêne, Cyrus Cooper, George Davey-Smith, Erik von Elm, Matthias Egger, France Gagnon, Peter C. Gøtzsche, Philip Greenland, Sander Greenland, Claire Infante-Rivard, John Ioannidis, Astrid James, Giselle Jones, Bruno Ledergerber, Julian Little, Margaret May, David Moher, Hooman Momen, Alfredo Morabia, Hal Morgenstern, Cynthia D. Mulrow, Fred Paccaud, Stuart J. Pocock, Charles Poole, Martin Röösli, Dietrich Rothenbacher, Kenneth Rothman, Caroline Sabin, Willi Sauerbrei, Lale Say, James J. Schlesselman, Jonathan Sterne, Holly Sydall, Jan P. Vandenbroucke, Ian White, Susan Wieland, Hywel Williams, and Guang Yong Zou.

Acknowledgments: The authors thank Gerd Antes, Kay Dickersin, Shah Ebrahim, Richard Lilford, and Drummond Rennie for supporting the STROBE Initiative. They also thank the following institutions that have hosted working meetings of the coordinating group: Institute of Social and Preventive Medicine, University of Bern, Bern, Switzerland; Department of Social Medicine, University of Bristol, Bristol, United Kingdom; London School of Hygiene & Tropical Medicine, London, United Kingdom; Nordic Cochrane Centre, Copenhagen, Denmark; and Centre for Statistics in Medicine, University of Oxford, Oxford, United Kingdom. Finally, they thank the 4 anonymous reviewers who provided helpful comments on a previous draft of this paper.

Grant Support: The workshop was funded by the European Science Foundation. Additional funding was received from the Medical Research Council Health Services Research

Collaboration and the National Health Services Research & Development Methodology Programme. The funders had no role in study design, data collection and analysis, decision to publish, or preparation of the manuscript.

Potential Financial Conflicts of Interest: None disclosed.

REFERENCES FROM THE READING

1. Glasziou P, Vandenbroucke JP, Chalmers I. Assessing the quality of research. BMJ. 2004;328:39–41.

2. Funai EF, Rosenbush EJ, Lee MJ, Del Priore G. Distribution of study designs in four major US journals of obstetrics and gynecology. Gynecol Obstet Invest. 2001;51:8–11.

3. Scales CD Jr, Norris RD, Peterson BL, Preminger GM, Dahm P. Clinical research and statistical methods in the urology literature. J Urol. 2005;174:1374–9.

4. Pocock SJ, Collier TJ, Dandreo KJ, de Stavola BL, Goldman MB, Kalish LA, et al. Issues in the reporting of epidemiological studies: a survey of recent practice. BMJ. 2004;329:883.

5. Tooth L, Ware R, Bain C, Purdie DM, Dobson A. Quality of reporting of observational longitudinal research. Am J Epidemiol. 2005;161:280–8.

6. von Elm E, Altman DG, Egger M, Gotzsche PC, Pocock SJ, Vandenbroucke JP, STROBE Initiative. The Strengthening the Reporting of Observational Studies in Epidemiology (STROBE) Statement: guidelines for reporting observational studies. Ann Intern Med. 2007;147:573–7.

7. Mihailovic A, Bell CM, Urbach DR. Users' guide to the surgical literature. Case-control studies in surgical journals. Can J Surg. 2005;48:148–51.

8. Rushton L. Reporting of occupational and environmental research: use and misuse of statistical and epidemiological methods. Occup Environ Med. 2000;57:1–9.

9. Rothman KJ. No adjustments are needed for multiple comparisons. Epidemiology. 1990;1:43–6.

10. Moonesinghe R, Khoury MJ, Janssens AC. Most published research findings are false—but a little replication goes a long way. PLoS Med. 2007;4:e28.

11. Jenicek M. Clinical Case Reporting. Evidence-Based Medicine. Oxford: Butterworth-Heinemann; 1999:117.

12. Vandenbroucke JP. In defense of case reports and case series. Ann Intern Med. 2001;134:330–4.

13. Bossuyt PM, Reitsma JB, Bruns DE, Gatsonis CA, Glasziou PP, Irwig LM, Standards for Reporting of Diagnostic Accuracy. Towards complete and accurate reporting of studies of diagnostic accuracy: The STARD Initiative. Ann Intern Med. 2003;138:40–4.

14. McShane LM, Altman DG, Sauerbrei W, Taube SE, Gion M, Clark GM, Statistics Subcommittee of the NCI-EORTC Working Group on Cancer Diagnostics. REporting recommendations for tumour MARKer prognostic studies (REMARK). Br J Cancer. 2005;93:387–91.

15. Ioannidis JP, Gwinn M, Little J, Higgins JP, Bernstein JL, Boffetta P, Human Genome Epidemiology Network and the Network of Investigator Networks. A road map for efficient and reliable human genome epidemiology. Nat Genet. 2006;38:3–5.

16. Rodrigues L, Kirkwood BR. Case-control designs in the study of common diseases: updates on the demise of the rare disease assumption and the choice of sampling scheme for controls. Int J Epidemiol. 1990;19:205–13.

17. Rothman KJ, Greenland S. Case-control studies. In: Rothman KJ, Greenland S, ed. Modern Epidemiology. 2nd ed. Philadelphia: Lippincott Raven; 1998:93–114.

18. Forand SP. Leukaemia incidence among workers in the shoe and boot manufacturing industry: a case-control study. Environ Health. 2004;3:7.

19. Benson K, Hartz AJ. A comparison of observational studies and randomized, controlled trials. N Engl J Med. 2000;342:1878–86.

20. Gøtzsche PC, Harden A. Searching for non-randomised studies. Draft chapter 3. Cochrane Non-Randomised Studies Methods Group, 26 July 2002 Accessed at www.cochrane.dk/nrsmg on 10 September, 2007.

21. Lohse N, Hansen AB, Pedersen G, Kronborg G, Gerstoft J, Sørensen HT, et al. Survival of persons with and without HIV infection in Denmark, 1995–2005. Ann Intern Med. 2007;146:87–95.

22. American Journal of Epidemiology. Information for authors. Accessed at www.oxfordjournals.org/aje/for_authors/index.html on 30 August, 2007.

23. Haynes RB, Mulrow CD, Huth EJ, Altman DG, Gardner MJ. More informative abstracts revisited. Ann Intern Med. 1990;113:69–76.

24. Taddio A, Pain T, Fassos FF, Boon H, Ilersich AL, Einarson TR. Quality of nonstructured and structured abstracts of original research articles in the British Medical Journal, the Canadian Medical Association Journal and the Journal of the American Medical Association. CMAJ. 1994;150:1611–5.

25. Hartley J, Sydes M. Which layout do you prefer? An analysis of readers' preferences for different typographic layouts of structured abstracts. J Inf Sci. 1996;22:27–37.

26. Viner RM, Cole TJ. Adult socioeconomic, educational, social, and psychological outcomes of childhood obesity: a national birth cohort study. BMJ. 2005;330:1354.

27. McCauley J, Kern DE, Kolodner K, Dill L, Schroeder AF, DeChant HK, et al. The "battering syndrome": prevalence and clinical characteristics of domestic violence in primary care internal medicine practices. Ann Intern Med. 1995;123:737–46.

28. McEvoy SP, Stevenson MR, McCartt AT, Woodward M, Haworth C, Palamara P, et al. Role of mobile phones in motor vehicle crashes resulting in hospital attendance: a case-crossover study. BMJ. 2005;331:428.

29. Vandenbroucke JP. Prospective or retrospective: what's in a name? [Editorial]. BMJ. 1991;302:249–50.

30. Last JM. A Dictionary of Epidemiology. New York: Oxford Univ Pr: 2000.

31. Miettinen OS. Theoretical Epidemiology: Principles of Occurrence Research in Medicine. New York: Wiley; 1985:64–6.

32. Rothman KJ, Greenland S. Types of Epidemiologic Studies. In: Rothman KJ, Greenland S, eds. Modern Epidemiology. 2nd ed. Philadelphia: Lippincott Raven; 1998:74–5.

33. MacMahon B, Trichopoulos D. Epidemiology, Principles and Methods. 2nd ed. Boston: Little, Brown; 1996:81.

34. Lilienfeld AM. Foundations of Epidemiology. New York: Oxford Univ Pr; 1976.

35. Ridker PM, Hennekens CH, Lindpaintner K, Stampfer MJ, Eisenberg PR, Miletich JP. Mutation in the gene coding for coagulation factor V and the risk of myocardial infarction, stroke, and venous thrombosis in apparently healthy men. N Engl J Med. 1995;332:912–7.

36. Goodman KJ, O'Rourke K, Day RS, Wang C, Nurgalieva Z, Phillips CV, et al. Dynamics of Helicobacter pylori infection in a US–Mexico cohort during the first two years of life. Int J Epidemiol. 2005;34:1348–55.

37. Altman DG, De Stavola BL, Love SB, Stepniewska KA. Review of survival analyses published in cancer journals. Br J Cancer. 1995;72:511–8.

38. Cerhan JR, Wallace RB, Folsom AR, Potter JD, Munger RG, Prineas RJ. Transfusion history and cancer risk in older women. Ann Intern Med. 1993;119:8–15.

39. Beane Freeman LE, Dennis LK, Lynch CF, Thorne PS, Just CL. Toenail arsenic content and cutaneous melanoma in Iowa. Am J Epidemiol. 2004;160:679–87.

40. Canto JG, Allison JJ, Kiefe CI, Fincher C, Farmer R, Sekar P, et al. Relation of race and sex to the use of reperfusion therapy in Medicare beneficiaries with acute myocardial infarction. N Engl J Med. 2000;342:1094–100.

41. Metzkor-Cotter E, Kletter Y, Avidor B, Varon M, Golan Y, Ephros M, et al. Long-term serological analysis and clinical follow-up of patients with cat scratch disease. Clin Infect Dis. 2003;37:1149–54.

42. Johnson ES. Bias on withdrawing lost subjects from the analysis at the time of loss, in cohort mortality studies, and in follow-up methods. J Occup Med. 1990;32:250–4.

43. Berkson J. Limitations of the application of fourfold table analysis to hospital data. Biometrics Bulletin. 1946;2:53.

44. Feinstein AR, Walter SD, Horwitz RI. An analysis of Berkson's bias in case-control studies. J Chronic Dis. 1986;39:495–504.

45. Jick H, Vessey MP. Case-control studies in the evaluation of drug-induced illness. Am J Epidemiol. 1978;107:1–7.

46. Hackam DG, Mamdani M, Li P, Redelmeier DA. Statins and sepsis in patients with cardiovascular disease: a population-based cohort analysis. Lancet. 2006;367:413–8.

47. Smeeth L, Cook C, Fombonne E, Heavey L, Rodrigues LC, Smith PG, et al. MMR vaccination and pervasive developmental disorders: a case-control study. Lancet. 2004;364:963–9.

48. Costanza MC. Matching. Prev Med. 1995;24:425–33.

49. Stürmer T, Brenner H. Flexible matching strategies to increase power and efficiency to detect and estimate gene-environment interactions in case-control studies. Am J Epidemiol. 2002;155:593–602.

50. Rothman KJ, Greenland S. Matching. In: Rothman KJ, Greenland S, eds. Modern Epidemiology. 2nd ed. Philadelphia: Lippincott Raven; 1998:147–61.

51. Szklo MF, Nieto J. Epidemiology, Beyond the Basics. Sudbury, United Kingdom: Jones and Bartlett; 2000:40–51.

52. Cole P, MacMahon B. Attributable risk percent in case-control studies. Br J Prev Soc Med. 1971;25:242–4.

53. Gissler M, Hemminki E. The danger of overmatching in studies of the perinatal mortality and birthweight of infants born after assisted conception. Eur J Obstet Gynecol Reprod Biol. 1996;69:73–5.

54. Gefeller O, Pfahlberg A, Brenner H, Windeler J. An empirical investigation on matching in published case-control studies. Eur J Epidemiol. 1998;14:321–5.

55. Artama M, Ritvanen A, Gissler M, Isojärvi J, Auvinen A. Congenital structural anomalies in offspring of women with epilepsy—a population-based cohort study in Finland. Int J Epidemiol. 2006;35:280–7.

56. Ebrahim S. Cohorts, infants and children. Int J Epidemiol. 2004;33:1165–1166.

57. Walker M, Whincup PH, Shaper AG. The British Regional Heart Study 1975–2004. Int J Epidemiol. 2004;33:1185–92.

58. Wieland S, Dickersin K. Selective exposure reporting and Medline indexing limited the search sensitivity for observational studies of the adverse effects of oral contraceptives. J Clin Epidemiol. 2005;58:560–7.

59. Anderson HR, Atkinson RW, Peacock JL, Sweeting MJ, Marston L. Ambient particulate matter and health effects: publication bias in studies of short-term associations. Epidemiology. 2005;16:155–63.

60. Winkelmayer WC, Stampfer MJ, Willett WC, Curhan GC. Habitual caffeine intake and the risk of hypertension in women. JAMA. 2005;294:2330–5.

61. Lukanova A, Söderberg S, Kaaks R, Jellum E, Stattin P. Serum adiponectin is not associated with risk of colorectal cancer. Cancer Epidemiol Biomarkers Prev. 2006;15:401–2.

62. Becher H. The concept of residual confounding in regression models and some applications. Stat Med. 1992;11:1747–58.

63. Brenner H, Blettner M. Controlling for continuous confounders in epidemiologic research. Epidemiology. 1997;8:429–34.

64. Phillips MR, Yang G, Zhang Y, Wang L, Ji H, Zhou M. Risk factors for suicide in China: a national case-control psychological autopsy study. Lancet. 2002;360:1728–36.

65. Pasquale LR, Kang JH, Manson JE, Willett WC, Rosner BA, Hankinson SE. Prospective study of type 2 diabetes mellitus and risk of primary open-angle glaucoma in women. Ophthalmology. 2006;113:1081–6.

66. Craig SL, Feinstein AR. Antecedent therapy versus detection bias as causes of neoplastic multimorbidity. Am J Clin Oncol. 1999;22:51–6.

67. Rogler LH, Mroczek DK, Fellows M, Loftus ST. The neglect of response bias in mental health research. J Nerv Ment Dis. 2001;189:182–7.

68. Murphy EA. The logic of medicine. Baltimore: Johns Hopkins Univ Pr; 1976.

69. Sackett DL. Bias in analytic research. J Chronic Dis. 1979;32:51–63.

70. Johannes CB, Crawford SL, McKinlay JB. Interviewer effects in a cohort study. Results from the Massachusetts Women's Health Study. Am J Epidemiol. 1997;146:429–38.

71. Bloemenkamp KW, Rosendaal FR, Büller HR, Helmerhorst FM, Colly LP, Vandenbroucke JP. Risk of venous thrombosis with use of current low-dose oral contraceptives is not explained by diagnostic suspicion and referral bias. Arch Intern Med. 1999;159:65–70.

72. Feinstein AR. Clinical Epidemiology: The Architecture of Clinical Research. Philadelphia: W.B. Saunders: 1985.

73. Yadon ZE, Rodrigues LC, Davies CR, Quigley MA. Indoor and peridomestic transmission of American cutaneous leishmaniasis in northwestern Argentina: a retrospective case-control study. Am J Trop Med Hyg. 2003;68:519–26.

74. Anoop S, Saravanan B, Joseph A, Cherian A, Jacob KS. Maternal depression and low maternal intelligence as risk factors for malnutrition in children: a community based case-control study from South India. Arch Dis Child. 2004;89:325–9.

75. Carlin JB, Doyle LW. Sample size. J Paediatr Child Health. 2002;38:300–4.

76. Rigby AS, Vail A. Statistical methods in epidemiology. II: A common-sense approach to sample size estimation. Disabil Rehabil. 1998;20:405–10.

77. Schulz KF, Grimes DA. Sample size calculations in randomised trials: mandatory and mystical. Lancet. 2005;365:1348–53.

78. Drescher K, Timm J, Jöckel KH. The design of case-control studies: the effect of confounding on sample size requirements. Stat Med. 1990;9:765–76.

79. Devine OJ, Smith JM. Estimating sample size for epidemiologic studies: the impact of ignoring exposure measurement uncertainty. Stat Med. 1998;17:1375–89.

80. Linn S, Levi L, Grunau PD, Zaidise I, Zarka S. Effect measure modification and confounding of severe head injury mortality by age and multiple organ injury severity. Ann Epidemiol. 2007;17:142–7.

81. Altman DG, Lausen B, Sauerbrei W, Schumacher M. Dangers of using "optimal" cutpoints in the evaluation of prognostic factors. J Natl Cancer Inst. 1994;86:829–35.

82. Royston P, Altman DG, Sauerbrei W. Dichotomizing continuous predictors in multiple regression: a bad idea. Stat Med. 2006;25:127–41.

83. Greenland S. Avoiding power loss associated with categorization and ordinal scores in dose-response and trend analysis. Epidemiology. 1995;6:450–4.

84. Royston P, Ambler G, Sauerbrei W. The use of fractional polynomials to model continuous risk variables in epidemiology. Int J Epidemiol. 1999;28:964–74.

85. MacCallum RC, Zhang S, Preacher KJ, Rucker DD. On the practice of dichotomization of quantitative variables. Psychol Methods. 2002;7:19–40.

86. Altman DG. Categorizing continuous variables. In: Armitage P, Colton T, ed. Encyclopedia of biostatistics, 2nd edition. Chichester, United Kingdom: John Wiley; 2005:708–11.

87. Cohen J. The cost of dichotomization. Appl Psychol Meas. 1983;7:249–53.

88. Zhao LP, Kolonel LN. Efficiency loss from categorizing quantitative exposures into qualitative exposures in case-control studies. Am J Epidemiol. 1992;136:464–74.

89. Cochran WG. The effectiveness of adjustment by subclassification in removing bias in observational studies. Biometrics. 1968;24:295–313.

90. Clayton D, Hills M. Models for dose-response. In: Statistical Models in Epidemiology. Oxford: Oxford Univ Pr 1993:249–60.

91. Cox DR. Note on grouping. J Am Stat Assoc. 1957;52:543–7.

92. Il'yasova D, Hertz-Picciotto I, Peters U, Berlin JA, Poole C. Choice of exposure scores for categorical regression in meta-analysis: a case study of a common problem. Cancer Causes Control. 2005;16:383–8.

93. Berglund A, Alfredsson L, Cassidy JD, Jensen I, Nygren A. The association between exposure to a rear-end collision and future neck or shoulder pain: a cohort study. J Clin Epidemiol. 2000;53:1089–94.

94. Slama R, Werwatz A. Controlling for continuous confounding factors: non- and semiparametric approaches. Rev Epidemiol Sante Publique. 2005;53 Spec No 2:2S65–80.

95. Greenland S. Introduction to regression modelling. In: Rothman KJ, Greenland S, eds. Modern Epidemiology. 2nd ed. Philadelphia: Lippincott Raven: 1998:401–32.

96. Thompson WD. Statistical analysis of case-control studies. Epidemiol Rev. 1994;16:33–50.

97. Schlesselman JJ. Logistic regression for case-control studies. In: Case-Control Studies: Design, Conduct, Analysis. New York: Oxford Univ Pr; 1982:235–41.

98. Clayton D, Hills M. Choice and interpretation of models. In: Statistical Models in Epidemiology. Oxford: Oxford Univ Pr; 1993:271–81.

99. Altman DG, Gore SM, Gardner MJ, Pocock SJ. Statistical guidelines for contributors to medical journals. Br Med J (Clin Res Ed). 1983;286:1489–93.

100. Uniform requirements for manuscripts submitted to biomedical journals. International Committee of Medical Journal Editors. N Engl J Med. 1997;336:309–15.

101. Müllner M, Matthews H, Altman DG. Reporting on statistical methods to adjust for confounding: a cross-sectional survey. Ann Intern Med. 2002;136:122–6.

102. Olsen J, Basso O. Re: Residual confounding [Letter]. Am J Epidemiol. 1999;149:290.

103. Hallan S, de Mutsert R, Carlsen S, Dekker FW, Aasarød K, Holmen J. Obesity, smoking, and physical inactivity as risk factors for CKD: are men more vulnerable? Am J Kidney Dis. 2006;47:396–405.

104. Gøtzsche PC. Believability of relative risks and odds ratios in abstracts: cross sectional study. BMJ. 2006;333:231–4.

105. Szklo MF, Nieto J. Communicating results of epidemiologic studies. In: Epidemiology, Beyond the Basics. Sudbury: Jones and Bartlett. 2000:408–30.

106. Chandola T, Brunner E, Marmot M. Chronic stress at work and the metabolic syndrome: prospective study. BMJ. 2006;332:521–5.

107. Vach W, Blettner M. Biased estimation of the odds ratio in case-control studies due to the use of ad hoc methods of correcting for missing values for confounding variables. Am J Epidemiol. 1991;134:895–907.

108. Little RJ, Rubin DB. A taxonomy of missing-data methods. In: Statistical Analysis with Missing Data. New York: Wiley; 2002:19–23.

109. Ware JH. Interpreting incomplete data in studies of diet and weight loss [Editorial]. N Engl J Med. 2003;348:2136–7.

110. Rubin DB. Inference and missing data. Biometrika. 1976;63:581–92.

111. Schafer JL. Analysis of Incomplete Multivariate Data. London: Chapman & Hall; 1997.

112. Lipsitz SR, Ibrahim JG, Chen MH, Peterson H. Non-ignorable missing covariates in generalized linear models. Stat Med. 1999;18:2435–48.

113. Rotnitzky A, Robins J. Analysis of semi-parametric regression models with non-ignorable non-response. Stat Med. 1997;16:81–102.

114. Rubin DB. Multiple Imputation for Nonresponse in Surveys. New York: Wiley; 1987.

115. Barnard J, Meng XL. Applications of multiple imputation in medical studies: from AIDS to NHANES. Stat Methods Med Res. 1999;8:17–36.

116. Braitstein P, Brinkhof MW, Dabis F, Schechter M, Boulle A, Miotti P, Antiretroviral Therapy in Lower Income Countries (ART-LINC) Collaboration. Mortality of HIV-1-infected patients in the first year of antiretroviral therapy: comparison between low-income and high-income countries. Lancet. 2006;367:817–24.

117. Purandare N, Burns A, Daly KJ, Hardicre J, Morris J, Macfarlane G, et al. Cerebral emboli as a potential cause of Alzheimer's disease and vascular dementia: case-control study. BMJ. 2006;332:1119–24.

118. South African Demographic and Health Coordinating Team. Hypertension in South African adults: results from the Demographic and Health Survey, 1998. J Hypertens. 2001;19:1717–25.

119. Lohr SL. Design effects. Sampling: Design and Analysis. Pacific Grove, CA: Duxbury Pr; 1999.

120. Dunn NR, Arscott A, Thorogood M. The relationship between use of oral contraceptives and myocardial infarction in young women with fatal outcome, compared to those who survive: results from the MICA case-control study. Contraception. 2001;63:65–9.

121. Rothman KJ, Greenland S. Basic methods for sensitivity analysis and external adjustment. In: Rothman KJ, Greenland S, ed. Modern Epidemiology. 2nd ed. Philadelphia: Lippincott Raven; 1998:343–57.

122. Custer B, Longstreth WT Jr, Phillips LE, Koepsell TD, Van Belle G. Hormonal exposures and the risk of intracranial meningioma in women: a population-based case-control study. BMC Cancer. 2006;6:152.

123. Wakefield MA, Chaloupka FJ, Kaufman NJ, Orleans CT, Barker DC, Ruel EE. Effect of restrictions on smoking at home, at school, and in public places on teenage smoking: cross sectional study. BMJ. 2000;321:333–7.

124. Greenland S. The impact of prior distributions for uncontrolled confounding and response bias: a case study of the relation of wire codes and magnetic fields to childhood leukemia. J Am Stat Assoc. 2003;98:47–54.

125. Lash TL, Fink AK. Semi-automated sensitivity analysis to assess systematic errors in observational data. Epidemiology. 2003;14:451–8.

126. Phillips CV. Quantifying and reporting uncertainty from systematic errors. Epidemiology. 2003;14:459–66.

127. Cornfield J, Haenszel W, Hammond EC, Lilienfeld AM, Shimkin MB, Wynder EL. Smoking and lung cancer: recent evidence and a discussion of some questions. J Natl Cancer Inst. 1959;22:173–203.

128. Langholz B. Factors that explain the power line configuration wiring code-childhood leukemia association: what would they look like? Bioelectromagnetics. 2001(suppl 5):S19–31.

129. Eisner MD, Smith AK, Blanc PD. Bartenders' respiratory health after establishment of smoke-free bars and taverns. JAMA. 1998;280:1909–14.

130. Dunne MP, Martin NG, Bailey JM, Heath AC, Bucholz KK, Madden PA, et al. Participation bias in a sexuality survey: psychological and behavioural characteristics of responders and non-responders. Int J Epidemiol. 1997;26:844–54.

131. Schüz J, Kaatsch P, Kaletsch U, Meinert R, Michaelis J. Association of childhood cancer with factors related to pregnancy and birth. Int J Epidemiol. 1999;28:631–9.

132. Cnattingius S, Zack M, Ekbom A, Gunnarskog J, Linet M, Adami HO. Prenatal and neonatal risk factors for childhood myeloid leukemia. Cancer Epidemiol Biomarkers Prev. 1995;4:441–5.

133. Schüz J. Non-response bias as a likely cause of the association between young maternal age at the time of delivery and the risk of cancer in the offspring. Paediatr Perinat Epidemiol. 2003;17:106–12.

134. Slattery ML, Edwards SL, Caan BJ, Kerber RA, Potter JD. Response rates among control subjects in case-control studies. Ann Epidemiol. 1995;5:245–9.

135. Schulz KF, Grimes DA. Case-control studies: research in reverse. Lancet. 2002;359:431–4.

136. Olson SH, Voigt LF, Begg CB, Weiss NS. Reporting participation in case-control studies. Epidemiology. 2002;13:123–6.

137. Morton LM, Cahill J, Hartge P. Reporting participation in epidemiologic studies: a survey of practice. Am J Epidemiol. 2006;163:197–203.

138. Olson SH. Reported participation in case-control studies: changes over time. Am J Epidemiol. 2001;154:574–81.

139. Sandler DP. On revealing what we'd rather hide: the problem of describing study participation [Editorial]. Epidemiology. 2002;13:117.

140. Hepworth SJ, Schoemaker MJ, Muir KR, Swerdlow AJ, van Tongeren MJ, McKinney PA. Mobile phone use and risk of glioma in adults: case-control study. BMJ. 2006;332:883–7.

141. Hay AD, Wilson A, Fahey T, Peters TJ. The duration of acute cough in pre-school children presenting to primary care: a prospective cohort study. Fam Pract. 2003;20:696–705.

142. Egger M, Jüni P, Bartlett C, CONSORT Group (Consolidated Standards of Reporting of Trials). Value of flow diagrams in reports of randomized controlled trials. JAMA. 2001;285:1996–9.

143. Osella AR, Misciagna G, Guerra VM, Chiloiro M, Cuppone R, Cavallini A, et al. Hepatitis C virus (HCV) infection and liver-related mortality: a population-based cohort study in southern Italy. The Association for the Study of Liver Disease in Puglia. Int J Epidemiol. 2000;29:922–7.

144. Dales LG, Ury HK. An improper use of statistical significance testing in studying covariables. Int J Epidemiol. 1978;7:373–5.

145. Maldonado G, Greenland S. Simulation study of confounder-selection strategies. Am J Epidemiol. 1993;138:923–36.

146. Tanis BC, van den Bosch MA, Kemmeren JM, Cats VM, Helmerhorst FM, Algra A, et al. Oral contraceptives and the risk of myocardial infarction. N Engl J Med. 2001;345:1787–93.

147. Rothman KJ, Greenland S. Precision and validity in epidemiologic studies. In: Rothman KJ, Greenland S, ed. Modern Epidemiology. 2nd ed. Philadelphia: Lippincott Raven; 1998:120–5.

148. Clark TG, Altman DG, De Stavola BL. Quantification of the completeness of follow-up. Lancet. 2002;359:1309–10.

149. Qiu C, Fratiglioni L, Karp A, Winblad B, Bellander T. Occupational exposure to electromagnetic fields and risk of Alzheimer's disease. Epidemiology. 2004;15:687–94.

150. Kengeya-Kayondo JF, Kamali A, Nunn AJ, Ruberantwari A, Wagner HU, Mulder DW. Incidence of HIV-1 infection in adults and socio-demographic characteristics of seroconverters in a rural population in Uganda: 1990–1994. Int J Epidemiol. 1996;25:1077–82.

151. Mastrangelo G, Fedeli U, Fadda E, Valentini F, Agnesi R, Magarotto G, et al. Increased risk of hepatocellular carcinoma and liver cirrhosis in vinyl chloride workers: synergistic effect of occupational exposure with alcohol intake. Environ Health Perspect. 2004;112:1188–92.

152. Salo PM, Arbes SJ Jr, Sever M, Jaramillo R, Cohn RD, London SJ, et al. Exposure to Alternaria alternata in US homes is associated with asthma symptoms. J Allergy Clin Immunol. 2006;118:892–8.

153. Pocock SJ, Clayton TC, Altman DG. Survival plots of time-to-event outcomes in clinical trials: good practice and pitfalls. Lancet. 2002;359:1686–9.

154. Sasieni P. A note on the presentation of matched case-control data. Stat Med. 1992;11:617–20.

155. Lee GM, Neutra RR, Hristova L, Yost M, Hiatt RA. A nested case-control study of residential and personal magnetic field measures and miscarriages. Epidemiology. 2002;13:21–31.

156. Tiihonen J, Walhbeck K, Lönnqvist J, Klaukka T, Ioannidis JP, Volavka J, et al. Effectiveness of antipsychotic treatments in a nationwide cohort of patients in community care after first hospitalisation due to schizophrenia and schizoaffective disorder: observational follow-up study. BMJ. 2006;333:224.

157. Christenfeld NJ, Sloan RP, Carroll D, Greenland S. Risk factors, confounding, and the illusion of statistical control. Psychosom Med. 2004;66:868–75.

158. Smith GD, Phillips A. Declaring independence: why we should be cautious [Editorial]. J Epidemiol Community Health. 1990;44:257–8.

159. Greenland S, Neutra R. Control of confounding in the assessment of medical technology. Int J Epidemiol. 1980;9:361–7.

160. Robins JM. Data, design, and background knowledge in etiologic inference. Epidemiology. 2001;12:313–20.

161. Sagiv SK, Tolbert PE, Altshul LM, Korrick SA. Organochlorine exposures during pregnancy and infant size at birth. Epidemiology. 2007;18:120–9.

162. World Health Organization. Body Mass Index (BMI). Accessed at www.euro.who.int/nutrition/20030507_1 on 10 September 2007.

163. Beral V, Million Women Study Collaborators. Breast cancer and hormone-replacement therapy in the Million Women Study. Lancet. 2003;362:419–27.

164. Hill AB. The environment and disease: association or causation? Proc R Soc Med. 1965;58:295–300.

165. Vineis P. Causality in epidemiology. Soz Praventivmed. 2003;48:80–7.

166. Empana JP, Ducimetière P, Arveiler D, Ferrières J, Evans A, Ruidavets JB, PRIME Study Group. Are the Framingham and PROCAM coronary heart disease risk functions applicable to different European populations? The PRIME Study. Eur Heart J. 2003;24:1903–11.

167. Tunstall-Pedoe H, Kuulasmaa K, Mähönen M, Tolonen H, Ruokokoski E, Amouyel P. Contribution of trends in survival and coronary-event rates to changes in coronary heart disease mortality: 10-year results from 37 WHO MONICA project populations. Monitoring trends and determinants in cardiovascular disease. Lancet. 1999;353:1547–57.

168. Cambien F, Chretien JM, Ducimetiere P, Guize L, Richard JL. Is the relationship between blood pressure and cardiovascular risk dependent on body mass index? Am J Epidemiol. 1985;122:434–42.

169. Hosmer DW, Taber S, Lemeshow S. The importance of assessing the fit of logistic regression models: a case study. Am J Public Health. 1991;81:1630–5.

170. Tibshirani R. A plain man's guide to the proportional hazards model. Clin Invest Med. 1982;5:63–8.

171. Rockhill B, Newman B, Weinberg C. Use and misuse of population attributable fractions. Am J Public Health. 1998;88:15–9.

172. Uter W, Pfahlberg A. The application of methods to quantify attributable risk in medical practice. Stat Methods Med Res. 2001;10:231–7.

173. Schwartz LM, Woloshin S, Dvorin EL, Welch HG. Ratio measures in leading medical journals: structured review of accessibility of underlying absolute risks. BMJ. 2006;333:1248.

174. Nakayama T, Zaman MM, Tanaka H. Reporting of attributable and relative risks, 1966–97 [Letter]. Lancet. 1998;351:1179.

175. Cornfield J. A method of estimating comparative rates from clinical data; applications to cancer of the lung, breast, and cervix. J Natl Cancer Inst. 1951;11:1269–75.

176. Pearce N. What does the odds ratio estimate in a case-control study? Int J Epidemiol. 1993;22:1189–92.

177. Rothman KJ, Greenland S. Measures of disease frequency. In: Rothman KJ, Greenland S, editors. Modern Epidemiology. 2nd ed. Philadelphia: Lippincott Raven; 1998:44–5.

178. Doll R, Hill AB. The mortality of doctors in relation to their smoking habits: a preliminary report. 1954. BMJ. 2004;328:1529–33; discussion 1533. [PMID: 15217868]. [Free Full Text]

179. Ezzati M, Lopez AD. Estimates of global mortality attributable to smoking in 2000. Lancet. 2003;362:847–52.

180. Greenland S. Applications of stratified analysis methods. In: Rothman KJ, Greenland S, eds. Modern Epidemiology. 2nd ed. Philadelphia: Lippincott Raven; 1998:295–7.

181. Rose G. Sick individuals and sick populations. Int J Epidemiol. 2001;30:427–32; discussion 433–4.

182. Vandenbroucke JP, Koster T, Briët E, Reitsma PH, Bertina RM, Rosendaal FR. Increased risk of venous thrombosis in oral-contraceptive users who are carriers of factor V Leiden mutation. Lancet. 1994;344:1453–7.

183. Botto LD, Khoury MJ. Commentary: facing the challenge of gene-environment interaction: the two-by-four table and beyond [Editorial]. Am J Epidemiol. 2001;153:1016–20.

184. Wei L, MacDonald TM, Walker BR. Taking glucocorticoids by prescription is associated with subsequent cardiovascular disease. Ann Intern Med. 2004;141:764–70.

185. Martinelli I, Taioli E, Battaglioli T, Podda GM, Passamonti SM, Pedotti P, et al. Risk of venous thromboembolism after air travel: interaction with thrombophilia and oral contraceptives. Arch Intern Med. 2003;163:2771–4.

186. Kyzas PA, Loizou KT, Ioannidis JP. Selective reporting biases in cancer prognostic factor studies. J Natl Cancer Inst. 2005;97:1043–55.

187. Rothman KJ, Greenland S, Walker AM. Concepts of interaction. Am J Epidemiol. 1980;112:467–70.

188. Saracci R. Interaction and synergism. Am J Epidemiol. 1980;112:465–6.

189. Rothman KJ. Epidemiology. An Introduction. Oxford: Oxford Univ Pr; 2002:168–80.

190. Rothman KJ. Interactions between causes. In: Modern Epidemiology. Boston: Little, Brown; 1986:311–26.

191. Hess DR. How to write an effective discussion. Respir Care. 2004;49:1238–41.

192. Horton R. The hidden research paper. JAMA. 2002;287:2775–8.

193. Horton R. The rhetoric of research. BMJ. 1995;310:985–7.

194. Docherty M, Smith R. The case for structuring the discussion of scientific papers [Editorial]. BMJ. 1999;318:1224–5.

195. Perneger TV, Hudelson PM. Writing a research article: advice to beginners [Editorial]. Int J Qual Health Care. 2004;16:191–2.

196. Annals of Internal Medicine. Information for authors. Accessed at www.annals.org/shared/author_info.html on 10 September 2007.

197. Maldonado G, Poole C. More research is needed [Editorial]. Ann Epidemiol. 1999;9:17–8.

198. Phillips CV. The economics of 'more research is needed'. Int J Epidemiol. 2001;30:771–6. [PMID: 11511601].

199. Winkleby MA, Kraemer HC, Ahn DK, Varady AN. Ethnic and socioeconomic differences in cardiovascular disease risk factors: findings for women from the Third National Health and Nutrition Examination Survey, 1988–1994. JAMA. 1998;280:356–62.

200. Galuska DA, Will JC, Serdula MK, Ford ES. Are health care professionals advising obese patients to lose weight? JAMA. 1999;282:1576–8.

201. Spearman C. The proof and measurement of association between two things. Am J Psychol. 1987;100:441–71.

202. Fuller WA, Hidiroglou MA. Regression estimates after correcting for attenuation. J Am Stat Assoc. 1978;73:99–104.

203. MacMahon S, Peto R, Cutler J, Collins R, Sorlie P, Neaton J, et al. Blood pressure, stroke, and coronary heart disease. Part 1, Prolonged differences in blood pressure: prospective observational studies corrected for the regression dilution bias. Lancet. 1990;335:765–74.

204. Phillips AN, Smith GD. How independent are "independent" effects? Relative risk estimation when correlated exposures are measured imprecisely. J Clin Epidemiol. 1991;44:1223–31.

205. Phillips AN, Smith GD. Bias in relative odds estimation owing to imprecise measurement of correlated exposures. Stat Med. 1992;11:953–61.

206. Greenland S. The effect of misclassification in the presence of covariates. Am J Epidemiol. 1980;112:564–9.

207. Poole C, Peters U, Il'yasova D, Arab L. Commentary: This study failed? Int J Epidemiol. 2003;32:534–5.

208. Kaufman JS, Cooper RS, McGee DL. Socioeconomic status and health in blacks and whites: the problem of residual confounding and the resiliency of race. Epidemiology. 1997;8:621–8.

209. Greenland S. Randomization, statistics, and causal inference. Epidemiology. 1990;1:421–9.

210. Taubes G. Epidemiology faces its limits. Science. 1995;269:164–9.

211. Temple R. Meta-analysis and epidemiologic studies in drug development and postmarketing surveillance. JAMA. 1999;281:841–4.

212. Greenberg RS, Shuster JL Jr. Epidemiology of cancer in children. Epidemiol Rev. 1985;7:22–48.

213. Kushi LH, Mink PJ, Folsom AR, Anderson KE, Zheng W, Lazovich D, et al. Prospective study of diet and ovarian cancer. Am J Epidemiol. 1999;149:21–31.

214. Kemmeren JM, Algra A, Meijers JC, Tans G, Bouma BN, Curvers J, et al. Effect of second- and third-generation oral contraceptives on the protein C system in the absence or presence of the factor V Leiden mutation: a randomized trial. Blood. 2004;103:927–33.

215. Egger M, May M, Chêne G, Phillips AN, Ledergerber B, Dabis F, ART Cohort Collaboration. Prognosis of HIV-1-infected patients starting highly active antiretroviral therapy: a collaborative analysis of prospective studies. Lancet. 2002;360:119–29.

216. Campbell DT. Factors relevant to the validity of experiments in social settings. Psychol Bull. 1957;54:297–312.

217. Justice AC, Covinsky KE, Berlin JA. Assessing the generalizability of prognostic information. Ann Intern Med. 1999;130:515–24.

218. Krimsky S, Rothenberg LS. Conflict of interest policies in science and medical journals: editorial practices and author disclosures. Sci Eng Ethics. 2001;7:205–18.

219. Bekelman JE, Li Y, Gross CP. Scope and impact of financial conflicts of interest in biomedical research: a systematic review. JAMA. 2003;289:454–65.

220. Davidson RA. Source of funding and outcome of clinical trials. J Gen Intern Med. 1986;1:155–8.

221. Stelfox HT, Chua G, O'Rourke K, Detsky AS. Conflict of interest in the debate over calcium-channel antagonists. N Engl J Med. 1998;338:101–6.

222. Lexchin J, Bero LA, Djulbegovic B, Clark O. Pharmaceutical industry sponsorship and research outcome and quality: systematic review. BMJ. 2003;326:1167–70. [PMID: 12775614].

223. Als-Nielsen B, Chen W, Gluud C, Kjaergard LL. Association of funding and conclusions in randomized drug trials: a reflection of treatment effect or adverse events? JAMA. 2003;290:921–8.

224. Barnes DE, Bero LA. Why review articles on the health effects of passive smoking reach different conclusions. JAMA. 1998;279:1566–70.

225. Barnes DE, Bero LA. Industry-funded research and conflict of interest: an analysis of research sponsored by the tobacco industry through the Center for Indoor Air Research. J Health Polit Policy Law. 1996;21:515–42.

226. Glantz SA, Barnes DE, Bero L, Hanauer P, Slade J. Looking through a keyhole at the tobacco industry. The Brown and Williamson documents. JAMA. 1995;274:219–24.

227. Huss A, Egger M, Hug K, Huwiler-Müntener K, Röösli M. Source of funding and results of studies of health effects of mobile phone use: systematic review of experimental studies. Environ Health Perspect. 2007;115:1–4.

228. Safer DJ. Design and reporting modifications in industry-sponsored comparative psychopharmacology trials. J Nerv Ment Dis. 2002;190:583–92.

229. Aspinall RL, Goodman NW. Denial of effective treatment and poor quality of clinical information in placebo controlled trials of ondansetron for postoperative nausea and vomiting: a review of published trials. BMJ. 1995;311:844–6.

230. Chan AW, Hróbjartsson A, Haahr MT, Gøtzsche PC, Altman DG. Empirical evidence for selective reporting of outcomes in randomized trials: comparison of protocols to published articles. JAMA. 2004;291:2457–65.

231. Melander H, Ahlqvist-Rastad J, Meijer G, Beermann B. Evidence b(i)ased medicine—selective reporting from studies sponsored by pharmaceutical industry: review of studies in new drug applications. BMJ. 2003;326:1171–3.

232. Scherer RW, Langenberg P, von Elm E. Full publication of results initially presented in abstracts. Cochrane Database Syst Rev. 2007:R000005.

233. Moher D, Schulz KF, Altman DG. The CONSORT statement: revised recommendations for improving the quality of reports of parallel-group randomised trials. Lancet. 2001;357:1191–4.

234. Stroup DF, Berlin JA, Morton SC, Olkin I, Williamson GD, Rennie D, et al. Meta-analysis of observational studies in epidemiology: a proposal for reporting. Meta-analysis Of Observational Studies in Epidemiology (MOOSE) group. JAMA. 2000;283:2008–12.

235. Altman DG, Schulz KF, Moher D, Egger M, Davidoff F, Elbourne D, CONSORT GROUP (Consolidated Standards of Reporting Trials). The revised CONSORT statement for reporting randomized trials: explanation and elaboration. Ann Intern Med. 2001;134:663–94.

236. Moher D. CONSORT: an evolving tool to help improve the quality of reports of randomized controlled trials. Consolidated Standards of Reporting Trials. JAMA. 1998;279:1489–91.

237. Begg C, Cho M, Eastwood S, Horton R, Moher D, Olkin I, et al. Improving the quality of reporting of randomized controlled trials. The CONSORT statement. JAMA. 1996;276:637–9.

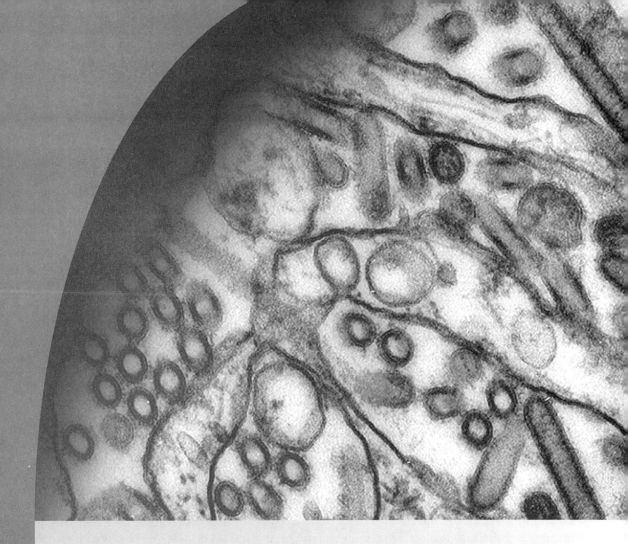

PART **XI**

Intention-to-Treat: Tough Idea Made Simple

The intention-to-treat principle is one of the more difficult methodological ideas to understand: Why should we compare outcomes among grouping of people on the basis of what they *were randomized to get* instead of *what they did get?* This basic question has haunted many researchers and more readers. Now more than ever, this principle is widely accepted—a very good thing. But you as the epidemiologist must understand this principle at its core. It affects not only RCTs but other studies as well. In fact, more and more observational studies are using this principle to assign exposures and evaluate their effects than in the past, with growing awareness about how valuable this can be especially in the presence of changing exposures or treatments. This article explains this concept very clearly so all can understand.

READING 29
Intention-to-Treat Principle

Victor M. Montori, Gordon H. Guyatt

Montori VM, Guyatt GH. Intention-to-treat principle. *CMAJ.* 2001;165:1339–41.

In deciding if a treatment is likely to work in an individual patient, clinicians need to know the effect of the intervention in patients who take the treatment as prescribed. However, participants in clinical trials may not adhere to the protocol, or clinicians may recommend withdrawal of the study medication because of apparent adverse effects. Should investigators exclude from the analysis any participants who violate the research protocol? In this article, we review how randomization reduces bias in clinical trials and then discuss the importance of including all eligible patients in the analysis, to ensure the validity of the results.

PREVENTING BIAS IN RANDOMIZED CONTROLLED TRIALS

The randomized controlled clinical trial is the best way to minimize bias in ascertaining treatment effects. The intent of randomization is to establish groups of patients with similar distributions of the characteristics that could determine whether they will suffer the adverse outcome of interest. If prognostic factors are balanced in the 2 (or more) groups and if the treatment has no effect, the proportion of participants experiencing the target outcome will be similar in the arms of the study. Conversely, if differences in outcome are observed, clinicians can confidently attribute those differences to the experimental intervention.

APPLYING THE INTENTION-TO-TREAT PRINCIPLE

How should investigators analyze study data if one or more patients have not adhered to the allocated management strat-

egy, for whatever reason? Some investigators deal with these protocol violations by excluding the participants from the analysis. This form of analysis, known as a per protocol, efficacy, explanatory analysis, or analysis by treatment administered, describes the outcomes of the participants who adhered to the research protocol. Although investigators can use information from such an analysis to estimate the intervention's efficacy in those who actually received it in the intended intensity or dose for the intended interval, this estimate is likely to be seriously flawed.

The problem arises because the reasons for nonadherence to the protocol may be related to prognosis. Empirical evidence suggests that participants who adhere tend to do better than those who do not adhere, even after adjustment for all known prognostic factors and irrespective of assignment to active treatment or placebo.[1,2] Excluding nonadherent participants from the analysis leaves those who may be destined to have a better outcome and destroys the unbiased comparison afforded by randomization.[3]

A hypothetical example will illustrate how excluding patients who do not receive the treatment to which they are assigned can introduce bias. Imagine a randomized trial of 200 patients with cerebrovascular disease, of whom 100 are assigned to receive acetylsalicylic acid (ASA) and a surgical intervention for which there is a 1-month waiting period and the other 100 are assigned to receive ASA alone (Figure 11-1). Let us assume that the surgery is ineffective in preventing stroke—that is, on average, the same proportion of patients in each of the 2 arms (surgery + ASA and ASA only) will suffer a stroke.

In the surgery + ASA arm, 10 of the 100 patients have a stroke, the primary outcome of the trial, in the 1-month waiting period between randomization and surgery. Of the 90 patients who go on to have the surgery, 10 have a stroke in the

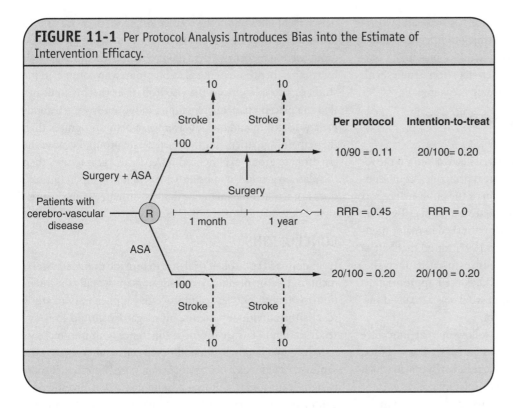

FIGURE 11-1 Per Protocol Analysis Introduces Bias into the Estimate of Intervention Efficacy.

However, clinicians make decisions at the level of the individual patient. Patients considering a treatment regimen and committed to complying with treatment wish to know how well the treatment will work when they use it at the intended dose for the intended duration. We have seen how per protocol analysis fails to answer this question and introduces bias. Unfortunately, applying the intention-to-treat principle doesn't solve the problem. When treatment is effective but nonadherence is substantial, the analysis following the intention-to-treat principle underestimates the magnitude of the treatment effect that will occur in adherent patients.

The solution involves conducting an intention-to-treat analysis, but only after using a protocol that ensures maximal adherence. For instance, studies may include run-in periods that identify nonadherent participants or participants intolerant to the experimental treatment, so they can be excluded before randomization.[4]

DEALING WITH LOSS TO FOLLOW-UP

Intention-to-treat analysis cannot minimize bias introduced by loss to follow-up, that is, patients whose outcome status is unknown. If investigators stop following patients who do not adhere to the study protocol, they will be unaware if those patients suffered the target outcome. If they conduct an intention-to-treat analysis and count events in all participants of whose outcomes they are aware (that is, those who followed the protocol), they will, de facto, be conducting a per protocol analysis.

Investigators often include patients lost to follow-up in the denominators in tables describing study results and in calculating estimates of effect. This approach assumes that none of those lost to follow-up suffered the target outcome. Making this unlikely assumption opens the door to a misleading presentation of study results. Alternative strategies are available that impute outcomes to those lost to follow-up. Some of these strategies include using multivariate analysis of prognostic factors to predict the most likely outcome in those lost to follow-up, imputation of outcomes by carrying the last known

subsequent year. Because in the absence of an effective intervention the patients in the ASA-only arm share the same destiny as those in the surgery + ASA arm, and because we have assumed that surgery is ineffective, we know that 10 patients in the ASA-only arm will have a stroke in the month after randomization and another 10 will do so in the subsequent year.

If we restrict the analysis in the surgery + ASA arm to the patients who underwent surgery (a per protocol analysis), the event rate would be 11% (10/90); however, the rate in the ASA-only arm would be 20% (20/100). These values represent a spurious (since we have assumed that surgery in fact has no effect on subsequent occurrence of stroke) reduction in stroke risk of close to 50%. Alternatively, if we count all events in all randomized patients, according to the intention-to-treat principle, we find that there were 20 events in each group and no evidence of a positive treatment effect. This analysis eliminates the misleading estimate of surgery's impact that is obtained with the per protocol analysis.

As illustrated by this example, applying the intention-to-treat principle provides an unbiased assessment of the efficacy of the intervention at the level of adherence observed in the trial. This level of adherence could be similar to that observed in the community, and the results could inform community-based decisions about the effectiveness of the experimental intervention.

outcome status forward and analysis of best-case and worst-case scenarios. Nonetheless, these strategies in general make unverifiable assumptions that may introduce bias in the estimates of treatment effect.[5] Thus, inferences from studies with appreciable loss to follow-up are usually weaker.

DETERMINING IF INTENTION-TO-TREAT ANALYSIS WAS USED

Clinicians evaluating a randomized trial need to know if the researchers applied the intention-to-treat principle. A quick approach is to scan the Methods section of the published report looking for the phrase "intention-to-treat analysis." Two surveys of randomized controlled trials published in major medical journals during 1993–1995[6] and 1997[5] found that half of the reports used the term "intention-to-treat analysis." Unfortunately, the term was not always used appropriately. Thus, readers must look carefully at what was actually done, rather than looking only for the term.

In particular, significant loss to follow-up may introduce exactly the same bias as a per protocol analysis. For instance, Silverstein and associates[7] reported the results of a trial in which 8843 patients taking nonsteroidal anti-inflammatory agents for rheumatoid arthritis were randomly assigned to receive misoprostol (4404 patients) or placebo (4439 patients) to prevent gastroduodenal complications, as judged by outcome assessors blinded to treatment assignment. The authors described their analysis as an intention-to-treat analysis. However, patients lost to follow-up were included in the denominator of event rates. Inclusion of these patients in the denominator without accounting for their outcomes in the numerator assumes that no patient lost to follow-up had gastroduodenal complications. The size of the groups lost to follow-up (1851 patients in the misoprostol group and 1617 in the placebo group) eclipsed the number of patients who experienced the primary end point in each group (25 in the misoprostol group and 42 in the placebo group), a situation that leaves the reader uncertain about the true magnitude of the treatment effect.

In another example, Harris and associates[8] reported the results of study in which 1628 postmenopausal women with a previous vertebral fracture were randomly assigned to receive risedronate (813 patients) or placebo (815 patients) to prevent another vertebral fracture, as judged by a radiologist blinded to treatment assignment. These authors also described their analysis as an intention-to-treat analysis. After 3 years, 324 patients in the risedronate arm and 365 patients in the placebo arm had been lost to follow-up. The authors reported outcomes up to the point of last follow-up (using survival analysis), including 61 in the risedronate group and 93 patients in the placebo group with

new vertebral fractures; the relative risk reduction was 41% in favour of risedronate. Those lost to follow-up from the placebo group were at higher risk (had more vertebral fractures) at baseline than either those in the placebo group who completed the study or those lost from the risedronate arm. This indicates that the placebo patients remaining in the study were a good-prognosis group and had, on average, a better prognosis than the remaining patients in the risedronate group. Because the risedronate group experienced fewer vertebral fractures than the placebo group, the substantial loss to follow-up in this case does not weaken the inference that risedronate results in a relative risk reduction of about 41%.

CONCLUSIONS

If randomized controlled trials are to provide unbiased assessments of treatment efficacy, investigators must apply the intention-to-treat principle. To improve the applicability of study results to individual patients, investigators should improve study design to ensure protocol adherence with minimal loss to follow-up. Finally, loss to follow-up can result in exactly the same sort of bias as a per protocol analysis. Therefore, if there is significant loss to follow-up, statements that investigators conducted an "intention-to-treat analysis" generally provide little reassurance.

Dr. Montori is with the Division of Endocrinology, Metabolism, and Nutrition, Department of Internal Medicine, Mayo Clinic and Foundation, Rochester, Minn. Dr. Guyatt is with the Departments of Medicine and of Clinical Epidemiology and Biostatistics, McMaster University, Hamilton, Ont.

This article has been peer reviewed.

ACKNOWLEDGMENT

This work was supported in part by the American Medical Association.

Competing interests: None declared.

REFERENCES FROM THE READING

1. Coronary Drug Project Research Group. Influence of adherence to treatment and response of cholesterol on mortality in the Coronary Drug Project. *N Engl J Med* 1980;303:1038–41.

2. Horwitz R, Viscoli C, Berkman L. Treatment adherence and risk of death after myocardial infarction. *Lancet* 1990;336:542–5.

3. Altman D. Clinical trials. In: *Practical statistics for medical research.* London: Chapman & Hall; 1991. p. 440–4761.

4. Heart Outcomes Prevention Evaluation Study Investigators. Effects of an angiotensin-converting-enzyme inhibitor, ramipril, on cardiovascular events in high-risk patients. *N Engl J Med* 2000;342:145–53.

5. Hollis S, Campbell F. What is meant by intention to treat analysis? Survey of published randomised controlled trials. *BMJ* 1999;319:670–47.

6. Ruiz-Canela M, Martinez-Gonzalez MA, de Irala-Estevez J. Intention to treat analysis is related to methodological quality. *BMJ* 2000;320:1007–8.

7. Silverstein FE, Graham DY, Senior JR, Davies HW, Struthers BJ, Bittman RM, et al. Misoprostol reduces serious gastrointestinal complications in patients with rheumatoid arthritis receiving nonsteroidal anti-inflammatory drugs: a randomized, double-blind placebo-controlled trial. *Ann Intern Med* 1995;123:241–9.

8. Harris ST, Watts NB, Genant HK, McKeever CD, Hangartner T, Keller M, et al, for the Vertebral Efficacy with Risedronate Therapy (VERT) Study Group. Effects of risedronate treatment on vertebral and nonvertebral fractures in women with postmenopausal osteoporosis: a randomized controlled trial. *JAMA* 1999;282:1344–52.

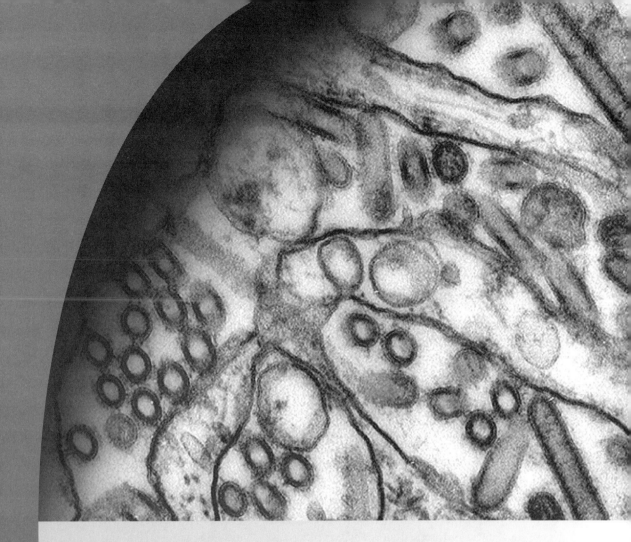

PART XII

Assessing Misclassification: Surveillance Meets Methods

The following article demonstrates the importance and relative ease of assessing for the presence of misclassification. The findings have critical implications for surveillance of syphilis.

READING 30
Misclassification of the Stages of Syphilis: Implications for Surveillance

Thomas A. Peterman, MD, MSc, Richard H. Kahn, MS, Carol A. Ciesielski, MD, Elizabeth Ortiz-Rios, MD, Mph, Bruce W. Furness, MD, MPH, Susan Blank, MD, MPH, Julia A. Schillinger, MD, MSc, Robert A. Gunn, MD, Mph, Melanie Taylor, MD, MPH, and Stuart M. Berman, MD, ScM

Peterson TA, Kahn RH, Ciesielski CA, et al. Misclassification of the Stages of Syphilis: Implications for Surveillance [From the CDC]. Sexually Transmitted Diseases. 2005;32:144–9.

Short summary: Syphilis cases were reviewed to see if reported stages met the Centers for Disease Control and Prevention case definition. Classification was excellent for primary and secondary and good for late latent, but half of early latent and unknown duration were misclassified. New surveillance definitions are suggested, comments requested.

Background: Uncertainty when staging latent syphilis should lead clinicians to call it late latent (requires more treatment) and disease investigators to call it early latent (priority for partner investigation). Accurate surveillance requires consistent case definitions.

Objective: Assess validity of reported syphilis stages.

Methods: Record reviews in 6 jurisdictions to determine if reported cases met the Centers for Disease Control and Prevention case definitions.

Results: Nine hundred seventy-three records from 6 jurisdictions in 2002 showed excellent agreement for reported primary (94.0%) and secondary (95.4%), good agreement for late latent (80.2%), and poor agreement for early latent (48.4%) and unknown duration (49.7%). Unknown duration (age <35 and nontreponemal test titer >32) was often misinterpreted to mean "not known." Early latent (within the past year, documented: seroconversion, fourfold titer increase, symptoms, or contact with an independently documented early syphilis case) was often misinterpreted to include patients with risky behavior, young age, or high nontreponemal test titers.

Conclusions: The unknown duration stage should be dropped. Surveillance of latent syphilis would be more consistent if cases were reported as having high or low titers on nontreponemal test. Alternative approaches are solicited from readers.

Syphilis has a complicated natural history with a multitude of possible disease manifestations in the decades following infection.[1] These manifestations have been divided into stages. Primary syphilis occurs 10 to 90 days after infection and is usually characterized by a painless ulcer (chancre) at the site of infection. Secondary syphilis occurs a few weeks or months later, with a variety of possible systemic symptoms, including a general body rash (often including the palmar and plantar surfaces), alopecia, and others. Latent syphilis is detectable only by serologic testing. For the first year (previously 4 years[2] and still 2 in some countries[3]) latent syphilis is staged as early latent and may lapse or relapse into the secondary stage. Following this, syphilis is classified as late latent, during which sexual transmission is unlikely, but persons may develop tertiary syphilis, which can include neurologic, cardiovascular, and other life-threatening complications. These stages of syphilis have important clinical, public health, and surveillance implications. Clinicians treat early infections (primary, secondary, or early latent) with 1 dose of benzathine penicillin G (2.4 million units), while late latent infections are treated with 3 doses, each a week apart.[3,4] Health department disease-intervention specialists are charged with interrupting syphilis transmission in their communities. Because transmission usually occurs during the primary and secondary stages when lesions are present, effective interruption of transmission requires treating infected persons with early infection. Thus, health departments concentrate on reaching partners of persons who have been infected for a year or less. Syphilis surveillance monitors cases by stage to identify trends in transmission (primary and secondary cases and sometimes also early latent) and how effectively early cases of syphilis are being detected and treated (comparison of primary, secondary, and early latent vs. late latent). Differentiating between early and late latent syphilis can be difficult because it requires knowing whether a patient has been infected for more or less than a year. Health workers should have conflicting responses when there is uncertainty about the duration of infection. When faced with uncertainty, clinicians should act conservatively and treat latent syphilis as if it were a late infection, with 3 doses of benzathine penicillin. In contrast, disease-intervention specialists acting conservatively should consider the same person to have an early latent infection and search for partners who may have been recently infected. Syphilis surveillance could consider such a case as early or late but above all else should be consistent because inconsistent classification can obscure important changes in disease rates.

Our experience suggested that surveillance stages were not consistently applied. Many people working in surveillance seemed confused by the stage definitions; others, for various reasons, appeared to be using their own definitions. We reviewed syphilis staging in 6 cities to identify and quantify variations from the Centers for Disease Control and Prevention (CDC) case definitions.

METHODS

We evaluated syphilis cases reported in New York City; Washington, DC; Puerto Rico (San Juan and Ponce); Chicago; San Diego; and Los Angeles. In each city, syphilis interview records were abstracted beginning with the first case of each stage in January 2002 and moving forward in time. We attempted to review 30 cases for each stage of syphilis at each site.

For surveillance purposes, the CDC defines a latent infection as early (less than a year) if there is a documented negative serologic test in the previous year followed by a positive test (or if previously infected and adequately treated, a documented fourfold increase in nontreponemal titer).[5] Alternatively, a person is considered to have early latent infection if they recall symptoms of primary or secondary syphilis within the past year or if a sex partner from the previous year was diagnosed with primary, secondary, or early latent syphilis. In 1990, an additional surveillance category was added to identify persons who likely had recent infections but did not meet the criteria for early latent infection.[6] This group consists of persons aged 35 years or less who have a titer of 1:32 or higher on a nontreponemal syphilis test and was named "syphilis of unknown duration."

Cases reported as primary, secondary, early latent, unknown duration, and late latent were evaluated to determine correspondence between the stage assigned locally and staging according to CDC case definitions.[5] Cases were reviewed by 2 authors (TAP and RHK); questionable cases were discussed before agreeing on a final classification. When the correct classification was unclear from available information, we accepted the classification listed in the chart. For example, a rash was considered to be manifestation of secondary syphilis if the clinician or disease investigator classified it as a syphilis rash but was considered to be due to other causes if the notes on the chart stated that the rash was not secondary syphilis.

The amount of information available for review varied considerably by stage of disease and by jurisdiction. Clinician's notes were generally available for cases that were diagnosed in public STD clinics (except in Los Angeles). Records from private practitioners were generally not available. Notes from disease-intervention specialists were usually available for early infections but often limited or absent for late latent infections. Disease interventionists recorded notes on signs or symptoms based on conversations with clinicians and patients. Many disease interventionists had shown pictures to patients to help them identify the sores and rashes. Patients were often interviewed to identify partners who might be infected. Notes from these partner investigations were also reviewed. Positive syphilis test results are reportable by law in each jurisdiction and are routinely entered into local databases where comparison to past titers helped us distinguish old from new infections. These old laboratory results were also reviewed. Adjusted overall case rates for 2002 were calculated by assuming all cases reported during the year were misclassified in the same way as the sample we reviewed. We also estimated the effect of using a titer-based reporting system for latent syphilis by assuming the titers for cases we reviewed were representative of all cases from the jurisdiction and considering high titer to be ≥ 16. We compared syphilis treatment regimens used for persons in different stages who did or did not have documented HIV infection, using the stage reported by the health departments.

RESULTS

We reviewed 973 records from the 6 jurisdictions (Table 12-1). Primary and secondary cases almost always (>94%) met the CDC definitions. Early latent cases met the CDC definitions only about half of the time, with 14.4% meeting the CDC definition for unknown duration and 31.6% considered late latent. Cases classified by sites as unknown duration also met the CDC definition only half of the time, with 41.3% meeting the case definition for late latent. Most (80.2%) of the cases called late latent by the sites met the CDC definition, though 11.8% did not meet the CDC definition for any stage of syphilis. Overall, 40 cases did not meet the definition for syphilis because nontreponemal tests were negative (26), the patient was previously treated for syphilis and there was no subsequent increase in titer (10), or treponemal tests were negative or not

TABLE 12-1 Stage of Syphilis as Classified by the Sites and Reclassified by the Authors Using the CDC Case Definition.

Sites' Stage (n)	Reclassified Stage Using CDC Definition (%)					
	Primary	Secondary	Early Latent	Unknown Duration	Late Latent	Not Syphilis
Primary (150)	94.0		3.3			2.7
Secondary (218)		95.4	2.8	0.5	0.5	0.5
Early L (250)	2.8	1.6	48.4	14.4	31.6	1.2
Unknown duration (143)			4.2	49.7	41.3	4.9
Late L (212)	0.5	1.4	3.8	2.4	80.2	11.8

L = latent.

done (4). Classification also varied by site (Table 12-2). Many (28.6%) of the cases called primary in Puerto Rico did not meet the CDC definition, because there was no mention of a lesion in the chart. In San Diego, 4 cases were called primary syphilis based on an ulcer, but there were no positive laboratory tests, so they did not meet the CDC case definition.

For latent syphilis, the San Diego and Los Angeles programs used a form for recording the stage and the rationale for the classification and had more records that agreed with the CDC definition than the other sites. However, the Los Angeles cases had only 68.8% agreement with the CDC definition for early latent. The Los Angeles program had intentionally changed their definition for early latent to include patients who had a fourfold titer decrease in the year after treatment. Many cases at the other sites were apparently called early latent because they seemed to be recently infected due to a high titer, young age, or a history of many recent partners, but they did not meet the CDC case definition.

The unknown duration category was not used in Puerto Rico. The New York program began using it midway through the year and had their own definition, including cases as old as 45. Others apparently thought that "unknown" meant "not known" because many cases had low titers, were over 35 years old, or both. Although the forms used in San Diego and Los Angeles increased the accuracy of this classification, all the health department personnel we talked to thought this stage was confusing, unhelpful, and should be dropped.

Finally, some of the cases that were called late latent in Washington, DC, met the CDC definitions for each of the other stages. In New York, most discrepancies were cases that had positive treponemal tests but negative RPRs or were previously treated and did not have evidence of a rising titer, so would not be considered a case of syphilis by the CDC.

The criteria that cases met to qualify as early latent syphilis varied by site (Table 12-3). In some areas, the most common reason was having had a partner with early syphilis (Chicago;

TABLE 12-2 Percent Agreement Between the Local Stage and the CDC Stage Definitions, by Site.

	Chicago	Puerto Rico	Washington, DC	New York	San Diego	Los Angeles
Primary	100.0	71.4	100.0	96.8	88.2	100.0
Secondary	100.0	87.5	90.9	100.0	100.0	100.0
Early latent	50.0	51.8	26.3	23.7	85.7	68.8
Unknown duration	12.9	na	23.1	17.2	85.7	82.9
Late latent	80.0	86.1	66.7	71.4	84.6	91.7

TABLE 12-3 Characteristics that Qualified Cases as Early Latent Syphilis, by Site (%).

Site (n)	Documented Seroconversion	Documented Titer Increase	Partner with Early Syphilis	History of Symptoms
Chicago (19)	26.3	21.1	52.6	5.3
Puerto Rico (37)	8.1	5.4	73.0	35.1
Washington, DC (20)*	20.0	5.0	45.0	30.0
New York (14)*	21.4	28.6	21.4	28.6
San Diego (33)	42.4	12.1	36.4	24.2
Los Angeles (23)	21.7	43.5	17.4	30.4

*One case had only 1 opportunity for exposure. Cases may meet more than 1 criterion, so row percentages do not add up to 100.

Puerto Rico; Washington, DC). For other programs, the most common reason was a documented change in serology, either seroconversion or an increase in titer (New York, Los Angeles, San Diego). Restaging all reported cases from 2002 based on the distribution of cases we reviewed had a very large impact on rates in some areas (Table 4). For example, in Washington, DC, early latent decreased from 33.6 to 11.3 per 100,000, while late latent increased from 17.8 to 37.9 per 100,000. Similarly, in New York City, the rate of early latent dropped by 58.2%.

We also considered the impact of changing surveillance definitions to classify latent syphilis cases based on nontreponemal test titers rather than duration of infection. Cases were considered high titer if any nontreponemal titer was ≥1:16. High-titer cases were much more common than low-titer cases in Chicago; Washington, DC; New York City; and San Diego (Table 12-4).

Treatment of early syphilis for persons who were not known to be HIV infected was usually a single dose of benzathine penicillin G, including 84 (79.2%) of 106 with primary, 92 (71.3%) of 129 with secondary, and 86 (45.3%) of 190 infections listed by the sites as early latent. In contrast, persons with documented HIV infection were less likely to receive a single dose of benzathine penicillin G for early syphilis, including only 17 (40.5%) of 42 with primary, 37 (41.6%) of 89 with secondary, and 18 (30.0%) of 60 with infections listed by the sites as early latent.

DISCUSSION

Classification of primary and secondary syphilis was excellent. However, we found many errors in the classification of latent syphilis, especially syphilis of unknown duration (50.3% misclassified) and early latent syphilis (51.6% misclassified). While

all programs had some review of syphilis cases to see that partner management and syphilis staging were done correctly, classification was much more consistent in the 2 programs that used forms for recording the stage and rationale for the classification. Two programs were intentionally using definitions that differed from the definitions used by CDC and the National Association of STD Directors, and the Council of State and Territorial Epidemiologists.[5] The New York City program expanded the unknown duration category to include persons up to the age of 45 years. The rationale for this expansion was that the median age for primary and secondary syphilis cases was 35 years,[7] so a cutoff at age 35 years would be expected to miss half of the early cases. In Los Angeles, the definition of early latent syphilis was expanded to include persons with nontreponemal titers that fell fourfold or more in the year following treatment. The rationale for this was that nontreponemal test titers are known to fall at a faster rate after treatment of early syphilis than for late syphilis. This definition of early latent syphilis has also been used in South Australia.[8] Although both of these definitions may be rational, they make it difficult to compare trends between areas that use different definitions and prohibit aggregation of cases at the state or national level.

Variations in case definitions can also make it difficult to interpret surveillance data at the site level. While we did not study differences in classification over time, a misclassification rate of 70% suggests a program will have difficulty identifying real changes in disease rates over time. Surveillance systems can accommodate consistent misclassification to a much greater extent than inconsistent misclassification. Thus, systematically expanding an age cutoff is easier to adjust for than changing a definition to include persons who, for whatever

TABLE 12-4 Changes in Reported Syphilis Rates (per 100,000) After Adjusting for Differences with the CDC Definitions and After Reclassification of Latent Syphilis as High and Low Titer, by Site.

Site	Primary and Secondary	Early	Latent			
			Unknown Duration	Late	High Titer	Low Titer
Chicago: reported	11.4	14.2	5.2	4.3		
Adjusted to CDC definition	12.0	7.6	3.3	11.0		
Adjusted, latent classified by titer	12.0				12.8	9.1
Puerto Rico: reported	7.0	21.0	0.2	14.3		
Adjusted to CDC definition	6.3	11.8	3.5	18.7		
Adjusted, latent classified by titer	6.3				16.1	17.9
Washington, DC: reported	10.1	33.6	12.2	17.8		
Adjusted to CDC definition	12.6	11.3	8.9	37.9		
Adjusted, latent classified by titer	12.6				41.6	16.5
New York: reported	5.4	9.1	0.3	28.4		
Adjusted to CDC definition	5.5	3.8	2.9	24.5		
Adjusted, latent classified by titer	5.5				18.1	13.1
San Diego: reported	1.3	1.2	0.6	2.5		
Adjusted to CDC definition	1.3	1.2	0.6	2.2		
Adjusted, latent classified by titer	1.3				2.9	1.1
Los Angeles: reported	4.0	3.9	0.9	9.0		
Adjusted to CDC definition	4.4	2.7	1.0	9.0		
Adjusted, latent classified by titer	4.4				5.4	7.3

reason, seem to have been infected in the past year. Most of the misclassifications that we observed were not due to systematically applied criteria, so they are likely to be highly variable over time. For example, some staff members told us they classified cases as early latent if they reported risky sexual behaviors in the previous year. The descriptions of what constituted risky behavior were vague and variable.

Others classified cases as early latent based on young age. These behavior and age criteria may well be associated to some extent with early infection but would need to be consistently applied to be viable surveillance definitions. They were not written down, so are likely to vary, depending on who reviews the cases, and may even vary in the same reviewer over time.

We saw several instances where there were conflicts between the perspectives of the clinicians, disease investigators, and surveillance. These conflicts are inevitable, and when they occur, both perspectives should be acknowledged and accepted rather than trying to force clinicians to use the surveillance definition or force surveillance to use the clinician's stage. For example, we saw 4 cases that were called primary syphilis by clinicians treating ulcers, but they did not meet the case definition because serologic tests were negative. On the other hand, we reviewed records of patients who returned with secondary syphilis after they had been seen for evaluation of an ulcer; the ulcers had apparently not been considered syphilitic because their serologic tests were negative and neither darkfield microscopy nor direct florescent antibody testing was done. Clinicians should treat suspicious ulcers as though they are syphilis, even if serologic tests are negative because serologic tests are insensitive in early primary syphilis.[9] Such cases should be reported to the health department, and disease investigators should search for partners who may have been exposed, but surveillance should not consider these ulcers to be syphilis, because they do not meet the case definition. Some classification errors appear to be due to a conflict between partner notification activities and surveillance. Disease control programs generally will not investigate partners of late latent cases because such investigations are unlikely to interrupt transmission. Although it is not possible to be sure that a case is late latent without interviewing the patient and examining the partners, high case loads may necessitate triaging cases for investigation. In some programs, once a case is labeled as late latent, investigation stops. Thus, some disease investigators who really believed a case should be investigated labeled it as early latent despite the surveillance definitions. In many instances, these erroneous classifications stuck all the way through reporting.

Adjusting the reported rates from the sites to reflect the CDC classification had minor effects on primary and secondary syphilis but very large effects on latent syphilis, causing some rates to fall or rise by more than half. Most analyses of syphilis at the national level have been confined to primary and secondary syphilis, so have not been greatly affected by misclassification. However, early latent cases have often been included in local surveillance reports, program evaluations, and research studies, especially when there were relatively few cases of primary and secondary syphilis.[10–27] Rates of correctly classified early latent syphilis would help reflect syphilis incidence rates. Our study was limited to the 6 jurisdictions that had CDC assigned medical epidemiologists working within the STD control program. Although we reviewed 973 cases, the number from each stage at each jurisdiction was fairly small. Furthermore, our design limited the analysis to how often reported cases met the CDC definition (positive predictive value). We could not measure how often cases that met a particular CDC stage definition were reported as being in that stage (sensitivity). Despite these limitations, our study has important implications for syphilis surveillance in the United States.

The "unknown duration" stage of syphilis is poorly named because it implies it is the stage for all latent cases where the duration is not known. Second, the age cutoff is inappropriate because 35 is now the median age for all cases of primary and secondary syphilis,[7] and therefore it would miss half of the early cases. Finally, the significance of this category was not clear to anyone we talked with. Most (including the CDC surveillance report) just combine unknown duration cases with late latent cases.

Given the confusion and absence of any significant influence on programs, we believe this stage should be dropped. The early latent stage was also quite confusing and was misclassified as often as the cases of unknown duration. The definition of early latent infection requires identification of a recently infected partner, a history of symptoms, or laboratory evidence of seroconversion. Information on partners is increasingly difficult to obtain. For example, the number of partners contacted and treated for newly identified syphilis fell from 0.55 per case in 1961[28] to 0.19 in 1991[29] and may be even lower

in the recent epidemics among persons with anonymous partners. Documenting seroconversion can also be quite difficult because it requires frequent testing and easily retrievable results. Syphilis testing frequency has declined in many areas. Health departments have very good record systems for tracking positive tests, which are reportable by law, but negative tests are not reportable. Changes in availability of information on partners and past serostatus can lead to artifactual trends in reported syphilis. We suspect, in some areas, most latent infections of less than 1 year's duration would be erroneously classified as late latent due to the lack of evidence. We suggest considering a change in syphilis surveillance so that latent syphilis is classified as high-titer or low-titer instead of early, late, and unknown duration. While it would be nice to be able to track trends in early infections, in reality it is too often impossible to accurately determine the duration of an asymptomatic infection. High nontreponemal titers are strongly associated with recent infection.[9] Thus, we believe this change would facilitate consistent reporting and would also more closely reflect the true duration of infections for persons with incomplete partner evaluations and limited past serologic information. Indeed, we believe tracking high-titer latent syphilis would more accurately reflect trends in recently acquired infection than the current approach of tracking early latent.

Titer-based surveillance would be subject to some limitations. A definition that depends on a laboratory test would need to change if the test was changed. Also, titers can vary from laboratory to laboratory, VDRL titers are slightly different from RPR titers, and there is some evidence that HIV infection may slightly increase nontreponemal titers.[20] However, this variability would only influence classification of cases with titers that are near the cutoff. From a surveillance perspective, we believe these disadvantages are outweighed by the advantages of consistent availability and objectivity of titers. Treatment of syphilis should not be changed by this change in surveillance definitions. Clinicians who are sure that a latent infection was acquired within a year should continue to treat patients with 2.4 million units of benzathine penicillin G4. In practice, clinicians rarely have the dates of previous negative tests or the results of partner investigations needed to determine that an infection was recently acquired. Thus, as seen in our study, many infections reported as early latent by health departments had been treated for late latent syphilis. Many HIV-infected patients with early syphilis were treated with a total of 7.2 million units of benzathine penicillin G regardless of their stage.

Disease control programs should be better off if latent syphilis were tracked in a more consistent fashion that allows comparison with other programs or within a program over time. High-titer latent infections would also provide a more consistent estimate of recently infected persons who were not detected in the primary or secondary stages. Thus, evaluations of syphilis-control strategies such as partner notification or screening would benefit from the proposed surveillance changes. Partner investigations could continue to focus on partners of persons thought to have early syphilis, including persons with primary or secondary, recent seroconversion, recent symptoms, high titer, or other factors that are deemed important based on local evidence.

Changes in surveillance definitions make it difficult to compare rates before and after the new definitions, so any suggestion to change case definitions should be carefully considered. However, for the unknown duration and early latent stages, half of the cases have been misclassified, so trends have already been obscured. We believe changing these definitions would result in more accurate and more consistent staging and will therefore clarify surveillance trends. We would appreciate hearing the thoughts of interested readers.

DISCUSSION QUESTIONS

1. How do you think this methodology could be applied to other diseases? Select a disease of interest to you, and design a hypothetical study on the basis of these methods to assess the degree of misclassification.

2. Why do the authors stress that treatment recommendations should not be changed on the basis of these findings and their interpretation? Why is this important?

REFERENCES FROM THE READING

1. Sparling PF. The natural history of syphilis. In: Holmes KK et al, eds. *Sexually Transmitted Diseases.* 3rd ed. New York: McGraw-Hill; 1999:473–485.

2. US Department of Health, Education, and Welfare. *Public Health Service. Notes on Modern Management of VD.* US Government Printing Office; 1962. Publication No. 859.

3. Parkes R, Renton A, Meheus A, Laukamm-Josten U. Review of current evidence and comparison of guidelines for effective syphilis treatment in Europe. Int J STD AIDS 2004;15:73–88.

4. Centers for Disease Control and Prevention. Sexually transmitted diseases treatment guidelines 2002. MMWR Morb Mortal Wkly Rep 2002;51:21–25.

5. Centers for Disease Control and Prevention. *Recommendations for Public Health Surveillance of Syphilis in the United States.* Atlanta GA: US Department of Health and Human Services; 2003.

6. Centers for Disease Control and Prevention. Case definitions for public health surveillance. MMWR Morb Mortal Wkly Rep 1990;39:37.

7. Centers for Disease Control and Prevention. *Sexually Transmitted Disease Surveillance, 2002.* Atlanta GA: US Department of Health and Human Services; 2003:117.

8. Available at: http://www.stdservices.on.net/notification/surveillance_system.htm. Accessed April 7, 2004.

9. Hart G. Syphilis tests in diagnostic and therapeutic decision making. Ann Intern Med 1986;104:368–376.

10. Sexually Transmitted Disease Program; Los Angeles County Department of Health Services. *Annual Sexually Transmitted Disease Morbidity Report, 2000–2001.* pp. 1–56.

11. STD Control Section. *San Francisco Sexually Transmitted Disease Annual Summary, 1999.* San Francisco, CA: San Francisco Department of Public Health; 2000.

12. Louisiana Department of Health and Hospitals. *Louisiana Department of Health and Hospitals, Office of Public Health: Annual Epidemiology Report 1997.* Baton Rouge, LA: Bourque Printing.

13. Chen JL, Kodagoda D, Lawrence AM, Kerndt PR. Rapid public health interventions in response to an outbreak of syphilis in Los Angeles. Sex Transm Dis 2002;29:277–284.

14. Koumans EH, Farley TA, Gibson JJ, et al. Characteristics of persons with syphilis in areas of persisting syphilis in the United States: sustained transmission associated with concurrent partnerships. Sex Transm Dis 2001;28:487–503.

15. Rolfs RT, Goldberg M, Sharrar RG. Risk factors for syphilis: cocaine use and prostitution. Am J Public Health 1990;80:853–857.

16. Paz-Bailey G, Teran S, Levine W, Markowitz LE. Syphilis outbreak among Hispanic immigrants in Decatur, Alabama: association with commercial sex. Sex Transm Dis 2004;31:20–25.

17. Garnett GP, Aral SO, Hoyle DV, Cates W Jr, Anderson RM. The natural history of syphilis: implications for the transmission dynamics and control of infection. Sex Transm Dis 1997;24:185–200.

18. Rompalo AM, Joesoef MR, O'Donnell JA, et al, and the Syphilis and HIV Study Group. Clinical manifestations of early syphilis by HIV status and gender: results of the syphilis and HIV study. Sex Transm Dis 2001;28:158–165.

19. Huchinson CM, Hook EW III, Sheperd M, Verley J, Rompalo AM. Altered clinical presentation of early syphilis in patients with human immunodeficiency virus infection. Ann Intern Med 1994;121:94–100.

20. Rolfs RT, Joesoef MR, Hendershot EF, et al. A randomized trial of enhanced therapy for early syphilis in patients with and without human immunodeficiency virus infection. N Engl J Med 1997;337:307–314.

21. Hook EW III, Martin DH, Stephens J, Smith BS, Smith K. A randomized, comparative pilot study of azithromycin versus benzathine penicillin G for treatment of early syphilis. Sex Transm Dis 2002;29:486–490.

22. Kohl KS, Farley TA, Ewell J, Scioneaux J. Usefulness of partner notification for syphilis control. Sex Transm Dis 1999;26:201–207.

23. Hibbs JR, Ceglawski WS, Goldberg M, Kaufman F. Emergency department-based surveillance for syphilis during an outbreak in Philadelphia. Ann Emerg Med 1993;22:1286–1290.

24. Farley TA, Kahn RH, Johnson G, Cohen DA. Strategies for syphilis prevention: findings from surveys in a high-incidence area. Sex Transm Dis 2000;27:305–310.

25. Hibbs JR, Gunn RA. Public health intervention in a cocaine-related syphilis outbreak. Am J Public Health 1991;81:1259–1262.

26. Centers for Disease Control and Prevention. Internet use and early syphilis infection among men who have sex with men: San Francisco, California, 1999–2003. MMWR Morb Mortal Wkly Rep 2003;52:1229–1232.

27. Farley TA, Hadler JL, Gunn RA. The syphilis epidemic in Connecticut: relationship to drug use and prostitution. Sex Transm Dis 1990;17:163–168.

28. Communicable Disease Center. *VD Fact Sheet 1961, Eighteenth Revision.* Atlanta GA: US Department of Health, Education, and Welfare; 14.

29. Peterman TA, Toomey KE, Dicker LW, Zaidi AA, Wroten JE, Carolina J. Partner notification for syphilis: a randomized, controlled trial of three approaches. Sex Transm Dis 1997;24:511–518.

READING 31
Interim Within-Season Estimate of the Effectiveness of Trivalent Inactivated Influenza Vaccine—Marshfield, Wisconsin, 2007–08 Influenza Season

Centers for Disease Control and Prevention. Interim Within-Season Estimate of the Effectiveness of Trivalent Inactivated Influenza Vaccine—Marshfield, Wisconsin, 2007–08 Influenza Season. *MMWR.* 2008;57:393–398.

USING CASE-CONTROL METHODOLOGY TO ASSESS VACCINE EFFICACY DURING 2007–08 INFLUENZA SEASON

You will recall from the first section that we continue the battle with influenza. Read the below article to learn about an interesting case-control approach to assessing vaccine efficacy during a season when there was a less than optimal match—as can happen simply due to the way that the virus circulates and replicates globally—between the most prevalent strain and the vaccine from the previous season.

INTERIM WITHIN-SEASON ESTIMATE OF THE EFFECTIVENESS OF TRIVALENT INACTIVATED INFLUENZA VACCINE—MARSHFIELD, WISCONSIN, 2007–08 INFLUENZA SEASON

During clinical trials, the efficacy of vaccination with inactivated influenza vaccines for the prevention of serologically confirmed influenza infection has been estimated as high as 70%–90% among healthier adults. However, the effectiveness of annual influenza vaccination typically is lower during those influenza seasons when a suboptimal match between the vaccine strains and circulating influenza strains is observed. For example, in a 4-year randomized study of influenza vaccine among healthy persons aged 1–65 years, the predominant strain was drifted from the vaccine strain in 2 of the 4 years. Inactivated vaccine effectiveness (VE) against culture-confirmed influenza ranged from 71% to 79% when the vaccine and circulating strains were suboptimally matched to 74% to 79% when the matches were well matched (1). In contrast, a 2-year study of inactivated influenza vaccine among healthy adults aged 18–64 years found no measurable VE during a year when a poorly matched strain circulated, but found VE of 86% against labo-

ratory-confirmed influenza during the following year when the vaccine and circulating strains were well matched (2). Although laboratory data on the antigenic characteristics of circulating influenza viruses compared with vaccine strains are available during influenza seasons, estimates of VE usually have not been made until months after the conclusion of the season. This report summarizes interim results of a 2008 case-control study to estimate the effectiveness of trivalent inactivated influenza vaccine for prevention of medically attended, laboratory-confirmed influenza during the 2007–08 influenza season, when most circulating influenza A (H3N2) and B viruses were suboptimally matched to the vaccine strains. Despite the suboptimal match between two of three vaccine strains and circulating influenza strains, overall VE in the study population during January 21–February 8, 2008, was 44%. These findings demonstrate that, in any season, assessment of the clinical effectiveness of influenza vaccines cannot be determined solely by laboratory evaluation of the degree of antigenic match between vaccine and circulation strains.

Patients living in a 14 postal-code area surrounding Marshfield, Wisconsin, were eligible to participate in this study. Nearly all residents in this area receive outpatient and inpatient care from Marshfield Clinic health-care providers. Study enrollment began on January 21, 2008, based on laboratory evidence of influenza circulation from both Marshfield Clinic laboratories and the Wisconsin State Laboratory of Hygiene and continued through March 28, 2008. Patients who visited a Marshfield Clinic facility with medically attended illnesses were screened for study eligibility during outpatient or inpatient visits. Patients who reported feverishness, chills, or cough were eligible for enrollment. Those who reported symptoms for 8 or more days were not eligible for enrollment because influenza virus shedding decreases with illness duration, making detection of the virus unlikely after 8 days of symptoms. The majority of ill patients not approached during a clinical encounter were identified the next day by using electronic diagnosis codes entered by the clinician; these patients were contacted by telephone and enrolled at home if they met eligibility criteria. The Marshfield Clinic Research Foundation institutional review board approved this study.

Nasal or nasopharyngeal swabs were obtained from consenting patients and were tested for influenza A or B infection by reverse transcription-polymerase chain reaction (RT-PCR) at the Marshfield Clinic Research Foundation using CDC-recommended probes and primers. Viral culture was performed on all samples that were RT-PCR positive to provide virus isolates for antigenic characterization. Influenza vaccination status was determined through an immunization information system (Regional Early Childhood Immunization Network*) used by all public and private immunization providers for vaccines administered to adults and children. Previous validations have demonstrated that the system captures 96%–98% of influenza vaccines administered to area residents (Marshfield Clinic Research Foundation, unpublished data, 2005–2007). Trivalent inactivated influenza vaccine from Sanofi-Pasteur ([Fluzone®], Swiftwater, Pennsylvania) was the only influenza vaccine used by Marshfield Clinic during the 2007–08 influenza season.

For this case-control study, a case of medically attended influenza was defined as an acute illness in a patient with feverishness, chills, or cough and documentation of influenza infection by RT-PCR. Controls were defined as patients with the same symptoms who had a negative RT-PCR test for influenza. Using persons with acute respiratory symptoms who test negative for influenza as controls is a method that in modeling studies has compared favorably with cohort studies and traditional case-control designs for the assessment of vaccine effectiveness (3). Patients were categorized as immunized if they had received influenza vaccine 14 days or more before enrollment; in addition, children aged <9 years were categorized as immunized if they had received 2 doses of influenza vaccine. Twenty-three children were excluded because they had received only 1 of the 2 recommended doses; this subgroup was too small to permit a separate analysis of VE for partial immunization.

VE was estimated by using logistic regression to compare patients with laboratory-confirmed influenza with patients who tested negative for influenza. The likelihood of receiving influenza vaccination in this population is associated with a propensity to seek health care, and use of test-negative controls helped adjust for this source of bias by estimating VE for medically attended influenza illness. Comparisons of this study design to traditional cohort and case-control methods for assessing VE have been published recently (3). For this analysis, the enrolled patients were categorized into two groups:

persons for whom influenza vaccine was recommended by the Advisory Committee on Immunization Practices (ACIP) for the 2007–08 season based on age or an existing chronic medical condition[†] that increased their risk for influenza-related complications (i.e., the ACIP recommended group), and healthy children and adults aged 5–49 years (i.e., the healthy group).

Logistic regression models were adjusted for age, week of enrollment, and presence of a chronic medical condition. The last variable was not included in the models restricted to healthy patients aged 5–49 years. VE was estimated as 100 × [1—adjusted odds ratio]) and was interpreted as zero if the percentage was negative. The first 59 influenza virus isolates obtained during the study were submitted to CDC for detailed antigenic characterization.

During January 21–February 8, 2008, a total of 1,779 patients were assessed for study eligibility after a clinical encounter for acute respiratory illness or febrile illness. A total of 850 (48%) did not meet eligibility criteria; 773 (91%) of exclusions resulted from absence of feverishness, chills, or cough or an illness duration 8 days or longer. Of the 929 eligible patients, 639 (69%) consented to the study and were tested for influenza infection. Final enrollment for this interim analysis was reduced to 616 patients after exclusion of 23 partially immunized children who had received only 1 of 2 recommended vaccine doses.

Influenza was detected by RT-PCR in 191 (31%) enrollees; 75% of influenza infections were type A. Distribution by sex was similar for patients who tested positive and patients who tested negative for influenza (Table 12-5); however, the median age was higher for patients who tested positive (21 years) than those who tested negative (10 years). Approximately 19% of patients who tested positive and 39% of those who tested negative had been vaccinated against influenza.

The overall interim estimate of VE was 44% (Table 12-6); the estimate was higher among persons in the healthy group aged 5–49 years (54%). The overall estimate of VE for prevention of medically attended influenza A infections was 58%. No VE was observed for prevention of medically attended influenza B infections.

Subtyping by RT-PCR performed at CDC demonstrated that 40 of 41 influenza A specimens were influenza A (H3N2) viruses; the remaining specimen was an H3N2 and B virus mixture. Preliminary data on antigenic characterizations were

---

*Available at http://www.recin.org/default.asp.

†Defined as existing if the patient had two or more health-care visits with relevant International Classification of Diseases, Ninth Revision, Clinical Modification diagnosis codes during 2007. Diagnosis codes were based on ACIP criteria, including cardiac, pulmonary, renal, neurological/musculoskeletal, metabolic, cerebrovascular, immunosuppressive, circulatory system, and liver disorders; diabetes mellitus; and malignancies.

TABLE 12-5 Number and Percentage of Patients with Medically Attended Acute Respiratory Illness Who Were Enrolled* in a Study and Tested for Influenza, by Selected Characteristics—Marshfield, Wisconsin, January 21–February 8, 2008.

Characteristic	Patients Testing Positive for Influenza[†] (n = 191) No.	(%)	Patients Testing Negative for Influenza (n = 425) No.	(%)	Total (n = 616) No.	(%)
Sex						
Male	94	(49)	188	(44)	282	(46)
Female	97	(51)	237	(56)	334	(54)
Age group						
6–59 mos	23	(12)	148	(35)	171	(28)
5–49 yrs	139	(73)	219	(52)	358	(58)
50–64 yrs	24	(13)	39	(9)	63	(10)
≥ 65 yrs	5	(3)	19	(4)	24	(4)
Existing chronic medical condition[§]						
Yes	17	(9)	62	(15)	79	(13)

*Patients who reported having feverishness, chills, or cough for <8 days were eligible for enrollment.
[†]By reverse transcription-polymerase chain reaction.
[§]Defined as existing if the patient had two or more healthcare visits with relevant *International Classification of Diseases, Ninth Revision, Clinical Modification* diagnosis codes during 2007. Diagnosis codes were based on Advisory Committee on Immunization Practices (ACIP) criteria, including cardiac, pulmonary, renal, neurological/musculoskeletal, metabolic, cerebrovascular, immunosuppressive, circulatory system, and liver disorders; diabetes mellitus; and malignancies.

available for nine influenza A (H3N2) viruses and 18 of 20 influenza B viruses. Two of nine influenza A (H3N2) viruses were A/Wisconsin/67/2005-like, the H3N2 component of the 2007–08 Northern Hemisphere vaccine; the other seven were A/Brisbane/10/2007-like (H3N2) viruses, a strain that is drifted from the A/Wisconsin/76/2005 strain. All 18 influenza B viruses were B/Florida/04/2006-like, belonging to the B/Yamagata/16/88 lineage of viruses. B/Yamagata-like viruses are antigenically distinct from the B/Victoria-like lineage virus that was included in the 2007–08 influenza vaccine.

Reported by: E Belongia, MD, B Kieke, L Coleman, PhD, J Donahue, DVM, PhD, S Irving, J Meece, PhD, M Vandermause, Marshfield Clinic Research Foundation, Marshfield, Wisconsin. D Shay, MD, P Gargiullo, PhD, A Balish, A Foust, MA, L Guo, MD, S Lindstrom, PhD, X Xu, MD, A Klimov, PhD, J Bresee, MD, N Cox, PhD Influenza Div, National Center for Immunization and Respiratory Disease, CDC.

Editorial Note

Influenza infections result in substantial morbidity and mortality each year in the United States (4, 5). Because of the sizeable burden of influenza-associated disease, annual influenza vaccination was recommended by ACIP for the 2007–08 season for children aged 6–59 months, adults aged >50 years, persons with chronic medical conditions that place them at high risk for serious influenza-related complications, and close contacts of these groups and of children aged <6 months (6).

Viral data reported to World Health Organization (WHO) and National Respiratory and Enteric Virus Surveillance System (NREVSS) laboratories in the United States during the 2007–08 influenza season through April 5, 2008, demonstrated that influenza A and B viruses accounted for 74% and 26%, respectively, of influenza viruses characterized in the United States (7). Of influenza A viruses subtyped, 27% were influenza A (H1N1) viruses, and 73% were influenza A (H3N2) viruses. Antigenic characterization of a subset of these viruses by CDC indicated that 69% of A (H1N1) viruses were A/Solomon Islands/3/2006-like, the A (H1N1) vaccine component, but that 71% of A (H3N2) viruses were A/Brisbane/10/2007-like, a recent antigenic variant of the A/Wisconsin/67/2005-like virus, the A (H3N2) vaccine component. In addition, 95% of antigenically characterized B viruses belonged to the B/Yamagata lineage. Viruses in this lineage are antigenically distinct from the B/Malaysia/2506/2004-like component of the 2007–08 vaccine, which is in the B/Victoria lineage. These viral surveillance data suggested that the effectiveness of the 2007–08

TABLE 12-6 Interim Vaccine Effectiveness (VE) Estimates Among Patients with Medically Attended Acute Respiratory Illness Who Were Enrolled* in a Study and Tested for Influenza, by Influenza Type and Selected Categories—Marshfield, Wisconsin, January 21–February 8, 2008.

Influenza type/Patient group	Patients Testing Positive for Influenza[†] (n = 191)		Patients Testing Negative for Influenza (n = 425)		Adjusted VE	
	Vaccinated[§]	Not Vaccinated	Vaccinated	Not Vaccinated	%	(95% CI[‡])
All Influenza						
All Influenza						
All enrollees	36	155	165	260	44**	(11–65)
ACIP recommended[††]	21	39	120	114	34	(−31–67)
Healthy persons aged 5–49 yrs[§§]	15	116	45	146	54**	(12–76)
Influenza A						
All enrollees	22	122	179	293	58**	(28–76)
ACIP recommended	14	28	127	125	49	(−14–77)
Healthy persons aged 5–49 yrs	8	94	52	168	68**	(29–86)
Influenza B						
All enrollees	14	33	187	382	−35	(−172–33)
ACIP recommended	7	11	134	142	−32	(−287–55)
Healthy persons aged 5–49 yrs	7	22	53	240	−33	(−241–48)

*Patients who reported having feverishness, chills, or cough for < 8 days were eligible for enrollment.

[†]By reverse transcription-polymerase chain reaction.

[§]Patients were categorized as vaccinated if they had received influenza vaccine ≥ 14 days before enrollment; in addition, children aged < 9 years were categorized as vaccinated if they had received 2 doses of influenza vaccine. Twenty-three children were excluded because they had received only 1 of the 2 recommended doses.

[‡]Confidence interval.

**Statistically significant.

[††]All children aged 6–59 months, all adults aged ≥ 50 years, and persons aged 5–49 years with an existing chronic medical condition for whom influenza vaccination is recommended by the Advisory Committee on Immunization Practices (ACIP).

[§§]Persons aged 5–49 years with no chronic medical conditions for which ACIP recommends influenza vaccination.

influenza vaccine might be reduced against circulating influenza A (H3N2) and B viruses. However, in this analysis, preliminary VE results indicated that, despite the antigenic differences between vaccine and circulating H3N2 strains, the effectiveness of vaccine in preventing medically attended respiratory illnesses from influenza A infections was 58%. In contrast, no VE could be demonstrated against influenza B.

Multiple previous studies of the effectiveness of influenza vaccines have been reported (i.e., observational studies of the clinical effects of vaccination as opposed to randomized clinical trials) (8). VE varies from influenza season to season, based in part on the degree of antigenic match between vaccine and circulating influenza strains. VE previously has been assessed sporadically in different populations and by using different methods. Annual systematic assessments of VE using laboratory-confirmed outcomes have not been available within an influenza season. Furthermore, antigenic characterization data rarely have been available for influenza viruses isolated from participants of VE studies, and not previously from the population for whom annual vaccination is recommended by ACIP. Despite a mismatch between the vaccine influenza A (H3N2) strain and seven of nine influenza A (H3N2) viruses isolated from study participants, the data in this report are consistent with results obtained in seasons with a moderate antigenic mismatch between vaccine and circulating strains of H3N2 viruses (1, 8).

Based on preliminary analyses of A/Brisbane/10/2007-like (H3N2) viruses and the 2007–08 vaccine H3N2 strain using the method of antigenic mapping (9), an average four-fold difference was observed between the homologous titer for the vaccine strain and average titers for circulating strains. These differences were measured with hemagglutination inhibition tests by using a panel of reference postinfection ferret antisera. The degree of mismatch between the A/Wisconsin/67/2005 vaccine strain and H3N2 viruses tested at CDC thus far during the U.S. 2007–08 influenza season can be described as moderate in relation to antigenic distances seen over time for H3N2 viruses (10). By contrast, all the influenza B viruses isolated in the Marshfield Clinic study this season and antigenically characterized thus far belong to the B lineage not contained in this season's vaccine. Viruses from the B/Victoria-like lineage and B/Yamagata-like lineage are substantially more antigenically distinct from each other than A/Wisconsin/67/2005-like and A/Brisbane/10/2007-like H3N2 viruses are from each other.

The findings in this report are subject to at least four limitations. First, analyses were conducted while enrollment and laboratory testing were ongoing, and not all RT-PCR positive samples had yet been confirmed by culture. Thus, the preliminary subtype distribution and antigenic characterization results might not be representative of all patients in the study with influenza. Second, VE was estimated only for prevention of influenza among persons who sought care for acute respiratory illness, comparing patients who tested positive for influenza with patients who tested negative. Certain patients who tested negative for influenza might actually have had influenza virus infections, although RT-PCR is the most sensitive diagnostic test available. In addition, although simulation models have demonstrated that VE estimated with test-negative controls was close to the actual VE when test specificity was high, as is also the case with RT-PCR (3), this method is only beginning to be used in studies. VE was assessed against medically attended influenza and not against more severe outcomes of influenza infection, such as influenza hospitalizations; VE might vary with severity of the outcome studied. Third, if the antigenic characteristics of influenza viruses circulating in other regions of the United States differ substantially from viruses isolated from the Marshfield, Wisconsin, study participants, VE might vary by region. Finally, enrollment of patients continued in this study thorough March 28, and final analyses might differ from these interim assessments of VE.

These preliminary data based on study enrollment during January 21–February 8 suggest several conclusions. First, when assessing VE, laboratory data on antigenic characterization of circulating influenza viruses compared with vaccine strains should be interpreted together with data on the clinical effectiveness of vaccination in preventing laboratory-confirmed influenza illnesses. Although two of three vaccine strains were not optimally matched with circulating viruses this season, an interim VE estimate suggests that vaccination provided substantial protection against medically attended acute respiratory illness in this study population. In addition, intraseason estimates of VE, such as those from this analysis, might be useful to public health authorities and medical practitioners in their communications about the benefits of vaccination, especially late in the influenza season. Such data also might be helpful to practitioners when evaluating the need for antiviral treatment and prophylaxis for their patients. Therefore, creating systems that enable collection and dissemination of timely VE data during an influenza season are a priority for CDC. Finally, healthcare providers should be aware of the types and subtypes of influenza circulating in their communities over the course of each influenza season. If influenza B strains predominate during the remainder of this season, providers can anticipate an increased risk for vaccine failures and should consider early use of antiviral medications for treatment and prophylaxis of persons at high risk for complications from influenza infection.

ACKNOWLEDGMENTS

The findings in this report are based, in part, on contributions from V Allison, J Anderson, E Bergmann, C Beyer, L Bennetti, N Berger, C Becker, A Bernitt, A Brockman, K Buedding, D Cole, A Deedon, J Frahmann, D Gamble, L Gavigan, D Gentz, G Greenwald, N Hartl, J Herr, D Hilgemann, L Ivacic, D Johnson, D Kempf, T Kronenwetter-Koeppel, D Marx, C Meyer, C Reis, S Reisner, J Salzwedel, S Strey, P Siegler, P Stockwell, L Verhagen, D York, J Zygarlicke, Marshfield Clinic Research Foundation, Marshfield, Wisconsin.

DISCUSSION QUESTIONS

1. Identify at least three each strengths and limitations of the case-control design in assessing vaccine efficacy. Why do you think the authors used the case-control approach for this study?
2. What other designs could have been used and what would their strengths and limitations be?
3. This study represents the intersection between research, surveillance, and care. Describe this intersection and how it is important in the advancing of public health.
4. Imagine that you are responsible for designing a prospective study to assess this same research question next year: What type of study design would you use? What surveillance system infrastructure would you wish to develop before the season begins?

REFERENCES FROM THE READING

1. Edwards KM, DuPont WD, Westrich MK, Plummer WD, Palmer PS, Wright PF. A randomized controlled trial of cold-adapted and inactivated vaccines for the prevention of influenza A disease. J Infect Dis 1994;169:68–76.

2. Bridges CB, Thompson WW, Meltzer MI, et al. Effectiveness and cost-benefit of influenza vaccination of healthy working adults: a randomized controlled trial. JAMA 2000;284:1655–63.

3. Orenstein EW, De Serres G, Haber MJ, et al. Methodologic issues regarding the use of three observational study designs to assess influenza vaccine effectiveness. Int J Epidemiol 2007;36:623–31.

4. Thompson WW, Shay DK, Weintraub E, et al. Mortality associated with influenza and respiratory syncytial virus in the United States. JAMA 2003;289:179–86.

5. Thompson WW, Shay DK, Weintraub E, et al. Influenza-associated hospitalizations in the United States. JAMA 2004;292:1333–40.

6. CDC. Prevention and control of influenza: recommendations of the Advisory Committee on Immunization Practices (ACIP), 2007. MMWR 2007;56(No. RR-6).

7. CDC. Update: influenza activity—United States, September 30, 2007–April 5, 2008, and composition of the 2008–09 influenza vaccine. MMWR 2008;57:404–9.

8. Nichol KL, Nordin JD, Nelson DB, Mullooly JP, Hak E. Effectiveness of influenza vaccine in the community-dwelling elderly. N Engl J Med 2007;357:1373–81.

9. Smith DJ, Lapedes AS, de Jong JC, et al. Mapping the antigenic and genetic evolution of influenza virus. Science 2004;305:371–6.

10. Russell CA, Jones TC, Barr IG, et al. The global circulation of seasonal influenza A(H3N2) viruses. Science. In press 2008.

DISCLAIMER

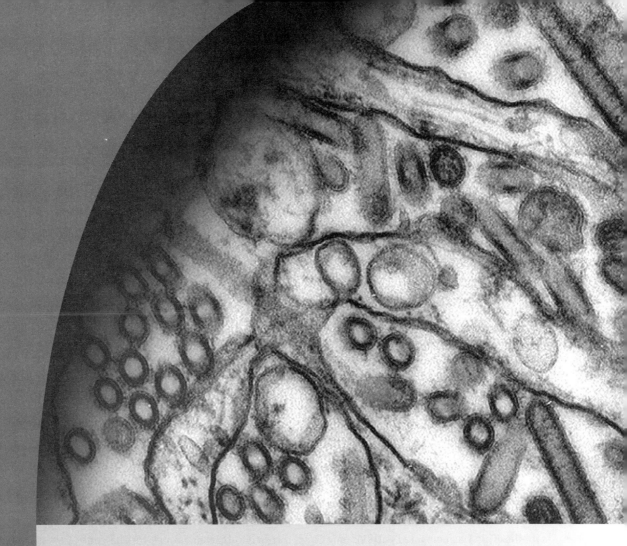

PART XIII

Understanding Results

In all studies, we begin with a research question and null and alternative hypotheses. We operationalize our independent and dependent variables, do formative, preliminary work to understand the milieu in which we are researching, work with a multidisciplinary team, create instrumentation and protocols to collect data, then clean, manage, and analyze those data to provide insight—putative "answers"—to our research questions. This information is then incorporated into our future research, and so goes the scientific process.

When we develop our null hypothesis, we must be committed to listening to what our data say—at least to an appropriate degree. If our null hypothesis is, "there is no association between X and Y," and we reject this hypothesis, then we should be able to accept that there is—in the way it was specified—an association between X and Y. But it is our methods and analysis of these methods that need also to be incorporated into our understanding of what it means to reject or to fail to reject a null hypothesis. If we ask the wrong question, if we define the variable inappropriately for the given research question, if we design a study that is not capable of answering the question, then our analysis may not be telling the whole story. The beauty of the scientific process is that it takes many, many studies of different types and methods and approaches to develop theories—it is never just one approach, but many, that provide an understanding of the phenomena under study. (Note the many resources on causality, Bradford Hill criteria for causality, etc.)

In the 1990s two community-based randomized trials were conducted to assess the role of sexually transmitted infections (STIs) in the transmission of HIV. On the basis of the hypothesis (now well-accepted) that ulcerative and non-ulcerative STIs are associated with an increased risk of HIV transmission (sometimes referred to as the STI/HIV co-factor hypothesis), these two studies strove to assess the impact of two interventions. In Mwanza, Tanzania, improved treatment for STDs using a syndromic treatment approach was compared with the standard of care. In Rakai, Uganda, all individuals in the treatment communities were given directly observed therapy of highly active antibiotics with activity against STIs and penicillin for those that had syphilis. This was compared with vitamins and anti-helminth medications for the control areas. Under the alternative hypothesis that reduction of STIs will be associated with a reduction in HIV transmission, one would expect certain findings. In this section you will read a media release from CDC that summarizes some of the differences between the two studies and alludes to reasons why the expected findings were not exactly what was found:

Here are summaries of the two studies:

- The Mwanza study
  - 12 matched communities
  - Randomized six to intervention and six to control group
    - Intervention: syndromic STD management to symptomatic persons
    - Training to existing providers, supervision, increased drugs and supplies, social marketing
  - Findings: 38% reduction in HIV incidence over 2 years in adult population (adjusted rate ratio 0.62, 95% CI 0.45–0.85)
  - No significant reductions in STDs at antenatal clinics or in STDs other than newly acquired syphilis and symptomatic urethritis in men
- The Rakai study
  - Randomized community-based clusters to home-based intervention or control groups every ten months
    - Intervention (n = 7871 clusters): single broad spectrum antibiotics for gonarrhea (Gc), Chlamydia (Ct), trichomonas (Tv), Vaginosis (BV), chancroid, syphilis
    - Control (n = 7256 clusters): referral for care if found to be infected plus anti-parasite drug and vitamins
  - All participants screened and either treated (I) or referred; project mobile clinics provided in communities for symptomatic STDs
  - Significant reductions in prevalence of BV, Tv, syphilis and incidence of Tv. In pregnant women significant reductions in Tv, Gc, Ct, BV

REFERENCES

Grosskurth H, et al. Impact of improved treatment of sexually transmitted diseases on HIV infection in rural Tanzania: randomized controlled trial. Lancet 1995; 346:530–36.

Orroth KK, Korenromp EL, White RG, et al. Comparison of STD prevalences in the Mwanza, Rakai, and Masaka trial populations: the role of selection bias and diagnostic errors. Sex Transm Infect 2003;79:98–105.

Wawer MJ, Sewankambo NK, Serwadda D, et al. Control of sexually transmitted diseases for AID prevention in Uganda: a randomized community trial. Lancet 1999; 353:525–35.

READING 32
STD Treatment to Prevent HIV Infection: Implications of Recent Community-Level Studies

Centers for Disease Control. Media Release July 1998; *STD Treatment to Prevent HIV Infection: Implications of Recent Community-Level Studies*. Available at: http://www.cdc.gov/nchstp/dstd/Facts_Treatment_Prevent_HIV_Infection.htm.

CDC MEDIA RELEASE JULY 1998

STD TREATMENT TO PREVENT HIV INFECTION: IMPLICATIONS OF RECENT COMMUNITY-LEVEL STUDIES

Evidence from two major community-level, randomized trials has begun to clarify conditions under which STD treatment is likely to be most successful in reducing HIV transmission. The trials were conducted to examine the potential impact of STD treatment on HIV prevention. While both were community-level, randomized, controlled trials, there were differences in the design and the conditions under which the trials were carried out.

The first trial, conducted in Mwanza, a rural area of Tanzania, demonstrated a decrease of about 40% in new, heterosexually transmitted HIV infections in communities with continuous access to improved treatment of symptomatic STDs, as compared to communities with minimal STD services, where incidence remained about the same (Grosskurth et al., 1995). However, in the second trial, conducted in Rakai, Uganda, a reduction in HIV transmission was not demonstrated when the STD control approach was community-wide mass treatment administered to everyone every 10 months in the absence of ongoing access to improved STD services (Wawer, 1998).

What were some of the important differences in the two interventions?

- In Rakai, the intervention was STD mass treatment carried out in all households, regardless of symptom status, as compared to Mwanza where the intervention was the treatment of symptomatic STDs provided through improved clinic-based services.
- In Rakai, mass treatment was offered intermittently every 10 months, whereas in Mwanza, treatment was available on a continuous basis.
- In Mwanza, STD treatment was only for symptomatic STDs, whereas the mass treatment approach in Rakai treated both symptomatic and asymptomatic STDs.
- In Rakai, there was no referral for partners since it was presumed that partners were reached during mass treatment; in Mwanza, patients referred partners to clinics, although less than 30% actually presented for treatment.

What were some of the key differences in the two communities when they were studied?

- Rakai was at a much later stage of the HIV epidemic than Mwanza. Mwanza was experiencing a relatively early HIV epidemic, with community HIV prevalence of about 4%, whereas Rakai represented one of the world's most mature epidemics, with a community HIV prevalence of approximately 16%.
- Rakai had relatively low prevalence of curable STDs, and Mwanza's prevalence was slightly higher.

WHAT DO THESE DIFFERENCES MEAN FOR HIV PREVENTION?

While additional research is needed, results of these two studies provide some direction for how STD prevention efforts can be best targeted as a tool to prevent HIV transmission. Toward this end, communities should consider the following:

- Continuous access to improved STD services is likely to have greater impact on HIV transmission than an intermittent mass treatment approach to STD control.

- In later stages of the HIV epidemic, the contribution of curable STDs to increasing HIV transmission may decline.
- Treating symptomatic STDs may be more important in reducing HIV transmission than treating asymptomatic STDs. However, treatment of asymptomatic STDs is critical to reducing rates of other STDs and their serious complications.
- STD treatment is especially critical in populations with substantial rates of curable STDs and early or growing HIV epidemics.

DISCUSSION QUESTIONS

1. Go to the original articles (referenced in the study) and to the Orroth study, and review each of them with respect to the research question, methods, specific strengths and limitations, and biases present (and how/if they were assessed). Examine the articles and describe each of the following:

   a. Internal validity
   b. External validity
   c. Specific biases (referenced and not)
   d. Presence of confounders (and how examined)
   e. Presence of effect modifiers (and how examined)
   f. Power
   g. Use of intention to treat analysis vs. per protocol or on treatment analysis
   h. Relationship between findings and interpretation.

3. Catalogue each of the issues discussed in the above article; now go to the source articles and highlight each issue/finding. Do you agree with the assessment of Orroth and colleagues?

REFERENCES FROM THE READING

Grosskurth H, et al. Impact of improved treatment of sexually transmitted diseases on HIV infection in rural Tanzania: randomized controlled trial. Lancet 1995; 346:530–36.

Kassler W, et al. STD control for HIV prevention in the US: Is there likely to be an impact? [Abstract No. 33238]. In: Conference Supplement of the 12th World AIDS Conference. Geneva, Switzerland, June 28–July 3, 1998.

Wawer MJ. The Rakai randomized, community-based trial of STD control for AIDS prevention: no effect on HIV incidence despite reductions in STDs [Abstract no. 12473]. In: Conference Supplement of the 12th World AIDS Conference. Geneva, Switzerland, June 28–July 3, 1998.

If you think about this, it is fascinating: If there was a reduction of STIs in Rakai, under the STD/HIV co-factor hypothesis, what would you have expected the effect on HIV to be? Reduced, right? That is where the methods come in. There were several critical differences in the communities under study, and those differences, described in the table below, may be why the findings were not what were originally expected. This table (adapted from UNAIDS) summarizes some of the differences between the two studies with regard to where and how they were performed.

TABLE 13-1 Study Comparison.

	Rakai	Mwanza
Design	Community based randomized controlled single-blinded open cohort	Community based randomized controlled unblinded trial in cohort
Intervention	STD mass treatment in home, directly observed; baseline, q10m	Syndromic tx of STDs through access to improved clinic-based services (incl. syph tx to all at baseline); continuous
Partner treatment	Mass treatment of community, incl. partners	Patient referral (~30% turned up for care)
Participation	77% of eligible	85% of eligible
Follow up	73–75%	71%
HIV prevalence	15.9%	4.1%
STD prevalence	Relatively high	Relatively low
STD reduction	Substantial	Not substantial
HIV reduction	No difference in HIV incidence between arms (adjusted rate ratio 0.97, 95% CI 0.81–1.16)	38% over 2 years (adjusted rate ratio 0.62, 95% CI 0.45–0.85)

FOR MORE INFORMATION

Please contact the NCHSTP Office of Communications at (404) 639-8063.

Source: CDC Media Release July 1998; STD Treatment to Prevent HIV Infection: Implications of Recent Community-Level Studies. http://www.cdc.gov/nchstp/dstd/Facts_Treatment_Prevent_HIV_Infection.htm [accessed 3-30-08].

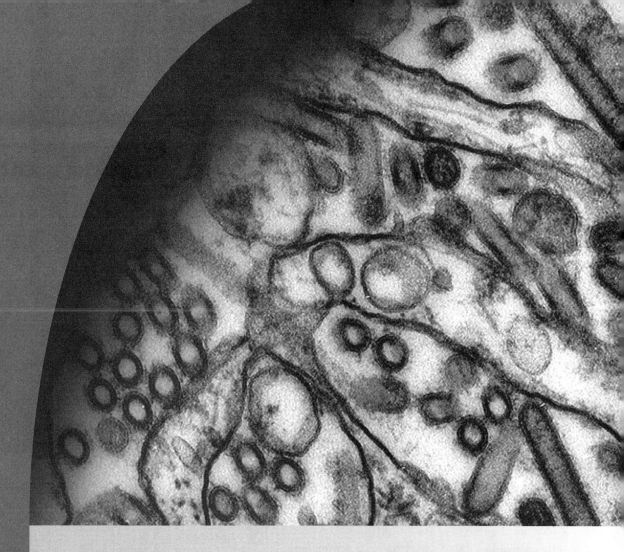

PART XIV

Different Approaches to Examining Bias in Infectious Disease Epidemiology

The methods section excerpts from the two studies below examine methodological issues concerning study of infectious disease, against a background of a serious infection that is frequently found in hospitalized patients and that complicates their care. The first uses a case-control approach to examine two biases—severity of illness and control group misclassification bias. This study demonstrates the power of methods themselves to explicate and expand our understanding of bias and how it impacts our understanding of public health phenomena. The second study uses three methods—epidemiologic investigation, environmental assessment, and an ambidirectional cohort method—to examine an outbreak of *Pseudomonas aeruginosa*. This study highlights the way in which multiple methods and "thinking outside the box" sometimes needs to be used to triangulate infectious disease explorations.

For the first study, a specific bias—severity of illness bias—was proposed and evaluated. The methods are able to compare/contrast two different approaches and then quantify the differing results:

READING 33
Excerpt from: Impact of Severity of Illness Bias and Control Group Misclassification Bias in Case-Control Studies of Antimicrobial-Resistant Organisms

Harris AD, Carmeli Y, Samore MH, et al.

Impact of Severity of Illness Bias and Control Group Misclassification Bias in Case-Control Studies of Antimicrobial-Resistant Organisms. *Infect Control Hosp Epidemiol.* 2005;26:342–5.

We hypothesize that although this refined criterion would help eliminate control group misclassification, it may introduce a selection bias by eliminating patients with the least severe illness (ie, patients who have no cultures performed during their hospital stay may receive fewer antibiotics, have fewer comorbid conditions, and have less severe illness). This selection bias, hereon referred to as severity of illness bias, would bias the OR closer to 1 and the ORs of risk factors would again be falsely decreased. In this study, we aimed to analyze the potential biases that arise due to control group misclassification and severity of illness selection. This was done by performing parallel case-control studies with two different control groups to determine how the selection of control-patients affects the results of risk factor analyses for imipenem-resistant *Pseudomonas aeruginosa*.

METHODS
Study Design and Definition of Cases and Controls
Two retrospective case-control studies were concurrently performed at the University of Maryland Medical System, which has a 609-bed acute care hospital that includes the R. Adams Cowley Shock Trauma Center and the Greenbaum Cancer Center. Cases were defined as patients from whom imipenem-resistant *P. aeruginosa* was nosocomially isolated in clinical cultures. Microbiologic identification methods have been outlined previously.

The microbiology laboratory database was electronically searched to identify all clinical cultures positive for imipenem-resistant *P. aeruginosa* from patients admitted to the hospital from January 1, 1998, to July 1, 2000. Patients who had imipenem-resistant *P. aeruginosa* isolates recovered within 48 hours of admission were excluded from the study, as were those who had isolates recovered from surveillance cultures. These cases were compared with two different control groups. Control-patients in group 1 (study 1) were randomly selected among patients receiving care from the same medical or surgical services from which case-patients were receiving care on the date that imipenem-resistant *P. aeruginosa* was isolated (ie, the base population of interest). Control-patients in group 1 did not have imipenem-resistant *P. aeruginosa* isolated during their hospital stay. Control-patients in group 2 (study 2) were identical to control-patients in group 1 except that they had to have had at least one specimen for clinical culture sent to the microbiology laboratory during their time at risk (ie, their length of stay in the hospital).

Data were collected from administrative, pharmacy, and laboratory computerized databases by means of a relational database management system. The relational database was maintained by the Information Technology Group of the University of Maryland. The pharmacy, microbiology, and medical demographics tables in the relational database have been validated against medical records of more than 400 patients admitted between October 1997 and January 2003. In addition, data for a 10% sample of case-patients and a 5% sample of control patients in this study were validated with medical charts. The positive and negative predictive values of the data are greater than 99%. In study 1, case-patients who had clinical cultures positive for imipenem-resistant *P. aeruginosa* were compared with control-patients in group 1. In study 2, the same case-patients were compared with the control patients in group 2 (i.e., control-patients who had at least one clinical culture).

Risk Factors Analyzed

We were particularly interested in the effect that control group misclassification bias and severity of illness selection bias had on the measurement of the effect of exposure to individual antimicrobial agents on the isolation of an antimicrobial-resistant organism, in this case imipenem-resistant *P. aeruginosa*. The

categories of antimicrobials analyzed were as follows: any antibiotic, cephalosporins, piperacillin–tazobactam, imipenem, vancomycin, quinolones, and aminoglycosides. For case patients, the antimicrobials analyzed had been received during the 14 days before clinical culture positivity. For both groups of control-patients, the antimicrobials analyzed had been received during the 14 days before discharge from the hospital. However, because the 14-day period was chosen arbitrarily, statistical analyses were repeated with the use of data on antibiotics that were received during the entire time that the patient was at risk before the event and the results obtained were the same. Thus, only data from the 14-day exposure period are presented. Co-morbid conditions for case-patients and control-patients were represented by the Charlson score. Further details regarding the central data repository at the University of Maryland Medical System that was used to obtain the variables are outlined in other studies.

This is an example in which existing specimens were put to good use to assess predictors of infection in an ICU, using a unique ambidirectional cohort design.

READING 34
Excerpt from: An Outbreak of Multidrug-Resistant *Pseudomonas Aeruginosa* Associated with Increased Risk of Patient Death in an Intensive Care Unit

Bukholm G, Tannæs T, Bye Kjelsberg ABB, et al.

An Outbreak of Multidrug-Resistant *Pseudomonas Aeruginosa* Associated with Increased Risk of Patient Death in an Intensive Care Unit. *Infect Control Hosp Epidemiol.* 2002;23:441–446.

STUDY DESIGN

The study period was from December 1, 1999, to September 1, 2000. From the start of the study period, all clinical isolates of *P. aeruginosa* were stored. The end of the study period was when the outbreak was stopped. This was an epidemiologic investigation and environmental assessment study. Risk factors were evaluated in an ambidirectional cohort design (ie, retrospective from March 1, 2000, and prospective from March 1, 2000).

PATIENTS

All patients admitted to the ICU from December 1, 1999, through September 1, 2000, receiving mechanical ventilation treatment were included in the study. The inclusion criteria did not contain clinical characteristics. Age, length of treatment with a ventilator, Simplified Acute Physiology Score (SAPS II),expected mortality, infection with *P. aeruginosa*, and colonization with *P. aeruginosa* were recorded for each patient (Table 14-1). An infected patient was defined as a patient with clinical symptoms of lower respiratory tract infection or bloodstream infection, and from whom a clinical culture from bronchoalveolar lavage, expectorate, or blood culture yielded a dominant growth of *P. aeruginosa*. A colonized patient was defined as a patient from whom only surveillance cultures were positive for *P.aeruginosa*.

TABLE 14-1 Baseline Data of the Patients in the Cohort And Data of the Noninfected and Infected Groups.

Sample (No.)	Age, y			SAPS II			Ventilator Days		
	Mean	Range	Median	Mean	Range	Median	Mean	Range	Median
Whole cohort (95)	63.3	18.1 to 86.1	67.4	46.8	0 to 103	46	14.6	0.04 to 78.8	6.54
Control (82)	63.1	18.1 to 86.1	67.7	46.3	0 to 103	46	12.24	0.04 to 61.4	4.6
Infected (13)	63.6	38.9 to 81	63.9	49.7	30 to 75	49	29.5	1.7 to 78.8	27.4

SAPS II = Simplified Acute Physiology Score

SURVEILLANCE CULTURES OF PATIENTS AND ENVIRONMENTAL CULTURES

From March 1, surveillance cultures were taken from all patients in the ICU. Three cultures were taken from patients every week as long as they stayed in the ICU: tracheal aspirate, gastric tube, and rectal swab. Environmental brush samples were taken from all ventilators before patient use and from liquid soap containers, water sinks, and water taps in the patient rooms and all other rooms in the ICU. From July, water samples were taken from all water taps. Five hundred milliliters of water was passed through filters with a 0.45-μm pore size. The filters were cultivated on blood agar for 3 days and examined for bacterial growth.

DISCUSSION QUESTIONS

1. Compare and contrast the two methods above. How are they the same? How do they differ? Do either or both impact the way that you view the study infectious diseases in the hospital setting?

2. How do you think these findings may be generalized to other studies or outbreak investigations?

3. Practice is essential: The more you read and critically evaluate, the more you will be able to understand methods, identify biases if they are present, and incorporate the biases into the way that you view the findings. As you did before, examine each of the excerpts and describe the following:

   a. Internal validity
   b. External validity
   c. Specific biases (referenced and not)
   d. Presence of confounders (and how examined)
   e. Presence of effect modifiers (and how examined)

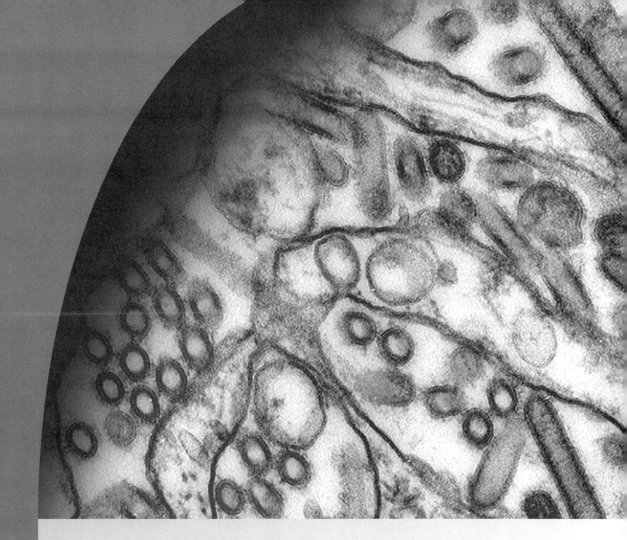

PART **XV**

Challenges in Studying Behavior

As the *Onion* (a parody newspaper) announces in one of its headlines, "Study: Casual Sex Only Rewarding For First Few Decades." The joke goes on to say, "An alarming new study published in the *International Journal of Sexual Health* reveals that casual sex, the practice of engaging in frequent, spontaneous sexual encounters with new and exciting partners, may only provide unimaginable pleasure and heart-pounding exhilaration for, at most, 25 to 30 years." In some way, this sums up why changing behavior is so difficult: many public health dangers—smoking, drug use, alcohol, risk taking, unsafe sexual behaviors—can be exhilarating. And if only it were only the changing! Studying and measuring behavior change are enormously difficult tasks. In creating interventions to improve behavior, we must be able to measure whether the interventions work. The following article discusses the myriad challenges involved in studying sexual behavior.

READING 35
Measuring Sexual Behavior: Methodological Challenges in Survey Research

Fenton, et al.

Fenton KA, Johnson AM, McManus S, Erens B. Measuring Sexual Behaviour: Methodological Challenges in Survey Research. *Sex Transm Inf*. 2001;77:84–92.

INTRODUCTION

The study of sexual behaviour lies at the heart of understanding the transmission dynamics of sexually transmitted infections (STIs). Academic investigation into sexual behaviour dates back to the 18th century and, over time, has employed a variety of approaches including the medical and psychiatric investigation of sexual disorders, anthropological investigations, and survey research based largely on volunteer samples. More recent studies, driven largely by the public health response to HIV/AIDS, have focused on large scale probability sample survey research.[1–5] Key areas of inquiry have shifted towards describing population patterns of risk behaviours for STI/HIV transmission, understanding how epidemics of STIs are generated, and informing disease control strategies.

Sexual behaviour is a largely private activity, subject to varying degrees of social, cultural, religious, moral and legal norms and constraints. A key challenge for all sex survey research is to generate unbiased and precise measures of individual and population behaviour patterns. Methods are needed to minimize measurement error which may be introduced by participation bias, recall and comprehension problems, and respondents' willingness to report sensitive and sometimes socially censured attitudes or behaviours.[6,7] This paper briefly considers the role of different types of study in understanding STI epidemiology. It then focuses on potential sources of measurement error in survey research and strategies for assessing and limiting them.

TYPES OF STUDY

The type of study chosen will depend on the purpose of the investigation. However, studies generally fall into four main groups: general population surveys, studies on population subgroups, partner and network studies, ethnographic and qualitative studies.

General Population Probability Sample Surveys

Cross sectional population surveys aim to describe the overall distribution of behaviours in populations. By using probability sampling techniques and maximising response rates, large scale behavioural surveys can provide robust estimates of the prevalence of behaviours and their determinants in the population. However, they are frequently not large enough to determine the prevalence of behaviours among small population subgroups (for example, homosexual men) or among individuals with relatively rare experiences (for example, injecting drug use) which may be particularly important in transmission of infection. Since cross sectional surveys provide a snapshot in time, multiple surveys are required to measure and monitor behaviour change over time. Data from Switzerland[8] and Sweden[9] have shown temporal changes in partner change and condom use over time. In Britain, although two successive national surveys of sexual attitudes and lifestyles (NATSAL)[3,10] have been carried out a decade apart, there are few robust data for the interim period. In order to supplement data from intermittently commissioned large scale sex surveys, sexual behaviour questions (as key indictors or modules) may be added to probability sample general social surveys.[11,12]

Surveys on Small Subgroups at High Risk

Sexual behaviour studies often focus on epidemiologically important core groups that maintain STI transmission in the population such as commercial sex workers, homosexual men, injecting drug users, and STD clinic attenders. With very rare exceptions,[13] difficulties in accessing these groups make probability sampling costly and challenging, and more cost effective sampling strategies are required, including advertising, snowballing, recruiting from STD clinics, social and commercial venues. However, findings from these studies may not be representative of the wider target population. Thus, homosexual men who attend STD clinics have higher risk behaviours than those who do not[14] and STD clinic surveys will therefore tend to overestimate the prevalence of these behaviours. Prospective monitoring of behaviours in high risk groups may be achieved through cohort investigations or serial surveying. Probability samples from the general population can also be followed up to provide repeated behavioural measurements over time.[15] Cohort studies enable estimation of disease incidence and monitoring of behavioural risk over time.[15–19] In these instances, attributing lifestyle changes to behavioural interventions can be difficult, since significant age confounding (associated with decreasing sexual activity) may occur. Attrition rates can also be problematic in cohort studies, if those with high risk behaviours are more likely to drop out, leaving more compliant individuals. Behavioural surveillance, involving serial cross sectional surveys of a target group using the same sampling strategy over time, provides an alternative mechanism for prospective behavioural monitoring.[12] In London, annual surveys of homosexual men in social venues, STD clinics,[14,20] and Gay Pride events[21] use a stable set of behavioural indicators—for example, unprotected anal intercourse in the past 3 months, which are then monitored repeatedly. Both have demonstrated increasing risk behaviour among homosexual men and have provided useful behavioural trend data to inform public health interventions.

Partner and Network Studies

Partner studies are concerned with studying transmission probabilities for STIs and their association with specific sexual behaviours. In the 1980s, a series of partner studies examined the transmission probability of heterosexual transmission of HIV.[22,23] These relied on detailed behavioural data to exclude other sources of exposure than the index case, and to identify risk factors for transmission. These studies established the role of unprotected vaginal intercourse in heterosexual transmission; the protective role of condoms; the increased risk of unprotected anal intercourse; and the poor association between the number of acts of intercourse and the probability of transmission. Other studies have utilised partner notification data to estimate transmission probabilities for STIs[24] and to determine the role of sexual networks in maintaining endemic STI transmission.[24–26] These studies have highlighted the importance of "core groups"[27] and of particular individuals within networks, in maintaining chains of transmission.

Such studies are however highly intensive, with many practical difficulties. Nevertheless, epidemiological research on STI transmission is increasingly focusing on the importance of understanding mixing matrices, particularly in "core" populations. More detailed considerations of these important developments are beyond the scope of this paper.

Ethnographic and Qualitative Studies

Ethnographic and qualitative studies on sexual behaviour have made significant contributions to our understanding of STI transmission dynamics.[28] Studies exploring the social context of sexual behaviour—for example, the importance of San Francisco "bath houses"[29] where homosexual men had large numbers of anonymous sexual contacts, were key to understanding the early evolution of the AIDS epidemic.[30] Qualitative research has enabled the exploration of concepts within communities[31,32] and revealed behaviours or cultural factors which are relevant for developing prevention strategies. For example, understanding the relevance of and preference for "dry sex" in different African communities has been an important consideration in developing vaginal microbicides.[33,34] Qualitative research has also been used to inform the design and development of quantitative research instruments and methods. Cognitive and in-depth interviewing have been used to inform the use of appropriate language in surveys and to identify factors which influence willingness to report such as privacy, sex of interviewers, and use of computer assisted self completion interviews.[29,32,35]

SOURCES OF MEASUREMENT ERROR IN SEXUAL BEHAVIOUR SURVEY RESEARCH

All epidemiological research aims to achieve accuracy in estimation. This requires minimizing measurement error, which may occur at any stage of the survey from sample selection, to questionnaire content, design, and administration. Potential sources are discussed in detail below.

Sampling Procedures

Many early sexual behaviour studies, including those of Kinsey,[36,37] relied on volunteer samples with little attempt to achieve representativeness of the demographic and behavioural characteristics of the target population. A number of studies have since shown that volunteers tend to be more sexually experienced, sensation seeking, and unconventional, and to have more relaxed sexual attitudes and behaviours than those randomly recruited from the general population.[38–40]

Random probability sampling methods can reduce volunteer bias by yielding unbiased samples of the target population. Commonly used sampling frames for general population surveys include electoral registers, postcode files, and telephone numbers; however, all may systematically underrepresent certain groups whose behaviours may differ from the general population. In many countries, no sampling frames of households, addresses, or individuals exist. A common strategy in these circumstances is to use a multistage clustered sampling technique in which census enumeration areas are first selected, all contained households listed, and then sampled. Homeless and prison populations are missed in most population samples, yet they have high prevalence of epidemiologically important behaviours such as injecting drug use or commercial sex.[41] Similarly, telephone samples often underrepresent young people and poorer populations.[42]

Respondent Variables

Survey non-response and representativeness

Achieving good response rates in sex survey research is essential to improve the representativeness of the survey and reduce participation bias (see below). Obtaining a representative sample increases our ability to make robust inferences about the source population—that is, to generalise survey findings. Generally, between 25–35% of people refuse to engage in telephone or face to face interviews designed to investigate sexual attitudes and lifestyles, and non-return rates of 40% in postal surveys of this nature are common.[38] However, others have argued that non-response rates are no greater for sex research than for other studies of sensitive issues, which would suggest that the *sexual* nature of the questionnaire does not necessarily bias the responses.[4,43] Survey nonresponse may become more problematic if public interest in survey participation declines, particularly in studies perceived to be intrusive, sensitive, or of no immediate relevance. Reasons for non-participation vary but include non-contact with selected addressees, refusals in person or by proxy, respondent being ill or unable to speak the appropriate language. Methods that rely on high levels of literacy may also exclude groups particularly vulnerable to poor sexual health outcomes. Refusal to participate may occur at any stage of the interview but is most likely at the point of initial contact or invitation.[6] In the National AIDS Behavioral Survey, over 80% of refusals occurred before respondents heard that the survey concerned AIDS related issues.[44]

Participation bias

Participation bias describes error arising from systematic differences in the characteristics (for example, sexual behaviour) of those who agree to participate in a study compared with those who do not. Even in well designed studies, achieving response rates in excess of 80% may be difficult, although higher response rates are often achieved in developing countries.[2] Therefore participation bias has the potential to introduce significant error in measuring estimates of behavioural risk. Participation bias has been documented in a variety of sexual behaviour studies, and is associated with the respondents' characteristics (for example, sex, age, social class), beliefs, and sexual behaviour.[45] Clement[46] argues that the more intrusive a survey, the higher the barrier to intimacy, and the more likely we are to encounter participation bias that overestimates variability and frequency of sexual behaviour (since those with conservative or normative lifestyles are less likely to participate). However, Biggar and Melbye[47] found little difference in the sexual behaviour of those who responded early and late to a sexual behaviour survey, and Laumann et al[5] drew similar conclusions. Item response bias is another type of participation bias in which respondents refusing to answer a particular question(s) are systematically more or less likely to have experience of the relevant behaviour. Copas et al[48] found older age, problems of comprehension, and ethnicity to be associated with refusal to complete more detailed and sensitive questions contained in a self completion booklet in the British NATSAL survey, but concluded that those who declined to answer the more intimate questions were, if anything, likely to be at lower HIV risk. Dunne et al[49] reached similar conclusions with a cohort study of twins, but concluded that the effect on most measures was small. In both cases, participation bias may have led to an overestimation of HIV risk behaviours which counteracts the observed tendency for survey respondents to minimise or underreport the frequency and diversity of their sexual behaviour.[39,42,50]

Reporting and recall bias

Sexual behaviour is most commonly studied using self reported recall of behaviours across some retrospective time frame. Even among respondents who attempt to "accurately" report their past behaviours, problems with recall can distort the reported incidence and frequency of specific behaviours.[6,42,51–53] Studies have found that the reliability of self reported sexual behaviour varies with a variety of factors including age,[54–56] ethnicity,[57] the number of sexual partners,[42] and the time frame for recall.[45] *Incidence reports* (for example, first sexual intercourse) are generally more reliably reported than *frequency reports* (for example, number of partners, frequency of sex). The reliability of frequency reports decreases with longer recall periods and more frequent behaviours (for example, vaginal sex).[54,58–60] Other reliability studies have found that recall of the number of partners tended to be less variable than the number of acts.[61–63] In general, longer recall intervals result in either underreporting or inaccurate recall of sexual practices and partners, because a more elaborate reconstruction of events rather than a simple scanning of more recent events is required.[64–66] Sex related bias in self reported behaviours may also occur. In a closed population with a balanced sex ratio, men and women should report the same population mean number of partners over a defined period. However, men consistently report a higher mean number of partners in nearly all surveys.[67] Wadsworth et al[68] explored this relation in data from NATSAL and concluded that the discrepancy could be reduced but not eliminated by accounting for age mixing in partnership formation, underrepresentation of prostitutes, and modest assumptions about response bias introduced by lower response rates among men than women. Similarly, evidence from other surveys indicates that men and women may differ in what they count as "sex," with men more likely to include non-penetrative sex than women.[62,69] However, it is likely that there remains some social desirability bias in the direction of overreporting by men and/or underreporting by women. Other examples of social desirability bias include the general tendency for women to underreport their premarital sexual experiences.[70,71] In the 1980s, Potterat[72] and Stoneburner et al[73] showed that HIV positive military personnel were initially more likely to report sexual encounters with prostitutes to be the source of infection than in later interviews with civilian counsellors when they were more willing to admit to homosexual exposure. Social desirability bias may also be influenced by data collection modes, with self completion modules typically eliciting higher rates of sensitive behaviours than face to face interviews (see below).

Questionnaire Design, Content, and Delivery

The design, content, and mode of administration of the survey questionnaire, whether by interviewer or self completed, may contribute to measurement error. Pen and paper methods may exclude those with poor literacy, and long questionnaires may lead to poor data quality with missing data and inconsistent answers. Detailed behavioural surveys may require elaborate skip and filtering instructions, which are difficult to follow. Words that might be considered offensive and "big words" may lead to significant item non-response and, as the meanings and use of terms used in surveys vary across sexes and cultures, they should never be assumed. For example, Sanders and Reinisch[69] found that 60% of a sample of college students did not consider oral sex alone to be "having sex." Development work for NATSAL[31] encountered different assumptions about the nature of a "sexual partner." Some married respondents felt the term was too casual to refer to their married partner, while single respondents thought it implied a steady relationship rather than a casual encounter. A sexual partner was carefully defined to all respondents in NATSAL, as were all behaviours reported in the survey. Although postal self completion surveys are less expensive, and may reach respondents in rural areas or who are hard to find at home, most studies have found response rates to be poorer on postal surveys than interviewer administered surveys, despite reminders.[42] While respondents have time to reflect on their answers, there is no motivational effect of the interviewer. Additionally, there is little control over how, in what order, or by whom the questionnaire is completed. Face to face (and to some extent, telephone) contact with respondents is often used in sex survey research. Interviewers can explain the rationale and format of a survey directly, and they may have a motivating effect on the respondent, by providing full, clear definitions, probing ambiguous responses, or querying inconsistent answers.[74] However, interviewers can also introduce reporting bias, leading to reduced disclosure of socially proscribed attitudes or behaviours (even when done in coded fashion). Research has shown that people tend to report more sexual information to female interviewers, and that in this regard, women may be more influenced than men by interviewer sex diVerences.[52,67] Delamater[51] found that females were more likely to underreport proscribed behaviours to male interviewers than to female interviewers whereas Johnson and Delamater[75] found male interviewees with good rapport with the interviewer also reported more frequent sexual activity.

ASSESSING MEASUREMENT ERROR

Response Rates and Representatives

Strategies for assessing the extent and magnitude of participation bias remain relatively undeveloped. Checking the overall study response rates provides some indication of the representativeness and the likely magnitude of participation bias in the survey. However, formal assessment of sample representativeness usually involves comparing demographic characteristics such as age, sex, socioeconomic group, and geographic location with census data or other large scale studies on less sensitive topics.[3,76] Data from probability sample surveys consistently suggest that non-responders are more likely to be male, older, urban residents, with lower educational attainment than responders, with no consistent relation being noted with marital status, occupational status, and ethnicity.[38,42,48] NATSAL obtained a 65% response rate and the achieved sample was broadly representative of the population of Great Britain aged 16–59 years. In common with other surveys, response rates were lower among men than women, and those least likely to respond were in the oldest age group. Parameter estimates could have been affected if recruited males were younger (therefore reporting more sexual activity) and if non-participation was related to sexual behaviours.

Validity Checks

Validity describes the extent to which an instrument measures what it purports to measure. It is extremely difficult to determine the absolute validity of self reported sexual behaviours and therefore a number of indirect measures (internal and external) are used instead. External validation of reports may be achieved by using independent data sources as external references. For example, in NATSAL, self reported abortion showed a good approximation to national statutory reports, although there was some evidence of underreporting of STD clinic attendance.[3] Similarly, data from studies among high risk population subgroups may be triangulated for consistency with similar information on the overall spectrum of behaviour from general population surveys. Validation of survey results with those obtained from in-depth interviewing has also been used.[77]

Other methods of validation include interviewing the respondents and their sexual partners separately.[36] These reports may vary with the stability of the relationship, degree of substance abuse, type of sexual behaviour within the relationship, and time interval asked about.[6] Padian et al[78] found high levels of agreement in couples with one HIV infected partner on levels of frequency of sex, sex practices, and condom use. Others have found only fair agreement in couples attending STD clinics, which tends to decrease as recall periods increase.[79]

Biological methods using incident STIs or urinary testing for HIV, *Chlamydia trachomatis*, and pregnancy are being increasingly used to assess the validity of self reports. However further evaluation of this strategy is needed. Zenilman et al[80] in an STD clinic population, found similar levels of incident STI in "always" condom users to "never users" suggesting evidence of reporting bias (assuming high condom effectiveness in preventing STIs).

Internal Consistency

The internal consistency of questionnaire responses, where responses to questions asked in one part of an individual's ques-

tionnaire are checked for logical agreement with related questions, may be used to assess the reliability and validity of self reports. NATSAL[3] included 158 consistency checks, and around 80% of respondents had no inconsistencies. Where differences occurred in different parts of the interview, the most common inconsistencies were greater reporting of multiple heterosexual partners and of homosexual experiences in questions completed in a self completion booklet compared with those in face to face interviews.

Test–Retest Reliability

Readministration of the same items after a brief time interval has been used to assess optimal recall time frames or the stability of responses (test–retest reliability)[42,58,64] and to compare different techniques for enhancing memory. This provides an index of the stability of people's estimates of their sexual behaviours over time. A variety of studies have examined the reliability of reports of a range of behaviours across different populations. Factors increasing reliability include age (adolescents have higher test-retest coefficients than adults), rarity of events, incidence reports compared with frequency reports, and shorter period of recall.[42,45,58,64] In 1990, Catania argued that existing test-retest data represented a "mixed bag" and called for studies which examine reliability for different reporting periods across specific sexual behaviours, in different population subgroups.

REDUCING MEASUREMENT ERROR

Improve Sample Design

In a probability sample survey, increasing the size of the study can reduce sampling error and increase study precision (thereby providing more robust parameter estimates). However, this must be balanced against increasing research costs. Stratifying the sample, or sorting the sampling frame before selection, ensures that the sample proportion from any particular stratum equals the population proportion. Variable sampling fractions can also be applied to increase the sample size of small groups of particular interest—for example, to achieve acceptable confidence intervals for estimates based on different ethnic or regional groups, and to increase the precision of estimates by oversampling more variable strata. Weighting can be applied to correct for different selection probabilities resulting from the use of variable sampling fractions or to control for random variations in the sample numbers across strata.

Reduce Participation Bias

Any intervention that improves response rates will reduce participation bias. Respondent callbacks, re-invitations to participate, and postal reminders have been used to obtain interviews with the selected participant. Laumann et al[5] used incremental payments to encourage participation in those initially declining to participate. Interviewer characteristics and training, and the perceived public health importance of the survey topic may also influence response rates.[81] Methods that make the interview process less invasive or more private (for example, use of computer assisted self interviewing techniques) may reduce participation bias since embarrassment and worries about confidentiality, often of primary concern to participants, are reduced. However, even if very high response rates were achieved, estimates of rarer behaviours remain sensitive to participation bias and there are no simple techniques to reduce their effect in analysis. If the demographic differences between the sample and the population are known then statistical weighting techniques can be used to adjust for differential nonresponse. Typically, results are weighted to the known demographic structure (age, marital status, region, etc) of the target population to provide population estimates. However, this method assumes that the prevalence of behaviours is the same as in responders (at least within demographic classes). It cannot overcome participation bias that arises independently of demographic factors. Alternatively, special studies with nonparticipants may be undertaken to characterise the magnitude of, and subsequently adjust for, participation bias.[38,48] A sensitivity analysis approach may then be employed to calculate and present parameter estimates, which take into account different assumptions of this (participation bias) effect.[48]

Improve Questionnaire Design and Content

The terms used to describe or investigate sexual behaviour may influence respondents' willingness to participate in the study or to provide accurate and reliable answers. Items should be specific, clear, and use defined time periods to inquire about sexual behaviour. They should also avoid acquiescence bias (implying a "mid point" or "norm") and undue embarrassment.[82]

Using appropriate and comprehensible language and terminology is important. Binson and Catania[83] state that one approach to establishing appropriate language is to ask each respondent to select the sexual terminology they would prefer the interviewer to use.[36,37,74] This technique has been shown to elicit higher reporting of sensitive behaviours[83]; however, tailoring language to each respondent is less feasible on a large scale, heterogeneous, general population sample. It also places demands on the interviewer, and may create problems in quantifying precise and standardised behaviours. Spencer et al[31] also found general population respondents felt awkward about providing their own definitions for sexual practices. While colloquial or street language has been found suitable for specific populations, such as bar attending homosexual men, drug users, and prostitutes, general population surveys have tended to-

wards the formal. NATSAL development work found a strong preference for "formal rather than street language"[31] and ACSF used "technical anatomical terms."[50] Finally, care in the ordering of questions is also important. Spencer et al[31] found that both interviewers and respondents preferred the questionnaire to begin with neutral questions, leading in to more intimate and sensitive ones once rapport had been developed. General questions also provided a "contextual framework" into which life events could be situated to aid recall. However, beginning with first sexual experiences may be particularly sensitive if the age was perceived by the respondent to be very early or late, or involved abuse. In NATSAL[3] and the American NHSLS,[5] attitude questions are asked towards the end of the interview and after the sexual behaviour questions to avoid possible reinforcement of social norms in reporting on partners and practices.

Telephone Interviewing

Telephone surveys have gained increasing popularity over the past two decades and are a mainstay of market oriented research. Telephone interviews were used for the French (ACSF),[4] other national sex surveys and others.[62,84-86] Telephone interviewing allows for an unclustered sample at a lower cost than could be achieved face to face. It allows faster data collection, greater control over and monitoring of the interview process. However, telephone interviews need to be shorter, require simple questions, and do not allow the use of show cards or long lists. It may also be more difficult to guarantee privacy as other household members may be listening in. Nevertheless, in the French survey, Bajos and Spira[87] compared telephone interviewing and face to face interviewing with pen and paper self completion and found that questions were "more easily answered" and answers were more coherent in the telephone study. New systems are available for both private call-in and call-out telephone interviews. With a call-in system, respondents telephone a live interviewer; with call-out, live interviewers screen households and recruit participants. Some of the questionnaire is administered directly, with respondents transferred to an automated system for the sensitive sections.

Self Completion Questionnaires

Self completion questionnaires reduce the need for respondents to disclose sensitive behaviours to the interviewer and may result in more valid reports than interviews.[6] Paper self completions should be simple and short with limited filtering and few open ended questions. Combinations of pen and paper self completion and interviewer techniques have been used in many of the large surveys and combine the benefits of face to face interviewing with the privacy of self completion for more sensitive questions. Johnson et al[3] reported increased disclosure of censured behaviours (for example, homosexual experience) in self completion compared with face to face questioning. Davoli et al[88] reported good correlation between self completion and face to face interviews among Italian adolescents for reported coital experience and age at first intercourse; however, interviews underreported coitus and overreported condom use when administered before the questionnaire. Despite good reproducibility, social desirability bias had occurred.

Computer Assisted Interviews

In the past decade there have been major developments in the use of technologies for undertaking computer assisted personal interviews (CAPI) and self completion interviews.

Face to face and telephone interviews are undertaken with responses keyed directly into computers by interviewers. Computer assisted self interviews (CASI) are increasingly being used where the respondents key their response to questions on the screen directly into a laptop computer. These methods are well suited to complex questionnaires since skips and routing can be automatically programmed without respondents having to follow complex instructions on paper.

In audio-CASI, respondents listen to prerecorded questions on headphones and key in appropriate responses. All respondents can hear the same standardised delivery of questions (with voice quality, not computer generated words). Audio-CASI helps overcome literacy problems and can provide prerecorded questionnaires in different languages and can also be used for telephone interviews. In comparing CAPI, CASI, and audio-CASI, Tourangeau and Smith[89] found audio-CASI elicited highest mean number of reported partners and highest reporting of anal sex. They found that respondents felt a greater sense of privacy, that CASI gave the study an air of "legitimate and scientific value," and that audio input (whether on face to face or audio-CASI) facilitated comprehension. Des Jarlais et al[90] assessed audio-CASI as a method of reducing underreporting of HIV risk behaviour among injecting drug users and noted significantly increased reporting of HIV risk and sensitive behaviours, such as borrowing or renting used injecting equipment, in audio-CASI than in face to face interviews.

Studies comparing CASI with identical questions using pen and paper self completion have demonstrated the potential of CASI to improve the quality of data, and to increase respondents' willingness to report sensitive behaviours.[91,92] Turner et al[92] reported significant audio-CASI effects for the reporting of several sensitive behaviours. However, their sample was restricted to adolescent males, many from disadvantaged backgrounds, and the study used audio-CASI to get over potential literacy problems in this group. Johnson et al,[10] in a methodological experiment in a British general population sample, found no consistent evidence of increased reporting of

risk behaviour when comparing CASI with pen and paper self completion, although item response and data consistency were improved using CASI. Method effects may be related to the degree of perceived social censure of particular behaviours and these vary between cultures and demographic groups.

Sexual Diaries

Sexual diaries have been proposed as a means of improving reliability of reported behaviours.

If kept regularly they can allow prospective collection of data and minimise problems associated with long term recall.[42] Verbal diaries, regularly collected by an interviewer, have also been used with poorly literate respondents. This may be particularly useful given that recall of sexual partners is more likely to be cited as a difficulty by the most sexually active respondents, and that infrequent practices are easier to remember than frequent ones.[93] In a study among commercial sex workers, Ramjee et al[94] found a significantly greater mean number of clients, condoms used, vaginal acts and anal acts reported in diary format compared with recall questionnaire.

While McLaws et al[93] found most respondents preferred using the diary to the recall questionnaire, their sample of homosexual men, like Coxon's,[95] may have been particularly well motivated. The burden of a regular diary may be too time consuming a task to expect of most respondents, and measuring behaviours may in turn produce changes in the behaviour being measured (monitoring effects). Consequently McLaws concluded that data collected by recall were, in fact, more consistently reliable than data collected by diary.[93]

CONCLUSIONS

Reliable data on sexual behaviour remain difficult to collect. Nevertheless, many of the methodological challenges of sexual behaviour research are common to other areas of self reported behaviour including diet, smoking, and alcohol consumption. Improvements in social research methods provide a number of strategies for reducing measurement error. Computer assisted techniques, by improving internal consistency and increasing privacy and interviewee control, offer exciting possibilities for improving survey validity. So too does our increasing ability to triangulate survey results with focused qualitative investigations and a variety of social research and surveillance data. Increasingly available non-invasive diagnostic techniques provide biological outcome measures, which in turn offer new opportunities for studying the relation between behaviours and STI epidemiology.

Continued methodological research is needed to better identify the sources and magnitude of measurement error. Achieving high response rates in population based studies remains a challenge, despite technological developments, increasing public discourse about sex, and greater awareness of sexual health matters. In many developed countries, this is further compounded by a reduction in the perceived threat posed by the HIV/AIDS epidemic, undoubtedly a stimulant for much progress over the past two decades. As a result, waning public interest and changing political prioritisation can only serve to increase these difficulties. Spiraling research costs mean that large scale studies of sexual behaviour are becoming less attractive to policy makers. Cost effective and robust strategies for monitoring sexual behaviour are required, and behavioural surveillance programmes (ongoing population based prospective monitoring of sexual behaviour) are urgently needed. A potential way to develop this surveillance in the United Kingdom and elsewhere may involve adding a small module of key sexual behaviour questions to other routine surveys (for example, general health surveys). Such surveillance programmes would not obviate the need for targeted or in-depth studies of sexual behaviours but would, in concert, continue to increase our understanding of disease epidemiology and strategies to promote sexual health.

DISCUSSION QUESTIONS

1. Select any article that uses survey research to assess sexual behavior from the literature. Remember that often, the exposure and/or outcome variables that are being analyzed are collected through interview or other survey methods—even if that is not the *point* of the study. You may wish to look for data from the Behavioral Risk Factor Surveillance System, NHANES, or any survey of your liking. Examine this article in light of the topics outlined above. Does this critical evaluation affect how you view the findings?

2. See what instrumentation you either have available to you or can obtain online. Give the survey to a friend and then have the friend give it to you. Are there any issues with the instrumentation or the administration that you can point out, on the basis of this thoughtful examination of challenges in survey research? Did you know it would be so hard to ask questions?

REFERENCES FROM THE READING

1. Catania JA, Moskowitz JT, Ruiz M, *et al.* A review of national AIDS-related behavioral surveys. *AIDS* 1996;10:S183–90.

2. Cleland J, Ferry B. *Sexual behaviour and AIDS in the developing world.* London: Taylor Francis, 1995.

3. Johnson AM, Wadsworth J, Wellings K, *et al. Sexual attitudes and lifestyles.* Oxford: Blackwell Scientific Press, 1994.

4. ASCF principal investigators and their associates. Analysis of sexual behaviour in France (ACSF). A comparison between two modes of investigation: telephone survey and face-to-face survey. *AIDS* 1992;6:315–23.

5. Laumann EO, Gagnon JH, Michael RT, *et al. The social organization of sexuality: sexual practices in the United States.* Chicago and London: University of Chicago Press, 1994.

6. Catania JA, Binson D, Van der Straten A, *et al.* Methodological research on sexual behavior in the AIDS era. *Annual Review of Sex Research* 1995;6:77–125.

7. McLaws M, Oldenburg B, Ross MW, *et al.* Sexual behaviour in AIDS-related research: reliability and validity of recall and diary measures. *Journal of Sex Research* 1990;27:265–81.

8. Hausser D, Zimmerman E, Dubois-Arber F, *et al.* Evaluation of the AIDS Prevention Strategy in Switzerland: third assessment report, 1989–1990. Lausanne: Institut Universitaire de Medicine Sociale et Preventive, 1991.

9. Herlitz CA, Steel JL. A decade of HIV/AIDS prevention in Sweden: changes in attitudes associated with HIV and sexual risk behaviour from 1987 to 1997. *AIDS* 2000;14: 881–90.

10. Johnson AM, Copas A, Field J, *et al.* Do computerised self completion interviews influence the reporting of sexual behaviours? A methodological experiment. Proceedings of the Thirteenth Meeting of the International Society for Sexually Transmitted Diseases Research, Denver Colorado, 11–14 July, 1999.

11. Smith TW. A methodological analysis of the sexual behaviour questions on the general social surveys. *Journal of Official Statistics* 1992;8:309–25.

12. World Health Organization and Joint United Nations Programme on HIV/AIDS. *Second generation surveillance for HIV: the next decade.* Geneva: WHO, 2000.

13. Schneider J, King J, Macnab GM, *et al.* Hepatitis-B surface antigen and antibody in black and white patients with venereal diseases. *Br J Vener Dis* 1977;53:372–4.

14. Nardone A, Dodds JP, Mercey DE, *et al.* Active surveillance of sexual behaviour among homosexual men in London. *Communicable Disease and Public Health* 1998;1:197–201.

15. Choi K-H, Catania JA. Changes in multiple sexual partnerships, HIV testing and condom use among US heterosexuals 18 to 49 years of age, 1990 and 1992. *Am J Public Health* 1996;86:554–6.

16. Adib SM, Joseph JG, Ostrow DG, *et al.* Relapse in sexual behavior among homosexual men: a 2-year follow-up from the Chicago MACS/CCS. *AIDS* 1991;5:757–60.

17. Hutchinson GA, Simeon DT. HIV infection rates and associated factors in high risk patients admitted to a psychiatric hospital in Trinidad and Tobago. *West Indian Med J* 1999;48:129–31.

18. Loveday C, Kaye S, Tenant-Flowers M, *et al.* Viral load rebound and viral resistance are independent of each other in a cohort of patients with HIV disease on open zidovudine therapy. *Lancet* 1995;345:820–4.

19. Ng'weshemi JZL, Ties Boerma J, Pool R, *et al.* Changes in male sexual behaviour in response to AIDS epidemic: evidence from a cohort study in urban Tanzania. *AIDS* 1996;10:1415–20.

20. Dodds JP, Nardone A, Mercey DE, *et al.* Increase in high risk sexual behaviour among homosexual men, London 1996–8: cross sectional, questionnaire study. *BMJ* 2000;320:1510–1.

21. Weatherburn P, Stephens M, Reid D, *et al.* Vital statistics. *Findings from the national gay men's sex survey 1999.* London: Sigma Research, 2000, chaps 1–70.

22. Carael M, Van De Perre PH, Lepage PH, *et al.* Human immunodeficiency virus transmission among heterosexual couples in central Africa. *AIDS* 1988;2:201–5.

23. De Vincenzi I, for the European Study Group on Heterosexual Transmission of HIV. A longitudinal study of human immunodeficiency virus transmission by heterosexual partners. *N Engl J Med* 1994;331:341–6.

24. Ghani A, Ison CA, Ward H, *et al.* Sexual partner networks in the transmission of sexually transmitted diseases. An analysis of gonorrhoea cases in Sheffield, UK. *Sex Transm Dis* 1996;23:498–503.

25. Day S, Ward H, Ghani A, *et al.* Sexual histories, partnerships and networks associated with the transmission of gonorrhoea. *Int J STD AIDS* 1998;9:666–71.

26. Ghani A, Swinton J, Garnett GP. The role of sexual partnership networks in the epidemiology of gonorrhoea. *Sex Transm Dis* 1997;24:1–12.

27. Rothenberg RR, Potterat JJ, Woodhouse DE. Personal risk taking and the spread of disease: beyond core groups. *J Infect Dis* 1996;174:S144–9.

28. Power R. The role of qualitative research in HIV/AIDS [editorial]. *AIDS* 1998;12:687–95.

29. McKusick L, Horstman W, Coates TJ. AIDS and sexual behavior reported by gay men in San Francisco. *Am J Public Health* 1985;75:493–6.

30. Parker RG, Carballo M. Qualitative research on homosexual and bisexual behavior relevant to HIV/AIDS. *J Sex Res* 1990;27:497–525.

31. Spencer L, Faulkner A, Keegan J. *Talking about sex.* London: SCPR, 1988.

32. Elam G, Fenton K, Johnson A, *et al. Exploring ethnicity and sexual health.* London: Social and Community Planning Research, 1999:1–116.

33. Civic D, Wilson D. Dry sex in Zimbabwe and implications for condom use. *Soc Sci Med* 1996;42:91–8.

34. Pool R, Whitworth JA, Green G, *et al.* An acceptability study of female-controlled methods of protection against HIV and STDs in southwestern Uganda. *Int J STD AIDS* 2000;11:162–7.

35. Mitchell K, Wellings K, Elam G. NSSAL II survey design and implementation report of the qualitative stage. Report to Medical Research Council. London: MRC, June, 1998:1–40.

36. Ostrow DG, Vanable PA, McKirnan DJ, *et al.* Hepatitis and HIV risk among drug-using men who have sex with men: demonstration of Hart's law of inverse access and application to HIV. *J Gay Lesbian Med Assoc* 2000;3/4:136.

37. Seal DW, Kelly JA, Bloom FR, *et al.* HIV prevention with young men who have sex with men: what young men themselves say is needed. *Aids Care Psychol Socio Med Asp AIDS HIV* 2000;12/1:26.

38. Dunne MP, Martin NG, Bailey JM, *et al.* Participation bias in a sexuality survey: psychological and behavioural characteristics of responders and non-responders. *Int J Epidem* 1997;26:844–54.

39. Strassberg D, Lowe K. Volunteer bias in sexuality research. *Arch Sex Behav* 1995;24:369–82.

40. Catania J, McDermott L, Pollack L. Questionnaire response bias and face to face interview sample bias in sexuality research. *J Sex Res* 1986;22:52–72.

41. Bird AG, Gore SM, Burns SM, *et al.* Study of infection with HIV and related risk factors in young offenders' institution. *BMJ* 1993;307:228–31.

42. Catania JA, Gibson DR, Chitwood DD, *et al.* Methodological problems in AIDS behavioral research: influences on measurement error and participation bias in studies of sexual behavior. *Psychol Bull* 1990;108:339–62.

43. Biggar RJ, Brinton LA, Rosenthal MD. Trends in the number of sexual partners among American women. *J Acquir Immune Defic Syndr* 1989;2: 497–502.

44. Catania JA, Coates TJ, Stall R, *et al.* Prevalence of AIDS-related risk factors and condom use in the United States. *Science* 1992;258:1101–6.

45. Catania JA, Gibson DR, Marin B, *et al.* Response bias in assessing sexual behaviors relevant to HIV transmission. *Evaluation and Program Planning* 1990;13:19–29.

46. Clement U. Surveys of heterosexual behaviour. *Annual Review of Sex Research* 1990;1:45–74.

47. Biggar RJ, Melbye M. Responses to anonymous questionnaires concerning sexual behavior: A method to examine potential biases. *Am J Public Health* 1992;82:1–7.

48. Copas A, Johnson AM, Wadsworth J. Assessing participation bias in a sexual behaviour survey: implications for measuring HIV risk. *AIDS* 1997;11: 783–90.

49. Dunne MP, Martin NG, Bailey JM, *et al.* Participation bias in a sexuality survey: Psychological and behavioural characteristics of responders and non-responders. *Int J Epidem* 1997;26:844–53.

50. Horner RD, Oddone EZ, Matchar DB. Theories explaining racial differences in the utilization of diagnostic and therapeutic procedures for cerebrovascular disease. *Millbank Q* 1995;73:443–62.

51. James NJ, Bignell CJ, Gillies PA. The reliability of self reported sexual behaviour. *AIDS* 1991;5:333–6.

52. Delamater J. Methodological issues in the study of pre-marital sexuality. *Sociol Methods Res* 1974;3:30–61.

53. Anderson B, Broffitt B. Is there a reliable and valid self-report measure of sexual behaviour? *Arch Sex Behav* 1988;17:509–25.

54. McFarlane M, St Lawrence JS. Adolescents' recall of sexual behaviour: consistency of self-report and effect of variations in recall duration. *J Adolesc Health* 1999;25:199–206.

55. Clark LR, Brasseux C, Richmond D, *et al.* Are adolescents accurate in self-report of frequencies of sexually transmitted diseases and pregnancies? *J Adolesc Health* 1997;21:91–6.

56. Capaldi D. The reliability of retrospective report for timing first sexual intercourse for adolescent males. *J Adolesc Health* 1999;11:375–87.

57. Rogers J. The rescission of behaviours: inconsistent responses in adolescent sexuality data. *Soc Sci Res* 1982;11:280–96.

58. Saltzman SP, Stoddard AM, McCusker J, *et al.* Reliability of self-reported sexual behavior risk factors for HIV infection in homosexual men. *Public Health Rep* 1987;102:692–7.

59. Bellak AS, Herson M. Self-report inventories in behavioural assessment. In: Cone JD, Hakins RP, eds. *Behavioral assessment: new directions in clinical psychology.* New York: Brunner Mazel, 1977.

60. Reading A. A comparison of the accuracy and reactivity of methods for monitoring male sexual behaviour. *J Sex Res* 1983;36:11–23.

61. Becker S, Begum S. Reliability study of reporting of days since last sexual intercourse in Matlab, Bangladesh. *J Biosoc Sci* 1994;26:291–9.

62. Jeannin A, Konings E, Dubois-Arber F, *et al.* Validity and reliability in reporting sexual partners and condom use in a swiss population survey. *Eur J Epidemiol* 1998;14: 139–46.

63. Van Duynhoven YTHP, Nagelkerke NJD, Van De Laar MJW. Reliability of self-reported sexual histories: test-retest and interpartner comparison in a sexually transmitted diseases clinic. *Sex Transm Dis* 1999;26:33–42.

64. Blake SM, Sharp SS, Temoshok L, *et al.* Methodological considerations in developing measures of HIV risk-relevant behaviours and attitudes; an empirical illustration. *Psychology and Health* 1992;6:265–80.

65. Coates RA, Soskolne CL, Calzavara L, *et al.* The reliability of sexual histories in AIDS-related research: evaluation of an interview-administered questionnaire. *Can J Public Health* 1986;77:343–8.

66. Kauth MR, St Lawrence JS, Kelly JA. Reliability of retrospective assessments of sexual HIV risk behavior: a comparison of biweekly, three-month, and twelve-month self-reports. *AIDS Educ Prev* 1991;3:207–14.

67. Catania JA, Binson D, Canchola J, *et al.* Effects of interviewer gender, interviewer choice, and item wording on responses to questions concerning sexual behaviour. *Public Opin Q* 1996;60:345–75.

68. Wadsworth J, Johnson AM, Wellings K, *et al.* What's in a mean?—an examination of the inconsistency between men and women reporting sexual partnerships. *J Roy Stat Soc* 1996;159:111–23.

69. Sanders SA, Reinisch JM. Would you say you "had sex" if. . .? *JAMA* 1999;281:275–7.

70. Abraham HD, Degli ES, Marino L. Seroprevalence of hepatitis C in a sample of middle class substance abusers. *J Addict Dis* 2000;18:77–87.

71. Appleby J. Poor control of AIDS spending. *BMJ* 1990;301: 509.

72. Potterat JJ, Phillips L, Muth JB. Lying to military physicians about risk factors for HIV infections. *JAMA* 1987;257: 1727.

73. Stoneburner RL, Chiasson MA, Solomon K, *et al.* Risk factors in military recruits positive for HIV antibody. *N Engl J Med* 1986;315:1355.

74. Gribble JN, Miller HG, Rogers SM, *et al.* Interview mode and measurement of sexual behaviors: methodological issues. *J Sex Res* 1999;36:16–24.

75. Johnson W, Delamater J. Response effects in sex surveys. *Public Opin Q* 1976;40:165–81.

76. Michael R, Ganon J, Laumann E, *et al. Sex in America: a definitive survey.* Boston: Little, Brown, 1994.

77. Konings E, Bantebya G, Carael M, *et al.* Validating population surveys for the measurement of HIV/STD prevention indicators. *AIDS* 1995;9: 375–82.

78. Padian NS, Shiboski SC, Glass SO, *et al.* Heterosexual transmission of human immunodeficiency virus (HIV) in Northern California: results from a ten year study. *Am J Epidemiol* 1997;146:350–7.

79. Ellish NJ, Weisman CS, Celentano D, *et al.* Reliability of partner reports of sexual history in a heterosexual population at a sexually transmitted diseases clinic. *Sex Transm Dis* 1996;23:446–52.

80. Zenilman JM, Weisman CS, Rompalo AM, *et al.* Condom use to prevent incident STDS: the validity of self-reported condom use. *Sex Transm Dis* 1995;22:15–21.

81. Herlitz CA, Steel JL. A decade of HIV/AIDS prevention in Sweden: changes in attitudes associated with HIV and sexual risk behaviour from 1987 to 1997. *AIDS* 2000;14:881–90.

82. Martin J, Ashworth K, Heath A. "Question wording effects on the British General Election Studies" Joint Centre for Survey Methods and Joint Unit for the Study of Social Trends, Occasional Paper, Number 1. 1991.

83. Binson D, Catania JA. Respondents understanding of the words used in sexual behavior questions. *Public Opin Q* 1998;62:190–208.

84. Bray F, Chapman S. Community knowledge, attitudes and media recall about AIDS, Sydney 1988 and 1989. *Aust J Public Health* 1991;15:107–13.

85. Paul C, Dickson N, Davis PB, *et al.* Heterosexual behaviour and HIV risk in New Zealand: data from a national survey. *Aust J Public Health* 1995;19:13–8.

86. Davis PB, Yee RL, Chetwynd J, *et al.* The New Zealand partner relations survey: methodological results of a national telephone survey. *AIDS* 1993;7:1509–16.

87. Bajos N, Spira A. Analysis of sexual behaviour in France (ACSF). A comparison between two modes of investigation: telephone survey and face-to-face survey. *AIDS* 1992;6:315–23.

88. Davoli M, Perucci CA, Sangalli M, *et al.* Reliability of sexual behavior data among high school students in Rome. *Epidemiology* 1992;3:531–5.

89. Tourangeau R, Smith TW. Asking sensitive questions. The impact of data collection mode, question format, and question context. *Public Opin Q* 1996;60:275–304.

90. Des Jarlais DC, Paone D, Milliken J, *et al.* Audio-computer interviewing to measure risk behaviour for HIV among injecting drug users: a quasi-randomised trial. *Lancet* 1999;353:1657–61.

91. Weeks MF. Computer assisted survey information collection: a review of CASIC methods and their implications for survey operations. *Journal of Official Statistics* 1992;8:445–65.

92. Turner CF, Ku L, Rogers SM, *et al.* Adolescent sexual behaviour, drug use and violence: increased reporting with computer survey technology. *Science* 1998;280:867–73.

93. McLaws M, Oldenburg B, Ross MW, *et al.* Sexual behaviour in AIDS-related research: reliability and validity of recall and diary measures. *J Sex Res* 1990;27:265–81.

94. Ramjee G, Weber AE, Morar NS. Recording sexual behaviour: comparison of recall questionnaires with a coital diary. *Sex Transm Dis* 1999;26:374–80.

95. Coxon APM. Parallel accounts? Discrepancies between self-report (diary) and recall (questionnaire) measures of the same sexual behaviour. *AIDS Care* 1999;11: 221–34.

READING 36
HIV Prevalence, Unrecognized Infection, and HIV Testing Among Men Who Have Sex with Men—Five U.S. Cities, June 2004–April 2005

Reported by: F Sifakis, PhD, Johns Hopkins Bloomberg School of Public Health, Baltimore; CP Flynn, ScM, Maryland Dept of Health and Mental Hygiene. L Metsch, PhD, Univ of Miami; M LaLota, MPH, Florida Dept of Health. C Murrill, PhD, New York City Dept of Health; BA Koblin, PhD, New York Blood Center, New York. T Bingham, MPH, Los Angeles County Dept of Health Svcs; W McFarland, MD, H Raymond, San Francisco Dept of Public Health, California. S Behel, MPH, A Lansky, PhD, B Byers, PhD, D MacKellar, MPH, A Drake, MPH, K Gallagher, DSc, Div of HIV/AIDS Prevention, National Center for HIV, STD, and TB Prevention, CDC.

Centers for Disease Control and Prevention. HIV Prevalence, Unrecognized Infection, and HIV Testing Among Men Who Have Sex with Men—Five U.S. Cities, June 2004—April 2005. *MMWR*. 2005;54:597–601. Available from http://www.cdc.gov/mmwr/preview/mmwrhtml/mm5424a2.htm.

Well into the third decade of the human immunodeficiency virus (HIV) epidemic, rates of HIV infection remain high, especially among minority populations. Of newly diagnosed HIV infections in the United States during 2003, CDC estimated that approximately 63% were among men who were infected through sexual contact with other men, 50% were among blacks, 32% were among whites, and 16% were among Hispanics (1). Studies of HIV infection among young men who have sex with men (MSM) in the mid to late 1990s revealed high rates of HIV prevalence, incidence, and unrecognized infection, particularly among young black MSM (2–4). To reassess those findings and previous HIV testing behaviors among MSM, CDC analyzed data from five of 17 cities participating in the National HIV Behavioral Surveillance (NHBS) system. This report summarizes preliminary findings from the HIV-testing component of NHBS, which indicated that, of MSM surveyed, 25% were infected with HIV, and 48% of those infected were unaware of their infection. To decrease HIV transmission, MSM should be encouraged to receive an HIV test at least annually, and prevention programs should improve means of reaching persons unaware of their HIV status, especially those in populations disproportionately at risk.

NHBS is an ongoing behavioral surveillance system that collects cross-sectional data among populations at high risk for acquiring HIV, including MSM, injection-drug users, and heterosexuals at high risk. Men aged ≥18 years were sampled systematically from randomly selected venues where MSM congregated (e.g., bars/clubs, organizations, and street locations). Formative research was conducted to identify venues and days and times when MSM frequented these venues (2–4). Men eligible for the survey were aged ≥18 years and residents of the metropolitan statistical area (MSA). Using a standardized questionnaire, men were interviewed about their sexual and drug-use behaviors, HIV-testing behavior, and use of -HIV-prevention services. During June 2004–April 2005, participants in five NHBS cities (Baltimore, Maryland; Los Angeles, California; Miami, Florida; New York, New York; and San Francisco, California) were also tested for HIV infection after informed consent.

The OraQuick® rapid test or an enzyme immunoassay (EIA) was used to screen blood specimens for HIV antibody, and initially reactive specimens were tested by Western blot for confirmation. To estimate HIV incidence, CDC used a serologic testing algorithm for recent HIV seroconversion (STARHS) (5). Specimens that were confirmed positive were tested further with the Vironostika-Less Sensitive (LS) EIA, which detects HIV infection approximately 170 days after initial infection by using a 1.0 standard optical density cutoff (95% confidence interval [CI] = 145–200 days) (6). A specimen confirmed positive by Western blot and nonreactive on the Vironostika-LS assay was categorized as an incident infection. Persons self-reporting a previous positive test result and HIV-positive participants reporting use of antiretroviral therapy were excluded from the incidence estimate.

Participants were asked about the date and result of their most recent HIV test before having their blood drawn as part of NHBS. Men who had not been tested during the preceding year were asked about their reasons for not being tested. MSM with unrecognized infection were defined as those who reported being HIV negative, indeterminate, or not knowing their HIV status, but who tested HIV positive at the time of their interview. Prevalence ratios and 95% CIs were calculated to evaluate characteristics associated with testing during the preceding year. Differences in reasons for not testing between HIV-negative MSM and MSM with unrecognized infection were assessed by using chi-square tests (p<0.05).

In the five cities, 2,261 men sampled from 258 venues participated in NHBS. The participation rate among eligible men was 83% (range by city: 69%–99%). A total of 1,767 (78%) were men who had one or more male sex partners and agreed to the survey, HIV test, and STARHS test (range by city:

222–462). Of these 1,767 participants, the median age was 32 years (range: 18–81 years); 35% were white, 27% Hispanic, 25% black, 7% multiracial/other, and 6% Asian/Pacific Islander. Participants were recruited at bars (30%), street locations (20%), dance clubs (19%), cafes/retail stores (10%), Gay Pride events (6%), social organizations (5%), gyms (5%), sex establishments (3%), and parks (1%).

Of the 1,767 MSM, 450 (25%) tested positive for HIV (range by city: 18%–40%). HIV prevalence was 46% among blacks, 21% among whites, and 17% among Hispanics. A total of 340 (76%) of those who were HIV positive were aged ≥30 years (Table 1). Of the 449 HIV-antibody–positive specimens tested by Vironostika-LS, 80 were nonreactive; of these, 31 were considered incident infections, and 49 were excluded from the incidence estimate. HIV incidence among MSM by city was as follows: Baltimore, 8.0% (95% CI = 4.2%–11.8%); Los Angeles, 1.4% (95% CI = 0.0%–2.9%); Miami, 2.6% (95% CI = 0.0%–5.6%); New York City, 2.3% (95% CI = 0.28%–4.2%); and San Francisco, 1.2% (95% CI = 0.0%–2.6%).

Of the 450 HIV-infected MSM, 217 (48%) were unaware of their HIV infections. The proportion of unrecognized HIV infection was highest among MSM who were aged <30 years, nonwhite, and surveyed in the four cities other than San Francisco (Table 1). Of the 217 MSM with unrecognized HIV infections, 64% were black, 18% Hispanic, 11% white, and 6% multiracial/other. The majority (184 [84%]) of the 217 MSM with unrecognized HIV infection had previously been tested for HIV; 145 (79%) reported that their most recent test result was negative, 33 (18%) were unknown, and six (3%) were indeterminate. Approximately 58% of MSM with unrecognized infections had not been tested during the preceding year. Compared with MSM who were HIV negative, proportionally more MSM with unrecognized infections had not been tested during the preceding year because they were afraid of learning they had HIV (34% versus 68%; p<0.0001) and were worried others would find out the result (14% versus 35%; p<0.0001) (Figure).

Nearly all participants (92%) reported previously being tested for HIV, and 64% reported being tested during the preceding year. MSM were more likely to have been tested during the preceding year if they had visited a health-care provider and their provider recommended an HIV test (Table 2). Sexual and drug-use behaviors were not associated with testing during the preceding year.

EDITORIAL NOTE

Consistent with previous studies of young MSM conducted in the same cities using similar sampling methods (2–4, 7, 8), this study revealed that 1) prevalence and incidence of HIV

TABLE 15-1 HIV Prevalence and Proportion of Unrecognized HIV Infection Among Men Who Have Sex with Men, by City, Age Group, and Race/Ethnicity— Five NHBS* Cities, June 2004–April 2005.

Characteristic	Total tested	HIV Prevalence		Unrecognized HIV Infection	
		No.	(%)	No.	(%)
City					
Baltimore	462	186	(40)	115	(62)
Los Angeles	382	73	(19)	31	(42)
Miami	222	41	(18)	19	(46)
New York City	336	62	(18)	32	(52)
San Francisco	365	88	(24)	20	(23)
Age group (yrs)					
18–24	410	57	(14)	45	(79)
25–29	303	53	(17)	37	(70)
30–39	585	171	(29)	83	(49)
40–49	367	137	(37)	41	(30)
≥ 50	102	32	(31)	11	(34)
Race/Ethnicity†					
White, non-Hispanic	616	127	(21)	23	(18)
Black, non-Hispanic	444	206	(46)	139	(67)
Hispanic	466	80	(17)	38	(48)
Multiracial	86	16	(19)	8	(50)
Other§	139	18	(13)	9	(50)
Total	**1,767**	**450**	**(25)**	**217**	**(48)**

*National HIV Behavioral Surveillance.

†Numbers for HIV prevalence do not add to 450 because of missing data in three records.

§Because of small sample sizes, category includes Asian/Pacific Islander, Native American/Alaska Native, and other.

infection in this population were high; 2) many HIV-infected MSM, particularly younger and black MSM, were unaware they were HIV-infected; and 3) among MSM with unrecognized infection, nearly half presumably acquired HIV during the preceding year, and many had not been tested recently because of fears of testing positive. These findings underscore the need to increase testing and improve primary prevention practices for MSM.

Although a majority of MSM had been tested during the preceding year, more than half with unrecognized infections had not had an annual test. The results of this study support CDC guidelines recommending at least annual testing for sexually active MSM (8), especially among younger MSM and minority populations (7).

The findings in this report are subject to at least four limitations. First, the date of a participant's most recent HIV test is self-reported and might be subject to reporting inaccuracies.

Second, given the sensitive nature of some questions, HIV status might have been underreported during the interview, thereby inflating estimates of unrecognized infections. Third, these findings are limited to men who frequented MSM-identified venues in the five selected cities during the survey period. Although similar rates of HIV incidence were observed compared with previous surveys (2), the limited number of incident cases prevents comparisons by race and age. Finally, data are preliminary and have not been weighted by venue-selection probability.

The 2004 NHBS system was conducted in 17 MSAs with the highest AIDS prevalence. Although this report focuses on testing results from five selected cities, behavioral data are forthcoming from all participating cities. NHBS is an important tool for monitoring the impact of the HIV epidemic and informing prevention efforts.

HIV incidence and prevalence are high among MSM, and many are unaware they are HIV positive. The high level of unrecognized HIV infections among MSM is a public health concern. Persons aware of their HIV infection often take steps to reduce their risk behaviors, which could reduce HIV transmission (9). To increase the proportion of HIV-positive persons who know they are infected, sexually active MSM should be encouraged to have an HIV test at least annually. Corresponding efforts should be developed to address barriers to testing, particularly those related to fear, and to increase the availability of testing in clinical and nonclinical settings (10). Testing programs should target both younger MSM and black MSM to reach populations disproportionately unaware they are HIV positive.

DISCUSSION QUESTIONS

1. Given the type of study NHBS is, what strengths and limitations do you see in the study design?

FIGURE 15-1 Reasons For Not Having an HIV Test During the Preceding 12 Months Among Men Who Have Sex With Men (MSM), by HIV-infected Status*—Five NHBS†, Cities§, June 2004–April 2005.

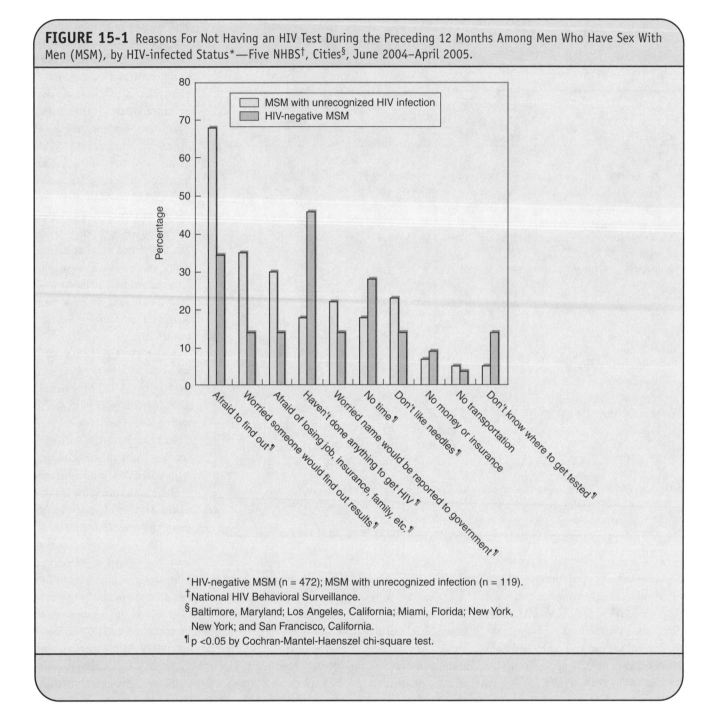

*HIV-negative MSM (n = 472); MSM with unrecognized infection (n = 119).
†National HIV Behavioral Surveillance.
§ Baltimore, Maryland; Los Angeles, California; Miami, Florida; New York,
   New York; and San Francisco, California.
¶ p <0.05 by Cochran-Mantel-Haenszel chi-square test.

2. Discuss the NHBS sampling strategy. Describe and then list strengths and limitations of this sampling scheme. What biases may emerge from this strategy? If you could quantitatively estimate the direction of this bias, what would you imagine could occur?

3. Looking at the incidence estimates by city, which of the cities statistically differ from the others? Rank the cities from lowest (1) to highest (5), and indicate statistically significant differences with an asterisk (*).

4. Information was collected by NHBS on respondent knowledge of HIV status. How did NHBS operationalize (define) "unrecognized infection"? Which biases may come into play when considering this factor?

5. Looking at the figure regarding reasons for not having an HIV test during the preceding 12 months, identify three potential public health actions you could take (as a public health provider) to increase counseling and testing behavior.

TABLE 15-2 Prevalence of HIV Testing During the Preceding Year Among Men Who Have Sex with Men, by Selected Characteristics—Five NHBS* Cities, June 2004–April 2005.

Characteristic	Total Previously Tested	Last HIV Test During Preceding Year No.	(%)	Prevalence Ratio	(95% CI†)
City					
Baltimore	404	260	64	1.00	Referent
Los Angeles	358	231	64	1.00	(0.90–1.11)
Miami	230	136	67	1.04	(0.92–1.17)
New York City	306	202	66	1.03	(0.92–1.14)
San Francisco	351	206	59	0.91	(0.81–1.02)
Age Group (yrs)					
18–24	350	285	81	1.00	Referent
25–29	285	200	70	0.86	(0.79–0.94)
30–39	547	330	60	0.74	(0.68–0.81)
40–49	346	180	52	0.64	(0.57–0.72)
≥ 50	94	40	43	0.52	(0.41–0.66)
Race/Ethnicity					
White, non-Hispanic	589	345	58	1.00	Referent
Black, non-Hispanic	391	254	65	1.11	(1.00–1.23)
Hispanic	422	289	68	1.17	(1.06–1.28)
Asian/Pacific Islander	85	55	65	1.10	(0.93–1.31)
Native American/Alaska Native	7	6	86	1.46	(1.07–2.00)
Multiracial	79	52	66	1.12	(0.95–1.34)
Other	34	25	74	1.26	(0.36–1.13)
Education					
< High School	142	97	68	1.00	Referent
High School or equivalent	343	227	66	0.97	(0.85–1.11)
> High School	1,135	709	62	0.91	(0.81–1.03)
Sexual Identity					
Homosexual	1,256	787	63	1.00	Referent
Bisexual	320	219	68	1.09	(1.00–1.19)
Health-insurance Status					
Private physician or HMO§	954	616	65	1.00	Referent
Public	149	91	61	0.95	(0.83–1.08)
None	495	312	63	0.98	(0.90–1.06)
Health-care Use					
Visited provider during Preceding Year					
No	317	156	49	1.00	Referent
Yes	1,305	879	67	1.37	(1.22–1.54)
Provider recommended HIV Test					
No	809	476	59	1.00	Referent
Yes	496	403	81	1.38	(1.29–1.48)
Most Recent HIV Test Result**					
Negative	1,285	874	68	1.00	Referent
Unknown	95	72	76	0.90	(0.80–1.01)
Total	**1,622**	**1,035**	**64**	—	—

*National HIV Behavioral Surveillance.
†Confidence interval.
§Health maintenance organization.
ˀAmong those who visited a health-care provider during the preceding year.
**Result of last HIV test before participation in NHBS.

REFERENCES FROM THE READING

1. CDC. HIV/AIDS surveillance report; 2003 (Vol. 15). Atlanta, GA: US Department of Health and Human Services, CDC; 2004. Available at http://www.cdc.gov/hiv/stats/2003SurveillanceReport.pdf.

2. CDC. HIV incidence among young men who have sex with men—seven U.S. cities, 1994–2000. MMWR 2001;50:440–4.

3. Valleroy LA, MacKellar DA, Karon JM, et al. HIV prevalence and associated risks in young men who have sex with men. JAMA 2000;284:198–204.

4. MacKellar DA, Valleroy LA, Secura GM, et al. Unrecognized HIV infection, risk behaviors, and perceptions of risk among young men who have sex with men: opportunities for advancing HIV prevention in the third decade of HIV/AIDS. J Acquir Immune Defic Syndr 2005;38:603–14.

5. Janssen RS, Satten GA, Stramer SL, et al. New testing strategy to detect early HIV-1 infection for use in incidence estimates and for clinical and prevention purposes. JAMA 1998;280:42–8.

6. Kothe D, Byers R, Caudill S, et al. Performance characteristics of a new less sensitive HIV-1 enzyme immunoassay for use in estimating HIV seroincidence. J Acquir Immune Defic Syndr 2003;33:625–34.

7. CDC. Unrecognized HIV infection, risk behaviors, and perceptions of risk among young black men who have sex with men—six U.S. cities, 1994–1998. MMWR 2002;51:733–6.

8. CDC. Revised guidelines for HIV counseling, testing, and referral. MMWR 2001;50(No. RR-19).

9. CDC. Advancing HIV prevention: new strategies for a changing epidemic—United States, 2003. MMWR 2003;52:329–32.

10. Spielberg F, Branson BM, Goldbaum GM, et al. Overcoming barriers to HIV testing: preferences for new strategies among clients of a needle exchange, a sexually transmitted disease clinic, and sex venues for men who have sex with men. J Acquir Immune Defic Syndr 2003;32:318–27.

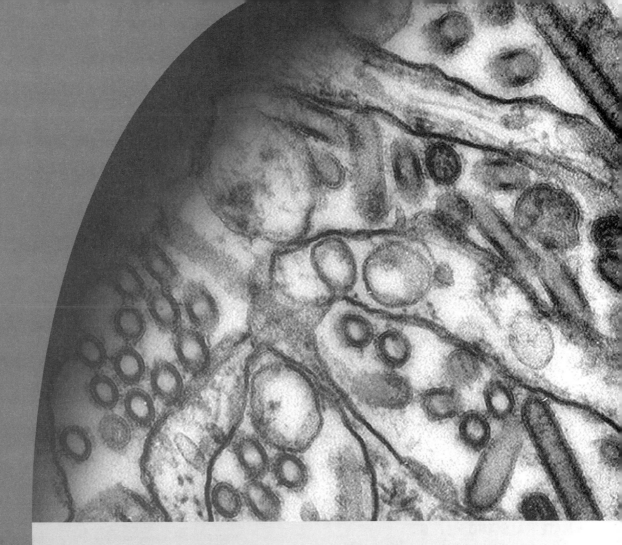

PART **XVI**

Using Computers to Improve Validity of Data Collection while Studying Behavior

Computers offer a potential approach to reducing social desirability bias, prevarication bias, misclassification, interviewer bias, and many, many more. Particularly in the arena of behavioral research—where the respondent's response is often the only way to obtain information and direct observation is impractical—computer-assisted approaches can be very valuable. Here are excerpted methods from three studies that evaluated the ability of computer-assisted self-interviewing (CASI) techniques to improve data validity.

READING 37
A Comparison Between Audio Computer-Assisted Self-Interviews and Clinician Interviews for Obtaining the Sexual History

Kurth, et al

Excerpted from Kurth AE, Martin DP, Golden MA, et al. A Comparison Between Audio Computer-Assisted Self-Interviews and Clinician Interviews for Obtaining the Sexual History. *Sexually Transmitted Diseases*. 2004;31:719–26.

MATERIALS AND METHODS

Study Design and Population

From June 2002 to February 2003, this cross-sectional study enrolled 609 attendees of the Seattle, Washington, public STD clinic who were 14 to 65 years old, being seen for assessment of a new problem, and able to understand spoken English. Participants completed an ACASI sexual history before their clinical examinations. During the clinical evaluation, nurse practitioners, physician assistants, or physicians (n = 15) conducted a standard-of-care sexual history using a checklist form but not scripted wording (some questions may not have been consistently asked by all clinicians). The responses charted during the clinician interview were later entered into an electronic clinic database. In addition to any clinician-ordered tests, evidence of gonococcal, chlamydial, or herpes simplex virus-2 infections and of vaginal trichomoniasis was ascertained using blood, urine, and vaginal fluid specimens collected from all respondents using standardized procedures. Participants were paid $25. The study was approved by the University of Washington Human Subjects Review Committee. The ACASI tool was explicitly designed to include the 177 parameters in the clinic's standard sexual history (CH), including queries about reasons for the visit, current symptoms, prior STIs, recent sexual activities (specific behaviors with main and other partners in the last 2 and 12 months), obstetric and gynecologic

history, and HIV risk questions. The ACASI and CH thus examined the same content. The ACASI assessment contained some additional items based on our theoretical model of STI risk. These included information about the last 3 sexual partners, condom use problems and stage of change, and brief screens for substance abuse (CAGE-AID) and depression (PRIME-MD). For the CH, separate behavioral risk modules were used for women, men who acknowledged sex only with women, and men who reported having sex with men (MSM). Patients themselves indicated their race and income on a self-administered clinic registration form. These designations were labeled on the CH form and became part of the clinic database but were not ascertained by any clinic staff.

Six of the clinical staff reviewed the content validity of the ACASI to ensure that the sequence of questions and question wording approximated typical use in this clinic. We first reviewed the current clinic form with key clinicians to capture how they "usually" asked the questions (e.g., "Tell me in your own words how you usually describe the 'symptoms' list."). We also solicited introductory, transitional, and normalizing language and a variety of verbal probes for particularly sensitive questions. Clinicians then reviewed the draft ACASI tool. Once this was completed, the final ACASI tool was programmed in Ci3 software (Sawtooth Technologies, Northbrook, IL). It was pilot-tested by 12 clinic patients (6 men and 6 women ranging in age from teens to 50s) to assess acceptability, comprehension, and navigation. Minor revisions from these debriefings were incorporated into the final instrument. Both the clinic form and the ACASI instrument can be viewed at http://depts.washington.edu/cfar/riskassess.

The ACASI presented 162 main items to all participants, with additional questions depending on participant characteristics and risk behaviors such as same-sex behavior or substance use. The sessions were completed on average within 36 minutes (range, 14–87 minutes; mode, 32 minutes). The participant completed several debriefing questions on the computer to assess interview preference and perceived reporting honesty. Research assistants approached clinic attendees in the waiting room using quota sampling to attain a 1:1 sex ratio for the first 100 participants. Thereafter, probability sampling was undertaken through a random selection algorithm whereby a quadrant of the room and a chair within that quadrant were selected to approach for the study using a random number assignment. Of 1705 individuals approached, 1134 were eligible. Reasons for ineligibility included not getting a full examination (generally these individuals had appointments for HIV testing only, partner notification follow up, or wart

treatment) and inability to understand English. Among those eligible, 626 (55.2%) agreed to participate. The main reason given for study refusal was lack of time. The research assistant reviewed the study purpose, obtained informed consent, and assisted the participant in an initial ACASI tutorial on a laptop computer in an examination room with a closed door. Participants were assured verbally, in the consent form, and during the ACASI itself that no one in the clinic would have access to the ACASI answers. After the tutorial, the assistant left the room to maximize participant privacy. On completion of the ACASI, participants underwent their clinical examination, during which the clinicians conducted the sexual history interview without access to ACASI results.

READING 38
Randomized Controlled Trial of Audio Computer-Assisted Self-Interviewing: Utility and Acceptability in Longitudinal Studies

Metzger, et al

Excerpted from Metzger DS, Koblin B, Turner C, et al. Randomized Controlled Trial of Audio Computer-Assisted Self-Interviewing: Utility and Acceptability in Longitudinal Studies. *Am J Epidemiol.* 2000;152:99–106.

MATERIALS AND METHODS

The Vaccine Preparedness Study (VPS) followed 3,257 gay men and 1,124 injection drug users. Enrollment took place in eight US cities between April and November 1995. To be eligible, gay men had to report anal intercourse during the previous year and drug users had to report injecting during the previous 6 months. Using a common protocol and uniform instruments, participants completed behavioral assessments, HIV testing, and risk reduction counseling at 6-month intervals during the 18-month study. Because this was a multisite study, it was also possible to examine the feasibility of using ACASI in a variety of settings and to test its acceptability among participants from two risk groups (gay men and IDUs) representing a broad range of sociodemographic characteristics.

Study participants were drawn from six of the VPS sites: two IDU sites (New York City, New York, and Philadelphia,

Pennsylvania) and four gay men's sites (New York City, New York; Chicago, Illinois; Seattle, Washington; and San Francisco, California). A total of 600 gay men (150 from each site) and 500 IDUs (250 from each site) were randomly selected for ACASI assessment. All subjects from these sites who were not selected for ACASI assessment served as controls. These sample sizes provided 95 percent power to reject the null within each risk group.

The IAQ version of the month 12 VPS questionnaire was used as the model for programming the ACASI. This questionnaire included nine demographic items, eight health questions, 31 questions about sexual activity, seven alcohol and noninjection drug use questions, and seven questions about injection drug use. Since many of these items had multiple questions incorporated within them, the questionnaire included more than 258 individual items and a complex skip pattern. The questionnaire was designed for administration in about 30 minutes by trained interviewers. The ACASI version incorporated identical question sequence and skip patterns using a wording as similar as possible to those found in the IAQ version. Several items that required text responses were dropped from the ACASI, and some optional probes were not included. For estimation of the frequency of specific sexual activities during the follow-up interval, the ACASI offered assistance to participants who desired help in calculating the frequency. This help was modeled after the manner in which interviewers had been trained to provide such assistance by calculating a total frequency based upon estimates of frequency during a shorter time interval (e.g., per week) and then examining the total and recalculating if warranted. The ACASI interviews were completed using desktop computers located in private areas of the study sites.

At the data collection visit, a standardized administration protocol was implemented. After confirmation of group assignment, this protocol required trained staff to provide participants with a brief orientation to the system and to complete the registration of the participant by entering the subject's study identification and date of administration. All participants then completed five practice questions with staff present. These practice questions were designed to provide examples of each type of response (continuous, categorical, dichotomous) contained in the interview. After successful completion of the practice questions, the participant was left alone to complete the assessment and was told to contact staff who remained easily accessible in case of questions or problems. Research staff were instructed to remain available but not to directly observe the respondent during the ACASI completion.

Data were saved on the hard drive of the computer as the respondent moved from one section of the questionnaire to another. At the end of the interview, the data were saved onto a diskette, and all data from the hard drive were copied onto tape backups at the close of each day in which data had been collected. Data from all sites were regularly transferred via modem to a central database.

At the close of the ACASI interview, subjects were asked to complete a two-page, self-administered acceptability questionnaire, which asked about problems they might have encountered in using the ACASI. The acceptability questionnaire also asked respondents to indicate which mode of questionnaire administration they would prefer for future assessments, which mode they felt best protected the privacy of their responses, and which mode would elicit the most honest responses.

To test the hypothesis of equivalence, responses from subjects assigned to the ACASI condition were compared with responses from controls who completed the questionnaire via interviewer administration. For this test, a limited set of risk-related items were selected prior to study implementation. These items assessed behaviors considered to be the most sensitive to response biases and socially desirable reporting. For the gay men, the following questions were selected: 1) any unprotected receptive anal intercourse; and 2) sexual activity with any HIV-positive partner. For the IDUs, the questions were 1) injecting at a rate equal to or greater than one time per week; 2) any sharing of syringes; 3) use of a syringe after another person without cleaning it; and 4) not using the needle exchange program. As stated, equivalence between the two modes of administration was defined as ACASI reports of equal or greater frequency. Thus, the null hypotheses for these analyses was that the ACASI would yield significantly lower rates of reporting on these items. The null specified a minimum tolerable odds ratio of 0.80 and thus would be rejected if the odds ratio for the collection of key variables was greater than 0.80. Secondary objectives of feasibility and acceptability were assessed by descriptive analyses of participant responses to the acceptability questionnaire.

READING 39
Application of Computer-Assisted Interviews to Sexual Behavior Research

Kissinger, et al

Excerpted from Kissinger P, Rice J, Farley T, et al. Application of Computer-assisted Interviews to Sexual Behavior Research. *Am J Epidemiol.* 1999;149:950–4.

MATERIALS AND METHODS

Women attending a New Orleans, Louisiana, public family planning or sexually transmitted disease clinic from July 1995 to July 1996, who were enrolled in an infertility prevention co-

hort study and who provided consent were included. Enrollment criteria for the cohort study were ages 15–50 years; *Chlamydia trachomatis-positive* by GenProbe (San Diego, California), Chlamydiazyme (Abbott Laboratories, North Chicago, Illinois) or urine ligase chain reaction test; and no prior treatment for that episode of *C. trachomatis* infection. Women were administered a closed-ended survey via both FTFI and touch-screen V-CASI in a crossover design. Eight questions (four socially undesirable, two socially desirable, and two neutral behaviors) were chosen for analysis. Women were randomized to receive either FTFT or V-CASI first by using a randomized systematic allocation method. Upon completion of that interview, the other type of interview was immediately administered.

The questionnaire was developed by a multicenter group of investigators from New Orleans, Louisiana; Birmingham, Alabama; Seattle, Washington; San Francisco, California; and Indianapolis, Indiana, working on the Centers for Disease Control and Prevention Infertility Prevention Study. The purpose of that study was to determine factors associated with recurrent *C. trachomatis* infection. According to the SMOG technique, the survey was at a fourth-grade reading level.

FACE-TO-FACE INTERVIEWS

The FTFT was administered by a study staff composed of six female interviewers aged 21–30 years, of whom four were African American and two were Caucasian. All of the interviewers received training using a multicentered protocol, and the quality of interview technique was monitored through weekly meetings and data integrity checks.

COMPUTER INTERVIEW

Toolbook development software was used to create the video-assisted questionnaire with questions used verbatim from the FTFT questionnaire. Possible responses were printed on the screen and read by an audible voice with a video picture of the reader (a young African-American woman) in the top right corner of the screen, and responses were highlighted as read to assist the viewer.

The respondents chose their answers either by touching the touch-sensitive video monitor or by using the computer mouse. An introductory question was included for training purposes, allowing the participant to practice operating the computer before beginning the real questionnaire. A response was required for each question before the subject could go to the next question. Study personnel were available to respond to any questions about the video questionnaire.

DISCUSSION QUESTIONS

1. Compare and contrast the three approaches above, based on the methods shown. How are they similar? How do they differ?

2. Each of the studies uses a different "gold standard" for the "truth"—what is each of them? What are the strengths/limitations for each?

3. Design two hypothetical studies:

   a. The first study to examine the utility of CASI to improve the collection of data regarding adherence to medication for tuberculosis (in the absence of directly observed therapy).

   b. The second to compare audio CASI to video CASI in the collection of sexual and illicit drug use behavior among adolescent males. What might be some of the strengths and weaknesses of this study? What are specific concerns based on the target population?

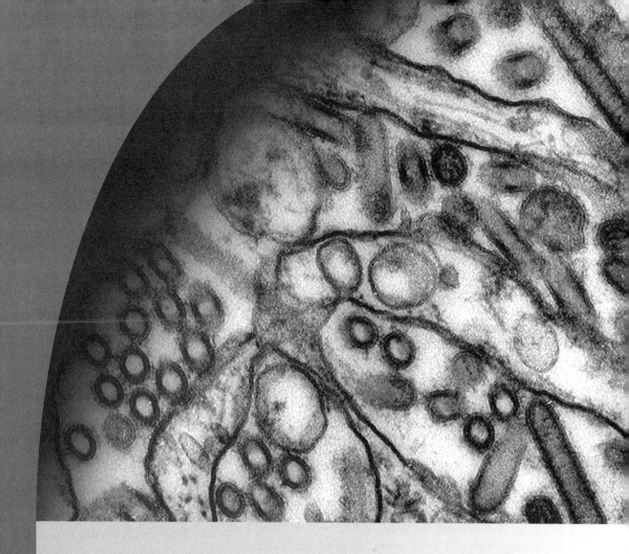

Exercises

EXERCISE 1
Creating an HIV Prevention Program

Your mission:

You and your research team have been asked to create an HIV prevention plan for a mid-sized city. You will need to develop a specific program for each of the target populations listed here. Describe your program comprehensively so that the details are clear and presentable. Also describe an evaluation plan for your program. This plan should include study design and handling of the relevant epidemiologic methods issues (e.g., bias). This exercise can be done alone but works particularly well as a group exercise with three to five participants.

Characteristics of the city are as follows:

- There is currently only very weak, incomplete AIDS surveillance in this region, with no HIV surveillance.
- HIV prevalence (based on estimation models) is thought to be high (approximately 4%); incidence differs by target population.
- Anecdotally, the most common mode of HIV transmission is heterosexual transmission. Maternal to child transmission (MTCT) is concomitantly high. Injecting drug user (IDU) is also thought to be a problem; however, IDU is highly stigmatized in this area, and most users are unlikely to access medical care. Estimates of transmission via this mode are thought to be invalid. Similarly, religious concerns have made homosexual HIV transmission highly stigmatized as well.
- You cannot establish/recreate the entire surveillance system, but you can use your program to augment/expand it if you think it wise or if it is necessary for evaluation of your prevention program.
- You have $350,000 annually to spend on your program (assume that these approximate US dollars). This in-

cludes salaries, fringe benefits, buildings, transportation, incentives infrastructure, and supplies, etc.*

- Primary health care and antenatal care are well used in this community; however, there are no public sexually transmitted disease (STD) clinics, and STDs are heavily stigmatized.

Groups will develop prevention programs specific to each of the following:

Group 1:   IDU
Group 2:   heterosexual transmission
Group 3:   MTCT
Group 4:   homosexual transmission

Your goals are to do the following:

- Develop and implement a program designed to reduce HIV transmission among your target population.
- Develop and implement a means of evaluating whether your program "works" to reduce HIV transmission.

For each population, cover the following issues:

- Type of program (category, e.g., biomedical, behavioral, and structural, as well as specifics)
- Rationale for selecting this type of prevention program
- Goals and objectives (be specific!)
- Program plan (what you will be doing)
- Staffing/resources
- Method of evaluation (can include revision/expansion of surveillance system, within your budget)
- Strengths
- Limitations/challenges

---

*You do not have to cost out your program, but be mindful that this isn't a lot of money; thus, you need to be aware of cost constraints, have specific goals and objectives, and so forth.

EXERCISE 2
Logic Model Development

Your mission:

For each of the programs developed in Exercise 1, create an accompanying logic model. You may use any format you choose; here is a sample of a United Way logic model as a reference. In case you need additional resources, here are several easily accessible ones:

The American Journal of Evaluation: http://aje.sagepub.com/.

A Practical Guide to Evaluation and Evaluation Terms for Ryan White CARE Act Grantees, Report #4, September 1999.

CDC Evaluation Working Group has listed multiple evaluation resources and references: www.cdc.gov/eval/index.htm.

Centers for Disease Control and Prevention. Framework for Program Evaluation in Public Health. *MMWR* 1999;48: 1–40, http://www.cdc.gov/eval/framework.htm.

Centers for Disease Control and Prevention. Evaluating CDC HIV Prevention Programs—Volume 2: Supplemental Handbook 1999. www.cdc.gov.

Outcomes Evaluation Technical Assistance Guide: Primary Medical Care Outcomes, developed for the HIV/AIDS Bureau, Division of Service Systems, 1999.

Outcomes Evaluation Technical Assistance Guide. Getting Started: Titles I and II of the Ryan White CARE Act, 2001. Available through the HRSA/HAB website at http://www.hab.hrsa.gov.

Outcomes Evaluation Technical Assistance Guide Case. Management Outcomes: Titles I and II of the Ryan White CARE Act, 2001. Available through the HRSA/HAB website at http://www.hab.hrsa.gov.

U.S. Department of Health and Human Services. Centers for Disease Control and Prevention. Office of the Director, Office of Strategy and Innovation. Introduction to program evaluation for public health programs: A self-study guide. Atlanta, GA: Centers for Disease Control and Prevention, 2005.

Evaluation Guidance Handbook: Strategies for Implementing the Evaluation Guidance for CDC-Funded HIV Prevention Programs; March 2002.

Medical Outcomes Trust Instruments: http://www.outcomes-trust.org

United Way of America. Measuring Program Outcomes: A Practical Approach. 1996; Alexandria, Virginia.

United Way's Outcome Measurement Resource Network, http://national.unitedway.org/outcomes.

W.K. Kellogg Foundation Evaluation Handbook. Battle Creek, Michigan: W.K. Kellogg Foundation, 1998. http://wkkf.org/Publications/evalhdbk.

EXERCISE 2. TABLE: Sample United Way Logic Model for Hypothetical HIV/AIDS Program for Adolescents

Inputs	Activities	Outputs	Outcomes
Inputs are the resources dedicated to or consumed by program: • Dollars from grant • Donations to this nonprofit • Staff time and expertise • Peer educators • Condoms • Outreach brochures • Mobile van and personnel • Adolescent-specific HIV primary care clinic • 24 hour on-call providers, including mental health staff	**Activities** are services the program provides; how the program will use the inputs it has to achieve its goals: • Innovative outreach program using vans to go outside of schools, with consent of school system • Culturally competent print media and condoms, developed by peer educators, and assessed by target population • Linkage agreement with adolescent-specific HIV primary care clinic	**Outputs** are the products of the program's activities and services, in a tangible, day-to-day sense: • Mobile outreach • Peer education • Adolescent males aged 13 to 24 given condoms, brochures, outreach • Peer education contacts • HIV tests (including pre- and post-test counseling) • Number of new HIV+ clients identified • Referrals made to clinical partner • Number of clients engaged in care • Number of clients retained in care	**Outcomes** are benefits or changes in participants during or after involvement in program activities. These may be divided into program- and client-level. On the basis of the nature of this example, client-level outcomes are provided. These are generally broken down into initial, intermediate, and long-term outcomes, and quantified where possible: **Initial:** • Expose at least 100 adolescents per month to culturally appropriate HIV 101 materials • Provide condom packets to at least 100 new adolescent males per month • Screen at least 50 adolescent males for HIV each month • Identify at least one HIV+ male aged 13 to 24 years identified per quarter and link into adolescent-specific HIV care **Intermediate:** • Increased safer sex behavior among adolescent males, based on survey data • For HIV+, adherence with recommended treatments and retention in care **Long-term:** • Improvements in condom use and drug use behavior • Reduced HIV (and other STD) risk • Improvements in health care utilization demonstrated by engagement and retention in care (for HIV+) • Improvements in adherence to antiretroviral regimens

EXERCISE 3
Identifying Study Designs

Your mission:

Below is an assortment of abstracts obtained from a literature search. For each of the following studies:
Identify the study design.

1. Identify the outcome (dependent variable) and exposure (independent variable).
2. Suggest at least one other study design that could address same question, and discuss the relative strengths and limitations versus what was presented.
3. Suggest one possible bias that may be present.
4. Suggest potential confounders.
5. Suggest potential effect modifiers.

For some of these you may not be able to answer some of these questions. Try going to the original source (citations are provided) and looking at each study in its entirety. Can you improve on the abstract that was provided? This is an enjoyable exercise to work on in pairs or small groups for those of you who are interested in doing so.

(For some of these, the reference to the study design in the titles has been removed to force you to look at the information provided and not simply on what the authors named their article. There are varying usages—not just epidemiologic study design references—for some words, such as cases, con- trols, cohort, prospective, and others. Do not let these distract you from what study design you are looking at: The design is what counts, more even than what it is being dubbed.)

Looking only at the abstracts is never enough! One should always read the whole article in order to understand the methods, the strengths and limitations, and the findings of the study. These are for practice only to help you become more comfortable and fluid with looking at study design and brainstorming about potential limitations. It is important that whenever citing the literature you always go to the source: It is not enough to go to an abstract or even to go to another article where the research was cited. You need to con- sult the original source to be sure that you are seeing all there is to see and understanding all the methods, findings, and implications. (It is also worth mentioning that abstracts fre- quently incorrectly portray the research. This often occurs because the abstracts are not updated after the article is com- pleted, space considerations prevent a full explication of the work, or for other reasons.) Always trust yourself and your own critical evaluation instead of relying on an abstract (or another author) alone.

As a refresher, here are the study designs at a glance table, as you think through each of these designs.

EXERCISE 3. TABLE: Study Designs at a Glance

Categorization based on:	Exposure of interest is:	Direction	Design type	Measure of association*
Exposure	Randomly assigned by study	Prospective; follow forward in time for outcomes of interest.	Randomized controlled trial	Relative risk (RR)
Exposure	Self-selected by participant	Prospective; follow forward in time for outcomes of interset.	Concurrent cohort (aka prospective cohort)	Relative risk (RR)
Exposure	Self-selected by participant	Retrospective; both exposures *and* outcomes have occurred at the time the study starts; however, at the time of the exposure, the outcome has NOT yet occurred.	Nonconcurrent cohort (aka retrospective cohort)	Relative risk (RR)
Disease	Self-selected by participant	Retrospective; both exposures *and* outcomes have occurred at the time the study starts; in almost every case, at the time of the exposure assessment, the outcome HAS already occurred.	Case-control	Odds ratio (OR)
Disease	Self-selected by participant	Snapshot; data on exposure and outcome collected simultaneously. Exposure assessment may inquire about temporal sequence, but no additional timepoint data are available.	Cross-sectional	Prevalence odds ratio (POR)
Exposure	Self-selected by participant	Snapshot; data on exposure and outcome collected simultaneously. Exposure assessment can inquire about temporal sequence, but no additional timepoint data are available.	Cross-sectional	Prevalence Ratio (PR)

*Depending on analysis, other measures may also be used. These come from the 2×2 table, however.

INCREASED RISK OF INCIDENT HIV DURING PREGNANCY IN RAKAI, UGANDA: A [   ] STUDY

Gray RH, Li X, Kigozi G, et al.

Summary

Background. HIV acquisition is significantly higher during pregnancy than in the postpartum period. We did a [   ] study to estimate HIV incidence rates during pregnancy and lactation.

Methods. We assessed 2188 HIV-negative sexually active women with 2625 exposure intervals during pregnancy and 2887 intervals during breastfeeding, and 8473 non-pregnant and non-lactating women with 24 258 exposure intervals. Outcomes were HIV incidence rates per 100 person years and incidence rate ratios estimated by Poisson multivariate regression, with the non-pregnant or non-lactating women as the reference group. We also assessed the husbands of the married women to study male risk behaviours.

Findings. HIV incidence rates were 2·3 per 100 person years during pregnancy, 1·3 per 100 person years during breast-feeding, and 1·1 per 100 person years in the non-pregnant and non-lactating women. The adjusted incidence rate ratios were 2·16 (95% CI 1·39–3·37) during pregnancy and 1·16 (0·82–1·63) during breastfeeding. Pregnant women and their male partners reported significantly fewer external sexual partners than did the other groups. In married pregnant women who had a sexual relationship with their male spouses, the HIV incidence rate ratio was 1·36 (0·63–2·93). In married pregnant women in HIV-discordant relationships (ie, with HIV-positive men) the incidence rate ratio was 1·76 (0·62–4·03).

Interpretation. The risk of HIV acquisition rises during pregnancy. This change is unlikely to be due to sexual risk behaviours, but might be attributable to hormonal changes affecting the genital tract mucosa or immune responses. HIV prevention efforts are needed during pregnancy to protect mothers and their infants.

Lancet 2005;366:1182–88.

PSYCHOLOGICAL RESPONSES OF PREGNANT WOMEN TO AN INFECTIOUS OUTBREAK: A [   ] STUDY OF THE 2003 SARS OUTBREAK IN HONG KONG

Lee DTS, Sahota D, Leung TN, et al.

Objective: The aim of the present study was to examine the behavioral and psychological responses of pregnant women during the 2003 severe acute respiratory syndrome (SARS) outbreak in Hong Kong. Methods: Ethnographic interviews were first conducted to identify the common psychological and behavioral responses to the outbreak. This was followed by a [   ] study of 235 consecutive pregnant women recruited during the SARS epidemic, and a historical cohort of 939 pregnant women recruited a year before the outbreak. Both cohorts completed standardized rating scales on depression, anxiety, and social support. Results: Women in the SARS cohort adopted behavioral strategies to mitigate their risk of contracting infection. However, pregnant women tended to overestimate the risk of contracting SARS and nearly a third of the women were homebound. The anxiety level of the SARS cohort was slightly higher than that of the pre-SARS control. No statistical difference was found between the depression levels of the two cohorts. Conclusion: The improved social support experienced by pregnant women during SARS might have buffered the stress associated with an outbreak. However, clinicians should monitor for overestimation of infectious risk among pregnant women.

Journal of Psychosomatic Research 2006;61:707–713.

HIGH RATES OF SYPHILIS AMONG STI PATIENTS ARE CONTRIBUTING TO THE SPREAD OF HIV-1 IN INDIA

Reynolds SJ, Risbud AR, Shepherd ME, et al.

Background: Recent syphilis outbreaks have raised concern regarding the potential enhancement of HIV transmission. The incidence of syphilis and its association with HIV-1 infection rates among a cohort of sexually transmitted infection (STI) clinic attendees was investigated.

Methods: 2732 HIV-1 seronegative patients attending three STI and one gynaecology clinic, were enrolled from 1993–2000 in an ongoing [   ] study of acute HIV-1 infection in Pune, India. At screening and quarterly follow up visits, participants underwent HIV-1 risk reduction counseling, risk behaviour assessment and HIV/STI screening that included testing for serological evidence of syphilis by RPR with TPHA confirmation. Patients with genital ulcers were screened with dark field microscopy.

Results: Among 2324 participants who were HIV-1 and RPR seronegative at baseline, 172 participants were found to have clinical or laboratory evidence of syphilis during follow up (5.4 per 100 person years, 95% CI 4.8 to 6.5 per 100 person years). Independent predictors of syphilis acquisition based on a Cox proportional hazards model included age less than 20 years, lack of formal education, earlier calendar year of follow up, and recent HIV-1 infection. Based on a median follow up time of 11 months, the incidence of HIV-1 was 5.8 per 100 person years (95% CI 5.0 to 6.6 per 100 person years). Using a Cox proportional hazards model to adjust for known HIV risk factors, the adjusted hazard ratio of HIV-1 infection associated with incident syphilis was 4.44 (95% CI 2.96 to 6.65; p, 0.001).

Conclusions: A high incidence rate of syphilis was observed among STI clinic attendees. The elevated risk of HIV-1 infection that was observed among participants with incident syphilis supports the hypothesis that syphilis enhances the sexual transmission of HIV-1 and highlights the importance of early diagnosis and treatment of syphilis.

Sex Transm Infect 2006;82:121–126.

STANDARDIZED INCIDENCE RATES OF SURGICAL SITE INFECTION: A MULTICENTER STUDY IN THAILAND

Kasatpibal N, Jamulitrat S, Chongsuvivatwong V for The Surgical Site Infection Study Group.

Background: No previous multicenter data regarding the incidence of surgical site infection (SSI) are available in Thailand. The magnitude of the problem resulting from SSI at the national level could not be assessed. The purpose of this study was to estimate the incidence of SSI in 9 hospitals, together with patterns of surgical antibiotic prophylaxis, risk factors for SSI, and common causative pathogens.

Methods: A prospective data collection among patients undergoing surgery in 9 hospitals in Thailand was conducted. The National Nosocomial Infection Surveillance (NNIS) system criteria and method were used for identifying and diagnosing SSI. The SSI rates were benchmarked with the NNIS report by means of indirect standardization and reported in terms of standardized infection ratio (SIR). Antibiotic prophylaxis was categorized into preoperative, intraoperative, and postoperative. Risk factors for SSI were evaluated using multiple logistic regression models.

Results: From July 1, 2003, to February 29, 2004, the study included 8764 patients with 8854 major operations and identified 127 SSIs, yielding an SSI rate of 1.4 infections/100 operations and a corresponding SIR of 0.6 (95% CI: 0.5–0.8). Of these, 35 SSIs (27.6%)were detected postdischarge. The 3 most common operative procedures were cesarean section, appendectomy, and hysterectomy. The 3 most common pathogens isolated were Escherichia coli, Staphylococcus aureus, and Pseudomonas aeruginosa, which accounted for 15.3%, 8.5%, and 6.8% of infections, respectively. The 3 most common antibiotics used for prophylaxis were ampicillin/amoxicillin, cefazolin, and gentamicin. The proportion of types of antibiotic prophylaxis administered were 51.6% preoperative, 24.3% intraoperative, and 24.1% postoperative. Factors significantly associated with SSI were high degree of wound contamination, prolonged preoperative hospital stay, emergency operation, and prolonged duration of operation.

Conclusion: Overall SSI rates were less than the average NNIS rates. The causative pathogens of SSI were different from those of other reports. There was a crucial proportion of operations that did not comply with the antibiotic guidelines. The risk factors for SSI identified in this study were consistent with most other reports.

Am J Infect Control 2005;33:587–94.

INVASIVE GROUP B STREPTOCOCCAL DISEASE IN MARYLAND NURSING HOME RESIDENTS

Henning KJ, Hall EL, Dwyer DM, et al. Kelly J. Henning,1,a Elvira L. Hall,1,5,a

Between 1991 and 1995, among 999 nonpregnant adult Maryland residents with group B Streptococcus (GBS) isolated from a normally sterile site, 84 resided in nursing homes (NHs). The age-adjusted annual incidence of GBS infection (per 100,000 population) among those > 65 years old was 72.3 for NH residents and 17.5 for community residents (relative risk, 4.1;). < P .001 Thirty-four case patients resided in 11 NHs with > 2 cases; 1 NH had 8 case patients within 22 months. Six of 8 case patients from 3 NHs had serotype V GBS. Molecular sub-

typing of several isolates identified 2 case patients in 1 NH with identical subtype patterns. NH residents have a markedly higher incidence of invasive GBS than do community residents > 65 years old and may serve as a target group for immunization when GBS vaccines become available. Further evaluation of intra-NH transmission of GBS is warranted.

Journal of Infectious Diseases 2001;183:1138–42.

OUTBREAK OF HEPATITIS B IN A NURSING HOME ASSOCIATED WITH CAPILLARY BLOOD SAMPLING

Dreesman JM, Bailloti A, Hamschmidt L, et al.

In 2001, two residents of a nursing home in Lower Saxony, Germany, were diagnosed with acute hepatitis B virus (HBV) infection. A systematic contact investigation of 188 residents yielded 19 confirmed or probable cases of acute or recent HBV infection and three persistent asymptomatic HBsAg carriers. Sequence analysis revealed that one carrier had high viraemia (109 genomes/ml), HBV genotype A2, and the same S gene and/or X gene sequence as 16 acutely infected persons. An unmatched case-control study was conducted with the 17 cases that had sequence identity together with 26 controls. The strongest association was found for treatment by a particular general practitioner (GP) (OR > 11, $P < 0.001$) and blood sampling for glucose monitoring on a particular day by the GP's staff (OR 13.6, $P < 0.001$, adjusted OR 8.5, $P = 0.017$). Control measures were implemented. Serological controls after 6 and 18 months revealed that the outbreak was brought under control.

Epidemiol Infect 2006;134:1102–1113.

DECLINE IN INVASIVE PNEUMOCOCCAL DISEASE AFTER THE INTRODUCTION OF PROTEIN–POLYSACCHARIDE CONJUGATE VACCINE

Whitney CG, Farley MM, Hadler J, et al.

Background

In early 2000, a protein–polysaccharide conjugate vaccine targeting seven pneumococcal serotypes was licensed in the United States for use in young children.

Methods

We examined population-based data from the Active Bacterial Core Surveillance of the Centers for Disease Control and Prevention to evaluate changes in the burden of invasive disease, defined by isolation of Streptococcus pneumoniae from a normally sterile site. Serotyping and susceptibility testing of isolates were performed. We assessed trends using data from seven geographic areas with continuous participation from 1998 through 2001 (population, 16 million).

Results

The rate of invasive disease dropped from an average of 24.3 cases per 100,000 persons in 1998 and 1999 to 17.3 per 100,000 in 2001. The largest decline was in children under two years of age. In this group, the rate of disease was 69 percent lower in 2001 than the base-line rate (59.0 cases per 100,000 vs. 188.0 per 100,000, P < 0.001); the rate of disease caused by vaccine and vaccine-related serotypes declined by 78 percent (P < 0.001) and 50 percent (P < 0.001), respectively. Disease rates also fell for adults; as compared with base line, the rate of disease in 2001 was 32 percent lower for adults 20 to 39 years of age (7.6 cases per 100,000 vs. 11.2 per 100,000, P < 0.001), 8 percent lower for those 40 to 64 years of age (19.7 per 100,000 vs. 21.5 per 100,000, P = 0.03), and 18 percent lower for those 65 years of age or more (49.5 per 100,000 vs. 60.1 per 100,000, P < 0.001).

The rate of disease caused by strains that were not susceptible to penicillin was 35 percent lower in 2001 than in 1999 (4.1 cases per 100,000 vs. 6.3 per 100,000, P < 0.001).

Conclusions

The use of the pneumococcal conjugate vaccine is preventing disease in young children, for whom the vaccine is indicated, and may be reducing the rate of disease in adults. The vaccine provides an effective new tool for reducing disease caused by drug-resistant strains.

N Engl J Med 2003;348:1737–46.

IMPACT OF *ACINETOBACTER* INFECTION ON THE MORTALITY OF BURN PATIENTS

Albrecht MA, Griffith ME, Murray CK, et al.

Background: *Acinetobacter calcoaceticus-baumannii* complex (Acb) is recognized as an important cause of nosocomial infections. Although Acb can be associated with multidrug resistance, its impact on mortality in burn patients has not been fully elucidated.

Study Design: In a [   ] study assessing medical records and microbiology laboratory data at a US military tertiary care burn center, we evaluated all patients admitted to the burn center between January 2003 and November 2005. Data collected included age, severity of burn, comorbidities, length of stay, and survival to hospital discharge. In addition, microbiology data were reviewed to determine which patients were infected with Acb during this time frame. These data were then used to compare patients infected with Acb to patients not infected. Multivariate analysis using logistic regression was performed to determine which patient characteristics were associated with increased mortality.

Results: There were 802 patients included in the study. Fifty-nine patients met the case definition for infection. An ad-

ditional 52 patients were found to be colonized with Acb. Patients with Acb infection had more severe burns and comorbidities, and had longer lengths of stay compared with patients without Acb or those with Acb colonization. Mortality in infected patients was higher compared with those without infection (relative risk 2.86, < 0.001). On multivariate analysis, infection with Acb was not statistically associated with mortality.

Conclusions: Multidrug-resistant Acb is a common cause of nosocomial infection in the burn patient population. Despite this, it does not independently affect mortality.

J Am Coll Surg 2006;203:546–550.

PROLONGED OUTBREAK OF GIARDIASIS WITH TWO MODES OF TRANSMISSION

Katz DE, Heisey-Grove D, Beach M, et al.

Large outbreaks of giardiasis caused by person-to-person transmission, or a combination of transmission routes, have not previously been reported. A large, prolonged giardiasis outbreak affected families belonging to a country club in a suburb of Boston, Massachusetts, during June–December 2003. We conducted a [   ] study to determine the source of this outbreak. Giardiasis-compatible illness was experienced by 149 (25%) respondents to a questionnaire, and was laboratory confirmed in 97 (65%) of these cases. Of the 30 primary cases, exposure to the children's pool at the country club was significantly associated with illness (risk ratio 3.3, 95% confidence interval 1.7–6.5). In addition, 105 secondary cases probably resulted from person-to-person spread; 14 cases did not report an onset date. This outbreak illustrates the potential for Giardia to spread through multiple modes of transmission, with a common-source outbreak caused by exposure to a contaminated water source resulting in subsequent prolonged propagation through person-to-person transmission in the community. This capacity for a common-source outbreak to continue propagation through secondary person-to-person spread has been reported with Shigella and Cryptosporidium and may also be a feature of other enteric pathogens having low infectious doses.

Epidemiol Infect 2006;134:935–941.

SAFETY OF TRIVALENT INACTIVATED INFLUENZA VACCINE IN CHILDREN 6 TO 23 MONTHS OLD

Hambidge SJ, Glanz JM, France EK, et al.

Context. Beginning with the winter season of 2004–2005, influenza vaccination has been recommended for all children 6 to 23 months old in the United States. However, its safety in young children has not been adequately studied in large populations.

Objective. To screen for medically attended events in the clinic, emergency department, or hospital after administration of trivalent inactivated influenza vaccine in children 6 to 23 months old.

Design, Setting, and Participants. [   ] Using self-control analysis, with chart review of significant medically attended events at 8 managed care organizations in the United States that comprise the Vaccine Safety Datalink. Participants were all children in the Vaccine Safety Datalink cohort 6 to 23 months old who received trivalent inactivated influenza vaccine between January 1, 1991, and May 31, 2003 (45 356 children with 69 359 vaccinations).

Main Outcome Measure. Any medically attended event significantly associated with trivalent inactivated influenza vaccine in risk windows 0 to 3 days, 1 to 14 days (primary analysis), 1 to 42 days, or 15 to 42 days after vaccination, compared with 2 control periods, one before vaccination and the second after the risk window. All individual *ICD-9* codes as well as predefined aggregate codes were examined.

Results. Before chart review, only 1 diagnosis, gastritis/duodenitis, was more likely to occur in the 14 days after trivalent inactivated influenza vaccine (matched odds ratio [OR], 5.50; 95% confidence interval [CI], 1.22–24.81 for control period 1, and matched OR, 4.33; 95% CI, 1.23–15.21 for control period 2). Thirteen medically attended events were less likely to occur after trivalent inactivated influenza vaccine, including acute upper respiratory tract infection, asthma, bronchiolitis, and otitis media. After chart review, gastritis/duodenitis was not significantly associated with trivalent inactivated influenza vaccine (matched OR, 4.00; 95% CI, 0.85–18.84 for control period 1; matched OR, 3.34; 95% CI, 0.92–12.11 for control period 2).

Conclusions. In the largest population-based study to date of the safety of trivalent inactivated influenza vaccine in young children, there were very few medically attended events, none of which were serious, significantly associated with the vaccine. This study provides additional evidence supporting the safety of universally immunizing all children 6 to 23 months old with influenza vaccine.

JAMA 2006;296:1990–1997.

EFFECT OF HIGHLY ACTIVE ANTIRETROVIRAL THERAPY ON MULTIPLE AIDS-DEFINING ILLNESSES AMONG MALE HIV SEROCONVERTERS

Cain LE, Cole SR, Chmiel JS, et al.

The effect of highly active antiretroviral therapy (HAART) on multiple acquired immunodeficiency syndrome (AIDS)–defining illnesses remains unclear. Between 1984 and 2005, 573 male human immunodeficiency virus seroconverters in four US urban centers were followed for a median of 9.7 years. During follow-up, 345, 113, 50, and 65 men incurred 0, 1, 2, and > 2 AIDS-defining illnesses, respectively. The authors extend the Cox proportional hazards model to determine whether the effect of HAART, as measured by calendar periods, persists beyond the first AIDS-defining illness. After adjustment for race and age at seroconversion, the hazards of a first through third AIDS-defining illness in the HAART calendar period (beyond July 1995) were 0.31 (95% confidence interval (CI): 0.21, 0.46), 0.39 (95% CI: 0.22, 0.74), and 0.33 (95% CI: 0.14, 0.79), respectively, relative to the monotherapy and combination therapy reference calendar period (January 1990–July 1995) and therefore did not attenuate with the number of prior AIDS-defining illnesses (p for homogeneity = 0.83). After the authors averaged over multiple AIDS-defining illnesses, the hazard of an AIDS-defining illness in the HAART calendar period was 0.34 (95% CI: 0.25, 0.45) relative to the reference calendar period. HAART protects against initial and subsequent AIDS-defining illnesses, whose inclusion in analysis markedly increased the precision of the estimated hazard ratio.

Am J Epidemiol 2006;163:310–315.

IMPACT OF PERMETHRIN-TREATED BED NETS ON MALARIA, ANEMIA, AND GROWTH IN INFANTS IN AN AREA OF INTENSE PERENNIAL MALARIA TRANSMISSION IN WESTERN KENYA

Ter Kuile FO, Terlouw DJ, Kariuki SK, et al.

As part of a community-based, [   ] trial of insecticide-treated bed nets (ITNs) in an area with intense malaria transmission in western Kenya, a birth cohort(n = 833) was followed monthly until the age of 24 months to determine the potential beneficial and adverse effects of reduced malaria exposure during pregnancy and infancy. Malaria transmission and morbidity were comparable pre-intervention. The ITNs reduced malaria attack rates (force of infection) in infancy by 74%, and delayed the median time-to-first parasitemia (4.5 to 10.7 months; $P < 0.0001$). The incidence of both clinical malaria and moderate-severe anemia (hemoglobin level < 7 g/dL) were reduced by 60% ($P < 0.001$ for both). Protective efficacy was greatest in infants less than three months old and similar in older infants and one-year-old children. Efficacy was lowest in the dry season. Infants from ITN villages experienced better height and weight gain. In areas of intense perennial malaria transmission, ITNs substantially reduce exposure to malaria and subsequent malaria-associated morbidity in children less than 24 months old. Reduced malaria exposure during infancy did not result, with continued ITN use, in increased malaria morbidity in one-year-old children.

Am J Trop Med Hyg 2003;68(Suppl 4):68–77.

EFFICACY OF AN ACELLULAR PERTUSSIS VACCINE AMONG ADOLESCENTS AND ADULTS WARD

Ward JI, Cherry JD, Chang S-J, et al.

Background: Pertussis immunization of adults may be necessary to improve the control of a rising burden of disease and infection. This trial of an acellular pertussis vaccine among adolescents and adults evaluated the incidence of pertussis, vaccine safety, immunogenicity, and protective efficacy.

Methods: Bordetella pertussis infections and illnesses were prospectively assessed in 2781 healthy subjects between the ages of 15 and 65 years who were enrolled in a national multicenter, randomized, double-blind trial of an acellular pertussis vaccine. Subjects received either a dose of a tricomponent acellular pertussis vaccine or a hepatitis A vaccine (control) and were monitored for 2.5 years for illnesses with cough that lasted for more than 5 days. Each illness was evaluated with use of a nasopharyngeal aspirate for culture and polymerase-chain-reaction assay, and serum samples from patients in both acute and convalescent stages of illness were analyzed for changes in antibodies to nine B. pertussis antigens.

Results: Of the 2781 subjects, 1391 received the acellular pertussis vaccine and 1390 received the control vaccine. The groups had similar ages and demographic characteristics, and the median duration of follow-up was 22 months. The acellular pertussis vaccine was safe and immunogenic. There were 2672 prolonged illnesses with cough, but the incidence of this nonspecific outcome did not vary between the groups, even when stratified according to age, season, and duration of cough. On the basis of the primary pertussis case definition, vaccine protection was 92 percent (95 percent confidence interval, 32 to 99 percent). Among unimmunized controls with illness, 0.7 percent to 5.7 percent had B. pertussis infection, and the percentage increased with the duration of cough. On the basis of other case definitions, the incidence of pertussis in the controls ranged from 370 to 450 cases per 100,000 person-years.

Conclusions: The acellular pertussis vaccine was protective among adolescents and adults, and its routine use might reduce the overall disease burden and transmission to children.

N Engl J Med 2005;353: 1555–63.

PREVALENCE TRENDS IN CHLAMYDIAL INFECTIONS AMONG YOUNG WOMEN ENTERING THE NATIONAL JOB TRAINING PROGRAM, 1998–2004

Joesoef MR, Mosure DJ.

Objectives: To assess the trends and risk factors of chlamydial infections in disadvantaged women aged 16 to 24 years entering a national job training program.

Goal: To assess the impact of chlamydia screening program on chlamydia trend.

Study Design: The authors calculated the prevalence of Chlamydia by demographic and geographic characteristics from 106,377 women who were screened from 1998 through 2004.

Results: Chlamydia prevalence was inversely associated with age, decreasing from 12.7% in women aged 16 to 17 years to 6.6% in women aged 22 to 24 years. Blacks had the highest prevalence (13.1%). Chlamydia prevalence significantly decreased from 11.7% in 1998 to 10.0% in 2003 and then slightly increased to 10.3% in 2004. After direct standardization and adjustment for the laboratory test type, a similar trend was observed by age and race/ethnicities.

Conclusions: Among disadvantaged women aged 16 to 24 years entering a national job training program, the chlamydia prevalence and racial disparities in prevalence were consistently high from 1998 to 2004, especially among younger black women.

Sexually Transmitted Diseases 2006;33:571–575.

ENDEMICALLY ACQUIRED FOODBORNE OUTBREAK OF ENTEROTOXIN-PRODUCING *ESCHERICHIA COLI* Serotype O169:H41

Devasia RA, Jones TF, Ward J, et al.

Purpose: Enterotoxigenic *Escherichia coli* (ETEC) is traditionally recognized as a common cause of traveler's diarrhea, but is becoming a more frequent cause of foodborne disease outbreaks in the United States. It is important for public health practitioners and clinicians to be aware of ETEC as a domestic cause of gastroenteritis. We investigated a foodborne disease outbreak to understand the epidemiology of ETEC in this setting.

[   ] Methods: We conducted a study of 63 employees of Company A. A case was defined as an employee who experienced diarrhea or vomiting or fever and cramps after eating a catered meal at Company A from August 14th-15th. A standardized questionnaire was administered to cases and controls.

Results: Of 63 employees, 36 met the case definition (attack rate 57.1%). Diarrhea (94%) and cramps (74%) were common, whereas vomiting was not (3%). Mean duration of illness was 2.7 days. Coleslaw at the August 15th lunch was significantly associated with illness (odds ratio 4.4, 95% CI 1.1–17). Stool specimens were positive for heat-stable enterotoxin-producing *E. coli* O169:H41. Contamination likely occurred at the point of service.

Conclusions: This outbreak illustrates the changing epidemiology of enterotoxigenic *E. coli* and the importance for healthcare practitioners to consider ETEC as a potential cause of domestically acquired gastroenteritis.

American Journal of Medicine 2006;119:168.e7–168.e10.

AN OUTBREAK OF MULTIDRUG-RESISTANT *PSEUDOMONAS AERUGINOSA* ASSOCIATED WITH INCREASED RISK OF PATIENT DEATH IN AN INTENSIVE CARE UNIT

Bukholm G, Tannæs T, Kjelsberg ABB, Smith-Erichsen N

Objective: To investigate an outbreak of multidrug resistant. *Pseudomonas aeruginosa* in an intensive care unit (ICU).

Design: Epidemiologic investigation, environmental assessment, and [   ] study.

Setting: A secondary-care university hospital with a 10-bed ICU.

Patients: All patients admitted to the ICU receiving ventilator treatment from December 1, 1999, to September 1, 2000.

Results: An outbreak in an ICU with multidrug-resistant isolates of *P. aeruginosa* belonging to one amplified fragment length polymorphism (AFLP)–defined genetic cluster was identified, characterized, and cleared. Molecular typing of bacterial isolates with AFLP made it possible to identify the outbreak and make rational decisions during the outbreak period. The outbreak included 19 patients during the study period. Infection with bacterial isolates belonging to the AFLP cluster was associated with reduced survival (odds ratio, 5.26; 95% confidence interval, 1.14 to 24.26). Enhanced barrier and hygiene precautions, cohorting of patients, and altered antibiotic policy were not sufficient to eliminate the outbreak. At the end of the study period (in July), there was a change in the outbreak pattern from long (December to June) to short (July) incubation times before colonization and from primarily tracheal colonization (December to June) to primarily gastric or enteral (July) colonization. In this period, the bacterium was also isolated from water taps.

Conclusion: Complete elimination of the outbreak was achieved after weekly pasteurization of the water taps of the ICU and use of sterile water as a solvent in the gastric tubes.

Infect Control Hosp Epidemiol 2002;23:441–446.

RISK FACTORS FOR HOSPITAL-ACQUIRED METHICILLIN-RESISTANT STAPHYLOCOCCUS AUREUS BACTERAEMIA: A [   ] STUDY

Carnicer-Pont D, Bailey KA, Masoni BW, et al.

A [   ] study was undertaken in an acute district general hospital to identify risk factors for hospital-acquired bacteraemia caused by methicillin-resistant Staphylococcus aureus (MRSA). Cases of hospital-acquired MRSA bacteraemia were defined as consecutive patients from whom MRSA was isolated from a blood sample taken on the third or subsequent day after admission. Controls were randomly selected from patients admitted to the hospital over the same time period with a length of stay of more than 2 days who did not have bacteraemia. Data

on 42 of the 46 cases of hospital-acquired bacteraemia and 90 of the 92 controls were available for analysis. There were no significant differences in the age or sex of cases and controls. After adjusting for confounding factors, insertion of a central line [adjusted odds ratio (aOR) 35.3, 95% confidence interval (CI) 3.8–325.5] or urinary catheter (aOR 37.1, 95% CI 7.1–193.2) during the admission, and surgical site infection (aOR 4.3, 95% CI 1.2–14.6) all remained independent risk factors for MRSA bacteraemia. The adjusted population attributable fraction, showed that 51% of hospital-acquired MRSA bacteraemia cases were attributable to a urinary catheter, 39% to a central line, and 16% to a surgical site infection. In the United Kingdom, measures to reduce the incidence of hospital-acquired MRSA bacteraemia in acute general hospitals should focus on improving infection control procedures for the insertion and, most importantly, care of central lines and urinary catheters.

Epidemiol Infect 2006;134:1167–1173.

EBOLA HEMORRHAGIC FEVER IN KIKWIT, DEMOCRATIC REPUBLIC OF THE CONGO: CLINICAL OBSERVATIONS IN 103 PATIENTS

Bwaka MA, Bonnet M-J, Calain P, et al.

During the 1995 outbreak of Ebola hemorrhagic fever in the Democratic Republic of the Congo, a series of 103 cases (one-third of the total number of cases) had clinical symptoms and signs accurately recorded by medical workers, mainly in the setting of the urban hospital in Kikwit. Clinical diagnosis was confirmed retrospectively in cases for which serum samples were available ($n = 63$, 61% of the cases). The disease began unspecifically with fever, asthenia, diarrhea, headaches, myalgia, arthralgia, vomiting, and abdominal pain. Early inconsistent signs and symptoms included conjunctival injection, sore throat, and rash. Overall, bleeding signs were observed in .45% of the cases. Typically, terminally ill patients presented with obtundation, anuria, shock, tachypnea, and normothermia. Late manifestations, most frequently arthralgia and ocular diseases, occurred in convalescent patients. This series is the most extensive number of cases of Ebola hemorrhagic fever observed during an outbreak.

Journal of Infectious Diseases 1999;179:(Suppl 1):S1–7.

WHEN TO INITIATE HIGHLY ACTIVE ANTI-RETROVIRAL THERAPY: A [   ] APPROACH

Ahdieh-Grant L, Yamashita TE, Phair JP, et al.

The appropriate immunologic stage of human immunodeficiency virus infection at which to initiate highly active anti-retroviral therapy (HAART) among asymptomatic persons is a core question. A [   ] approach using longitudinal data from the US Multicenter AIDS Cohort Study was used to mimic a clinical trial to assess the risk of acquired immunodeficiency syndrome (AIDS) by timing of therapy. Three treatment groups were defined according to CD4 + count (cells/l) at HAART initiation between July 1995 and January 2000: < 200 (deferral to < 200, n = 127), 200–349 (deferral to 200–349, n = 130), and 350–499 (immediate treatment, n = 92). Survival analysis was used to compare time to AIDS between groups from the index visit until July 2000. The index visit for the immediate group was the one prior to HAART initiation. For the deferral groups, the index visit was a randomly selected, pre-HAART, AIDS-free visit after July 1990 at which CD4+ counts were 350–499 cells/mm^3. This strategy accounted for lead time bias. Compared with immediate treatment, the relative hazards of AIDS were 2.68 (p = 0.003) and 1.05 (p = 0.897) for deferral to < 200 cells/mm^{3}l and 200–349 cells/mm^3, respectively. These results support recent US public health guidelines for deferring HAART initiation until a count of < 350 cells/mm^3. Furthermore, results suggest a potential threshold for HAART initiation in the neighborhood of 275 cells/mm^3.

Am J Epidemiol 2003;157:738–746.

INCREASE IN CONDOM USE AND DECLINE IN HIV AND SEXUALLY TRANSMITTED DISEASES AMONG FEMALE SEX WORKERS IN ABIDJAN, COTE D'IVOIRE, 1991–1998

Ghys PD, Diallo MO, Ettiegne-Traore V, et al.

Objective: To assess clinic- and community-based trends in demographic and behavioral characteristics and clinic-based trends in HIV infection and other sexually transmitted diseases (STD) in female sex workers in Abidjan, Cote d'Ivoire.

Design: Multiyear [   ] study of first-time attenders in Clinique de Confiance, a confidential STD clinic; biannual community-based behavioral surveys.

Methods: From 1992 to 1998, female sex workers were invited to attend Clinique de Confiance, where they were counseled, interviewed, clinically examined during their first visit and tested for STD and HIV infection. Community-based surveys, conducted in 1991, 1993, 1995, and 1997, interviewed women regarding socio-demographic characteristics and HIV/STD-related knowledge, attitudes and behavior.

Results: Among female sex workers in Abidjan, there was a trend toward shorter duration of sex work, higher prices, and more condom use. Among sex workers attending Clinique de Confiance for the first time, significant declines were found in the prevalence of HIV infection (from 89 to 32%), gonorrhoea (from 33 to 11%), genital ulcers (from 21 to 4%), and syphilis (from 21 to 2%). In a logistic regression model that controlled for socio-demographic and behavioral changes, the year of screening remained significantly associated with HIV infection.

Conclusion: The increase in condom use and the decline in prevalence of HIV infection and other STD may well have resulted from the prevention campaign for female sex workers, and such campaigns should therefore be continued, strengthened, and expanded.

AIDS 2002;16:251–8.

EXERCISE 4
Getting Started with Critical Evaluation of the Literature

After you have read the STROBE statement, select your favorite article in infectious disease and dissect it, assessing it for the criteria discussed in the article. Then answer the following questions comprehensively. Do not evaluate it superficially or consider the *obvious* methodological issues at hand; delve deeply into the methods used and consider every element of research question at hand, study design, program or study implementation, data collection instruments and techniques (e.g., CASI vs. face-to-face interview), analytic techniques, and interpretation. Then address each of the following points in the context of the STROBE statement:

1. Comprehensively describe
   a. The study methods

   b. Null and alternative hypotheses
   c. Research questions
   d. Dependent and independent variables selected for study
   e. Confounders and effect modifiers (explored, actual)
   f. Operationalization of all variables
   g. Study design
   h. Biases emerging from methodological approach
   i. Analytic approach (if there are terms you do not understand, consult a biostatics text book, or even the internet so that you understand the basics of it. For this exercise, you do not need to be an expert in the analytic methods undertaken, but you

should always know basically what each technique is doing. For example, is it evaluating categorical, count, scaled, nonnormally or normally distributed continuous variables? Does it assess survival, panel, or time-series data? If you understand the basics of what the technique is looking at—even in broad strokes—you will understand the paper's epidemiologic methods far better than if you skip over the statistical considerations section. As you become more familiar with reading the literature, this section will matter to you more and more: As many biases or problems can be had in the study design, so, too, can there be in the analysis. Also in the interpretation!)

    j. Limitations

    k. And how they were assessed. For example, if selection bias is a limitation, how was it demonstrated to be present/absent? If there were refusals to enter the study, were individuals who refused to participate different from those that did participate?

    l. Strengths

    m. How the study either did or did not reduce any biases present

    n. Cow this bias might be expected to affect estimates deriving from the study

2. Propose another study that will overcome the bias addressed by the study (e.g., same research question with a better design). Do not use the same design the authors already used!

EXERCISE 5
Name That Study Design

Your mission:

For each of the following study descriptions, identify the study design, exposure, and outcome. Each of the designs has many potential biases (some which would emerge of course in the methods section of the article more than may be apparent here). For each, identify at least one primary potential bias the reader should be alert for.

1. It is 2000, and a study is initiated. The study includes 4,000 women and is designed to evaluate the association between *Trichomonas vaginalis* (a sexually transmitted disease) and transmission of Hepatitis B. Women were followed for three years. 2,000 had *T vaginalis* at baseline; 2,000 did not. Those that had the STD were treated. Women were all Hepatitis B-negative at the baseline study visit (via serologic testing). The women were followed every three months and given clinical and laboratory evaluations, including screening for *T vaginalis*, behavioral questionnaires, and repeated serology. Women who became infected with Hepatitis B were provided with primary care and safer sex counseling. All women consented to participate in the study.

2. A new screening test has been developed to identify HIV+ people at risk for lipodystrophy as a side effect of HAART. A study to assess the screening test is developed, and 2,000 HIV+ individuals participate in a study, while at their routine primary care visits. Among the 500 who screen positive, 150 had a screen indicating at least some degree of risk. Among those who screened negative, 50 were diagnosed with the condition.

3. Parents of 75 HIV+ children with developmental delay and 150 without developmental delay are interviewed to assess their exposure to malaria prophylaxis *in utero*. Exposure assessment is conducted via interview and medical record abstraction.

4. Investigators were concerned that increased formula availability in a developing country would result in decreased breastfeeding of newborns, which could result in increased morbidity and mortality associated with lack of passive immunity through breast milk. Sales of formula and admits to local hospitals and deaths related to diarrheal illnesses of infants ≤ 6 months of age are compared between provinces with/without formula to evaluate this question.

5. A cohort of 1,800 HIV+ males who have been seen in a clinic-based cohort since 1990 is followed. Semen and blood specimens taken at baseline were banked. A new genotyping test is available to assess ARV resistance patterns and their association with time to progression to AIDS.

6. A survey is conducted in which participants are asked about their condom use and sexual behavior. The participants were randomly sampled from the voter

registration and DMV databases and contacted by telephone.

7. HIV+ women are recommended to have Pap smears (screening for cervical cancer) every six months because of their increased risk of this cancer. Some HIV+ women (like their uninfected counterparts) are on hormone replacement therapy. A prospective study is done to see whether there is an association between HRT and cervical or endometrial cancer. Women with signs or symptoms of cancer are given Pap smears as needed, even if not during the six month visits.

8. A new birth defect potentially associated with prenatal exposure to an experimental drug to mitigate symptoms of influenza has been proposed. Infants are categorized on the basis of presence/absence of the defect. At the time of birth women are asked whether they took the medication and, if so, how much. They are also asked about x-rays, alcohol, tobacco, illicit drug use, and exercise behavior and nutrition during pregnancy.

9. A cohort of adolescents IDUs with Hepatitis C is assembled at ten different centers throughout the U.S. The study accepts all infected persons < 25 years of age and will treat and follow them forward until age 34. Investigators are interested in exploring the "hit early—hit hard" approach to therapy.

10. Investigators are conducting a study of a new behavioral intervention to increase risk reduction behavior among African American males who have sex with males (MSM). Following provisions of informed consent, participants are randomly assigned to a control group—where they discuss general issues—and a motivational interviewing condition in which participants learn, through the MI technique, how to improve condom negotiation skills. Participants that do not come for at least two of the group sessions are excluded from the analysis as they did not receive the "treatment." Of the 456 eligible individuals contacted, only 80 wish to participate.

EXERCISE 6
Evaluating a Public Health Surveillance Program

In 2001, the Centers for Disease Control and Prevention issued updated guidelines for the evaluation of public health surveillance systems. These guidelines offer concrete guidance for evaluating surveillance programs in general. Given that infectious disease represents one major domain under domestic and international surveillance, working to improve surveillance systems is of critical concern. Looking to the full document (available at www.cdc.gov; see below citation) is strongly encouraged. Here are definitions of the key attributes—simplicity, flexibility, data quality, acceptability, sensitivity, predictive value positive, representativeness, timeliness, and stability—that guide the evaluation of surveillance programs. These attributes are defined below (excerpted from the guidelines themselves) and may be used in evaluating a public health surveillance system.

Indicate the Level of Usefulness

Definition

A public health surveillance system is useful if it contributes to the prevention and control of adverse health-related events, including an improved understanding of the public health implications of such events. A public health surveillance system can also be useful if it helps to determine that an adverse health-related event previously thought to be unimportant is actually important. In addition, data from a surveillance system can be useful in contributing to performance measures, including health indicators that are used in needs assessments and accountability systems. . . .

Does the system

- Detect diseases, injuries, or adverse or protective exposures of public importance in a timely way to permit accurate diagnosis or identification, prevention or treatment, and handling of contacts when appropriate?

- Provide estimates of the magnitude of morbidity and mortality related to the health-related event under surveillance, including the identification of factors associated with the event?

- Detect trends that signal changes in the occurrence of disease, injury, or adverse or protective exposure, including detection of epidemics (or outbreaks)?

- Permit assessment of the effect of prevention and control programs?

- Lead to improved clinical, behavioral, social, policy, or environmental practices? or
- Stimulate research intended to lead to prevention or control?

Describe Each System Attribute

Simplicity

Definition

The simplicity of a public health surveillance system refers to both its structure and ease of operation. Surveillance systems should be as simple as possible while still meeting their objectives.

Flexibility

Definition

A flexible public health surveillance system can adapt to changing information needs or operating conditions with little additional time, personnel, or allocated funds. Flexible systems can accommodate, for example, new health-related events, changes in case definitions or technology, and variations in funding or reporting sources. In addition, systems that use standard data formats (e.g., in electronic data interchange) can be easily integrated with other systems and thus might be considered flexible.

Data Quality

Definition

Data quality reflects the completeness and validity of the data recorded in the public health surveillance system.

Acceptability

Definition

Acceptability reflects the willingness of persons and organizations to participate in the surveillance system.

Sensitivity

Definition

The sensitivity of a surveillance system can be considered on two levels. First, at the level of case reporting, sensitivity refers to the proportion of cases of a disease (or other health-related event) detected by the surveillance system. Second, sensitivity can refer to the ability to detect outbreaks, including the ability to monitor changes in the number of cases over time.

Predictive Value Positive

Definition

Predictive value positive (PVP) is the proportion of reported cases that actually have the health-related event under surveillance.

Representativeness

Definition

A public health surveillance system that is representative accurately describes the occurrence of a health-related event over time and its distribution in the population by place and person.

Timeliness

Definition

Timeliness reflects the speed between steps in a public health surveillance system.

Stability

Definition

Stability refers to the reliability (i.e., the ability to collect, manage, and provide data properly without failure) and availability (the ability to be operational when it is needed) of the public health surveillance system.

Exercise 6. TABLE: Checklist for Evaluating Public Health Surveillance Systems

Tasks for evaluating a surveillance system*	Page(s) in this report
☐ Task A. Engage the stakeholders in the evaluation	
☐ Task B. Describe the surveillance system to be evaluated	
☐ 1. Describe the public health importance of the health-related event under surveillance	
☐ a. Indices of frequency	
☐ b. Indices of severity	
☐ c. Disparities or inequities associated with the health-related event	
☐ d. Costs associated with the health-related event	
☐ e. Preventability	
☐ f. Potential future clinical course in the absence of an intervention	
☐ g. Public interest	
☐ 2. Describe the purpose and operation of the surveillance system	
☐ a. Purpose and objectives of the system	
☐ b. Planned uses of the data from the system	
☐ c. Health-related event under surveillance, including case definition	
☐ d. Legal authority for data collection	
☐ e. The system resides where in organization(s)	
☐ f. Level of integration with other systems, if appropriate	
☐ g. Flow chart of system	
☐ h. Components of system	
☐ 1) Population under surveillance	
☐ 2) Period of time or data collection	
☐ 3) Data collection	
☐ 4) Reporting sources of data	
☐ 5) Data management	
☐ 6) Data analysis and dissemination	
☐ 7) Patient privacy, data confidentiality, and system security	
☐ 8) Records management program	
☐ 3. Describe the resources used to operate the surveillance system	
☐ a. Funding source(s)	
☐ b. Personnel requirements	
☐ c. Other resources	
☐ Task C. Focus the evaluation design	
☐ 1. Determine the specific purpose of the evaluation	
☐ 2. Identify stakeholders who will receive the findings and recommendations of the evaluation	
☐ 3. Consider what will be done with the information generated from the evaluation	
☐ 4. Specify the questions that will be answered by the evaluation	
☐ 5. Determine standards for assessing the performance of the system	
☐ Task D. Gather credible evidence regarding the performance of the surveillance system	
☐ 1. Indicate the level of usefulness	
☐ 2. Describe each system attribute	
☐ a. Simplicity	
☐ b. Flexibility	
☐ c. Data quality	
☐ d. Acceptability	
☐ e. Sensitivity	

continues

Exercise 6. TABLE: Checklist for Evaluating Public Health Surveillance Systems (continued)

Tasks for evaluating a surveillance system*	Page(s) in this report
☐ f. Predictive value positive	
☐ g. Representativeness	
☐ h. Timeliness	
☐ i. Stability	
☐ Task E. Justify and state conclusions, and make recommendations	
☐ Task F. Ensure use of evaluation findings and share lessons learned	

*Adapted from *Framework for Program Evaluation in Public Health* [CDC. Framework for program evaluation in public health. MMWR 1999;48(RR-11)] and the original guidelines [CDC. Guidelines for evaluation surveillance systems. MMWR 1988;37(No. S-5)].

Source: MMWR 2001;50(No. RR-13);1–36.

Your mission:

Go to www.cdc.gov and search under *Surveillance.* Identify any one disease of your liking for which there is an existing surveillance system. Evaluate the information provided, including forms, reports, description, evaluations, etc., and summarize that system with regard to each of the aforementioned key attributes. On the basis of your first impression, would your evaluation reveal the surveillance system to be useful? What do you think needs to be addressed in order to increase the system's usefulness?

Now take a disease for which you do not see a national (U.S. or other) surveillance system described. Create the skeleton of the system and consult the full guidelines to develop measures and outcomes, in order to evaluate it.

Index

A

absolute risk, translating relative risk estimates into, 195–196

abstract, in observational studies, STROBE recommendations, 176–177

acquiescence bias, 243

additive model, 187

AIDS (acquired immune deficiency syndrome), 88. *See also* HIV (human immunodeficiency virus)

alert, automated, in public health surveillance system, 78

alternative hypothesis, 228

Althomsons, S., 116–121

Altman, D. G., 172–202

American Dental Association, 46

American Medical Association, 46

American Public Health Association, 46

American Red Cross, 46

analytic methods. *See also* STROBE Statement

Anderson, K., 127–131

Annals of Internal Medicine, 198

antimicrobials, 235

antimony, and vomiting, 164

antiviral medications, resistance to, in 2007–2008, 39–40

applicability, 200

Archer, D. L., 143

Arnold, K., 127–131

association, measures of, 197

Astrovirus, 150

    foodborne illness statistics, 137, 138

audio computer-assisted self-interviews (ACASI)

    vs. clinician interviews, for obtaining sexual history, 254–255

    randomized control trials, in longitudinal studies, 255–256

automated alert, in public health surveillance system, 78

B

Bacillus cereus, 144–145, 153

    and diarrhea, 164

    foodborne illness statistics, 137, 138

    and vomiting, 164

background rate, establishing in outbreak investigations, 69–70

backward deletion strategy, 195

bacterial pathogens, foodborne illness from, 144–148

Baigent, C., 62

Bajos, N., 243

Barthell, E., 108–114

behavior, onset in disease outbreak, 77–78

Behel, S., 247–249

Belmont Report

    applications, 54–57

        informed consent, 54–55

        risks and benefits assessment, 55–56

        selection of subjects, 56–57

    basic ethical principles

        beneficence, 53

        justice, 53–54, 57

        respect for persons, 52–53

    boundaries between practice and research, 52

comprehension and informed consent, 55

and injustice, 57

justice, 57

risks and benefits assessment, 55–56

beneficence, Belmont Report on, 53

benefits assessment, Belmont Report on, 55–56

Bennett, J., 143

Berman, S. M., 214–220

bias

    case-control studies of, 234–235

    vs. confounding, 183

    missing data and, 188

    in observational studies, STROBE recommendations, 182–183

    from per protocol analysis, 208–209, *209*

    preventing in randomized controlled trials, 208

    in sexual behavior surveys

        acquiescence bias, 243

        participation bias, 240, 242–243

        reporting and recall, 240–241

Biedrzycki, P., 108–114

Biggar, R. J., 240

Bingham, T., 247–249

Binson, D., 243

BioSense, 36*n*

Blank, S., 214–220

botulism, 166–167

    foodborne illness statistics, 137, 138

Brammer, L., 127–131

Braun, C., 8

Bresee, J. S., 134–150

Brewer, G., 108–114

Brucella spp., 145

    foodborne illness statistics, 137, 138

Brunkard, J., 127–131

Buehler, J. W., 74–84

Bukholm, G., 235–236

Bulens, S., 127–131

Burton, S., 127–131

Bye Kjelsberg, A. B. B., 235–236

Byers, B., 247–249

C

cadmium, and vomiting, 164

Campylobacter jejuni, 136

    foodborne illness from, 134

Campylobacter spp., 145, 153

    estimated food-related deaths, 139

    foodborne illness statistics, 137, 138

deaths, 143

    hospitalizations and deaths from, 143

Carmeli, Y., 234–235

case-control studies, 45, 175, 187–188, 197

    confounders in, 192

    to examine severity of illness and control group misclassification bias, 234

    for influenza vaccine efficacy assessment, 40, 221

    matching criteria, 180

    outcome data, 193

    participants description, 190

    providing eligibility criteria for, 179

case definition and confirmation, in outbreak investigations, 69

case study, on gastrointestinal illness, 157–163

Castro, K. G., 116–121

Catania, J. A., 243

categorizing. *See* grouping continuous data

causality, conclusions about, 200

cause-effect relationships, 197

Cegielski, J. P., 116–121

Centers for Disease Control and Prevention, 45, 47. *See also Morbidity and Mortality Weekly Report*

    and FoodNet, 134

    syphilis cases review for stage classification, 214

childbed fever, 4

children

    hospitalizations associated with influenza, 37–38

    influenza-related mortality, 39

Chinese Ministry of Health, and SARS, 98

chlorina liquida, 8

Ciesielski, C. A., 214–220

Clarke, M. D., 100–101

classic swine flu, 23

Clement, U., 240

Cleveland study, 136, 140

clinician inteviews, vs. audio computer-assisted self-interviews, for obtaining sexual history, 254–255

closed cohort studies, 175

Clostridium botulinum, 145, 166

Clostridium perfringens, 145, 153

    and diarrhea, 164

    foodborne illness statistics, 137, 138

coal-face commitment, 61

    application of, 62

cohort studies, 175, 192

    follow-up information, 193

    matching criteria, 180

    outcome data, 193

participant information in, 179
  of sexual behavior, 239
Coles, R., 108–114
colleges, schools of public health, 45–46
Communicable Disease Center, 45
community-acquired pneumonia, associated with influenza, *Staphylococcus aureus* as cause, 127–131
community-level studies, on STD treatment to prevent HIV, 229–231
comprehension, and informed consent, 55
computer-assisted interviews (CASI), 244
  audio self-interviews vs. clinician interviews for obtaining history, 254–255
  in sexual behavior survey research, 256–257
conditional logistic regression, 188
confidence intervals, 192, 197
confounding, 185
  vs. bias, 183
  explanation, 195
  residual, 199
confounding factor, 185
The Contagiousness of Puerperal Fever (Holmes), 8–11
continuous data, grouping, 182
control group misclassification bias, case-control study of, 234–235
control measures, outbreak investigations, 73
Copas, A., 240
Cope, J., 127–131
copper, and vomiting, 164
coronavirus, *99*
costs, of public health surveillance system, 83
Council for Agricultural Science and Technology (CAST), 143
Council of State and Territorial Epidemiologists (CSTE), 45
county health departments, 46
Cox proportional hazard regression, 185
critical evaluation, 172
cross-sectional studies, 175, 188–189
  outcome data, 193, 194
  providing eligibility criteria for, 179–180
  of sexual behavior, 238–239
Cryptosporidium parvum, 148, 167
  and diarrhea, 166
  foodborne illness statistics, 137, 138
cumulative incidences, 197
  in closed cohort, 175
Cyclospora cayetanensis, 148–149, 167
  and diarrhea, 166

foodborne illness from, 134
foodborne illness statistics, 137, 138

D

data capture, in public health surveillance system, 78
data sources
  in observational studies, STROBE recommendations, 181–182
  quality and validity of syndromic surveillance system, 81–82
deaths
  from foodborne illness, 139
    from Norwalk-like viruses, 143
    from unknown pathogens, 141–142
  from influenza and pneumonia, 2007–2008, 38, *39*
    in children, 39
  risk from multidrug-resistant *Pseudomonas aeruginosa*, 235–236
  Vienna maternity hospital (1841–1946), 5–6
De Foe, D., *A Journal of the Plague Year*, 14–20
Delamater, J., 241
Department of Health and Human Services, 47
dependent variable, 181
Des Jarlais, D. C., 244
descriptive epidemiology, outbreak investigations, 70
design effect, 189
detection bias, 183
"determinant", in studies, 181
Dhara, R., 127–131
diarrhea
  diseases typified by, 164–166
  from *E. coli* infection, *135*
Discussion section, in observational studies, STROBE recommendations, 198–201
Dietz, V., 134–150
disease registers, and selection bias, 183
disproportionate stratification, 188
Drake, A., 247–249

E

early latent syphilis, 219
Eby, E., 108–114
"effect modification", 186
Egger, M., 172–202
eligibility criteria, in observational studies, 179
emergency department, prototypical surveillance data flow chart for encounters, *78*
EMSystem Regional Emergency Medicine Internet (REMI), 109

"end points", in studies, 181
environmental investigation, outbreak investigations, 72
Environmental Protection Agency, 47
Epidemic Intelligence Service (EIS), 46
epidemiology, 44
    in outbreak investigations, 69, 70
equipoise, 61–62, 63
Erens, B., 238–245
Erme, M., 108–114
Escherichia coli
    enteroinvasive, and diarrhea, 165
    enterotoxigenic, 146
        and diarrhea, 165
        foodborne illness statistics, 137, 138
    non-O157 STEC, foodborne illness statistics, 137, 138
    O157:H7, *135*, 144, 145–146
        and diarrhea, 166
        estimated food-related deaths, 139
        foodborne illness from, 134
        foodborne illness statistics, 137, 138
        underreporting estimates, 136
    Shiga toxin-producing serogroups, 146
ethics. *See also* Belmont Report
    in research, 50
    violations in syphilis study at Tuskegee, 58–60
ethnographic studies, of sexual behavior, 239
explanatory variable, 181
exposure to disease, onset, 77
external validity, 200

F

Farley, T., 256–257
Federal Register, Belmont Report in, 51
Federal Security Agency, 47
Federal Venereal Diseases Control Act, 47
Felton, C., 108–114
Fenton, K. A., 238–245
Fleischauer, A. T., 98–100
flexibility, of public health surveillance system, 82
flow diagram, in observational studies, STROBE
        recommendations, 190, *191*
flu. *See* influenza
fluoroquinolone, tuberculosis resistant to treatment with, 116
Flynn, C. P., 247–249
Foldy, S. L., 108–114
follow-up
    loss to, 209–210
    study details on procedures, 179

Food and Drug Administration, 47
    and FoodNet, 134
    Vaccines and Related Biological Products Advisory
        Committee, 36
Foodborne Disease Outbreak Surveillance System, 134, 135
Foodborne Diseases Active Surveillance Network, 134
foodborne illness
    from bacterial pathogens, 144–148
    causes, 134
    compendium, 163–167
    conclusions, 143–144
    data sources, 134–136
    deaths, 139
        from unknown pathogens, 141–142
    estimated frequency, *142*
    hospitalizations, 139
        from unknown pathogens, 141
    limits on estimating, 153–154
    statistics, 137, 138
    total cases estimate, 136–139
    underreporting, 134
        reasons for, 136
    from unknown pathogens, 140–142
        assumptions, 154
    U.S. statistics, 134
forward inclusion strategy, 195
Fosheim, G., 127–131
foundling homes, 8
Framingham Heart Study, 44–45
frequency matching, 180
frequency reports, 241
Frontlines of Medicine, 108
Frost, W. H., 31–33
Fry, A., 127–131
funding, in observational studies, STROBE
        recommendations, 200–201
Furness, B. W., 214–220

G

Gallagher, K., 247–249
gastrointestinal illness. *See also* foodborne illness
    age-adjusted rate, 140
    CDC case study, 157–163
    frequency in general population, 140
    frequency of acute, 144
    of unknown etiology, 141–142
general population probability sample surveys, of sexual
        behavior, 238–239

generalizability, in observational studies, STROBE
        recommendations, 200
Giardia lamblia, 149, 167
    and diarrhea, 166
    foodborne illness statistics, 137, 138
Golden, M. A., 254–255
Gorwitz, R., 127–131
Gøtzsche, P. C., 172–202
Griffin, P. M., 134–150
group matching, 180
grouping continuous data, 182, 195
    choices, 184
Guarner, J., 127–131
Guillain-Barré syndrome, 145
Gulf Coast States Vibrio Surveillance System, 134, 135
Gunn, R. A., 214–220
Guyatt, G. H., 208–210

H

HA protein binding, and influenza virus infection, 26
Hageman, J., 127–131
Hamilton, C., 108–114
handwashing, history, 4
Harris, A. D., 234–235
health services, withholding of treatment in Tuskegee study,
        58–60
heavy metals, and vomiting, 164
hepatitis A, 150
    foodborne illness statistics, 138
hepatitis A virus
    foodborne illness from, 139
    foodborne illness statistics, 137
Hill, H. A., 122–126
HIV (human immunodeficiency virus), *88*
    deaths from toxoplasmosis, 143
    estimating incidence, 248
    first reports
        Kaposi's sarcoma and *Pneumocystis* pneumonia, 90–91,
            94–95
        Kaposi's sarcoma and *Pneumocystis* pneumonia,
            follow-up, 92–93
        Pneumocystis carinii pneumonia, 88–89
    prevalence of testing among men who have sex with men,
        251
    prevalence, unrecognized infection and testing, men who
        have sex with men, 247–251
    reasons for not having test, 250
    STD treatment to prevent infection, 229–231

Holmes, Oliver Wendell, *The Contagiousness of Puerperal
        Fever*, 8–11, 14
Hopkins, R. S., 74–84
Hospital Services and Construction Act (Hill-Burton) of
        1946, 47
hospitalizations
    of children, influenza and, 37–38
    from foodborne illness, 139
        from Norwalk-like viruses, 143
        from unknown pathogens, 141
Howe, D., 108–114
Human Genomic Epidemiology Network (HuGENet), 187
hypotheses
    null and alternative, 228
    in outbreak investigations
        generating, 70–71
        testing, 71–72

I

illness severity bias, case-control study of, 234–235
Imperial Foundling Home (Vienna), 8
imprecision of results, 199
imputation, 188
incidence, 197
incidence rates, in closed cohort, 175
incidence reports, 241
independent variable, 181
indicator data types, in syndromic surveillance systems,
        75–76
individual matching, 180
infectious disease, methodological issues in study, 234
influenza, 22
    death rates per 100,000, 1887–1916, 32, *33*
    death rates per 100,000, 1910–1918, *33*
    defining for case-control study, 222
    epidemiology, 31–33
    methicillin-resistant *Staphylococcus aureus* and, 127–131
    pandemic 1918, 22–29
        animal host origin, 25–26
        beginnings, 23–24
        biological basis for pathogenicity, 26–27
        efforts to understand, 23
        impact, 23
        impact on young adults, 27, *27*, 29
        likelihood of pandemic re-occurrence, 29
        waves, *24*, 24–25
    and pneumonia, age-specific incidence rates, *28*
    relationship to vaccine composition 2007–8, 34–41

statistics, 22
surveillance 2007–2008, *35*, 35–36
    estimated activity levels by state, *38*
    mortality rates, 38, *39*
    outpatient visits, 36, *37*
    pediatric hospitalizations, 37–38
    resistance to antiviral medications, 39–40
    state-specific activity levels, 36–37
types, 22
virus shedding, 221
influenza vaccine, 22
    case-control studies for efficacy assessment, 221
    composition 2008–09, 36
    influenza activity in U.S. and vaccine composition 2008,
        34–41
    interim within-season estimate of effectiveness of
        trivalent inactivated, 221–225
    limitations of report, 225
influenza virus
    H1N1 strain, 23, 40
    H2N2 strain, 23, 27, 39–40
    H3N2 strain, 23, 40
    H5N1 strain, 23, 24, 29
    H7N7 strain, 23
information
    Belmont Report on, 54–55
    learning to describe, 68
information bias, 183
informed consent, Belmont Report on, 54–55
Institute of Medicine, 46
intensive care unit, multidrug-resistant *Pseudomonas
        aeruginosa*, and risk of patient death, 235–236
intention-to-treat principle, 208–210
    determining use, 210
interaction, 186, 187
    between risk factors, evaluating, 197
internal consistency, in survey responses, 242
International Classification of Diseases, 9th Revision,
        Clinical Modifications (ICD-9-CM,18), 135
International Journal of Epidemiology, 181
interpretation, in observational studies, STROBE
        recommendations, 199–200
interviewer bias, 183
interviews
    clinician vs. audio computer-assisted self-interviews,
        254–255
    computer assisted, 244
    in sexual behavior surveys, 256–257
introduction, in observational studies, STROBE
        recommendations, 177

iron, and vomiting, 164
isoniazid, tuberculosis resistant to treatment with, 116

J

Jernigan, D. B., 122–126
Johns Hopkins School of Hygiene and Public Health, 45
Johnson, A. M., 244, 238–245
Johnson, W., 241
joint effects, 197
    analysis of, 187
A Journal of the Plague Year (De Foe), 14–20
justice, Belmont Report on, 53–54, 57

K

Kahn, R. H., 214–220
Kallen, A., 127–131
Kaposi's sarcoma, 88, *93*
    and *Pneumocystis* pneumonia, 90–91, 94–95
        follow-up, 92–93
Keaton, B., 108–114
key results, in observational studies, STROBE
        recommendations, 198–199
kidney failure, from *E. coli* infection, *135*
Kinsey, A., 240
Kissinger, P., 256–257
Koblin, B. A., 247–249, 255–256
Kolletschka, J., 10
Kuehnert, M. J., 122–126
Kupronis, B. A., 122–126
Kurth, A. E., 254–255
Kvenberg, J. E., 143

L

labor unions, 46
Ladson, J., 127–131
LaLota, M., 247–249
The Lancet, 199
Langmuir, A., 45
language, street vs. formal, for sexual behavior survey, 243
Lansky, A., 247–249
late latent syphilis, 214
latent syphilis, 214
Laumann, E. O., 240, 243
legionellosis, 70–71
Limbago, B., 127–131
limitations, in observational studies, STROBE
        recommendations, 199
Listeria
    estimated food-related deaths, 139
    foodborne illness from, 134, 139

Listeria monocytogenes, 146–147
  and diarrhea, 165
    foodborne illness from, 134
    foodborne illness statistics, 137, 138
local health departments, 46
logistic regression, 185
longitudinal studies, randomized control trials of audio
    computer-assisted self-interview, 255–256
Lyme disease, 14

M

MacKellar, D., 247–249
Mantel-Haenszel method, 188
March of Dimes, 46
Marine Hospital Service, 47
Martin, D. P., 254–255
Massachusetts Sanitary Commission, report 1850, 46
matched analysis, 187
matching criteria, 180
  in case-control studies, 181
McAllister, S., 127–131
McCaig, L. F., 134–150
McFarland, W., 247–249
McLaws, M., 244
McManus, S., 238–245
Mead, P. S., 134–150
measles import-associated outbreak, post-exposure
    prophylaxis, isolation and quarantine, 114–116
measures of association, 197
Medicaid, 47
medical surveillance bias, 183
Medicare, 47
Melbye, M., 240
methicillin-resistant *Staphylococcus aureus*, 121
  community-acquired pneumonia associated with
     influenza, 127–131
  hospitalizations, 122–126
Metzger, D. S., 255–256
Metsch, L., 247–249
Miller, G., 108–114
missing data in observational studies
  approach to, 188
  STROBE recommendations, 192–193
Montori, V. M., 208–210
morbidity and mortality surveillance, 45
Morbidity and Mortality Weekly Report, 88
  Kaposi's sarcoma and *Pneumocystis* pneumonia among
    homosexual men, 90–91
    cluster among homosexual males, 94–95
    follow-up, 92–93

measles import-associated outbreak, post-exposure
    prophylaxis, isolation and quarantine, 114–116
Pneumocystis pneumonia, 88–89
Severe Acute Respiratory Syndrome (SARS)
  outbreak, 98–100
    preliminary clinical description, 100–101
    revised U.S. surveillance case definition, 104–107
    surveillance project, 108–114
    updated interim surveillance case definition, 2003,
     101–103
Morens, D. M., 22–29
mortality rates. *See* deaths
Mothers Against Drunk Driving, 46
Motin, R., 59
Mulrow, C. D., 172–202
multiplicative modeling, 187
multiplier for estimating underreporting, 136, 154
  problems applying, 153
multivariant analysis, 185
Murrill, C., 247–249
Mwanza study (Tanzania), 228, 229
Mycobacterium tuberculosis, 117

N

Naponick, J., 127–131
National Action Plan to Combat Multidrug-Resistant
  Tuberculosis, 120
National Ambulatory Medical Care Survey, 134, 135, 141
National Bioethics Advisory Commission, 60
National Commission for the Protection of Human Subjects
  of Biomedical and Behavioral Research, 59
National Health Care Survey, 135
National Health Survey, 45
National HIV Behavioral Surveillance (NHBS), 247–248
National Hospital Ambulatory Medical Care Survey, 134,
  135, 141
National Hospital Discharge Survey, 122, 134, 136, 141
National Institutes of Health, 47
National Nosocomial Infections Surveillance (NNIS)
  System, 123
National Notifiable Disease Surveillance System, 75, 134, 135
National Research Act, 59
National Respiratory and Enteric Virus Surveillance System
  (NREVSS), 223
  influenza surveillance, *35*, 35
National Tuberculosis Association, 46
National Vital Statistics System, 134
Navin, T., 116–121
New York State Department of Public Health Division, 157
newborns, puerperal fever, 4, 5–9

nongovernment organizations, 46
nonparticipation, giving reasons for, 190
Norovirus. *See* Norwalk-like viruses
Norwalk-like viruses, 144, 150
    and diarrhea, 165
    estimated food-related deaths, 139
    foodborne illness statistics, 137, 138
    hospitalizations and deaths from, 143
The Notifiable Diseases (1912), 45
null hypothesis, 228

O

objectives, in observational studies, STROBE
        recommendations, 177
observational studies. *See also* STROBE Statement
        (Strengthening the Reporting of Observational
        Studies in Epidemiology recommendations)
    quality of reporting, 172
    scope, 175
    types, 173, 175
Occupational Safety and Health Administration, 47
odds ratio, 197
Onion, 238
open cohort studies, 175
OraQuick rapid test, 248
organizations, in public health system, 46–47
Ortiz-Rios, E., 214–220
oseltamivir, resistance to, in 2007–2008, 39–40
outbreak investigations, 68–73. *See also* public health
        system, surveillance
    case confirmation, 69
    case definition, 69
    control measures, 73
    descriptive epidemiology, 70
    environmental investigation, 72
    epidemiologic investigation, 69
    establishing background rate and finding cases, 69–70
    hypothesis generation, 70–71
    hypothesis testing, 71–72
    interactions with public and press, 73
    process model for early detection, *77*
    reasons for investigating, 68–69
    recognition of outbreaks, 68
    timeline milestones for early detection, *79*
Overhage, J. M., 74–84
oxacillin, *S. aureus* resistance to, 123

P

Padian, N. S., 242
parasitic pathogens, 148–149

Park, B., 100–101
participants in observational studies
    missing data, 192–193
    STROBE recommendations, 179–180, 189–190
participation bias
    and measurement error reduction, 242–243
    in sexual behavior surveys, 240
partner studies, of sexual behavior, 239
Patel, J., 127–131
pathogens
    bacterial, 144–148
    parasitic, 148–149
    unidentified, and foodborne illness, 134, 140–142
    viral, 149–150
patient care, vs. research, 61
pattern recognition, in public health surveillance system, 75,
        78
pediatrics. *See* children
Pemble, K., 108–114
penicillins
    randomized control trials, 61
    S. aureus resistance to, 123
per protocol analysis, bias from, 208–209, *209*
periodic standardized surveys, 45
Perkins, B. A., 153
Peterman, T. A., 214–220
Peto, R., 62
plague, 14
Pneumocystis carinii pneumonia, 88–89
Pneumocystis pneumonia, and Kaposi's sarcoma, 90–91,
        94–95
    follow-up, 92–93
pneumonia
    death rates per 100,000
        1887–1916, 32, *33*
        1910–1918, *33*
    and influenza, age-specific incidence rates, *28*
    methicillin-resistant *Staphylococcus aureus* and, 127–131
    mortality related to, 2007–2008, 38, *39*
Pocock, S. J., 172–202
Pogue, M., 127–131
polio surveillance program, 45
Poole, C., 172–202
portability, of public health surveillance system, 83
Potterat, J. J., 241
practice, vs. research, 52
Pratt, R., 116–121
"predictor", in studies, 181
prevalence, 197
primary syphilis, 214

professional organizations, 46

proportionate stratification, 188

"prospective" study, 178

protocol violations, and analysis, 208–209

Pseudomonas aeruginosa, 234

   multidrug-resistant, and patient death risk in intensive care unit, 235–236

Public Health Laboratory Information System, 134, 135

Public Health Service, 47

   syphilis study at Tuskegee, ethics violations, 58–60

public health system

   achievements 1900–1999, 44–47

      morbidity and mortality surveillance, 45

      nongovernment and government organizations, 46–47

      periodic standardized surveys, 45

      quantitative analytic techniques, 44–45

      training, 45–46

   surveillance system evaluation framework, 74–84

      background, 75

      costs, 83

      data quality, 81–84

      disease case reports, 75

      flexibility, 82

      new data types, 75–76

      outbreak detection, 76–80, *77*

      pattern recognition, 75

      portability, 83

      stability, 83

      statistical assessment of validity, 81

      system description, 76

      usefulness of system, 82

      validation approaches, 80–81

Public Health Weekly Report, epidemiology of influenza 1919, 31–33

puerperal fever, 4, 5–10

Q

qualitative studies, of sexual behavior, 239

quantitative analytic techniques, 44–45

quantitative variables, in observational studies, STROBE recommendations, 184–185

quarantine

   to control import-associated measles outbreak, 114–116

   principles of modern, 115

   questions to review regarding authority, 116

questionnaire

   design and content, 243

   design, content, and delivery, 241

   self completion, 243–244

R

racism, in syphilis study at Tuskegee, 58–60

Rakai study (Uganda), 228, 229

Ramjee, G., 244

random probability sampling methods, in sexual behavior surveys, 240

randomized control trials

   audio computer-assisted self-interviews, in longitudinal studies, 255–256

   bias prevention in, 208

   failure to gain coal-face commitment, 60–63

   preventing failure, 63

Ratard, R., 127–131

rate difference, 187

rate ratio, 187

Raymond, H., 247–249

recall bias, 183

   in sexual behavior surveys, 240–241

Reingold, A. L., 68–73

Reinisch, J. M., 241

Relative Excess Risk from Interaction (RERI), 197

relative risk, 187, 197, 200

   translating estimates into absolute risk, 195–196

reporting bias, in sexual behavior surveys, 240–241

representativeness, and data quality in surveillance system, 81

research. *See also specific study types*

   ethics in, 50. *See also* Belmont Report

   vs. practice, 52

   study design, 60

   Tuskegee impact on methods, 59–60

research question, 228

residual confounding, 199

respect for persons, Belmont Report on, 52–53

respiratory symptoms, in acute gastroenteritis, 140

respiratory syndrome. *See* Severe Acute Respiratory Syndrome (SARS)

respondent variables, in sexual behavior surveys, 240–241

response bias, 183

results section, in observational studies, STROBE recommendations, 189–198

"retrospective" study, 178

Rice, J., 256–257

rifampin, tuberculosis resistant to treatment with, 116

rimantadine, resistance to, in 2007–2008, 39–40

risk difference, 187

risks and benefits assessment, Belmont Report on, 55–56

Robison, V. A., 116–121

Rockefeller Foundation, 45

Rockefeller Sanitary Committee, Hookworm Eradication
        Project, 46
Rosenwald, J., 59
Rotavirus, 149–150
    and diarrhea, 165
    foodborne illness statistics, 137, 138

S

Sackett, D. L., 60–63
Salmonella, 147, 153
    and diarrhea, 165
    estimated food-related deaths, 139
    foodborne diseases from, 134
    foodborne illness statistics, 137, 138
    hospitalizations and deaths from, 143
    underreporting estimates, 136
Salmonella infantis, 139
salmonellosis, 70
    clinical features, *139*
Samore, M. H., 234–235
sample design, and measurement error reduction, 242
sample size, determination in observation studies, 184
sampling
        for cross-sectional studies, 188
        errors from procedures, 240
Sanders, S. A., 241
SARS. *See* Severe Acute Respiratory Syndrome (SARS)
Schillinger, J. A., 214–220
Schlesselman, J. J., 172–202
scientific background, in observational studies, 177
scientific process, 228
secondary syphilis, 214
selection bias, 183
self completion questionnaires, 243–244
Semmelweis, I. P., 4–8, 10, 14
sensitivity analysis, 197–198
    in observational studies, STROBE recommendations, 189
sepsis, from *Salmonella*, 139
setting, in observational studies, STROBE
        recommendations, 178–179
Severe Acute Respiratory Syndrome (SARS)
    CDC preliminary case definition, 99
    outbreak, 98–100
    preliminary clinical description, 100–101
    quarantine to control, 115
    revised U.S. surveillance case definition, 104–107
    SARs-CoV classification before and after laboratory
        testing, 107
    surveillance project, 108–114

    case-finding triage forms, 109–110
    conclusions, 113–114
    daily emergency department visits, *112*
    discussion, 112–113
    results, 111–112
    surveys, 110
    syndromic surveillance, 110
    workflow, *110*
    suspected and probable cases and deaths, 2003, 98
    updated interim surveillance case definition, 2003,
        101–103
sex related bias, in self-reported behaviours, 241
sexual behavior survey research
    audio computer-assisted self-interviews vs. clinician
        interviews for obtaining history, 254–255
    computer assisted interviews, 256–257
    conclusions, 244–245
    measurement challenges, 238–245
        error sources, 239–241
        internal consistency, 242
        response rates and representatives, 241–242
        study types, 238–239
        test-retest reliability, 242
        validity checks, 242
    measurement error reduction, 242–244
sexual diaries, 244
sexual partner, defining, 241
sexually transmitted infections (STIs), 228
    sexual behavior and transmission dynamics, 238
    treatment to prevent HIV infection, 229–231
Shah, N. S., 116–121
Shapiro, C., 134–150
Shattuck, L., 46
Shay, D., 127–131
Shigella spp., 147
    and diarrhea, 165
    foodborne illness statistics, 137, 138
Sifakis, F., 247–249
significance tests, 192
Silva, J., 108–114
Slutsker, L., 134–150
Smith, T. W., 244
Smithsonian Institution, Belmont Conference Center, 51
social desirability bias, in sexual behavior surveys, 241
Social Security Act of 1935, 47
Solomon, S. L., 122–126
Sosin, D. M., 74–84
"Spanish" influenza pandemic of 1918–1919, 22–29
Speaker, A., 121

Spencer, L., 243

Spira, A., 243

stability, of public health surveillance system, 83

stakeholders, in public health surveillance system, 76

standard errors, 192

Staphylococcus aureus, 147, 153

    methicillin-resistant, 121

        community-acquired pneumonia associated with influenza, 127–131

        hospitalizations, 122–126

    and vomiting, 163

Staphylococcus food poisoning

    deaths due to, 143

    statistics, 137, 138

state health departments, 46

statistical methods

    for assessing validity of surveillance systems, 81

    to examine subgroups, 186

    in observational studies, STROBE recommendations, 185–189

    weighting techniques, 243

Stefanski, J., 127–131

STI/HIV co-factor hypothesis, 228

Stoneburner, R. I., 241

stratification, 185

Streptococcus algalactiae (Streptococcus group B), 4

Streptococcus, foodborne illness statistics, 137, 138

Streptococcus pyogenes (Streptococcus group A), 4, 147–148

Streptococcus zooepidemicus, 71

STROBE Statement (Strengthening the Reporting of Observational Studies in Epidemiology recommendations), 172–201

    checklist of items to be addressed, 173–174

        bias, 182–183

        data sources, 181–182

        Discussion section, 198–201

        flow diagram, 190, *191*

        funding, 200–201

        generalizability, 200

        interpretation, 199–200

        introduction, 177

        key results, 198–199

        limitations, 199

        missing data, 192–193

        objectives, 177

        participants, 179–180, 189–190

        quantitative variables, 184–185

        results section, 189–198

        sensitivity analysis, 189

        setting, locations and relevant dates, 178–179

        statistical methods, 185–189

        study design, 177

        study size, 183–184

        title and abstract, 176–177

        variables, 180–181

    concluding remarks about, 201

    main study designs covered, 175

    study designs covered by, 175

study design in observational studies, 175

    STROBE recommendations, 177

study size in observational studies, STROBE recommendations, 183–184

subgroups

    analysis in observational studies, 196

    at high risk, surveys of sexual behavior, 239

    statistical methods to examine, 186

subjects of research, selection, Belmont Report on, 56–57

surveillance system evaluation framework for public health system, 74–84

    background, 75

    costs, 83

    data quality, 81–84

    disease case reports, 75

    flexibility, 82

    new data types, 75–76

    outbreak detection, 76–80, *77*

    pattern recognition, 75

    portability, 83

    stability, 83

    statistical assessment of validity, 81

    system description, 76

    usefulness of system, 82

    validation approaches, 80–81

survey research on sexual behavior. *See also* questionnaire

    conclusions, 244–245

    measurement challenges, 238–245

        error sources, 239–241

        internal consistency, 242

        response rates and representatives, 241–242

        study types, 238–239

        test-retest reliability, 242

        validity checks, 242

surveys, periodic standardized, 45

swine flu, 23

symptoms, onset in disease outbreak, 77

syndromic surveillance systems, 75–76

    validity of, 81

syphilis

misclassification of stages, 214–220
  discussion, 217–220
  methods, 215
  results, 215–217
  unknown duration stage, 219

T

Tannæs, T., 235–236
Taubenberger, J. K., 22–29
Tauxe, R. V., 134–150
Taxoplasma gondii, foodborne illness statistics, 137, 138
Taylor, M., 214–220
Tecumseh study, 136, 140
telephone interview, for sexual behavior survey, 243
terrorism threat, and public health surveillance systems, 74
test-retest reliability, of questionnaire responses, 242
timeliness, of surveillance, 77
tin, and vomiting, 164
titer-based surveillance, 219
title, in observational studies, STROBE recommendations, 176–177
Tobin-D'Angelo, M., 127–131
Todd, E. C. D., 143
Tokars, J. I., 122–126
Tong, V., 74–84
Tourangeau, R., 244
Toxoplasma
  estimated food-related deaths, 139
  foodborne diseases from, 134, 139
Toxoplasma gondii, 149
toxoplasmosis, deaths from, 143
training in public health, 45–46
Trichinella spiralis, 149
  foodborne illness statistics, 137, 138
trichinosis, deaths from, 143
tuberculosis
  extensively drug-resistant, 116–121
    reported cases in U.S. 1993–2006, *118*
    statistics, 118–119
    travel timeline for person with, 121
    Mycobacterium tuberculosis, *117*
Turner, C. F., 244, 255–256
Tuskegee Health Benefit Program (THBP), 59
Tuskegee syphilis study, 58–60
Tuttle, J., 127–131

U

uncertainty principle, 61–62
  applying when patient enters randomized control trials, 62–63

underreporting
  assumptions on, 143
  of foodborne illness, 134
  multiplier for estimating, 136
U.S. Department of Agriculture, and FoodNet, 134
U.S. federal government, health services, 47
U.S. Food and Drug Administration, 47
  and FoodNet, 134
  Vaccines and Related Biological Products Advisory Committee, 36
unknown pathogens, foodborne illness from, 140–142

V

vaccination. *See* influenza vaccine
Vaccine Preparedness Study, 255–256
validity checks, 242
validity, measuring for outbreak detection system, 79–80
vancomycin, *S. aureus* resistance to, 123
Vandenbroucke, J. P., 172–202
variables
  in observational studies, STROBE recommendations, 180–181
  respondent, in sexual behavior surveys, 240–241
Vibrio spp., 148
Vibrio cholerae
  and diarrhea, 165
  toxigenic, 148
    foodborne illness statistics, 137, 138
Vibrio parahemolyticus, and diarrhea, 164
Vibrio vulnificus, 148
  foodborne illness statistics, 137, 138
Vienna, Imperial Foundling Home, 8
Vienna maternity hospital (1841–1846)
  births, deaths and mortality rates 1841–1846, *4*
  mortality rates
    all patients, *5*
    newborns, *5–6*
viral pathogens, 149–150
Vironostika-Less Sensitive (LS) EIA, 248
voluntariness, and informed consent, 55
volunteer samples, 240
vomiting, diseases typified by, 163–164
von Elm, E., 172–202

W

Wadsworth, J., 241
Washington, B. T., 59
waterborne disease, compendium, 163–167
World Health Organization, 223

influenza surveillance, *35*, 35
and SARS, 98

X

XDR TB. *See* tuberculosis, extensively drug-resistant

Y

Yersinia enterocolitica, 71, 148, 167
  and diarrhea, 166
  foodborne illness statistics, 137, 138
Yersinia pestis, 14, *15*

Z

Zaki, S., 127–131
Zenilman, J. M., 242
zinc, and vomiting, 164